Global Issues

Politics, Economics, and Culture

Richard J. Payne
Illinois State University

PEARSON
Longman

New York • San Francisco • Boston
London • Toronto • Sydney • Tokyo • Singapore • Madrid
Mexico City • Munich • Paris • Cape Town • Hong Kong • Montreal

Editor in Chief: Eric Stano
Acquisitions Editor: Vikram Mukhija
Senior Marketing Manager: Elizabeth Fogarty
Production Manager: Savoula Amanatidis
Project Coordination, Text Design, and Electronic Page Makeup: GGS Book Services
Cover Design Manager: Wendy Ann Fredericks
Cover Designer: Kay Petronio
Cover Photos: (Left to right) Copyright © Reuters/CORBIS; AP Photo/Chien-min Chung; and Robert
    Harbison/Christian Science Monitor/Getty Images
Photo Researcher: Christine A. Pullo
Senior Manufacturing Buyer: Dennis Para
Printer and Binder: R.R. Donnelley and Sons Company—Crawfordsville
Cover Printer: Phoenix Color

Library of Congress Cataloging-in-Publication Data

Payne, Richard J., 1949–
    Global issues : politics, economics, and culture / Richard J. Payne.
        p. cm.
    Includes bibliographical references and index.
    ISBN 0-321-08957-X
    1. Globalization—Textbooks. 2. World politics—Textbooks. I. Title.
    JZ1318.P39 2007
    303.48'2—dc22

                                                    2006039049

Please visit us at http://www.ablongman.com

ISBN 0-321-08957-X

1 2 3 4 5 6 7 8 9 10—DOC—09 08 07 06

BRIEF CONTENTS

To Elaine Cook Graybill
and
Alyson Sue Figge

DETAILED CONTENTS

PREFACE

Throughout history, pivotal events have significantly altered perspectives on, and approaches to, academic disciplines. Terrorist attacks on the United States, the world's dominant power, constituted the most dramatic development at the beginning of the twenty-first century. They reinforced the need for scholars, political leaders, policymakers, international organizations, nonstate actors, and individuals to focus even more on global issues in an age of increasing globalization. For many years, there has been a growing recognition that we need to pay more attention to the interdependence of problems and their global implications, regardless of where they originate. Globalization links the fates of countries, intergovernmental organizations, nonstate actors, and individuals to an unprecedented degree. The proliferation of books, journal articles, professional conferences, and discussions on globalization clearly demonstrates a profound transition toward global issues and global studies. Many universities and colleges have developed courses on global issues. They have also created centers composed of departments representing many disciplines that concentrate on globalization. College students consistently demonstrate a strong and growing interest in global issues, and many high schools offer courses on global studies.

My decision to write this textbook was strongly influenced by the need for a comprehensive, accessible, and student-oriented introductory textbook for undergraduates that focuses specifically on global issues. For many years, those of us who teach global issues courses have generally relied on compilations of journal articles, book chapters, and supplementary scholarly books, many of which are too advanced and theoretically complex for most students in introductory courses. Many textbooks on global politics are essentially traditional international relations texts that include a few chapters on selected global challenges and are written primarily for students interested in political science. Other global politics texts are collections of previously published articles. They often lack a unified approach and are therefore not suitable for introductory undergraduate courses on global issues. In both cases, global issues are considered secondarily. This text concentrates on global issues that students around the world are passionate about because they are directly related to the forces of globalization that are integral components of their lives. The issues discussed in this book are both primary global concerns as well as those in which students have shown great interest. This book's pedagogical features are based on classroom experiences that demonstrate how to help students understand complex concepts and develop the critical thinking skills and abilities necessary to engage in problem-solving.

TEXT PHILOSOPHY

Global Issues: Politics, Economics, and Culture is based on ten philosophical components that are interwoven into each chapter and throughout this book in order to provide students with:

1. A clearer understanding of how the powerful forces of economic, financial, cultural, political, environmental, and military globalization are affecting governments, nonstate actors, and individuals.
2. A deeper awareness of the growing inability of governments, nonstate actors, and individuals to neatly compartmentalize problems within countries outside broader global developments.
3. An appreciation for the complexities of global problems and their interdependence.
4. A broader sense of the global issues and problems in developing countries.
5. An historical background to many global issues that enables students to see continuity and change in human experiences.
6. A deeper awareness of how globalization is profoundly challenging the state-centric emphasis that dominates international relations and world politics.
7. A foundation for more advanced courses on globalization and global affairs.
8. An understanding of basic concepts and theories and an ability to evaluate and apply them to real-life events and problems.
9. An ability to think critically, develop independent judgment, and sharpen intellectual curiosity and imagination.
10. A recognition of the power of individuals, including students, to have a positive impact on global problems.

TEXT ORGANIZATION

Global Issues: Politics, Economics, and Culture is composed of twelve chapters, each focusing on a specific topic and related subtopics. The global issues covered in this book are widely regarded to be of critical importance by both the global community and instructors. In addition to providing instructors with the flexibility to stimulate student participation, the range of issues allows sufficient time during a semester to cover each chapter and to incorporate various pedagogical approaches. Instructors will have enough time to review for exams, administer at least three exams, and allow students to present research papers and other projects. This book can be easily supplemented with subscriptions to publications such as the *New York Times*, the *Washington Post*, the *Wall Street Journal*, or *Foreign Affairs*, enabling students to obtain more current examples of the global issues discussed in these pages.

Chapter 1 provides a theoretical framework and broad historical background to help students understand the specific issues discussed in later chapters. It examines the growth of the modern state, the concept of sovereignty, the emergence and proliferation of nonstate actors, interdependence and globalization, and various forms and periods of globalization. Chapter 2 addresses the ongoing struggle for international primacy in a global society and how this competition is affected by globalization. It provides background on the rise and fall of earlier empires and concentrates on America's rise to global dominance as well as challenges to its power. Focusing on the defeat of Nazi Germany, Italy, and Japan in World War II, the rise of the United States as the dominant power, and the end of the Cold War, Chapter 3 concentrates on how human rights have become an integral component of the general forces of globalization. It examines the philosophical foundations of human rights, controversies and different perspectives on human rights, the problem of genocide, the relationship between terrorism and human rights, and global efforts to promote and protect human rights. Chapter 4 discusses the complex, uncertain, and challenging process of democratization, paying special attention to specific transitions to democracy. This chapter also shows how globalization is leading to increased demands for increased democratic governance within global institutions.

Global terrorism is a dominant global issue that occupies the attention of the United States and other major countries, nonstate actors, global institutions, and individuals. No other issue has had a greater impact on the United States in the twenty-first century. Chapter 5 shows the problems involved in defining terrorism and gives students insights into the causes of terrorism, various types of terrorism, and strategies for dealing with terrorism. Global trade profoundly challenges perceptions of countries as independent and autonomous units that exercise virtually complete control over their territory, population, and domestic and foreign policies. Our lives are increasingly affected by global trade. Chapter 6 deals with the growth of free trade, concerns about trade deficits and surpluses, the emergence of global companies and global factories, the impact of global trade on labor unions and the environment, and the formation of global institutions to deal with trade disputes. Chapter 7 explores global and domestic inequality, discussing the many debates about and struggles for equality among countries, groups, and individuals.

Environmental issues are central to debates about preserving life on earth. Chapter 8 analyzes the globalization of environmental problems, biodiversity, deforestation, invasive species, pollution, global warming, and the connection between global trade and environmental issues. Chapter 9 focuses on population growth and shows that population and migration issues will likely determine the future of humanity. Chapter 10 gives background information on global criminal activities, particularly the globalization of illegal drugs and the different approaches used by Europeans and Americans to deal with drug problems. Chapter 11 examines the globalization of infectious diseases and how threats of pandemics have increased. Finally, we look at globalization's ability to attract and repel, to unify and divide, and to integrate and separate. Chapter 12 focuses on the role of culture in global conflicts. It analyzes theories on the clashes of civilizations, international conflicts, and ethnic conflicts within countries. After discussing various cases, this chapter examines approaches to conflict resolution, such as negotiations, humanitarian intervention, peacemaking, and peacebuilding.

PEDAGOGICAL FEATURES

The pedagogical features in this book are designed for students. As a comprehensive introduction to global issues for students from different academic disciplines, *Global Issues* is written in a style that makes information very accessible. A more conversational writing style engages students, encourages them to relate what they read to global developments and their own lives, facilitates the development of analytical skills, and makes it easier for them to engage in discussions. Above all, it attempts to present a clear, straightforward discussion of interesting and important global issues without obscuring their complexity. The complexity and overlapping nature of global issues require an interdisciplinary or multidisciplinary approach, one that includes politics, economics, science, sociology, history, and psychology. By providing a global theoretical framework, historical background, and many examples, this book enables students to develop a broad and coherent understanding of contemporary issues and developments.

The following pedagogical features underscore an emphasis on generating student involvement in classroom discussions and on helping them to develop skills for success beyond the classroom. I hope that students will find these features informative, intellectually stimulating, and enjoyable.

Chapter Introductions

The introduction provides a brief overview of the main points in the chapter, tells students what is covered, and provides examples of controversial issues included in the chapter to stimulate students' interest in the material.

Current Examples

Consistent with the decision to adopt an accessible writing style, I have included many brief and current examples of global issues throughout the book. These examples make global issues more immediately relevant for students and encourages them to develop a concrete understanding of specific problems.

Historical Background

Each chapter provides practical historical background information to give students an understanding of the issue's broader context.

Cross-Referenced Issues

Chapters are cross-referenced to help students see the interrelatedness and interdependence of global issues. For example, by reading Chapter 8 "Environmental Issues," students will explore the impact of economic globalization on the environment and culture as well as the relationships among environmental issues, global and domestic inequality, economic development, migration, cultural conflicts, and the spread of infectious diseases.

"You Decide" Boxes

These boxes encourage students to be active participants. They discuss controversial issues and then ask students to evaluate them and make a decision. They engage students in problem-solving activities, help them develop critical thinking skills, and encourage classroom discussions.

Maps and Photographs

Maps help to put issues in context and enable students to better grasp essential points discussed in the text. Carefully selected photographs portray specific developments and capture students' attention.

Tables

Tables throughout the book help students understand important points discussed in the text.

Boldfaced Key Terms and Definitions

These are designed to draw students' attention to definitions, concepts, key terms, and main points. Stressing their importance reinforces the point that they are the building blocks of the chapter.

Marginal Glossaries

Small boxes in the margins define key terms and give students a quick reference to important definitions and concepts.

End-of-Chapter Summaries

These provide a brief review of the chapter. They focus students' attention on major points and help them to improve their comprehension and retention of the information.

End-of-Chapter Questions and List of Key Terms

These questions and key terms are designed to improve students' retention of information, stimulate discussions in study groups, and help students prepare for exams.

Suggested Readings

A list of suggested readings is included at the end of each chapter to familiarize students with scholarly literature and to help them gain additional information.

Addresses and Websites

Names, addresses, telephone numbers, and websites are provided for major organizations and groups involved in issues discussed in each chapter, thereby enabling students to obtain additional information.

Index

This listing allows students to quickly find key terms, concepts, names, and subjects discussed throughout the text. Many students find the index especially helpful when reviewing for exams.

ACKNOWLEDGMENTS

I am deeply indebted to many students and colleagues who made significant contributions to this collaborative and interdisciplinary project. Feedback from students in my Global Issues courses over the years has been invaluable and has contributed to making the book accessible to other students. I am also indebted to many research assistants, especially Yu Bo, Lara Saba, Brian Zednick, Janet Schultz, Natalie Mullen, Anthony DiMaggio, Nadejda Negroustoueva, Vanda Rajcan, Sean Zears, and James M. Trask.

I am grateful to many colleagues who read the manuscript, made useful suggestions, and shared their insights. I would like to thank Michele Ganschow, Jamal Nassar, and Cherie Valentine of the Department of Politics and Government at Illinois State University; Laura Berk of the Department of Psychology at Illinois State University; Kelly Keogh of Normal Community High School; Carole J. Cosimano of the Illinois Humanities Council; Mikhail Alexseev of San Diego State University; Lindsey Back of Morehead State University; Brad T. Clark and M. Dawn King of Colorado State University; Mark E. Denham and Richard F. Weisfelder of the University of Toledo, Erich Frankland of Casper College; Mark Haas of Duquesne University; Barbara Hufker of Webster University; Mark Martinez of California State University at Bakersfield; Anjana Mishra at Florida International University; Luis Antonio Payan at the University of Texas at El Paso; George Quester of the University of Maryland; Timothy Russell of the University of Memphis; Houman Sadri of the University of Central Florida; Tom Schrand of Philadelphia University; Mark Schroeder of the University of Kentucky, and Thomas J. Volgy of the University of Arizona.

I would also like to thank Michele Ganschow for her invaluable assistance; as well as Kay Stultz of Institutional Technology Service; and Edward Costello, Eric Stano, Sarah Orzalli, Lucy Silberman, Elizabeth Fogarty, and Vikram Mukhija at Pearson Longman. Above all, I am especially indebted to Elaine Cook Graybill for her support, insights, and suggestions throughout the process of writing this book.

RICHARD J. PAYNE

CHAPTER 1

Global Issues: Challenges of Globalization

INTRODUCTION

Although the terrorist attack on the United States on September 11, 2001 is often compared to the Japanese bombing of Pearl Harbor on December 7, 1941, there are fundamental differences between the two that have a significant impact on how Americans, and much of the world, think about national security and their government's ability to protect them. A general sense of global insecurity has underscored how easily national boundaries are crossed and the difficulty of distinguishing between external and internal threats in an age of increasing globalization. The attack on Pearl Harbor was carried out by an identifiable enemy that controlled a society with a government, an identifiable population, and well-defined national boundaries. The tragedy of September 11, 2001, was inflicted on the United States by a small group of terrorists that had no government or territory. When Japan was defeated, the war was over and the United States regained its sense of security. But the war President George W. Bush declared on terrorism is a war without a foreseeable end, and America's military might is now less effective than it was in World War II in achieving the enemy's surrender. Wars among countries dominate the history and theories of international relations. The terrorist attacks on the United States crystallized the global nature of new threats and underscored the links between national security and global security. They also reinforced the need to understand the nature and challenges of globalization.

Revolutions in technology, transportation, and communication, and the different ways of thinking that characterize interdependence and globalization are exerting pressures on nation-states that strengthen them in some ways but weaken them in others. Globalization—especially economic, cultural, and environmental globalization—has spawned debates around the world. These debates illustrate both the significant resistance to and widespread acceptance of globalization. Although some aspects of globalization are embraced as positive, others are rejected as destructive to cultures, the environment, and political and economic institutions, especially in poorer countries. Distinct lines in this debate are sometimes difficult to discern.

This chapter illustrates the economic, political, and cultural aspects of globalization. Like all the chapters in this book, it demonstrates how politics, economics, and culture are intricately linked in an increasingly complex global society. This is evident in discussions of the transition from the traditional emphasis on international relations to contemporary global issues, pluralism and interdependence, the growth of the modern state and the concept of sovereignty, and the proliferation of intergovernmental organizations as well as nonstate actors. This chapter also examines the causes of globalization, various forms of globalization, periods of globalization, and the debates about globalization.

International Relations

The relations among the world's state governments and other actors

Peace of Westphalia

The treaty that concluded the Thirty Years' War in 1648

State

A legal and political unit that must be internationally recognized, be politically organized, and be a populated geographic area that has sovereignty

Sovereignty

The ability of a state to be independent and free from the control of another state

Nation

A group of people who identify as a political community based on common territory, culture, and other similar bonds

Nation-State

Nations and states that have similar boundaries where the people identify with the nation and establish a state for themselves

FROM INTERNATIONAL RELATIONS TO GLOBAL ISSUES

International relations is essentially concerned with the interaction of states. Such interactions are almost as old as human societies, although the oldest states are traced back to China and Ethiopia. The modern state emerged in Western Europe in 1648, following the **Peace of Westphalia**, which ended thirty years of war among various groups of princes and between political leaders and the Catholic Church. International relations, international politics, and world politics, which are all closely related, focus on states as the main actors. States are often referred to as nations, and most students of international relations use the terms states and nations interchangeably. They also use the term nation-state. The terms state and nation are related, but they are not exactly the same. A **state** is essentially a political unit composed of people, a well-defined territory, and a set of governing institutions. It is regarded as **sovereign**. This means that it is recognized by other states as having the exclusive right to make its own domestic and foreign policies. In other words, it is an independent actor in world politics. A **nation** is generally defined as a group of people who have strong emotional, cultural, linguistic, religious, and historical ties. They may live within the boundaries of one or several states. Unlike a state—which includes people who may not share the same cultural, linguistic, or religious background and may not particularly like each other—a nation is characterized by commonality and strong feelings of identity. Despite these differences between states and nations, the two concepts have become linked in everyday usage, and many scholars and practitioners of international relations use the term **nation-state** to capture this linkage.[1]

International relations focuses on three main questions:

1. What are the contexts in which states operate, and how do these contexts shape or influence the decisions governments make?
2. What are the major objectives and interests of states in international politics, and what strategies do they employ to achieve them?
3. How are the choices made by states explained?[2]

At the heart of these questions is the concept of power. Power is defined as the ability to get others to do things they would not ordinarily do or to behave in ways they would prefer to avoid. This definition clearly implies that power is relative and is, to a large extent, a psychological relationship because it aims at changing the way people think. Power is also contextual, meaning that a country may exercise power over another country in one context but not in another. Central to an understanding of international relations is the view that the interactions among countries are characterized by a struggle for power.[3] This emphasis on states as the dominant, almost exclusive, actors in world politics is referred to as the **state-centric model**.

All fields of study are concerned with theories. Human beings develop theories as they deal with various problems. There are theories about how things should work or why they don't work. Parents and psychologists develop theories on how children should be raised, and financial analysts develop theories about how the stock market will perform. The general purpose of a **theory** is to describe, explain, and predict how humans behave or how things work in the real world under certain circumstances. A theory is generally defined as an orderly, logical, integrated set of ideas or statements about human behavior or things in our environment. All theories provide conceptual frameworks and simplify complex realities. Because humans create theories, there are inevitably inconsistencies in theories and conflicts among them. Theories not only compete, they also overlap. Most scholars realize that there are usually valuable insights in most theories and avoid thinking that there is one best theory.

PLURALISM AND INTERDEPENDENCE

A theory marking the transition from traditional international relations to global issues is pluralism and interdependence. Although this approach views states as the most important actors in world politics, it takes **nonstate actors** (i.e., organizations that are not formally associated with governments) into consideration. Its main concern is with how human activities are intertwined and interconnected across national boundaries. Nonstate actors are increasingly independent of countries and play a crucial role in setting the international agenda and solving international problems. An important point of the pluralist-interdependence approach is that the growing economic interdependence of states has linked the fates of most countries together.

It is increasingly clear to both practitioners and observers of international affairs that new and far-reaching forces of globalization are having such profound effects on the world that how we approach international relations must also be significantly transformed. James N. Rosenau and Mary Durfee have concluded that "daily occurrences of complex and uncertain developments in every region of the world are so pervasive as to cast doubt on the viability of the long-established ways in which international affairs have been conducted and analyzed."[4] The rapid proliferation of states as well as nonstate actors, revolutions in technology and communications, the growing sophistication and global views of many ordinary citizens, and the changing nature of conflicts are all contributing to the complex environments in which we live.[5]

The formative experiences of individuals influence their behavior even late in their lives. The same can be said of states. The violence and threat of violence that accompanied the emergence of modern states led to the pervasive emphasis on military power as the highest priority of states. The fear of losing territory or being eliminated was very real. It is estimated that 95 percent of the state-units in Europe at the beginning of the sixteenth century have been destroyed or combined to make other countries.[6] The devastating effectiveness of military force and the development of nuclear weapons that threatened the extinction of most of the world made countries, especially the superpowers, extremely reluctant to use military force.

In addition to terrorism, there are other nontraditional threats to national security. Economic competition, population growth and migration, organized crime, drug trafficking, environmental problems, poverty, inequality, and ethnic conflicts are among the threats to security. Recognition of these threats is strengthening the concept of human security in an increasingly global society. **Human security** is

State-Centric Model
The view that world politics is dominated almost exclusively by state actors

Theory
Predicts how humans behave or how things work in the real world under specific circumstances

Nonstate Actors
Organizations that are not formally associated with governments and play a crucial role in setting the international agenda

Human Security
A concept of security that deals with the everyday challenges humans face that don't involve military issues

viewed as being linked to challenges that human beings face every day, most of which are not primarily related to military power. The concept of human security focuses on seven categories of threats.[7] They are

1. **Economic security** (an assured basic income)
2. **Food security** (access to an adequate supply of food)
3. **Health security** (access to basic health care)
4. **Environmental security** (access to clean water, clean air, etc.)
5. **Personal security** (safety from physical violence and threats)
6. **Community security** (safety from ethnic cleansing and genocide)
7. **Political security** (protection of basic human rights and freedoms)

This concept of human security shifts the emphasis from the state to the dignity and freedom of human beings, regardless of national boundaries. The focus on human security diminishes the perception of states as sovereign, discrete units. In fact, human security transcends the state. In some cases, the pursuit of human security requires humanitarian intervention in sovereign states.

The growing complexity of our world is generally viewed as giving rise to a new period in international relations, or postinternational politics.[8] This transition is characterized by greater attention to interdependence and globalization, and a stronger emphasis on global politics in particular and global issues in general. **Global politics** refers to political issues and activities by states and nonstate actors that extend across national boundaries and that have implications for most of the world. The concepts of interdependence and globalization are at the heart of global politics. But globalization itself is a hotly debated concept. Global politics captures the complexity of the connections and interactions among states, nonstate actors, national groups, and individuals. Global politics calls attention to the need for cooperation, rather than conflict, to deal with many of the world's problems. But the concept of global politics inadequately portrays how economic, cultural, environmental, and demographic factors, among others, are creating a global society with **global norms** (i.e., a set of basic values that are increasingly common to human societies). This book focuses on **global issues**. The term global issues conveys concerns with problems that go beyond the narrower focus on politics. Stressing global issues indicates a recognition of how globalization intertwines many aspects of human activities and how essential it is to adopt an interdisciplinary approach in order to understand our world and its impact on our daily lives. A global issue can be economic, political, cultural, strategic, environmental, scientific, or technological in nature. The essential aspect of a global issue is its impact on the world community and the widespread response to the issue. Where the problem originated is not the primary concern. Instead, we must look at its global implications. For example, the spread of AIDS, avian flu, and other infectious diseases has serious implications for all of us, directly and indirectly, regardless of where the diseases originated. Global warming, global crime, weapons proliferation, terrorism, global inequality, population and migration, and cultural conflicts occupy the attention of individuals, governments, international organizations, the media, and nonstate actors around the world.

Global Politics

Political issues and activities that have implications for most of the world

Global Norms

A set of basic values that are increasingly common to human societies

Global Issues

Encompass traditional international relations and worldwide politics

THE GROWTH OF THE MODERN STATE

The state as we know it emerged over several centuries through struggles for power among institutions, groups, and individuals with military, economic, cultural, religious, and political interests. As we will see, the power of ideas played a pivotal role in the process. The spread of **humanism**—with its emphasis on the study of ancient Greek and Hebrew texts, which concentrated on the Bible—strengthened individualism and critical thinking. Humanism was accompanied by the **Renaissance**, which evolved in Italy in the fourteenth century and marked the transition from the Middle Ages to modern times. Like humanism, the Renaissance concentrated on the individual, self-consciousness, creativity, exploration, and science. The combination of ideas, technological developments, ambition, the quest for freedom, and the constant struggle for power radically altered accepted practices, institutions, and patterns of authority. Because the Catholic Church was the dominant institution in Western Europe following the decline and fall of the Roman Empire, it was inevitably the target of those advocating change. Challenges to the Catholic Church were strengthened by the development of technology, namely, the printing press. **Johann Gutenberg** (1397–1468) invented the printing press around 1436, just as the Chinese and Koreans had done earlier. Together with a growing body of literature and the questioning of authority, the printing press facilitated the distribution of information about papal corruption and weakened the Church's ability to exercise almost exclusive control over ideas and ways of thinking. As the Church's influence eroded, queens, princes, and kings in Europe attempted to enhance their own power by promoting national consciousness and territorial independence.

They were assisted in their efforts to consolidate their secular authority within their territories by the Protestant Reformation. This does not mean that European royalty emerged with an antireligious character. In fact, a clear separation of church and state within European countries is still a subject of debate today. This religious transformation was gradual. The most outspoken critic of the Catholic Church was **Martin Luther** (1483–1546), a professor of theology at the University of Wittenberg who had been motivated to act by the campaign for selling indulgences (i.e., pardons of temporal or secular punishment due to sin) in Germany.[9] European monarchs also formed alliances with merchants to weaken the Catholic Church and the Holy Roman Empire. The existence of numerous small political units made it extremely difficult to engage in profitable trade and other economic transactions beyond their limited boundaries. Larger, unified political systems were beneficial to businesses because of the existence of uniform regulations and fewer taxing jurisdictions, and the enhanced ability of larger areas to enforce the laws. These economic interests coincided with the various monarchs' desire to collect more taxes in order to acquire military technology and build larger armies.

Traveling through Europe, one notices that many towns are dominated by old castles. These castles symbolized not only military strength by also the political and economic independence of local barons, many of whom were loyal to the Holy Roman emperor and the Catholic Church. Refinement of cannons and the availability of gunpowder enabled Europe's kings and queens to effectively challenge barons and

Humanism

A system of thought that centers on human beings and their values, capacities, and worth

Renaissance

The humanistic revival in Europe of classical art, architecture, literature, and learning

Johann Gutenberg

(1397–1468); German inventor of the printing press

Martin Luther

(1483–1546); German theologian and Reformation leader

FIGURE 1.1 Europe in the Sixteenth Century

others, and to consolidate their power over increasingly larger areas. Between 1400 and 1600, large numbers of the smaller political entities lost their independence.[10] An excellent example of how Europe's monarchs strengthened internal control as they tried to weaken the power of the Catholic Church is provided by England's King Henry VIII in 1534. Named Defender of the Faith in 1521 for his strong support of the Catholic Church, the king clashed with Rome when he decided to divorce his first wife, Catherine of Aragon, on the grounds that she could not produce a son. Instead of retreating after being excommunicated by the pope, King Henry VIII persuaded England's Parliament to make him Protector and Only Supreme Head of the Church and Clergy of England, thereby creating the Anglican Church. By taking control of England's Catholic Church and its assets, the king ignited the spark of English nationalism and increased his own economic, political, and religious power.

Religious, cultural, political, economic, and technological developments ultimately led to the outbreak of the Thirty Years' War in 1618. The German Protestant princes, who also fought each other, were allied with France, Sweden, Denmark, and England against the Holy Roman Empire, represented by the Hapsburgs of Spain and the Catholic princes. The Hapsburgs, also concerned about maintaining their own power, often clashed with each other.[11] The Thirty Years' War had devastating consequences for Germany. It is estimated that two-thirds of the population perished and that five-sixths of the villages in the empire were destroyed. Those who survived experienced great hardship.[12]

SOVEREIGNTY

The concept of sovereignty was first articulated in ancient Rome where ongoing, widespread violence and disorder demonstrated the need for stronger government. Freeing the ruler from restraint was regarded as being a lesser evil than the existence of violence and disorder.[13]

Pressures for change that spread across Europe were accompanied by the formulation of new philosophies. The interaction of the power of ideas and change is demonstrated by **Jean Bodin** (1530–1596) and his major contribution to the modern idea of sovereignty. Bodin was a French social and political philosopher and lawyer. During the last half of the sixteenth century France was experiencing severe disorder, caused primarily by conflicts between Roman Catholics and the **Huguenots** (i.e., French Protestants who were followers of John Calvin). Bodin believed that order could be restored through a combination of greater religious tolerance and the establishment of a fully sovereign monarch. In his **Six Books on the Commonwealth** (or state), Bodin stressed that the state, represented by the king, was sovereign. Sovereignty, from Bodin's viewpoint, was the absolute and perpetual power of the state.

Jean Bodin

(1530–1596); French social and political philosopher and lawyer

Universal Catholic laws that governed Europe were replaced by **international law**. Leaders and scholars realized that states also needed a system of rules and norms to govern their interaction and to establish order and predictability. This view was articulated by **Hugo Grotius** (1583–1645). Grotius was a Dutch lawyer, author, strong advocate of natural law, and is regarded as the father of international law. Grotius stressed that sovereign states were governed by natural law because they were composed of human beings who were ruled by nature and because it was in the interest of sovereign states to support an international legal system. A second component of the new international system was **diplomacy**. Diplomats, their possessions, and their embassies were regarded as extensions of sovereign states and accorded extraordinary legal protections. A third component of the system for maintaining international order was the **balance of power**, which attempted to prevent a state or group of states from becoming strong enough to dominate Europe. Finally, the new international system would rely on common cultural values and family connections to avoid disorder.[14]

International Law

An international system of rules created to govern the interaction of states and to establish order

Diplomacy

The practice of conducting international relations

There has always been a gap between the ideal of sovereignty and the actual practice and realization of sovereignty. In a world characterized by a struggle for power, there will always be unequal power and unequal results. Legal sovereignty and operational sovereignty are not always the same. Although legal sovereignty recognizes the rights of states to do certain things, those rights are usually compromised by the various

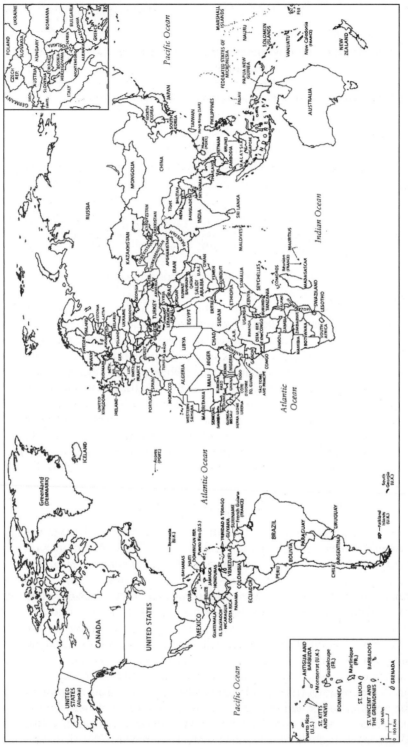

FIGURE 1.2 Political Map of the World

countries' ability to secure those rights in practice. Sovereignty is used in at least four ways:

International legal sovereignty, which focuses on the recognition of a state's independence by other states and respect for its territorial boundaries.

Westphalian sovereignty, which focuses on the exclusion of other states from the affairs of the government that exists within a given territory.

Internal or domestic sovereignty, which refers to the rights of the government or formal organization of political authority within a state to exercise a monopoly of power over social, economic, political, and other activities within its borders.

Interdependence sovereignty, which reflects the realities of globalization. It is concerned with the ability of governments to control or regulate the flow of people, money, trade, environmental hazards, information, and ideas across national boundaries.[15]

The Decline of Sovereignty

Global realities today demand that states share power with nonstate actors, that they cooperate to deal with threats they cannot control by themselves, and that they pay attention to global public opinion and the forces of economic, cultural, financial, political, criminal, and environmental globalization. Information and technological revolutions and the ease of international travel are contributing to the erosion of a state's control over its population as well as to the decline of citizens' identification with the state, two of the key components of sovereignty. Although most governments continue to exert significant influence over their domestic economies, many governments are perceived as "mere salesmen, promoting the fortunes of their own multinational corporations in the hope that this will provide a core prosperity that keeps everyone afloat."[16]

THE EUROPEAN UNION: REDEFINING SOVEREIGNTY

Klaus Schroeder grew up in Donaustauf, a small German town overlooking the Danube. The German mark evoked strong emotions in Klaus. But in 2001 the mark was replaced with the **euro,** the common currency of most countries of the European Union. Just as the dollar is a symbol of American power and independence, the mark symbolized German power and sovereignty. Although Karl and other ordinary Germans preferred to keep the mark, German leaders regarded the adoption of a common European currency as an essential step toward strengthening European political union and firmly anchoring a reunified and bigger Germany into a bigger Europe. Compared with America, where sovereignty remains a powerful and positive idea, European states are voluntarily relinquishing some of their sovereignty to achieve political and economic objectives. On December 13, 2002, European leaders redrew the map of Europe by extending the fifteen-member European Union eastward to include ten additional countries, most of them former Communist bloc countries. This unprecedented European expansion created a new Europe that has a

Euro

Common European currency established by the European Union

Jean Monnet

French statesman and distinguished economist

Robert Schuman

French Prime Minister after WWII who proposed the Schuman plan for pooling the coal and steel resources of West Europe

Paul Henri Spaak

Foreign Minister of Belgium who was elected first president of the General Assembly of the United Nations

Treaty of Rome

Established the European Economic Community as an economic alliance

European Court of Justice

A judicial arm of the European Union, based in Luxembourg

NGOs

Organizations that are not part of a government

population of 480 million and an economy that exceeds $10 trillion. The general view is that European countries are modifying their sovereignty on a scale not seen since the Emperor Charlemagne tried to unify Europe 1,200 years ago.[17]

Devastating wars, as we have seen, were instrumental in the growth of sovereignty and the rise of the modern state. But many Europeans began to believe that excessive sovereignty and nationalism were leading causes of wars that engulfed the continent and destroyed the most basic aspects of security and independence. This was especially the case in World War II. Statesmen such as **Jean Monnet** and **Robert Schuman** of France and **Paul Henri Spaak** of Belgium were visionaries who believed that a united Europe, in which traditional sovereignty would be redefined, was essential to preserving peace and security and preventing another European holocaust. The basic idea was that controlling coal and steel (materials essential for war) would ultimately result in the reconciliation of Europe. France and Germany, the two principal antagonists, would combine their coal and steel production. In 1957, France, Germany, Italy, Belgium, the Netherlands, and Luxembourg signed a treaty that led to the creation of the Coal and Steel Community, the first major European institution. The Europeans signed the **Treaty of Rome** in 1957, which established both the European Economic Community and the European Atomic Energy Community (EURATOM). Since then, in many areas of political and economic life, power has been gradually transferred from the state level to the European Union and its various institutions.[18] For example, the **European Court of Justice** has powers that are similar to those of the U.S. Supreme Court. It has weakened the sovereignty of states by declaring that the laws of the European Union are supreme in relation to the laws of individual states. So, in addition to losing the mark as his national currency, Klaus Schroeder is also affected by a wide array of European regulations and institutions.

THE RISE OF NONSTATE ACTORS

Nonstate actors, or **nongovernmental organizations (NGOs),** are not formally associated with states or the authority structures of states, although they often cooperate with the government to achieve their goals. Transnational NGOs operate across national boundaries and have achieved significant influence in world affairs. Their rapid proliferation, from around 200 in 1909 to more than 26,000 today, and their wide range of activities have led many observers to conclude that their emergence is almost as important as the rise of the nation-state. *Several factors have contributed to their growth.* These include (1) the spread of democracy around the world, (2) an increase in global problems that states are ill equipped to solve unilaterally, (3) problems created by the proliferation of weak states, (4) the computer and telecommunications revolutions, and (5) relatively easy and inexpensive transportation. It has become easier for groups of people to organize and interact across national boundaries.

There are several types of NGOs. These include:

Economic organizations, such as transnational corporations;

Advocacy organizations, such as Greenpeace and Amnesty International;

Service organizations, such as the International Red Cross, and Doctors Without Borders;

Transnational terrorist organizations that seek to undermine governments; and

Transnational criminal organizations that focus on profiting from illegal activities.

With the exception of terrorist and criminal NGOs, nonstate actors have played **four main roles** that are generally accepted by states and international governmental institutions. They are as follows:

1. **Setting Agendas.** NGOs often force national policymakers to include certain issues on their agendas. For example, the British and Foreign Anti-Slavery Society in the early 1800s persuaded the British government to act to end the slave trade. Similarly, the Anglo-Oriental Society for the Suppression of the Opium Trade (trading in opium was legal) was instrumental in the passage of the Hague Opium Convention in 1912, which outlawed the opium trade.
2. **Negotiating Outcomes.** NGOs work with governments to solve global problems. Environmental groups often collaborate with business groups and governments on such issues as sustainable development and climate change.
3. **Conferring Legitimacy.** Organizations, such as the World Bank, and transnational corporations derive legitimacy from the support or approval of various NGOs.
4. **Making Solutions Work.** Many governments and intergovernmental organizations rely on NGOs to implement their decisions in such areas as humanitarian relief and economic development.[19] Two of the oldest and most significant nonstate actors are the Catholic Church and transnational corporations.

The Catholic Church

On the streets outside the Palazzo Montecitorio, where the lower house of Italy's Parliament meets, crowds gathered to participate in an historic event on November 14, 2002. Pope John Paul II was scheduled to address 800 lawmakers and national leaders, including Prime Minister Silvio Berlusconi. Given the fact that Italy is predominantly Catholic, you are probably wondering why such an address would be significant. The pope's speech marked the first time a head of the Catholic Church had ever made an appearance in the Italian Parliament.[20] The geographic proximity between the Vatican and Italians has engendered strong emotional attachments to the Catholic Church on the one hand and deep suspicions of the Vatican on the other. While many Catholics in the Americas strongly oppose abortion, for example, Italy legalized abortion and divorce there is common. The turbulent relationship between the Italians and the Vatican has its roots in the historical struggles between church and state. Much of Italy, unlike the rest of Europe, continued to be ruled by popes until the middle of the nineteenth century. In 1871, Italy was largely free of control by the papal authorities and popes were deprived of almost all their land. A compromise between the Vatican and the Italian government was reached in 1929, when the **Lateran Treaty**, negotiated

Lateran Treaty

A compromise between the Vatican and the Italian government

Pope addressing
Italy's Parliament

Benito Mussolini

Italian fascist
dictator and prime
minister from
1922–1943

with **Benito Mussolini**, the Italian dictator and leader of the fascist movement, was signed. The Italian government recognized Vatican City as fully sovereign and independent, and the Vatican recognized the Italian government.

The Vatican has voiced strong opinions on social, economic, political, and military issues, especially under the leadership of Pope John Paul II. For many years the Catholic Church strongly opposed communism and reached out to Catholics in Poland and other Communist bloc countries in an effort to undermine communist rule. Pope John Paul, a native of Poland, played a major role in the fall of communism in Eastern Europe. But the pope also criticized the West for its extreme materialism and individualism, as well as for its tolerance of poverty and inequality in the developing countries. The Catholic Church consistently condemned the proliferation of nuclear weapons in the United States, Russia, and other countries and strongly opposed America's military action against Iraq. Human rights concerns, which were sometimes overlooked historically, have also been a priority for the Catholic Church. Pope John Paul visited more than 120 countries in an attempt to spread his church's message. An important part of that message has been reconciliation among different religions. The Vatican has quietly but persistently attempted to bring an end to the conflict between Israelis and Palestinians. But the Catholic Church was besieged with its own problems, especially in 2002 when widespread sexual abuse by Catholic priests became a global issue. The death of Pope John Paul II on April 2, 2005, and the selection of Cardinal Joseph Ratzinger of Germany as the new pope (Benedict XVI) have raised new challenges for the Catholic Church. These include the growth of Islam

MNC

A companys that
operates in more
than one country
and depends on
interdependence
for the operation of
its enterprise

and the decline of Catholicism in Europe, an increase in the number of Catholics in Africa and Asia, and a decline in applicants for the priesthood.

Transnational Corporations

Whether one is putting gas in a car or buying shoes, it is very difficult to avoid being affected by transnational corporations. The origins of products are increasingly hard to determine, and companies' bargaining power vis-à-vis governments in relation to manufacturing and selling these products is growing. A **multinational corporation** is generally defined as a national company that has many foreign subsidiaries. These subsidiaries are basically self-contained, making what they sell in a particular country, buying their supplies from that country, and employing that country's citizens. **Transnational corporations** are structurally different from multinational corporations. A transnational corporation is organized as a global entity. While selling, servicing, public relations, and legal matters are local, planning, research, finance, pricing, marketing, and management are conducted with the world market in mind.[21] Companies were instrumental in the conquest and settlement of North America, India, Southern Africa, and elsewhere. The **British East India Company** was in effect the government of British-controlled areas of India for a long time. The **Dutch West India Company** was granted a charter that allowed it to make agreements and alliances with leaders of conquered areas, to construct fortifications, to appoint and discharge governors, to raise armies, to provide administrative services, and to maintain order.[22] Transnational corporations are among the driving forces of globalization.

Transnational Corporations

Organizations with a global outlook and operations

British East India Company

Established under a royal charter of Queen Elizabeth I for the purposes of spice trading; it launched British rule of India

Dutch West India Company

Trading and colonizing company, chartered by the States-General of the Dutch republic in 1621 and organized in 1623

You DECIDE | ## Multinational Companies and Patriotism

While many of you think of the Caribbean islands as sunny places that provide a refuge from winter, many corporations have long regarded Bermuda, the Cayman Islands, the Bahamas, and elsewhere as tax havens, places of refuge from the U.S. Internal Revenue Service. Compared with many Caribbean islands, the United States is not an especially friendly tax environment. But under U.S. tax law, a company can have its headquarters in the Cayman Islands without having any operations or management there. Prior to September 11, 2001, President George W. Bush pressured the thirty members of the Organization for Economic

Cooperation and Development (OECD) to end their opposition to such offshore tax havens. But when Stanley Works of Connecticut proposed to reincorporate in Bermuda in February 2002, it ran into strong opposition. Many Americans regarded the practice of moving to Bermuda and elsewhere to avoid taxes as unpatriotic.

Do you consider it unpatriotic to move a company's headquarters overseas to avoid paying taxes?

Source: Jonathan Weisman, "A Question of Patriotism," *The Washington Post National Weekly Edition*, 2–8 September 2002, 19.

INTERDEPENDENCE AND GLOBALIZATION

Human societies have always been characterized by varying degrees of interdependence. Most of us do not grow the food we eat, make the clothes we wear, manufacture the cars we drive, produce the water we drink, build the homes we live in, or take care of many of our basic needs. We depend on each other to accomplish both profound and mundane objectives. **Interdependence** in world affairs, as it is in private life, involves mutual dependence and cooperation. This mutual dependence means that what happens in one place usually has consequences elsewhere. A war in Iraq, for example, drives up the price of gas at your neighborhood gas station. Countries rely on each other for raw materials, security, trade, and environmental protection. Their fates are intertwined, and they share a sense of mutual vulnerability, although some states are clearly more vulnerable than others in some areas. At the heart of the concept of interdependence is reciprocity.[23]

Globalization is a complex and far-reaching form of interdependence. Globalization not only creates more obvious and extensive webs of interdependence, it also makes their impact more immediate and more widespread. Globalization refers to the shrinking of distances among the various continents, a wider geographic sense of vulnerability, and a worldwide interconnectedness of important aspects of human life, including religion, migration, war, finance, trade, diseases, drugs, sex, food, and music. Globalization implies a significant and obvious blurring of distinctions between the internal and external affairs of countries and the weakening of differences among countries. Some countries, and groups within countries, are more entangled in the networks of globalization than others. Not everyone has access to the Internet, television, or telephones, and many people around the world cannot afford to consume many of the products of globalization. Although globalization is generally regarded as the Americanization of the world, America itself is profoundly shaped by the forces of globalization.[24]

Interdependence

A political and economic situation in which two states are simultaneously dependent on each other for their well-being

Globalization

The integration of markets, politics, values, and environmental concerns across borders

CAUSES OF GLOBALIZATION

The process of globalization has been occurring for a long time and, like most changes, it has been marked by advances and retreats, by hope and disappointment. But it marches on. The causes of globalization are inseparable from the human desire to explore, to gain greater physical and economic security, to be creative and curious, and to move from one place to another. Migration, as we will discuss, is as old as human societies. When some of our ancestors left Africa they began the process of globalization. But migration, like other causes of globalization, did not occur without the assistance of some basic forms of technology. The movement of large numbers of people from one part of the world to another over a relatively short period of time was facilitated by improvements in transportation. Canal building, the development of navigational equipment (such as the compass), the ability to construct stable oceangoing vessels, and the development and improvement of railways helped to speed up migration. Improved transportation also made it easier to conduct trade over long distances and to colonize new areas. Rapid and inexpensive transportation is a major cause of globalization today.

Together with revolutions in communications, transportation plays a crucial role in shrinking distances and in creating greater interdependence among people and nations. Container ships in Long Beach, California, for example, are visible and constant reminders of how transportation links cultures and economies. Inexpensive airline travel has made migration a global reality and constantly reminds us how small the world is becoming and how problems in a distant country can spread to our own.

Advances in military and medical technologies have also driven globalization. Military technology, as we have seen, allowed states to consolidate power internally and subsequently to challenge other states for power and dominance. The ability to mount a canon on a ship gave a country a decisive advantage over its opponents and also allowed the countries possessing them to expand commerce and to acquire territories. The spread of empires is inseparable from innovations in military power. Perhaps nothing reminds us more about our interdependence than nuclear weapons and other weapons of mass destruction. Our security is still greatly determined by the ability of nuclear powers to preserve the strategic balance and to prevent the use of nuclear weapons. Our sensitivity to how military weapons link our fates was heightened during the **Cold War** (i.e., the competition between the United States and the Soviet Union that occurred after World War II). In addition to the threat posed by state-controlled nuclear weapons, we have entered into an age of uncertainty heralded in by the use of both conventional and unconventional weapons by terrorist organizations. Medical technology, like military technology, has assisted globalization, and its inability to successfully control infectious diseases, such as AIDS, increases our sense of vulnerability in a global society. Advances in medical technology have played a crucial role in virtually all aspects of globalization. By enabling people to live longer and healthier lives, medical technology has contributed to improvements in other areas of technology, advances in commerce, and developments in culture. For example, imagine how much talent would be wasted without the availability of eyeglasses and contact lenses.

Cold War

The hostile relations between the two superpowers, the U.S. and the U.S.S.R., from 1945–1990

While we tend to focus on revolutions in telecommunications and computer technologies as driving forces of globalization, the progress we are experiencing today is based on older scientific and technological innovations that are mostly overlooked and forgotten. As Table 1.1 indicates, commerce and finance provided the foundation for many of these advances. A major cause of globalization is **financial market expansion**. The availability of finance encouraged more economic interactions, innovation, entrepreneurship, and the development of new technologies. New technologies made it easier to conduct trade, migrate, conquer territories, and resist diseases. These new technologies have now spread around the world, speeding up innovation and strengthening competition. Michael Pettis argues that globalization takes place largely because investors are willing to take risks.[25]

Financial Market Expansion

The global expansion of national markets

The emphasis on revolutions in telecommunications and computers as a major cause of globalization is due in part to the obvious implications that these new technologies have on all of us on a daily basis. While the impact of CNN and other global television networks on the majority of the world's population is overrated—especially since almost four-fifths of the world's population does not have access to television—the speed with which news travels around the world makes news networks a potent symbol of globalization.

TABLE 1.1 PERIODS OF MONETARY EXPANSION AND GLOBALIZATION

Period	New Technologies and Commercial Applications
1807–1844	Extensive canal building, railway boom, steam power used in manufacturing, improved machine tool design, invention of McCormick's reaper, commercial gas-lighting, and development of the telegraph
1851–1873	Advances in mining, railways and shipping, and rapid growth of corporations
1881–1914	Increased productivity in Europe and the United States, improvements in steel production and heavy chemical manufacturing, first power station, spread of electricity, development of the internal combustion engine, and developments in canning and refrigeration
1922–1930	Commercialization of automobiles and aircraft, spread of artificial fibers and plastics, new electrical appliances invented, and telephone ownership grows
1960–1973	Development and application of transistor technology, advances in commercial flying and shipping, and the spread of telecommunications and software
1985–Present	Rapid growth in computer memory and information processing, advances in biotechnology and medical technologies, and commercial use of the Internet

Source: Michael Pettis, "Will Globalization Go Bankrupt?" *Foreign Policy*, No. 126 (September/October 2001), 56–57.

National leaders, policymakers, citizens who participate in important government decisions, and groups involved in nonstate actors are linked by global news networks and respond to developments almost simultaneously. This global network of communications underscores our sense of interdependence. Computers, telephones, and fax machines have augmented global communication. Individuals and groups around the world communicate instantaneously, and at very low cost. Fiber-optic cable and microwave and satellite systems have made it easier, cheaper, and faster to communicate. For example, in 1960, transatlantic telephone lines were capable of carrying a maximum of 138 conversations at once, compared with the fiber-optic cables that handle more than 1.5 million conversations today. Table 1.2 shows the huge growth in communication between 1990 and 2000.

Global communications have been facilitated by the spread of the English language around the world during an earlier period of globalization. America's dominant technological, economic, military, and cultural position in the world helps to reinforce the centrality of English in all aspects of global life. The communications revolution is regarded as the major cause of globalization because it directly affects economic, financial, military, cultural, environmental, and criminal globalization. For example, in May 2000, e-mail users around the world received an e-mail with a subject line that read, "I LOVE YOU." With it came an attached document labeled "LOVE-LETTER-FOR-YOU.TXT.VBS." When many e-mail users opened the attachment they contributed to spreading a computer virus created by a 23-year-old student in the Philippines. The "LOVE BUG" virus caused computers worldwide to crash at lightning speed, with devastating effects on communications, businesses, education, and medical care around the world. The "LOVE BUG" even penetrated the secret computer system of the code breakers at the U.S. National Security Agency, as

TABLE 1.2 GROWTH IN COMMUNICATION

Country	Telephone Mainlines (per 1,000 people)		Cellular Mobile Subscribers (per 1,000 people)		Internet Users (per 1,000 people)	
High Human Development	**1990**	**2002**	**1990**	**2002**	**1990**	**2002**
Norway	502	734	46	844	7.1	502.6
Sweden	681	736	54	889	5.8	573.1
Canada	565	635	22	377	3.7	512.8
United States	545	646	21	488	8	551.4
Netherlands	464	618	5	745	3.3	506.3
Japan	441	558	7	637	0.2	448.9
Finland	534	523	52	867	4	508.9
France	495	569	5	647	0.5	313.8
United Kingdom	441	591	19	841	0.9	423.1
Germany	441	651	5	727	1.4	411.9
Italy	388	481	5	939	0.2	352.4
New Zealand	434	448	16	622	0	484.4
Spain	316	506	1	824	0.1	156.3
Greece	389	491	0	845	0	154.7
Medium Human Development						
Mexico	65	147	1	255	0	98.5
Russian Federation	140	242	0	120	0	40.9
Thailand	24	105	1	260	0	77.6
Philippines	10	42	0	191	0	0.3
Turkey	121	281	1	347	0	72.8
China	6	167	0	161	0	46
India	6	40	0	12	0	15.9
Low Human Development						
Pakistan	8	25	0	8	0	10.3
Bangladesh	2	5	0	8	0	1.5
Zambia	9	8	0	13	0	4.8
Mali	1	5	0	5	0	2.4
Niger	1	2	0	1	0	1.3
Sierra Leone	3	5	0	4	0	1.6

Source: United Nations Development Program, Human Development Report 2004
(New York: Oxford University Press, 2004), 180–183.

well as some classified systems at the Pentagon.[26] Many terrorist groups, criminal gangs, and individuals rely on global communications to conduct their activities.

FORMS OF GLOBALIZATION

Among the most important forms of globalization are (1) economic and trade globalization, (2) financial globalization, (3) political globalization, (4) military globalization, (5) cultural globalization, (6) environmental globalization, and (7) criminal globalization.

Although we will discuss each of these forms separately, they cannot be neatly separated from each other in the real world. All forms of globalization soon become interdependent. For example, economic globalization and financial globalization facilitate the spread of criminal globalization and environmental globalization, which, in turn, focus attention on the need for greater political globalization, and so on.

Economic Globalization

Economic Globalization

Free trade, open markets, and competition in the world economy

Economic globalization generally receives the most attention by scholars, the media, and political leaders. **Economic globalization** may be defined as the intercontinental exchange of products, services, and labor. This form of globalization has a long history, and has intensified with the emergence of new technologies and their diffusion to major parts of the world. Multinational corporations have been instrumental in globalization of both production and distribution networks. Consumers worldwide use similar products made by the same corporations. Buying an American brand or any other national brand is complicated by the nature of economic globalization.

Economies around the world develop greater capability to produce and export goods as they obtain capital, technology, and access to distribution networks. As trade increases, competition intensifies, leading to lower prices and the elimination of companies that cannot effectively compete in the global market. Global competition and the shrinking of space due to revolutions in communications technology and transportation combine to divide the world into areas that specialize in making products that require low-skilled labor.[27] But the speed of technological changes and the ease

TABLE 1.3 FOREIGN-OWNED AMERICAN BRANDS

Brand	Company	Country
Universal Studios, Sci-Fi Channel	Vivendi	France
Amoco	BP Amoco	United Kingdom
Snapple, Dr. Pepper, 7-Up	Cadbury Schweppes	United Kingdom
Shell	Royal Dutch Shell	United Kingdom/Netherlands
Holiday Inn	Six Continents Hotels	United Kingdom
Baby Ruth, Taster's Choice	Nestlé	Switzerland
Random House, RCA Records	Bertelsmann	Germany
Brooks Brothers	Retail Brand Alliance	Italy
Vaseline, Slim-Fast	Unilever	United Kingdom
Jeep	Daimler Chrysler	Germany
Giant Food, Stop and Shop	Royal Ahold	Netherlands
Mellon Bank	Royal Bank of Scotland	United Kingdom
Kent Cigarettes	British American Tobacco	United Kingdom
Burger King	Diageo	United Kingdom
Credit Suisse First Boston	Credit Suisse Group	Switzerland
Eureka Vacuum	ABElectrolux	Sweden

Source: The Washington Post National Weekly Edition, 2 June 2002, 20.

with which new technologies are transferred around the world make it hard for countries to maintain a competitive edge. Consumers are benefiting from low prices resulting from this intense competition. Economic globalization is manifested by the growth of regional economies, especially in North America, Europe, and the Asia Pacific region. Leading countries in these regions integrate less economically powerful countries, thereby expanding trade. These regions, in turn, develop stronger economic ties, deepening their interdependence. Many of the companies based in these regions form alliances in response to competition.

Economic globalization also includes the movement of people and the exchange of ideas. The most innovative companies encourage the formation of **global teams** that operate across national borders. This process is aided not only by rapid, easy, and inexpensive communication but also by the fact that employees have similar education and training. Multinationals usually have training camps that help to create a common corporate culture. Engineers from India, Japan, Germany, Australia, and elsewhere who work for Hewlett-Packard, for example, work with their American counterparts in Los Gatos, California.[28] Economic globalization has also stimulated the development of **global cities**, such as New York, London, Tokyo, Shanghai, Hong Kong, Milan, Sidney, Zurich, and Chicago. Companies put their headquarters in major cities to take advantage of the services of lawyers, accountants, consultants, and advertising firms. Global cities concentrate talent in a relatively small area and allow companies to have easy access to the rest of the world.

Global Teams

Groups of employees who work across national boarders in multinational corporations

Global Cities

Major financial cities where companies place their headquarters

FINANCIAL GLOBALIZATION

Terrorist attacks on the World Trade Center and the Pentagon on September 11, 2001, sent shock waves through financial markets worldwide, painfully demonstrating direct linkages among American, European, Asian, and Latin American economies. The financial world reacted in a synchronized manner, with each market that opened the day following the attacks falling precipitously in the first few minutes. A flood of sell orders

TABLE 1.4 GLOBAL AIRLINE ALLIANCES, AIRLINE GROUPS (2002)

Group	Members (Airlines)	Global Market Share (%)
Star	Air Canada, Air New Zealand, ANA, Austrian Airlines, Lufthansa, SAS, Singapore Airlines, Thai Airways, United Airlines, Varig	21.7
Oneworld Alliance	Aer Lingus, American Airlines, British Airways, Cathay Pacific, Finnair, Iberia, Lan Chile, Qantas	16.1
Sky Team	Aeromexico, Air France, Alitalia, CSA Czech Airlines, Delta Airlines, Korean Airlines	12.0
Wings	KLM, Northwest Airlines	6.0

Sources: Airline Business and the *Economist*, 30 November 2002.

inundated the Tokyo Stock Exchange, delaying the opening and pushing the benchmark Nikkei index down 6 percent. All of the major stock markets declined dramatically in the week after the terrorist attacks, as Figure 1.3 shows. The decline in the U.S. housing market in 2006 had both domestic and global ramifications, given America's economic power.

Global financial markets, even under ordinary circumstances, are likely to experience unpredictable changes and to be affected by each other. Instability, as we have seen, cannot be confined to a few markets. Instead, financial problems spread across the world almost instantaneously, reflecting how revolutions in telecommunications and computers have linked financial institutions. Rapid increases in financial flows from rich countries to developing societies—rising from $10 billion to $20 billion a year in the 1980s to $280 billion in 1997—have integrated financial markets to an unprecedented degree.[29]

Four basic developments drive **financial globalization**, leading to the expansion and deepening of global finance. The first is the *consolidation of financial institutions* in most countries. Local banks were, until about two decades ago, largely locally owned and operated. Today, the local bank is likely to be owned by a much larger bank in a major city. The number of independent financial institutions is declining as mergers and acquisitions result in larger financial institutions. The second development is the *globalization of operations*, which is evident everywhere as banking conglomerates extend their reach by forming strategic alliances with similar institutions in different countries. European, American, and Asian financial institutions are increasingly linked, and major banks in the industrial world are acquiring banks in developing countries. A third development is the emergence of *new technologies* that are familiar to all of us. Money moves across national boundaries at the touch of a button. Internet banking and brokerage services compete with more traditional financial conglomerates. Taking advantage of advances in telecommunications, many financial institutions are using their online operation to expand into foreign markets without having branches there. The fourth development is the *universalization of banking*. Growing competition in financial markets, the increasing irrelevance of national borders, and the increasingly complex relationships among businesses have contributed to a blurring of bank and nonbank financial services.[30]

Financial globalization, as we have discussed, has been the catalyst for the growth of other forms of globalization. But other forms of globalization have also strengthened financial globalization. When the British Empire stretched across much of the world, the British pound became the strongest and most desirable international currency. As British power receded, America rose to international prominence and the U.S. dollar became the leading global currency. In 1944, the United States, Britain, and other countries held a conference at Bretton Woods, New Hampshire, to determine the international financial order. The conference established the **Bretton Woods System**, which required the currencies of other countries to

STOCK INDEXES	PERCENT CHANGE
Britain	- 2.7%
S. and P. 500	- 4.9
Canada	- 5.9
Argentina	- 6.8
Nasdaq	- 6.8
Dow Jones ind. avg.	- 7.1
Spain	- 7.6
Japan	- 7.7
France	- 8.5
New Zealand	- 8.8
Australia	- 9.0
Germany	- 9.3
Hong Kong	-10.5
Brazil	-11.6
Italy	-11.9
South Korea	-13.3
Mexico	-14.7
Singapore	-14.8
Thailand	-18.1

FIGURE 1.3 Financial Markets Response to Terrorists' Attack on September 11, 2001
Source: The New York Times, 18 September 2001, C3

have an exchange rate fixed to the dollar, with the dollar fixed in terms of gold at $35 an ounce. This arrangement gave the United States significant influence over the international money supply.

The Bretton Woods System set up the **World Bank** (also known as the International Bank for Reconstruction and Development) to help stimulate Europe's economic recovery after the devastation of World War II. It also created the **International Monetary Fund (IMF)** to implement the rules of the international financial system and to help countries experiencing short-term balance-of-payment and liquidity problems. IMF loans, which now go primarily to developing countries, are given with certain conditions attached, (e.g., reducing government spending, eliminating trade barriers, cutting social subsidies, devaluing currencies, and removing artificial barriers to foreign investment). As Europe recovered, and as the Soviet Union and other countries deposited their dollar holdings in West European banks, European banks receiving deposits in dollars simply kept them instead of changing them into the national currencies. The practice resulted in the growth of **Eurodollar** funds. Large U.S. budget deficits—caused partly by the Vietnam War, domestic inflation, and the practice of many American companies of depositing their foreign currency earnings in European banks—weakened the U.S. dollar and strengthened the Eurodollar. These developments eventually contributed to the collapse of the Bretton Woods System. On August 15, 1971, President Richard M. Nixon decided that the dollar was no longer to be freely convertible into gold, thereby ending fixed exchange rates. Furthermore, large financial surpluses accumulated by oil-exporting countries as a result of the quadrupling of oil prices by the **Organization of Petroleum Exporting Countries (OPEC)** in 1973 increased the liquidity of international banks. These financial institutions had approximately $50 billion to recycle through the world economy.[31] These developments provided the foundation for the current wave of financial globalization. Rapid economic growth in China, India, and other Asian countries, as well as in several countries in the Middle East and Latin America, has engendered capital movements between rich and poor countries. The United States, which has significant trade and budget deficits, is dependent on financial flows from developing countries, especially China and India.

Political Globalization

The growth of sovereignty in Europe marks the beginning of the modern period of political globalization in the sense that it created widespread recognition of states as the dominant political institutions. When European powers conquered areas in Asia, Africa, and Latin America, they brought with them the idea of the sovereign state, despite the colonial status given to areas under their control. An important aspect of political globalization is the worldwide acceptance of states. States share common characteristics, engage in similar behaviors, and are generally preoccupied with similar international and domestic policies. **Political globalization** is characterized by the acceptance of states, the relative power of states, the proliferation of international and regional organizations composed of states, and the spread of nonstate political actors. Political issues in one part of the world directly or indirectly affect many other areas. For example, conflicts in the Middle East have important ramifications for Europe,

Bretton Woods System
A post-WWII arrangement for managing the world economy; its main components are the World Bank and the International Monetary Fund

World Bank
A UN agency that deals with monetary aid transfers to developing nations, usually via a loan program varying from nation to nation

IMF
Established in 1944 to prevent countries from defaulting on their loans and to make financing available

Eurodollar
The process of European banks accepting dollars and not changing them into national currency

OPEC
Formed by major oil-producing nations in response to the control of the world oil market by seven major oil companies

Political Globalization

The proliferation of international and regional organizations composed of states and the spread of nonstate political actors

Multilateral Institutions

Organizations composed of many states pursuing common objectives

the United States, and Japan. The competition that dominated relations between the United States and the Soviet Union during the Cold War is an example of political globalization. The behavior of these superpowers had global implications, including the threat of a global nuclear holocaust. Most of the emphasis on political globalization is concentrated on the spread of **multilateral institutions**. These are organizations composed of many states pursuing common objectives, and include both international intergovernmental organizations (IGOs), such as the United Nations, the European Union, the Organization of American States, and the British Commonwealth. Some international organizations are universal in their mission and membership. An example is the United Nations. Others are limited in both their objectives and membership. Examples include the Organization of American States and the British Commonwealth. Although multilateral organizations are created by sovereign countries, they often develop their own institutional identities and act as independent entities, often in opposition to some of the states that formed them.

Political globalization is clearly intertwined with other forms of globalization and is a reflection of the realities of an increasingly global society. All societies are concerned with the authoritative allocation of values, the provision of public or collective goods, and legal norms that help to provide security and justice. Political globalization is evidence of eroding national boundaries. *Four developments have contributed to the spread of political globalization*:

1. **The revolutions in telecommunications and transportation,** which help to shrink distances and strengthen interdependence.
2. **The need to regulate various interactions and transactions** across national boundaries, which has led to the creation of legal norms and institutions.
3. **The growth of democratic values and institutions** and increased economic prosperity and educational opportunities for people worldwide, which augment demands for governments to be accountable and responsible not only to their own citizens but also to the global community.
4. **The increased monitoring of governments** by the media, individuals, and nonstate actors.

Policy Interdependence

National policies of one country are intertwined with those of other countries

International Regimes

International institutions designed to regulate the behavior of their members

Politics is both local and global. Many policies that were once considered to be primarily of local or national concern are now global, which suggests the strengthening of **policy interdependence**. In other words, national policies of one country are intertwined with those of other countries, and many national problems can be solved only through global cooperation. States form **international regimes** to cope with problems generated by complex interdependence. Regimes are essentially institutions designed to regulate the behavior of their members. The basic goal is to establish orderly and predictable interactions to secure the interests of those participating in these international institutions. At the heart of most international regimes is the concept of **global governance**, which refers to collective actions taken to establish international institutions and norms to deal with national and global issues.[32] For example, John Bolton, America's Ambassador to the UN, made reforming that organization a major priority in 2006. He believed that the UN was ineffective in dealing with significant global challenges.

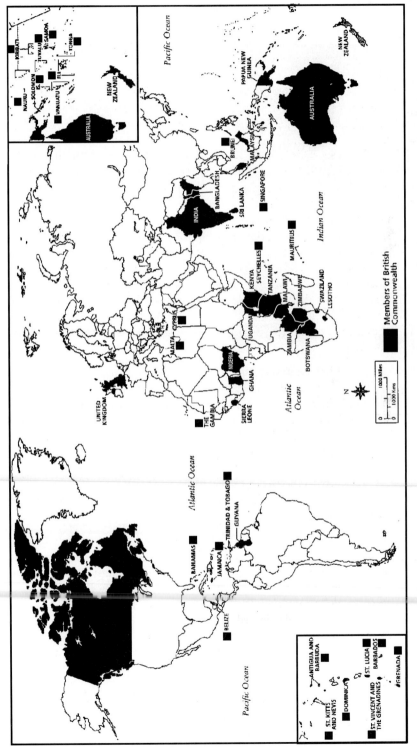

FIGURE 1.4 The British Commonwealth

23

UN Secretary General Kofi Annan

Military Globalization

Human societies have generally relied on the use of force to achieve certain objectives. The ability of one group to organize and to develop weapons gave that group significant advantages over groups that were disorganized and had less sophisticated weapons. It is not an exaggeration to say that force has always been a central component of human relations. The rise of great powers, the spread of civilizations, the age of imperialism, the dominance of one nation over others, and the rise of the nation-state itself, as we have seen, were inseparable from the application of military force. In a very real sense, military globalization is an integral part of other forms of globalization. **Military globalization** is characterized by extensive as well as intensive networks of military force. This includes both the actual use of force and threats to use violence. The most obvious example of military globalization is the nuclear age and the proliferation of weapons of mass destruction. The balance of terror created by nuclear weapons threatens the future of not only the countries that have them but also of all human existence on the earth. In less than thirty minutes the entire world can be completely destroyed by nuclear weapons, controlled primarily by the United States and Russia. The reality that we share a common destiny regardless of where we live or who we are makes military globalization the most potent form of globalization. *Military globalization is demonstrated by several developments in modern history*. These include

1. The *competition among European powers and territorial expansion* that resulted in the colonization of Asia, Africa, and the Americas;
2. The emergence *of international alliances and international security regimes*, such as the Concert of Europe and the North Atlantic Treaty Organization (NATO);
3. The *proliferation of weapons and military technologies worldwide*; and
4. The *creation of global institutions to deal with military issues*, such as the nuclear nonproliferation regime.[33]

Cultural Globalization

Alyson, an American toddler, is fascinated with Barney and enjoys being read *Barney's Color Surprise*. Older American children watch the Teletubbies, and both children and adults have made Harry Potter one of the world's most famous characters. Although these are British products, few Americans are concerned about their national origins. Looking at the shelves in the local grocery store, one is likely to find more salsa than ketchup. Indian curry dishes have replaced fish and chips as Britain's most popular fast food. Management

Global Governance

Collective actions taken to establish international institutions and norms to deal with national and global issues

Military Globalization

Networks of military force that operate internationally

meetings at big banks like Deutsche Bank in Germany and Credit Suisse in Switzerland are routinely conducted in English. Airbus, the European aircraft manufacturer, uses English as its official language. In fact, from Asia to Europe, English is the dominant language of business, entertainment, and finance. These examples show that societies are increasingly linked culturally and socially. But human beings have interacted from the earliest times, and there has long been extensive borrowing from different civilizations.

As we will discuss in Chapter 2, the transregional and transcontinental flow of cultural influences usually accompanies the expansion of economic and military power. In other words, **cultural globalization**—which involves the exchange of food, people, products, ideas, and technology across national boundaries—has very deep roots. Few people in Europe stop to think that potatoes came from South America, and few Americans realize that their cattle came from Europe and their corn came from Mexico. The spread of ideas, technology, and products from China and other parts of Asia through the Middle East to Western Europe profoundly influenced the development of Western civilization. Imagine America without Christianity. Christianity, like Islam, originated in the Middle East and later spread across the world. Although cultural globalization is often equated with Americanization, it is a very complex development. America is shaped by other cultures even as it seems to dominate other societies.

Cultural Globalization

The spread of one cultural across national borders

Cultural globalization affects the consciousness of individuals and their attitudes toward politics, religion, economics, and broader cultural values. It also influences their sense of identity, belonging, and nationalism. Sports, which have generally been associated with nationalism, are one of the most obvious and emotional aspects of cultural globalization. World Cup soccer (football) in 2006, watched by billions of people around the world, demonstrates the global passion for sport. Ghana's defeat of the United States also showed that nationalism continues to be important. Cricket, for example, is as much an Indian or a Pakistani game as it is British. American baseball and basketball teams now compete with players from Latin America, Japan, and China. Many American sports are dominated by foreigners or naturalized American citizens. The globalization of sports has been accompanied by the development and enforcement of rules for athletes around the world.[34] Using drugs and blood for performance-enhancing transfusions has long been a major issue in global sport. Lance Armstrong and Floyd Landis, for example, were accused in 2006 of using banned substances to win the Tour de France.

FIGURE 1.5 NATO Expansion

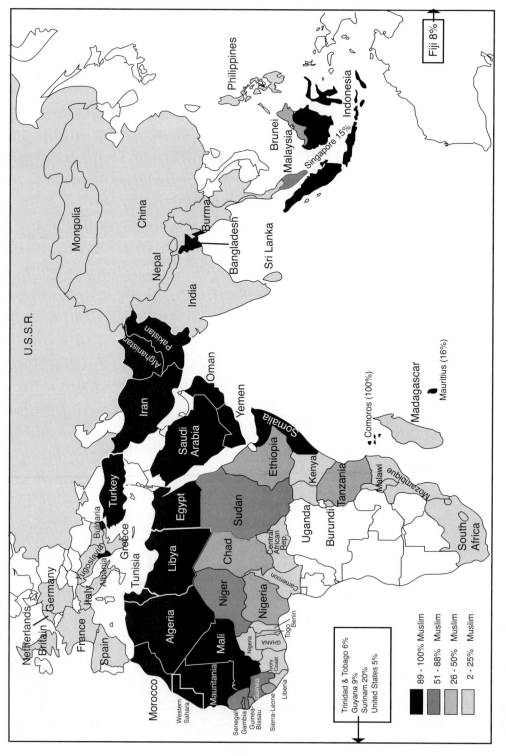

FIGURE 1.6 The Spread of Islam

Fiji 8%

Singapore 15%

Mauritius (16%)

Comoros (100%)

Trinidad & Tobago 6%
Guyana 9%
Surinam 20%
United States 5%

89 - 100% Muslim
51 - 88% Muslim
26 - 50% Muslim
2 - 25% Muslim

Environmental Globalization

Visitors to Boston generally observe that extremely valuable land in the center of the city has been preserved as a public park. The Boston Common was originally used by the city's residents as a place where their cattle could graze. When discussing the environment, it is useful to think of our planet as a common. We are all affected by what happens to it, and the problems can be solved only through the cooperation of the global community. **Environmental globalization** focuses on the interdependence among countries in relation to such problems as global warming, the spread of infectious diseases, air and water pollution, deforestation, the loss of biodiversity, and threats to endangered species. Environmental globalization refers to the impact that environmental problems in one part of the world have on distant places. Virtually all forms of globalization have an impact on the environment. For example, military globalization has had disastrous consequences for people, animals, forests, air quality, and the oceans. Economic globalization is often perceived as directly contributing to deforestation, pollution, and the degradation of the land. Oil pollution caused by Israeli military action in Lebanon in July and August 2006 generated global concerns about its impact not only on Lebanon but also on neighboring Mediterranean countries. It also demonstrated the impact of environmental globalization on the economic, military, cultural, and other aspects of globalization.

Environmental Globalization

The interdependence of countries to work together to solve environmental problems

Criminal Globalization

Terrorist attacks in the United States on September 11, 2001, represented an extreme form of **criminal globalization** and diminished the attention given to less dramatic but almost equally dangerous transnational criminal activities. The terrorists used the instruments of globalization to achieve their objectives. Criminal globalization is the intercontinental spread of global crime and its impact on governments and individuals. As Chapter 11 shows, criminal globalization includes transborder crimes, such as drug trafficking, money laundering, prostitution, alien smuggling, arms

You DECIDE | ## Exporting E-waste to China

In the Chinese city of Guiyu, entire communities, including children, try to earn a living by scavenging for metals, glass, and plastics from dumps, disregarding the harm to the environment and to themselves. At the heart of the problem is an unwillingness of wealthy societies to bear the expense of recycling computers to keep them out of landfills. In the United States, where more than 40 million computers become obsolete each year,

the general approach to solving environmental problems associated with the disposal of computers is to sell them to China. Because the United States has not ratified the Basel Convention (i.e., an international agreement that limits the export of hazardous wastes), the practice of shipping used computers to China is legal.

Should the United States ratify the Basel Convention and prevent the export of e-waste?

trafficking, and counterfeiting. Criminal globalization poses severe challenges to national and global security. Global cooperation is essential to reduce its negative consequences.

National boundaries have never been effective barriers to the conduct of transnational crimes. As globalization has expanded, criminal organizations have deepened and widened their activities. Furthermore, globalization has imposed on governments certain burdens, such as smaller public budgets, decentralization, privatization, deregulation, and an open environment that is more conducive to criminal globalization.[35]

PERIODS OF GLOBALIZATION

Because globalization is a process that advances and retreats, that is more intense at some points than at others, it is artificial to divide it into distinct periods. However, for discussion, we can identify *five waves of globalization* in the constant sea of change that defines human experience.

The *first wave of globalization* is as old as human civilization. For more than five thousand years human beings from different places have interacted, mostly through trade, migration, and conquest. The growth of urban areas provided spaces for people from different places to exchange ideas and engage in commerce. As we mentioned, the spread of Christianity and Islam from the Middle East clearly shows that globalization has deep foundations. In other words, globalization was occurring long before the language of globalization came into existence.[36]

The *second wave of globalization* is closely associated with the Western European conquest of Asia, Latin America, and Africa and the spread of capitalism to these areas. Colonization, slavery, trade, the spread of religion, and concerted efforts to impose European ways and values on the conquered territories marked a fundamental shift toward creating a more interdependent world. The development of new technologies, faster transportation, and the availability of finance enabled Europeans to connect distant areas to European countries. This wave of globalization continues to influence developments within and among societies today. **Dependency** theorists view this period of globalization as being profoundly influential on global politics and trade.

The *third wave of globalization*, which began around 1870 and declined around 1914, was marked by breakthroughs in technological development, the global production of primary commodities as well as manufactured products, and mass migration. Less expensive transportation costs, the switch from sails to steam power, the development of railways, the availability of capital, and the reduction of trade barriers combined to fuel global economic growth. Vast areas of land in North America, Argentina, Australia, and elsewhere were cultivated and agricultural products were exported. The production of primary products led to the demand for labor. In addition to the Africans and others who were already providing labor, about 60 million Europeans migrated to North America and Australia to work on farms. Argentina, Australia, New Zealand, and the United States became some of the richest countries in the world by exporting primary commodities and importing people, institutions, capital, and manufactured products.[37] This explosion of global activities was followed by a retreat into nationalism from 1914 to 1945. World War I was followed by the Great Depression and a wave of protectionism,

Dependency

Belief that industrialized countries benefit from the present capitalist economic system at the expense of poor countries

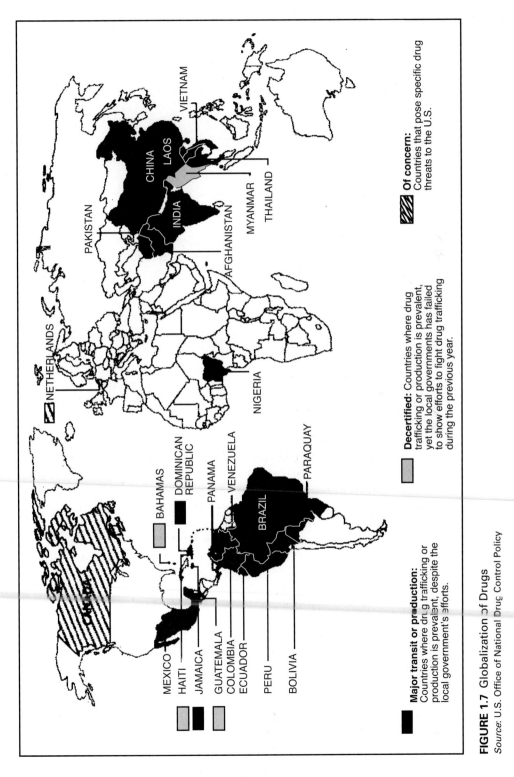

FIGURE 1.7 Globalization of Drugs

Source: U.S. Office of National Drug Control Policy

The following labels appear on the map:

VIETNAM
LAOS
CHINA
INDIA
PAKISTAN
AFGHANISTAN
MYANMAR
THAILAND
NETHERLANDS
NIGERIA

MEXICO
HAITI
JAMAICA
GUATEMALA
COLOMBIA
ECUADOR
PERU
BOLIVIA
BAHAMAS
DOMINICAN REPUBLIC
PANAMA
VENEZUELA
BRAZIL
PARAQUAY

Major transit or production: Countries where drug trafficking or production is prevalent, despite the local government's efforts.

Decertified: Countries where drug trafficking or production is prevalent, yet the local governments has failed to show efforts to fight drug trafficking during the previous year.

Of concern: Countries that pose specific drug threats to the U.S.

led by the United States. America attempted to protect its economy by enacting the **Smoot-Hawley Tariff Act** in 1930, a move that led to retaliation abroad. Between 1929 and 1933, U.S. imports fell by 30 percent and exports fell by almost 40 percent.[38]

The *fourth wave of globalization*, from 1945 to 1980, was spurred by the retreat of nationalism and protectionism and the strengthening of internationalism and global cooperation, led by the United States. The removal of trade barriers was selective, but institutions—such as the World Bank, the International Monetary Fund, and the General Agreement on Tariffs and Trade (GATT)—were formed to encourage global trade and development. Many developing countries, relying on the exports of primary commodities, continued to be marginalized and disadvantaged in the global economy. This period of globalization was characterized by both cooperation and conflict. Efforts to encourage nations to work together in the United Nations were weakened by the rivalry between the United States and the Soviet Union. While the economic aspects of globalization are usually emphasized, the most important form of globalization during this period was military globalization, dominated by the constant threat of a nuclear war between the superpowers.

The *fifth wave of globalization*, which is the current period, is characterized by unprecedented interdependence among nations and the explosive growth of powerful nonstate actors. As we have discussed, telecommunications and computer technologies and inexpensive transportation have allowed the global production and sale of goods. Financial transactions occur with the touch of a button, foreign investment ignores national boundaries, and services are now an integral component of international trade. The various forms of globalization now combine to link the fate of humanity to an unprecedented degree.

Smoot-Hawley Tariff Act

Act that brought the U.S. tariff to the highest protective level in the history of the U.S.

RESISTANCE TO GLOBALIZATION

On most American college campuses there are groups protesting against globalization, even as they fully participate in the process of globalization. Globalization, in other words, engenders complex and conflicting emotions as well as contradictory and inconsistent behavior. Many students who protest the homogenization of cultures that results from globalization are more connected than any previous generation of American students to the rest of the world through the Internet, telephones, and travel. They also consume a wide variety of products made in foreign countries by the same companies they usually protest against. Part of their dilemma is that globalization has inextricably linked so many aspects of ordinary life to products, problems, and issues in other parts of the world that it is very difficult to reject most aspects of globalization in practice. From Seattle, Washington, to Davos, Switzerland, students, members of labor unions, environmentalists, and anarchists are resisting globalization. Many societies perceive globalization as a threat to their cultures, while others view globalization as a danger to their economies. Overall, many countries, groups, and individuals who resist globalization do so because they equate it with westernization in general and Americanization in particular. Many see such problems as global inequality and conflict as direct results of globalization. However, much resistance to globalization comes from France and the United States, two countries that play a pivotal role in the process of globalization.

France's opposition to globalization is strongly linked to its desire to retain control over its borders and to preserve its culture. Although France has been instrumental in creating European organizations that clearly diminish national sovereignty, France also sees a weakening of sovereignty as a factor that facilitates the invasion of France by immigrants, most of whom are Muslims from North Africa. **Jean-Marie Le Pen**, the leader of France's far-right National Front Party, views these immigrants as threats to his country's economy, culture, and national identity. Widespread violent protests by Muslim youths in 2005 and 2006 confirmed these fears. But France also resists globalization because it perceives it as an Anglo-Saxon threat to the French cultural model, which is portrayed as a "high-brow" culture of philosophers, fine dining, and intellectual films. Globalization is equated with the "low-brow" uniformity of American culture—fast food, bad clothing, and, even worse, sitcoms.[39] Globalization is also seen as promoting American individualism. France, on the other hand, values a strong centralized government that can provide essential benefits for the people as a whole. Equally important to the French is the impact that globalization is having on the French language, which declines in prominence as English spreads across the globe.

Jean-Marie Le Pen

Leader of France's far-right National Front Party

Consider America's resistance to globalization. On several fronts, Americans are increasingly embracing a view of sovereignty that rejects participation in a number of international regimes dealing with the environment, war crimes, land mines, arms control, and human rights. Even as President George W. Bush reiterated his confidence in the United Nations, he treated the organization as largely irrelevant to the achievement of America's objectives in the Persian Gulf, the Middle East, and elsewhere. Many American intellectuals and policymakers defend American institutions from the encroachment of international institutions. They resist abiding by international norms, draping "the power to do so in the mantle of constitutional legitimacy."[40] At a more general level, many regard globalization as a threat to their jobs, wages, and culture, despite obvious benefits from globalization (e.g., low inflation and greater economic opportunities for most Americans).

DEBATING GLOBALIZATION

Throughout this chapter, globalization has been discussed as a fact, as reality. However, there is disagreement about the extent to which globalization exists. The *three dominant positions* in this debate are assumed by: (1) the hyperglobalizers and the transformationalists, (2) the weak globalizers, and (3) the skeptics and rejectionists. The *hyperglobalizers and transformationalists* see profound changes in the international system, such as the erosion of sovereignty and the weakening of nation-states, a borderless economy that integrates people everywhere in the global marketplace, and the emergence of new forms of social and economic organizations that challenge traditional states. Contemporary patterns of globalization are viewed as being unprecedented. The *weak globalizers*, while acknowledging that there are many important changes in the international system, argue that this increased internationalization is not altering the world to the extent claimed by the hyperglobalizers and transformationalists. States remain sovereign and people around the world, while living in the "global village," continue to jealously guard their own huts. Culture, nationalism, and geography continue to divide us. Finally, the *skeptics and rejectionists* basically argue that globalization is largely a myth that disguises the reality of the existence of powerful sovereign states and major economic divisions in the world. National governments remain in control of their domestic economies as well as the regulation of international economic activities. National governments determine the nature of global interactions. Inequality continues to fuel nationalism and, instead of cultural homogenization, the world is dividing into cultures that remain suspicious of each other.[41]

At another level, there is the debate about the nature and impact of globalization and whether it is temporary or reversible. Some groups see globalization as homogenization, while others view it as promoting diversity and greater tolerance of differences. Many nonstate actors view globalization as conducive to their efforts to improve social conditions, protect the environment, and promote democracy. Globalization is linked to the toppling of dictators and the spread of human rights and democratic government. By removing restraints on people's movement, globalization is perceived as instrumental in giving to the individual the power to choose. People are free to shape their identities, pursue an education anywhere in the world, and upgrade their standard of living.[42] On the other side, critics of globalization focus on how cultural homogenization imposes Western values on others and destroys their traditions, religious beliefs, identities, and sense of community and belonging. Many believe that globalization is a threat to national sovereignty and autonomy. Environmentalists, for example, believe that globalization contributes to environmental degradation, and labor unions and students contend that globalization lowers wages, creates greater inequality, and allows rich countries to maintain their dominant position in relation to poor countries.

Summary and Review

This chapter discussed the foundations of international relations and provided a general view of how interdependence and the forces of globalization are creating serious challenges to governments as the almost exclusive major actors in world politics. It examined

You
DECIDE   ## Does Globalization Improve Lives?

Free trade, an important part of economic globalization, is generally viewed as beneficial. However, many opponents of globalization argue that benefits from free trade are often derived at the expense of poorly paid workers in developing countries, such as China, Indonesia, and Thailand. Those supporting globalization point out that the countries that have narrowed the economic gap with the industrial countries embraced free trade and globalization.

They argue that globalization is not the evil force that street protestors claim it is, that the idea that American workers or workers in foreign countries will gain from reducing trade is irrational, and that globalization has created opportunities that raised hundreds of millions of people from poverty.

Do you think that globalization, overall, contributes to improved standards of living around the world?

how technological, economic, social, political, and philosophical developments in Europe contributed to the rise of the modern state, the concept of sovereignty, the system of relations among states, and the decline of the Catholic Church as the dominant political and cultural institution in Europe. It illustrated how political, economic, and cultural forces contributed to the rise of the modern nation-state and how they continue to be integral components of contemporary globalization. We looked at interdependence and globalization. Just as interdependence plays a role in our private lives (e.g., most of us do not grow the food we eat), it also plays a role in world affairs. Globalization creates more obvious and extensive webs of interdependence. The causes of globalization can range from social issues (e.g., migration) to technological advances (e.g., in fields such as communication and transportation) to economic issues (e.g., market expansion). The major forms of globalization are (1) economic and trade, (2) financial, (3) political, (4) military, (5) cultural, (6) environmental, and (7) criminal. Finally, we discussed the five historical waves of globalization and the current debate that exists between groups that have resisted it and those that have been more accepting of it.

Key Terms

international relations 2
Peace of Westphalia 2
state 2
sovereign 2
nation 2
nation-state 2
state-centric model 2
theory 3
nonstate actors 3
human security 3
global politics 4
global norms 4
global issues 4

humanism 5
Huguenots 7
Six Books on the Commonwealth 7
international law 7
Hugo Grotius 7
diplomacy 7
balance of power 7
Nongovernmental organizations (NGOs) 10
multinational corporation 13
transnational corporations 13

interdependence 14
globalization 14
Cold War 15
economic globalization 18
financial globalization 20
World Bank 21
International Monetary Fund (IMF) 21
Organization of Petroleum Exporting Countries (OPEC) 21

political globalization 21
global governance 22
military globalization 24
cultural globalization 25
environmental globalization 27
criminal globalization 27
dependency 28

Discussion Questions

1. As stated in this chapter, even people involved with international relations often use the terms state and nation interchangeably. What are the differences between a state, a nation, and a nation-state? How are the technical definitions of these terms different from your everyday usage of them?
2. What roles do nonstate actors play in international relations?
3. This chapter discusses the five waves of globalization and provides examples of globalization for each

time period. What are some additional examples of globalization within some of these periods?
4. What is the difference between a multinational corporation and a transnational corporation?
5. "Interdependence is the foundation of society." What does this mean? How does it relate to the concept of globalization?
6. What are some of the advances in technology that have contributed to globalization? What are some of the new problems we face because of these advances?

7. What are global cities and global teams? How do they help companies achieve their goals?
8. What are some of the arguments made against globalization? Do you agree or disagree with any of these arguments? Explain.
9. Some observers of international relations say the movement against globalization is actually another example of globalization. Through advances in communications and other technologies, many nonstate actors have been able to oppose the spread of certain economic forces that they say are harmful to such things as workers' rights and the environment. Does saying that these organizations are participating in globalization delegitimize the arguments they present? Explain.

Suggested Readings

Barber, Benjamin. *Jihad vs. McWorld*. New York: Ballantine Books, 1996.

Barnett, Michael, and Martha Finnmore. *Rules for the World*. Ithaca: Cornell University Press, 2006.

Bhagwati, Jagdish. *In Defense of Globalization*. New York: Oxford University Press, 2004.

Cohen, Daniel. *Globalization and Its Enemies*. Cambridge, MA: MIT Press, 2006.

Dervis, Kemal. *A Better Globalization*. Washington, D.C.: Brookings Institution Press, 2005.

Friedman, Thomas. *The World Is Flat*. New York: Farrar Straus and Giroux, 2005.

Huntington, Samuel P. *The Clash of Civilizations and the Remaking of World Order*. New York: Simon and Schuster, 1996.

James, Harold. *The End of Globalization: Lessons From the Great Depression*. Cambridge, MA: Harvard University Press, 2001.

Keck, Margaret, and Kathryn Sikkink. *Activists Beyond Borders*. Ithaca: Cornell University Press, 1998.

Kindleberger, Charles P. *A Financial History of Western Europe*. New York: Oxford University Press, 1993.

Krasner, Stephen D. *Sovereignty: Organized Hypocrisy*. Princeton: Princeton University Press, 1999.

O'Rourke, Kevin H., and Jeffrey G. Williamson. *Globalization and History*. Cambridge, MA: MIT Press, 1999.

Pettis, Michael. *The Volatility Machine: Emerging Economies and the Threat of Financial Collapse*. New York: Oxford University Press, 2001.

Ruggie, John. *Constructing the World Policy*. London: Routledge, 1998.

Wapner, Paul. *Environmental Activism and World Civil Politics*. Albany: State University of New York Press, 1996.

Weinstein, Michael, ed. *Globalization: What's New*. New York: Columbia University Press, 2005.

Weiss, Thomas, and Leon Gordenker, eds. *NGOs, the UN, and Global Governance*. Boulder: Lynne Rienner, 1996.

Williams, Michael. *The Realist Tradition and the Limits of International Relations*. Cambridge: Cambridge University Press, 2005.

Addresses and Websites

The International Forum on Globalization
The Thoreau Center for Sustainability
1009 General Kennedy Ave., No. 2
San Francisco, CA 94129
Tel: (415) 561–7650
Fax: (415) 561–7651
www.ifg.org/index.html

This website for the International Forum on Globalization provides special reports, lists upcoming events, and has information on the World Trade Organization and the International Monetary Fund. It also provides United Nations resources.

www.polity.co.uk/global

This website, Global Transformations, contains extensive information on exploring what globalization is and how to research it. Other sections include interviews and a debate on realism versus cosmopolitanism. The links to governmental and NGO webpages are especially good.

www.worldbank.org/economicpolicy/globalization/

The globalization part of the World Bank webpage features key readings, data and statistics, learning programs, news, presentations, and speeches.
It is interesting and educational to look at globalization through the eyes of the World Bank.

http://globalization.about.com

About.com has a wonderful globalization section that shows the pros of globalization and the complaints about it. It provides articles as well as information on how globalization affects such things as human rights and the environment.

The World Bank
1818 H St. NW
Washington, D.C. 20433
Tel: (202) 473–1000
Fax: (202) 477–6391
www.worldbank.org/globalization

The World Bank is an international organization that deals with worldwide financial issues. This website, sponsored by the World Bank, offers information on globalization, including data and statistics, readings, news, research, and links to other useful sites.

International Monetary Fund
700 19th St. NW
Washington, D.C. 20431
Tel: (202) 623–7000
www.imf.org

The International Monetary Fund's goals are "to promote international monetary cooperation, exchange stability, and orderly exchange arrangements; to foster economic growth and high levels of employment; and to provide temporary financial assistance to countries to help ease balance of payments adjustment." This website offers information on globalization, specifically briefs of previous years and publications on globalization.

International Forum of Globalization
1009 General Kennedy Ave., No. 2
San Francisco, CA 94129
Tel: (415) 561–7650
E-mail: info@ifg.org
www.ifg.org

The International Forum of Globalization, a think tank formed in 1994 in response to the North America Free Trade Agreement, it wants globalization to be understood as a global process. The goal of the IFG, therefore, is twofold: (1) to expose the multiple effects of economic globalization in order to stimulate debate, and (2) to reverse the globalization process by encouraging ideas and activities that revitalize local economies and communities, and ensure long-term ecological stability. This website offers a variety of information on globalization.

Global Interdependence Center
Fels Center of Government
University of Pennsylvania
3814 Walnut St.
Philadelphia, PA 19104
Tel: (202) 898–9453
www.interdependence.org

This website is home for the Global Interdependence Center, which is sponsored by the University of Pennsylvania. The GIC is dedicated to the expansion of global trade and finance within a free-trade environment and to the development of well-reasoned policy analysis on critical economic issues. GIC's main focus is on international trade, international finance, and monetary policy, since these have social, political, and economic impacts on societies. The website offers information on topics relating to global economic problems and their solutions.

North-South Centre of the Council of Europe
Avenida da Liberdade, 229-4
1250-142 Lisbon
Portugal
Tel: 00 351 21 358 40 58
Fax: 00 351 21 352 49 66/21 358 40 37
E-mail: nscifo@coe.int
www.nscentre.org

The European Centre for Global Interdependence and Solidarity, better known as the North-South Centre, was established to encourage North-South cooperation and solidarity and to improve education and information on the ties of interdependence that bind the world's inhabitants. This website focuses mainly on respect for human rights, democracy, and social cohesion.

Endnotes

1. Richard J. Payne and Jamal R. Nassar, *Politics and Culture in the Developing World* (New York: Longman, 2003), 8–9.
2. K. J. Holsti, *International Politics: A Framework for Analysis* (Englewood Cliffs, NJ: Prentice Hall, 1995), xi.
3. Hans Morgenthau, *Politics Among Nations* (New York: Knoff, 1948), 23.
4. James N. Rosenau and Mary Durfee, *Thinking Theory Thoroughly* (Boulder: Westview Press, 2000), 48.
5. James N. Rosenau, *Along the Domestic-Foreign Frontier: Exploring Governance in a Turbulent World* (Cambridge: Cambridge University Press, 1997), 58–60.
6. Richard Rosencrance, "Trade and Power," in *Conflict After the Cold War*, ed. Richard K. Betts (New York: Longman, 2002), 281.
7. Steve Lonergan, "Human Security, Environmental Security, and Sustainable Development," in *Environment and Security*, eds. Miriam R. Lowi and Brian R. Shaw (New York: St. Martin's Press, 2000), 70.
8. Rosenau and Durfee, *Thinking Theory Thoroughly*, 47.
9. Charles W. Kegley and Gregory A. Raymond, *Exorcising the Ghosts of Westphalia* (Upper Saddle River, NJ: Prentice Hall, 2002), 30.
10. James Lee Ray, *Global Politics* (Boston: Houghton Mifflin, 1998), 165.
11. Richard Cavendish, "The Treaty of Westphalia," *History Today* 48 (November 1998): 50–52.
12. Carlton Hayes, *A Political and Social History of Modern Europe* (New York: Macmillan, 1921), 231.
13. F. H. Hinsely, *Sovereignty* (Cambridge: Cambridge University Press, 1986), 126.
14. Geoffrey Stern, *The Structure of International Society* (London: Printer, 2000), 78.
15. Stephen D. Krasner, *Sovereignty* (Princeton: Princeton University Press, 1999), 4.
16. William Greider, *One World, Ready or Not: The Manic Logic of Global Capitalism* (New York: Simon and Schuster, 1997), 24.
17. Elaine Sciolino, "European Union Acts to Admit 10 Nations," *The New York Times*, 14 December 2002, A7.
18. Solange Villas, "The Path to Unity," in *Europe in the New Century*, ed. Robert J. Guttman (Boulder: Lynne Rienner, 2001), 17.
19. P. J. Simmons, "Learning to Live With NGOs," *Foreign Policy*, No. 112 (Fall 1998), 84–87.
20. Frank Bruni, "John Paul Makes First Papal Address to Italy's Parliament," *The New York Times*, 15 November 2002, A3.
21. Peter Drucker, "The Global Economy and the Nation-State," *Foreign Affairs* 79, No. 5 (September/October 1997), 8.
22. Marina Ottaway, "Reluctant Missionaries," *Foreign Policy*, No. 125 (July/August 2001), 45.
23. Robert O. Keohane and Joseph S. Nye, *Power and Interdependence* (Boston: Little, Brown and Company, 1977).
24. David Held, et al. *Global Transformations* (Stanford: Stanford University Press, 1999), 28; and James H. Mittleman, *The Globalization Syndrome* (Princeton: Princeton University Press, 2000), 15.
25. Michael Pettis, "Will Globalization Go Bankrupt?" *Foreign Policy*, No. 126 (September/October 2001), 55.
26. George Wehrfity, "Raiding the Love Bug," *Newsweek*, 22 May 2000, 44.
27. Held, et al., *Global Transformations*, 186.
28. G. Pascal Zachary, "The Rage for Global Team," *Technology Review* 101, No. 4 (July/August 1998), 33.
29. Malcolm D. Knight, "Developing and Transition Countries Confront Financial Globalization," *Finance and Development* 36, No. 2 (June 1999), 32.
30. Thomas Balion and Angel Ubide, "The New World of Banking," *Finance and Development* 37, No. 2 (June 2000), 41.
31. Held, et al., *Global Transformations*, 202.
32. Raimo Vayrynen, "Norms, Compliance, and Enforcement in Global Governance," in *Globalization and Global Governance*, ed. Raimo Vayrynen (Lanham: Romman and Littlefield, 1999), 25.
33. Held, et al., *Global Transformations*, 88.
34. Robert O. Keohane and Joseph S. Nye, "Globalization," *Foreign Policy*, No. 118 (Spring 2000), 107.
35. Toby Miller, et al., *Globalization and Sport* (London: Sage Publications, 2001), 11–12.
36. Moises Naim, "The Five Wars of Globalization," *Foreign Policy*, No. 134 (January-February 2003), 30.
37. Mittelman, *The Globalization Syndrome*, 18.
38. Paul Collier and David Dollar, *Globalization, Growth, and Poverty* (New York: Oxford University Press, 2002), 25.
39. Paul Collier and David Dollar, *Globalization, Growth, and Poverty*, 27.
40. Sophie Meunier, "The French Exception," *Foreign Affairs* 79, No. 6 (November/December 2000), 9
41. Peter J. Spiro, "The New Sovereigntists," *Foreign Affairs* 79, No. 6 (November/December 2000), 9.
42. R. J. Barry Jones, *The World Turned Upside Down?* (Manchester: Manchester University Press, 2000), 11; and Held, et al., *Global Transformations*, 5; and John Micklethwait and Adrian Wooldridge, *A Future Perfect: The Essentials of Globalization* (New York: Crown Publishers, 2000), xxvi.

CHAPTER 2

The Struggle for Primacy in a Global Society

INTRODUCTION

Throughout history great powers—such as Rome, Spain, and Britain—have gone through growth and decline, through competition and internal weakness. **Power transition theory,** which is an offshoot of Cycle theories, stresses that the distribution-of-power changes in countries will rise and fall. Dominant countries are often referred to as great powers, hegemonies, superpowers, or states that enjoy primacy in the international system. Often, these terms are used interchangeably. They generally refer to the ability of a country or a small group of countries to have extraordinary influence over the behavior of the other states.[1] These dominant countries have economic, military, political, technological, and cultural resources that enable them to influence developments in distant places and to persuade or coerce other countries to do or to refrain from doing certain things. This chapter shows how political, economic, and cultural factors combine to influence both the emergence of great powers and their maintenance of power in the global system. It also demonstrates that the struggle for power among states continues to have profound implications for the global system. Punishments and rewards, or sticks and carrots, are instrumental in achieving the objectives of dominant powers.

A country enjoying international primacy, or hegemony, is generally regarded as having diverse interests. It affects many countries' behavior on a wide range of issues without having to significantly change its own behavior. When there are several hegemons, dominant states, or great powers, the international system is defined as being **multipolar**. An example is the international system that existed before World War II, when the United States, Britain, France, Germany, Japan, Italy, and the Soviet Union were considered great powers. Following World War II, there were clearly two dominant countries: the United States and the Soviet Union. The new structure was **bipolar**. The disintegration of the Soviet Union created a **unipolar** world, dominated by the United States. In his essay, "Why We Will Soon Miss the Cold War," John J. Mearsheimer argues that the Cold War provided a degree of order in a world characterized by anarchy. The end of the Cold War, he argues, engenders greater anarchy in international relations.

Implicit in the discussion of great powers is the existence of a hierarchical system of power and that positions often change within this hierarchy. In theory, the leading country, or **hegemon**, can single-handedly control the actions of other powerful countries. The United States is often perceived as a hegemon. A dominant country exercises significant power, has few potential rivals, and leads an international system that benefits other powerful countries. Below the dominant countries are great powers, which help to maintain the international system. Then there are regional powers. But most

Power Transition Theory

Stresses that the distribution-of-power changes in countries will rise and fall

Multipolar

The international system that includes several hegemons, dominant states, or great powers

Bipolar

The international system that includes two hegemons, dominant states, or great powers

Unipolar

The international system that has only one hegemon, dominant state, or great power

Hegemon

The leading country in an international system

Antonio Gramsci

(1891–1937); leading Marxist theoretician and a founder of the Italian Communist Party

Power

The ability to get others—individuals, groups, or nations—to behave in ways that they ordinarily would not

countries are at the bottom of the pyramid of power.[2] While it is often assumed that the hegemon, or dominant power, can make decisions unilaterally and be dismissive of other countries, the strongest nation needs the cooperation of others. The concept of hegemony was developed by **Antonio Gramsci** (1891–1937), a leading Marxist theoretician and a founder of the Italian Communist Party, to describe relations, classes, and social groups within countries. Gramsci focused on how the ruling class legitimized its power; that is, how that class managed to get others to accept the existing order because they view the ruling class as having moral authority.[3] This moral authority is an essential component of the hegemon's economic, military, and political power.

This chapter shows that great powers rise and fall. There have been challengers to dominant powers throughout history. However, while the rivalry among states is the primary focus of international relations, the growing interdependence of states and the emergence of powerful nonstate actors must also be considered when discussing international primacy. Furthermore, globalization, as we have seen, weakens hierarchies in several ways and challenges traditional views on the rise and fall of dominant countries. This chapter examines the nature of power, factors that influence the rise and fall of nations, and the strategies countries use to maintain their dominant position. As we discuss these ideas, we will examine the rise and fall of countries in the ancient world, China, the Islamic world, Western Europe (including Britain), and the Soviet Union. Given its unprecedented power, the rise of the United States will be of special interest in our discussion.

POWER AND LEADERSHIP

Central to concerns about the rise and fall of dominant nations is the concept of power. Despite human preoccupation with power, measuring power is difficult. Because power is essentially a psychological relationship, there are numerous reasons for the failure of even great nations to exercise it effectively. **Power** is generally understood as the ability to get others—individuals, groups, or nations—to behave in ways that they would ordinarily try to avoid. *Power capabilities* are usually determined by economic strength, military strength, and political effectiveness. *Elements of power* include a country's geographic area and location, its population, and its natural resources. Other elements of power are intelligence capabilities, the quality of national leadership, the level of educational and technological achievement, the openness of the political system, the character of the people, transportation and communication capabilities, ideology, and a country's culture (generally referred to as "soft power").[4]

Economic power is often seen as the foundation of military and political power. It is measured in terms of the **gross national product (GNP)** or the **gross domestic product (GDP)**. The GNP measures the total market value of all goods and services produced by resources supplied by the residents and businesses of a particular country, regardless of where those residents and businesses are located. The GDP measures the total market value of all goods and services produced within a country. Military power is often the most visible and impressive manifestation of national power. Great powers generally have large, healthy, and relatively well-educated populations, which enable them to build large and technologically sophisticated militaries.[5] As we will discuss, a major challenge for great powers is to maintain a balance between economic strength and military might. Too much emphasis on the military often weakens the economy, and ultimately the military itself.

A nation's strength goes beyond simply possessing the various resources that are sources of power. Countries, like individuals, must be skilled at converting these resources into effective influence. **Power conversion** is defined as the capacity to change potential power, as measured by available resources, into realized power, which is determined by the changed behavior of others.[6] Knowing what resources to use, when, and how will also affect the exercise of power. Certain factors—such as globalization, domestic support for policies, and the willingness of citizens to support activities associated with international primacy—must also be considered. Even though a country, such as Japan, is strong economically, its ability to be a great power is determined by its economic vulnerability to resource shortages and the reluctance of its population to play a significant military role in world affairs. Furthermore, the horrific consequences of war in a nuclear age deter the use of force by great powers in cases where smaller countries can retaliate with nuclear weapons. For example, North Korea's limited nuclear capabilities deter the United States from using military force to resolve problems between the two countries. Globalization, which links states, also constrains them. It restrains even powerful nations from using force unilaterally in many cases, partly because of the high costs and unintended negative consequences for themselves and their allies.

An important component of power is leadership. In fact, leadership is about power. Leadership is the ability to persuade others to behave in certain ways, to shape their interest, and to influence their thinking. Leadership implies a capability to get others to cooperate to achieve particular objectives.[7] At the foundation of leadership is the ability to get others to follow. It is impossible to be an effective hegemon without followers. Leadership can be structural, institutional, or situational. **Structural leadership** is derived largely from the control of economic resources, military power, technology, and other sources of power that enable a small group of countries to shape the international system. Structural leadership is often augmented by **institutional leadership**; that is, the ability to determine the rules, principles, procedures, and practices that guide the behavior of members of the global community. Institutions provide order and predictability and allow the dominant power to exercise control. Finally, **situational leadership** is primarily the ability to seize opportunities to build or reorient the global system, apart from the distribution of power and the building of institutions. Often, this kind of leadership is associated with a specific individual.[8]

THE RISE AND FALL OF GREAT POWERS

Several complex and interrelated factors influence the rise and fall of great powers. Because states compete for power and position in the international system, today's dominant country is likely to be replaced by an aspiring state.

GNP

Measures the total market value of all goods and services produced by resources supplied by residents and businesses of a particular country, regardless of where the residents and businesses are located

GDP

Measures the total market value of all goods and services produced within a country

Power Conversion

The capacity to change potential power, as measured by available resources, into realized power, which is determined by the changed behavior of others

Structural Leadership

The possession of economic resources, military power, technology, and other sources of power that enable a small group of countries to shape the international system

**Institutional
Leadership**

The ability to deter-
mine the rules,
principles, proce-
dures, and prac-
tices that guide the
behavior of mem-
bers of the global
community.

**Situational
Leadership**

The ability to seize
opportunities to
build or reorient the
global system, apart
from the distribu-
tion of power and
the building of
institutions

**Uneven Economic
Growth**

A factor that
enables countries
to enhance their
power while that
of other countries
declines

States generally expand because of *threats* and *opportunities* in their international system. States fear power vacuums because rival states are likely to take advantage of them if they fail to act. Weaker states tend to gravitate toward a rising power and to move away from a declining power.[9] Failure to demonstrate strength causes a band-wagoning effect, which benefits the rising power. These dynamics strongly influence states to expand to protect their interests and security. **Population pressures** influence the rise of great powers. Population growth puts pressure on available domestic resources. To address this problem, countries that are capable of expanding will venture across oceans or land boundaries to obtain raw materials, markets for their products, and living space for their people. European expansion was, to some extent, fueled by population pressures. Such expansion is usually accomplished through military force, which depends on a strong economic base. This means that economic factors are also very important. Countries with access to finance can build strong armies and navies. In fact, many countries expand because they can afford to do so. As states accumulate wealth, they define their interests more broadly and attempt to match their economic power with political influence. **Uneven economic growth** enables some countries to enhance their power while other countries decline. Some of the engines behind economic growth are technological change, organizational advances, innovations, educational opportunities, urbanization, tolerance, an environment that promotes freedom, and the development of trust. But leading powers spread these engines of growth to other countries, ultimately strengthening their rivals.

Urbanization has usually been associated with freedom and innovation. Urban areas attract diverse groups of people with differing ideas. They also improve the wealth-generating, administrative, and political capabilities of a rising power. The efficient functioning of great cities depends on a commitment to tolerance, freedom, and trust. These characteristics, in turn, attract more talent, wealth, innovation, and technology to cities. Trust, for example, is essential for commercial transactions as well as for mundane, routine interactions. Cities like London and Amsterdam attracted refugees from religious intolerance and persecution. During the seventeenth-century religious wars, Protestants and Jews migrated to Amsterdam and other Dutch cities that were more tolerant of religious diversity. Repression and persecution in France after the French Revolution, for example, forced many French citizens—especially those who were young, educated, and had entrepreneurial skills—to seek refuge in a much freer England.[10]

Geography is another factor that influences the rise and fall of great powers. Britain, Russia, and the United States have benefited from their geographic location and, in the case of Russia and the United States, their continental-size territory. None of these countries is located in the middle of warring states, and they usually refrained from getting involved in other nations' conflicts until it was to their advantage to do so. They could fight in other countries and avoid destroying their own. Their geography also enabled them to concentrate resources on internal consolidation, which ultimately increased their power vis-à-vis other states. Equally important, their separation by water and expanses of land made it more difficult for countries to invade them.

War, which played a crucial role in making states, has been a major factor in the rise and fall of great powers. It usually increased the power of some nations at the detriment of others. Even when countries emerged victorious from war, some were so weakened that the countries that had avoided major damage rose to the top. An example is Britain after World War II: It experienced declining power as America's global dominance grew. Historically, war has been instrumental in strengthening patriotism and nationalism. Historically, Britain went to war against France and Spain to engender cohesion among England, Scotland, Wales, and Ireland.

In addition to the competition among states that ultimately weakens some and strengthens others, several other factors contribute to the decline and fall of great powers. Many great powers decline because of **hubris**, (i.e., excessive pride) and imperial arrogance. They tend to overestimate their power and expand their military power so much that they ultimately erode their economic base. In other words, believing that their power is virtually limitless, they allow a gap to grow between their global ambitions and the resources they have to fulfill those ambitions. This disparity is referred to as the **Lippmann Gap** because Walter Lippmann clearly articulated the problem as early as 1943; Paul Kennedy, writing in the late 1980s, referred to this problem as **imperial overstretch**.[11] Taking resources away from domestic programs for military activities abroad often leads to the unraveling of domestic political cohesion. It may even force allies to find ways to balance against the power of the dominant state in order to protect their own interests and security. For example, even as the United States increased spending on the war in Iraq in 2006, the country faced rising budget deficits and growing concerns about the viability of the Social Security program and rising costs for Medicare. At a more fundamental level, the arrogance of power leads to erosion of trust at home and abroad. *Trust* enables great powers to dominate the international system at relatively low costs. When trust declines, the fall of a great power is almost assured.

STRATEGIES FOR MAINTAINING POWER

Leading powers, facing challenges from rising countries that are dissatisfied with the status quo, adopt several strategies to preserve their position in the international system. Although all great powers rely on varying degrees of military force to acquire and retain dominance, many of them attempt to legitimize their control. In other words, great powers try to find ways to get others to believe that they have the right to lead and to persuade them to accept the status quo. *Democratic enlargement* is a prominent strategy in this effort. Potential challengers are restrained when they internalize the values, beliefs, and norms articulated by the dominant power. The United States, for example, has emphasized spreading democracy. But the dissemination of values and beliefs by great powers does not guarantee indefinite control, a reality that Britain had to face as India and other colonies demanded for themselves the rights enjoyed by people in Britain, including the right to self-government. Great powers also build institutions to legitimize their control. They articulate concepts of an international normative order, concepts that involve principles of order and change within the international system as well as normative claims about the role of the leading power within that order.[12] The Dutch used this approach in the seventeenth century, the British in the eighteenth and nineteenth centuries, and it is currently being used by the United States.

Hubris

A term used to stress the dangers of excessive pride and arrogance

Lippmann Gap

The disparity between the global ambitions of countries and their resources to fulfill those ambitions

Imperial Overstretch

The disparity between the global ambitions of countries and their resources to fulfill those ambitions

Another strategy used to prevent rising powers from creating disorder in the international system is *offshore balancing*. Following Napoleon's final defeat in 1815, European powers created the **Concert of Europe** to maintain stability by preserving a relatively equal distribution of power among them. The main goal was to prevent one country from gaining so much power that it would dominate the others. The balance of power relied on the willingness of a group of powerful countries to cooperate militarily, if necessary, against a rising hegemon. *Balancing*—which basically means opposing the stronger or more threatening side in a conflict—can be achieved through efforts by individual states to strengthen themselves and by building alliances to preserve the balance of power.[13] Closely related to balancing is the strategy of **containment**, which attempts to prevent ambitious powers from expanding and destroying order and balance in the international system. When the Soviet Union marched through Eastern Europe and subjugated the countries there, the United States and its European allies responded by implementing a policy of containment.

Binding and *engagement* are also important state responses to rising powers. The European Union, as we have seen, has its origins in efforts by France and other countries after World War II to avoid the nightmare of another war in Europe by forming economic and political alliances with Germany, which had initiated the conflict. *Binding* aims at controlling the behavior of the rising or threatening country by embedding it into bilateral or multilateral alliances. By making the rising state a member of the alliance, dominant countries allow it to participate in decisions and to contribute to building the institutions that maintain the status quo. Binding makes it more difficult for the rising state to take unilateral actions that could weaken leading powers. West Germany and East Germany, belonging to the North Atlantic Treaty Organization (NATO) and the Warsaw pact, respectively, are examples of countries that were included in alliances to prevent them from creating problems for the leading countries in each alliance. Many Europeans perceive the continuation and expansion of NATO in the absence of the Soviet threat as part of America's binding strategy. *Engagement* attempts to minimize conflict with a rising power and to strengthen those aspects of its behavior that are consistent with the status quo and the interests of the great powers.[14] Eventually the rising power will have too great a stake in preserving the international order to challenge it. Finally, a hegemon could resort to *preventive war* to preserve its position in the international system. However, wars against major powers in a nuclear age and in an era of increasing globalization are almost unthinkable because of their devastating consequences for the world, including the hegemon. The following discussion shows that throughout history great powers have gone through growth and decline.

THE RISE AND FALL OF GREAT POWERS—CASE STUDIES

The Ancient World

Empires in the ancient world were in many ways remarkably similar to more recent empires, both in the strategies they used to expand their power and consolidate their position and in the reasons for their decline. The Persian Empire, based primarily in

---

Concert of Europe

Created by European powers to prevent one country from gaining so much power that it would dominate the others

Containment

A strategy that attempts to prevent ambitious powers from expanding and destroying order and balance in the international system

what is now Iran, was built on the Assyrian Empire, which rose in the seventeenth century B.C., quickly declined, and emerged stronger around the ninth century B.C. The Assyrian Empire, which expanded from the Mediterranean to Arabia and Egypt, borrowed extensively from the earlier Babylonian civilization. The **Persian Empire** extended from the eastern Mediterranean south to Egypt and as far as the western borders of India. The Persians practiced a balance-of-power strategy in relation to the Greeks in order to prevent any one Greek city-state from becoming strong enough to challenge Persia.[15] Later empires adopted strategies used by the Persians to maintain their power.

Among the empires of the ancient world, the various **Greek city-states** have most profoundly shaped Western civilization in particular and the world in general through the power of their ideas. Two of these city-states, Athens and Sparta, emerged as the dominant powers in the fifth century B.C. and exercised a dual hegemony. Sparta, principally a land power, was preoccupied with maintaining stability on the Greek peninsula south of Athens known as the Pelopannese. Athens, on the other hand, was predominantly a naval power that dominated central Greece. Athens became the most prominent power because of its larger territory and population and because of its success in resisting Persian invasions of Greek territory. Both Sparta and Athens formed alliances with other city-states to secure their power. Athens created the **Delian League** to contain Persian expansion, a development that greatly enhanced Athenian power and civilization. But Athens' success threatened Sparta, and eventually the two hegemons clashed in 457 B.C. in the **Peloponnesian War**. Conflicts continued until 404 B.C., ending with Athens' defeat. **Thucydides**, the preeminent Greek historian and the first prominent scholar of international relations, observed that "what made war inevitable was the growth of Athenian power and the fear which this caused in Sparta."[16] Thucydides was the first to clearly articulate what is now known as the power transition theory. As the Greeks were weakening themselves with incessant warfare, Rome was getting stronger; by 146 B.C., Rome controlled Greece.

Building on Greek foundations, Rome created an empire that included most of the world known to Europeans, West Asians, and North Africans. The Roman Empire, at its zenith, stretched from North Africa to England and Scotland, and from Spain to Egypt and Turkey. Rome was unique in that it dominated the world as the lone superpower and had no serious challengers. Once it defeated such rivals as Carthage and Macedonia, Rome worried only about rebellious tribes, such as the Germans and the Gauls (French). Rome was, in a very real sense, the international system. No country balanced against the Roman Empire because no balancers existed.[17] But competition for power among leaders, the costs of expansion, and internal chaos eventually weakened the Roman Empire. The Visigoths in 440 A.D. and the Vandals in 455 A.D. plundered Rome. In 476 A.D., the German Odoacer overthrew the last Roman emperor, the child Romulus Augustulus, thereby ending the western half of the Roman Empire. However, the eastern half, based in Constantinople (now Istanbul, Turkey) remained strong until around 1453 A.D. But Rome, unique in the extent and degree of its power, had fallen.

Persian Empire

The empire that extended from the eastern Mediterranean south to Egypt and as far as the western borders of India

Greek City-States

Ancient empires that profoundly shaped Western civilization in particular and the world in general through the power of their ideas

Delian League

Created by Athens to contain Persian expansion, thereby greatly enhancing Athenian power and civilization

Peloponnesian War

The war between Athens and Sparta that started in 457 B.C.

Thucydides

The preeminent Greek historian and the first prominent scholar of international relations

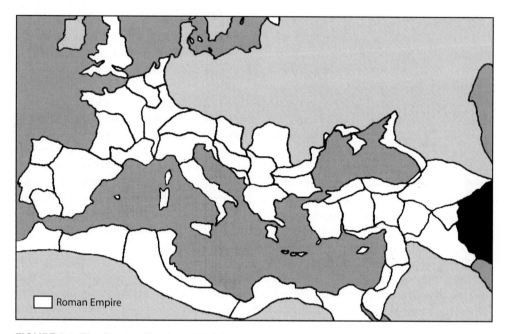

FIGURE 2.1 The Roman Empire, 116 A.D.

China

China clearly dominated the premodern world. Directly and indirectly, it contributed to the scientific, military, administrative, and cultural development of Western Europe, especially through its impact on the Islamic societies that later directly influenced European civilization. Marco Polo, the Venetian who traveled to China around 1275, was impressed by Chinese achievements in virtually every human endeavor. By the eleventh century, China had an extensive system of canals, huge libraries, printing by movable type, paper money to facilitate commerce, a well-educated bureaucracy, an iron ore industry with an output larger than that of Britain seven centuries later, gunpowder, the clock, the magnetic compass, and the wheelbarrow, among other things. In the twelfth century, the Chinese produced textiles by using a water-driven machine for spinning hemp which was almost 500 years before England developed this technique in its Industrial Revolution. China engaged in long-distance maritime trade long before Europe. Its ships reached the Pacific Islands, Africa, and Southeast Asia. The Ming navy in 1420 had an estimated 1,350 combat vessels, including 400 large floating fortresses and 200 ships designed to sail long distances.[18] Despite these remarkable achievements, China declined as a great power.

Like many other great civilizations, China was challenged by a rising power; in its case, the Mongols. Concerned about the vulnerability of its extensive northern border, the Chinese turned their attention to building fortifications to prevent an invasion. Part of this effort involved the construction of the massive Great Wall, around

1,500 miles long and an average of 25 feet high and 15-to-30 feet wide. Partly due to threats from the Mongols, China turned inward, abandoning most of its overseas exploration and trade. The Chinese government's actions contributed to China's decline. Government officials opposed the accumulation of wealth, derived largely from overseas trade, because it threatened their power, was regarded as a divisive influence, and created significant income inequality. The values of Chinese society, based on **Confucianism**, stressed traditionalism, a rigid hierarchy, obedience to authority, consensus, and centralization of power. Women were confined to the home and prevented from having free access to public spaces, a practice that seriously reduced their contributions to the society.[19] This preoccupation with control also stifled technological innovations, and many technological breakthroughs were abandoned. However, many of China's inventions and ideas reached the West through the expansion of the Islamic Empire.

Confucianism

Chinese philosophy that emphasized a rigid hierarchy and obedience to authority

The Islamic World

Originating in Mecca on the Arabian peninsula in 622, Islam was spread to Africa, Asia, and Europe by Arabs, Ottomans, Turks, Persians, and others. The area under Islam's control and influence was larger than that of the Roman Empire. Islamic civilization expanded from what is now Saudi Arabia, across the Red Sea into North Africa, and from Africa into Spain. For almost seven centuries, some Muslims (the Moors) ruled parts of Spain and profoundly influenced all aspects of Spanish culture and society. The Ottoman Turks dismantled the Venetian Empire, pushed into the Red Sea, and challenged the Portuguese in the Indian Ocean around 1516. The Turks controlled Bulgaria, Serbia, and Hungary, and they threatened to subdue Vienna as late as 1683.[20] Islam spread to India, China, and Indonesia, and other parts of Asia. Although the Islamic world is widely perceived today as part of the developing world, for several centuries before the emergence of Western Europe as a center of power, the Islamic world had great libraries, universities, great architecture, advanced mathematics, and significant achievements in science, medicine, cartography, and philosophy. In fact, the infusion of knowledge from the Islamic world into Europe fueled the Renaissance and the scientific revolution.[21]

Yet internal problems and external challenges eventually led to the decline of the Islamic Empire. From as early as the thirteenth century, the Islamic world was confronted by Crusaders from the West and the Mongols from the East. Spain, in 1492, successfully ended Muslim control in that country, thereby depriving Islam of great centers of learning in Cordoba and Toledo. Like most empires, the Islamic Empire overextended its military resources and was unable to sustain numerous military operations simultaneously. This problem was exacerbated by increasing centralization of power; diminishing freedom to innovate, think, and engage in commerce; and growing despotism. Serious divisions within Islam in Iraq and Persia (now Iran) between the Shi'ite and the dominant Sunnis hardened religious views and intolerance of dissent. These divisions and conflicts within Islam became more obvious in 2006, due partly to the war in Iraq. Turning inward, the Turks, for example, were so resistant to European ideas that they refused to implement advanced methods for containing the

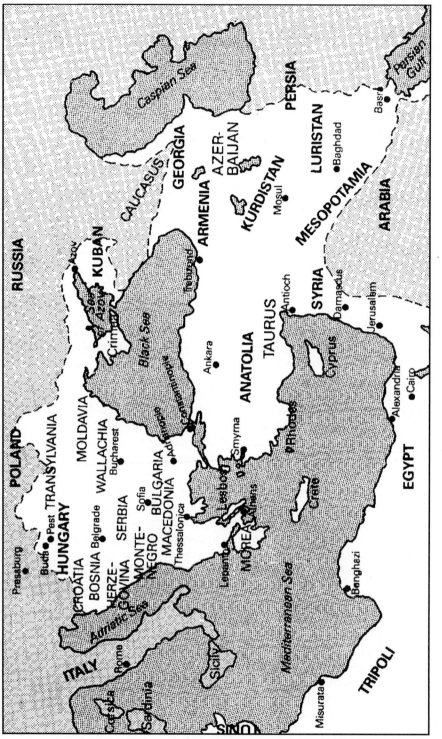

FIGURE 2.2 The Ottoman Empire, 1680

spread infectious diseases.[22] The Muslims became so conservative that they prevented business practices from evolving to meet new challenges. For example, both Islamic and European law required a business partnership to dissolve if one partner died or was incapacitated. However, European inheritance law permitted a person to designate heirs and to have only one heir. Although the partnership had to be dissolved, it could be rebuilt easily. Under Islamic law, inheritance could not be limited to one person. Because the law was based on the **Koran** (i.e., the Islamic holy book), it was fairly rigid, especially in light of the general hardening of religious positions. As a result, businesses remained small and were unable to compete effectively with larger European companies.[23] Conservatism also manifested itself, with devastating consequences, in the military. Despite their awareness of advances in European weaponry, the Turks refused to modernize their weapons. For example, they did not replace heavy cannons with lighter guns, and their ships, constructed for the calmer waters of the Red Sea and the Persian Gulf, were no match for oceangoing European ships.

Koran
The Islamic holy book upon which Islamic law was based

Western Europe

Based on our discussion of the rise and fall of great powers so far, it is not surprising that the European world also built on the achievements of previous civilizations. From the sixteenth century onward, European influence and power around the world surpassed that of any other major empire. Several factors contributed to Europe's emergence as the dominant power center. One of the most prominent was geographic fragmentation. Europe—unlike China, India, and the Middle East—lacked the large plains and fertile river valleys that made conquest relatively easy. In fact, Europe's rivers, mountains, forests, and rugged terrain impeded conquering armies. These geographical features led to great diversity and made centralized control very difficult. Geographic fragmentation fostered a deep sense of independence and separateness in politics, economics, culture, technology, and ideas, which all contributed to the cross-fertilization of societies that ultimately made Europe the dominant power. An important component of this geographic fragmentation was the range of climates that enabled different regions in Europe to produce various commodities that could be traded. The existence of navigable rivers and the building of canals encouraged commerce and intercultural exchanges. Countries with access to the sea had to develop increasingly stronger and more sophisticated ships to transport their products. In sum, Europe's geographic diversity contributed to the emergence of political fragmentation and, eventually, to political freedom.[24]

Political fragmentation allowed diverse approaches to governing to develop, with consequences that could be observed and rejected or adopted by others. Inherent in political diversity were competition and the availability of options to migrate from the countryside to cities, from one city to another, and from one country to another. Freedom of movement moderated authoritarian tendencies and made political authority more circumscribed and accountable. Crucial to the growth of political freedom was the recognition and protection of property rights. Economic freedom was fostered by the development of the semi-autonomous city, known as a commune.

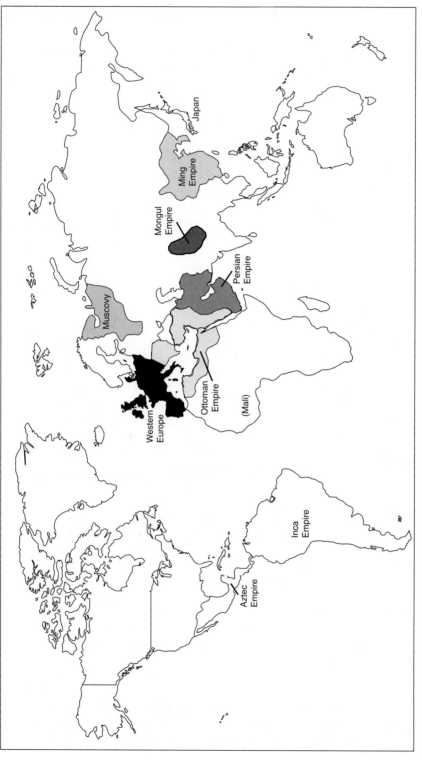

FIGURE 2.3 Great Powers in the Sixteenth Century

Communes were governed principally by the merchants who inhabited them. These residents had political and economic rights that enabled them to engage in commerce without the interference of centralized governments. Freedoms and cities have long been synonymous. In fact, cities liberated individuals from the oppressive hierarchical systems often found in the countryside.[25] Cities also served as gathering places for people from different places who had diverse talents and financial resources. Cities generally provided more economic opportunities, which augmented political freedom. Political, geographic, and cultural diversity along with economic freedom are among the factors that combined to challenge religious domination and conformity. This decline in religious authority in many European countries further fostered freedom of thought and the spirit of experimentation and innovation.

The **cultivation of invention** was another significant factor that propelled Europe ahead of other empires. Many of the inventions usually attributed to Europe were refinements of inventions by China and the Muslim world. But what distinguished Europe from previous empires was the commitment to innovation by government, groups, and individuals in an environment that was also increasingly committed to freedom in its broadest sense. Instead of discouraging invention, as the Chinese and Muslims did, Europeans rewarded inventions that were pivotal to Europe's progress. The waterwheel, used by the Romans, was revived by the Europeans, who had abundant water supplies. They invented devices, such as gears and cranks, to make greater use of the power generated by the waterwheel. The mechanical clock was invented in England and Italy almost simultaneously in the late thirteenth century; it brought the order, control, and precision needed for the development of industry and society. It also expanded personal autonomy by undermining the Church's control over time by removing its monopoly. The invention of eyeglasses not only lengthened the productive lives of craftsmen, but also led to the invention of fine instruments, such as gauges, micrometers, and fine wheel cutters.[26] Advancements in printing increased the dissemination of knowledge. The refinement of both gunpowder and the cannon helped to consolidate power both internally and abroad.

Economic, political, and intellectual freedom encouraged the development of a strong financial system. The availability of credit, insurance, and a sound banking system enabled merchants to expand their businesses. But the globalization of Europe's power depended heavily on advances in military organization and weaponry. While armies played a crucial role in Europe's power, countries such as Portugal, Spain, Holland, France, and Britain stressed naval supremacy. Among the factors that gave rise to impressive navies were the roughness of the North Sea and the Atlantic Ocean, fierce competition among the Europeans, the growth of commerce, an avid interest in exploration, and, unlike China, a drive to acquire colonies in the Americas, Asia, and Africa. Among Europeans, Britain stands out as a builder of a global empire.

Britain

The British Empire at its zenith in the late nineteenth and early twentieth centuries covered far more territory and had global reach far greater than the Roman Empire. What is truly remarkable about the British Empire is that such a small country

Communes

Semi-autonomous cities governed principally by the merchants who inhabited them

Cultivation of Invention

The factor that propelled Europe ahead of other empires

(see Figure 2.4) could control an area that was roughly ninety-six times its size. British rule covered a fifth of the earth's land and a quarter of its population, clearly surpassing all of its imperial competitors' combined territories and populations. How could an island the size of Oregon acquire enough power to dominate so much of the world? Its population was smaller than that of France or Spain, and it had fewer natural resources.

There are many *reasons for Britain's rise* as a great power. First, Britain's *geographic location*, an island apart from Europe's troubles, was an important factor. It generally avoided costly involvement in many of Europe's wars, and its location impeded invasions. Second, Britain had easy *access to transportation routes* because of its navigable rivers and canals and its numerous harbors. Surrounded by the sea, Britain naturally developed a strong interest in shipbuilding, navigation, and trade. Third, building *a strong navy* not only strengthened Britain's security against Spain, France, and other countries, but also enabled it to expand and acquire its vast empire. Fourth, the *protection of property rights* helped to create an environment conducive to the promotion of political freedom and checks on political power as far back as 1215, when the **Magna Carta** limited the power of the king. The growth of constitutional government and respect for the rule of law became the foundation of British power at home and abroad. Fifth, economic and political freedom encouraged *scientific and intellectual freedom* and reduced the power of religious authorities. Freedom to think and innovate was essential to the growth of economic power, especially the Industrial Revolution in the mid-eighteenth century. Sixth, an *emphasis on learning* created widespread literacy, which augmented economic growth and political development. Finally, Britain recognized the crucial importance of *diplomacy* as an instrument of power. These factors, among others, contributed to Britain's international primacy.[27]

After defeating Napoleon at Waterloo in 1815 with the help of its allies and imprisoning him on the island of Saint Helena, Britain enjoyed a long period of global supremacy. Advances in military organization and technology, rapid technological innovation in general, the navy's dominant position, rising economic production, population growth, political stability at home, the decline of warfare among European countries, the preoccupation of potential challengers (such as the United States and Russia) with domestic instability, and a relatively stable international environment helped to consolidate Britain's leadership in the international system. However, by the end of the nineteenth century, signs of Britain's decline were evident. The United States emerged united and stronger from its devastating Civil War; the rest of Europe was also industrializing; Japan was rising; and Germany, following its unification in 1871 under **Otto Von Bismarck** (1815–1898) of Prussia, developed global ambitions.

Otto Von Bismarck (1815–1898); Prussian (German) statesman, known as the Iron Chancellor; implemented the unification of Germany in 1871

Both the United States and Germany, with growing populations and increasing technical and economic might, challenged Britain. Ireland's struggle for autonomy, domestic dissatisfaction in Britain among the working classes, and a relative decline in intellectual, technological, and economic power further weakened Britain. In an attempt to diminish Germany's challenge, Britain formed alliances, such as the

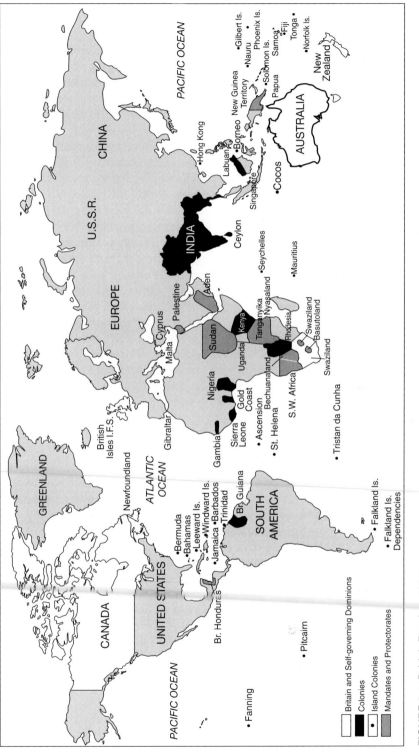

FIGURE 2.4 British Empire, 1930

51

Triple Entente

The alliance of Britain, France, and Russia

Triple Alliance

The alliance of Germany, Austria-Hungary, and Italy

Triple Entente (1891) with France and Russia. Germany was a member of the **Triple Alliance** (1882) along with Austria-Hungary and Italy. Britain allocated substantial resources to defense. Tensions between these alliances, together with the assassination of Archduke Francis Ferdinand of Austria-Hungary by a Serbian nationalist in 1914, culminated in the outbreak of World War I. The conflict significantly eroded Britain's global position. Four years of trench warfare left roughly a million British soldiers dead and several millions wounded. These were some of Britain's best and brightest citizens. Such a huge loss of human resources, combined with deep political and economic divisions in Britain following the war, weakened the country.

Problems in Britain resulting from World War I were compounded by World War II. The war was extremely costly, the colonies were demanding independence, the United States and Russia had emerged as superpowers, and Britain was slow to adjust to changing economic realities. The British Empire had declined.

Catherine the Great

Or Catherine II (1729–1796); empress of Russia who expanded her vast country's borders south to the Black Sea and west into Europe while continuing the westernization begun by Peter the Great

Yet Britain managed to retain significant worldwide influence through its participation in the building of international institutions, such as the United Nations, the World Bank, the International Monetary Fund, NATO, the General Agreement on Tariffs and Trade, and the Commonwealth. It also strengthened its alliance with the United States, developed a potent nuclear arsenal, and relied more on diplomacy than on military might and on its power as one of the five permanent members of the UN Security Council. Britain's membership in the European Union and its economic revitalization under Prime Ministers Margaret Thatcher and Tony Blair have also contributed to its ability to remain a significant global power. Britain's support of the American-led war in Iraq in 2003 raised questions about Britain's power and the wisdom of British foreign policy.

Peter the Great

Or Peter I (1672–1725); tsar and later emperor of Russia; who challenged the Ottoman Empire, made Russia a maritime power, and attempted to westernize the country

Russia (The Soviet Union)

Straddling Asia and Europe, Russia's vast territory and abundant natural resources gave it many advantages over a small country such as Britain. However, the case of Russia demonstrates that freedom is a crucial ingredient in gaining and, more important, maintaining power. Whereas Britain encouraged individualization, entrepreneurship, and freedom of thought, Russia discouraged all of these. Russia looked inward, deprived its people of basic freedoms, legalized serfdom, distrusted foreign ways and innovations, and isolated its people. Repression led to revolts, which justified further repression. These habits undermined Russia's quest for great-power status. Despite these drawbacks, Russia emerged as the leading power on the European continent under the leadership of **Catherine the Great** (1762–1796). The foundations for Russia's rise were built by **Peter the Great** (1672–1725), who challenged the Ottoman Empire, made Russia a maritime power, and attempted to westernize the country. As Table 2.1 shows, Russia (the Soviet Union) remained a great power from around 1713 to 1989. Like many empires, Russia expanded its territory at its neighbors' expense and faced threats to its territory from other countries. Russia's weakness in World War I contributed to the Russian Revolution in 1917 and to the rise of the communists, led by **V. I. Lenin** (1870–1924), after which Russia was renamed the Union of Soviet Socialist Republics (U.S.S.R), or the Soviet Union.

V. I. Lenin

Vladimir Ilich (1870–1924); Russian revolutionary leader and theorist; presided over the first government of Soviet Russia and then that of the U.S.S.R.

Anglo-American alliance; Tony Blair and George W. Bush

The Soviet Union experienced gains in economic and military power after World War I. Its population was at least twice as large as those of major European countries and its manufacturing sector expanded greatly to move ahead of France's and just behind Britain's by the late 1930s. Threatened by Nazi Germany, the Soviet Union concentrated on strengthening its military. World War II had devastating consequences for both the Soviet Union and Germany. Germany suffered roughly 13 million casualties in its conflict with the Soviet Union. But the Soviet Union lost between 20 million and 25 million people in this war. German-occupied parts of the country suffered incalculable damage. Agriculture, livestock, railways, and buildings were

TABLE 2.1 GREAT POWERS FROM 1495–PRESENT

Period	Great Powers
1495–1521	France, England, Austrian Hapsburgs, Spain, Ottoman Empire, Portugal
1604–1618	France, England, Austria, Spain, Ottoman Empire, Holland, Sweden
1648–1702	France, England, Austrian Hapsburgs, Spain, Ottoman Empire, Holland, Sweden
1713–1792	France, Great Britain, Austrian Hapsburgs, Spain, Sweden, Russia, Prussia
1815–1914	France, Great Britain, Austria-Hungary, Russia, Prussia/Germany, Italy, United States, Japan
1919–1939	France, Great Britain, Soviet Union, Germany, Italy, United States, Japan
1945–1989	Soviet Union, United States
1989–Present	United States

Joseph Stalin

(1879–1953);
general secretary of
the Communist
Party of the
U.S.S.R; directly
challenged the
West through
Soviet expansion

**Cuban Missile
Crisis**

A major
confrontation
between the U.S.
and U.S.S.R. in
1962; started when
Soviet leader Nikita
Krushchev decided
to station nuclear
missiles in Cuba

Mikhail Gorbachev

The last leader
of the U.S.S.R.
(from 1985 to 1991);
believed that decen-
tralization of power,
economic reforms,
and greater polit-
ical freedoms were
essential to improv-
ing Soviet society

Glasnost

Soviet reforms
aimed at fostering
openness, political
freedom, and
truthfulness

Perestroika

Soviet reforms
aimed at economic
restructuring

destroyed. So complete was the destruction that many people lived in holes in the ground.[28] Nevertheless, the Soviet Union emerged militarily stronger than other European countries and Japan at the end of the war and became, along with the United States, a dominant power. Military technology (specifically the development of nuclear weapons), communist ideology, and geographic location and size contributed to Soviet power. Germany and Japan were defeated, paving the way for Soviet expansion in the West, East, and North. The Baltic states of Latvia, Estonia, and Lithuania were inte-grated into the Soviet Empire; and Poland, East Germany, Czechoslovakia, Hungary, Romania, Albania, Bulgaria, and Yugoslavia came under Soviet control and influence. Soviet leader **Joseph Stalin** (1879–1953)—who had allied with the United States, Britain, France, China, and other countries, against Germany—directly challenged the West through his expansion of communism and territorial acquisitions. The Cold War had started even before Germany was totally defeated, and an Iron Curtain descended between the Soviet Union and Western Europe and the United States. The power of the Soviet Union and the United States dwarfed that of nearest rivals, thus their desig-nation as superpowers. The Soviet Union challenged the United States around the world, including in America's sphere of influence—Latin America and the Caribbean. The most dangerous confrontation during the Cold War was the **Cuban missile crisis** in October 1962, which started with Soviet leader Nikita Krushchev's decision to sta-tion nuclear weapons in Cuba, ninety miles from the United States.

While the Soviet Union's deadly nuclear arsenal and its ideological appeal demon-strated its military might, *numerous weaknesses* were steadily eroding its power. A major problem was an overconcentration of resources on the military and the forging of expen-sive alliances with developing countries. The lack of economic and political freedom stifled innovation, eliminated entrepreneurship, isolated Soviet citizens from the revolu-tionary breakthroughs in technology occurring in the West, and deprived the country of globalization's benefits. Increasing access to information technologies, greater exposure to prosperity in the West, and concerted efforts by various countries and organizations to free countries under Soviet domination contributed to the fall of communism and the disintegration of the Soviet Empire. An emphasis on centrally planned economic growth, articulated by Stalin, proved to be exceedingly rigid and inefficient, thereby weakening the economic base of the Soviet Union's military power. Equally important to the fall of the Soviet Union were efforts by reformists, such as **Mikhail Gorbachev**. Gorbachev, the last leader of the Soviet Union, believed that decentralization of power, economic reforms, and greater political freedoms were essential to improving Soviet society. The cornerstones of these reforms were **glasnost** (i.e., openness, political freedom, and telling the truth) and **perestroika** (i.e., economic restructuring and reforms). The impact of these changes finally led to the demise of the Soviet Union.[29]

America

America's decision to launch a preemptive war against Iraq in March 2003 without broad international support and with significant domestic opposition to war demon-strated its power to ignore world opinion. Its awesome military power was evident in its "shock and awe" campaign against Iraq. However, although there was strong disagreement about America's decision to engage in a preemptive war, there was global consensus about America's military predominance. By 2006 it was increasingly clear that the war in Iraq had weakened American power and that ways should be found to remove American troops from Iraq. The strength of the U.S. military is unprecedented in the history of great powers. The United States accounts for roughly half of global defense spending. America spends more on its military than the next twenty powers combined and three as much times on military research and development as the next six powers combined. America's economic might is also undisputed. With less than 6 percent of the world's population, the United States produces almost a third of the world's gross domestic product. Culturally, intellectually, scientifically, and politically America dominates the global system, a reality that came into sharper focus when President George W. Bush employed America's unprecedented power against Iraq to effectuate regime change. Subsequent developments in Iraq, however, demonstrated both the limits of American power and the perilous difficulties involved in changing regimes.

Aircraft Carrier

America's emergence as the most powerful country in history was a complex and relatively gradual process. Often overlooked in political analysis of America's rise to great-power status is that the United States, like previous civilizations, borrowed heavily from others and built on foundations created by others. America, in many ways, was a continuation of British society in the New World. The Pilgrims who arrived in 1620 on the *Mayflower* at Plymouth in Massachusetts were English people who brought English values and institutions with them. The United States utilized strategies very similar to those used by other great powers to achieve its dominant position. It also benefited from the protection of the Pacific and Atlantic Oceans and unthreatening neighbors on its borders. The expansion of the United States occurred over land through the acquisition of Native American territories. Similar to other great powers, America relied heavily on military force to expand and consolidate its power. Believing in the concept of **manifest destiny**, it eventually expanded its territory from the Atlantic to the Pacific. The **Mexican-American War** (1846–1848) resulted in America's acquisition of two-fifths of Mexico's territory, including California and the present American Southwest, in the Treaty of Guadalupe-Hidalgo, which ended the conflict. However, the issue of slavery divided the United States into two warring factions, leading to the bloodiest war in American history. Even so, the American Civil War removed a serious obstacle to the United States' rise as a great power. In essence, the Civil War forged a common American culture and internal unification.[30]

Manifest Destiny

Jingoistic tenet that the U.S. expansion is reinforced through God's will

Mexican-American War

The war between Mexico and the U.S. (1846–1848) that resulted in the U.S. acquisition of two-fifths of Mexico's territory, including California and the present American Southwest

Internal stability enabled the United States to concentrate on building its economy and broadening its interests. The Civil War produced advancements in American military organization and technologies. However, after the war the United States demobilized the army, scrapped over half its warships, and allowed the rest to rot. The government declined to remain ahead of other countries in construction of iron-clad steamships.[31] As a continental-size power, the United States remained largely preoccupied with domestic and regional affairs. Furthermore, America believed that it could be "a City on a Hill" and an example to other nations, albeit from a distance and without getting entangled in their problems. This proclivity toward isolationism has always been an essential component of American foreign policy. But isolationism also emanated from the reality that until the late 1880s America was far behind such great powers as Britain, France, Germany, Austria-Hungary, Russia, and Italy. In fact, when the Sultan of Turkey decided to reduce expenses in 1880, he closed Turkey's diplomatic missions in Sweden, Belgium, the Netherlands, and the United States.[32] Yet America's vast territory, abundant natural resources, spirit of freedom and innovation, ability to attract immigrants and investments, institutional stability, and cultural values contributed to its phenomenal growth in the 1880s. The United States became a leading producer of agricultural products, coal, iron, and steel. Its banking and manufacturing sectors surpassed those of the major countries. By 1890 the United States had decided to strengthen its navy to be competitive with European navies. This development was fueled partly by America's imperial ambitions, evidenced by its conquest of the Philippines, Puerto Rico, and Guam and its increased influence in Cuba and Hawaii as a consequence of its victory in the **Spanish American War** in 1898. By ending Spain's declining position in the Americas and the Pacific, the United States established itself as the hegemon of the Western Hemisphere, thereby achieving the objective of the **Monroe Doctrine** of 1823, namely, diminishing European involvement in the Americas.

Reluctantly, America began abandoning its policy of isolationism during WWI in response to dangers of war in Europe and indiscriminate German submarine warfare. President Woodrow Wilson accelerated the construction of military weapons and warships, drafted young men, and trained them to fight. World War I stimulated a rapid growth in the foreign-policy establishment and brought out a strong American commitment to free trade, the promotion of democracy, support for national self-determination, and an emphasis on international cooperation to achieve world peace through such organizations as the **League of Nations**. American power was applied to protect its growing interests abroad. The United States' rise to global prominence meant that it could no longer avoid entanglement in European affairs, a reality made clearer by World War II. President Franklin D. Roosevelt, even before Japan bombed the American fleet at **Pearl Harbor** on December 7, 1941, expressed an urgent need to strengthen the military. He created the U.S. Air Force in 1939 and a two-ocean navy in 1940. The military draft was reinstated, military cooperation with Britain was enhanced, and military assistance was extended to Britain, the Soviet Union, and China. America's entry into World War II unleashed unprecedented military growth. By the end of the war, the United States was indisputably the dominant global power. But the Soviet Union, especially after it acquired intercontinental nuclear weapons, also gained superpower status. As Table 2.1

Spanish American War

The war between Spain and the U.S. (1898)

Monroe Doctrine

The statement of U.S. policy made by President James Monroe in 1823 that resulted in diminished European involvement in the Americas

League of Nations

International alliance created in 1920 to promote international peace and security

Pearl Harbor

Bombed by Japanese submarines and carrier-based planes in 1941

shows, the major European powers and Japan, destroyed by war, declined. And, as we discussed, the Soviet Union finally collapsed in 1989 under the weight of its ideological rigidity, denial of basic freedoms and fundamental rights, stagnant economy, and expenditures on global ambitions. America emerged as the sole superpower.

America's hegemony or primacy rests not only on its dominant power but also on its ability to legitimize that power by making it acceptable to potential challengers in particular and members of the global community in general. Cooperation, integration, and multilateralism became cornerstones of the American-led postwar order. Certain institutions—such as the United Nations, the World Bank, the International Monetary Fund, and the General Agreement on Tariffs and Trade—benefited most countries and induced them to accept American leadership. Institutionalization and increasing globalization meant that the United States and other countries would be constrained to varying degrees and would embrace multilateralism and cooperation instead of unilateralism. As the global leader, America would play a major role in providing collective benefits or **public goods** (i.e., services such as security, stability, open markets, and economic opportunities). By so doing, the United States would minimize the possibility of envy and resentment that could escalate into the fear and loathing that spawn hostile alliances designed to balance power.[33]

> **Public Goods**
> Collective benefits, such as security, stability, open markets, and economic opportunities

Terrorist attacks on the United States, on September 11, 2001, demonstrated the country's vulnerabilities to nonstate actors as well as its military might. In the Gulf War against Iraq in 1991, the United States' use of very sophisticated weapons stunned many countries and prompted them to upgrade their own military technologies. Ten years later, the war in Afghanistan was fought with even more advanced weapons. For example, American commandos using binoculars with laser range finders could spot distant enemy targets and relay the coordinates to satellite telephones or laptop computers in U.S. warplanes. Bombs weighing 2,000 pounds and guided by lasers and global positioning systems that improved their precision were dropped on targets in Afghanistan. Bombs weighing 4,700 pounds were used against Baghdad in the 2003 war. New technologies allowed American forces to detect heat, magnetic fields, and vibrations through as much as one hundred feet of solid rock, and thermobaric weapons could be used to penetrate rock and concrete to destroy underground targets.[34] The Predator, an unmanned reconnaissance and surveillance plane that is controlled by a ground team from a remote location, can be equipped with Hellfire missiles to strike targets. In addition to breakthroughs in military technology, America's strength was evidenced by the scope of its global military activities.

CHALLENGERS TO AMERICAN HEGEMONY

The U.S. military superiority, combined with what many countries viewed as unilateralism, deepened fissures between America and other countries, such as France, Germany, Russia, and China. Instead of being perceived as promoting the global welfare, American foreign policy was increasingly seen as being preoccupied with narrowly defined American interests. Instead of consulting, Washington was perceived to be issuing

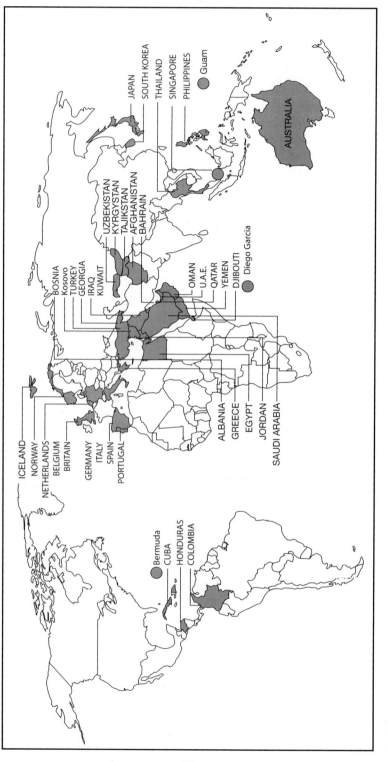

FIGURE 2.5 Location of U.S. Military Forces (2006)

demands and ultimatums. America's preference for a unipolar system and American global hegemony threatened other great powers, most of which favored a multipolar system.[35] Even before the schisms caused by debates on Iraq, American power was being challenged. This section discusses the principal challengers to American power.

Japan

Throughout the 1980s and during the early 1990s, scholars, political leaders, and most of the business sector were preoccupied with Japan as an economic juggernaut that was poised to dominate industries that produce such products as automobiles, cameras, ships, robotics, biotechnology, semiconductors, steel, musical instruments, and electronics. At the heart of their concerns was a growing realization that American hegemony was being challenged by a country that had been defeated by the United States in World War II. The U.S. occupation of Japan after the war enabled Japan to acquire American technology, organizational skills, political institutions and values, and access to American markets. Now America was looking at Japan's success as an indicator of its own failures. Many ordinary Americans and their political leaders admired Japan's achievements, even as they grew increasingly fearful and resentful of the rising Pacific power. The strong religious tradition that permeates American thinking and foreign policy reinforced the perception of the United States as an exceptional country that was exempt from the logic of historical forces faced by the other great powers. The fact that Japan had achieved such unprecedented economic power in just twenty-five years and was widely viewed as the model for the world shook Americans' confidence in their belief that the United States was destined to be the global redeemer. This doubt was reinforced by the failures in Vietnam, declining trust in political institutions after the Watergate crisis, and a prolonged economic recession.[36] Japan's economy grew at an annual average of 10 percent between 1950 and 1973, much faster than the economies of its competitors, and continued to be robust when most countries were experiencing recessionary pressures.

Japan's extraordinary rise as an economic power is the result of at least eleven complex factors. *First*, Japan already had an industrial infrastructure and a well-educated, talented, and cohesive population. *Second*, because the United States feared a militarized Japan, it made strenuous efforts to disarm the country and to focus on economic reconstruction and international trade. *Third*, Japan's cultural values emphasized cooperation and consensus in labor-management relations as well as economic security for workers. *Fourth*, Japan took advantage of America's military involvement in Korea and Vietnam by supplying trucks and other defense-related products to the United States. These wars stimulated Japanese exports, strengthening such companies as Toyota. *Fifth*, in addition to reducing government defense spending, Japan concentrated on encouraging high levels of personal savings. The availability of money at low interest rates enabled companies to borrow for investment both at home and abroad. *Sixth*, Japan created the **Ministry of International Trade and Industry (MITI)** to promote the country's industrial expansion and technological development and exports, thereby giving the government a direct role in the economy and helping Japanese companies to be

MITI

Created by Japanese to promote Japan's Industrial expansion, technological development, and exports

more globally competitive. *Seventh*, Japan used nontariff barriers to imports in order to protect its domestic industries. Although foreign products were imported, Japanese officials impeded their flow through extraordinary inspections. For example, baseball bats were drilled to ascertain that they were solid wood. Similarly, the Japanese attempted to exclude French skis by claiming that Japanese snow was different. The French responded by threatening to exclude Japanese motorcycles on the grounds that French roads were different. The Japanese dropped their plans.[37] *Eighth*, the Japanese borrowed ideas and technology from the United States and improved them to make Japanese industries more efficient and products more reliable. For example, workers were encouraged to inspect all products to avoid defects. This commitment to perfection gave the Japanese significant advantages over American companies, especially automobile makers. Japanese products became widely known for their durability and high quality. *Ninth*, Japanese companies built modern industrial plants that were far more efficient than plants in other industrialized countries. *Tenth*, the Japanese developed flexible production strategies that allowed them to develop products tailored for specific markets. *Finally*, the Japanese implemented the *just-in-time* system to minimize accumulating large inventories of components and products required in manufacturing. Their ability to reduce stockpiling was facilitated by their reliance on telecommunications and computer technologies as well as on their ability to diminish conflicts between labor and management and the probability of strikes.

Ideology

Set of beliefs and principles

Japanese Exceptionalism

Embodies homogeneity, insularity, and the exclusion of others who are not genetically and culturally Japanese

Despite Japan's economic superpower status, its ability to emerge as a hegemonic power is hindered by serious drawbacks. Compared with America, whose values are generally regarded as universally applicable, Japan is generally perceived as not having an **ideology** (i.e., set of beliefs and principles) that is widely relevant beyond Japan. More importantly, Japanese exceptionalism stresses that the uniqueness of Japanese culture is genetically based. In other words, **Japanese exceptionalism** embodies homogeneity, insularity, and the exclusion of others who are not genetically and culturally Japanese. Furthermore, Japan's expansion in the 1930s and 1940s has engendered deep suspicions, among other Asians in particular, about Japan's intentions. Japan's actions in World War II have essentially limited its ability to gain the legitimacy required to emerge as a great power. Widespread protests in China in 2005 against Japan for its refusal to acknowledge its atrocities in World War II and China's determination to prevent Japan from gaining a permanent seat on the UN Security Council underscore the challenge facing Japan. David Rapkin argues that within Japan and externally, Japan is generally considered deficient in the universal norms, values, beliefs, and principles that could form the foundation of world order.[38] Most countries do not expect Japan to exercise global leadership beyond the economic sphere. Japanese power remains largely unidimensional, even though it has the technological ability to develop nuclear weapons and to strengthen its military. Because Japan depends heavily on international trade and investment, it is highly vulnerable to pressures by powerful countries, such as the United States, France, and Britain. A major beneficiary of globalization, Japan is also restrained by interdependence. Japan's small territory and lack of vital natural resources put it at disadvantage in competition with large and resource-rich countries, such as the United States, China, and Russia, especially in a nuclear age and in a world in which acquiring territory forcefully is unacceptable.[39]

Finally, Japan's economy, once viewed as a juggernaut, has been steadily declining. Japan's aging population and its restrictive immigration policies combine to weaken its competitiveness. Moreover, the Japanese model has been successfully adopted by Taiwan, South Korea, China, and other countries. These countries manufacture many products that Japan exports for less without compromising quality. China's competitiveness, low wages, and huge potential market influenced many Japanese companies to invest in China in order to avoid Japan's high labor costs. Japan is also exporting technology, engineering, business, and organizational skills to China, which will help China to more effectively challenge Japan economically. Japan is viewed as having too many vulnerabilities and limitations to successfully challenge America's dominance. Furthermore, Japan's concerns about the emergence of China as a dominant power influence it to increase its cooperation with the United States.

China

China has been one of the world's leading powers for at least four thousand years. As we saw in our earlier discussion, China was once far superior to Western Europe in virtually every human endeavor. These historical achievements reinforce China's self-perception as a great power. China's many contributions to human civilization, its population of more than 1.2 billion, its rapid economic growth, and the spread of its culture across continents combine to strengthen its view that it is entitled to play a major role in world affairs. Just as an individual's identity helps to influence his or her perception of his or her role in the world, a nation's identity is crucial in its determination of its global status. China's identity is that of a great power.[40] China has traditionally emphasized protecting its borders, fostering domestic integration and stability, and reducing regional threats. Unlike other great powers, China did not systematically conquer other countries, despite its ability to do so. It has remained primarily a regional power.

But China is now widely viewed as a major challenger to America's dominance of the global system. An example of America's fear of a rising China was its strong opposition in 2005 to efforts by Crook, the Chinese government-owned oil company, to buy Unocal, an American oil company. China has established strong economic ties with oil-producing countries in Latin America, the Middle East, and Africa. Prior to the terrorist attacks on September 11, 2001, the United States perceived China as its most potent strategic competitor and embarked on a more confrontational policy toward the country to underscore its concerns. China's rapid and sustained economic development, its abundant natural resources, the vastness of its territory, its huge population, its growing technological progress, its significant military capabilities, and its historical international role are widely seen as the foundations of China's reemergence as a great power. China's military is seen as replacing that of Russia, and its economy is viewed as becoming as competitive as Japan's and even surpassing it. This combination of military and economic power is perceived as a threat to American global leadership. As the United States became preoccupied with wars in Iraq and Afghanistan, fighting global terrorism, and preventing nuclear proliferation in Iran and Korea, China, in 2005, strengthened its navy and increased its defense spending.[41]

China's economic growth has been spectacular since it implemented far-reaching economic reforms and improved relations with the United States in the 1970s. The economy has consistently grown by around 10 percent a year, even during periods when the American economy experienced recession. China's economic growth was spurred by deliberate and often draconian policies to reduce population growth, by the adoption of the free market, by increased privatization of the economy, by promotion of entrepreneurship, and by the efforts to attract foreign investments through the creation of special enterprise zones.

Companies from around the world established subsidiaries in China to take advantage of low production costs as well as the growing Chinese market. Many American companies manufacture their products in China and export them to the United States and other countries, helping to make China the factory of the world. Numerous Japanese companies—such as Honda Motor, Sony, Toshiba, Yamaha, Mitsubishi, and Hitachi—are transferring investments as well as technological and scientific skills to China. Despite strained relations with Taiwan, which China claims to be part of its territory, many Taiwanese engineers and high-technology companies have moved to China to take advantage of business opportunities. China's own engineering and technological schools and universities are producing experts in information technology. China's goal is to replace India as the world's second largest producer of software, after the United States.[42] Such advantages in technology improve China's economic competitiveness as well as its military capabilities. But China, a major beneficiary of globalization, has a vested interest in maintaining and strengthening the current global system.

Although largely preoccupied with regional security, especially the significant U.S. military presence in the area, China developed nuclear weapons as a deterrent to threats from the Soviet Union and the United States. India's acquisition of nuclear weapons and America's display of its awesome military power in the Persian Gulf wars have influenced China to modernize and expand its military capabilities. America's

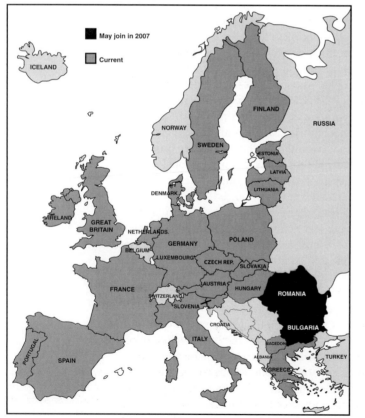

FIGURE 2.6 The European Union

predominant military power is perceived by China as an essential component of its strategy to maintain its hegemonic position in Asia. China also worries about the possibility of Japan developing its own nuclear weapons to deter threats from North Korea, which declared its intention to produce nuclear missiles in early 2003 and tested a nuclear weapon in 2006. In addition to acquiring advanced Russian military technology, China is making a concerted effort to build a new generation of nuclear-powered submarines that can launch intercontinental nuclear missiles. It is also modernizing its air force and reorganizing its army to enable it to be a "mobile and technologically competent force able to fight limited wars under high-technology conditions."[43]

China is building alliances with Russia, symbolized by the **Treaty of Friendship and Cooperation** of July 2001 to challenge the American framework for international security. It is also increasing economic ties with India through an agreement reached in 2005 to resolve the border dispute between the two countries. In July 2006 they reopened the Nathu La Pass, which was closed for 44 years, to facilitate trade. With a third of the world's population, the alliance between China and India has the potential to significantly impact global affairs. The United States attempted to strengthen its ties with India in 2006 with the signing of a nuclear agreement, discussed in Chapter 6. Growing perceptions of America's unilateralism and its willingness to use its military might reinforce China's determination to balance American power, especially in Asia. However, China is also careful not to jeopardize its strong economic links with the United States or its rapid economic development by allocating an overwhelming share of its resources to expanding its military. China's strategy underscores the reality of the declining utility of a massive military in an age of globalization. Nonstate actors, such as terrorist organizations and insurgents, seriously challenge the United States' military power, as was clearly demonstrated by Iraq in 2006.

> **Treaty of Friendship and Cooperation**
> Chinese-Russian alliance designed to challenge the U.S. framework for international security

The European Union

Although Europe's major powers were devastated by World War II, the vision of a united Europe gained greater impetus due to the perception that only European political and economic cooperation could diminish the outbreak of other such destructive wars on the continent. Attempts at European unification can be traced back to the Roman Empire. Charlemagne, Napoleon Bonaparte, Adolph Hitler, and others relied on force to achieve their vision of a united Europe. Despite deep religious, political, and cultural schisms in Europe, the idea of a "United States of Europe" persisted. The success of the European unification was strongly supported by America, which implemented the **Marshall Plan** in June 1947 to rebuild the devastated economies of Western countries. Furthermore, the United States played a pivotal role in the formation of *NATO* in April 1949 to prevent the expansion of the Soviet Union beyond Central and Eastern Europe. Europe's success in avoiding war and achieving economic and political integration has enabled it not only to emerge as a united continent but also to be perceived as a serious challenger to American hegemony.

> **Marshall Plan**
> Post-WW II plan to rebuild the devastated economies of Europe

The European Union possesses *seven key ingredients essential for great power status*:

1. Economic power, and political and diplomatic influence;
2. Advanced technological and scientific capabilities;
3. Soft power (i.e., cultural appeal);
4. A combined population of more than 480 million (larger than those of the United States, Canada, and Mexico combined);
5. Extensive links with most of the world because of colonialism;
6. Growing military capabilities; and
7. An emerging common identity.

A common currency (the euro), a parliament, courts, passports, a flag, a capital city, and free movement of people, capital, and products reinforce the acceptance of a European identity.

European unification heightened U.S. concern about the construction of a "fortress Europe" that would exclude American products and ultimately rise as a super-power to challenge the United States. Several developments helped to strengthen the perception that Europe and America are growing apart and becoming competitors. *First*, the end of the Cold War diminished European military and psychological dependence on the United States and influenced the United States to shift its attention from Europe in order to deal with domestic problems and emerging global threats. *Second*, Europeans are becoming more conscious of their European identity and more willing to differentiate themselves from Americans. *Third*, there are fundamental differences about the concept of power on each side of the Atlantic. Whereas the United States embraces an almost Westphalian concept of sovereignty and unilateralism, Europeans strongly support relinquishing important aspects of their sovereignty to achieve political, economic, monetary, and military unification, and they embrace multilateralism. *Fourth*, America's unprecedented power is influencing it to reject cooperation and consultation with Europeans on important issues. Europeans believe that American leaders show a growing disdain for the "old Europe," as U.S. Secretary of Defense Donald Rumsfeld called it. Visits to Europe in early 2005 by U.S. Secretary of State Condoleezza Rice and President George W. Bush attempted to repair the damage to U.S.-European relations caused by Rumsfeld and America's invasion and occupation of Iraq. *Fifth*, positions on both sides of the Atlantic are hardening, as evidenced by sharp divisions between the United States and Europe over U.S. military actions in Iraq. *Sixth*, there is growing acceptance in America of the view that Europe is no longer an indispensable partner. *Finally*, Americans and Europeans have divergent positions on major issues, including the use of military power, the power of the International Criminal Court, the role of the United Nations, the environment, the treatment of terrorist suspects, and the death penalty. These differences—together with Europe's increasing economic, political, military, and technological power—are seen as providing the foundation for the emergence of a united Europe to balance American power. Equally important, most Europeans, about 65 percent, believe that the European Union should become a superpower like the United States.

TABLE 2.2 DIVERGING U.S. AND EUROPEAN POSITIONS

Issue	U.S. Position	European Position
International Criminal Court	Opposed	Ratified
Kyoto Protocol	Opposed	Ratified
Comprehensive Test Ban Treaty	Opposed	Ratified
Land Mines Ban	Opposed	Signed
Biodiversity Treaty	Opposed	Approved
Anti-Ballistic Missile Treaty	Unilaterally withdrew	Preferred a multilateral decision
U.S. National Missile Defense	Strongly supports	Skeptical
Treaty Limiting Small Arms Exports	Opposed	Supports
Death Penalty	Exists in 38 states	Does not exist in Europe
Israeli-Palestinian Conflict	Strongly supports Israel	More supportive of Palestinians
Invasion of Iraq	Initiated/Led	Generally strongly opposed
U.S. Farm Bill	Signed by Bush, May 13, 2002	Opposed
U.S. Quotas on Steel	Implemented by Bush	Opposed

Source: Chicago Tribune, 28 July 2002, Sect. I, II.

Arguments supporting the view that the European Union will become a super-power and challenge the United States focus on the continent's economic strength and the desire of many countries to be included in the EU. Europe is widely seen as having the potential to become the dominant global economic power within two or three decades. This assumption is based on the following:

1. Europe is prosperous and technologically advanced.
2. Europe has four of the world's seven leading economic powers: Germany, Britain, France, and Italy.
3. The EU is likely to expand to include Russia.
4. The EU will have more than 800 million relatively rich consumers, thereby creating a huge internal market.
5. Europe attracts immigrants from around the world.
6. The adoption of the euro as a single currency for most EU countries will challenge the international financial dominance of the U.S. dollar and facilitate economic growth and commerce within Europe.[44]

The **Treaty of Nice**—approved in October 2002 by unanimous consent after Ireland finally voted in favor of it—set the rules for an orderly expansion of the EU.

Treaty of Nice
Provides for the EU's orderly expansion

Europe's economic power and technological and scientific achievements could enable it to develop stronger military capabilities. Both Britain and France possess nuclear weapons and advanced weapons systems. European political and economic integration is influencing the leading countries to coordinate the building and purchasing of military weapons. Instead of continuing to rely on the United States for the most technologically advanced weapons, the Europeans are making their own and competing more vigorously with American defense companies. These trends were accelerated not only by European integration but also by the end of the Cold War and

TABLE 2.3 JOINT EUROPEAN MILITARY PROJECTS

Project	What It Is	Project's Value	Countries Involved
Eurofighter	Fighter jet	$12 billion (208 orders)	Germany, Italy, Spain, U.K.
NH-90	Military transport helicopter	$4 billion (298 orders)	France, Germany, Italy, Netherlands
Tiger	Combat helicopter	$1.5 billion (160 orders)	France, Germany
Scalp/ Stormshadow	Cruise missile	$1.5 billion	France, Italy, U.K., Belgium, Germany, Netherlands, Portugal, Spain, Turkey
A400M	Military transport plane	$20 billion (projected)	Portugal, Spain, Turkey
Meteor	Air-to-air missile	$1.5 billion	France, Germany, Italy, Spain, Sweden, U.K., U.S.
Galileo	Global positioning system	N.A.	France, Germany, Italy, U.K.
Sostar	Airborne ground surveillance	N.A.	France, Germany, Italy, Netherlands

Sources: Wall Street Journal, 9 March 2001, A11; and "EU Ministers to Increase Defense R and T Investment and Collaboration," *US FedNews*, 15 May 2006, 1–2.

the decision by leading countries, including the United States, to reduce defense expenditures partly by merging defense companies.

Joint European Military Projects

Helsinki Declaration

Transfers responsibility for defense and security to the EU, thereby consolidating European military initiatives

European military weakness in Bosnia, Kosovo, and elsewhere, and the United States' ability to invade Iraq despite widespread European opposition, underscored the need for Europe to consolidate its military power. As early as December 1999, EU leaders met in Helsinki, Finland, to create a rapid deployment force capable of acting independently of NATO. They also created a new political and security committee, appointed a military staff to advise EU leaders, and created a military committee composed of defense chiefs, modeled on NATO's. The **Helsinki Declaration** transfers responsibility for defense and security to the EU, thereby consolidating European military initiatives.[45] However, Britain's strong relationship with the United States and the ongoing disagreement between the British and the French on defense and other issues threaten to weaken Europe's efforts to become more independent militarily of the United States. Furthermore, discussions of Europe's efforts to develop stronger military capabilities must take into consideration Europe's desire to preserve the current global system and to limit American hegemony by strengthening multilateralism and global institutions.

Nonstate Actors

Asymmetrical Warfare

Strategy of counteracting the dominant power of a hegemon through unorthodox ways

When faced with overwhelming power, represented by the giant Goliath, the Israelites employed a boy, David, with a slingshot to counteract that power. In Jonathan Swift's *Gulliver's Travels*, the Lilliputians are able to restrain the giant through cooperation. These stories illustrate the paradox of being a superpower. Instead of engaging a country that possesses overwhelming power with conventional weapons, the weak usually confront the strong in unorthodox ways. This strategy of counteracting the dominant power of a hegemon is called **asymmetrical warfare**. It enables the weaker side to gain military advantages and level the playing field to some extent by using comparatively unsophisticated weapons and strategies. Increasing globalization facilitates the proliferation of challenges from nonstate actors.

Almost 98 percent of Americans view terrorist organizations as the most potent nonstate challengers to American dominance. Their ability to effectively utilize asymmetrical power has been facilitated by globalization. The United States has many interests around the world, which generate resentments that can escalate into violence. For example, in 1983 a suicide bomber drove a truck loaded with explosives into a U.S. Marine barracks in Beirut, Lebanon, killing 241 Americans. In 1996 a truck bomb destroyed part of the Khobar Towers housing complex near Dhahran, Saudi Arabia, killing 19 American soldiers. The following year American embassies in Kenya and Tanzania were bombed, killing 224 people, including 12 Americans. In 2000, a major military symbol, the USS *Cole*, a destroyer, was badly damaged by suicide bombers in Aden, Yemen.[46] Finally, the openness of American society has allowed terrorist organizations to operate without being easily detected, even with the increased security measures implemented after the devastating terrorist attacks in New York and Washington, D.C., on September 11, 2001. Despite its superior military forces, America found itself bogged down in a war against insurgents in Iraq armed with road-side bombs and suicide bombers. Violence escalated in 2005 and 2006, at a time when the U.S. military was clearly overextended.

Domestic Challenges to American Hegemony

As the Pentagon prepared a postwar plan in early 2003 for a short-term military occupation of Iraq, followed by an indefinite period of a U.S.-run civil administration that would determine the form and time frame of an eventual resumption of Iraqi control, Americans appeared to be ambivalent about their country's new role as an occupying power. By 2006, a majority of Americans opposed the war in Iraq. Our discussion of previous empires has shown that empires decline not only because of challenges from rising powers, but also because of decisions made by their leaders and general attitudes and beliefs of ordinary citizens. In other words, empires are usually their own worst enemy. More important than what others do to them is what they often do to themselves that ultimately hastens their fall. Historically, America's hegemonic impulses have been largely restrained by its isolationist instincts.

Public opinion polls consistently show that Americans have a definite lack of sustained interest in the rest of the world and in foreign relations. This attitude was especially prevalent prior to the terrorist attacks in 2001. A majority of Americans, ranging from 55 to 66 percent, believed that what happened in Western Europe, Asia, and even Canada and Mexico had little impact on their lives. This reality influenced Samuel P. Huntington, an astute observer of American international and domestic affairs to conclude that "however much foreign policy elites may ignore or deplore it, the United States lacks the domestic political base to create a unipolar world."[47] Public opinion polls taken after the terrorist attacks showed an increased interest in global issues among Americans but ambivalence toward America's hegemony. While 52 percent of

You
DECIDE | ## Responding to Asymmetrical Power

Focusing primarily on nations as the principal challengers to U.S. power, American leaders have concentrated on constructing even more technologically advanced weapons. The terrorist attacks on the United States in Lebanon, Saudi Arabia, Kenya, Tanzania, Yemen, and America itself show that despite possessing the most powerful military in the world, the country is vulnerable to attacks by nonstate actors.

What should the U.S. government do to diminish the occurrence of such attacks?

Americans believed the United States should remain the only superpower, compared with 14 percent of Europeans who held this view, 62 percent of Americans rejected the idea that their country has the responsibility to be the world's policeman.[48] This deeply rooted view was reflected in the growing opposition in 2006 to America's long involvement in the war in Iraq.

Most Americans support a volunteer army, one composed of people who generally come from less privileged economic backgrounds. The country as a whole has demonstrated a low tolerance for combat fatalities and long-term military involvement in dangerous regions. Charles William Maynes observed that empires need to have either **Hessians** (i.e., mercenary soldiers from the region of Hesse in Germany) or citizens who, like the Romans, are anxious to go to war in distant places. America has neither.[49] Moreover, Americans, increasingly more affluent and better educated, are having smaller families and are unwilling to encourage their sons and daughters to join the military. Despite strong public support for the war against terrorism and short-term conflicts, Americans remain primarily concerned with economic issues and the implications of economic globalization. They have constantly viewed economic rather than military power as the more important determinant of global dominance, thus their preoccupation with Japan's economic success during the 1980s and early 1990s. In 1999, roughly 66 percent of the public believed that economic strength was more important than military might. Leaders (89 percent) were even more convinced in the centrality of economic power as the most critical measure of a country's strength.[50]

Hessians

Mercenary soldiers
from Hesse region
in Germany

Will the United States Remain the Dominant Power?

As American troops marched across Iraq and its planes and ships bombed Baghdad to effectuate what the Pentagon called "shock and awe," the rest of the world watched the most awesome military force the world has ever known unilaterally impose its will on another country. The war against terrorism continued in Afghanistan and elsewhere, and North Korea threatened to accelerate its production of nuclear weapons and to destabilize the Korean peninsula. America clearly demonstrated that it is a hegemon with a preponderance of power. On the other hand, some scholars, such as Paul Kennedy, caution that overwhelming power often leads a country to engage in imperial overstretch or to expand its interests and obligations to such a great degree that it overburdens its resource base and is unable to defend all of its interests simultaneously.[51] America's difficulties in Iraq made this obvious by 2006. Another concern was America's emphasis on unilateralism. Stanley Hoffmann, a leading scholar of international relations, argued that there is nothing more dangerous for a hyperpower than the temptation of unilateralism. It may well believe that the constraints of international agreements and organizations are not necessary. But those constraints provide for better opportunities for leadership than does the arrogant demonstration of contempt for the behavior of other states.[52] The danger for the United States, it is argued, is that its unprecedented power is likely to influence it to become insensitive to other nations' fear and interests. Great powers often succumb to hubris. This hubris often leads the dominant nation to believe that it is a benevolent hegemon and that it is immunized from a backlash against its preponderance by the attractiveness of its ideology and culture. But because states are competitive and worry about the predominant country's capabilities, they are likely to coalesce against what they perceive to be a threat.[53]

Many scholars argue that discussions of America's decline are routine and wrong and that the country is likely to remain the dominant power for the foreseeable future. Samuel P. Huntington, for example, identified *five waves of declinism* that turned out to be wrong. The *first wave* occurred with the launch of *Sputnik* by the Soviets in 1957. The *second wave* was at the end of the 1960s, when the United States and the Soviet Union were perceived to be losing to rising economic powers, such as Japan and Western Europe. The *third declinist wave* came with the oil embargo by **the Organization of Petroleum Exporting Countries (OPEC)** in 1973. The *fourth wave* was marked by America's defeat in Vietnam, the Watergate crisis that undermined public confidence in U.S. government and institutions, and the upsurge in Soviet-Cuban expansion in Angola, Afghanistan, Nicaragua, Ethiopia, and Mozambique. Finally, the *fifth wave* came in the late 1980s as a result of growing U.S. trade and budget deficits and Japan's economic might.[54] All of these waves subsided, leaving the United States as a dominant power.

OPEC

Group of oil-exporting states that collaborate to elevate their export power

TABLE 2.4 VIEWS OF DETERMINANTS OF GLOBAL POWER (PUBLIC OPINION POLL)

Which of the following do you think is more important in determining a country's overall power and influence in the world? Economic strength or military strength?

Country	Economic Strength	Military Strength
Great Britain	81%	15%
France	89%	9%
Germany	80%	16%
The Netherlands	89%	7%
Italy	88%	10%
Poland	83%	11%
Europe	84%	12%
United States	66%	27%

Source: "Public Opinion Poll," *Chicago Tribune*, 8 September 2002, Sect. 2, 4.

Huntington and Joseph S. Nye contend that the United States will remain the dominant power. Huntington states that the ultimate test of a great power is its ability to renew itself, and that the United States meets this test to a far greater extent than past or present great powers. The *forces of renewal* are competition, mobility, and immigration. Furthermore, America's strength is multidimensional, meaning that it is based on military might, economic power, technological capabilities, cultural appeal, political leadership and influence in international institutions, an abundance of natural resources, and social cohesion and political stability at home.[55] Nye argues that the American problem is different from that of Britain, which faced challenges from a rising Germany and the United States itself. Instead, the United States will remain the dominant power but will have to cope with unprecedented problems of globalization that cannot be solved unilaterally.[56]

Advocates of American dominance or primacy stress that rising powers are the greatest threat to international security. China and countries in Europe are viewed as the major challengers to American leadership. Advocates of primacy believe that American supremacy must be maintained by politically, economically, and military outdistancing any challenger.[57] Advocates of primacy argue that force should be used sparingly and strategically in defense of concrete American interests. They also recognize the need to prevent the proliferation of weapons of mass destruction because of the direct threats they pose to American primacy.[58]

DOES PRIMACY MATTER IN A GLOBAL SOCIETY?

Have nuclear weapons, globalization, and other developments changed the world enough to render preoccupation with international primacy largely irrelevant and counterproductive? Has the world moved sufficiently beyond traditional great power politics and into a more complicated and interdependent global age to make historical patterns in international relations less applicable? As we have seen, wars for global dominance were fought for specific reasons, many of which are no longer as potent in this age of globalization.

Samuel P. Huntington represents those who argue for primacy. He contends that primacy matters because power, a central reality of human existence, matters, and will always matter. He rejects the widely held assumption that because wars among great powers are unlikely today, primacy is not important. In his view, states pursue primacy to enhance their security, to promote and protect their interests, to build international institutions that reinforce their security interests, and to shape the global environment in ways that are consistent with their values and objectives.[59] Primacy when legitimized, as we discussed earlier in this chapter, enables countries to dominate without having to rely primarily on force. In other words, hegemons usually attempt to maintain primacy principally through peaceful means, not war. America's decision to launch a preemptive war on Iraq weakened its position as the hegemon. Some argue that primacy is important because billions of people think it is important to have one country instead of another influencing global society. For example, it makes a difference whether Russia or China, instead of the United States, has dominant power.[60] However, complex webs of interdependence and increasing globalization, especially economic globalization, challenge fundamental assumptions about the importance of primacy.

Summary and Review

This chapter examined the rise and fall of great powers and the essential role of politics, economics, and culture in that process. Countries with strong economies and well-managed political systems are able to spread their culture globally and to exercise power over other states. A state, or in some cases a small group of states, that has extraordinary influence over the behavior of other states is said to have international primacy. States that enjoy international primacy are generally said to have diverse interests. When several great powers are in the international system, it is defined as being multipolar. During the Cold War, when the United States and the Soviet Union were superpowers, the system was bipolar. Today, the United States remains the world's only superpower, which makes the current system unipolar.

States and groups of states become powerful and lose their power for many reasons. War is one major factor. While investing in military power can help turn a state into a great power, it can also lead to its fall as a great nation. Many great powers decline because of hubris, or excessive pride, and imperial arrogance. These nations tend to overestimate their power and expand their military power so much that they ultimately erode their economic base. We discussed some challenges to the U.S. status as the world's lone great power. Some of these challenges come from nations that are quickly advancing economically, such as Japan and China. A second challenge to American hegemony is the consolidation of power in Europe under one European Union. Finally, we discussed the challenge to American power from nonstate actors, such as terrorist organizations, that try to undermine the strength of great nations.

Key Terms

power transition theory 37	population pressures 40	Magna Carta 50	Pearl Harbor 56
multipolar 37	uneven economic growth 40	Otto Von Bismarck 50	public goods 57
bipolar 37	hubris 41	Triple Entente 52	Ministry of International Trade and Industry (MITI) 59
unipolar 37	Lippmann Gap 41	Triple Alliance 52	ideology 60
hegemon 37	imperial overstretch 41	Catherine the Great 52	Japanese exceptionalism 60
Antonio Gramsci 38	Concert of Europe 42	Peter the Great 52	
power 38	containment 42	V. I. Lenin 52	Treaty of Friendship and Cooperation 63
gross national product (GNP) 38	Persian Empire 43	Cuban missile crisis 54	Marshall Plan 63
gross domestic product (GDP) 38	Greek city-states 43	Mikhail Gorbachev 54	Treaty of Nice 65
power conversion 39	Delian League 43	glasnost 54	Helsinki Declaration 66
structural leadership 39	Peloponnesian War 43	perestroika 54	asymmetrical warfare 66
institutional leadership 39	Thucydides 43	manifest destiny 55	Organization of Petroleum Exporting Countries (OPEC) 69
situational leadership 39	Confucianism 45	Mexican-American War 55	
	Koran 47	Spanish American War 56	
	communes 49	Monroe Doctrine 56	
	cultivation of invention 49	League of Nations 56	

Discussion Questions

1. Economic power and military power are often discussed as the two most important factors that make up a great power. What are some other elements of power? How might they contribute to a nation's rise to superpower status?

2. What are the three types of leadership? Provide some examples of how the United States and past world powers have exercised these types of leadership.

3. As explained in this chapter, war is a major factor in the rise and fall of great powers. How did war play a role in the rise and fall of some of the great powers discussed in this chapter? How does the Lippmann Gap play a role in the fall of great powers?

4. What are some strategies for maintaining power and preventing rising powers from creating disorder in the international system? Provide some examples of countries that have used some of these strategies.

5. This chapter provided several case studies of the rise and fall of past great powers. Pick one great power and discuss how some of the key terms in this chapter apply to its rise and fall. For example, what elements of power contributed to its rise?

6. This chapter stated that the United States borrowed from past great powers in becoming a world power itself. Provide some examples of how the United States did this.

7. What are some current examples of challenges to American hegemony? What are the strongest challenges the United States faces to maintain its status as a great power? Explain.

8. What are some ways that globalization makes it difficult for the United States to maintain its status as a great power?

9. Many observers of international affairs argue that the U.S. status as a dominant power is not likely to change for a long time. What are some points to support this argument? Do you agree? Explain.

10. What are some reasons that states pursue primacy? Do these pursuits matter in today's world of globalization?

Suggested Readings

Brzezinski, Zhigniew. *The Choice: Global Domination or Global Leadership*. New York: Basic Books, 2005.

Dunlop, John B. *The Rise of Russia and the Fall of the Soviet Empire*. Princeton: Princeton University Press, 1993.

Dunne, Michael. "U.S. Foreign Relations in the Twentieth Century: From World Power to Global Hegemon," *International Affairs* 76, No. 8 (2000): 25–40.

Huntington, Samuel P. "Why International Primacy Matters," *International Security* 17, No. 4 (Spring 1993): 68–83.

Ikenberry, G. John, ed. *America Unrivaled: The Future of the Balance of Power*. Ithaca: Cornell University Press, 2002.

Jervis, Robert. *American Foreign Policy in a New Era*. New York: Routledge, 2006.

Keohane, Robert O. *After Hegemony*. Princeton: Princeton University Press, 1984.

Kristof, Nicholas. "The Rise of China," *Foreign Affairs* 72, No. 5 (November/December 1993): 59–74.

Layne, Christopher. "The Unipolar Illusion: Why New Great Powers Will Rise," *International Security* 17, No. 4 (Spring 1993): 5–15.

Legro, Jeffrey. *Rethinking the World: Great Power Strategies and International Order*. Ithaca: Cornell University Press, 2005.

Mandelbaum, Michael. "David's Friend Goliath," *Foreign Policy* 152 (January/February 2006): 50–57.

Patten, Chris. *Cousins and Strangers: America, Britain, and Europe in a New Century*. New York: Times Books, 2006.

Schwartau, Winn. "Asymmetrical Adversaries," *Orbis* 44, No. 2 (Spring 2000): 197–205.

Walt, Stephen M. *Taming American Power: The Global Response to U.S. Primacy*. New York: Norton, 2005.

Addresses and Websites

AsiaSource
725 Park Ave.
New York, NY 10021
Tel: (212) 288–6400
Fax: (212) 744–8825
E-mail: webmaster@asiasource.org
www.asiasource.org

This website is devoted to topics relating to the continent of Asia. It offers numerous links to other Asia-related websites, including government and economics, as well as information on individual Asian countries.

Asian Development Bank
Headquarters:
6 ADB Ave.
Mandaluyong City
0401 Metro Manila
Philippines
Tel: +632 632 4444
Fax: +632 636 2444
www.adb.org

The Asian Development Bank is a sixty-one-member multilateral economic institution devoted to ending poverty in Asian countries and the Pacific region. The ADB lends money mainly to underdeveloped countries in the region, and focuses on sustainable development, social development, and good governance. This website provides information on topics relating to underdeveloped nations in Asia and the Pacific region.

European Parliament
Rue Wiertz
B-1047 Brussels
Tel: 322–284–2111
www.europarl.eu.int

The European Parliament represents 375 million Europeans in fifteen nations. Its website offers information on all member states of the European Union, as well as information on legal concerns that affect each member state. Links to other European parliamentary websites are also provided.

CIA Factbook

www.cia.gov/cia/publications

The *CIA Factbook* is a yearly publication of the U.S. Central Intelligence Agency. It is available online as well as in hard copy. This website offers information on almost every country in the world, including information on a country's geography, people, economy, and historical facts.

The European Union

http://europa.eu.int/

The European Union, a federation of many European states, has a large website that provides detailed information on the activities in which the EU is involved. The institutions within the EU, such as the Court of Justice, all have special sections. Official documents are also available.

China Internet Information Center
24 Baiwanzhuang Rd.
Beijing 100037
China
Tel: 86–10–68996217
Fax: 86–10–68997796
www.china.org.cn/english

This government website offers news about China and has special sections for topics such as Tibet and Taiwan. Government position papers as well as information on Chinese culture are also available.

Endnotes

1. Samuel P. Huntington, "Why International Primacy Matters," *International Security* 17, No. 4 (Spring 1993), 68.
2. Ronald L. Tammen, et al., *Power Transitions* (New York: Seven Bridges Press, 2000), 6.
3. Alan W. Cafruny, "A Gramscian Concept of Declining Hegemony," in *World Leadership and Hegemony*, ed. David R. Rapkin (Boulder: Lynne Rienner, 1990), 103.
4. Joseph S. Nye, *Bound to Lead: The Changing Nature of American Power* (New York: Basic Books, 1990), 32.

5. John J. Mearsheimer, *The Tragedy of Great Power Politics* (New York: W. W. Norton, 2001), 61.
6. Nye, *Bound to Lead*, 27.
7. G. John Ikenberry, "The Future of International Leadership," *Political Science Quarterly* III (Fall 1996), 388.
8. Ikenberry, "The Future of International Leadership," 389.
9. Randall Schweller, "Managing the Rise of Great Powers," in *Engaging China*, eds. Alastair Johnston and Robert Ross (London: Routledge, 1999), 2.
10. Torbjorn L. Knutsen, *The Rise and Fall of World Orders* (Manchester: Manchester University Press, 1999), 24.
11. Walter Lippmann, *U.S. Foreign Policy* (London: Hanish Hamilton, 1943), 5; and Paul Kennedy, *The Rise and Fall of Great Powers* (New York: Vintage Books, 1987), xvi.
12. G. John Ikenberry and Charles Kupchan, "The Legitimation of Hegemonic Power," in *World Leadership and Hegemony*, 49.
13. Schweller, "Managing the Rise of Great Powers," in *Engaging China*, 9.
14. Schweller, "Managing the Rise of Great Powers," in *Engaging China*, 14.
15. Paul R. Viotti and Mark V. Kauppi, *International Relations and World Politics* (Upper Saddle River, NJ: Prentice Hall, 1997), 39.
16. Thucydides, *History of the Peloponnesian War*, translated by Rex Warner (Baltimore: Penguin, 1954), 25.
17. Josef Joffe, "How America Does It," *Foreign Affairs* 76, No. 5 (September/October 1997), 14.
18. Kennedy, *The Rise and Fall of Great Powers*, 6.
19. David S. Landes, *The Wealth and Poverty of Nations* (New York: W. W. Norton, 1998), 56.
20. Kennedy, *The Rise and Fall of Great Powers*, 10.
21. Dennis Overbye, "How Islam Won, and Lost, the Lead in Science," *The New York Times*, 30 October 2001, D1.
22. Kennedy, *The Rise and Fall of Great Powers*, 12.
23. Virginia Postrel, "The Decline of the Muslim Middle East," *The New York Times*, 8 November 2001, C2.
24. Kennedy, *The Rise and Fall of Great Powers*, 17.
25. Landes, *The Wealth and Poverty of Nations*, 36.
26. Landes, *The Wealth and Poverty of Nations*, 47.
27. Robert J. Lieber, "Great Britain: Decline and Recovery," in *A Century's Journey*, ed. Robert A. Pastor (New York: Basic Books, 1999), 36.
28. Kennedy, *The Rise and Fall of Great Powers*, 362.
29. Robert G. Kaiser, "The USSR in Decline," *Foreign Affairs* 79, No. 2 (Winter 1988/89), 98; and William Robinson, *Promoting Polyarchy: Globalization, U.S. Intervention, and Hegemony* (Cambridge: Cambridge University Press, 1996), 320–323.
30. Knutsen, *The Rise and Fall of World Orders*, 175.
31. Ernest R. May, *Imperial Democracy: The Emergence of America as a Great Power* (Chicago: Imprint Publications, 1991), 7.
32. May, *Imperial Democracy*, 3.
33. Joffe, "How America Does It," 27; and G. John Ikenberry, "Institutions, Strategic Restraint, and the Persistence of American Postwar Order," *International Security* 23, No. 3 (Winter 1998–99), 71.
34. Andrew C. Revkin, "U.S. Making Weapons to Blast Underground Hide-outs," *The New York Times*, 3 December 2001, B4.
35. Samuel P. Huntington, "The Lonely Superpower," *Foreign Affairs* 78, No. 2 (March/April 1999), 37.
36. Hugh De Santis, *Beyond Progress* (Chicago: University of Chicago Press, 1996), 33.
37. Landes, *The Wealth and Poverty of Nations*, 474.
38. David Rapkin, "Japan and World Leadership," in *World Leadership*, 199.
39. Michael M. May, "Japan as a Superpower?" *International Security* 18, No. 3 (Winter 1993/94), 183.
40. Gilbert Royman, "China's Quest for Great Power Identity," *Orbis* 43, No. 3 (Winter 1993/94), 183.
41. Thomas J. Christensen, "Posing Problems Without Catching Up: China's Rise and Challenges for U.S. Security Policy," *International Security* 25, No. 4 (Spring 2001), 5; and Jim Yardley and Thom Shanker, "Chinese Navy Buildup Gives Pentagon New Worries," *The New York Times*, 8 April 2005, A3.
42. Saritha Rai, "Chinese Race to Supplant India in Software," *The New York Times*, 5 January 2002, B1.
43. Craig S. Smith, "China Reshaping Military to Toughen Its Muscle in the Region," *The New York Times*, 16 October 2002, A14.
44. Andrew Reding, "EU in Position to Be the Next Superpower," *Chicago Tribune*, 6 January 2002, Sect. 1, 19; and C. Fred Bergsten, "America and Europe: A Clash of the Titans," *Foreign Affairs* 78, No. 2 (March/April 1999), 20.
45. Philip H. Gordon, "Their Own Army? Making European Defense Work," *Foreign Affairs* 79, No. 4 (July/August 2000), 12; and Roger Cohen, "Europe's Shifting Role Poses Challenge to U.S.," *The New York Times*, 11 February 2001, A1.
46. Michael R. Gordon, "Superpower Suddenly Finds Itself Threatened by Sophisticated Terrorists," *The New York Times*, 14 October 2000, A9.
47. Huntington, "The Lonely Superpower," 40.
48. Marshall M. Bouton and Benjamin I. Page, "Vulnerable, Vigilant, Engaged," *Chicago Tribune*, 8 September 2002, Sect. 2, 3.
49. Charles William Maynes, "The Perils of (and for) an Imperial America," *Foreign Policy*, No. 111 (Summer 1998), 42.
50. John E. Rielly, "Americans and the World," *Foreign Policy*, No. 114 (Spring 1999), 105.
51. Kennedy, *The Rise and Fall of Great Powers*, 515.
52. Stanley Hoffmann, "Clash of Globalizations," *Foreign Affairs* 81, No. 4 (July/August 2002), 113.

53. Benjamin Schwarz and Christopher Layne, "A New Grand Strategy," *The Atlantic Monthly*, January 2002, 38; and David P. Calleo, "The United States and the Great Powers," *World Policy Journal* 16, No. 3 (Fall 1999), 13.

54. Samuel P. Huntington, "The U.S.—Decline or Renewal?" *Foreign Affairs* 67, No. 2 (Winter 1988/89), 94–95.

55. Huntington, "The U.S.—Decline or Renewal?" 90–91.

56. Nye, *Bound to Lead*, 21.

57. Barry R. Rosen and Andrew L. Ross, "Competing Visions for U.S. Grand Strategy," in *America's Strategic Choices*, eds. Michael E. Brown, et al. (Cambridge, MA: The MIT Press, 2000), 30.

58. Rosen and Ross, "Competing Visions," 39.

59. Huntington, "Why International Primacy Matters," 70.

60. Huntington, "Why International Primacy Matters," 69.

CHAPTER 3

Human Rights

INTRODUCTION

Each culture or society has a moral sense, a set of feelings and beliefs about what is right and wrong. Although cultural values differ significantly from one society to another, our common humanity has equipped us with many shared ideas about how human beings should treat each other. However, as this chapter shows, many societies, including our own, engage in practices that others condemn as violations of human rights. In general, there is global agreement that human beings, simply because we exist, are entitled to at least three types of rights. One is **civil rights**, which include personal liberties, such as freedom of speech, religion, and thought; the right to own property; and the right to equal treatment under the laws. Second is **political rights**, including the right to vote, to voice political opinions, and to participate in the political process. Third is **social rights**, including the right to be secure from violence and other physical danger, the right to a decent standard of living, and the right to health care and education. Societies differ in terms of which rights they emphasize.

As a society that originated from a revolution, the United States often stresses rights and deemphasizes responsibilities. But rights do not exist apart from duties and responsibilities. A right is a claim that individuals may expect others to respect. When individuals claim the right to free speech, they are in essence saying that others are obligated to respect their right to speak freely. Their assertion of a right clearly implies that others have responsibilities. **Positive rights** require others to behave in a certain way. These include the right to a certain level of economic well-being, health, education, and cultural amenities. **Negative rights** include rights or claims of individuals and groups against governments and other institutions. Freedom of speech, of religion, of the press, and the right to a fair trial are examples of negative rights. *Four types of human rights claims* that dominate global politics are

1. Accusations that governments are abusing individuals.
2. Demands by ethnic, racial, and religious communities for autonomy or independence.
3. Claims in what is generally regarded as private life, including rights and obligations within families, and the demands for equality by minority groups with unconventional lifestyles.
4. Demands by governments for protection against powerful governments and nonstate actors, as well as the right to economic development.[1]

This chapter discusses human rights as an integral component of the political, economic, and cultural forces of globalization. We will examine historical and philosophical foundations undergirding the development of human rights as a central component of

76

modern civilizations. The issues involved in implementing human rights are essential to any discussion of securing freedom. Economic and political sanctions are often used to achieve compliance with human rights commitments. In extreme cases, countries support humanitarian intervention to terminate violations of human rights. One of the most significant developments is the emphasis on women's human rights. All societies, to varying degrees, confer on women an inferior status that makes them vulnerable to discrimination and abuse. In this chapter, we will look closely at issues like forced marriages, honor killings, and rape as a weapon of war. Closely related to women's rights is the contemporary debate on human rights in Islamic countries. In fighting terrorism, many governments violate human rights, which we will also discuss. Finally, we will briefly examine the death penalty issue, contemporary slavery, and the treatment of gays and lesbians.

GLOBALIZATION AND HUMAN RIGHTS

The different waves of globalization we discussed in Chapter 1 were accompanied by both positive and negative consequences for human rights. While some people benefited from global change, others paid an extremely high price for progress. The rise of the modern state in Western Europe and the European expansion into the Americas, Asia, and Africa increased both freedom and oppression. The modern state provided increased security, but often it also became a cold instrument for systematically abusing human rights. In fact, it was due to violence against Jews, gypsies, gays and lesbians, communists, religious groups, and others in Nazi Germany, which culminated in the **Holocaust**, that human rights became so prominent in global affairs.

The current wave of globalization has undoubtedly enhanced the observance of human rights. Telecommunications, trade, migration, travel, the weakening of national boundaries, the decline of **Westphalian** sovereignty, and growing interdependence have strengthened a commitment to human rights. Information is now relayed instantaneously, which helps to limit governments' ability to engage in secrecy and brutality. China, for example, uses telecommunications technologies to control its population, but many Chinese also use these technologies to diminish the government's ability to limit their freedom. In fact, globalization complicates efforts by governments to abuse human rights. Because their interests are intertwined with those of leading global actors, countries must consider the costs and benefits of decisions concerning their treatment of citizens. For example, China risks jeopardizing trade with the United States if it engages in gross violations of human rights. In March 2001, China decided to ratify the International Convention on Economic, Social, and Cultural Rights (ICESCR), partly because it was competing to host the 2008 Olympics.[2] This decision demonstrates how sports, which are a component of cultural globalization, often pressure governments to comply with global humanitarian values. However, other aspects of globalization contribute to abuses of human rights. For example, many human rights activists argue that America's war against drugs in Colombia has contributed to widespread brutality by Colombia's armed forces and right-wing militias.[3] America's war on terrorism is also widely perceived as endangering human rights. As we will see in this chapter, competing national interests often lead to mixed results relating to human rights.

Civil Rights
Personal liberties, such as freedom of speech, thought, and religion

Political Rights
Right to vote, voice political opinions, and participate in the political process

Social Rights
Right to health care, education, and other social benefits

Positive Rights
Rights a government/society is supposed to provide

Negative Rights
Rights a government may not infringe upon

Holocaust
Mass murder of millions of Jews driven by ethnic and religious hate and discrimination

Westphalian
Concept of state sovereignty developed over 350 years ago

The horrors of the Holocaust and World War II marked a turning point in the struggle to obtain global respect for human rights. Equally important was the rise of the United States to global power and its competition with the Soviet Union for the hearts and minds of people around the world, especially in the developing countries. This period of globalization radically transformed the perception that domestic affairs could be automatically separated from international politics. A deeper awareness of the indivisibility of humanity and of our problems weakened the idea that governments are essentially free to treat their citizens as they wish. America's self-definition as a redeemer nation and a positive force made human rights a central global issue. But the Soviet Union also helped to further this process by emphasizing basic human needs, such as food, shelter, and medicine as essential human rights. While human rights under communism suffered severe setbacks, the idea that human rights should be respected was firmly established as an integral component of global politics. The superpower struggle led to the signing of international agreements that protected both civil and political rights (strongly advocated by the United States) and social and economic rights (endorsed by the Soviet Union). To these were added the right of minority groups to equal treatment and a cultural identity; humanitarian treatment of civilians in internal conflicts; and the right to economic development, security, and a healthy environment. In addition to the influence of the United States and the Soviet Union, several other factors contributed to the expansion of and commitment to the human rights agenda. These include

1. The *creation of global institutions* to protect human rights. The legitimacy of this human rights system gave states as well as nonstate actors a forum for protecting human rights.
2. A growing *acceptance of the interdependence and indivisibility of rights*. Violations of rights in one country have implications for people in other countries.
3. An *emphasis on promoting democracy*. The idea that democracy is essential to peaceful international relations became a central part of U.S. foreign policy. This helped to elevate human rights in global affairs, especially during President Jimmy Carter's administration.
4. The view that *respect for human rights facilitated market-based economic development*. Political liberalization, which included values associated with the American system of government, became an integral part of the new wave of globalization in the 1980s.[4]
5. *The effectiveness of nonstate actors*. Revolutions in telecommunications and computer technologies greatly enhanced the ability of human rights activists to exchange information, organize global support for human rights, and to exert considerable pressure on governments at all levels.

Nongovernmental Organizations and Human Rights

Because many governments violate human rights, responsibility for protecting individual freedoms was taken up by numerous nonstate actors at the local, national, and global levels. As citizens became more politically sophisticated, they challenged the

DEVELOPMENT OF HUMAN RIGHTS

Inventors of Western democracy, the Greeks profoundly believed that humans have fundamental rights and freedoms, although these rights were not enjoyed by women and slaves in Greek society. Humans have always had a moral sense and have practiced, to varying degrees, rights embraced by the Greeks. But the Greeks clearly articulated and systematically practiced such rights as *isogoria* (equal freedom of speech) and *isonomia* (equality before the law). Greek philosophers, known as **Stoics**, developed the idea that rights enjoyed by Greeks were **universal rights**, freedoms that humans everywhere were entitled to simply because humans exist. These rights emanated from a law that was higher and more permanent than civil law—a universal law that was equated with the laws of gods. These laws were natural laws, which embodied elementary principles of justice that rational human beings could understand. Greek philosophy, like many other Greek inventions, was adopted by the Romans. Roman Stoics were primarily lawyers who attempted to implement the ideas of Greek philosophers in an expanding Roman Empire that encompassed diverse peoples. Marcus Tullius Cicero, Lucius Annaeus Seneca, and Marcus Aurelius were some of the leading Roman Stoics. **Cicero** (106–43 B.C.) was the leading Stoic. The most prominent lawyer and philosopher of the Roman Empire, Cicero wrote that "true law is right reason in agreement with nature; it is of universal application, unchanging and everlasting."[9] This *natural law concept* was consistent with Rome's universal or cosmopolitan perception of humanity. Like other Greek and Roman institutions and ideas, Stoic philosophy profoundly shaped European societies. John Locke in England, Hugo Grotius in Holland, and Immanuel Kant in Germany were influenced by the Stoics.

Stoics

Ancient Greek and Roman philosophers

Universal Rights

Freedoms to which all humans are automatically entitled

Cicero

The leading Stoic, and Rome's greatest lawyer and orator

Social Contract Theories and Human Rights

A major step toward widespread acceptance and practice of natural rights, which are closely associated with universal human rights, was the significant recognition by England's king, barons, and others that citizens were entitled to exercise basic freedoms without interference from their leaders, and that such leaders' powers were limited by law and a sense of justice and fairness. The signing of the **Magna Carta** in 1215 was followed by England's King Edward III's acceptance in 1354 of the concept of **due process of law**, which means that a person cannot be deprived of life, liberty, or property without a fair trial based on fair procedures and rules. Another important step toward consolidating human rights was the decision of King Charles I of England, in his Petition of Rights in 1628, to guarantee the right of **habeas corpus**; that is, the right of a person to be brought before a judge or a court to determine whether or not he or she should be imprisoned. Because human rights are largely concerned with restraining governments, these governments were crucial to the articulation of natural rights and social contract theories.

Natural rights theories flourished during a period of revolutions, beginning with the English Revolution of 1688, then the American Revolution of 1776, and the French Revolution of 1789. These revolutions stressed that individuals' freedoms

Magna Carta

The first written legal protections for the British people

Due Process of Law

Protection of individual life, liberty, and property through a fair trial system

Habeas Corpus

The right to be brought before a judge or court to determine guilt or innocence

were natural and that governments could not violate them. Restrictions on governments emerged from various historical experiences, but more directly from social contract theories. *Thomas Hobbes*, an English philosopher, justified the absolute power of monarchs by arguing that in the state of nature, before governments existed, life was unbearably violent and insecure. The creation of a powerful state or ruler, which he called **Leviathan**, to provide security in exchange for obedience was a social contract. *John Locke*, another English philosopher, argued in his *Second Treatise on Government* (1690) that the state of nature was governed by natural law. People were relatively secure and free and could acquire property. From Locke's perspective, the social contract between citizens and government protected these natural rights. In sharp contrast with the obedience advocated by Hobbes, Locke believed that people had the right to overthrow governments that failed to honor freedoms promised in the social contract. Nowhere are Locke's ideas expressed more forcefully than in the American Declaration of Independence, authored principally by *Thomas Jefferson* in 1776.

Another advocate of the social contract was the French philosopher *Jean-Jacques Rousseau*. He was convinced that civilization corrupts human beings, who are naturally good. Nonetheless, he stressed in the **social contract** that through their total and equal subordination to the government, which is based on and functions according to the *general will* of all its citizens, humans could regain some of their natural goodness and freedoms. In essence, however, Rousseau ended up supporting a social contract that subordinates individual freedoms to the tyranny of the majority. His philosophy justified the government's absolute power over citizens.[10] The French Revolution, despite its embrace of human rights in the Declaration of the Rights of Man and of Citizens (1789), soon degenerated into the **Reign of Terror**, a period that became a hallmark of the systematic, pervasive, and extreme abuse of human rights by the French government. Drawing on the works of social contract theorists, *Immanuel Kant* developed the idea that human rights are directly linked to an inviolable obligation that we have to ourselves and to others. Kant believed that these obligations are universal, binding on all of us no matter where we live, thereby underscoring the concept of the indivisibility of humanity and universal nature of human rights. The most profound of these obligations is what Kant called the *categorical imperative;* that is, the absolute obligation that each of us should always treat humanity never simply as a means but always at the same time as an end.[11]

Utilitarianism, Libertarianism, and Marxism

Jeremy Bentham, James Mill, and John Stuart Mill were among those who developed the theory of **utilitarianism**, directly challenging the idea that human beings have natural rights. The utilitarians, led by **Jeremy Bentham**, believed that individuals determine what is good for them and what they want. Conversely, they avoid the things that cause them pain. In his *Principles of Morals and Legislation* (1789), Bentham used his training as an Oxford-educated lawyer to develop a scientific analysis of morals and legislation. His theory of utilitarianism held that the greatest happiness of the largest

Leviathan

A powerful state or ruler

Second Treatise on Government

By John Locke; addressed the state of nature and natural law

Social Contract

Government sovereignty over its people in exchange for protecting individual rights

Reign of Terror

Terrorism committed by the French government after the French Revolution

Utilitarianism

Theory contradicting the idea that humans have natural rights

Principles of Morals and Legislation

Bentham's scientific analysis of morals and legislation

number of people is the fundamental and self-evident principle of morality. Utilitarianism was regarded as the standard by which we should measure institutions and actions. In a nutshell, Bentham and the other utilitarians argued that self-interests are generally harmonious with the general welfare. The state should be designed to enable individuals to achieve their objectives. Through the careful balancing of individual interests, individual rights arise and are protected. From the utilitarians' perspective, rights are derived from laws. Individual rights, according to the utilitarians, are neither natural nor unalienable, and they cannot be allowed to frustrate the principle and practice of the greatest happiness for the greatest number.

But **John Stuart Mill**—a utilitarian advocate and the son of James Mill, a leading utilitarian—questioned major assumptions of utilitarianism. He stressed that the government, representing the majority, can brutally suppress the rights of individuals. This fear of the tyranny of the majority is what motivated Jefferson and others to insist on the inclusion of the **Bill of Rights** in the U.S. Constitution to protect individuals who disagree with the majority. In other words, John Stuart Mill believed that focusing on the greatest happiness for the greatest number could easily result in the suppression of speech, religion, private morality, artistic endeavors, and nonconformist behavior that were not acceptable to the majority. Mill articulated his philosophy in *On Liberty* (1859). He argued that one could justify interfering with an individual's liberty only to prevent that person from harming others, an assumption that must be proven by government authorities. Mill believed that individual freedoms, such as freedom of speech, benefited society as a whole by providing different viewpoints that could expose problems in the positions held by the majority. The rights of women, for example, were championed by Mill, partly because of the influence of his wife, Harriet Taylor, at a time when the majority strongly and violently opposed such rights.

Another challenge to prevailing perspectives on human rights came from socialist philosophers, such as *Saint Simon* and *Karl Marx*. Marx, the most famous socialist, believed that the history of society is essentially a history of class struggle. Capitalists, while producing unprecedented profits for the few, created high levels of unemployment, subsistence wages, and successively more serious economic crises. Marx and Saint Simon argued that traditional human rights were largely irrelevant to the majority who lived in poverty. They advocated that governments should develop policies that give people economic and social rights. Their perspective was embraced by the former Soviet Union, China, Cuba, and many other communist countries. Social and economic rights are now integral components of global human rights.

Bill of Rights

Constitutional protections of individual political rights

On Liberty

Stated that an individual's civil liberties can be violated only in order to protect others' rights

Legal Positivism and Human Rights

Closely related to utilitarianism are the positivistic theories and conservatism. Some conservatives, such as **Edmund Burke**, strongly opposed natural rights theories and Rousseau's views on the social contract and the general will. Strongly influenced by the Reign of Terror that followed the French Revolution, Burke believed that individuals derived whatever rights they have from tradition and concrete laws, not from

Legal Positivists

Demand absolute court and legal authority over the individual

abstract philosophical theories of natural laws.[12] What distinguished the **legal positivists** from the utilitarians was the extent to which the former insisted on the absolute supremacy of laws and courts in determining rights. After World War I, the legal positivists became more extremist, arguing that law was what courts upheld and that justice was the correct enforcement of the law. Yet those bound to honor specific laws had to have given their consent. In many ways, the legal positivists embraced Hobbes' view that law was essentially the command of the sovereign. Legal positivism was taken to its logical and devastatingly destructive conclusion in Germany under the Nazis. When **Adolf Hitler** came to power in Germany, he made the courts subservient to him and used them as a tool of legal positivism to an extent unparalleled by even the most ardent proponents of legal positivism. Hitler enacted laws suppressing freedom of speech, as well as laws requiring children to spy on their parents and Germans to spy on each other. Individuals could be imprisoned and executed without public trials. Ultimately, laws were enacted that authorized the Jewish Holocaust.[13] Hitler's absolute power, backed by law, demonstrated legal positivism's dangerous consequences and shocked the global community into embracing human rights.

Adolf Hitler

Mastermind of the Nazi cause and the Holocaust

Globalization of Human Rights: The Universal Declaration of Human Rights

Concerns about human rights occurred largely within the context of domestic politics. An overriding emphasis on state sovereignty, which included a preoccupation with independence and control over citizens' lives, prevented broader applications of human rights philosophies from emerging. But increasing globalization—especially European colonization of the Americas and the enslavement of Africans and others—engendered greater global attention to human rights issues that transcended national boundaries. The horrors of slavery shocked people in Europe and the Americas and led to an antislavery campaign in the nineteenth century. Leading countries generally supported abolishing the slave trade at the Congress of Vienna in 1815, seven years after the United States had ceased importing enslaved Africans as required by the U.S. Constitution. *The First Anti-Slavery Convention* was held in London in 1840 by the **Anti-Slavery Society**, the oldest global human rights NGO. Wars also helped to globalize human rights. Horrified by the death and suffering of soldiers at the battle of Solferino in Italy in 1859, *Jean Henry Dunant*, a Swiss citizen, decided to publicize what he saw and to "humanize" war. These efforts resulted in the creation of the **International Committee of the Red Cross** in 1863, followed by the approval of the First Geneva Convention in 1864. The convention was designed to humanize war by making rules for the treatment of wounded and sick soldiers and sailors, prisoners of war, and medical personnel. World War I led to the creation of the **League of Nations** in 1919, which made protecting inhabitants of dependent territories and the trafficking in children and women international human rights issues.[14] The covenant of the League of Nations also made the protection and treatment of workers an international human rights concern. But it wasn't until the global catastrophe of World War II that human rights became a dominant global issue.

Anti-Slavery Society

The oldest global human rights NGO

Nazi Germany's brutal march across Europe and the rise of the United States as the leading global power under the leadership of President Franklin Delano Roosevelt combined to give the impetus to making human rights global. America's self-perception as a nation with a universal message facilitated this development. Addressing Congress in January 1941, President Roosevelt committed the United States to securing **four freedoms** for the world: freedom of speech and expression, freedom of religion, freedom from economic hardship, and freedom from fear. Achieving these freedoms became the centerpiece of the *Atlantic Declaration* made by President Roosevelt and Britain's Prime Minister Winston Churchill in August 1941. The allies met in Washington, D.C., under the auspices of the American Law Institute to draft a declaration or bill of international human rights.[15] These developments laid the foundation for including human rights in the charter of the United Nations (UN) when it was founded in 1945 in San Francisco. The UN Charter provided for the formation of the Human Rights Commission, with the major responsibility for drafting global human rights standards. The final result of these efforts was the adoption by the UN General Assembly of the **Universal Declaration of Human Rights (UDHR)** in 1948. *Eleanor Roosevelt* played a crucial role in this accomplishment. She was largely responsible for promoting the use of the term human rights instead of the traditional emphasis on the rights of man, which actually meant just that. It is also important to point out that the Convention on the Prevention and Punishment of the Crime of Genocide (the Genocide Convention), a direct response to the Holocaust, was adopted by the UN General Assembly the day before it adopted the Universal Declaration of Human Rights. Although the world was united in its determination to promote human rights, differences between the United States and the Soviet Union later led to the adoption in 1966 of two separate international covenants: The **International Covenant on Civil and Political Rights (ICCPR)**, which stressed negative rights and was favored by the United States, and the **International Covenant on Economic, Social, and Cultural Rights (ICESCR)**, which focused on positive rights and was favored by the Soviet Union.

The Universal Declaration of Human Rights helped to unleash global demands for national self-determination by stating that all peoples have this right. Defining "a people" would become more complex than imagined and would lead to numerous conflicts in which human rights were and are still being violated. Newly independent countries in Africa, Asia, and the Caribbean succeeded in getting the UN General Assembly to adopt the International Convention on the Elimination of All Forms of Racial Discrimination in 1965. The global human rights agenda expanded to include the Convention on the Elimination of All Forms of Discrimination Against Women (1981), the Convention on the Rights of the Child (1990), the Convention Concerning Indigenous and Tribal Peoples in Independent Countries (1991), and the International Convention on the Protection of the Rights of All Migrant Workers and Members of Their Families (1991). Human rights issues often became entangled in political disputes between the United States and the Soviet Union during the Cold War. The end of this confrontation in the late 1980s renewed global interest in enforcing human rights.

Four Freedoms

Freedoms espoused by FDR which are necessary for a just society

UDHR

Universal rights entitled to all humankind

ICCPR

Stressed protection of negative political and civil rights from government infringement

ICESCR

Stressed protection and promotion of positive economic, cultural, and social rights that government should provide its people

PHILOSOPHICAL CONTROVERSIES OVER HUMAN RIGHTS

The question on justice or torture in Saudi Arabia raises a fundamental philosophical controversy over human rights, one that persists and grows as societies feel increasingly threatened by the realities of cultural globalization. Other such controversies involve (1) the relationship between individuals and the communities in which they live, (2) the relationship between rights and obligations, (3) the prioritizing of rights and responsibilities, and (4) the absolute or conditional quality of various human rights.[16]

Universalism vs. Cultural Relativism

As we have seen, Greek and Roman Stoics articulated the view that people have natural rights no matter where they live. This idea was more clearly developed by Locke, Jefferson, and others, and has become the dominant view of human rights. But even in societies that stress universal human rights, cultural factors often complicate these theories. The United States, for example, simultaneously embraced natural rights and slavery. In other words, countries modify their support of universal rights by practicing **cultural relativism**. Often, leaders and ordinary citizens do not recognize their own biases in this regard. Proponents of cultural relativism believe that rights enjoyed by individuals are determined by each country's specific cultural and historical experiences. Consequently, what is acceptable behavior in one country could be a violation of human rights in another. Amputating limbs in Saudi Arabia, for example, is viewed in that society as reasonable punishment. Americans reject that punishment as barbaric. On the other hand, America's support of the death penalty is widely regarded in Europe as barbaric. Conservatives and traditionalists in virtually all societies strongly support national cultural relativism. Often, cultural relativism sustains power relations in a society and draws artificial distinctions between societies, instead of emphasizing common values across cultures and the cross-fertilization among cultures. One version of cultural relativism that was popular when Japan was viewed as a rising superpower was

Cultural Relativism

Idea that culture determines the degree of human rights protections in each country

---

You **DECIDE** | ## Justice or Torture in Saudi Arabia?

Shari'a law, the Islamic legal code that governs Saudi Arabia, allows amputations of limbs for theft and floggings for certain sexual offenses and for drinking alcohol. Shari'a also allows murderers, rapists, and drug dealers to be executed. For most Saudis, cutting off a person's hand is acceptable because although that action harms the criminal it protects society. However, the 1987 Convention Against Torture, signed by Saudi Arabia, outlaws floggings and amputations. The Saudis argue that Shari'a takes precedence over international agreements.

Are the Saudis justified in following their religious beliefs even if those beliefs violate human rights? Are their actions justice or torture?

Confucianism. Some argued that Asians were successful because their cultures embrace the Confucianism values of obedience to authority and intense allegiance to groups, and stress collective identities over individual identities. Based on this perspective, the assumption was that universalism was essentially Western and largely incompatible with Asian values.[17] This treatment of Asian values as monolithic has since been widely rejected as being overly simplistic.

Individuals and Communities

Complicating discussions of human rights are varying perspectives on the relationship between the individual and the community to which she or he belongs. As you travel through China, Africa, or the Middle East, you quickly observe that the individualism so prevalent in the United States is subordinated to the needs and values of the community. In societies strongly influenced by Buddhism, Hinduism, or Confucianism, individualism is discouraged and community solidarity is a virtue. The individual is inseparable from the community and enjoys certain benefits from belonging to the community. However, the danger of denying individual rights is that the least powerful in these societies are often brutally suppressed by elites. Many authoritarian governments have justified violating human rights by stressing the need to promote the common good over individual rights and democratic values.

Relationship Between Rights and Obligations

Earlier in this chapter we discussed the connection between rights and responsibilities or obligations. The basic argument is that rights are simply corresponding obligations. In other words, failing to act to prevent human rights violations is in itself a violation of human rights. This argument assumes that we are capable of doing something to either prevent such violations or to mitigate their severity. The idea that we are responsible for what happens to others, to varying degrees, goes back to the idea that we have a moral responsibility for both acts of omission and acts of commission.

Prioritizing Human Rights

As American and British troops entered Baghdad in April 2003, many Americans and Iraqis celebrated the destruction of Saddam Hussein's regime and the idea of restoring fundamental freedoms to the Iraqis. But as chaos and violence escalated, many people worldwide, including the Iraqis, emphasized the urgency of providing electricity, medical supplies, petroleum, and basic services. Above all, the Iraqis wanted security, food, and clean water. American democracy and individual rights were not the most important priority. This situation demonstrates the philosophical controversy over prioritizing human rights. Freedom of religion, speech, assembly, and the press are often elevated above other concerns in the United States. But many other societies, even some groups in the United States, place a much higher priority on satisfying basic economic needs.

You
DECIDE | **Torturing Terrorist Suspects**

After the terrorist attacks in the United States on September 11, 2001, the U.S. government imposed many restrictions on Muslims and Arabs. People accused of having links to terrorist organizations were routinely imprisoned without being granted access to lawyers or being informed of specific charges against them. To most Americans, these actions were easily justified based on national security concerns. But other actions worried some Americans. Suspects, for example, were taken to countries known to use torture to extract confessions. Some Americans have advocated using torture in the United States in order to obtain information about terrorism.

Do you think that the use of torture by governments is ever justified?

Absolutism vs. Consequentialism

Finally, there is the debate about whether we should be willing to compromise on upholding human rights under certain circumstances. Some human rights advocates believe that some rights are absolute; that is, they can never be violated. On the other hand, many of these same advocates would agree that some rights are sometimes limited because exercising them under specific circumstances could endanger the rights of others. In practice, limiting rights under any circumstances can be extremely controversial.

HUMAN RIGHTS REGIMES

UNCHR

Commission responsible for monitoring human rights on a global level

Regimes, as defined in Chapter 1, are institutions, rules, and regulations governing particular types of behavior and interactions. *Human rights regimes* consist of global, regional, national, and local institutions and rules designed to protect human rights, as well as the activities of numerous nonstate human rights organizations and grassroots campaigns. The **UN Commission on Human Rights (UNCHR)** is charged with the responsibility of monitoring human rights globally and for informing the UN Security Council of human rights violations. Previously, we also noted that nations and NGOs, especially after World War I and World War II, succeeded in developing international laws concerning the treatment of national minorities and laborers. These are all components of the global human rights regimes. In this section we will examine regional human rights regimes, focusing on those in Europe. The main institutions dealing with human rights in Europe are the European Commission for Human Rights, the European Court of Justice, and the Organization for Security and Cooperation in Europe (OSCE). Latin America, Africa, and other regions have essentially adopted Europe's regime.[18]

Council of Europe

Created in 1949 to promote democracy and human rights

Meeting in The Hague in 1948, European representatives laid the foundations for establishing the **Council of Europe** in 1949 to promote democracy and protect human rights. Recent events in Europe propelled the states belonging to the council to sign the *European Convention for the Protection of Human Rights and Fundamental Freedoms* in 1950. This agreement focused on safeguarding civil and political rights.

The European Social Charter, signed in 1961, dealt with economic and social rights.[19] Continuing abuses of human rights in Europe, especially in countries under Soviet domination, influenced German Chancellor *Willy Brandt* to promote dialogue across ideological divisions. These efforts led to the adoption of the Helsinki Final Act in 1975 and the creation of the OSCE. The **Helsinki Final Act** provided for the dissemination of the agreement and information about it within countries that originated it. This allowed people in Eastern Europe and the Soviet Union to learn more about human rights initiatives and sparked debate within the communist countries. Combined internal and external pressure influenced Soviet leader Mikhail Gorbachev to adopt policies conducive to the exercise of both civil and political rights and economic and social rights.[20] Eventually, the Soviet domination of Eastern Europe collapsed in 1989 and the Soviet Union disintegrated in 1991. Nevertheless, human rights violations remain a serious issue in many parts of Europe. Jews and immigrants, for example, continue to be targets of violence by extremist groups in Germany and France.

Helsinki Final Act
Created to implement civil and political rights throughout Europe and the Soviet Union

Latin Americans have adopted many features of the European human rights regime but have been less successful in implementing human rights protections. The two most important agreements that established the **Inter-American regime** are the charter of the Organization of American States (OAS) and the American Human Rights Convention. Like Europeans, Latin Americans have a human rights commission (the Inter-American Commission on Human Rights) and a court (the Inter-American Court of Human Rights). However, unlike Europeans, who are willing to relinquish some of their sovereignty, Latin Americans cling so tightly to theirs that they impede the effectiveness of the human rights regime. In fact, governments that are the worst violators of human rights have generally refused to cooperate with investigations by the Inter-American Commission on Human Rights.

Inter-American Regime
Attempt to establish regional protections for human rights in Latin America

ENFORCING HUMAN RIGHTS GLOBALLY

Although much of the responsibility for enforcing human rights is placed on global institutions, governments, and various NGOs, we as individuals have the ultimate obligation for protecting human rights. Crimes against humanity are generally seen as crimes against all of us, a viewpoint supported by the widespread acceptance of the universal nature of human rights. Yet, as individuals, our effectiveness to combat major human rights violations, especially when they occur in distant countries and are carried out by governments, is limited. Consequently, government institutions and various organizations that represent individuals are regarded as bearing most of the responsibility for implementing human rights. The extent to which various global actors and individuals are morally obligated to take action depends on three factors: (1) the nature of the relationship with the rights being violated, (2) the degree of effectiveness, and (3) capacity. The nature of the *relationship* involves such issues as geographic, economic, cultural, or political ties and the depth and duration of those connections. Countries closest to where human rights abuses are taking place are generally expected to act to prevent them, although geographic proximity in an age of globalization is declining in importance. More stress is placed on the *degree of effectiveness* and *capacity*. Powerful countries and institutions can be far more effective than individuals and groups in responding to human rights violations. Similarly, some global actors have greater capacity to act and can absorb the costs associated with such action. These three factors are integral to the concept of a *fair allocation of responsibility*.[21] Generally, there are two approaches to implementing human rights. One is the soft systems of implementation, which concentrate primarily on conducting inquiries, exposing human rights violations, empowering the victims, and finding ways to damage the violating state's reputation. The other is the *hard*, or *coercive*, *enforcement measures*, which include making interventions, setting up international tribunals to prosecute violators, and establishing a permanent international criminal court.[22] This section will focus on economic sanctions, humanitarian intervention, the establishment of international tribunals in cases of genocide, and the creation of the International Criminal Court.

Sanctions

Sanctions

Punishments or penalties imposed on one or more states by another state, group of states, or the global community

Economic Sanctions

Designed to limit or freeze a state's trade, investments, or financing

Diplomatic and Political Sanctions

Designed to isolate and embarrass a state on a political level

Sanctions are punishments or penalties imposed by one state, a group of states, or the global community on another state or group of states in order to gain compliance with widely accepted global standards of behavior. Because political, economic, and military-strategic considerations affect decisions to impose sanctions, there are usually inconsistencies in how sanctions are imposed. For example, allies often escape sanctions even though their behavior is similar to that of the states being sanctioned. The complexity of the factors involved in imposing sanctions results in much controversy about using them in order to force a country to comply with global rules for protecting and promoting human rights. Sanctions can be nonviolent or violent; most are nonviolent. Nonviolent sanctions include economic, diplomatic, political, and cultural measures. **Economic sanctions**, the most prevalent, often limit trade, reduce access to international investments and financing, and freeze or confiscate bank deposits of both countries and individuals. **Diplomatic and political sanctions** include actions that aim at embarrassing a government and its leaders and reducing its interactions with the global community. **Cultural sanctions** usually try to reduce or stop cultural exchanges, tourism, educational ties, and sporting activities with the target country.[23] Imposing sanctions to punish a government and force it to change its behavior without causing much harm to the civilian population that the sanctions are intended to assist is a difficult challenge. Often, sanctions not only fail to change the government's practices, but turn out to have devastating consequences for innocent civilians. So, in the process of imposing sanctions to safeguard human rights, governments sometimes undermine human rights and create humanitarian crises instead. For example, U.S. sanctions against Cuba, strengthened by the Bush administration in 2004, were widely perceived as being counterproductive as well as harmful to ordinary Cubans.

Sanctions can be imposed unilaterally or multilaterally. **Unilateral sanctions**, imposed by one country, were used more often than multilateral sanctions and by several countries before the end of the Cold War. Since 1990, however, the use of **multilateral sanctions** has increased as the ideological conflicts that penalized the UN and other international organizations ended. Increased international cooperation has also encouraged using sanctions as an alternative to military force. At the same time, however, the spread of globalization, which engenders global cooperation, complicates efforts to impose sanctions that are ultimately successful.[24] In an interdependent world, one country's loss due to sanctions can easily become another country's loss as well. In other words, sanctions aimed at an enemy often damage a friend. The United States, the dominant global power, uses sanctions far more often than any other country, and it often influences other countries to do the same. While U.S. sanctions are often designed to punish other countries, to encourage the promotion of democracy and human rights, to set an example for other countries, and to avoid military conflict, domestic factors often have significant influence on America's reliance on sanctions. The inherent competition and conflict between Congress and the president, built into the system of separation of powers, often motivates Congress to act quickly in response to growing domestic pressures. For largely political reasons, the president also supports imposing sanctions.[25]

Although some sanctions have achieved their objectives, such as those applied against the apartheid regime in South Africa, the consensus is that they are usually ineffective. *Sanctions fail for several reasons.* One reason is that nationalism, present in all countries, spawns a rally-round-the-flag effect. Another is that globalization makes it extremely difficult to effectively isolate a state economically. Third, sanctions may enable repressive governments to use external threats to justify cracking down on domestic opponents and to avoid responsibility for deteriorating economic, health, and social conditions. Fourth, sanctions are costly to countries that impose them. Over time, domestic pressures build to support removing sanctions against the targeted country. Finally, sanctions reduce the availability of resources in the target state, thereby strengthening its power to allocate scarce resources strategically to maintain support for its policies.[26] In fact, few leaders change their behavior because of sanctions.

Humanitarian Intervention

Increasing globalization, as we discussed in Chapter 1, is weakening traditional sovereignty and strengthening the idea that the global community has a responsibility to protect individuals from abuse by their governments and others. In extreme cases, when human rights violations shock human conscience, **humanitarian intervention** is regarded as a collective global responsibility. Humanitarian intervention usually involves deploying military forces to prevent or stop a country or group from engaging in gross violations of human rights.[27] It also includes efforts to provide humanitarian relief, to evacuate individuals, and to separate and monitor forces involved in conflicts. Humanitarian interventions fall into two basic categories: consensual and imposed. **Consensual interventions** are agreed to by those in control of a country or region. There is little need for military force. Uniformed forces are involved primarily

Cultural Sanctions
Seek to limit cultural exchanges, tourism, sports, and other interactions with a sanctioned state

Unilateral Sanctions
Sanctions imposed by only one country

Multilateral Sanctions
Sanctions imposed by more than one country

Humanitarian Intervention
The use of military force in order to protect human rights

Consensual Intervention
Interventions agreed upon by all states involved in the conflict

Imposed Intervention

Intervention conducted against the wishes of the occupied state/territory

because they have essential skills and technical capabilities that facilitate rescue operations or the provision of humanitarian supplies. **Imposed interventions** are conducted in a far more hostile environment and often against the wishes of governments or armed groups. Significant military force is required to reduce hostilities, protect civilians, and protect individuals who are delivering humanitarian assistance.[28]

Peacekeeping

Intervention involving impartial monitors and lightly armed observers

Peacemaking

Intervention by heavily armed military forces

Closely related to humanitarian intervention are peacekeeping and peacemaking operations. **Peacekeeping**, provided by Chapter 6 of the UN Charter, occurs within a consensual type of intervention. It involves largely impartial monitors and observers who are unarmed or lightly armed. They are generally required to monitor a separation of forces, verify and monitor troop withdrawals, provide some security, and supervise elections. Force is used as a last resort and only for self-defense.[29] **Peacemaking**, on the other hand, involves military forces that are heavily armed, well trained, and prepared to fight. But peacemaking is a far more circumscribed activity compared with standard military operations. Peacemaking occurs in situations in which most of the forces involved are friendly. The basic objective of peacemaking is to reduce the fighting and to restore or create an environment that will enable peacekeeping forces to function effectively.[30] Increasingly, humanitarian interventions—such as those in Haiti, Bosnia, Kosovo, East Timor, the Congo, and Sierra Leone—involve a mixture of peacekeeping and peacemaking operations.

Responding to Genocide

Genocide

Systematic mass murder of an ethnic, religious, or national group based on discriminatory preconceptions

In 1948, the United Nations adopted the Genocide Convention, which defines **genocide** as the intent to destroy, in whole or in part, a national, ethnic, racial, or religious group. Throughout history, people have attempted to destroy others who they perceived to be different, threatening, or in their way. Whole populations have been displaced or destroyed as others expanded their control over areas, usually through military force. Such behavior was largely justified in terms of progress and civilization. Often, only a small minority was concerned with the crime of genocide. Convinced that human beings were divided into different races and that some races were inherently superior to others, Europeans expanded their rule to Asia, the Americas, and Africa. In the process, they destroyed many indigenous peoples. The genocide committed by Nazi Germany marked a turning point in the human rights debate, as we have seen. The victorious allies united against such crimes and punished those most directly involved in carrying them out. However, genocide continued and is still going on. For example, between 1975 and 1979, the **Khmer Rouge** in Cambodia killed more than a million people. Another million people died in Rwanda's genocide. Genocide was part of the conflict in the former Yugoslavia. Sudan's actions in Darfur were declared to be genocide in 2004. However, the global community, especially the UN, continued to debate what actions should be taken against Sudan in 2006. Many countries refrain from declaring atrocities to be genocide partly because the Genocide Convention requires them to act to prevent and punish genocide.

Khmer Rouge

Communist government of Cambodia that slaughtered over 9 million people in its rural pacification programs

A big step toward holding individuals and governments responsible for gross violations of human rights, including genocide, came at the end of World War I. Britain and France attempted to punish Germany for violating the neutrality of Belgium and Luxembourg by destroying their cities and creating large numbers of refugees and for using poison gas. The *Commission on the Responsibility of the Authors of War and the Enforcement of Penalties* was established at the Paris Peace Conference in 1919. Its main objective was to prosecute those accused of committing war crimes and crimes against humanity, including government leaders. While France and Britain strongly supported prosecuting leaders, the United States, Italy, and Japan opposed such trials, principally on the grounds that such actions would violate the principle of national sovereignty.[31]

After World War II, however, the United States changed its position. It played the leading role in setting up the **Nuremberg Tribunal** to prosecute Nazi war crimes and the *Tokyo Tribunal* to prosecute crimes committed by Japan. Britain had also changed its position: Instead of trying the Nazis, Prime Minister Winston Churchill advocated shooting Nazi war criminals on sight. The United States, under Harry S. Truman's leadership, persuaded the allies to try the Nazis. The **London Agreement**—signed in 1945 by the United States, Britain, France, and the Soviet Union—provided for the creation of an international military tribunal for war criminals. This led to the establishment of the Nuremberg Tribunal, which focused on prosecuting high-level German officials. The tribunal held *individuals* responsible for (1) *crimes against peace*, which included planning, initiating, and launching a war of aggression; (2) **war crimes**, such as murder, abuse, and the destruction of private property and residential areas; and (3) **crimes against humanity**, including the murder, enslavement, extermination, deportation, and other inhumane acts against civilians based on their political, racial, or religious identities. The *Genocide Convention*, adopted by the UN Geneva Assembly in 1948, was a direct outgrowth of the Nuremberg Tribunal.[32]

Similar to Nazi Germany, Japan committed numerous atrocities, including the murder of prisoners, the extermination of civilians, sexual slavery, forced labor, the use of humans in deadly medical experiments, and the use of prisoners of war as live targets for bayonet practice. Following America's defeat in the Philippines, Japan forced U.S. and Filipino troops to participate in the gruesome *Bataan Death March*, which resulted in the deaths of around 10,000 Filipino troops and 600 American troops. Japan also committed crimes against Chinese civilians and soldiers. Even today, many Chinese continue to be suspicious of Japan. They talk about the indiscriminate bombings on Shanghai and other cities. But they are especially emotional when they recall the *Rape of Nanking*. Japanese soldiers, in October 1937, randomly raped, murdered, and executed Chinese civilians. Estimates of those killed range from 42,000 to 100,000. On July 26, 1945, the United States, China, Britain, and the Soviet Union issued the **Potsdam Declaration**, stating their decision to prosecute Japanese war criminals. *U.S. General Douglas MacArthur*, the Supreme Commander for the Allied Powers in Japan, acting under the authority of the United States, established the *International Military Tribunal for the Far East* (Tokyo Tribunal) to try individuals for crimes against peace. Because the United States was primarily responsible for defeating Japan, Americans unilaterally created the Tokyo Tribunal.[33]

Nuremberg Tribunal

Created after World War II in order to punish Nazi aggression and genocide

London Agreement

Created an international war tribunal after World War II

War Crimes

Include murder, destruction of public property, and other abuses

Crimes Against Humanity

Inhuman acts committed against civilians by states and individuals

Potsdam Declaration

Announced the prosecution of Japanese war criminals after World War II

The Nuremberg and Tokyo Tribunals set the precedent for prosecuting war criminals in the former Yugoslavia and Rwanda. The disintegration of Yugoslavia in the 1990s and escalating conflicts among the Serbs, Croats, and Muslims culminated in widespread atrocities. While the three ethnic groups committed war crimes and crimes against humanity, the dominant Serbs were clearly the most responsible for atrocities that included summary executions, torture, raping women as a weapon of war, mass internments, deportation and displacement of civilians, the inhumane treatment of prisoners, and the indiscriminate shelling of cities and villages. More than 7,000 unarmed Muslim men and boys were systematically executed near the Bosnian town of **Srebrenica** in July 1995. Roughly 740,000 ethnic Albanians were forcibly deported from Kosovo in 1999, and hundreds of Albanians disappeared or were murdered. These atrocities were the worst in Europe since World War II. Shocked by such widespread brutality, the UN Security Council responded by establishing the *International Criminal Tribunal for the Former Yugoslavia* on May 25, 1993.[34] Based in The Hague, in the Netherlands, the tribunal indicted leading Serbians, including Serbian President **Slobodan Milosevic**, Radovan Karadzic, General Ratko Mladic, and Radislav Krstic for committing war crimes. Similarly, ethnic conflicts, primarily between **Hutu extremists** and **Tutsis** and moderate Hutus, in 1993 and 1994 stunned the world. Hutus systematically killed and raped. Almost one million people were slaughtered. Genocide in Rwanda led to the creation of the *International Tribunal for the Prosecution of Persons Responsible for Genocide in Rwanda* (*the Rwanda Tribunal*). Outbreaks of ethnic conflicts and the accompanying atrocities have influenced the global community to establish the **International Criminal Court (ICC)** as a permanent institution to prosecute those accused of war crimes and genocide.

The International Criminal Court

On April 11, 2002—more than fifty years after the victorious allies in World War II proposed the creation of a permanent international court to prosecute war criminals and others who engage in gross violations of human rights—the International Criminal Court (ICC) was created. The **International Court of Justice (ICJ)**, or World Court, based in The Hague, had been created in 1945 to adjudicate disputes between states. Individuals, however, came before tribunals established on an *ad hoc basis* to try specific crimes against humanity. Examples are the Nuremberg and Tokyo Tribunals and the tribunals for Yugoslavia and Rwanda.[35]

The globalization of human rights—strengthened by the proliferation of human rights NGOs and increased economic, cultural, military, and political interdependence—laid the foundation of new thinking about bringing violators of human rights to justice, regardless of where they committed their crimes. The world, less preoccupied by ideological rivalries, turned its attention to issues ordinary people confront daily, including widespread atrocities. Small countries, unable to unilaterally deal with crimes against humanity, stressed the need to create a permanent international criminal court. At the request of Trinidad and Tobago and several other Caribbean and Latin American countries, the UN General Assembly asked the International Law

Srebrenica

Bosnian town where over 7,000 unarmed Muslims were executed in 1995

Slobodan Milosevic

Former Serbian president prosecuted for war crimes

Hutu Extremists

Responsible for the genocide committed against over a million Rwandans in the early 1990s

ICC

Created to try and punish individuals responsible for crimes against humanity

ICJ

World Court created to adjudicate disputes between states

Commission to return to the work it had started in 1948 to create an international criminal court.[36] Drawbacks of the country-by-country approach to prosecuting war crimes, genocide, and crimes against humanity had become increasingly obvious with increasing atrocities occurring worldwide, and the growing determination of the global community to terminate them. The *two major drawbacks* were (1) it was expensive and time-consuming to create new tribunals; and (2) securing the unanimous consent of the five permanent members of the UN Security Council (the United States, Britain, France, Russia, and China) was very difficult. More than 160 countries and numerous NGOs, many of which worked closely with smaller states, gathered in Rome in 1998 to create a tribunal with universal jurisdiction.[37] The United States, which had initially signed the agreement under the Clinton administration, later renounced its involvement in creating the court under the Bush administration.

WOMEN AND HUMAN RIGHTS

Images of Brazil, especially of sophisticated cities like Rio de Janeiro, portray women as enjoying equal rights and personal freedoms. But images can be deceptive. It took the Brazilian Congress twenty-six years to change the country's legal code to make women equal to men under the law. The new code, adopted in 2001, outlaws a provision that had allowed a husband to annul a marriage if he discovered that his wife was not a virgin when they were married. It also eliminates laws that allowed Brazilian fathers to have unrestricted legal rights to make decisions for their family.[38] While women are clearly not a monolithic group and do not face the same restrictions across all societies, even where laws support hierarchical patriarchy, the global community embraces the view that most women face violations of their rights. Women's rights are widely regarded as a category of human rights that deserve special attention. However, discussions of women's rights are usually complicated by cultural differences and by the general perception that many violations of women's rights are private in nature. Furthermore, women disagree about which rights are important. For example, some women in Islamic countries protest against wearing a veil, while others insist on wearing it. While Western women view themselves as liberated—because they are free to wear what they want—many Islamic, and some Western, women do not perceive this as freedom.

Human rights for women are directly and strongly influenced by how women perceive themselves and how others perceive them. Parents, teachers, friends, religious teachings, and the media through the process of socialization shape these perceptions. Perceptions help to determine our role in society. **Roles** can be defined as expectations regarding the skills, rights, and responsibilities of individuals. Roles influence how we see ourselves and how others see us, as well as what we expect from ourselves and what others expect from us.

Women's roles are closely connected to their lower status (compared with men) in virtually all societies, including those in the industrialized world, a reality that

Status

Refers to one's social, economic, or political position in society

complicates discussions of human rights regarding women. **Status** refers to one's position in the social, economic, and political hierarchy. These positions are largely *socially constructed* by men who want to protect their own power, privileges, and position in society. Violations of women's rights are closely linked to women's status. The most extreme abuses occur in societies where women are widely perceived as inferior to men. Veiling, dowries, female genital mutilation, forced marriages, polygamy, forced prostitution, sexual violence, and honor killings are examples of abuses associated with women's status. Universal rights for women include freedom from being subjected to these abuses. The struggle for women's rights is as old as the struggle for human rights in general. Some people have always advocated equal treatment of men and women. International organizations composed primarily of women led the struggle for suffrage and various social policies. Women were instrumental in getting protections for women written into the UN Charter and in the establishment of the UN Commission on the Status of Women. Increased emphasis was placed on women's rights as human rights in the 1970s. The UN Fund for Women was created by the UN General Assembly to support women in grassroots organizations. In 1981, the UN Convention on the Elimination of All Forms of Discrimination Against Women was adopted, thereby reaffirming the view that women's rights should receive special attention within broader discussions of human rights. The Women's Conference in Beijing in 1995 and the UN Forum of Women in New York in 2000, among others, underscore a growing global consensus on women's rights. A major concern among human rights advocates is sexual violence against women, especially the use of rape as a weapon of war.

Sexual Violence: Rape as a Weapon of War

Coming from communities where grinding poverty and hopelessness are oppressive realities, many young women worldwide are easily seduced by promises of job opportunities and a chance to better their lives in places far from home. Lena, a beautiful Russian woman, was told by a friendly, middle-aged woman that her own daughter had migrated to another country, was very happy, and was able to send remittances to her family. The older woman told Lena that she could help her migrate to Greece, where she would work as a domestic servant. When Lena arrived in Greece, her employers seized her passport, beat her, and forced her into prostitution.[39] Sexual violence against women has always been an integral part of most societies. Trafficking in women and children (i.e., buying and selling women as sex slaves), was outlawed at the global level by the *Convention for the Suppression of the Traffic in Persons and of the Exploitation of the Prostitution of Others* in 1949. Carol Bellamy, executive director of the UN International Children's Relief Fund, stated that "millions of children are bought and sold like fresh produce, commodities in a global sex industry steeped in greed and unspeakable cruelty."[40] Millions of women and children are victims of sexual violence within their own societies and millions more are trafficked across national borders. Globalization has facilitated sex trafficking. Networks of trafficking transport women from Asia, Russia, Latin America, Africa, and elsewhere to Western Europe, the United States, Canada, Japan, Australia, and the Middle East, where women and children are bought and sold as sex slaves. Sex tourism, especially in Southern Asia, is an important component of the sexual exploitation of women and children.[41] These abuses of human rights are extremely difficult to eliminate because poverty, tradition, and entrenched global criminal networks perpetuate them.

Sexual violence against women is often built into the legal system as well as the social structure of many countries. In many societies, men routinely kill women to protect the family honor or their own. In Jordan, Pakistan, and other Islamic countries, honor killing, though illegal, is sustained by tradition and religion. Rape is often treated as a crime against the family, an approach that makes the woman who was raped guilty of dishonoring her family. Only recently (1996) did Italy change its laws to emphasize that rape is a crime against the woman as opposed to being an offense against her family. Italy also recently abolished laws that enabled a rapist to avoid punishment by agreeing to marry the woman he had raped. Another example of how tradition, religion, and the law perpetuate sexual violence against women is the case of Zafran Bibi in Pakistan. While Zafran's husband was in prison, his brother raped her repeatedly. When she gave birth to a daughter, she was charged with adultery and sentenced to death by stoning. No charges were brought against her brother-in-law because, under Islamic laws in Pakistan, rape can be proved only with the testimony of four male witnesses. Domestic and global pressure persuaded General Pervez Musharraf, Pakistan's president, to force the court to overturn Zafran's death sentence.[42]

Rape has generally been considered part of war. Throughout history armies have killed male civilians and raped women and children. The emergence of rape during conflicts as a direct human rights issue reflects the growth of humanitarian international law as well as the willingness of women, especially the victims, to demand justice. For example, Koreans who were used as "comfort women" and subjected to sexual slavery by the Japanese military during World War II demanded justice from the Japanese government. These experiences fueled protests in China and Korea against Japan in 2005. Rape as a weapon of war is receiving increased attention partly because of the frequency of such atrocities in numerous civil wars and ethnic conflicts worldwide. Sexual enslavement is often used as an instrument of **ethnic cleansing**. Sexual violence is used to humiliate and destroy families and communities, to terrorize members of a particular ethnic group, and to force people to flee an area. The devastating nature of sexual violence makes it attractive as part of an overall military strategy. For example, the use of rape caused many Chinese to flee to Indonesia during the ethnic conflicts in 1998. The Hutus raped and deliberately infected Tutsi women with AIDS as part of their genocidal campaign in Rwanda. Serb troops raped more than 20,000 Muslim women in the former Yugoslavia as part of their ethnic-cleansing campaign.[43] Rape of girls and women in the Democratic Republic of the Congo escalated in 2005 as that country's ethnic warfare continued to rage. These atrocities helped to firmly establish global recognition of rape as a crime against humanity and as a war crime. Zoran Vukovic, Dragoljub Kunarac, and Radomir Kovac (Bosnian Serbs) were found guilty of such crimes by the Tribunal for Yugoslavia in The Hague in 2001. Genocidal rape is recognized as a crime against humanity by the International Criminal Court.

Ethnic Cleansing
Violence based upon race, ethnicity, sex, religion, or other social issues

ISLAM AND HUMAN RIGHTS

Negative stereotypes of Muslims and Islam are so prevalent and so profound in most Western societies that even isolated cases of human rights violations are perceived as reflections of a profound inability of Islamic countries to respect human rights. Such images are reinforced by extremists in Saudi Arabia, Afghanistan under the Taliban, Iran, and Northern Nigeria, for example. The general lack of a clear separation of religion and government and the dominance of Shari'a law as the foundation for legal codes in Islamic countries convey the impression of traditional societies that are fossilized, changing very little since the Prophet Muhammad (570–632 A.D.) founded the religion. But compared with Western societies, Islamic countries are far more repressive and disrespectful of fundamental rights and freedoms. Saudi Arabia—Muhammad's birthplace and keeper of Islam's holiest places, Mecca and Medina, that are sacred to Muslims worldwide—is perhaps the most repressive Islamic society. But Islam's spread made it a global religion long before the emergence of Western Europe as a dominant power and the subsequent spread of Christianity. Consequently, Islam is diverse and complex, reflecting how very different cultures interpret and practice the religion. The decentralization of Islam undermines efforts to portray the Islamic world, especially regarding human rights, as monolithic. It is also useful to distinguish the policies of governments from the aspirations of ordinary citizens to enjoy basic freedoms. As in many Western societies, religion is so often instrumental in maintaining the status quo and in preserving the power, privilege, and position for the few against the welfare and concerns of the majority. Many Western countries, including the United States, have benefited from this arrangement in, for example, Saudi Arabia and Kuwait.

Although Islamic cultures are composed of numerous beliefs and values that promote humanitarianism and respect for some forms of human rights, the religion emphasizes the priority of the Islamic community over the individual. Under the Koran, the ruler and the ruled are equal before God. However, unlike in Britain, for example, where limitations on the monarch were formalized into contracts, such as the Magna Carta, most Islamic countries did not develop formal institutions to restrain leaders and define their powers and responsibilities or to make them accountable to the people. This enabled rulers to interpret the Koran in ways that served their own interests. As we discussed in Chapter 2, the emergence of Europe as a global power was directly linked to the spread of freedom. Freedom to invent, freedom of thought, freedom of the press, freedom to engage in commerce, freedom to travel, and freedom of religion formed the foundation of the development of human rights. Chapter 1 showed how the Peace of Westphalia formalized the separation of church and state, a separation that Islam rejected. The separation of religion and politics, together with certain freedoms, fostered the growth of rationalism and scientific thinking. The dominance of theology in the Islamic world generally impeded freedom of thought and encouraged conformity and rigidity. However, Islam—like Judaism, Christianity, and other religions—has both fundamentalists and mainstream members. Instead of being free to challenge Islamic thinking, most Muslims had to try to be consistent with it. Just as this problem contributed to the decline and fall of the

Islamic Empire, it also created serious barriers to the development of democratic societies in which a wide range of human rights flourish. The Western belief that each individual has natural rights stood in sharp contrast to the Islamic belief that the community mattered most and that God's law did not permit individuals to think for themselves. Justice, in Islam, is derived from obedience to God's commands as expressed in the Koran. In effect, challenging political authorities is tantamount to challenging the supremacy of religious thinking.[44] Even so, Islam has been challenged by forces within Muslim societies and by the forces of colonization, westernization, and globalization. In 2003, Shirin Ebadi won the Nobel Peace Prize for her efforts to promote human rights in Iran.

The best example of a Muslim society that rejected the fusion of politics and religion and embraced freedoms prevalent in Western societies is Turkey. As the Ottoman Empire contracted and finally fragmented, and after Turkey's defeat in World War I, it was clear that to modernize Turkey wide-ranging reforms had to be implemented. **Mustafa Kemal Ataturk**, founder of the modern Turkish state in 1923, deliberately and systematically dismantled much of the old system, abolishing Islamic control and secularizing the country. Secular movements are deeply rooted in the Islamic world, despite their relative lack of success in countries like Saudi Arabia.

Throughout the Islamic world, clashes occur between the conservatives who stress communitarianism and cultural relativism and the reformers who focus on the universality of human rights and their country's participation in organizations that

Shirin Ebadi –
Nobel Peace Prize
winner

promote and strengthen fundamental rights and freedoms worldwide. This confrontation highlights the reality that there are many different interpretations of Islam, especially in relation to individual freedom. While cultural relativists and traditionalists argue that global human rights are inapplicable to Islamic societies, many Muslims are aware that governments often use Islam to justify abusing them, especially those who threaten their power. As in most societies dominated by religion, women suffer most from violations of human rights in Islamic societies. Ironically, the U.S. invasion and occupation of Iraq contributed to the strengthening of religious groups and the erosion of human rights for women. Although women comprised nearly a third of the Iraqi Parliament that was elected in 2005, women's rights were threatened. But even as Islamic religious leaders and institutions endeavor to maintain the subordinate status of women and their unequal treatment, secular forces also operate to challenge traditional ideas and behavior. In many Islamic societies, women occupy significant professional and political positions, including head of state. Globalization, education, and a deeper sense of empowerment combine to enable women to effectively challenge traditions and institutions that undergird human rights violations.

FIGHTING TERRORISM AND PROTECTING HUMAN RIGHTS

Democratic societies confronted with terrorism face an enduring dilemma, namely, how to provide security for the country while avoiding taking measures that violate the fundamental rights and freedoms that define democratic states and distinguish them from nondemocratic regimes. Believing that short-term restrictions on civil and political rights are essential to combat terrorism, many governments find themselves on a slippery slope that leads to more durable infringements on democratic freedoms. Britain, for example, responded in the early 1970s to Northern Ireland's Troubles, as the conflicts between the Protestants and Catholics are called, with increased arrests, essentially arbitrary detentions, increased surveillance capabilities, the creation of a special court to prosecute terrorist suspects, approval of inhumane treatment of prisoners, and excessive military force. Apart from having the unintended consequence of inflaming passions and escalating terrorism, British actions were scrutinized and severely criticized by the global community and within Britain itself. The European Court of Human Rights ruled against Britain in several cases, contending that it had violated the European Convention on Human Rights.[45] Following the terrorist attacks in London in 2005, Britain adopted several policies that were perceived as threats to human rights.

Alan Dershowitz
Argued for the use of nonlethal torture to gather information from terrorists

Catastrophic terrorist attacks in the United States in 2001 influenced **Alan Dershowitz**, a Harvard University law professor and a leading criminal defense lawyer, to argue in favor of using nonlethal torture in extreme cases and of issuing torture warrants by judges.[46] Dershowitz posed the "ticking bomb" scenario. Imagine that you are a government official and you know that a bomb capable of killing thousands of people is about to be used by terrorists. You are almost certain that a suspect knows where the bomb is and believe that by torturing the suspect you can extract crucial information to save lives. Would you torture or support this suspect's torturing under these circumstances? Democratic societies routinely condemn other societies that torture people. No country, not even authoritarian regimes, openly admits to torturing its citizens. Some argue that legalization of torture in the United States would encourage its wider use and seriously erode democratic principles that are the country's foundations. Furthermore, the effectiveness of torturing individuals in the long- and short-term is highly debatable. Those who are tortured obviously attempt to avoid being tortured. *Mary Robinson*, former head of the UN Commission for Human Rights, criticized the United States for eroding civil liberties at home and human rights globally after it was attacked. Like many others, Robinson cited measures used by the United States in its war on terrorism to illustrate her point.[47] These include detaining foreigners for indefinite periods; racial profiling citizens as enemy combatants; allowing authorities to conduct searches without the approval or knowledge of those being searched; implementing the Terrorist and Information System to use postal workers, meter readers, and others to report suspicious behavior; and using the Total Information Awareness program, which enables authorities to examine consumer transactions to locate possible terrorists. While most Americans regard these actions as reasonable responses to terrorist threats, others view them as dangerous precedents that could ultimately erode human rights both at home and abroad.

In the war against terrorism, the United States significantly altered its policy on human rights abroad. Prisoners taken during the war in Afghanistan were subject to "stress and duress" techniques, including sleep deprivation, physical abuse, hooding, and being forced to hold awkward positions for long periods of time. Many prisoners held at the U.S. military base in Guantanamo Bay in Cuba were denied access to lawyers and their families. Some prisoners were transferred to countries that are strategically located but are also known to violate human rights, including Pakistan and Uzbekistan. Widespread abuse of prisoners held at **Abu Ghraib** in Iraq was vividly demonstrated by numerous photographs and videotapes that shocked the world in 2004 and undermined American credibility in promoting human rights, especially in the Islamic world. Some prisoners were killed, tortured, or suffered from inhumane treatment and degradation. U.S. Army dogs were used to abuse Iraqi prisoners. Many human rights NGOs also drew attention to how other countries were justifying what are generally regarded as violations of human security. For example, India pushed the Prevention of Terrorism Ordinance to detain terrorist suspects for up to ninety days without a trial. China suddenly began to call the **Uighurs** (i.e., an ethnic separatist group that had been fighting the government for many years) terrorists. The Russians also called their conflict with the ethnic Chechens a war against terrorism. America's emphasis on the war against terrorism raised concerns about balancing national security concerns against a strong commitment to upholding human rights.

Abu Ghraib
U.S.-run prison in Iraq infamous for abuse committed against Iraqi war detainees

Uighurs
An ethnic separatist group labeled a terrorist group by the Chinese government

THE DEATH PENALTY AND HUMAN RIGHTS

On January 31, 2000, Governor George Ryan of Illinois shocked Americans by announcing his decision to impose a moratorium on capital punishment. Ryan, a strong advocate of the death penalty, was persuaded by growing evidence that several prisoners on death row were wrongfully convicted. One problem with the criminal justice system was that many of those sentenced to die were represented by incompetent lawyers. Another was that evidence used to convict some of them came from unreliable prisoners. Furthermore, many police officers obtained evidence illegally and courts often relied on tainted evidence. Several murder defendants who had been sentenced to die were released from death row because of work by students at Northwestern University's Center for Wrongful Convictions, as well as investigative reports by journalists who had uncovered evidence showing that police tortured defendants to extract confessions and coerced witnesses into falsely identifying suspects. But despite his ban on executions, Ryan continued to support the death penalty.[48]

While many countries impose the death penalty, there is a growing consensus that this practice violates the most fundamental human right: the right to life. Several countries have outlawed the execution of teenagers. In Yemen, often criticized for violating human rights, the government abolished the death penalty for individuals under 18 years. Only Saudi Arabia, Iran, Nigeria, and Pakistan allow teenagers to be executed. The United States executed teenagers until 2005, when the U.S. Supreme Court outlawed the practice. Within Europe, only Yugoslavia has the death penalty. Japan, which typically executes five or six prisoners each year, has been criticized by Amnesty International and other groups for its secretive and sometimes sudden executions. Many prisoners are told of their execution only moments before they are hanged.[49] Europeans are generally shocked by Americans' strong endorsement of the death penalty. European societies abolished the death penalty in the latter half of the twentieth century, mostly in the early 1960s.

CONTEMPORARY SLAVERY

In March 2001, a Nigerian-registered ship called the *Etireno* set sail from Benin in West Africa and attempted to stop in Cameroon and Gabon. Its cargo consisted of roughly 200 children who were being sold as slaves. Between 1996 and 2000, more than 3,000 children destined to live as slaves in neighboring countries were intercepted by Benin's border police. Benin is a clearinghouse in the West Africa slave trade. Due primarily to grinding poverty in Benin and the relative wealth and economic opportunities of neighboring Gabon and Ivory Coast, many parents sell their children for as little as $14 to agents who promise to find employment and educational opportunities for them. These agents are really slave traders who sell the children to farmers in Gabon, Ivory Coast, Cameroon, and elsewhere for between $27 and $400. Boys are forced to work on plantations, and most girls are forced to work as domestic servants and prostitutes.[50]

Global concerns about human rights emanated from efforts by various humanitarian organizations to abolish the slave trade and the institution of slavery in the Americas and other parts of the world. Consequently, it is surprising to see that slavery continues to be a significant global problem. Often, forced labor in Pakistan, India, Thailand, Brazil, and countries in Africa is seen as the modern version of slavery. Like slaves before them, slaves today are forced to work and are inadequately compensated for their labor. They work in agriculture, mining, land clearing, charcoal making, the jewelry industry, clothing factories, and carpet weaving, among other areas. Modern slavery is often disguised by fraudulent contracts. In some countries—such as Saudi Arabia, Kuwait, Britain, and the United States—many people find themselves living in conditions similar to slavery. Many of the estimated 27 million slaves are in the system of bonded labor prevalent in India, Pakistan, Bangladesh, Nepal, and other countries. Globalization, which increases competition, is viewed as a major factor influencing the growth of modern slavery. Kevin Bales argues that the new slavery "focuses on big profits and cheap lives. It is not about owning people in the traditional sense of the old slavery, but about controlling them completely. People become dispensable tools for making money."[51]

Summary and Review

The promotion of universal human rights worldwide has become an increasingly contentious topic. This chapter examined how the progression and promotion of human rights have occurred within the broader political, economic, and cultural aspects of globalization. The concept of human rights has been significantly strengthened in recent history, especially with the growth of multilateral human rights NGOs, such as Amnesty International and Human Rights Watch, and international human rights-based institutions, such as the International Criminal Court and the UN Commission on Human Rights. Protecting human rights is no longer seen as an exclusively national issue, but one of global magnitude and scope. We examined the importance of

You DECIDE | **Homosexuality and Human Rights**

At the Holocaust Memorial Museum in Washington, D.C., which is visited by more than 2 million people each year, emphasis is placed on the less-discussed Nazi victims, including homosexuals. Many gays and lesbians were beaten, imprisoned, used as slave labor, castrated, and sent to concentration camps to be exterminated. Nazi Germany's genocidal campaigns motivated the world to embrace universal human rights agreements shortly after World War II. Nevertheless, gays and lesbians continue to experience discrimination and violence throughout the world. For example, in 2000, Egyptian police arrested fifty-two men who were suspected of being homosexual. Transgendered people are often beaten by police or ignored when they are beaten by others. Gay men can be hanged in certain Middle Eastern countries. On the other hand, in 1998, the European Court of Human Rights ruled that Britain's treatment of gays in the military violated the fundamental right to privacy. In 2000, Britain officially ended its ban on gays in the military, thereby conforming to the practice of most NATO countries, including Canada, France, the Netherlands, and Germany. The Netherlands enacted groundbreaking laws in 2002 that allow gays and lesbians to marry and adopt children. In 2005, the Spanish Parliament passed legislation allowing same-sex couples to marry. In many parts of the world, however, the idea that homosexuals should be treated the same as heterosexuals remains very controversial. In fact, this was an issue in the 2004 U.S. presidential campaign and continues to influence American politics.

Do you think that treating gays and lesbians differently is a violation of human rights?

and distinctions among political, economic, and political rights, as well as the distinction between positive and negative human rights. We also identified factors that have contributed to the expansion of human rights globally, including the globalization of human rights through the creation and strengthening of international institutions;, the growing acceptance of interdependence among states, the international proliferation of democracy, the strengthening of human rights through economic development and corporate globalization, and the increasing effectiveness of nonstate actors dedicated to promoting human rights.

Key Terms

civil rights 76
political rights 76
social rights 76
positive rights 76
negative rights 76
Holocaust 77
Amnesty
    International 79
prisoners of
    conscience 79
universal rights 81
Magna Carta 81
due process of law 81
habeas corpus 81
social contract 82
Reign of Terror 82
utilitarianism 82
Jeremy Bentham 82

John Stuart Mill 83
Bill of Rights 83
Edmund Burke 83
International Committee
    of the Red Cross 84
League of Nations 84
four freedoms 85
Universal Declaration
    of Human Rights
    (UDHR) 85
International Covenant
    on Civil and Political
    Rights (ICCPR) 85
International Covenant
    on Economic, Social,
    and Cultural Rights
    (ICESCR) 85
cultural relativism 86

Confucianism 87
regimes 88
Council of Europe 88
Helsinki Final Act 89
sanctions 90
economic sanctions 90
diplomatic and political
    sanctions 90
cultural sanctions 90
unilateral sanctions 90
multilateral sanctions 91
humanitarian
    intervention 91
consensual
    interventions 91
imposed
    interventions 92
peacekeeping 92

peacemaking 92
genocide 92
war crimes 93
crimes against
    humanity 93
Hutu extremists 94
Tutsis 94
International Criminal
    Court (ICC) 94
International Court of
    Justice (ICJ) 94
Roles 95
ethnic cleansing 97
Mustafa Kemal
    Ataturk 99
Abu Ghraib 101

Discussion Questions

1. Can you explain the differences between relativistic and universal human rights? How are they different in their scope and normative assumptions?
2. What are the differences among civil/political rights, economic rights, and social rights? What specific areas of human rights does each of these concepts cover?
3. What are the differences between positive and negative human rights? How are positive and negative human rights related to the International Covenant on Civil and Political Rights and the

International Covenant on Economic, Social, and Cultural Rights?
4. Can you explain some of the important legal protections built into the U.S. Constitution (Bill of Rights) and Britain's Magna Carta that we discussed in this chapter?
5. What are the implications of utilitarianism concerning attempts to promote universal human rights?
6. What did the Helsinki Final Act do to promote human rights?

7. What are the different forms of sanctions used in international politics and relations?
8. Are sanctions an effective weapon for promoting human rights? If so, how are they effective? If not, how do they hurt human rights?

9. What is the difference between peacekeeping and peacemaking?
10. What is ethnic cleansing? How was it used in Rwanda and Yugoslavia?

Suggested Readings

Alston, Philip. *Non-State Actors and Human Rights*. New York: Oxford University Press, 2005.

Bales, Kevin. *Disposable People: New Slavery in the Global Economy*. Berkeley: University of California Press, 1999.

Coleman, Elizabeth, "Women, Islam, and the New Iraq," *Foreign Affairs* 85, No. 1 (January/February 2006): 24–38.

Cortright, David, and George A. Lopez. *The Sanctions Decade*. Boulder, CO: Lynne Rienner, 2000.

Feingold, David, "Human Trafficking," *Foreign Policy* 150 (September/October 2005): 26–32.

Greenberg, Karen, ed. *The Torture Debate in America*. Cambridge: Cambridge University Press, 2006.

Guilhot, Nicolas. *The Democracy Makers: Human Rights and International Order*. New York: Columbia University Press, 2005.

Hopgood, Stephen, *Keepers of the Flame: Understanding Amnesty International*. Ithaca: Cornell University Press, 2006.

Hunter, Shireen, and Huma Malik, eds. *Modernization, Democracy, and Islam*. Westport, CT: Praeger, 2005.

Kent, George. *Freedom From Want*. Washington, DC: Georgetown University Press, 2005.

Lockwood, Bert. *Women's Rights*. Baltimore: The Johns Hopkins University Press, 2006.

Mayer, Elizabeth Ann. *Islam and Human Rights*. Boulder, CO: Westview Press, 1999.

Otunnu, Olara. "The Secret Genocide," *Foreign Policy* 155 (July/August 2006): 45–46.

Outen, Nicholas, ed. *Human Rights and Human Wrongs*. New York: Oxford University Press. 2003.

Straus, Scott. "Darfur and the Genocide Debate," *Foreign Affairs* 84, No. 1 (January/February 2005): 123–133.

Wetzel, Janice Wood. *The World of Women: In Pursuit of Human Rights*. New York: New York University Press, 1999.

Addresses and Websites

Human Rights Watch
350 Fifth Ave., 34th floor
New York, NY 10118-3299
Tel.: (212) 290–4700
Fax: (212) 736–1300
E-mail: hrwnyc@hrw.org
www.hrw.org

Human Rights Watch seeks to protect the human rights of people worldwide. Its website provides breaking news, and information can be received by country or by a global issue topic. Commentaries, campaign information, an e-mail newsletter, and a special section on human rights after 9/11 are also available.

United Nations Economic and Social Development
E-mail: esa@un.org
www.ecosoc.org

This UN organization offers information on economic, social, and human rights issues. Multiple links to information on social and economic topics, and to UN-sponsored sites are also provided.

Office of High Commissioner for Human Rights
8-14 Avenue de la Paix
1211 Geneva 10
Switzerland
Tel.: 4122–917–9000
www.unhchr.ch

This website for the UN Office of the High Commissioner for Human Rights has highlights on seminars and meetings, a breakdown of human rights issues, and a list of its human rights organizations. Documents, treaties, and declarations (including the Universal Declaration of Human Rights in over 300 languages) are also available.

Amnesty International
322 Eighth Ave.
New York, NY 10001
Tel: (212) 807–8400
Fax: (212) 463–9193
E-mail: admin-us@aiusa.org

www.amnestyusa.org

Amnesty International is a worldwide campaigning organization that promotes internationally recognized human rights. This website contains a library, as well as a section on what you can do to fight human rights violations.

International Committee of the Red Cross

www.icrc.org/eng

The International Committee of the Red Cross is an impartial and independent organization whose exclusively humanitarian mission is to protect the lives and dignity of victims of war and internal violence and to provide them with assistance. The website lists information on the ICRC's activities and provides updates. Information can be obtained on humanitarian law, the Geneva conventions, and the Red Crescent Movement.

Endnotes

1. Seyom Brown, *Human Rights in World Politics* (New York: Longman, 2000), 22.
2. Elizabeth Rosenthal, "China Ratifies Major U.N. Rights Accord," *New York Times*, 1 March 2001, A9.
3. Pedro Ruz Guitierrez and E. A. Torriero, "Drug War Cash May Finance Brutality," *Chicago Tribune*, 22 September 2000, Sect. 1, 1.
4. Andrew Hurrell, "Power, Principles, and Prudence," in *Human Rights in Global Society*, ed. Tim Dunne and Nicholas J. Wheeler (Cambridge: Cambridge University Press, 1999), 279.
5. Tim Weiner, "Mexico's New Leader Vows to End Longstanding Impunity for Torture in Justice System," *New York Times*, 18 March 2001, A10.
6. Debora L. Spar, "The Spotlight and the Bottom Line," *Foreign Affairs* 77, No. 2 (March/April 1998), 12.
7. Michael A. Santoro, *Profits and Principles: Global Capitalism and Human Rights in China* (Ithaca: Cornell University Press, 2000), 29.
8. Laurent Belsie, "Companies Operating Abroad Pay Closer Attention to Human Rights," *Christian Science Monitor*, 3 April 2000, 11.
9. Marcus Tullius Cicero, *De Re Publica*, translated by Clinton Walker Keyes (Cambridge, MA: Harvard University Press, 1943), 385.
10. Maurice Cranston, "Are There Any Human Rights?" *Daedalus* 112, No. 4 (Fall 1983), 2; and Brown, *Human Rights*, 56.
11. Brown, *Human Rights*, 59.
12. Edmund Burke, *Reflections on the Revolution in France* (New York: Holt, Rinehart and Winston, 1959), 37.
13. Cranston, "Are There Any Human Rights?" 5.
14. Yves Beigbeder, *Judging War Criminals* (New York: St. Martin's Press, 1999), 18.
15. Asbjorn Eide, "The Historical Signficance of the Universal Declaration," *International Social Science Journal* 50, No. 4 (December 1998), 478.
16. Brown, *Human Rights*, 7.
17. Ken Booth, "Three Tyrannies," in *Human Rights in Global Politics*, 37; and Neil A. Englehart, "Rights and Culture in the Asian Values Argument," *Human Rights Quarterly* 22 (2000), 549.
18. Brown, *Human Rights*, 7; and Englehart, "Rights and Culture," 568.
19. Lammy Betten and Nicholas Grief, *EU Law and Human Rights* (New York: Longman, 1998), 27.
20. Eide, "Historical Significance of the Universal Declaration," 495.
21. Santoro, *Profits and Principles*, 155.
22. Hurrell, "Power, Principles, and Prudence," 283.
23. Margaret P. Doxey, *International Sanctions in Contemporary Perspective* (New York: St. Martin's Press, 1996), 14.
24. David Cortright and George Lopez, "Economic Sanctions in Contemporary Global Relations," in *Economic Sanctions*, ed. David Cortright and George Lopez (Boulder, CO: Westview Press, 1995), 5.

25. Center for Strategic International Studies, *Altering U.S. Sanctions Policy* (Washington, DC: CSIS Press, 1999), 5.

26. Daniel W. Drezner, *The Sanctions Paradox* (Cambridge: Cambridge University Press, 1999), 62.

27. Stephen A. Garrett, *Doing Good and Doing Well* (Westport, CT: Praeger, 1999), 4.

28. Richard N. Haass, *Intervention* (Washington, DC: Brookings Institution Press, 1999), 62.

29. Haass, *Intervention*, 57.

30. Haass, *Intervention*, 59.

31. Beigbeder, *Judging War Criminals*, 28.

32. Beigbeder, *Judging War Criminals*, 34.

33. Beigbeder, *Judging War Criminals*, 55.

34. Theodor Meron, "Answering for War Crimes," *Foreign Affairs* 76, No. 1 (January /February 1997), 2.

35. Barbara Crossette, "War Crimes Tribunal Becomes Reality, Without U.S. Role," *New York Times*, 12 April 2002, A3.

36. David Wippman, "Can an International Criminal Court Prevent and Punish Genocide?" in *Protection Against Genocide*, ed. Neal Riemer (Westport, CT: Praeger, 2000), 89.

37. Alton Frye, *Toward an International Criminal Court?* (New York: Council on Foreign Relations, 1999), 22.

38. Larry Rohter, "Brazil Passes Equal Rights for Its Women," *New York Times*, 19 August 2001, A9.

39. Fred Weir, "Russia Battles Its Sex Trade," *Christian Science Monitor*, 16 May 2001, 1.

40. James Brooke, "Sex Web Spun Worldwide Traps Children," *New York Times*, 23 December 2001, A8.

41. Andrea Marie Bertone, "Sexual Trafficking in Women," *Gender Issues* 18, No. 1 (Winter 2000), 5.

42. Seth Mydans, "Sentenced to Death, Rape Victim Is Freed by Pakistani Court," *New York Times*, 6 June 2002, A4.

43. Seth Mydans, "Sexual Violence as a Tool of War," *New York Times*, 1 March 2001, A1; Marlise Simons, "Bosnian War Trial Focuses on Sex Crimes," *New York Times*, 18 February 2001, A4; and Minh T. Vo, "Ending Rape as a Weapon of War," *Christian Science Monitor*, 25 April 2000, 6.

44. Ann Elizabeth Mayer, *Islam and Human Rights* (Boulder, CO: Westview Press, 1999), 49.

45. Laura K. Donohue, "A Lesson From the British," *Washington Post National Weekly Edition*, 14–20 April 2003, 22.

46. "Is Torture Ever Justified?" *Economist*, 11 January 2003, 9.

47. Julia Preston, "Departing Rights Commissioner Faults U.S.," *New York Times*, 12 September 2002, B22.

48. William Claiborne and Paul Duggan, "A Ban on Executions Ignites a Debate," *Washington Post National Weekly Edition*, 19–26 June 2000, 29.

49. Howard W. French, "Secrecy of Japan's Executions Is Criticized as Unduly Cruel," *New York Times*, 30 June 2002, A1; and Charles Lane, "A View to a Kill," *Foreign Policy* 148 (May/June 2005), 36.

50. "Wandering Ship Highlights African-Child Slave Trade," *Christian Science Monitor*, 16 April 2001, 7.

51. Kevin Bales, *Disposable People: New Slavery in the Global Economy* (Berkeley: University of California Press, 1999), 4.

CHAPTER 4

Promoting Democracy

INTRODUCTION

Many ancient societies throughout the world attempted to apply democratic principles to make decisions about war and peace, migration, the allocation of scarce resources, and how to govern themselves. Democracy is therefore inseparable from politics, economics, and culture, as this chapter shows. Democracy as a form of government is always evolving, is always incomplete, and is most accurately described as a work in progress. The United States as a democratic society wrestled with the issue of slavery, and was torn apart by a bloody civil war. It also faced severe economic crises, struggles for gender equality, and the challenges of racial equality and integration. The incomplete nature of democracy inevitably leads to the emergence of new issues, new challenges, efforts to undermine democracy, and attempts to consolidate democracy.

There is significant diversity among democratic societies, largely because each country or community responds to problems in ways that reflect different cultural values, economic and social realities, perceptions of problems, and ordering of priorities. Similarly, there are divergent paths to achieving a democratic society. Although many political scientists, government officials, development specialists, and others view economic development as an essential prerequisite for transitions to democracy, this view is contradicted by the persistence of democratic values and practices in many poor societies, such as India and the English-speaking Caribbean. On the other hand, wealthy societies in the Middle East, such as Saudi Arabia, resist democratization. Transitions to democracy are generally fraught with difficulty. Although societies might reject a dictatorship, they do not necessarily embrace liberal democratic values, such as freedom of speech, freedom of the press, the right to fully participate in politics, and the rule of law. This chapter shows that many transitions to democracy around the world remain incomplete. Some democratically elected governments often revert to dictatorial practices, generally ignoring constitutional restraints on their power.

Globalization has been, and remains, a potent force in the spread of democratic values and practices. The growth of the British Empire was accompanied by the spread of democracy to India, the English-speaking Caribbean, the United States, and Canada. America's rise as a superpower further consolidated the globalization of democracy, despite its embrace of some repressive regimes during the Cold War. But America's struggle against the Soviet Union ultimately helped to strengthen the emergence of democracy in Eastern Europe and in Russia itself. The "orange revolution" in Ukraine in 2004, during which millions of Ukrainians peacefully demonstrated against fraudulent elections and in support of opposition leader Viktor Yushchenko, was strongly supported by the United States. Global communications play a pivotal role in the globalization of democracy, largely by facilitating the flow of ideas, information, and strategies that promote democracy. Globalization also contributes to weakening the power of centralized government and helps to empower citizens by fostering economic prosperity, the acquisition of private property, and increased access to information. But globalization is also widely perceived as undermining democracy by weakening governments' control over many issues, thereby diminishing the effectiveness of citizen participation in the democratic process. Increasingly, at the global level, organizations that are not representative of the people are making decisions that have profound and global consequences for ordinary people.

This chapter discusses the complex, uncertain, and challenging process of promoting democracy in an increasingly global society. Although the concept of democracy is often equated with American practices, this chapter shows that there are variations of democracy, and that countries do not necessarily follow the same road map to achieve democratic societies. Within all democratic societies, however, there are restraints on the exercise of power and protections for the fundamental rights and freedoms. Globally, women's participation in the political process and their status in society are issues that are now inseparable from efforts to democratize. In this chapter, we will examine factors that contribute to the growth and maintenance of democratic societies. Both globalization and the focus on fighting global terrorism have significant ramifications for the promotion of democracy. We will analyze the roles of global civil society and of the United States in facilitating and encouraging transitions to democracy, paying special attention to America's decision to impose democracy through military intervention and by occupying Iraq. Transitions to democracy in Spain and Portugal; specific countries in Africa, Asia, and Latin America; and Russia are also discussed. Finally, we will discuss how globalization is leading to greater global governance and spawning demands for more democracy at the global level.

DEMOCRACY

Democracy has been practiced by many societies throughout the world, especially by small communities. The ancient world understood the importance of obtaining the consent of powerful individuals and groups to achieve various objectives. The word **democracy** is derived from the Greek words **demos** (meaning people, or populace) and kratia or kratis (meaning rule). A basic definition of democracy is rule by the people. Determining who the people are has always been a central challenge for democracy. Women, slaves, non-Greeks, and other individuals were not considered to be among the people who could participate in the political process. Democracy in ancient Greece was a form of **direct self-government**, meaning that people voted directly on issues that affected them. With the exception of some small New England towns that hold town meetings, direct democracy is not practiced in the United States. Modern democratic societies practice **indirect**, or **representative, democracy**. Citizens elect representatives who vote for them and safeguard their interests, usually in capital cities that are far away from most citizens. Usually, citizens are generally unaware of the issues or how their representatives voted on the issues. Fewer than half of the American

Democracy
Government that reflects the will of the people

Demos
Greek word for people

Direct Self-Government
Direct participation in the democratic process

Indirect/Representative Democracy
Democracy run through indirect means, such as elections and representatives

James Madison

Founding father advocating checks and balances and separation of powers

population votes for representatives, a reality that calls into question the strength of America's democracy. In the U.S. system of democracy, for example, **James Madison** strongly advocated the adoption of a system of checks and balances and the separation of legislative, executive, and judicial powers to prevent the abuse of power, to protect the rights of the minority, and to ensure the maintenance of democratic practices. Democracy is a system of government that is based on the consent of the governed, holds political leaders accountable, and allows individuals and groups to freely compete for power. This means that free and fair elections must be held frequently, and that adult citizens are entitled to participate in the political process.

Two questions that often arise are, who will govern, and how will the interests of various groups and segments of the population be protected and advanced? There are two dominant approaches to dealing with these questions. The first emphasizes that the majority of the people decide who will govern and who will benefit. Government by the people is synonymous with majority rule. This approach, practiced globally, is the **majoritarian model** of democracy. The second approach, also widely practiced,

Majoritarian Model

Government by the people on a global scale

Consensus Model

Focuses on achieving widespread support for government policies

Winner-Take-All System

System by which the candidate with the most votes wins

embraces the concept of majority rule, but attempts to include as many of the people as possible in the decision-making process. The underlying objectives are to enlarge the size of the majority and to obtain widespread support for government policies. This approach is called the **consensus model** of democracy. In countries with significant political and ethnic divisions, the consensus model—characterized by inclusiveness, bargaining, and compromise—is widely adopted. The majoritarian model of democracy relies on a plurality of votes in single-member districts. It embraces the **winner-take-all system**, which means that the candidate who receives the most votes, not necessarily a majority, wins. The consensus model, on the other hand, uses a system of **proportional representation** in which both majorities and minorities are represented, because seats in elective bodies are determined by the proportion or percentage of votes received. Smaller parties are generally more successful in this system because they have a better chance of getting enough votes to gain representation in government. The majoritarian model, by contrast, requires the winner to get just a plurality of votes, which leaves large numbers of voters unrepresented.[1] But neither the majoritarian nor the consensus model of democracy guarantees the functioning of **liberal democracy**, which is defined by limitations on the power of elected officials, freedom of speech, freedom of the press, the right to peacefully assemble, protection of private property, freedom of religion, protection of the rights of unpopular minorities, and respect for the rule of law. While free elections are often equated with democracy in many parts of the world, societies that do not restrain power and protect basic freedoms and human rights are not fully democratic. Such societies are often referred to as **illiberal democracies**.

Proportional Representation

Political and electoral system under which both majorities and minorities are represented

Liberal Democracy

Defined by limitations on power of government and protections of civil liberties

Fully developed democracies are characterized by **constitutional liberalism**; that is, a commitment to protecting individuals' rights, freedoms, and dignity from abuse by the government, institutions, society as a whole, and other individuals. Constitutional liberalism goes beyond simply having a constitution. The basis for constitutional liberalism can be found in many societies, the most prominent being the Magna Carta of 1215, the English Bill of Rights of 1688, and the American

Declaration of Independence and the American Constitution. The Helsinki Final Act of 1975—which focused on such basic human rights as freedom of speech, freedom of religion, and freedom of assembly—represents a continuation of the tradition of constitutional liberalism.[2]

A **constitution** is defined as the fundamental framework or basic law of a country. A constitution assigns powers and responsibilities to government institutions, indicates how decision-makers are to be selected, defines the scope of government authority, establishes the nature of the relationship between the people and their government, and has provisions for making political leaders accountable to the people. A constitution in a democratic society not only creates and distributes power, it also limits power. Central to democratic constitutions is the concept of the **rule of law**, which means that no person is above the law, that individuals are treated equally under the law, that basic freedoms are protected, and that the administration of justice is impartial. Constitutions embody the values of societies and reflect the wishes of the people about how they want to be governed. Although most modern constitutions are written documents, the British Constitution, for example, is largely unwritten and is composed of traditions, customs, general understandings, the Magna Carta, the Bill of Rights, the Parliament Acts of 1911 and 1949, legislative acts, precedents, and court decisions. Whether it is written or unwritten, the constitution is the supreme law within a society.

Democratic societies emphasize the political equality of all citizens and guarantee that their fundamental human rights and freedoms are protected by law. This means that people have the right to freely express their ideas; to offer dissenting and controversial opinions; to be left alone and have their privacy respected; to join and form political, social, economic, and other organizations; to worship or not worship as they see fit; and to live their lives free from unreasonable governmental interference. These freedoms are not absolute. Governments, groups, and individuals are constantly struggling to balance the rights of some individuals and groups against the rights of other individuals and groups. To secure these rights and to facilitate the proper functioning of democracy, the people must believe that their government is legitimate. **Legitimacy** is the power to govern based on the consent of the majority of the people. Table 4.1 shows some of the basic requirements societies must meet to be classified as democratic.

Most democratic societies have either a presidential or a parliamentary form of democracy. The United States is the best example of the **presidential democracy**. Partly in response to problems in the British parliamentary form of democracy, the framers of the U.S. Constitution decided to have a clear separation of executive, legislative, and judicial powers, and to provide for a system of checks and balances among these distinct branches of government. Both conflict and cooperation characterize the relationships among the three branches of government, a feature that was designed to prevent one branch from accumulating too much power. The presidential form of democracy, particularly the American system, makes conflict inevitable. The **parliamentary democracy** is most strongly associated with Britain. Unlike the presidential system, there is no clear separation of powers in the parliamentary system. The prime

Illiberal Democracies

Societies that fail to fully protect basic freedoms and human rights

Constitutional Liberalism

Government committed to ensuring individual rights and freedoms through constitutional protections

Constitution

Framework of laws designed to designate specific powers and responsibilities to governmental institutions

Rule of Law

Mandatory adherence to state laws

Legitimacy

Power to govern based on popular consent

Presidential Democracy

Democracy that elects a president to the executive level of government

Parliamentary Democracy

Governing system with no separation of powers

TABLE 4.1 CRITERIA FOR DEMOCRACY

Criteria	Explanation
Inclusive citizenship	Citizenship must be open to all residents in the country.
Rule of law	The government operates under the law, and minorities are protected against the "tyranny of the majority."
Freedom of expression	Freedom of religion, of speech, and of the press are essential aspects of democracy.
Free and fair elections	Citizens compete for elective office and government officials are selected in free, fair, and frequent elections.
Equality in voting	All votes are equal, with each person having one vote.
Citizen control of the agenda	Citizens, through elected representatives, ultimately decide the policies of the country.
Freedom of association	Citizens have the right to form and join political parties, interest groups, and other organizations.
Civilian control over the security forces	The armed forces, including the police, must be politically neutral and must be controlled by civilian authority.

Sources: Adapted from Robert A. Dahl, *Dilemmas of Pluralist Democracy* (New Haven: Yale University Press, 1983), 6; and Mary Kaldor and Ivan Vejvoda, *Democracy in Central and Eastern Europe* (London: Pinter, 1999), 4–5.

minister—the chief executive—is an elected member of parliament who is chosen by the majority party in parliament for the leadership position. Consequently, there is generally very little conflict between the majority in parliament and the prime minister. On the other hand, the prime minister, unlike the president, can be forced from office by a vote of no confidence in parliament. Whereas the president is clearly at the top of the administrative hierarchy, the prime minister has a more collegial relationship with the cabinet.[3] While the prime minister, like the president, is leader of a political party and the government, parliamentary systems differ from presidential systems in that the head of the country is politically neutral and is not connected to the legislative or executive branch of government. The British model, often referred to as the Westminster model, is found in many former British colonies.

Political Participation and Democracy

Conventional Participation
Traditional political activities, such as voting

Unconventional Participation
Engaging in less acceptable political activities, such as protesting

Political participation entails communicating with elected officials and others in government—expressing viewpoints and demanding certain actions or public policies from the government. Vehicles for political participation include political parties, interest groups, and a free press. Political participation can be either conventional or unconventional. **Conventional participation** includes voting, running for office, assisting with political campaigns, writing to elected officials, writing letters to newspapers about particular issues, and joining an interest group to influence public policies. **Unconventional participation** includes protests, mass demonstrations, civil disobedience, and sometimes even acts of violence. Freedom of the press and freedom of speech are essential components of a democratic society because they enable people to express different opinions, to criticize government policies and conduct, to offer solutions to problems, to keep the public informed, and to check the power of political institutions.

Political parties are coalitions of interests whose primary goal is to run the government by winning competitive elections. While some political parties represent narrow interests, and sometimes focus on just a single issue, political parties that are successful usually appeal to a wide range of interests and attempt to win a majority of the votes. In some societies minor parties form coalitions with each other or with a major party in order to exert greater influence on public policy and to gain more control over the government. The numerous *roles or functions of political parties* include (1) helping to provide a peaceful transfer of power from one political party to another, (2) giving the electorate choices by offering competing programs and candidates for office, (3) mobilizing public opinion, (4) serving as links between the people and the government, (5) providing people to run the government, and (6) serving as the loyal opposition to help keep the government accountable and responsible to the people. The functioning of the **loyal opposition** is important in democratic societies. It means that the party out of power criticizes the ruling majority and suggests alternative programs and policies.

Interest groups, like political parties, are critical players in established democracies and in countries that are becoming democratic. It is difficult to imagine democratic societies that lack politically active groups of citizens who consistently attempt to influence government policies. An **interest group**, or a pressure group, is composed of individuals who share common concerns and who believe that the most effective way to achieve their objectives is to organize and engage in political activities that exert pressure on government decision-makers. Among the numerous groups that promote democracy, college students tend to be the most active, largely because they come from middle-class families, are the best-educated citizens, and are usually concentrated in urban areas where government institutions and the mass media are located.

Interest groups are an essential component of **civil society**. Civil society—a concept that originated with Greek philosophers who were concerned with building democratic societies—refers to the networks of social relations and institutions that exist and act independently of government institutions. Civil society is generally seen as encompassing the wide range of settings that bring individuals together to exchange ideas; discuss issues; and organize to achieve social, political, and economic objectives.[4] Civil society, which exists within countries as well as at the global level, plays a crucial role in the growth and proper functioning of democracy. Individuals, groups, and organizations that operate across national boundaries and are linked together by common interests comprise what is referred to as **global civil society**. Forces of globalizations—especially telecommunications, computer technologies, and rapid and relatively inexpensive transportation—have facilitated the emergence and spread of global civil society. *Nongovernmental organizations (NGOs) use the Internet to promote and strengthen civil society in several ways.*[5] These include

1. Enhance interpersonal communication in order to develop and maintain social relationships;
2. Shape public opinion on various issues;

Political Parties

Competitive political groups that seek to win government positions and offices

Loyal Opposition

Antagonistic party in electoral politics that accepts the legitimacy of the ruling majority

Interest Group

Organization of individuals with common interests who attempt to influence public policy

Civil Society

Networks of social relations and structures that exist independently of the government

Global Civil Society

Individuals and organizations that operate across national borders

Women Elected to
the Palestinian
Parliament

3. Disseminate information, recruit members, and solicit support;
4. Mobilize grassroots organizations, which in turn help to generate public support for the groups' activities; and
5. Encourage individuals to become more active participants in political, economic, and social issues.

Increasing numbers of NGOs cooperate within nations and globally to promote democracy, thereby reinforcing the growth of both domestic civil society and global civil society.

Women's Political Participation and Democracy

Transitions to democracy are accompanied by rising levels of political participation for both men and women. However, even in advanced democracies, problems concerning women's participation remain a serious concern. In the vast majority of political systems, women's participation in politics is influenced to a large extent by their societies' perceptions of women, their roles, their status, and levels of economic development in the various countries. Another major barrier to women's involvement in politics is the widespread perception among both men and women that politics is a male activity. Najma Chowdhury and Barbara J. Nelson refer to this tendency as the "maleness of politics." They argue that politics has always been closely connected to the traditional fatherly connotation of patriarchy and to fraternalism, which essentially exclude women from political activities and power.[6] *Three main arguments are articulated in favor of increased participation of women in the democratic process*: (1) equity and democratic justice, (2) representation of women's interests, and (3) developing and making the maximum use of available human resources.[7] The *equity and democratic justice* argument rests on the widely accepted view that gender equality and fully including women in political life are prerequisites for democracy. Failure to remove impediments to women's political participation undermines the legitimacy of democratic governments and erodes public confidence in the democratic process. The *representation of women's interests* argument focuses on divergent interests between men and women and the need for women to protect and promote their interests themselves by becoming directly involved in the political system. Finally, the *using-all-available-talent* argument stresses the pragmatism of allowing women to contribute to all aspects of development, including the growth of democratic institutions and processes.

Women's political participation is increasing in mature democracies as well as in countries that are transitioning to democracy. An important indicator of this change is the growing number of women in national parliaments and in leadership positions. This development is due primarily to three factors. *First*, globalization has facilitated the emergence of global networks that heighten women's political awareness and enable them to mobilize politically at local, national, and global levels. *Second*, removing barriers to women's political participation, making deliberate efforts to recruit women into politics, modifying electoral systems, and adopting quotas have contributed to women's inclusion in political life. *Finally*, the proliferation of women in legislative and executive positions was facilitated by the termination of the Cold War. As traditional security issues receded and domestic challenges became a priority, women effectively articulated their ability to provide leadership.[8]

TABLE 4.2 WOMEN IN NATIONAL PARLIAMENTS (LOWER OR SINGLE HOUSE)

Rank	Country	Election Year	No. of Seats (Total)	No. of Women	% of Women
1	Rwanda	2003	80	39	48.8
2	Sweden	2002	349	158	45.3
3	Denmark	2001	179	68	38.0
4	Finland	2003	200	75	37.5
5	Netherlands	2003	150	55	36.7
6	Norway	2001	165	60	36.4
7	Cuba	2003	609	219	36.0
7	Spain	2004	350	126	36.0
8	Belgium	2003	150	53	35.3
9	Costa Rica	2002	57	20	35.1
10	Argentina	2001	256	87	34.0
11	Austria	2002	183	62	33.9
12	South Africa	2004	400	131	32.8
13	Germany	2002	603	194	32.2
14	Iceland	2003	63	19	30.2
61	**United States**	**2004**	**435**	**65**	**14.9**

Source: "Women in Parliaments: World Classification," *Inter-Parliamentary Union*, September 2004.

TABLE 4.3 WOMEN LEADERS

Name	Country	Position	Years in Power
Sirimavo Bandaranaike	Sri Lanka	Prime Minister	1960–65, 1970–77, 1992–2000
Indira Ghandi	India	Prime Minister	1966–77, 1980–84
Golda Meir	Israel	Prime Minister	1969–74
Isabel Peron	Argentina	President	1974–76
Elisabeth Domitien	Central African Republic	Prime Minister	1975–76
Maria de Lourdes Pintasilgo	Portugal	Prime Minister	1979–80
Lidia Gueiler Tejada	Bolivia	Prime Minister	1979–80
Mary Eugenia Charles	Commonwealth of Dominica	Prime Minister	1980–95
Vidgis Finnbogadottir	Iceland	President	1980–96
Gro Harlem Bruntland	Norway	Prime Minister	1981, 1986–89, 1990–96
Agatha Barbara	Malta	President	1982–87
Maria Liberia-Peters	Netherlands	Prime Minister	1984–86, 1988–93
Corazon Aquino	Philippines	President	1986–92
Benazir Bhutto	Pakistan	Prime Minister	1988–90, 1993–96
Kazimiera Prunskiene	Lithuania	Prime Minister	1990–91
Mary Robinson	Ireland	President	1990–97
Violeta Barrios de Chamarro	Nicaragua	Prime Minister	1990–96
Edith Cresson	France	Prime Minister	1991–92
Khaleda Zia	Bangladesh	Prime Minister	1991–96
Hanna Suchocka	Poland	Prime Minister	1992–93
Susanne Camelia-Romer	Netherlands	Prime Minister	1993, 1998–present
Sylvie Kinigi	Burundi	Prime Minister	1993–94
Tansu Ciller	Turkey	Prime Minister	1993–95
Chandrika Kumaratunga	Sri Lanka	Prime Minister/President	1994, 1999–present
Claudette Werleigh	Haiti	Prime Minister	1995–96
Mary McAleese	Ireland	President	1997–present
Jenny Shipley	New Zealand	Prime Minister	1997–99
Jennifer Smith	Bermuda	Prime Minister	1998–present
Mireya Elisa Moscoso de Arias	Panama	President	1999–present
Helen Clark	New Zealand	Prime Minister	1999–present
Vaira Vike-Freiberga	Latvia	President	1999–present
Tarja Halonen	Finland	President	2000–present
Gloria Macapagal-Arroyo	Philippines	President	2001–present
Megawati Sukarnoputri	Indonesia	President	2001–04
Angela Merkel	Germany	Chancellor	2005–present
Ellen Johnson Sirleaf	Liberia	President	2006–present
Michelle Bachelet	Chile	President	2006–present
Portia Simpson-Miller	Jamaica	Prime Minister	2006–present

Factors Conducive to Democracy

One of the most significant developments in global affairs at the beginning of the twenty-first century was the U.S. decision to launch a preemptive war against Iraq, partly to overthrow the Saddam Hussein regime and to establish democracy not only in Iraq but also throughout the Middle East. Although some observers were optimistic about democracy replacing authoritarianism and dictatorships, most remained unconvinced that democratic values and practices would flourish in a part of the world that both historically and culturally has been antagonistic toward democracy, especially the form of democracy practiced in the United States, Canada, and Western Europe. Central to this discussion on the spread of democracy in the Middle East, particularly in Iraq, is the assumption that a combination of factors—referred to as *preconditions for democracy*—are essential for the growth and consolidation of democracy.

Many observers concluded that the cultural values associated with Islam were almost insurmountable impediments to transitions to democracy in the majority of Muslim countries. At the heart of this debate is the assumption that **culture** (i.e., a set of values, beliefs, and attitudes) is one of the most important prerequisites for the growth of democracy. Cultures that foster democracy are generally characterized by toleration for divergent viewpoints and practices, bargaining, compromise, a commitment to pragmatism, flexibility, a willingness to accept the policies voted on by the majority of citizens, and commitment to protecting minority rights.

Culture
A set of values, beliefs, and attitudes

Cultural factors help to explain the existence of democratic governments in the English-speaking Caribbean as well as transitions to democracy in Botswana and Nigeria. The British brought many of their democratic institutions and values with them to their colonies in the Caribbean and implemented a process of decolonization aimed at deliberately preparing the new countries for democratic government. The **Westminster model** (i.e., the British model of government) had been practiced to a limited degree from as early as 1639, when the House of Assembly in Barbados was created, making it the third oldest legislative body in the Western Hemisphere, preceded only by Bermuda's legislature and Virginia's House of Burgesses.[9] British rule helped to create a culture that emphasizes the rule of law; constitutional government; civilian supremacy over the military; bureaucratic neutrality; a belief in a loyal opposition as a necessary and constructive component of democratic society, and respect for social, economic, religious, and political freedoms. Democratic competition was embraced, and attempts were made to use government as an instrument for promoting social welfare and economic equality.[10] Botswana and Nigeria also demonstrate that culture plays a significant role in determining democratic transitions. Botswana, a country with a population of 1.5 million, is a stable democracy, due in part to its political culture of toleration for freedom of expression, community consensus, and a tradition of peacefully resolving conflicts. Similarly, the political culture of Nigeria frustrated efforts by successive military regimes to gain legitimacy and institutionalize authoritarian rule. Despite ongoing political turbulence, Nigerians' strong commitment to political and personal liberty played a decisive role in persuading military regimes to promise a transition to civilian rule and democratic government.[11] Despite many broken promises, Nigeria periodically experienced democratic rule and is now consolidating its democratic transition.

Westminster Model
British model of government dating back to as early as 1639

The *global or regional environment* is widely perceived as playing a crucial role in either facilitating or impeding the growth of democracy. As we will see, the ideological rivalry between the East and the West essentially diminished the opportunities for countries under Soviet domination to embrace democracy. On the other hand, Spain and Portugal became democratic partly because economic, political, and cultural forces in Western Europe undermined support for authoritarian rule in those countries. The global environment in the aftermath of the terrorist attacks in the United States in 2001 enabled many governments to take advantage of the war against terrorism declared by the United States. Fighting terrorism was elevated to the primary preoccupation of the dominant power in the global system. This development not only relegated promoting democracy to a secondary priority but, more significantly, provided an opportunity for many governments to portray opposition to their policies as terrorism, thereby undermining democratic movements and individuals committed to effectuating democratic transitions.

Economic Development

Sometimes defined as greater economic growth and integration throughout the world

Another major factor that is conducive to democracy is **economic development**. As countries achieve greater economic prosperity, integration into global markets, exposure to democratic values, higher literacy rates and increased access to education, increased urbanization, and increased knowledge of other cultures through the global media and tourism, they tend to be more receptive to democracy. The forces of development bring people from diverse backgrounds together, encourage them to cooperate and compromise, and challenge as well as reinforce traditional beliefs that inhibit or support the development of democracy. This does not mean that poor countries cannot be democracies, or that all countries that have achieved economic prosperity are democratic. India, for example, is the world's largest democracy despite a history of widespread poverty. Other factors combine to determine the role of economic development in facilitating democracy. However, there is significant evidence supporting the view that poor countries are less likely to be democratic than countries that are relatively more prosperous.

Middle Class

Class in capitalist society between the lower and upper classes

Finally, the emergence of a strong **middle class** is perceived as an important factor conducive to the growth of democracy and is closely related to economic development. Increased national wealth generally expands the middle class, which many people believe is essential to the acquisition and maintenance of democratic values. As we will discuss, countries in Western Europe, Africa, Asia, and Latin America that have experienced rapid economic growth and the expansion of the middle class have adopted democratic values and practices. People who are middle class have greater economic security, are generally less dependent on governments, tend to participate in politics to protect their interests and to hold government accountable, are unwilling to allow governments to violate their rights, and have greater confidence in their abilities to govern themselves.

Promoting Democracy

When Nawadzaba Nasrullah Khan was a young man he was intrigued with the activities of Mohandas K. Gandhi, Jawaharlal Nehru, Ali Jinnah, and others who led independence movements against British control in India. Conflicts between Hindus and

Muslims gave impetus to the creation of Pakistan in 1947 under the leadership of Ali Jinnah as a separate state for Muslims. India has become the world's largest democracy, and Pakistan has been ruled mainly by military dictators and authoritarian civilian rulers. Living in Pakistan, Khan saw that decolonization there was not replaced by democracy. Consequently, he spent more than fifty years working to promote the implementation of a secular Western-style democracy that reflected indigenous influences, including respect for a moderate version of Islamic law. When General Mohammad Ayub Khan, Pakistan's army commander, seized power in a coup in 1958, Nawabzada Khan fought for the restoration of civilian rule by forming the **Democratic Action Committee**, the first of many opposition alliances. The fact that Pakistan continued to be ruled by a military ruler, General Pervez Musharraf, when Khan died in 2003, demonstrates how difficult promoting democracy can be in some societies.[12]

Democratic Action Committee
First oppositional alliance formed to oppose military rule in Pakistan

The disintegration of the Soviet Union removed a significant obstacle to creating and strengthening democratic practices globally. Although the United States had formed alliances with undemocratic governments during the Cold War, America became the primary proponent of exporting democracy when that conflict ended. Many Western governments made the promotion of democracy a prerequisite for financial, military, and other forms of assistance. In 2002, representatives from more than half of the world's countries met in Warsaw, Poland, to exchange ideas on how to create a global community of democracies. They signed the **Warsaw Declaration**, which committed them to promoting democracy in countries lacking it and strengthening democracy in countries that were building it. This development and other actions clearly underscored a growing global consensus that promoting democracy is a global priority.[13]

Warsaw Declaration
Global declaration made after the fall of the Soviet Union aiming at the proliferation of global democracy

Global Civil Society and the Promotion of Democracy

Domestic civil society helps to foster and perpetuate democratic society. But civil society also functions at the global level to promote democratization. Global civil society transcends national boundaries. It consists of organizations and individuals who attempt to influence politics both within countries and globally.[14] Economic, cultural, political, educational, technological, and other networks combine to constitute global civil society. These nonstate voluntary associations blur distinctions between domestic and global political activities. Many cooperate with grassroots activists to effectuate democratic change. Increasingly, they are uniting to maximize their impact on governments. For example, **CIVICUS** consists of more than five hundred NGOs. The World Forum for Democracy, the National Endowment for Democracy, and Transparency International also bring together many NGOs, a development reflecting the realities of globalization. Global civil society provides basic civic education, organizes and funds political parties and interest groups, assists with writing constitutions, observes and mediates elections, and lends credibility to the process of democratization among other activities. One of the most outspoken proponents of building global civil society and promoting democracy is former U.S. President Jimmy Carter.

CIVICUS
Organization of over five hundred NGOs

Jimmy Carter made strengthening human rights and democracy a central component of America's foreign policy while he was president. He championed these causes with even greater passion, energy, and commitment after leaving office. He has monitored elections around the world and has served as an interlocutor in international crises involving the United States in, for example, Haiti and North Korea. He was also the first U.S. president since Calvin Coolidge (1928) to visit Cuba. In 1982, he founded the **Carter Center**, which is affiliated with Emory University in Atlanta, Georgia, to assist in conflict resolution and global development, and to promote democracy globally. His pragmatism, courage, empathy, and willingness to concentrate on what countries or individuals have in common, instead of focusing on differences and conflict, have facilitated his interaction with leaders of authoritarian and dictatorial regimes, including Cuba's Fidel Castro. In 2002, Carter visited Cuba and, addressing the nation in Spanish on Cuba's only television network, he called on Castro and his government to implement democratic practices. While noting that the United States and Cuba had been trapped in a destructive state of belligerence and calling for an end to U.S. sanctions against Cuba, Carter urged Castro to recognize opposition movements and permit Cubans to enjoy democratic freedoms stated in the country's constitution. Carter contacted leading Cuban dissidents, such as Oswaldo Paya and Elizardo Sánchez, who launched the **Varela Project.** That prodemocracy grassroots campaign collected more than eleven thousand signatures supporting

Carter Center

Created to assist in global conflict resolution, development, and promotion of democracy

Varela Project

Cuban grassroots campaign demanding democratic reforms in Cuba

You
DECIDE

Multinational Corporations and the Promotion of Democracy

Although multinational or transnational corporations are often regarded as being so concerned with making profits that they pay little attention to democracy, some argue that these companies actually play a critical role in promoting democracy. By providing economic opportunities to poor communities, such companies are seen as contributing, both directly and indirectly, to the emergence of democratic principles and freedoms. Corporations often bring values into the workplace that challenge undemocratic practices. By providing economic benefits on the basis of individual accomplishment and merit, companies emphasize the principle of individual (as opposed to group or community) rights and responsibilities. Furthermore, individuals acquire a sense of empowerment and independence from the governments as they achieve middle-class status. Individual rights are inextricably linked to democracy. Another argument is that by stressing the need to share information and to cooperate, companies indirectly promote democracy. By demanding openness and accountability in the workplace, companies reinforce the idea that governments should also share information and be held accountable for their actions or failure to act. Finally, by encouraging employees to take initiative and become leaders, companies change ideas and perceptions regarding relationships between leaders and subordinates.

In your view, do companies promote or undermine democracy?

Source: Michael A. Santora, *Profits and Principles: Global Capitalism and Human Rights in China* (Ithaca: Cornell University Press, 2000), 43.

demands for the Cuban National Assembly to hold a referendum on democratic reforms. The Varela Project was named in honor of Felix Varela, a Cuban-born priest who opposed slavery and spent three decades in New York as an advocate of the poor until his death in 1853.[15] Castro's illness in 2006 sparked renewed discussions about transitions to democracy in Cuba under new leadership.

Private foundations, as well as foundations connected to governments, are components of civil society involved in building democracy. Foundations not only control significant financial resources, they also have experience working with other parts of civil society. Many private foundations use their own resources in conjunction with funds allocated by governments to support the growth of democracy. Examples of such foundations are the National Endowment for Democracy, the Adenauer Foundation, the Ebert Foundation, the Ford Foundation, and the Seidel Stiftungen Foundation. After the fall of communism in Central Europe, many foundations cooperated with grassroots democratic movements to rebuild civil society. **George Soros** and his foundations played a prominent role in assisting democratization projects in Central Europe. Soros decided to provide resources quickly and to involve people at the local levels in the decision-making process.[16]

The Promotion of Democracy by the United States

Perceiving itself to be established by divine providence and an exceptional country that has a unique responsibility to transform the world in its own image, the United States strongly believes that it has a divine destiny to expand freedom and American values globally. Throughout its history, America has vacillated between splendid isolation, believing that it was a beacon on a hill providing light and direction to less fortunate societies, and military intervention to enforce its version of democracy in other countries. From its inception, the United States equated its perception of morality with universal ideals and often mobilized its vast resources to implement its socially constructed reality elsewhere. **President Woodrow Wilson** articulated America's involvement in World War I as a mission for democracy, as a struggle to secure the rights of individuals and for self-determination in small countries, and as a fight to make the world free. From our discussion so far, it is obvious that American attempts to promote democracy are inextricably linked to an entrenched **ideology** (i.e., set of beliefs that are often impervious to objective reality and verifiable facts). An ideological approach invariably oversimplifies reality by ignoring or downplaying obvious historical and contemporary contradictory developments. But promoting democracy has also been perceived as an instrument for achieving well-defined national interests, reflecting a pragmatic aspect of American society and foreign policy. The combination of messianic impulses and pragmatism often results in practices that are not only inconsistent and contradictory but are also detrimental to U.S. democratization efforts.

The ideological polarization and military tensions that characterized the East-West struggle had many direct consequences for democratization. As Steven W. Hook observed, "The actual conduct of U.S. foreign policy reflected a **consequential ethic**

Woodrow Wilson

Idealist U.S. president who articulated the U.S. role throughout the world as one of a leader in democracy and self-determination

Ideology

A system of beliefs and values that influence one's activities and behavior

Consequential Ethic

Ethical system that prioritizes the end result of political actions

that regarded anticommunism as a moral end in itself, one that superseded the means by which the outcome was achieved."[17] In the Cold War context, the United States believed that preventing the spread of communism justified both abandoning support for democratic principles and forming alliances with undemocratic governments in Africa, Asia, the Middle East, and Latin America. For example, the United States allied itself with Iran under Shah Mohammed Reza Pahlavi (1953–1979) and successive authoritarian governments in Saudi Arabia. The United States also perceives democratization as an effective strategy for undermining global terrorism. But this strategy overlooks numerous examples of terrorism within the United States, as we will discuss in Chapter 5. Another pragmatic reason given for building democracy is that democracies do not fight one another. However, as we discussed in Chapters 1 and 2, countries protect their interests against real or perceived threats. Consequently, democracies will fight each other to safeguard their interests. Athens and Syracuse, Rome and Carthage, England and Holland, Britain and South Africa, Britain and the United States, and the American Civil War itself are examples of democracies fighting each other.[18]

Despite its longstanding commitment to building democracy abroad, the United States continues to confront several obstacles, including the following:

1. **Inadequate Resources.** In most cases, the United States does not allocate enough financial assistance to build the political institutions, economic and social environment, and civil society essential for promoting democracy.
2. **Lack of Domestic Consensus.** Although in theory most Americans support promoting democracy in foreign countries, democratization in practice has generally failed to engender a lasting commitment, partly because of an overriding preoccupation with domestic concerns.
3. **Conflicting Policy Objectives.** Promoting democracy must often compete with other conflicting national interests.
4. **Limitations of the U.S. Democratic Model.** Each society has its own historical, social, and economic realities, which mitigate the usefulness of the American model of democracy.[19]

The demise of communism in Central and Eastern Europe and the disintegration of the Soviet Union facilitated a resurgence of democratization activities by the United States. Further reinvigorating an emphasis on democracy was the proliferation of mass movements challenging authoritarian and totalitarian regimes and rule by minority governments. Popular uprisings in the Philippines and in Eastern and Central Europe led to the fall of undemocratic governments, and the prolonged struggle against **apartheid** (i.e., strict racial separation and a racial hierarchy) ended with relatively little violence in South Africa. The Berlin Wall was demolished, thereby uniting East and West Germany and signaling the unmistakable end of Soviet communism.

Undergirding and consolidating these developments were rapid economic changes that were integral components of economic globalization, dominated by

Apartheid
Strict racial segregation

You DECIDE | **The Promotion of Democracy by the United States**

A major criticism of U.S. efforts to promote democracy is that the United States is interested in superficial changes, such as elections, and not fundamental alterations of political systems, especially those with which it has significant military and economic ties. William I. Robinson argues that the United States promotes its version of democracy to relieve pressure from subordinate groups for more far-reaching and meaningful social, political, and economic transformations. The net result is that essentially undemocratic governments are allowed to continue denying their populations basic democratic freedoms. Instead of supporting popular aspirations for freedom and self-government, the United States suppresses efforts for more thorough democratization of social life.

Do you think the United States is more concerned with maintaining the status quo than with promoting democracy?

Source: William I. Robinson, *Promoting Polyarchy: Globalization, U.S. Intervention, and Hegemony* (Cambridge: Cambridge University Press, 1996), 6.

the United States. Pressure on countries to adopt market economies, which included privatization of state-owned economic activities, was widely regarded as an essential step toward democratization. The U.S. government enacted the **Support for Eastern European Democracy (SEED) Act** in 2001 to promote economic liberalization and privatization as well as democratic reforms. Foreign financial assistance—provided through the National Endowment for Democracy (NED) and the U.S. Agency for International Development (USAID)—was used to conduct free and fair competitive multiparty elections, draft constitutions, establish independent judicial systems, train police forces, and reduce, if not eliminate, competition in government. Financial assistance was also used to build the forces of civil society. Despite these efforts, much of the money that was allocated for building democracy was spent on aid consultants (many of them Americans) for salaries, airfare, rent, office equipment, cost-of-living allowances, cars, and a support staff in Washington, D.C.[20]

SEED Act

Designed to promote economic liberalization, privatization, and democratic reforms worldwide

Imposing Democracy by Force in Iraq

Achieving its own freedom and independence through revolution, the United States, compared with other great powers, is far more likely to resort to military force to change regimes and to spread democratic rule. Americans use the words "change," "newness," and "revolution" frequently, especially compared with Canada, Britain, and other Western European societies. In this regard, the United States remains a fervent disciple of *Thomas Paine*, who believed that Americans have it in their power to begin the world all over again. Revolutionary values and ideals are at the foundation of America's predilection to impose democracy by force. But strong democratic barriers also prevent the United States from intervening in other countries without clear and direct threats to its national security interests. Although humanitarian crises and ruthless dictators influence the United States to intervene, the size and power of the country involved is a factor in such decisions. At the heart of the debate is whether democracy can be successfully imposed by force. In addition to America's historical experiences, its unsurpassed economic and military power influences many of its leaders to believe that they can reshape the world in America's image. A different view is articulated by Dimitri K. Simes, who argues that "it is condescending to claim that America has the right to impose democracy on other nations and cultures. From the Roman Empire to the British Empire, civilization brought on the tips of swords and bayonets has never inspired lasting gratitude. Why should precision weapons be any more effective?"[21]

America's decision to invade Iraq in March 2003, partly to implement regime change and to impose democracy, raised many questions about the efficacy of using military force to effectuate democratic change. Following Iraq's invasion of Kuwait in 1990, the United States launched the first Gulf War to end Iraq's occupation. Iraq was bombed intensively, and much of its infrastructure and many of its industries were destroyed. Under pressure from the United States, the United Nations (UN) imposed comprehensive sanctions against Iraq and established two "no-fly zones" in Iraq: one in the North and the other in the South. The UN

TABLE 4.4 U.S. EFFORTS TO IMPOSE DEMOCRACY

Years	Country	Multilateral or Unilateral	Democracy Achieved?
2003–present	Iraq	Multilateral	?
2001–present	Afghanistan	Multilateral	?
1994	Haiti	Multilateral	No
1989	Panama	Unilateral	Yes
1983	Grenada	Multilateral	Yes
1970–73	Cambodia	Unilateral	No
1965–73	South Vietnam	Unilateral	No
1965–66	Dominican Republic	Unilateral	No
1945–52	Japan	Multilateral	Yes
1944–49	West Germany	Multilateral	Yes
1944–47	Italy	Multilateral	Yes
1924–25	Dominican Republic	Unilateral	No
1916–24	Cuba	Unilateral	No
1917–22	Haiti	Unilateral	No
1915–19	Mexico	Unilateral	No
1914	Nicaragua	Unilateral	No
1909–27	Nicaragua	Unilateral	No
1909	Cuba	Unilateral	No
1906–09	Honduras	Unilateral	No

Source: Minxim Pei and Sara Kasper, "Reconsider the U.S. Success Rate Before Forcing Democracy Again," *Christian Science Monitor,* 15 January 2003, 8.

inspections led to the destruction of many of Iraq's unconventional weapons, and the embargo against trade in military weapons severely weakened Iraq's military. A major objective of the sanctions was to destabilize Saddam Hussein's regime and render Iraq incapable of militarily threatening its neighbors. While this goal was achieved, sanctions also created widespread hardship and deprivation for most of Iraq's 25 million people, without significantly affecting Hussein and his supporters. Although invading Iraq was seriously considered during the first Gulf War, the risks of such an action were widely perceived as outweighing the benefits. The terrorist attacks in the United States in 2001 radically altered perceptions of the threat posed by Iraq, despite the lack of evidence linking Iraq to terrorism against the United States. President George W. Bush used the terrorist attacks to mobilize public support for invading and occupying Iraq to change the regime, destroy weapons of mass destruction, and build democracy.

FIGURE 4.1 Iraq

Following a swift and successful American military campaign against Iraq, U.S. forces captured Baghdad on April 9, 2003. Saddam Hussein's tyrannical rule ended, thousands of Iraqis greeted American troops, while other Iraqis looted government property and destroyed symbols of the old regime, especially the ubiquitous statues of Hussein. Optimism about regime change and spreading democracy not only in Iraq but throughout the Middle East was bolstered by the easy U.S. military victory, significant Iraqi support for the invasion, and the fact that Iraq contains large oil reserves, is comparatively secular and westernized, and has a well-educated population. But the commitment of the American population to paying the costs for promoting democracy, especially after no evidence of weapons of mass destruction was found, undermined efforts to impose democracy by force.

President Bush appointed **L. Paul Bremer III** as the senior civilian administrator in Iraq. As head of the **Coalition Provisional Authority**, Bremer faced the daunting responsibility of stabilizing Iraq, rebuilding the country's economy and infrastructure, and imposing democracy. Iraq's ethnic and religious divisions complicated the task. It was a major challenge to create political and economic institutions and processes acceptable to the vast majority of Sunnis and Shiites, Arabs and Kurds, religious fundamentalists and secularists, and men and women. Furthermore, as attacks against American troops continued and President Bush remained reluctant to internationalize the responsibility for Iraq's transformation, domestic support for imposing democracy declined precipitously. International opposition to the U.S. occupation of Iraq meant

L. Paul Bremer III
Senior U.S. civilian administrator in Iraq

Coalition Provisional Authority
Retained responsibility for stabilizing Iraq and helping the country transition from interim rule to upcoming elections

Marine Placing U.S. Flag on
Hussein's Statue

that most of the burden of reconstructing Iraq was assumed by the United States. By early November 2003, the Bush administration—faced with progressively sophisticated guerrilla attacks on U.S. forces and on international relief organizations, such as the United Nations and the Red Cross—decided to accelerate transferring responsibilities for security to the Iraqis. Despite widespread violence, elections for seats in a national assembly to draft Iraq's new constitution were held on January 30, 2005. In December 2005, elections were held for the 275 parliamentary seats and to form a government. These elections were viewed by the U.S. government as evidence of Iraq's transition to democracy and as the beginning of democratic change throughout the Middle East. By 2006 it was obvious that U.S. efforts to promote democracy had failed and that the Middle East faced continuing violence and instability. The election of *Hamas*, widely seen as a terrorist group, by the Palestinians in January 2006 created serious challenges to many of America's assumptions about promoting democracy. While Hamas won seventy-two of the 132 seats in the Palestinian legislature, the governing *Fatah* party, supported by the United States, won forty-three seats. The United States and Israel deliberately undermined Hamas. It was obvious that building institutions in the Middle East to ensure the rule of law, reconciling divergent and conflicting interests, protecting the rights of women and minority groups, developing effective market forces, and strengthening civilian control over the military and security forces required patience, substantial resources, and many years, if not decades. Violence and chaos in Iraq, conflicts between Palestinians and Israelis, and Israel's invasion of Lebanon in 2006 underscored the challenges to promoting democracy in the Middle East.

TRANSITIONS TO DEMOCRACY

In 1795, the philosopher Immanuel Kant, in his book, *Idea for a Universal History*, articulated the view that democratic government was destined to replace all other forms of government. The idea that progress was inevitable extended to beliefs about democracy. Despite history's cruel lessons, there was general optimism about a future characterized by justice, logic, and peace. But the auspicious beginnings of the twentieth century were destroyed by grave developments that threatened civilization and the survival of the human race. As Arthur Schlesinger Jr. put it, "Democracy, striding confidently into the 1900s, found itself almost at once on the defensive. The Great War shattered old structures of security and unleashed angry revolutions against democracy. Bolshevism in Russia, Fascism in Italy, Nazism in Germany, Militarism in Japan all despised, denounced, and, wherever they could, destroyed individual rights and the processes of self-government."[22] The Great Depression further eroded confidence in democracy's ability to engender prosperity for the majority of citizens. This economic devastation was quickly followed by World War II, in which antidemocratic forces triumphantly trampled democratic societies and forced Britain, the United States, and their allies to make unprecedented sacrifices to protect lives and liberties globally. It is estimated that by 1941 only twelve democracies had survived worldwide.[23] In his 1989 essay, "The End of History," Francis Fukuyama boldly asserted that with the end of the Cold War, democracy would inevitably spread to all countries. But the promise of liberal democracy encountered the harsh realities of antidemocratic forces.

Democratization (i.e., a transition to democracy) is a process of changing from an authoritarian or totalitarian system of government to a democratic government that is widely regarded by the population and the global community as legitimate and permanent. *A democratic transition* involves the negotiation and acceptance of democratic rules and procedures; the building or restructuring of political, social, and economic institutions; and the channeling of political competition along democratic lines.[24] An essential component of this transition is deciding on a new constitution that reflects political, religious, cultural, and economic realities within the society and its regional environment. *Constitutions* must create as well as limit power, help to legitimize political control, and unify, in many cases, very ethnically diverse populations. To a great extent, to be successful, constitutions must be widely accepted as a political creed or a secular belief system. Inevitably, compromises—which are at the heart of politics—must be incorporated into constitutions for them to embody the values, beliefs, interests, and aspirations of the population.

Democratic transitions often occur gradually over a long time. They usually begin with **liberalization** in what is essentially a predominantly nondemocratic environment. Liberalization includes implementing changes, such as imposing fewer restrictions on the freedom of the press and speech, recognizing the right of workers to unionize, moving away from arbitrarily arresting citizens, having greater respect for the rule of law, releasing political prisoners, and increasing tolerance for political opposition. *Democratization* includes liberalization but is a much broader concept. Democratization involves the right of citizens to compete in elections in order to gain control of the government and to determine the public policy agenda. But elections alone are not sufficient to bring about democratization. What is known as the **electoralist fallacy** (i.e., the view that free elections are a sufficient condition for democracy) is found in many societies transitioning to democracy. Even though nondemocratic leaders relinquish direct control of the government, they continue to exercise so much power that the democratically elected government is widely perceived as politically impotent.[25] Juan J. Linz and Alfred Stepan argue that a democratic transition is complete when there is a widespread agreement on how to elect a government; when the government has the authority to make decisions for the country; and when there is a legal separation of executive, legislature, and judicial powers.[26] Following a country's democratic transition, it faces the more difficult challenge of consolidating democracy.

Transitions to democracy generally do not occur in any specific order. Most countries allowed a degree of democracy to exist in societies that could not be classified as democratic. Some governments limited democratic freedoms to part of the population. For example, democracy in the United States emerged gradually and was initially limited

Liberalization

Traditionally equated with implementation of Western concepts of liberal republicanism

Electoralist Fallacy

The idea that elections are enough to foster democracy

to white males with property. Women and the country's large population of both enslaved and free Americans of African ancestry were excluded from the political process. Most countries transitioning to democracy seem to experience a serious national crisis. The United States, for example, endured a devastating civil war, while South Africa faced escalating internal violence and mounting global pressures for change. The disruption of the status quo often creates rivalries within the nondemocratic government, which eventually contribute to its disintegration. Confronted with unprecedented domestic and international pressures, most governments commit themselves to holding free elections and restoring some fundamental rights and freedoms to the people. Elections generally change the old government and install new leaders. The transitional phase of democracy contains both democratic and nondemocratic elements. Several free and fair elections must be held, civil society must be functioning effectively, the rule of law must be applied, and there must be a general societal consensus that no alternative to democracy exists before the transition to democracy occurs.[27] But democracies must deliver tangible benefits to demonstrate their superiority over nondemocratic systems. They must improve economic opportunities, maintain order, and provide an enhanced quality of life for their citizens in order to obtain legitimacy or acceptance by the people. A full transition to democracy, in summary, is accomplished when basic democratic rights and freedoms are an integral component of life and when the overwhelming majority of the citizens, despite problems in society, believe that democracy is better than its alternatives.

Managed Transitions

Attempt to create stable transitions of change throughout society

Many military regimes in Africa, Asia, and Latin America implemented **managed transitions** to democracy. These regimes try to control the process of change to protect their own interests, to ensure social stability, and to minimize concessions to those advocating political transformation. In managed transitions, the military often establishes a timetable for the restoration or creation of democratic rule and determines the process of democratic elections.[28] These managed transitions usually occur in response to widespread national unrest and severe economic crises. Some military leaders initiate transitions to democracy because of their own personal commitment to democracy or because developments in the country, regionally, and globally convince them that military rule is no longer a viable option.

Significant and persistent pressures for change prompt transitions to democracy. The global community, regional organizations, individual countries and NGOs, the local as well as global news media, the business community, women, labor unions, and students play crucial roles in engendering political reforms. Almost always, when nondemocratic governments implement some democratic changes, they face growing demands for more far-reaching and fundamental changes. Governments that relax restrictions on the press, for example, find themselves challenged by an emboldened press. The press plays an important role in creating conditions that eventually force governments to democratize. Widespread access to information and ideas provided by the media, especially the global media, ends the government's monopoly on information and ultimately weakens its ability to influence how people think and their perceptions of reality.

Consolidating democracy is a long-term process that involves behavioral, attitudinal, and institutional transformations. Behaviorally, a democratic regime is consolidated when there is widespread popular acceptance of the idea that governments should not be changed by force. Attitudinally, a democratic regime is consolidated when a strong majority of the population believes that democratic institutions and procedures are most appropriate for their society. Institutionally, a democratic regime is consolidated when society as a whole, including the government, believes that certain laws, procedures, and institutions must be used to govern society.[29] *For democracy to be consolidated, several conditions are believed to be essential. First*, conditions must exist that are conducive for the development and proper functioning of civil society. Individuals must be able to create organizations and engage in activities that are independent from the government in order to safeguard their interests, disseminate information to the public, and challenge government policies and procedures through legitimate processes. *Second*, specific arrangements must be made for groups and individuals to compete fairly and openly for political power. *Third*, society, including the government, must respect and uphold the rule of law, and an impartial and independent judiciary must be regarded as the ultimate authority, with the responsibility for interpreting the constitution and deciding what is lawful or unlawful. *Fourth*, there must be an institutionalized economic society or a significant degree of market autonomy and the right of individuals to own property.[30]

Waves of democratization have occurred since the eighteenth century and continue today. Samuel P. Huntington defines *a wave of democratization* as a group of transitions from nondemocratic to democratic regimes that happen within a specific period of time and that outnumber transitions away from democracy.[31] As you know, not all countries that are democratic were part of a wave of democratization. *Three* distinct waves of democratization can be identified in modern history. The *first wave* began with the American and French Revolutions and included parts of the British Empire (e.g., Canada, Australia, and New Zealand) and several small European countries (e.g., Switzerland). The *second wave* grew out of the retreat of democracy and the rise of Nazism, fascism, and totalitarianism in Europe and militarism in Japan. When these antidemocratic forces were defeated in World War II, democracy experienced a renewal or rebirth. Allied occupation of West Germany, Austria, Italy, and Japan led to the democratization of these former aggressive states. The *third wave* began with Portugal in 1974 and lasted until the late 1990s.[32] Because this wave was so expansive, we can subdivide it into *three distinct pathways to democracy* taken by various countries. The *first pathway* involved a movement away from military rule toward democracy in Greece, Spain, Portugal, Brazil, Argentina, and Chile. The *second pathway* toward democracy is characterized by a movement away from authoritarian regimes governed by a single dominant party. Examples are Taiwan, the Philippines, and South Africa. The *third pathway* toward democracy began in countries that had been dominated by communism and a communist oligarchy. Countries in Central and Eastern Europe and the former Soviet Union are the leading examples of this pathway.[33]

Western Europe—Portugal and Spain

Sharing many of the political, social, and economic characteristics of the developing world, Portugal and Spain were very different from the rest of Western Europe until relatively recently. Portugal was ruled by **Antonio de Oliveira Salazar** from 1928

Antonio de Oliveira Salazar

Former ruler of Portugal

Marcello Caetano

Salazar's successor

Revolution of the Carnations

Portugese revolution that overthrew Caetano

Francisco Franco

Fascist leader of Spain during and after World War II

Corporatism

Argument that government is inherently good but in need of checks and balances

Generational Change

Change in society based on radical transformation of norms and values as time progresses

until 1968, and by **Marcello Caetano**, who was selected by Salazar as his successor, from 1968 until 1974. In 1974, Caetano was overthrown in what the Portuguese call the **"Revolution of the Carnations,"** because soldiers involved in overthrowing the regime were greeted by cheering crowds who placed carnations in the barrels of their rifles. **Francisco Franco** ruled Spain from 1939 to 1975. Both Spain and Portugal were strongly influenced by Catholicism and the development of liberalism on the one hand and Marxist socialism on the other. Essentially, Portugal and Spain experienced authoritarianism that expressed itself in the ideology of **corporatism**. Corporatism, as practiced, was derived partly from ideas articulated by Aristotle and St. Thomas Aquinas. Corporatism emphasized that government is inherently good and natural and therefore a system of checks and balances is unnecessary. It also stressed that a well-ordered political system is integrated, disciplined, and hierarchical. Individuals and groups have their specific and relatively fixed roles and positions in a society that is dominated by the government.[34]

Neither Portugal nor Spain could escape dynamic forces in Western Europe, global developments, or the forces unleashed by the actions of their dictatorial regimes. Economic integration and military cooperation in Western Europe pressured Portugal and Spain to become more closely aligned with democratic governments in the region. Strongly influenced by Catholicism, both Portugal and Spain were staunchly opposed to communism, a fact that pushed them toward Western Europe and the United States in the global struggle that characterized the Cold War. Military and political alliances were reinforced by Europe's economic recovery after World War II and its rapidly expanding networks of economic cooperation, which ultimately spread to Portugal and Spain. Both Spain and, to a lesser extent, Portugal experienced rapid urbanization, with Spain going from being 70 percent rural to 70 percent urban, and Portugal becoming 60 percent urban, from 80 percent rural. Literacy increased, more women were employed outside the home, labor movements grew, a larger and more economically secure middle class emerged, and traditional elites were gradually replaced with individuals involved in business and industry. Economic transformation was accompanied by a **generational change**. The leaders of Portugal and Spain, who were in their late seventies and eighties, were widely perceived as belonging to a time that was no longer relevant. A younger generation of leaders wanted to change old economic and political arrangements and to bring their countries into the modern world. An even younger generation—exposed to American and European values and lifestyles through television, travel, books, movies, and magazines—wanted to adopt both the economic and political values and lifestyles of these democratic societies.[35] The authoritarian regimes, confronted with powerful agents of change, attempted to relax their control without relinquishing power. However, gradual changes led to deepening political, cultural, and economic fissures that eventually facilitated the demise of authoritarianism and paved the way for transitions to democracy in Portugal and Spain.

Portugal Portugal attempted to modernize its economy by encouraging foreign investment, lowering trade barriers, and creating an environment that was conducive to the growth of commerce and industry. Lower wages and fewer government regulations in Portugal, compared with those in the rest of Western Europe and the other industrialized countries, attracted foreign industry and contributed to Portugal's economic development. Salazar's economic reforms, which started in 1953, were continued by Caetano. Overall, economic improvements were impressive. Per capita income doubled between 1953 and the early 1960s, and doubled again by 1974. However, the oil embargo imposed on selected countries that imported petroleum from the Middle East as an outgrowth of the Arab-Israeli War of 1973 had severe negative economic implications for Portugal because of its heavy dependence on imported petroleum. Complicating the problems of the authoritarian regimes were developments in Portugal's African colonies (Angola, Mozambique, and Guinea-Bissau).

Long after most European countries had abandoned their colonial empires, Portugal continued to control African countries that were several times its size, regarding them as integral parts of Portugal. The waves of decolonization around the world, fueled by the radically altered political and strategic environment that grew out of World War II, engulfed Portugal, forcing it to fight destructive wars against colonies determined to achieve independence. These colonial struggles were strongly supported by Cuba and the Soviet Union, a reality that forced Portugal to allocate more than half of its national budget to military activities against liberation movements in its colonies. Portugal was also experiencing significant casualties, with its dead and wounded flown to Lisbon daily. Public sentiment turned against the wars and colonization, thereby emboldening both the military and civilian organizations to challenge the government. Shortly after midnight on April 25, 1974, a radio station in Lisbon began playing the song "Grando Vila Morena," which was a signal to military units to implement plans to overthrow the government. The **Armed Forces Movement (MFA)**, which was primarily responsible for the bloodless **coup d'etat**, initially attempted to govern Portugal but was gradually replaced by the Socialist Party, which was more moderate and more representative of mainstream Portuguese politics. The Socialist Party, headed by **Mario Soares**, was elected in 1975 and governed Portugal with the cooperation of the military, other political parties, and groups backed by the United States, Britain, West Germany, and others.[36]

Armed Forces Movement
Group that briefly governed Portugal until it was replaced by the Socialist Party

Coup d'etat
A military overthrow of government

Mario Soares
Leader of the Socialist Party elected into government in Portugal

Spain   Unlike Portugal, Spain's transition to democracy was more gradual, more carefully planned, and more institutionalized. Whereas Portugal looked more to Africa and Brazil, Spain became increasingly intertwined with Europe. Spain's emphasis on Europe in terms of trade, military alliances, and culture augmented its evolutionary transition to democracy. Francisco Franco, Spain's authoritarian leader, was instrumental in this process. Similar to Salazar in Portugal, Franco adopted economic reforms that dramatically improved the country's economy and standard of living. Economic liberalization, large inflows of foreign investment, an embrace of technological change as well as technocrats, and more participation of women in the economy were strongly supported by Franco, even as he attempted to maintain control of economic and political life. Spain rapidly changed from a developing country into an increasingly industrialized society. Growing by around 8 percent a year throughout

Spanish Miracle

Refers to growth in the Spanish economy during the rule of Franco

Political Reform Act

Called for elections in Spain to select a bicameral parliament and create a new constitution

the 1960s and into the early 1970s, Spain's growth rates were second only to those of Japan, a development called the **Spanish miracle**.[37]

Political transformations were equally important to Spain's democratization. Realizing that his health was failing, Franco instituted changes that he hoped would extend his influence in Spain after his death. He created the position of prime minister, which was subordinate to him. He also decided to restore the Spanish monarchy, which was abolished in 1931. Carlos Arias Navarro was designated prime minister, and **Juan Carlos**, the grandson of Spain's last king, Alfonso, was brought back to Spain and groomed by Franco to become the Spanish monarch. Despite Franco's efforts to influence Juan Carlos, the new king replaced the prime minister selected by Franco with Adolfo Suárez. He also enacted the **Political Reform Act**, which called for elections in order to select members of a new bicameral parliament and for the creation of a new constitution. A constitution was drafted by the parliament and approved by 90 percent of the population in a referendum in 1978. Spain's transition to democracy was achieved largely because the people supported it.

Latin America

Between 1978 and 1993, fifteen countries in Latin America transitioned from dictatorship and totalitarianism to democracy. Several factors contributed to these developments. *First*, given the historical and cultural relationships between Latin America and Spain and Portugal, the end of the Franco and Salazar regimes inspired democratic movements in Latin America. *Second*, economic difficulties, symbolized by the debt crisis, further eroded the legitimacy of nondemocratic governments, many of which justified their rule on the basis of the ability to develop the economy. *Third*, military conflicts in Nicaragua, El Salvador, Panama, and Argentina undermined dictatorships in those countries. The government in Argentina, for example, was weakened not only by economic problems but also by its defeat in the Falklands Malvinas by Britain. *Fourth*, the inability of governments to deal with the effects of natural disasters in such countries as Nicaragua and Bolivia contributed to their downfall. *Fifth*, some governments were pressured to democratize by sanctions, imposed primarily by the United States. *Sixth*, the demise of communism in the Soviet Union and Eastern Europe further weakened the credibility of dictatorships globally and highlighted democracy as the only viable alternative. *Finally*, the United States changed its approach to Latin America, becoming more reluctant to support dictators who were allies. These changes reinforced pressures within various Latin American countries for democracy.[38]

Salvador Allende

Chilean Marxist who became president

Augusto Pinochet

General responsible for the military overthrow of Allende

Chile, traditionally a stable democracy, is an example of a country in which democracy was replaced by authoritarian rule. In 1973, **Salvador Allende**, Chile's first democratically elected Marxist president, was overthrown and killed by **General Augusto Pinochet**, with the support of the United States. Pinochet and the military ruled Chile until the restoration of democracy in 1990. Domestic and international pressures, significant economic development under Pinochet, and the expansion of the middle class eventually influenced Pinochet to hold free and fair elections, which he lost. Although

Pinochet continued to play an influential role in the government and the military, Chile had returned to its democratic roots. Despite progress toward democracy, many Latin American societies are confronted with numerous problems that weaken the democratic process. Poverty remains widespread, economic inequality undermines political equality, and corruption continues to erode the legitimacy of political and economic institutions. Many ordinary citizens are not convinced that democracy can improve their lives.[39] For example, violent protests against economic and political conditions in Ecuador forced President Lucio Gutierrez from office in 2005.

Africa

Most African countries briefly experienced a degree of democracy following their independence from Britain and France in the early 1960s. However, the military, the strongest institution in the African states, soon dominated politics. Furthermore, Africa became a battleground for Cold War conflicts between the Soviet Union and the United States. Many African leaders used the rivalry between the superpowers to consolidate their own power and to postpone transitioning to democracy indefinitely. Transitions to democracy were also a low priority for the global powers. But many Africans continued to pressure military dictatorships to return their societies to civilian rule. For example, Nigeria embraced democracy in 1979, only to revert to military rule four years later. Nigeria eventually transitioned to democracy in early 1999. The end of Soviet communism, the termination of the Cold War, and a renewed interest in democracy globally influenced the majority of African countries to make tentative transitions to democracy. Several dictators, including **Mobutu Sese Seko** of Zaire, were overthrown and multiparty elections were held as the military retreated from government. Elections were held in the Congo in 2006, amid significant violence. While several countries—for example, Senegal, Ghana, and South Africa—have peacefully transferred power to opposition party rivals, most African states have experienced undemocratic practices. Leaders in Zimbabwe, for example, manipulated the electoral process to maintain a veneer of legitimacy and engaged in widespread violations of basic democratic freedoms. Led by Robert Mugabe, Zimbabwe, in 2006, retreated from democracy. Enduring poverty, escalating crime rates, endemic corruption, and the devastating spread of AIDS combine to weaken democratic transitions in Africa. In fact, democracy has generally been accompanied by deteriorating economic conditions, making Africans freer but poorer than they have been in decades.[40] South Africa represents Africa's most successful transition to democracy.

Settled by Dutch, French, German, and English immigrants and refugees, South Africa developed a system of rigid racial separation and inequality, known as apartheid. Apartheid became official policy in 1948, thereby legalizing racial discrimination and white minority rule. Although the white minority developed democratic institutions for themselves, they systematically oppressed the black majority and whites who opposed minority rule. Blacks responded by forming the **African National Congress (ANC)**, which was led by **Nelson Mandela**. After Mandela and other ANC leaders were imprisoned for resisting apartheid through peaceful means, black South Africans

Mobutu Sese Seko
Zairian dictator overthrown during the country's transition to elections

ANC
Black organization designed to resist South African apartheid

Nelson Mandela
Charismatic African leader who led the ANC

F. W. de Klerk

South African government leader who ended apartheid

Truth and Reconciliation Commission

Established to expose relevant information from the apartheid era and help transition South Africa into democratic government

resorted to a combination of armed struggle, trade union activity, mass demonstrations, and the mobilization of global pressures to influence the white minority to abandon apartheid and implement democracy for all South Africans. As South Africa achieved higher levels of economic development, it became increasingly dependent on black labor. Businesses eventually concluded that apartheid was unworkable and costly. International pressures, including economic sanctions against the apartheid regime, growing Soviet support for the ANC, and Portugal's withdrawal from neighboring Angola and Mozambique after its own transition to democracy, combined to convince the South African government, under the leadership of **F. W. de Klerk**, that apartheid was no longer viable.[41] Mandela and others were released from prison in 1990, free elections were held, and a new constitution was adopted. South Africans also established the **Truth and Reconciliation Commission** to try to repair some of the damage caused by apartheid and to unite the various South African groups. Mandela was elected in 1994 to lead South Africa, and the ANC gained control of the government. Although South Africa faces high crime rates, poverty, high levels of unemployment, and severe economic inequalities, its transition to democracy remains secure.

Asia

Rapid economic growth in such countries as Taiwan, South Korea, Thailand, Indonesia, and even China is a catalyst for transitions from authoritarianism or totalitarianism to democracy. However, despite economic growth in Thailand, the military seized control of the country in 2006 in a bloodless coup. Although China remains a communist country, its rapid economic growth and integration into the global economy and its leading role in global politics exert pressure on its government to implement far-reaching economic reforms and limited democratic freedoms. Taiwan and South Korea, for example, responded to pressure from prodemocracy movements, students, and labor unions by ending authoritarian rule. These countries' economic prosperity, their close relationships with the United States, and their rapid integration into the global economy weakened the old system. Many Asian countries adopted policies that reduced economic inequalities and provided adequate health care, education, housing, and employment for their citizens. The middle class, especially students, helped to push the world's largest Islamic country, Indonesia, to democratize during its economic crisis in the late 1990s.

Suharto

Dictatorial leader responsible for liberalizing the Indonesian economy

President Suharto of Indonesia, who seized power in 1965 by leading a military coup against the government, attempted to legitimize his authoritarian rule by strengthening the economy. Indonesians generally agreed to accept fewer democratic rights in exchange for improved economic conditions. When Indonesia's economy collapsed in the late 1990s, the government lacked a large enough reservoir of political legitimacy to convince the majority of the population to remain loyal and keep their side of the bargain. Ironically, Suharto had developed Indonesia sufficiently to enable Indonesians to demand democratic reforms. After two years of protests, Suharto's dictatorship ended, a new government was elected, and Indonesia's new leaders promised to implement democratic reforms.

You **DECIDE**   **Democracy in China**

Often, governments have been instrumental in developing their countries' economies. This has generally fostered the emergence and expansion of a strong middle class, diminished society's dependence on government programs, and enabled citizens to gain more exposure to other cultures and lifestyles. All of these developments strengthen demands for democracy. Similar to Spain in the 1960s and early 1970s, China is experiencing sustained high economic growth rates. With a population of more than 1.3 billion, China is becoming a major producer of exports for global markets as well as a major consumer market. China's membership in the World Trade Organization and its increasing westernization are regarded as posing significant challenges to the continuation of communism.

Do you think China will maintain a nondemocratic system despite the impact of globalization?

Source: Merle Goldman, *From Comrade to Citizen: The Struggle for Political Rights in China* (Cambridge, MA: Harvard University Press, 2006).

In many ways, China is a paradox. The Communist Party is simultaneously the initiator of comparatively revolutionary changes and the guardian of conservativism, stability, and political repression of opposition groups. Overall, China has adopted a cautious approach to democratic reforms, largely due to increased prosperity, a growing middle class, and pressure from the forces of globalization. Despite a veneer of democratic freedoms, the government controls China's judicial, economic, political, and social systems. Although the government initiated democracy at the village level in 1989 following its brutal repression of student protests for democracy in **Tiananmen Square**, political participation in rural areas has limited implications for the government in Beijing. Influenced partly by Russia's difficult transition to democracy, Chinese authorities are determined to carefully control the democratization process.

Tiananmen Square

Location where Chinese students were brutally repressed for demanding democratic reforms

Russia

Emerging as a superpower after World War II, the Soviet Union embarked on an expansionist foreign policy and directly competed with the United States and its allies to promote communism as the dominant ideology and way of life. Domestically, the **Communist Party of the Soviet Union (CPSU)** exercised complete control over the economy, politics, culture, and every aspect of Soviet life. Centrally planned economic activities excluded private enterprise and free markets. The government's control of the economy impeded the country's economic development and created many hardships for the population. Competition with the United States forced the Soviet Union to allocate a large proportion of its increasingly scarce resources to clients in the Third World and to military activities. Faced with a widening gap in living standards between themselves and the West, particularly the United States, Soviet citizens began to view global confrontation and the resources it required as undermining their own economic and social security. They began to turn their attention inward to domestic problems.

CPSU

Political party that exercised total economic, political, and cultural control over Soviet life

As Marshall Brement observed, it was difficult to convince the Soviet public that events in distant places were more important than their own basic needs and interests. Only the most conservative ideologues within the leadership failed to grasp that the Soviet system was in crisis and that a radical shake-up was desperately needed.[42]

Mikhail Gorbachev

Leader who inherited the economic, political, and social problems during the final days of the declining Soviet Union

Mikhail Gorbachev, who was selected by the Communist Party in 1985 to lead the Soviet Union, inherited a stagnating economy and a deteriorating social and political system. Food shortages were commonplace, crime was escalating, corruption was rampant, life expectancy was declining, interethnic violence was spreading, and the Communist Party was weakened by internal power struggles. What's more, the inefficiency, rigidity, corruption, and brutality of the system eroded the legitimacy of Soviet institutions. Most citizens stopped believing in the government. Mounting Soviet casualties in Afghanistan, which the Soviets had invaded in 1979, further demonstrated the seriousness of the challenges confronting the Soviet Union. Gorbachev equated Soviet involvement in Afghanistan with America's failure in Vietnam and decided to stanch the "bleeding wound" by withdrawing Soviet forces from Afghanistan. These problems influenced Gorbachev to adopt radical economic reforms and political liberalization in an effort to strengthen the Soviet Union. His program of *perestroika* (i.e., restructuring of the Soviet economy) challenged the idea of a centrally planned economy and advocated implementing a more open economy that stressed greater local autonomy, economic incentives, and market forces. Another reform was the program of *glasnost* (i.e., openness), which challenged the Communist Party's assumption that it had a monopoly on truth. Instead, Gorbachev strongly supported more freedom of speech and freedom of the press, believing that truth emerges through the exchange of ideas, discussions, and debates. Finally, Gorbachev advocated a program of **democratizatsiva** (i.e., democratization), a central component of which would be respect for the rule of law and the free and open election of government officials.

Democratizatsiva

Program of democratization implemented by Gorbachev

But Gorbachev's reforms, instead of strengthening the Soviet system, destroyed it. The Soviet Union disintegrated as the various republics declared their independence from Russia and communism itself fell. Hardliners were replaced by reformers, the military and the KGB (secret police) were reformed, and many Communist Party activities were abolished. When supporters of the old regime attempted to overthrow Gorbachev in 1991, Russians demonstrated against them in Moscow, helping to guarantee the failure of the coup. Although Gorbachev resigned as president in December 1991 when the Soviet Union was officially disbanded, he had been awarded the Nobel Peace Prize in 1990 for both his domestic and foreign policy reforms.

Boris Yeltsin

Former Communist Party chief who was elected president of Russia

Boris Yeltsin, the former Communist Party chief in Moscow, was elected to replace Gorbachev in Russia's first free presidential election. Opposition to change continued to frustrate efforts by Yeltsin to reform Russia. Yeltsin responded by disbanding the parliament, which was dominated by communist conservatives who opposed change. His decision to schedule new elections and to create a constitutional assembly to draft a new constitution, to be approved by the voters, prompted an armed revolt against the government, which was suppressed by the army. In 1995, Russia held its first fully constitutional parliamentary elections since the 1917 Bolshevik Revolution. Yeltsin was reelected president in 1996.[43] Despite ongoing problems with transitioning to democracy, Vladimir Putin, a former KGB agent, was appointed by Yeltsin to be his prime minister and acting president in January 2000; he was elected president later that year. During his inauguration, Putin held a red, leather-bound copy of the Russian Constitution and took an oath to "respect and guard the human and civil rights" of Russia. This event marked the first democratic transfer of executive power in Russia's 1,100–year history.[44]

Yeltsin and Putin at Inauguration

Developments in Russia demonstrate that elections and the creation of democratic institutions do not necessarily guarantee the practice of democracy. Although Russians travel freely, read what they want, and engage in free enterprise, the government continues to exercise power that is inconsistent with democracy. While in theory the press is free, in reality the government has consolidated its control over television. What's more, many government bureaucrats diminish freedom of the press by canceling leases, raising utility rates, abusing the government's taxation powers, denying access to printing plants, arresting reporters, and raising the cost of newsprint. The state also has a monopoly on distributing papers. Many newspapers, magazines, and television networks are closely affiliated with the government, and there is increasing consolidation of media ownership. Business is also concentrated in the hands of the oligarchs who are politically powerful. These realities undermine the role of the media as an essential component of democracy. Most Russians remain cynical and apathetic about political participation. Despite significant steps toward democracy, Russia remains at a crossroads, often leaning more toward authoritarianism than democracy. During her first visit to Russia in 2005 as U.S. Secretary of State, Condoleezza Rice emphasized that Russia should move closer toward democratic ideals, such as the rule of law and an independent news media.[45] Putin used the threat of terrorism to justify his retreat from democracy. By 2006, it was obvious that democracy in Russia, especially at the national level, had eroded.

Islam and Democracy in the Middle East

Americans' perceptions of the Middle East as predominantly undemocratic and their association of Islam with oppression emanated partly from the objective reality that most countries in the region are not democratic and partly from their negative experiences with the Arab oil embargo of 1973–1974; the Iranian Revolution in 1979, led by the **Ayatollah Khomeini**, in which American diplomats were held hostage at the American Embassy compound in Tehran for more than a year; and the terrorist attacks in the United States in 2001 by Islamic extremists. While most scholars do not believe that democracy is incompatible with Islam, the general perception is that Islamic societies are inherently undemocratic. Furthermore, there is a general tendency, especially in the United States, to think that all Muslims are the same. Islamists are obviously not a monolithic group, just as Christians and Jews are not monolithic. Islamists are conservative, radical, moderate, authoritarian, and democratic. Countries

Ayatollah Khomeini
Leader of the Iranian revolution and of the Iranian state

in which Islam is practiced have their own particular cultural practices and beliefs that differentiate them from each other and moderate religious influences on political life.

Given the many similarities among Judaism, Christianity and Islam—three monotheistic religions that have the same roots in the Middle East—just as there are democratic values in Christian thought, there are democratic values in Islamic thought. As Graham E. Fuller put it, "Democratic values are latent in Islamic thought if one wants to look for them."[46] The interpretation of the Christian holy book, the Bible, is often arbitrary and subject to debate. The prophet **Mohammad** (570–632 A.D.), the founder of Islam, called for **shura** (i.e., consultation between the ruler and the ruled), which, as we discussed earlier, is the essence of democracy. The concept of limited government, a cornerstone of democracy, is central to Islam. Both the rulers and the ruled are, according to Islamic teachings on the state, subject to God's law. This means that not even the most powerful leaders are above the law. But unlike Christianity, which stresses that we should give to "Caesar what is Caesar's and to God what is God's," Islam makes no distinction between the secular and the sacred or between state and mosque. Despite difficulties

Mohammad

(570–632); Founder of Islam

Shura

Concept of consultation between the ruler and the ruled

FIGURE 4.2 The Middle East

inherent in using the **Koran** as the foundation of laws for Muslims, the authoritarian governments in the Middle East are less a product of strict adherence to Islamic teachings than they are creations of modernization and the universal human struggle for power.

In an increasingly interdependent world, most Muslims aspire to have the same freedoms as people enjoy in the United States and Western Europe. Instead of viewing Islam as the primary obstacle to democratization, many citizens in the Middle East perceive U.S. policies that support authoritarian regimes as the most serious impediment to democracy.[47] Students in Iran, Egypt, and elsewhere in the Middle East routinely demonstrate against fundamentalist Islamic regimes and authoritarian governments and for democracy. In Iran, for example, students were instrumental in getting **Mohammad Khatami**, a moderate who advocated democratic changes, elected president. But powerful conservative clerics and their supporters prevented him from carrying out meaningful reforms. Many Iranian students have spearheaded protests against religious leaders. Apart from being concerned about corruption and growing unemployment, many students want more freedom in their private and social lives. They want the same freedoms that they know exist in the West because of their access to television, the Internet, and other aspects of globalization.[48] Most governments in the Muslim world respond to demands for democracy by creating a veneer of freedom, allowing token opposition parties to function, and stressing the need for economic development. But effective opposition movements—whether they advocate democracy, Islam, or socialism—are perceived as threats to the power and privileges of ruling elites.[49] Elections in Afghanistan in 2004, in Iraq in 2005, and in the Palestinian Territories in 2006 demonstrated that Muslims also value democracy. The Western countries' hostile response to democratic elections

Koran
Muslim holy book

Mohammad Khatami
Iranian president who has advocated moderate reforms

You **DECIDE** | ### Oil and Democracy

In a speech before the National Endowment for Democracy in November 2003, President George W. Bush attempted to change American and global perceptions of U.S. occupation of Iraq by stressing that the fall of Saddam Hussein was a "watershed event in the global democratic revolution." Pointing out that "sixty years of Western nations excusing and accommodating the lack of freedom in the Middle East did nothing to make Americans safe," President Bush concluded that "stability cannot be purchased at the expense of liberty." This speech underscored the concern of many advocates for democratic change in the Middle East that U.S. preoccupation with ensuring the flow of petroleum from the Middle East strengthened authoritarian governments in the region. At the heart of the lack of democracy in the Middle East, some argue, is the abundance of oil. The dependence of both exporting and importing countries on petroleum is seen as subverting democracy more than anything else. Countries with oil can flourish without having to provide the freedoms essential for developing human resources.

Do you think oil is a significant impediment to democratic transitions in the Middle East?

Sources: David E. Sanger, "Bush Asks Lands in Mideast to Try Democratic Ways," *New York Times*, 7 November 2003, A1. and Thomas L. Friedman, "The First Law of Petropolitics," *Foreign Policy*, No. 154 (May/June 2006), 31.

in Palestine and subsequent military actions by the Israelis against the Palestinians and Israel's invasion of Lebanon in July 2006 undermined the idea that the United States, in particular, is primarily concerned with promoting democracy.

GLOBAL GOVERNANCE AND DEMOCRACY

From Seattle to Prague, from Basel to Cancun, protesters are demanding that global institutions—such as the World Trade Organization (WTO), the World Bank, and the International Monetary Fund (IMF)—be more accountable, responsible, and responsive to ordinary citizens worldwide. In other words, they are demanding expanding democratic practices at the global level, just as individuals and groups are calling for transitions to democracy within countries. While power—economic, political, technological, and cultural—is becoming increasingly global, democracy continues to be associated with practices within the boundaries of nation-states. There is a growing perception that although globalization is having profound implications, both positive and negative, for people almost everywhere, global institutions and their activities remain essentially undemocratic because they are not accountable to the people. Globalization is often viewed as depriving democratically elected governments of their ability to determine public policies or to regulate the consequences of global decisions on the people who elected them. The gap between democracy at the national and global levels is most apparent in the area of **economic globalization**. There is a widespread fear, especially within developed societies, that the global economy is undermining democracy by shifting power from elected national governments to faceless and often secretive global bureaucracies.[50] In most cases citizens cannot use their votes to hold global institutions accountable, despite the fact that many global organizations were created and are controlled by nation-states. For example, many Europeans believe that the Council of the European Union—composed of presidents, prime ministers, and cabinet ministers who meet regularly to approve various public policies—has essentially diminished the power of elected parliaments to make economic decisions. This loss of power, the relative inability of governments and citizens to influence decisions by global institutions, is generally referred to as a **democratic deficit**.

International Regimes

Controversy surrounding the issue of a democratic deficit is a direct outgrowth of the proliferation of international regimes and global institutions as integral components of globalization. **International regimes** are basically institutions governing the behavior or actions of governmental as well as nongovernmental actors that are involved in specific activities. Regimes are characterized by complex interdependence and consist of rules, regulations, norms, and legal agreements that govern the behavior of those belonging to them.[51] International regimes reflect the interests and values of their members. However, because regimes also reflect power in the international system, the dominant actors or groups of actors often shape their organization, its functioning, and its policies. For example, although most countries are members of

Economic Globalization

Predominantly known as the spread of market values, institutions, and trade across state lines

Democratic Deficit

Loss of citizen and government power in challenging the agendas of global institutions

International Regimes

International institutions that govern the behavior of governmental and nongovernmental actors

the WTO and have a vote, actual decision-making occurs in the **green room**, which is the small group meeting convened by the director-general and is strongly influenced by the United States, the European Union, Canada, and Japan.[52]

The proliferation and increasing complexity of international regimes combine to create a global governance system. Global governance is not equated to a centralized global government or authority. In fact, global governance conveys a relatively orderly global community despite the lack of centralized power. Global governance reflects the transition from traditional international relations to the realities of globalization. **Global governance** is defined "as the formal institutions and organizations through which the rules governing world order are made and sustained as well as those organizations and pressure groups—from MNCs, transnational social movements to the plethora of nongovernmental organizations—which pursue goals and objectives that have a bearing on transnational rule and authority systems."[53] Global governance is based on cooperation as opposed to unilateralism. Coordination of actions occurs through governmental as well as nongovernmental organizations.

At the heart of global governance is the concept of global civil society, discussed earlier in this chapter. Global civil society is defined as a "decentralized network of autonomous social institutions that represent citizens and organized interests and engage in cooperative actions to achieve broad goals."[54] Just as the growth of civil society is essential to transitions to and consolidation of democracy within countries, global civil society plays a crucial role in promoting democracy at the global level. Global governance also reflects a growing awareness of the need to supply more global public goods as a consequence of increased globalization. Governments are no longer capable of addressing many issues, partly because these problems are globalized. *Global public goods* are characterized by nonrivalry in consumption and nonexcludability, as well as by the universal benefits they bestow on the majority of humanity.[55] Public goods are collective goods that are enjoyed by most of us, regardless of our contribution to efforts to achieve them. They include global financial stability, environmental protection, basic human security, and the nonproliferation of weapons of mass destruction.

Green Room

Small group meetings convened by the WTO director-general and strongly influenced by the U.S., the EU, Canada, and Japan

Global Governance

The institutions and structure that combine to govern many aspects of state policies, especially concerning international relations

Making Global Institutions More Democratic

Perceptions of a democratic deficit in global institutions and global governance have stimulated discussions about possible reforms to make the global system more accountable, transparent, and responsible to those affected by it. The *first suggestion* for the democratization of global institutions is changing the formulation and implementation of rules and procedures. This requires rethinking how interests are represented at the global level. Joseph S. Nye suggests that people could pressure their own governments to send representatives to meetings of global institutions, such as the WTO, to safeguard their interests; that legislators could hold hearings before or after meetings of global organizations; and that legislators themselves could become national delegates to various organizations.[56] A *second suggestion* is to make changes in the formal representation in global institutions, especially in relation to developing countries. The way seats and votes are allocated in many global organizations places developing countries at a disadvantage in terms of influence on decision-making. Countries that contribute more financially tend to determine global public policies. For example, decisions of the World Bank and the IMF are largely shaped by the United States and Western European countries. A *third suggestion* is to expand representation in them to include citizens' representatives, in addition to government representatives and bureaucrats. This means including civil society actors. A *fourth suggestion* is to increase transparency in global organizations. Just as interest groups and a free press play important roles in creating transparency in politics within countries, they can function in a similar manner globally. Transparency is crucial to accountability and requires access to both deliberations of global institutions and relevant information. Transparency can also be achieved through regular monitoring and evaluation of the operations and effectiveness of global organizations.[57] A final suggestion is to enforce judicial-style accountability. This form of accountability is designed to ensure that organizations act within their powers. Specific actions or decisions are examined and attention is drawn to violations of operating rules and procedures. Judicial-style accountability is exemplified by the World Bank's Inspection Panel (created in 1993 to deal with loans) and the Compliance Adviser/Ombudsman Office (established in 1999 to deal with the work of the International Finance Corporation and Multilateral Investment Guarantee Agency). The Inspection Panel investigates complaints from groups able to demonstrate that (1) they live in an area or represent people who live in an area that could be negatively affected by a World Bank project; (2) they have suffered from the World Bank's failure to adhere to its policies and procedures; and (3) their concerns were not resolved to their satisfaction by the World Bank's management.[58] These suggestions, while making global institutions more democratic, must be weighed against their impact on the effectiveness and efficiency of governance in a global society.

Summary and Review

This chapter focused on the spread of democracy at the global level. It shows how politics, economics, and culture are inextricably linked to the promotion of democracy on one hand, and are shaped by democracy on the other. Democracy is defined as government that reflects the will of the people. There is much diversity among the different forms of democracy throughout the world, and many divergent paths toward democratization exist. Competitive elections—where various political parties representing various political interests effectively and fairly compete—are vital in such a democratic system. Civil society and global civil society play an important role in the democratization process, as the individuals and groups involved exert pressure on autocratic regimes to initiate democratic reforms. This chapter reviewed the many global waves of democratization. The waves of democratization were split into (1) the American and French Revolutions; (2) World War II and the defeat of Nazism and fascism; and (3) the explosion of democratization from the 1970s to the 1990s throughout Africa, Asia, Europe, the former Soviet Republics, and Latin America. Specific countries were examined from each of these regions, as we saw how democratization proliferated in Indonesia, South Korea, Thailand, Zaire (now the

Democratic Republic of the Congo), South Africa, Nicaragua, Chile, Russia, Portugal, and Spain.

While democracy has not been universally accepted by all leaders throughout all nation-states, the strengthening of global civil society—as well as the rising expectations of those long deprived of democracy—have been driving factors in the growth of democratic developments and accountability in government. Democracy has increasingly becoming globalized, as many throughout the world continue to fight for universal human rights and for the establishment and consolidation of democratic government. With the success of the various waves of democratization, countries worldwide have been able to demand democratic reforms from their governments.

Key Terms

democracy 109
demos 109
direct self-
   government 109
indirect/representative
   democracy 109
majoritarian model 110
consensus model 110
winner-take-all
   system 110
proportional
   representation 110
liberal democracy 110
illiberal
   democracies 110
constitutional
   liberalism 110

constitution 111
rule of law 111
legitimacy 111
presidential
   democracy 111
parliamentary
   democracy 111
conventional
   participation 112
unconventional
   participation 112
political parties 113
loyal opposition 113
civil society 113
Westminster model 117
economic
   development 118

Warsaw
   Declaration 119
CIVICUS 119
Varela Project 120
George Soros 121
consequential ethic 121
apartheid 122
Support for Eastern
   European Democracy
   (SEED) Act 123
Coalition Provisional
   Authority 125
liberalization 127
electoralist fallacy 127
corporatism 130
generational change 130
coup d'etat 131

Political Reform
   Act 132
African National
   Congress (ANC) 133
Truth and Reconciliation
   Commission 134
Tiananmen Square 135
Koran 139
economic
   globalization 140
democratic deficit 140
international
   regimes 140
global governance 141

Discussion Questions

1. How would you define democracy? What are some of the basic elements that are needed for democracy to flourish?
2. Name some examples of how conventional and unconventional participation are implemented in real life. Can you name any strengths and weakness of both approaches?
3. Are there any pitfalls in trying to impose democracy, as in Iraq, by force? Can force be used

to impose democracy, or are the two concepts incompatible?
4. What is civil society?
5. How does culture impede or help to promote democracy? Can you give real-life examples from this chapter?
6. Can you name some ways that would help the United States better promote democracy throughout the world today?

7. How does liberalization help in the transition to democracy in traditionally undemocratic states?
8. What is electoralist fallacy? What are the weaknesses of relying predominantly on elections as a means of quantifying democracy?
9. Name some ways in which global institutions have undermined democratic developments in individual nation-states.
10. Does dramatic economic inequality between the rich and poor countries have negative implications for the proliferation of democracy throughout the world? If so, how?

Suggested Readings

Aslund, Anders, and Michael MeFaul, eds. *Revolution in Orange*. Washington, DC: Carnegie Endowment, 2006.

Barnett, Michael and Martha Finnemore. *Rules for the World: International Organizations in Global Politics*. Ithaca: Cornell University Press, 2006.

Carothers, Thomas. *Promoting the Rule of Law*. Washington, DC: Carnegie Endowment, 2006.

Chandrasekaran, Rajiv. "Who Killed Iraq?" *Foreign Policy*, No. 156 (September/October 2006): 36–45.

Fuller, Graham. *The Future of Political Islam*. New York: Palgrave, 2003.

Giller, Bruce. *China's Democratic Future*. New York: Columbia University Press, 2005.

Goldman, Merle. *From Comrade to Citizen: The Struggle for Political Rights in China*. Cambridge, MA: Harvard University Press, 2006.

Haggard, Stephan, and Robert R. Kaufman. *The Political Economy of Democratic Transitions*. Princeton: Princeton University Press, 1995.

Kahler, Miles, and David Lake, eds. *Governance in a Global Economy*. Princeton: Princeton University Press, 2003.

Keane, John. *Global Civil Society?* New York: Cambridge University Press, 2003.

Nye, Joseph S. "Globalization's Democratic Deficit," *Foreign Affairs* 80, No. 4 (July/August 2001): 2–6.

Ottaway, Marina. *Promoting Democracy in the Middle East: The Problem of U.S. Credibility*. Washington, DC: Carnegie Endowment Working Paper No. 35, 2003.

Shevtsova, Lilia. *Putin's Russia*. Washington, DC: Carnegie Endowment, 2005.

Suleiman, Ezra. *Dismantling Democratic States*. Princeton: Princeton University Press, 2003.

Zakaria, Fareed. *The Future of Freedom: The Rise of Illiberal Democracy at Home and Abroad*. New York: W. W. Norton, 2003.

Addresses and Websites

Organization of American States
17th St. and Constitution Ave. NW
Washington, DC 20006
Tel.: (202) 458–3000
www.oas.org

The website of the Organization of American States offers information on unity and cooperation among nations in both North and South America. It has in-depth information on the OAS and on the current missions of its members. Links to other sites with information on development and cooperation are also provided.

International Development Exchange
827 Valencia St., No. 101
San Francisco, CA 94110–1736
Tel.: (415) 824–8384
Fax: (415) 824–8387
www.idex.org

The International Development Exchange (IDEX) promotes economic justice for low-income communities in Asia, Africa, Latin America, and the United States. The website describes situations in different countries and by issues, such as micro-credit and food security.

Personal stories are available from those being helped and the volunteers.

Organization for Economic Co-Operation and Development
2001 L St., NW, No. 650
Washington, DC 20036–4922
Tel.: (202) 785–6323
Fax: (202) 785–0350
www.oecd.org/EN/home/0,,EN-home-0-nodirectorate-no-no-no-0,FF.html

The Organization for Economic Co-Operation and Development (OECD) is an international organization helping governments tackle the economic, social, and governance challenges of a globalized economy. News, statistics, and documentation are available on its website. The topics covered include competition, emerging and transition economies, international migration, and science and innovation.

World Movement for Democracy
c/o National Endowment for Democracy
1101 Fifteenth St., NW, No. 700
Washington, DC 20005–5000

Fax: (202) 293–0755
www.wmd.org

The World Movement for Democracy is a global network of democrats—including activists, practitioners, academics, policy makers, and funders—who cooperate in the promotion of democracy. Sections of its website include Democracy News, Regional Networking, Functional Networking, and resources, such as a research guide. A new section entitled, "What's being done on . . . ?" changes every two months.

International Institute for Democracy and Electoral Assistance
Stromsburg S-103 34
Stockholm, Sweden
Tel.: 46 8 698 3700
Fax: 46 8 20 24 22
www.idea.int

The International Institute for Democracy and Electoral Assistance (the International IDEA) promotes and advances sustainable democracy and improves and consolidates electoral processes worldwide. Its website provides news, reports from the field, and a democracy forum.

Endnotes

1. Arend Lijphart, *Patterns of Democracy* (New Haven: Yale University Press, 1999).
2. Fareed Zakaria, "The Rise of Illiberal Democracy," *Foreign Affairs* 76, No. 6 (November/December 1997), 26.
3. Lijphart, *Patterns of Democracy*, 105.
4. Craig Warkentin, *Reshaping World Politics* (Lanham: Rowman and Littlefield, 2001), 1: and Thomas Carothers, "Civil Society," *Foreign Policy*, No. 117 (Winter 1999–2000), 18.
5. Warkentin, *Reshaping World Politics*, 36–37.
6. Najma Chowdhury and Barbara J. Nelson, "Redefining Politics: Patterns of Women's Political Engagement From a Global Perspective," in *Women and Politics Worldwide*, ed. Barbara J. Nelson and Najma Chowdhury (New Haven: Yale University Press, 1994), 16.
7. Ruth Henig and Simon Henig, *Women and Political Power* (London: Routledge, 2001), 104.
8. Jane S. Jaquette, "Women in Power: From Tokenism to Critical Mass," *Foreign Policy*, No. 108 (Fall 1997), 27.
9. Richard J. Payne, *Opportunities and Dangers of Soviet-Cuban Expansion* (Albany: State University of New York Press, 1998), 125.
10. Jorge I. Dominquez, *Democratic Politics in Latin America and the Caribbean* (Baltimore: Johns Hopkins University Press, 1998), 26; and Enrique Krauze, "Furthering Democracy in Mexico," *Foreign Affairs* 85, No. 1 (January/February 2006), 54.
11. Larry Diamond, et al., "Introduction: Comparing Experiences With Democracy," in *Politics in Developing Countries*, ed. Larry Diamond, et al. (Boulder, CO: Lynne Rienner, 1990), 18; and Staffan Lindberg, *Democracy and Elections in Africa* (Baltimore: Johns Hopkins University Press, 2006).
12. David Rohde, "In One Man's Life, A Glimpse of Democracy's Agony," *New York Times*, 5 October 2003, A5.
13. Peter J. Schraeder, "Promoting an International Community of Democracies," in *Exporting Democracy*, ed. Peter J. Schraeder (Boulder, CO: Lynne Rienner, 2002), 1; and Larry Diamond, "Globalization of Democracy," in *The Globalization Reader*, ed. Frank J. Lechner and John Boli (Oxford: Blackwell, 2000), 247.
14. Paul Wapner, "Politics Beyond the State," *World Politics* 47, No. 3 (April 1995), 313.

15. Kevin Sullivan, "Carter Encourages Dissidents in Cuba," *Chicago Tribune*, 17 May 2002, Sect. 1, 3; and David Gonzalez, "Cuban Dissidents Put Hope in a Petition and Jimmy Carter," *The New York Times*, 14 May, 2002, A3.

16. Kevin F. F. Quigley, *For Democracy's Sake: Foundations and Democracy Assistance in Central Europe* (Washington, DC: Woodrow Wilson Center Press, 1999), 2.

17. Steven W. Hook, "Inconsistent U.S. Efforts to Promote Democracy Abroad," in *Exporting Democracy*, 111; and Thomas Carothers, "The Backlash Against Democracy Promotion," *Foreign Affairs* 85, No. 2 (March/April 2006): 55–56.

18. Dimitri K. Simes, "America's Imperial Dilemma," *Foreign Affairs* 82, No. 6 (November/December 2003), 98.

19. Hook, "Inconsistent U.S. Efforts," in *Exporting Democracy*, 125.

20. Michael Dobbs, "Overseas Aid: Big Business at Home," *Washington Post National Weekly Edition*, 12–18 February 2001, 10.

21. Simes, "America's Imperial Dilemma," 97.

22. Arthur Schlesinger Jr., "Has Democracy a Future?" *Foreign Affairs* 76, No. 5 (September/October 1997), 3–4.

23. Schlesinger, "Has Democracy a Future," 4.

24. Geoffrey Pridham, et al. "The International Dimension of Democratization," in *Building Democracy*, ed. Geoffrey Pridham, et al. (London: Leicester University Press, 1997), 2.

25. Juan J. Linz and Alfred Stepan, *Problems of Democratic Transitions and Consolidation* (Baltimore: Johns Hopkins University Press, 1996), 4.

26. Linz and Stepan, *Problems of Democratic Transitions*, 3.

27. George Sorenson, *Democracy and Democratization* (Boulder, CO: Westview Press, 1998), 39.

28. Michael Bratton and Nicolas van de Walle, *Democratic Experiments in Africa* (Cambridge: Cambridge University Press, 1997), 239.

29. Linz and Stepan, *Problems of Democratic Transitions*, 6.

30. Linz and Stepan, *Problems of Democratic Transitions*, 7–11.

31. Samuel P. Huntington, *The Third Wave: Democratization in the Late Twentieth Century* (Norman: University of Oklahoma Press, 1993), 15.

32. Huntington, *The Third Wave*, 27.

33. James F. Hollifield and Calvin Jilson, "Introduction," in *Pathways to Democracy: The Political Economy of Democratic Transitions*," ed. James F. Hollifield and Calvin Jilson (New York: Routledge, 2000), 10.

34. Howard J. Wiarda and Margaret McLeish Mott, *Catholic Roots and Democratic Flowers* (Westport, CT: Praeger, 2001), 43.

35. Wiarda and Mott, *Catholic Roots*, 56–57.

36. Wiarda and Mott, *Catholic Roots*, 66.

37. Wiarda and Mott, *Catholic Roots*, 55.

38. Robert K. Shaeffer, *Power to the People: Democratization Around the World* (Boulder: Westview Press, 1997), 124.

39. Peter Hakim, "Is Latin America Doomed to Failure?" *Foreign Policy* No. 117 (Winter 1999–2000), 107; Peter Smith, *Democracy in Latin America* (New York: Oxford University Press, 2005); and Luis Rubio and Jeffrey Davidow, "Mexico Disputed Election," *Foreign Affairs* 85, No. 5 (September/October 2006), 75.

40. Rachel L. Swarns and Norimitsu Onishi, "Africa Creeps Along Path to Democracy," *New York Times*, 2 June 2002, A1.

41. Richard J. Payne, *The Nonsuperpowers and South Africa* (Bloomington: Indiana University Press, 1990), 245.

42. Marshall Brement, "Reaching Out to Moscow," *Foreign Policy* No. 80 (Fall 1990), 58.

43. J. William Derleth, *The Transitions in Central and Eastern European Politics* (Upper Saddle River, NJ: Prentice Hall, 2000), 43.

44. Michael Wines, "Putin Is Made Russia's President," *New York Times*, 8 May 2000, A1; and Lilia Shevtsova, *Putin's Russia* (Washington, DC: Carnegie Endowment, 2005).

45. Alex Rodriguez, "Rice Offers Democratic Pitch During Visit With Russians," *Chicago Tribune*, 21 April 2005, Sect. 1, 4; Steven Fish, *Democracy Derailed in Russia* (Cambridge: Cambridge University Press, 2005), 1; and Dmitri Trenin, "Russia Leaves the West," *Foreign Affairs* 85, No. 4 (July/August 2006), 87.

46. Graham E. Fuller, "The Future of Political Islam," *Foreign Affairs*, 81, No. 2 (March/April 2002), 52; and Isobel Coleman, "Woman, Islam, and the New Iraq," *Foreign Affairs* 85, No. 1 (January/February 2006), 24.

47. Fuller, "The Future of Political Islam," 57.

48. Nazila Fathi, "Iran's Students Step Up Reform Drive," *New York Times*, 7 July 2002, A6.

49. John L. Esposito and John O. Voll, *Islam and Democracy* (New York: Oxford University Press, 1996), 20; and Zeyno Baran, "The Battle Within Islam: Fighting the War of Ideas," *Foreign Affairs* 84, No. 6 (November/December 2005), 68–77.

50. R. C. Longworth, "Resisting Globalization's Democratic Deficit," *Chicago Tribune*, 15 October 2000, Sect. 2, 1.

51. Marian A. L. Miller, *The Third World in Global Environmental Politics* (Buckingham: Open University Press, 1995), 53.

52. United Nations Development Program, *Human Development Report 2002* (New York: Oxford University Press, 2002), 118.

53. David Held, et al. *Global Transformations* (Stanford: Stanford University Press, 1999), 50.

54. Norman J. Vig, "Introduction," in *The Global Environment*, ed. Norman J. Vig and Regina S. Axelrod (Washington, DC: Congressional Quarterly Press, 1999), 5.

55. Inge Kaul, et al. *Global Public Goods* (New York: Oxford University Press, 1999), 3.

56. Joseph S. Nye, "Globalization's Democratic Deficit," *Foreign Affairs*, 80, No. 4 (July/August 2001), 5; and Barbara Crossette, "How to Defuse the Bolton Bomb," *Foreign Policy* No. 155 (July/August 2006), 68.

57. UN Development Program, *Human Development Report 2002*, 115.

58. UN Development Program, *Human Development Report 2002*, 116; and Jessica Einhorn, "Reforming the World Bank," *Foreign Affairs* 85, No. 1 (January/February 2006), 21–22.

CHAPTER 5

Global Terrorism

INTRODUCTION

Think about how the escalation of global terrorism affects our daily lives. This global problem is now virtually inseparable from personal concerns. Even traveling by plane from one city to another within the United States and Canada, which was once largely uneventful, has become much more complicated and stressful due to increased airport security, one of the most visible aspects of homeland security. National and global institutions have also been profoundly affected by this problem. The U.S. **Department of Homeland Security** was created in 2003 as a direct response to the terrorist attacks in September 2001. It brought together twenty-two government agencies with 180,000 workers, making it the largest government reorganization in forty years. Domestic security has been strengthened, especially around bridges, water supplies, government offices, nuclear power plants, scientific laboratories, food supplies, and industrial factories. As we will discuss, political, economic, and cultural components of globalization are intertwined with various aspects of global terrorism.

The assumption that superior military power and sophisticated technologies automatically ensure a high degree of national security was directly challenged by the terrorist attacks on the United States, the most powerful country in the world. This chapter emphasizes the growing importance of **asymmetrical power** in global affairs. When relatively weak groups use low-tech tools to inflict significant damage on very powerful countries they have the most advanced military technologies they are using asymmetrical power. Moises Naim argues that terrorism has destroyed the idea that technology can make the American homeland impregnable.[1] In fact, the challenges of confronting terrorism have forced the United States to rethink its approach to global issues, its priorities, and the implications of its foreign and domestic policies. For example, the dominant and largely unchallenged view in the United States prior to the terrorist attacks on September 11, 2001, was that nonstate threats to national security were relatively unimportant. In 2000, Condoleezza Rice, who became President George W. Bush's National Security Adviser and later the U.S. Secretary of State, clearly and forcefully articulated the *foreign policy priorities* of the United States:

1. To ensure that America's military could deter war, project power, and fight in defense of its interest;
2. To promote economic growth and political openness;
3. To renew strong and intimate relationships with allies;

4. To focus U.S. energies on comprehensive relationships with the big powers, particularly Russia and China; and

5. To deal decisively with the threat of rogue regimes and hostile powers, which is increasingly taking the forms of the potential for terrorism and the development of weapons of mass destruction.[2]

Department of Homeland Security

Combined 22 intelligence agencies in order to enhance national security against terrorist threats

Contemporary forces of globalization are weakening nation-states and strengthening nonstate actors, including terrorist groups and global criminals. Global migration, the growth of global cities, relatively inexpensive commercial airline travel, revolutions in telecommunications and computer technologies, the explosion of global trade, deregulation and privatization of most economic activities, and the general decentralization of power in a global system contribute to creating an environment conducive to terrorism and criminal activities. The growth of regional trading blocs, such as the European Union and the North American Free Trade Agreement, makes it easier to conduct both legal and illegal business. The centralization and cumbersome nature of government bureaucracies and their declining financial resources stand in sharp contrast to the nimbleness, decentralization, access to substantial financial resources, and freedom to operate unencumbered by respect for law or public opinion enjoyed by terrorists and criminal organizations. While states are generally impeded by national boundaries, their nonstate adversaries routinely disregard national borders. Naim contends that if nation-states have benefited from globalization, criminal networks have benefited even more.[3]

This chapter discusses difficulties involved in defining terrorism; factors conducive to the rise of terrorism; and goals, strategies, and weapons of terrorist groups. After examining specific cases of terrorism, we will discuss various responses to terrorism and the dilemmas democracies face in attempting to eliminate or reduce this threat. This chapter shows that taking a multifaceted and global approach is essential to diminishing the problem of terrorism.

Fires continued to burn a month after the terrorist attack or the World Trade Center.
Chicago Tribune, 12 October 2001, 1.

Asymmetrical Power

Form of conflict in which weaker groups or forces can inflict significant damage against more powerful states or forces

Edmund Burke

British philosopher who strongly criticized the French Reign of Terror

DEFINING TERRORISM

Many actions have been called terrorism: From the violence of the French Revolution, to the refusal of the National Education Association (NEA) to support federal policies. Proudly proclaiming their commitment to liberty, equality, and fraternity, the architects of the French Revolution instituted a **Reign of Terror** (1793–1794) to preserve the radical changes. Headed by **Maximilian Robespierre**, the Committee of Public Safety embraced terrorism in its effort to rule France during a period that was regarded as a national emergency. The French zeal for the *Terror*, the period of widespread violence, public executions, and intimidation of civilians, was strongly rejected by **Edmund Burke**, the British conservative philosopher who regarded French terrorists as hellhounds. In February 2004, U.S. Secretary of Education Rod Paige called the NEA, the country's largest teachers union, a terrorist organization because it opposed radical changes in federal education policies adopted by the Bush administration.[4] These two examples represent extreme definitions of terrorism. Although there is no universally accepted definition of terrorism, the standard view that one person's terrorist is another person's freedom fighter fails to distinguish among the various kinds and levels of terrorism and fails to acknowledge that freedom fighters' actions are not necessarily justified by their objectives. What is clear is that terrorism is a contentious issue that becomes hopelessly muddled by political considerations and the behavior of states and nonstate actors.

As American troops, tanks, and planes fought insurgents in the besieged city of Falluja in Iraq in early April 2004, opponents of the U.S. occupation kidnapped several foreign civilians and threatened to execute them. A group calling itself the Mujahedeen Brigades appeared on al-Jazeera television with three blindfolded Japanese civilians and threatened to kill them if Japan did not withdraw its 550 troops from Iraq within three days.[5] The horror the captives felt, evident from their screams, was made more palpable by guns pointed at them and knives and swords held to their throats. Many of the hostages were later beheaded. This example illustrates the nature of terrorism. *All acts of terrorism are designed to create fear*, to cause people to tremble. Our example of the hostages in Iraq points to another element of terrorism: communication with an audience that is far from the scene of violence. By using global communication, terrorists seek to frighten people in distant places in order to exert pressure on governments. *Terrorism is essentially a form of psychological warfare*. For most governments, acts of terrorism are *criminal behavior*. But our discussion will show that terrorism goes beyond ordinary criminal behavior and is thus in a separate category. Other characteristics of terrorism are that it is *systematic* and *protracted*. Unlike most conventional wars, terrorism lasts for generations, as we will see in our discussions of the Irish Republican Army, the Basques in Spain, and the Palestinians. Terrorism is also *indiscriminate*. Most terrorist activities aim to create uncertainty and general fear by communicating that anyone can be a target.[6] Virtually all acts of terrorism are justified by perpetrators and their supporters in terms of the *high moral purposes* they are intended to achieve. In many ways, terrorism is closely associated with ideology. This is clearly the case with al-Qaeda: It is less an organization than an

You **DECIDE** | **Defining Terrorism**

Martha Crenshaw, a leading expert on terrorism, argues that defining terrorism is difficult because terrorism is a social construction, which is relative to time and place. Because acts of terrorism generally occur within a political context, terrorism is essentially a political label. As such, this label reflects the struggle for power and the preferred approaches to solving the problem. Social construction helps to frame consciousness and to influence how behavior is perceived. Terrorism as a label is essentially subjective and judgmental. What Crenshaw is stressing is the politics of language: the struggle to define terms, and consequently to control behavior. Calling adversaries

terrorists, in her view, is a way of depicting them as fanatic and irrational. Doing so forecloses the possibility of compromise, draws attention to the real or imagined threat to security, and promotes solidarity among the threatened. In other words, terrorism is not a neutral descriptive term, and those who define terrorism are usually not neutral parties.

How would you arrive at an objective definition of terrorism?

Source: Martha Crenshaw, "Thoughts on Relating Terrorism to Historical Contexts," in *Terrorism in Context,* ed. Martha Crenshaw (University Park: Penn State University Press, 1995), 9–10.

ideology that inspires groups and people worldwide to engage in terrorist acts independent of any central organization.

Defining terrorism is complicated by historical experiences. Both revolutionary and conservative groups—people on the left and on the right of the ideological spectrum—have used various forms of terrorism to achieve their objectives. Many former terrorists become respectable leaders and their terrorist activities are downplayed or even justified as serving a larger purpose. Wars of liberation throughout history have generally been accompanied by actions that were defined as terrorism by those in favor of maintaining the status quo. Distinguishing terrorism from guerrilla warfare and insurgency is often challenging. **Guerrilla warfare**, which means little war, is the use of selective violence against military targets. But when societies experience extensive violence, distinctions between guerrilla warfare and terrorism tend to blur. Defining terrorism is also complicated by the tendency of governments to give different labels to essentially the same actions, applying the negative label of terrorism to their enemies and the more positive label of self-defense or national security measure to their friends. Following the 2001 attacks in the United States, many governments applied the label of terrorism to very old conflicts of their own that were previously regarded as insurgencies. For example, China annexed what is now Xinjiang in 1759. The inhabitants, known as **Uighurs**, practice Sufi Islam and speak a Turkic language. They resisted China's rule and launched their first uprising in 1865. The disintegration of the Soviet Union in 1991 and the independence gained by some Muslim communities in Central Asia inspired the Uighurs to renew their struggle to establish a separate state. But China was quick to label the Uighurs as terrorists after the global developments in 2001.[7] This raises the question: Who gets to define terrorism and

Guerilla Warfare

Use of selective violence against military targets by insurgency forces

Uighurs

Ethnic group that rebelled against China's annexation of Xinjiang in 1759

why? Complicating definitions of terrorism is the general acceptance of war as a legitimate instrument of governments. Paul Wilkinson argues that "terrorist campaigns inherently involve deliberate attacks on civilian targets and are therefore analogous to war crimes."[8] But who decides which military actions are war crimes?

FACTORS CONDUCIVE TO TERRORISM

The gruesome scenes left in the wake of terrorist attacks provoke such feelings of revulsion and horror that they often obscure the causes of or motivations for such bloodshed. Because their emotions often influence how people perceive and analyze terrorism, discussing the causes of terrorism is also likely to provoke controversy. Nonetheless, an objective assessment of most terrorist acts shows that such violence generally does not occur in a vacuum or randomly. Some societies experience more terrorism than others. Examining the factors that make terrorism a useful tool to accomplish certain objectives is essential to any pragmatic effort to eliminate or diminish terrorist threats. As we try to identify the dominant cause, we will see that terrorism has, in fact, many interrelated causes.

Poverty is widely perceived as the root of terrorism. Following the 2001 terrorist attacks in the United States, a consensus supported the view that poverty is a major cause of terrorism. As we will see in Chapter 7, global inequality became a major concern of the United States and other countries interested in fighting terrorism. A basic argument is that economic inequality and severe poverty in an increasingly globalized society foster resentment among the poor against rich countries, especially the United States. Poverty is closely linked to economic and political isolation, feelings of hopelessness, violations of human rights, and the lack of democracy, which all provide a fertile breeding ground for terrorism. In Pakistan, students enroll in religious seminaries, called **madrassas**. Supported by Muslim charities worldwide—especially those in Saudi Arabia—they feed, shelter, clothe, and educate students from poverty-stricken families. In addition to receiving training in the Koran, these students are

Madrassas

Religious seminaries supported by Muslim charities worldwide

You
DECIDE | **The Difference Between War and Terrorism**

In the documentary film, *The Fog of War*, former U.S. Secretary of Defense Robert McNamara discussed eleven lessons of war, using his experiences with World War II, the Cuban missile crisis, and the Vietnam War to illustrate his points. He talked about the extensive damage caused by the firebombing of Japanese cities by the United States. From his perspective, firebombing and dropping atomic bombs on Hiroshima and Nagasaki were meant to terrorize the Japanese people. Creating terror among civilians is an integral and inseparable component of war. Think of the widespread destruction caused by wars.

What is the difference between war and terrorism?

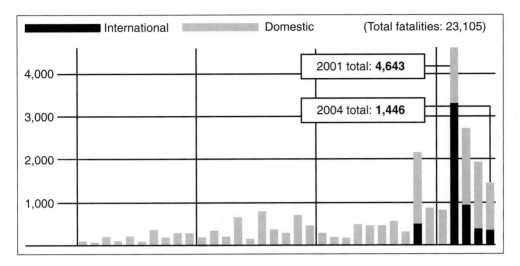

FIGURE 5.1 Deaths Caused by Terrorism, 1968–2004

Sources: National Memorial Institute for the Prevention of Terrorism; and Chicago Tribune, 10 October 2004. Sect. 1, 11.

indoctrinated to hate the West, especially the United States. Many terrorists graduate from madrassas.[11] However, terrorists who attacked the United States, Spain, and Britain were not poor. Many of them came from the middle class.

Globalization is a major factor in global terrorism. As we discussed in Chapter 1, globalization changes virtually every aspect of life. In many ways, terrorism is a product of resistance to change brought about by cultural, economic, political, military, and even environmental globalization. Revolutions in communication and transportation facilitate global terrorism. Individuals in distant places communicate instantaneously and are able to coordinate their activities on a global scale. Global transportation enables them to move easily from one country to another. Global cities provide an environment in which it is easy for people to be anonymous. While globalization helps to create webs of interdependence among countries and among individuals, it also fosters alienation and disconnectedness among individuals and communities. In fact, we often know very little about people who live in our neighborhoods. For example, the terrorists who attacked the United States in 2001 lived in American cities without raising suspicions among their neighbors. Groups and individuals opposed to globalization's impact on economics, religion, and culture can penetrate and inflict severe damage on the societies they believe are responsible for their problems.

Legitimate grievances and the failure of governments to adequately address these problems often foment terrorism. In fact, most terrorist organizations trace their origins to political, religious, social, economic, and ethnic problems that were ignored, downplayed, or dismissed by those in power and by society in general. In a world dominated by states and the state-centric model, few national leaders are pressured to accept responsibility for their contribution to causing terrorism. Why did the African National Congress (ANC) in South Africa, the Palestine Liberation Organization

(PLO), and the Irish Republican Army (IRA) become terrorist organizations? Specific grievances motivated individuals to form these groups and to use terrorism to achieve their objectives. Widespread and intolerable oppression by governments and the willingness of those in power to maintain the *status quo* create fertile ground for terrorism to grow. As we will see, terrorism is often embraced as an instrument of change only when other alternatives are unavailable. This was clearly the case in South Africa under apartheid.

Violence by governments also causes terrorism. Often overlooked by advocates of the state-centric model is that governments routinely abuse their monopoly on legitimate violence regarding to specific minority groups or majority groups that lack significant political, economic, and social power. Violence becomes an acceptable mode of behavior. The efficacy of official violence influences individuals and groups that want to change their circumstances to resort to violence. In other words, both sides believe that violence is an effective tool. Many groups that originally practiced nonviolence eventually become frustrated with the ineffectiveness of nonviolent methods and resort to terrorism.

Humiliation is another factor conducive to the use of terrorism. As we discussed in Chapter 5, the U.S. invasion of Iraq in 2003 was portrayed by the Bush administration in terms of destroying weapons of mass destruction and spreading democracy to Iraq and other countries in the Middle East. A year later, the United States found itself fighting some of the fiercest battles since the beginning of the war. Terrorism, which was not a problem in Iraq before the U.S. invasion, became widespread. Many Iraqis felt humiliated by intrusive American searches, by being occupied, and by being mistreated. **Thomas L. Friedman**, an outstanding journalist with the *New York Times*, stated: "If I've learned one thing covering world affairs, it is this: The single most under-appreciated force in international relations is humiliation."[9]

Thomas L. Friedman

New York Times columnist who writes on globalization, war, and terrorism

The lack of democracy, and widespread and systematic violations of human rights contribute to the rise of terrorism. The 2001 terrorist attacks in the United States drew attention to Saudi Arabia and Egypt, countries to which most of the terrorists belonged. As we will see, America's close ties with and military support of these countries made it the target of Muslim extremists. But the roots of terrorism are in the undemocratic and politically repressive practices of Egypt, Saudi Arabia, and many other Middle Eastern countries. Egypt and Saudi Arabia are authoritarian societies in which there is no free press, no freedom of expression, and no free elections. Dissent is not tolerated, individuals are routinely tortured, and fair trials are rare. Dissidents, such as **Osama bin Laden** (from Saudi Arabia) and **Mohammed Atta** (the Egyptian-born leader of the 2001 terrorist attacks), were unable to express dissent at home, so they went to Afghanistan to organize al-Qaeda, a global terrorist network.[10]

Foreign policies contribute to terrorism. Roman occupation of Israel generated strong resistance by the Jews, and some Jews adopted terrorism in a futile effort to end Roman oppression. European expansion and colonization laid the foundation for the emergence of national liberation movements that used terrorism to achieve independence. Throughout the Cold War, the United States and the Soviet Union ignored the terrorism that was used by the side they supported, preferring instead to see the terrorists as freedom fighters. Many foreign policy and terrorism analysts view U.S. foreign policies in the Middle East—especially those involving the Palestinian-Israeli conflict, Saudi Arabia, and Egypt—as being conducive to terrorism. For example, Osama bin Laden strongly opposed the stationing of American troops in Saudi Arabia during the 1991 Gulf War. The U.S. policies are widely seen in the Middle East and elsewhere as contributing to the oppression of the Palestinians by Israel. These perceptions were confirmed by President George W. Bush's decision in April 2004 to bypass the Palestinians and agree with Israel's Prime Minister Ariel Sharon's plan to withdraw from Gaza, retain major Jewish settlements in the West Bank, and reject the right of millions of Palestinian refugees to return to their homes and land in what is now Israel.[12] America's refusal to pressure Israel to exercise restraint when it invaded Lebanon in 2006 reinforced perceptions of the United States as oppressing Arabs in general.

Finally, *failed states provide an environment conducive to terrorism.* Failed states generally abuse human rights; are undemocratic; are governed by individuals who disregard the rule of law; are intolerant of ethnic, political, and religious diversity; and have weak economies. State failure is often accompanied by an increase in bureaucratic corruption and cooperation among government officials and criminals. In essence, state authority and civil society are severely undermined, and many regions within a country are lawless.[13] The most obvious example of how state failure breeds terrorism is **al-Qaeda** in Afghanistan. Ravaged by the Soviet Union invasion and years of war, the poverty-stricken country became a base for Islamic extremists and holy warriors. Under the leadership of the **Taliban** (i.e., a group of extreme Islamic fundamentalists), Afghanistan provided bin Laden with an ideal environment in which terrorism could grow and from which terrorist activities could be organized. By the end of 2006 Iraq was increasingly perceived as a failed state and the breeding ground of terrorists.

Taliban

Former government of Afganisthan that repressed its people and supported al-Qaeda

Self-Determination

Struggles for national independence that often motive terrorist attacks

GOALS, STRATEGIES, AND WEAPONS OF TERRORISM

The goals, strategies, and weapons of terrorism vary from group to group and from one period of history to another. What's more, terrorists are not a monolithic group. The goals of terrorists range from those that can be obtained through a combination of force and negotiation to those that are utopian and can never be achieved. *The goals of terrorism* include

1. **Social and political justice.** Terrorism (e.g., in Europe) has been used to achieve concrete political and social changes, including overthrowing repressive regimes.
2. **Self-determination.** Many terrorist organizations emerged as part of the struggle to gain national independence. The IRA, the Palestinian groups, the ANC, and the Basques are groups that adopted terrorism to achieve this goal.

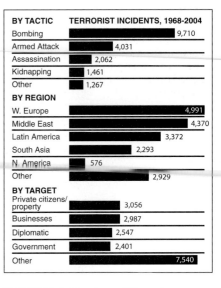

BY TACTIC	TERRORIST INCIDENTS, 1968-2004
Bombing	9,710
Armed Attack	4,031
Assassination	2,062
Kidnapping	1,461
Other	1,267
BY REGION	
W. Europe	4,991
Middle East	4,370
Latin America	3,372
South Asia	2,293
N. America	576
Other	2,929
BY TARGET	
Private citizens/ property	3,056
Businesses	2,987
Diplomatic	2,547
Government	2,401
Other	7,540

FIGURE 5.2 Number of Terrorists Attacks, 1968–2004

Sources: Chicago Tribune, 10 October 2004, Sect. 1, 11.

3. **New ideologies.** Many terrorist groups attempt to change the way people think and to replace old ideologies with their own. A major goal of the Reign of Terror was to change beliefs that supported the old system.

Utopianism

Image of a perfect society driving many terrorist individuals and groups

4. **Utopianism**. Many terrorist groups, especially those based on fundamentalist religious beliefs, aim to radically transform the world to fit their image of a perfect society.

5. **Nihilism.** European anarchists, such as **Mikhail Bakunin**, established a tradition that opposed all centralized governments and economic and social institutions.

6. **Racial superiority.** Many white supremacist groups attempt to preserve racial segregation and social, economic, and political power based on skin color.

7. **Foreign policies.** Terrorism is often used to influence governments to take or refrain from taking certain actions. Terrorist attacks on American and French barracks in Lebanon in 1983 forced the United States to withdraw its troops from that country. In April 2004, bin Laden offered to stop terrorist attacks against European countries that ended military actions in Muslim countries. That offer was clearly designed to influence European policies toward Iraq.[14]

8. **Publicity.** A central goal of most terrorist groups is to draw public attention to their cause.

9. **Demoralize governments.** By making governments appear weak and incompetent, terrorists believe they can undermine their legitimacy and policies.

10. **Provoke a violent response by the government.** Terrorists attempt to influence governments to use excessive force so that they can gain public support for their cause.

11. **Motivate followers and dominate the wider resistance movement.** Terrorism is often intended to inspire people to join the terrorist group, as well as to weaken challenges to the dominant group within the broader terrorist organization. Factional terrorism has long been part of the Palestinian terrorist movement.[15]

12. **Environmental protection.** As we will discuss in Chapter 8, fringe environmental groups resort to terrorism to prevent environmental degradation. Eco-terrorists are active in the United States and Europe.

Terrorist organizations adopt several *strategies* to achieve their objectives; all of those strategies include violence or threats of violence against governments and civilians. *Creating a climate of fear and insecurity*, partly to undermine people's confidence in their government, is an integral component of terrorists' strategies. But terrorism also depends on *cultivating popular support*. Terrorists are generally effective when they operate in an environment that enables them to hide, obtain resources (including weapons), gather information about government operations and plans, and communicate with each other. However, telecommunications and computer technologies have reduced the need for popular support as a component of strategy. As we have seen with al-Qaeda, terrorists use the Internet to communicate with each other and the world. They are now more decentralized in order to reduce their vulnerability to electronic surveillance by governments. They rely on **virtual networks**, a style of organization that is essentially leaderless and is facilitated by the Internet. American right-wing extremists developed this strategy to counteract the effectiveness of U.S. law enforcement agencies.[16]

Some terrorist groups *reject the terrorist label* in order to gain greater legitimacy or acceptance in society. Governments, on the other hand, refuse to confer any kind of legitimacy on terrorist groups and reject defining terrorism as warfare.[17] These terrorist groups are likely to select government targets, including embassies, military personnel and bases, and government officials. In Colombia, for example, terrorist groups launched a campaign of assassinations to get the attention of the government and its supporters. Judges, prosecutors, and elected officials were the main targets. This strategy attempts to undermine assumptions that government policies can ensure personal safety.[18] *Selective kidnappings* are also used by terrorists to achieve their goals. By taking government officials, soldiers, businesspeople, and prominent citizens hostage, the terrorists force the government to either take military action against them or bargain with them. Terrorists in Iraq adopted this strategy. Kidnappings of Israeli soldiers by Palestinians and Hezbollah in 2006 led to Israel's invasion of Lebanon.

Some terrorist groups engage in selective violence, but others are more indiscriminate. A familiar strategy of terrorist groups that use *indiscriminate violence* is to select high-profile targets that attract a large number of people, such as public transportation systems, airports, and office buildings. Bombings of the trains in India in 2006, in Britain in 2005, and in Spain in 2004, the World Trade Center and the Pentagon in 2001, and the Alfred E. Murrah Federal Building in Oklahoma City in 1995 are examples of indiscriminate violence designed to kill as many people as possible, especially innocent civilians. This strategy creates widespread fear, including among those who are far from the scene of terrorist attacks. Groups with specific grievances tend to be less likely to engage in indiscriminate killing, partly because they want to avoid alienating the public support needed for their cause.

Weapons used by terrorists vary according to their goals, available technology, and resources at their disposal. Apart from guns, knives, arson, and other traditional weapons, terrorists are taking advantage of new technologies to inflict maximum damage. Sarin gas, anthrax, and various poisons have been used in Japan and the United States. Motor vehicles packed with ammonium nitrate and fuel oil were used as bombs in Oklahoma City in 1995 and in Bali, Indonesia, in 2002. Suicide bombers are lethal weapons in many parts of the world, including Israel, Afghanistan, and Iraq. The use of airliners fully loaded with fuel as missiles to destroy the World Trade Center and damage the Pentagon focused global attention on a new terrorist weapon. As terrorists use the Internet to spread their message and organize their activities, there is growing awareness of cyberspace warfare as a weapon in the terrorists' arsenal.[19] Although few terrorists are capable of using weapons of mass destruction on a large scale, terrorist attacks in the United States in 2001 and the subsequent U.S. invasion of Iraq in 2003 put the issue of chemical and biological weapons in the possession of terrorists on the global agenda. Jessica Stern, a terrorism expert, discussed

Virtual Networks

A style of organization that is essentially leaderless and facilitated by the Internet

five interrelated developments that have increased the likelihood of terrorists acquiring and using weapons of mass destruction:

1. Nuclear, chemical, and biological weapons are attractive to terrorists seeking to conjure up a sense of divine retribution, to kill as many people as possible, and to retaliate against governments.
2. A new breed of terrorists, including religious and right-wing extremists, are more likely than earlier terrorists to commit mass murder.
3. The disintegration of the Soviet Union has contributed to the proliferation of weapons of mass destruction.
4. There is greater knowledge of these weapons and a willingness to share it with terrorists.
5. Advances in technology have facilitated the use of weapons of mass destruction by terrorists.[20]

FINANCING TERRORISM

Much emphasis has been placed on determining how terrorism is financed and on finding ways to disrupt, if not eliminate, financial support for terrorism. However, compared with conventional military activities, terrorism is relatively low-cost and very effective. Consider the attacks on the World Trade Center and the Pentagon. The terrorists involved lived middle-class lifestyles, took flying lessons, traveled around the country, and bought first-class tickets on the planes they hijacked. The cost of these activities relative to the damage the terrorists caused using American planes to bomb American buildings is almost insignificant. Bombings in Spain in 2004 and in Britain in 2005 also show that terrorists do not have to be well financed to launch destructive attacks. Nevertheless, knowing how terrorism is financed is an essential step toward developing effective counterterrorism responses. However, many terrorist cells are self-supporting, and many terrorists do not engage in financial activities that immediately draw attention, especially in increasingly global banking and financial markets. This makes it extremely difficult for governments to gather

Hawalas

Informal system of transferring money based primarily on trust and inter- personal relations

financial information. Furthermore, many terrorists use **hawalas** (i.e., an informal system of transferring money that is based primarily on trust and interpersonal relations). Developed in India before the arrival of Western banking, hawalas frustrate efforts to trace money because they leave no electronic and virtually no paper trail.[21]

Contributions from individuals and groups are a major source of money for terrorism. In the case of al-Qaeda, bin Laden used his considerable wealth to finance global terrorism. Many individuals make charitable contributions to organizations that are principally concerned with assisting the poor. However, some of this money is also used to support terrorism. Private donors give money directly to terrorist groups because they believe in their causes. Because some terrorist groups are also *de facto governments* that provide essential services, it is difficult to neatly separate contributions to terrorists from contributions to social programs. *Governments finance terrorism*, both directly and inadvertently. The most obvious way is by sponsoring their activities. For many years, Libya's leader, **Muammar Qaddafi**, openly financed and trained terrorist groups in the Middle East and Africa. In 2004, Qaddafi was embraced by Europe and the United States for his decision to fight terrorism and to compensate relatives of victims who were killed in the bombing of a Pan Am jet over Lockerbie, Scotland, in 1988. Libyan intelligence agents were blamed for that bombing. Libya eventually accepted responsibility and paid $2.7 billion to the families of the victims.[22] Governments, especially Saudi Arabia, provide substantial financial resources to charities and organizations that are indirectly linked to terrorism. As we saw earlier, many madrassas that are funded with charitable contributions from countries such as Saudi Arabia become the breeding ground for terrorists. When governments, such as the United States, give foreign assistance to other countries, such as Colombia and Israel, the money is sometimes used by these states to engage in activities that are regarded by others as state terrorism.

Diamonds, oil, and other natural resources provide revenues for terrorism. Many wars and terrorist activities, which are often indistinguishable, are fueled by money obtained from selling natural resources. Terrorists often prefer diamonds because they are easily transported, easily hidden, and easily converted into cash. Failed states in Africa often provide opportunities for rebel groups to cooperate with terrorist groups. One of the best examples is Sierra Leone in West Africa. Sierra Leone has some of the richest diamond fields in the world. It has also been plagued by political instability. The diamond trade helped to fund both Sierra Leone's civil wars and al-Qaeda. Senior members of Sierra Leone's **Revolutionary United Front (RUF)**, a rebel group that challenged the government and engaged in horrific acts of violence and terrorism, took diamonds, often wrapped in rags, across the border into Liberia and exchanged them for cash from al-Qaeda and **Hezbollah**, a Shiite terrorist group in Lebanon. With the cooperation of corrupt customs and immigration officials, the diamonds, which were bought at below-market prices, were then taken to Europe by terrorist organizations and sold at much higher prices.[23] These diamonds are widely known as *conflict diamonds* because of their inextricable links with brutal civil wars and terrorism.

Criminal activities are a major source of funding for terrorism. Terrorists are often involved in armed robbery, credit card fraud, identity theft, kidnapping, extortion, and other crimes. In the Philippines, for example, the terrorist group **Abu Sayyaf** routinely kidnaps people, including tourists, to finance its activities. The **Tamil Tigers** in Sri Lanka control and operate boats that smuggle contraband in the Indian Ocean region. Often, terrorist groups coerce civilians into paying protection money, sometimes called a revolutionary tax. The IRA is a group that used this method to finance terrorism. Other groups use money obtained from the sale of illegal drugs.

THE COSTS OF TERRORISM

Costs associated with terrorism are so widespread, complex, and intangible that they are virtually impossible to measure. Daily, individuals, families, governments, companies, and nonstate actors worldwide bear the costs of terrorism to varying degrees.

Muammar Qaddafi
Libyan leader accused of financing and training terrorist groups in the Middle East and Africa

RUF
Rebel group that challenged the government of Sierra Leone through acts of violence and terrorism

Hezbollah
Shiite terrorist group based in Lebanon

Abu Sayyaf
Terrorist group in the Philippines that regularly kidnaps to finance its activities

Tamil Tigers
Group in Sri Lanka that smuggles contraband in the Indian Ocean region

Time, money, and other resources are diverted from other global problems. Migration, trade, travel, and interpersonal relations are affected. In September 2001, a very small group of individuals, nineteen of them, caused incalculable damage to the United States as well as the global community. Almost three thousand people from roughly fifty countries were killed. Domestic terrorists, using anthrax, also damaged U.S. government offices, businesses, and individuals. For several weeks in the fall of 2002, two snipers, John Muhammad and Lee Malvo, almost paralyzed the Washington, D.C., area as they went on a rampage of indiscriminate violence, which left ten people dead. We will briefly discuss some of these costs of such actions.

Costs to Individuals The principal strategy of terrorism is to create fear in the general population. Consequently, individuals usually suffer the most from terrorist acts in terms of loss of lives and social, psychological, and physical problems. More than ten years after the Oklahoma City bombing, individuals continue to suffer. Many citizens are made ill by fear and a sudden loss of personal freedom. They restrict their activities, limit their travel, and often distrust their neighbors, thereby weakening community bonds and support. For example, the 2001 attacks undermined trust between most non-Muslim Americans and Muslims in general, especially Arabs.

Economic Costs Calculating the economic costs of terrorism and the responses to it is virtually impossible because they are so complex and far-reaching. For example, after the 2001 attacks, airlines suffered major financial losses and continue to feel the impact of terrorism. It is estimated that the global airline industry lost $18 billion in 2001 and $13 billion in 2002 following the attacks. Combined, these losses were more than the total profit of all the airlines since 1945.[24] The travel sector, the aerospace industry, and the tourism industry were severely damaged. Terrorism, especially in the Middle East, negatively affected the region's economy: stock markets generally decline, investments essential for economic development are severely restricted, consumers eventually pay higher prices for security measures, and governments lose tax revenues as unemployment grows. The global economy is still suffering from the 2001 terrorist attacks.

Costs to Governments Governments generally increase resources to fight terrorism and to provide their citizens with a heightened sense of security. For example, as you prepare to board an airline, the costs become obvious. There are more security guards, bags are carefully checked, and individuals are often searched. While airlines pay some of these costs, the U. S. federal government is primarily responsible for airport security. The federal, state, and local governments in the United States also spend money to guard bridges, nuclear power plants, train stations, and so on. The most obvious costs are associated with military actions against terrorists. The invasion of Afghanistan to destroy al-Qaeda and the Taliban, as well as the invasion, occupation, and rebuilding of Iraq has cost hundreds of billions of dollars and many lives.

Foreign Policy Costs Several times following the 2001 attacks, the United States closed its embassies in Saudi Arabia and elsewhere. These shutdowns meant that

America was paying a price for not being able to conduct normal diplomatic relations.[25] Furthermore, heightened security for embassies creates additional expenses. Finally, relations with countries are sometimes negatively affected in the process of fighting terrorism. America's decision to invade Iraq clearly hurt its relations with many countries, including close allies such as France and Germany.

Costs to Democracy People who are afraid, as Thomas Hobbes observed, are willing to turn to all-powerful rulers who promise to provide security. But part of the price for that security is less freedom. In a climate of fear, governments tighten controls on their own people and often justify violating of individuals' rights on the grounds of national security.[26]

KINDS OF TERRORISM

Although the types of terrorism tend to overlap, they vary in their implications and affect us in different ways. For example, the indiscriminate nature of global terrorism contrasts sharply with domestic terrorism aimed at specific groups or governments. In this section we will discuss *five kinds of terrorism:*

1. **Domestic terrorism** occurs within the borders of a particular country and is associated with extremist groups.
2. **Nationalist terrorism** is closely associated with struggles for political autonomy and independence.
3. **Religious terrorism** grows out of extreme fundamentalist religious groups that believe that God is on their side and that their violence is divinely inspired and approved.
4. **State terrorism** is a cold, calculated, efficient, and extremely destructive form of terrorism, partly because of the overwhelming power at the disposal of governments.
5. **Global terrorism** is partly an outgrowth of the forces of globalization, which enable the different kinds of terrorism to spread worldwide.

Domestic Terrorism

Occurs within borders of a state

Nationalist Terrorism

Occurs as a result of struggles for independence

Religious Terrorism

Occurs as a result of religious extremism

State Terrorism

Government repression targeted against civilians

Global Terrorism

Partly a result of increased globalization

Domestic Terrorism

On April 19, 1995, Americans watched with incredulity as bloodied bodies were pulled from the federal building in Oklahoma City that had been destroyed by a bomb in a Ryder truck. Most Americans quickly blamed Middle Eastern terrorists for the Oklahoma City bombing, which killed 168 people. They could not imagine that Americans would inflict such damage on the United States. But the leader of this terrorist act was Timothy McVeigh, an American and a decorated Gulf War veteran. Domestic terrorism has existed in the United States and other countries for hundreds of years. Unlike most countries, where terrorist activities have been carried out primarily against governments, terrorism in America has been used mostly against racial, ethnic, or religious minorities. American terrorists are predominantly right-wing extremists who embrace white supremacist, anti-Jewish, antiforeign, and antigovernment philosophies based on a religious doctrine known as *Christian identity*. This doctrine essentially holds that white people are chosen by God, whereas Jews, Americans with African ancestry, Asians, and other racial minorities are "mud people." These terrorists generally believe that the U.S. government is dominated by Jews and is an occupying power and that the United States should not participate in the United Nations and other international organizations. Based on these beliefs, they have formed heavily armed militias, strongly oppose gun control, and refuse to pay taxes.[27] Domestic terrorist groups include the **National Alliance**, the **Ku Klux Klan**, the **Aryan Nation**, **Posse Comitatus**, and the **Confederate Hammerskins**. Many American terrorists subscribe to the theory of **leaderless resistance**, which means that small groups of terrorists operate essentially independent of a hierarchical organization or central leadership.

Domestic terrorism has long been a significant problem in several European countries. Throughout the 1970s and 1980s, the **Red Brigades**, an Italian terrorist group, launched a campaign of bombings and assassinations of government officials. The terrorist act that received the most attention was the kidnapping and murder of former Prime Minister Aldo Moro by the Red Brigades in 1978. The widely published photograph of Moro's body slumped in the back seat of an abandoned car in Rome shocked many Italians.[28] Although most Red Brigades fled to France shortly after this terrorist act, in 2003 it was estimated that 140 members were still active in Italy. Germany, France, and Greece have also been plagued by domestic terrorism. In Greece, for example, the Marxist-Leninist terrorist group **Revolutionary Organization 17 November** (or **November 17**) has been involved in terrorist activities since 1975. November 17 took its name from the date of a student protest in 1973 that was violently crushed by Greece's military government. Embracing strong anti-American and anti-imperialist views, November 17 is believed to have killed several American and British citizens.[29] Many of the terrorist groups in Germany hold white supremacist, anti-Jewish, and antiforeigner views that are similar to those of their American counterparts. Bombings of trains in Spain in 2004 and in Britain in 2005 by Muslims, many of whom were born in these countries, underscored growing concerns about domestic terrorism. Furthermore, plans by British citizens to blow up airlines leaving Britain for the United States in 2006 reinforced the emphasis on domestic sources of terrorism.

Latin America has spawned many domestic terrorist organizations. Violence on both the left and the right, by terrorist groups and by governments, blurred distinctions between domestic terrorism and state terrorism. For example, left-wing terrorism in Argentina in the 1960s and 1970s was an integral component of a wider popular uprising. Growing violence and terrorist activities by such groups as the *Montoneros* and the *Ejercitos Revolucionares del Pueblo* were met with extreme violence from right-wing groups and the Peronist regime. Argentina's military dictatorship launched what became known as the **dirty war**, in which thousands of people disappeared or were killed. **Sendero Luminoso** (the **Shining Path**) in Peru and the **Revolutionary Armed Forces of Colombia (FARC)** are other examples of domestic terrorist groups in Latin America. Shining Path was formed by university students and professors who

Ku Klux Klan

Racist terrorist group operating in the United States

Leaderless Resistance

Where small groups of terrorists operate independently without hierarchal leadership

Red Brigades

An Italian terrorist group that attacked government officials

November 17

Marxist-Leninist group that committed terrorist acts in Greece

Dirty War

Terrorist campaign by the Argentine military dictatorship directed against those critical of their government

Shining Path

Peruvian terrorist group

subscribed to the philosophy of *Mao Zedong* (*Mao Tse-Tung*). They sought to weaken the government's authority by inspiring Indians and others to rebel. Violence by Shining Path and the Peruvian government resulted in more than 30,000 deaths. Many Asian countries also face constant threats from domestic terrorists. For example, in 2006 an Islamic group, Lashkar-e-Taiba, bombed trains in Mumbai, India, killing roughly 135 people and wounding another 800.

FARC

Colombian Marxist guerilla group practicing terrorism against civilians and government officials

Nationalist Terrorism

Many nationalist groups attempted to achieve nonviolent political change but were often brutally suppressed by governments. When Algerians resisted French colonialism in the late 1950s, the French government responded with extreme violence in an effort to maintain its control over its colony. Under these circumstances, there were few nonviolent options to ending French colonial rule and the privileges of the French minority in Algeria. Similarly, the apartheid regime in South Africa engaged in widespread terrorism against that country's black majority and its supporters, thereby eliminating peaceful alternatives to ending oppressive racial discrimination and inequality. Often, nationalist terrorism is accompanied by peaceful, legitimate political activities designed to achieve autonomy, political freedom and equality, or independence. It is often difficult, however, to distinguish the difference between the behavior of nationalist terrorists and that of governments. Nationalist groups are routinely labeled terrorists by the governments they oppose, and labeled national liberation movements or freedom fighters by their supporters, including other governments. For example, while the apartheid regime regarded the African National Congress and its supporters as terrorists, the dominant global view was that the South African government was the terrorist. Governments, international organizations, nonstate actors, and individuals opposed apartheid and worked for decades to abolish minority rule and racial inequality. In this section, we will discuss nationalist terrorism in the Middle East (focusing on the Palestinian-Israeli conflict), Northern Ireland, and Spain.

The Middle East Although nationalist terrorism was used in Egypt, Algeria, and other countries in the Middle East to achieve their independence from European colonial powers and the Ottoman Turks, the Palestinian-Israeli conflict stands out as the most prominent contemporary example of nationalist terrorism. This conflict has plunged the Middle East into four major wars and fuels ongoing violence in the region. Failure to resolve this conflict has global implications, largely because of the world's dependence on petroleum imports from the Middle East. Furthermore, global terrorists, such as al-Qaeda, use this conflict to justify their activities and to recruit members throughout the Islamic world. The spiritual and emotional components of this conflict, combined with the sufferings of both Jews and Palestinians, make any discussion of it highly controversial and often subjective. In many ways, the pain and humiliation of both Jews and Palestinians often prevent both sides from empathizing with each other and reaching mutually beneficial solutions to their problems. Instead, both sides

Holocaust

Mass murder of
millions of Jews
driven by ethnic
and religious hate
and discrimination

Menachem Begin

Leader of the Jew-
ish terrorist organi-
zation the Irgun,
committed to Israeli
independence

Irgun

Jewish terrorist
group committed to
driving the British
out of Palestine

Fedayeen

Small groups of
Palestinian
commandos

**Gamel Abdel
Nasser**

Egyptian leader
popular for his
resistance to israel

Six-Day War

1967 war in which
Israel seized the
Sinai, the West
Bank, Gaza,
Jerusalem, and the
Golan Heights

have been locked in an increasingly deadly embrace from which neither side is capable of extricating itself. To a large extent, the Palestinian-Israeli conflict is an outgrowth of virulent anti-Jewish practices in Europe that culminated in the **Holocaust**.

Nationalist terrorism, one could argue, began when Jews attempted to end Roman occupation of Israel by killing Roman soldiers and officials. The modern period of nationalist terrorism has its origin in the British efforts to establish a national homeland for Jews in Palestine under the Balfour Declaration. Palestine was controlled by the Ottoman Turks. However, after the Ottoman Empire disintegrated following Turkey's defeat in World War I, Palestine became a British mandate under the **League of Nations** in 1922. Britain's responsibility was to prepare Palestinians for independence. The persecution of Jews in Europe, especially in Nazi Germany, complicated the situation in Palestine and set the stage for conflict. Led by **Menachem Begin**, who later became Israel's prime minister and a winner of the Nobel Peace Prize, some Jews formed a terrorist organization, known as the *Irgun*, to drive the British out of Palestine and to establish a Jewish state. The Irgun and other groups created a climate of fear in Palestine that ultimately undermined the public's confidence in Britain's ability to maintain order and to protect civilians. The most significant terrorist act against the British was the 1946 bombing of the *King David Hotel* in Jerusalem, the headquarters of British military forces in Palestine. Ninety-one persons were killed and forty-five others were injured.[30] This act was condemned by many Jews and Jewish organizations. The division of Palestine into a Jewish and a Palestinian state by the United Nations in 1947 ended Jewish terrorism but set the stage for Palestinian terrorism.

The creation of Israel was accompanied by a large Palestinian refugee problem, discussed in Chapter 9. Palestinian terrorists began to organize in the refugee camps and to form small groups of **fedayeen** (i.e., commandos). With military and financial assistance from Egypt's leader, **Gamel Abdel Nasser**, they began to conduct hit-and-run attacks inside Israel. Palestinian terrorism escalated following the defeat of Arab armies that had attempted to regain Palestinian land in the **Six-Day War** with Israel in June 1967. Instead of pushing Israel out, the conflict left Israel with the Sinai, the West Bank, Gaza, Jerusalem, and the Golan Heights. Palestinian terrorists, concluding that they could achieve their objectives only by attacking Israel and Jews, initiated a violent wave of bombings, hijacking airlines, and killing civilians. In 1968, the *Popular Front for the Liberation of Palestine*—one of the groups belonging to the umbrella Palestinian terrorist group the **Palestine Liberation Organization (PLO)**, led by Yasser Arafat and his Fatah movement—hijacked an Israeli El Al commercial flight and held the passengers and crew hostage. Israel was forced to negotiate with the terrorists to secure their release.[31] One of the most serious terrorist attacks was launched by the **Black September Organization** (part of the PLO) in 1972 during which eleven Israeli athletes were seized and killed at the Olympic Games in Munich. This terrorist attack, together with the hijacking of airplanes, drew international attention to Palestinian nationalism and laid the foundation for increasing violence not only in the Middle East but also in other countries.

Despite numerous efforts to achieve a diplomatic settlement to the Palestinian-Israeli conflict, violence escalated. Israeli occupation of Palestinian areas and many counterterrorist activities contributed to the demise of many attempts to reach a peace agreement. Feeling abandoned by Arab states, Palestinians initiated a popular uprising, or **intifada**, in the late 1980s. During the second intifada, which began in September 2000, the Palestinian-Israeli conflict became even more violent as Palestinian terrorists from such groups as **Hamas**, **Islamic Jihad**, **Fatah**, and the **Popular Front for the Liberation of Palestine** decided to conduct devastating suicide bombings against innocent civilians and the government in Israel.[32] There were more than fifty suicide bombings in 2002, the height of this new wave of terrorism, which killed and wounded hundreds of Israelis. To prevent these attacks, Israel constructed a barrier or wall, much of which was built in disputed territory. From the Palestinian perspective, the barrier was essentially designed to seize their territory and make their lives even more difficult. In April 2004, Israel, under the leadership of Ariel Sharon, escalated its attacks on Palestinian terrorist leaders, killing Sheik Ahmed Yasin, the founder of Hamas, and Abdel Aziz Rantisi, who replaced Yasin as the leader of Hamas with rockets launched from helicopters. Kidnappings of Israeli soldiers by Hamas and Hezbollah in July 2006 led to Israel's invasion of Lebanon and escalation of violence in the Palestinian Territories. As is usually the case in nationalist terrorism, both sides were accused of conducting terrorist activities.

Northern Ireland When Peggy visited her relatives in Northern Ireland in 1995, she was terrified by the pervasive violence between Protestants and Catholics. Checkpoints, guard towers, damaged buildings, British troops, walls covered with portraits of masked gunmen, and sectarian graffiti were everywhere. Things could not have been more different when Peggy returned in 2006. Despite some violence and various criminal activities, Northern Ireland was now peaceful and prosperous, and terrorism was a thing of the past. Northern Ireland had managed to end terrorism through a strategy that combined force, negotiation, and economic incentives. Earlier in this chapter we mentioned that globalization is a major factor in terrorism. However, the case of Northern Ireland shows that globalization was also instrumental in helping to end one of the longest and most violent cases of nationalist terrorism.

Terrorism in Northern Ireland (also known as Ulster) was rooted in Ireland's resistance to English control, exploitation, and widespread violence that began in the twelfth century. Catholic Ireland, colonized by Protestants from Scotland and England, became engulfed in religious wars that characterized Europe for much of its recent history. Nationalist terrorism in Northern Ireland was essentially a struggle by Catholics to end Protestant political, economic, and social domination. Following numerous attempts to solve the "Irish problem," the **Anglo-Irish Treaty** was signed in 1921. It divided Ireland into the Republic of Ireland (an independent country) and Northern Ireland (which remained part of Britain). While the Republic of Ireland is predominantly Catholic, Northern Ireland has a Protestant majority. Catholics on both sides of this artificial border refused to accept the division of Ireland and maintained a strong sense of nationalism. Catholics in Northern Ireland, known as **Republicans**, remained committed to ending the British presence and reunifying the two parts of Ireland. The Protestants, known as **Loyalists**, or **Unionists**, were

PLO

Once considered a terrorist organization, committed to fighting Israel and its occupation of the West Bank and Gaza

Black September Organization

Part of the PLO responsible for some of the most serious terrorist attacks

Intifada

Collective Palestinian resistance to Israel's occupation of the West Bank and Gaza

Loyalists/Unionists

Protestants committed to retaining Northern Ireland's ties with Britain

determined to retain Northern Ireland's ties with Britain and to perpetuate their economic and political power. Both Catholics and Protestants used terrorism to achieve their respective objectives.

Although terrorism in Northern Ireland was deeply rooted in Ireland's long struggle to resist British domination, the contemporary problems began in 1922 when the Unionist government implemented the Special Powers Act to suppress opposition to its control. **The Irish Republican Army (IRA)**, founded by Michael Collins and composed of rebel units that had launched the **Easter Rebellion** in 1916 against British rule, became the military wing. **Sinn Fein**, a political party that represented Catholics in Ireland, was widely regarded as the political wing of the terrorist movement. Opposed to the division of Ireland and committed to reunifying it, the IRA engaged in terrorism in both the Republic of Ireland and Northern Ireland and was outlawed by the governments on both places. Terrorist attacks against the British in Northern Ireland continued, escalating between 1956 and 1962.[33] However, many Catholics in Northern Ireland were strongly influenced by the nonviolent Civil Rights movement in the United States under the leadership of *Dr. Martin Luther King*, a development that weakened the militant IRA. But the use of excessive violence against Catholic Civil Rights marchers and demonstrators in 1968 by the Royal Ulster Constabulary (RUC) and growing anti-Catholic hatred—inspired to a large degree by *Reverend Ian Paisley*, leader of the hard-line Protestant Democratic Unionists— rejuvenated the IRA and laid the foundation for terrorism that plagued Northern Ireland, London, and elsewhere in Britain. The IRA, widely perceived as ineffective in protecting Catholics, was challenged by the even more militant **Provisional IRA (PIRA)**, which was formed in 1970. As is often the case in conflicts, the most extreme groups gain the most support. Catholics in Northern Ireland rallied around the Provisional IRA.[34] Protestants formed their own terrorist groups to engage in violence against Catholics.

Similar to the Palestinians and Israelis, Catholics and Protestants seemed hopelessly locked in a cycle of deadly violence. Both the Republic of Ireland and Britain are strong democracies. Britain's use of violence against the IRA was checked by democratic processes and strong support for peacefully resolving the conflict. Close political, economic, and cultural links between Britain and Ireland also helped. Equally important was support among Irish-Americans for a negotiated settlement, despite the fact that the IRA received significant economic and military assistance from some of them. Another important factor was the growing unification of Europe and the declining nationalism that accompanied the process. The activities of the IRA were receiving less and less public support. Furthermore, European integration brought many economic opportunities, recognition, and responsibilities to Ireland, which influenced it to reduce its support for the IRA. Economic prosperity transformed Ireland and Northern Ireland. Their integration into the global economy significantly contributed to ending terrorism.

A major step toward ending sectarian violence was the 1985 **Anglo-Irish Agreement**, which gave Ireland increased responsibilities in Northern Ireland and provided greater security for the Unionists by requiring an electoral majority to change

IRA

Rebel forces opposed to Britain's presence in Northern Ireland

Easter Rebellion

IRA rebellion against British rule

Sinn Fein

Catholic party in Ireland regarded as a terrorist threat to Britain

PIRA

Militant outgrowth of IRA

Anglo-Irish Agreement

Gave Ireland increased responsibilities in Northern Ireland in exchange for security for the Unionists

Northern Ireland's political status. The major breakthrough came with the signing of the **Good Friday Agreement** in 1998. U.S. President Bill Clinton, British Prime Minister Tony Blair, Irish Prime Minister Bertie Ahern, Gerry Adams (head of Sinn Fein), and David Trimble (head of the Ulster Unionists) cooperated to achieve this agreement. While Britain will control Northern Ireland as long as that is the wish of the majority, Ireland is more involved in the affairs of Northern Ireland. Ireland had to terminate its territorial claim on Northern Ireland in exchange for an institutionalized voice in its government.[35] Sinn Fein and the IRA were persuaded to support the Good Friday Agreement by President Clinton and by British promises to reduce its troop presence in Northern Ireland and to support reforms of the police force to enable more Catholics to join. The 2001 terrorist attacks in the United States reinforced the peace process in Northern Ireland as many Americans pressured the IRA to abandon terrorism and disarm. For the first time, Sinn Fein supported disarming the IRA, the Independent Monitoring Commission was established to disarm it. Although this international panel concluded in April 2004 that Northern Irish paramilitaries continued to carry out violent attacks and were engaged in various criminal activities,[36] destruction of weapons, ammunition, and explosives underscored progress toward disarmament and ending terrorism in Northern Ireland. In 2005, the IRA renounced the armed struggle and committed itself to peaceful change. By 2006 terrorism in Northern Ireland ceased.

Good Friday Agreement Compromise that gave Britain control over Northern Ireland and the Irish a voice in government

Spain In sharp contrast with nationalist terrorism in the Middle East and Northern Ireland, Basque separatists in Spain attracted relatively little attention beyond Europe. However, massive bombings of trains in Madrid in early 2004—in which ninety-one people died and 1,700 were wounded—focused the spotlight on Basque terrorism, despite the fact that terrorists linked to al-Qaeda were responsible for the bombings. The 2.5 million Basques, who are concentrated in mountainous northern Spain on the Bay of Biscay and across the border into Southern France, are one of the most ancient peoples in Europe. They speak a distinct language, **Euskera**, and have their own culture. Basques resisted Roman occupiers to maintain their independence. Spanish rulers, unable to exercise effective control over the Basque region and other parts of Spain, recognized the political, cultural, and economic autonomy of the Basques as early as the Middle Ages. This linguistic, cultural, political, and economic independence laid the foundation for the emergence of Basque separatist movements, such as the **Basque Homeland and Freedom (ETA)**.

ETA Basque separatist movement operating in Spain

Determined to maintain their autonomy, the Basques participated in Spain's larger political and military struggle in the nineteenth century against the centralization of power in Madrid. Having joined the losing side in these conflicts, the Basques lost their autonomy and believed that their sense of identity was threatened. Between 1842 and 1868, the Basque provinces of Vizcaya and Guipuzcoa experienced rapid industrialization, urbanization, and significant population growth. While many Basques, especially the growing middle class and business leaders, strongly supported integrating the Basque region into Spain, resistance to these changes grew among the working class and others who wanted to preserve the status quo.[37] Prior to the Spanish Civil War (1936–1939), the government recognized the political and cultural

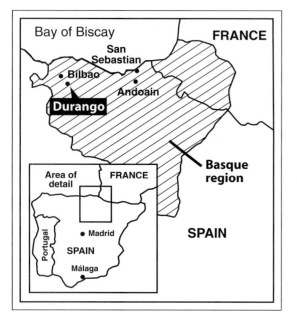

FIGURE 5.3 Basque Region of Spain

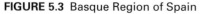

Francisco Franco

Former dictator of Spain who repressed Basque separatists

Lizarra Agreement

Committed the ETA to a cease-fire in its struggle for independence

autonomy of the Basque region. In return, Basques supported the government against insurgents led by **Generalissimo Francisco Franco**. Once again on the losing side in Spain's bloody struggle, the Basques were regarded as traitors by Franco, who centralized political power and abolished Basque autonomy. Any effort to maintain a separate Basque identity was severely repressed. Franco's authoritarianism, discussed in Chapter 4, fueled radicalization among the Basques. In 1959 a coalition of extremist youth groups separated from the more moderate Basque Nationalist Party to form ETA. Their principal objectives were achieving Basque independence from Spain and restoring Basque culture and language. ETA embraced a strategy of armed struggle against the Franco regime in 1962,[38] but refrained from engaging in major acts of terrorism until 1968.

Following Franco's death in 1975 and Spain's transition to democracy the Basques regained a significant degree of autonomy. They gained control over the police force, schools, and social welfare agencies. Basque language is taught in schools, and there are Basque radio and television stations. Despite this degree of autonomy, ETA continued to demand independence for the Basque region. But only about 30 percent of the Basques believed that independence was a viable option for them, compared with 60 percent who claimed both Spanish and Basque identities and preferred to maintain the status quo.[39] In fact, ETA's political wing, **Euskal Herritarrok**, is relatively weak and has never received more than 18 percent of the Basques' votes. These realities influenced Euskal Herritarrok to work out an agreement in 1998 with more moderate Basque nationalist parties. Known as the **Lizarra Agreement**, it committed ETA to a cease-fire and the moderates to achieving independence through the democratic process.[40]

Intransigence and political maneuvering by the government under Prime Minister Jose Maria Aznar and ETA contributed to the demise of the cease-fire in December 1999. The government continued to maintain its hard-line policy toward ETA during the cease-fire, refusing to negotiate with it, ignoring its demands to bring ETA prisoners from the Canary Islands so that their relatives could visit them, and continuing to arrest and detain suspected ETA members. ETA became impatient with peace initiatives and escalated its terrorist activities. In a major departure from its practice of primarily targeting government officials, police officers, and members of the military, ETA became more indiscriminate in its use of violence, targeting anyone who opposed its demands for an independent Basque state.[41] Following the 2001 terrorist attacks on the United States, Aznar equated ETA with al-Qaeda and intensified Spain's fight against the Basque separatists. However, when Aznar quickly blamed the 2004 train bombings on ETA instead of al-Qaeda, (the real terrorists), he lost the election that was held shortly thereafter, partly because the vast majority of Spaniards blamed his strong support for the U.S.-led invasion of Iraq for contributing to an escalation of terrorism in Europe. But the massive bombing in Madrid, Spain's consolidation of democracy and its integration into the European Union, and the sharp decline of terrorism in Northern Ireland weakened the public support for Basque terrorism and prompted the new government, led by Prime Minister Jose Luis Rodgriguez Zapatero, to aggressively pursue Basque terrorists. The arrests of many of ETA's leaders in 2004 and 2005 significantly weakened the terrorist group. In 2006 ETA announced a permanent cease-fire, thereby ending its campaign of terrorism.[42]

Religious Terrorism

Throughout history, religion has been used to justify committing acts of extreme cruelty and violence against human beings. Although religion is a major influence on some forms of terrorism, there are other issues at the core of religious terrorism.

Religious terrorism, especially that of al-Qaeda and other Islamic extremists, is widely perceived to be the most dangerous kind of terrorism, one that results in more destructive acts of indiscriminate violence. There are *four basic reasons for the extreme violence of religious terrorism*:

1. Violence is believed to be a sacramental act or divine duty in accordance with theology;
2. Religious terrorists view large-scale and indiscriminate violence as necessary for achieving their goals;
3. Religious terrorists do not feel constrained by public opinion or a need to gain popular support because they are engaged in a total war; and
4. Religious terrorists generally believe that modifying the system is insufficient; they seek fundamental changes in the existing order.[43]

You
DECIDE   ### Is Islam or Christianity More Supportive of Terrorism?

The rise of Islamic fundamentalism in Iran and elsewhere in the Middle East in the late 1970s, the escalation of suicide bombings from Beirut to Baghdad, and the 2001 attacks in the United States by Islamic extremists have led to a general and largely uncritical acceptance of the view that Islam inherently supports terrorism. However, there are many examples of terrorist acts carried out by Christian and Jewish extremists. For example, the 1995 bombing of the Oklahoma City federal office building was the work of Christian patriots. Colombia, a Catholic country, has experienced some of the bloodiest terrorist acts in the world. And, as we saw, the Reign of Terror occurred in Catholic France.

Do you think that Islam is more conducive to terrorism than Christianity is? Why or why not?

NOTES OF RELIGIOUS TERRORISTS WHO ATTACKED AMERICA

The Last Night

1. Read al-Tauba (a book of the Koran) and what God has prepared for the believers and the everlasting life for the martyrs.

2. Spend the night praying for victory and to smooth our affairs and that we will not be uncovered.

3. Cleanse your heart and purify it from impurities and forget anything related to this world for the time of play is past and the time of truth has come, for we have wasted much of our lives, shouldn't we spend those remaining hours in offering repentance and obedience?

4. You should be content for there are only a few moments before the beginning of happy life and eternal paradise with all righteous and martyrs.

5. Bring yourself, your suitcase, your clothes, the knife, your equipment, your identification, your passport, and all your papers.

6. Tighten your clothes well around your bodies, for this is what the righteous ones did before the battle and make sure your shoes are not ill fitting, and that your socks do not hang out of your shoes.

7. When you board the plane and before you step in, read your prayer and repeat the same prayers we mentioned before, when you take your seat. Read this verse from the Koran: "When you meet a group, be steadfast and remember God, you will be triumphant."

8. Apply the rules of prisoners of war. Take them prisoner and kill them as God said. No Prophet can have prisoners of war. . . .

9. Open your chest welcoming death in the path of God and utter your prayer seconds before you go to your target. Let your last words be, "There is no God but God and Mohammad is His messenger." Then, God willing, you will be in heavens.

Source: Excerpts from a document released by the FBI and reprinted in *New York Times*, 29 September 2001, B3.

Because religious terrorists are convinced not only that God is on their side but also that they are instruments of God's will, it is difficult to compromise with them. Unlike nationalist terrorism, which seeks to accomplish specific goals, religious terrorism is much more concerned with moral absolutes that are not negotiable.

In a hideaway in the shadow of Mount Fuji, members of the Japanese terrorist group **Aum Supreme Truth** developed and practiced to implement their deadly attacks on innocent Japanese in 1995 under the watchful eyes of *Shiva*, the Hindu god of destruction and rebirth. If you have visited Tokyo, you know how crowded the trains are that converge on Kasumigaseki, the center of power in Japan. Imagine the death and injury an attack on the subway system would cause. This is precisely why Aum Supreme Truth selected it to launch a preemptive attack on the Japanese government in order to implement its mission of world domination. Armed with bags containing a chemical solution that was about 30 percent *sarin gas* (i.e., a colorless, odorless, and deadly gas invented by the Nazis), the terrorists boarded the trains, determined to inflict catastrophic damage. Fortunately, their plan was not as successful as they had hoped. Nevertheless, twelve people were killed and more than 5,500 were injured in the sarin gas attack.[44]

In the heart of America, terrorist groups also believe that they are on a mission from God to destroy the U.S. government, create a racially pure society for whites only, and

Aum Supreme Truth

Japanese terrorist group fighting against the Japanese government

redeem the United States. The white supremacist Christian Identity movement and the Klu Klux Klan, among others, based their terrorist acts on Christianity. Their leaders often call themselves ministers. Muslim extremists also justify launching **jihads** (i.e., holy wars) on the basis of their religion. Many Islamic terrorists, including al-Qaeda, draw on medieval religious authorities to argue that killing innocents or even fellow Muslims is permitted if it serves the cause of jihad against the West.[45] As you can see, religious terrorists believe that they are acting in accordance with God's will and that the ends justify the means. Under these circumstances, human life is regarded as insignificant. Some Islamic terrorist organizations are closely tied to specific political and military developments in the Middle East. For example, Hezbollah in South Lebanon and Hamas in Gaza and the West Bank are directly linked to the Middle East conflict. However, a common influence on the emergence of Islamic terrorism was the Iranian Islamic revolution, led by Ayatollah Khomeini, which overthrew the shah in 1979.[46]

Jihad

Translated as "holy war" when described by Islamic terrorist groups

State Terrorism

Our definition of terrorism as the use of violence to coerce or intimidate and to generally create widespread fear among the population clearly covers many states, both historically and now. Think of Spain during the **Inquisition**, established by the pope in the fifteenth century at the request of the Spanish monarchy. Here is an obvious example of state terrorism, one of many to be found throughout history. During the Spanish Inquisition thousands of people were burned at the stake, torture was routinely used to extract confessions, and roughly 170,000 Spanish Jews who refused to convert to Christianity were expelled from the country. Imagine the terror that was generated by such violence. From the Spanish Inquisition to today, governments have relied on torture, both physical and psychological, as their ultimate instrument of terror to control the population. Nazi Germany, Stalinist Russia, Iraq under Saddam Hussein, China, North Korea, Argentina, Chile, Guatemala, Uganda, and many other countries have used terrorism, especially torture, to repress the population and stifle dissent.[47]

Inquisition

Spanish terrorist campaign directed against Jews refusing to convert to Christianity

Three levels of internal state terrorism are

1. **Intimidation.** The state uses its overwhelming power to discourage opposition and dissent, usually through excessive force by the police and paramilitary organizations.
2. **Coerced conversion.** This involves forcing the population to completely change its behavior, usually occurs after a revolution. The Soviet Union, China, and Iran are examples.
3. **Genocide.** This is the deliberate and systematic killing of an ethnic, religious, economic, intellectual, or any other group of people. Nazi Germany, Stalinist Russia, Cambodia under Pol Pot and his Khmer Rouge party, Uganda under Idi Amin, Bosnia, Sudan, and Rwanda are examples of internal state genocide.[48]

States also use terrorism against other states or nationalist groups to secure foreign policy objectives. A distinction is often made between *state-sponsored terrorism* and *state-supported terrorism*. Both types of state terrorism are usually clandestine. In state-sponsored terrorism, states are more directly involved in the terrorist activities of the groups they support. States act through client groups and proxies. Sometimes they send terrorists to assassinate dissidents and opposition leaders who live abroad. In state-supported terrorism, states have less influence over the terrorist group. They generally provide assistance and support the group's activities.[49]

Global Terrorism

Global terrorism encompasses activities by domestic, nationalist, religious, and state terrorists. It is characterized by its significant implications for a large number of major countries, nonstate actors, and individuals on several continents. It is covered routinely and extensively by the global media and engenders global responses to it. Global financial markets respond to terrorist acts or threats of terrorism, countries and nonstate actors cooperate to counter terrorism, airlines increase security and cancel flights, countries issue alerts to their citizens, businesses withdraw employees from areas threatened by terrorism, governments warn citizens to avoid traveling to certain places, and embassies reduce operations or close as diplomatic personnel and their families leave particular countries.

Sleeper Cells

Groups of terrorists who live what appear to be normal lives until instructed to commit terrorist attacks

Global terrorism is facilitated by various aspects of globalization. Terrorists take advantage of porous borders and their ability to blend into almost any major city in most parts of the world. Following al-Qaeda's 2001 attacks in the United States, it became increasingly obvious that global terrorists belonged to **sleeper cells**. Reminiscent of the Cold War, during which the Soviet Union relied heavily on sleeper agents to spy on the United States, global terrorists become part of a particular society, live what appear to be normal lives, and participate in terrorist activities against that society when instructed to do so. Sleeper terrorist cells have been found in the United States, Britain, Spain, Germany, Turkey, Belgium, Indonesia, Singapore, Malaysia, Italy, Pakistan, Morocco, the Philippines, and elsewhere. Global terrorism is also characterized by cooperation among different terrorist groups. The Internet, inexpensive transportation, and the global media contribute to global cooperation among terrorists.[50]

Mujahedeen

Group of Islamic holy warriors fighting the Soviet occupation of Afghanistan

Global terrorism is most often identified with Osama bin Laden and al-Qaeda. Al-Qaeda took advantage of globalization to build a global terrorist network. As we saw in our discussion of religious terrorism, al-Qaeda made a strong commitment to jihad as its principal objective. This struggle began in Afghanistan. Bin Laden and other holy warriors (or **mujahedeen**) were trained and supported by America's Central Intelligence Agency (CIA) to resist Soviet occupation of Afghanistan. However, this struggle evolved into a global jihad against the West, particularly the United States. By focusing on the United States as the country primarily responsible for creating problems for Muslims and as the common enemy of Muslims everywhere, leaders of al-Qaeda and other Islamic terrorist groups recruit and unite Islamic terrorists worldwide. Al-Qaeda evolved into an organization that is loosely hierarchical and very decentralized. Al-Qaeda, the organization, is based on an ideology articulated by Abdullah Azzam in 1987, which called for *Al-qaeda al-sulbah* (i.e., a vanguard of the strong). He envisioned Sunni Muslim radical activists who, through independent actions, would mobilize the *umma* (i.e., a global community of believers) to act against oppressors. The word *qaeda* is generally understood by Islamic militants as a precept or a method, as opposed to an organization. *Al-Qaedism* is essentially a worldview. The terrorist groups in Iraq, led by Abu al-Zarqawi acted independently of al-Qaeda led by bin Laden.[51]

Global terrorism is directed primarily against the United States, its close allies, and its global interests. There are several *reasons America is the target*:

1. The United States is the dominant global power. From the Roman Empire to the United States, leading countries have been targets.
2. America is widely regarded as the leader of globalization. Groups opposed to globalization target the United States.
3. Resentment of America's power, culture, and dominant position in the global system unites disparate terrorist groups.
4. America's global power means that America has many interests around the world. This provides numerous targets for terrorists.
5. Close ties between the United States and repressive governments—such as Saudi Arabia, Egypt, and Pakistan—motivate terrorists to attack it.
6. Many American foreign policies are regarded by terrorists as hostile to Muslims. The example most frequently cited is U.S. support for Israel and its indifference to Palestinian suffering.[52]

RESPONDING TO TERRORISM

In an age of increasing globalization, effective responses to terrorist threats take into consideration not only the interdependence of states and nonstate actors but also the difficulty of compartmentalizing domestic, regional, and global terrorist activities. Furthermore, the complexity of terrorism requires employing a wide variety of instruments to combat it. In addition to military, traditional law enforcement, and intelligence responses, there is growing support for the view that increased attention must also be given to the underlying causes of terrorism. The importance of global cooperation as a component of any counterterrorism policy became increasingly obvious in the wake of al-Qaeda's attacks on the United States and other countries. As Table 5.1 indicates, however, countries concluded several agreements dealing with terrorism before the 2001 attacks on the United States.

The most prevalent response to terrorism is the use of force, both domestically and internationally. Britain in Northern Ireland, Israel in the Palestinian territories, and the United States globally have relied on force, to varying degrees, to eliminate terrorism. Following the attacks on the United States, military action was taken in October 2001 against the Taliban regime and al-Qaeda in Afghanistan, a decision that was widely supported. President George W. Bush declared "war against terrorism" and stressed that America was engaged in a war of indefinite duration against a nonstate enemy that had no territory. As stated in the National Security Strategy of the

TABLE 5.1 MAJOR INTERNATIONAL AGREEMENTS ON TERRORISM

Year	Agreement
1963	Convention on Offenses Committed on Board Aircraft (Tokyo Convention)
1970	Convention for the Suppression of Unlawful Seizure of Aircraft (Hague Convention)
1971	Convention for the Suppression of Unlawful Acts Against the Safety of Civil Aviation (Montreal Convention)
1973	Convention on the Prevention and Punishment of Crimes Against Internationally Protected Persons, Including Diplomatic Agents
1979	International Convention Against the Taking of Hostages
1988	Protocol for the Suppression of Unlawful Acts of Violence at Airports Serving International Civil Aviation
1988	Convention for the Suppression of Unlawful Acts Against the Safety of Maritime Navigation
1988	Protocol for the Suppression of Unlawful Acts Against the Safety of Fixed Platforms Located on the Continental Shelf
1991	Convention on the Marking of Plastic Explosives for the Purpose of Detection
1997	International Convention for the Suppression of Terrorist Bombings
1999	International Convention for the Suppression of the Financing of Terrorism
2004	Creation of Counterterrorism Systems to Secure Ports and Ships (UN International Maritime Organization)
2004	UN Security Council Resolution Preventing Terrorist From Acquiring Chemical, Biological, and Nuclear Weapons

United States, the priority of the United States was to disrupt and destroy terrorist organizations of global reach and attack their leadership; command, control, and communications; material support, and finances.[53] Global support of military action was underscored by the response of the North Atlantic Treaty Organization (NATO). A day following the attacks on the United States, NATO's secretary general,

Prime Minister Tony Blair of Britain and Colonel Muammar Qaddafi of Libya. A combination of military action, economic sanctions, political isolation, and diplomatic and economic incentatives contributed to Qaddafi's decision to renounce terrorism and to join global efforts to combat it.

Lord Robertson, promised military assistance for America's campaign against terrorism. For the first time, NATO invoked the mutual defense clause in its treaty, that states that "any armed attack against allies in Europe or North America shall be considered an attack against them all."[54] America's invasion and occupation of Iraq in early 2003 was also designed, in part, to fight terrorism. Although there was no evidence linking the Iraqi leader Saddam Hussein to al-Qaeda, President Bush asserted that Hussein was involved in global terrorism and that his weapons of mass destruction could be used in terrorist attacks against the United States.

An essential aspect of combating terrorism is gathering intelligence and using it. The purpose of acquiring information and analyzing it is to learn about impending threats and to develop strategies to counteract them. As Table 5.2 shows, many U.S. agencies are involved in gathering intelligence related to terrorism and other threats to national security. Governments worldwide also engage in similar activities. There are essentially *four ways to acquire intelligence*: (1) take aerial and satellite photographs and conduct general photo reconnaissance; (2) use a wide variety of listening devices to record conversations, intercept radio and other signals, and monitor computer activities; (3) use spies and informants; and (4) collaborate with intelligence agencies from other countries and nonstate organizations. The first two ways are referred to as *technical intelligence* methods and the last two are called *human intelligence* methods.

Terrorists and their supporters have access to technology and can counteract the effectiveness of technology. They may know satellite overflight schedules, and how to use sophisticated encryption technologies. They also know not to use cell phones. In April 2002, terrorism investigators in Europe intercepted a cell phone call that lasted less than a minute, during which not a word was said. Suspecting that the call was a signal between

Lord Robertson

NATO's secretary general who offered military assistance for America's fight against terrorism.

TABLE 5.2 MAJOR U.S. INTELLIGENCE AGENCIES

Agency/Department	Functions Related to Terrorism
Defense Intelligence Agency	Provides military intelligence to the armed forces and policymakers. Each armed service has its own intelligence unit.
Central Intelligence Agency	Collects and analyzes foreign intelligence and conducts clandestine activities abroad.
National Security Agency	Intercepts, decodes, and translates foreign communications.
National Geospatial Intelligence Agency	Analyzes aerial and satellite photographs and prepares maps.
National Reconnaissance Office	Builds and operates spy satellites.
Federal Bureau of Investigation	Conducts domestic counterintelligence and counterterrorism activities and investigates international criminal cases.
Terrorism Threat Integration Center	Formed by the CIA, FBI, Homeland Security, and other agencies to analyze and share intelligence on terrorism.
Department of Energy	Office of Intelligence deals with nuclear weapons, nuclear energy, and energy-related areas.
Department of Treasury	Office of Intelligence Support studies intelligence relating to financial matters.
Department of Homeland Security	Determines domestic vulnerabilities to terrorist attacks.

Sources: CIA and *New York Times*, 16 April 2004, A16.

terrorists, the investigators followed the trail first to one terror suspect, then to others, and eventually to terrorist cells on three continents. What linked them was a computer chip that carried prepaid minutes and allowed phones to be used globally. Authorities monitored the conversations, arrested several suspected al-Qaeda members, and prevented attacks on Saudi Arabia and Indonesia. But terrorists adjusted their strategies. They abandoned cell phones, preferring instead to use e-mail, Internet phone calls, and hand-delivered messages.[55] Although technical intelligence is essential, the United States has relied too heavily on it and has allowed its human intelligence capabilities to deteriorate, partly by neglecting to learn foreign languages and about foreign cultures. Many terrorism experts believe that *human intelligence* is the most critical ingredient for rooting out terrorist groups because the essence of the terrorist threat is the capacity to conspire.[56]

As investigations of intelligence failures surrounding the terrorist attacks in the United States clearly demonstrate, simply acquiring information is insufficient to counteract terrorism. That information must be utilized and ways of thinking about threats to

Richard A. Clarke

Former chief anti-terrorism adviser under the Clinton and Bush administrations

national security must be critically examined. **Richard A. Clarke**, chief of counterterrorism in both the Clinton and Bush administrations, argued in his book, *Against All Enemies*, that the Bush administration essentially ignored the threat from al-Qaeda prior to the attacks on September 11, 2001. A major impediment to using intelligence effectively was inadequate communication between the FBI and the CIA. In an increasingly global society, distinctions between internal and external are becoming less relevant. In light of this reality, experts stressed the need to remove the barriers that divide domestic and foreign intelligence gathering.[57] Threats from global terrorism have influenced governments to strengthen their domestic security and to pay closer attention to how globalization and global terrorism intertwine. For example, water is the major link that countries have to the global economy. Almost all exports and imports are carried by ships. It is estimated that 95 percent of what comes into and goes out of America is by ships. Consequently, the global community, led by the United States, adopted a global code that requires the world's ships and ports to create counterterrorism systems, such as computers, communications gear, surveillance cameras, and security patrols. Ships that do not meet these standards or that have visited ports that do not meet these standards can be turned away from American waters.[58] Policing the seas, which comprise about 70 percent of the earth's surface, is a daunting undertaking. Countering terrorism in this way could seriously undermine global trade. A major domestic step toward protecting the United States against terrorism was the creation of the *Department of Homeland Security*. Its functions include controlling immigration and U.S. borders, monitoring foreign students, enhancing airport security, inspecting foreign ports, examining cargo containers, and cooperating with state and local governments to prevent terrorist attacks.

FIGHTING TERRORISM AND PROTECTING DEMOCRACY

Jose Padilla

American citizen detained as an "enemy combatant"

Jose Padilla, an American citizen, was arrested in the United States in 2002 at O'Hare International Airport in Chicago. Deemed an "enemy combatant," he was held incommunicado in a U.S. military prison without being charged. He was denied the right to counsel and visits from anyone, including his family, until he was released from the military prison to a civilian prison in late 2005, without an explanation from the U.S. government. President Bush justified Padilla's military detention on the grounds of protecting national security in a war against terrorism. Padilla, a former gang member, was believed to be working with operatives of al-Qaeda to detonate a "dirty" radiological bomb in the United States. These charges were suddenly dropped in 2006. During the U.S. invasion of Afghanistan in 2001, approximately 650 persons were arrested, transported to the U.S. naval base at **Guantanamo Bay** in Cuba, and imprisoned by the U.S. military without access to lawyers or visits from family members. In 2004, the U.S. Supreme Court ruled against President Bush and strongly supported an individual's right to due process of law.

Immediately following the terrorist attacks in September 2001, the U.S. Congress enacted the **USA Patriot Act** to protect the country from terrorist attacks. This law gave the federal government the power to conduct wiretaps, monitor books borrowed from libraries, demand access to financial records, and employ a wide range of investigative tools against people suspected of terrorism.[59] All of these cases raise fundamental questions about finding a balance between fighting terrorism and protecting democracy within the United States. Governments have extraordinary powers in wartime, including the power to detain or even kill suspects without trial. By defining the struggle against terrorism as a war in the conventional and literal sense of the word, President Bush essentially gave himself the power to disregard the basic due process rights that are essential components of democracy.[60] Furthermore, fighting terrorism collided with democratization efforts, which we discussed in Chapter 4. As we saw earlier in this chapter, many undemocratic governments collaborated with the U.S. war on terrorism and used the terrorist threat to justify their authoritarianism. But many people, including U.S. officials, scholars, and policy experts, stress that it is "precisely the lack of democracy in many of these countries that helps breed Islamic extremism."[61]

Guantanamo Bay

U.S. naval base where enemy prisoners of war are being held

USA Patriot Act

Controversial initiative passed by the Bush administrations to fight terrorist threats

---

You
DECIDE

Fighting Terrorism and Protecting Democracy

The war on terrorism has profound political, legal, social, and personal implications for people worldwide. While the vast majority believes that fighting terrorism is a global priority, there are disagreements on how to eliminate or diminish terrorist threats. Furthermore, there are questions about the extent to which counterterrorism strategies undermine democracy, weaken constitutional government, and ultimately create conditions that nourish the growth of terrorist activities. For example, the U.S. government routinely transferred terrorist suspects to secret prisons run by the CIA in Eastern Europe, where they were believed to be tortured. The Bush administration also defended its decision to use search warrants and the National Security Agency to listen in on the phone calls of Americans arguing that such action is necessary to protect U.S. national security interests.

How can governments fight terrorism without undermining democratic freedoms?

Summary and Review

This chapter addressed the problem of global terrorism. Since the September 2001 attacks in the United States the assumption that superior state military power ensures a high degree of national security has been seriously challenged. Specifically, we have seen a rise in what has become known as asymmetrical warfare, in which smaller, weaker groups—such as al-Qaeda—can inflict significant harm and damage against more powerful states, such as the United States. Increased globalization has created a global environment more conducive to international terrorism. Increased global migration, the growth of global cities, relatively inexpensive global and regional travel options, revolutions in communication technologies, and the explosion in global trade have all helped to create an environment in which global terrorism has gained prominence.

In this chapter we discussed the difficulties involved in accurately defining terrorism. As acts of terrorism incite emotional responses, it becomes increasingly difficult to agree on an objective definition of terrorism. Terrorist acts are designed to achieve specific, concrete goals. Often terrorists commit acts of violence against civilians in order to create fear and confusion. Terrorist acts are usually intended to be indiscriminate, in order to arouse a more fearful response from a population that does not know which public targets may be attacked next. In effect, terrorists are waging a form of psychological warfare against civilian populations. Another goal of terrorist acts is to humiliate governments, as we see in the example of Iraqi terrorists opposed to the U.S. presence in Iraq who have decided to target humanitarian aid workers in Iraq. In addition to the goals of terrorists, we also addressed the reasons and motivations for committing terrorist acts. We also discussed various forms of terrorism, including domestic terrorism, nationalist terrorism, religious terrorism, state terrorism, and global terrorism. Following the forms of terrorism, we examined some of the methods of financing terrorism, as well as various responses to terrorist acts.

Key Terms

asymmetrical power   148
Reign of Terror   150
Maximilian
     Robespierre   150
guerilla warfare   151
Osama bin Laden   154
Mohammed Atta   154
al-Qaeda   155
Taliban   155
Utopianism   156
Mikhail Bakunin   156
Hezbollah   159

domestic terrorism   161
nationalist
     terrorism   161
religious terrorism   161
state terrorism   161
global terrorism   161
National Alliance   162
Aryan Nation   162
Posse Comitatus   162
Confederate
     Hammerskins   162
dirty war   162

Sendero Luminoso   162
Revolutionary Armed
     Forces of Colombia
     (FARC)   162
Holocaust   164
League of Nations   164
fedayeen   164
Six-Day War   164
Palestine Liberation
     Organization
     (PLO)   164
intifada   165

Hamas   165
Isalmic Jihad   165
Fatah   165
Popular Front for the
     Liberation of
     Palestine   165
Anglo-Irish Treaty   165
Republicans   165
The Irish Republican
     Army (IRA)   166
Easter Rebellion   166
Sinn Fein   166

Discussion Questions

1. What are the main goals of the U.S. Department of Homeland Security?
2. What is asymmetrical power? How does it relate to the war on terror?
3. What is the main difference between guerilla warfare and terrorism?
4. Do you believe one can objectively define terrorism, or will such attempts always result in subjective, relative definitions?
5. What are some of the goals that drive terrorism discussed in this chapter?
6. Can you give an example of an act of domestic terrorism committed in the United States?
7. What are the four reasons for the extreme violence of religious terrorism addressed in this chapter?
8. What are some of the basic powers given to the U.S. government under the USA Patriot Act?

Suggested Readings

Ackerman, Bruce. *Before the Next Attack: Preserving Civil Liberties in an Age of Terrorism*. New Haven: Yale University Press, 2006.

Benjamin, Daniel, and Steven Simon. *The Age of Sacred Terror*. New York: Random House, 2002.

Bergen, Peter. *Holy War, Inc.: Inside the Secret World of Osama bin Laden*. New York: Free Press, 2001.

Burke, Jason. "Al Qaeda," *Foreign Policy* 142 (May/June 2004): 18–27.

Clarke, Richard A. *Against All Enemies*. New York: The Free Press, 2004.

Evans, Alexander. "Understanding Madrasahs," *Foreign Affairs* 85, No. 1 (January/February 2006) 9–16.

Gambretta, Diego, ed. *Making Sense of Suicide Missions*. New York: Oxford University Press, 2005.

Hewitt, Christopher. *Political Violence and Terror in Modern America*. Westport, CT: Praeger, 2005.

Heymann, Philip B. *Terrorism, Freedom, and Security*. Cambridge, MA: MIT Press, 2003.

Juergensmeyer, Mark. *Terror in the Mind of God*. Berkeley: University of California Press, 2000.

Kean, Thomas, and Lee Hamilton. *The 911 Report*. New York: St. Martin's Press, 2004.

Nassar, Jamal R. *Globalization and Terrorism*. Lanham: Rowman and Littlefield, 2005.

Primakov, Yevgeny M. *A World Challenged*. Washington, DC: Brookings Institution Press, 2004.

Richardson, Louise. *What Terrorists Want: Understanding the Enemy, Containing the Threat*. New York: Random House, 2006.

Schweitzer, Yoram, and Shaul Shay. *The Globalization of Terror*. New Brunswick, NJ: Transaction, 2003.

Weiman, Gabriel. *Terror on the Internet*. Washington, DC: U.S. Institute of Peace Press, 2006.

Addresses and Websites

The Interdisciplinary Center Herzlia
P.O. Box 167,
Herzlia, 46150
Israel
Fax: 972–9–9513073
www.ict.org.il

The *International Policy Institute* seeks to foster international cooperation in the global struggle against terrorism, paving the way for multilateral action against terrorist networks, benefactors, and states sponsoring terrorism. ICT is a research institute and think tank dedicated to developing innovative public policy solutions to international terrorism. This website provides information on the Arab-Israeli terrorism as well as international terrorism.

United Nations
Security Council Affairs Division
Room S–3520
New York, NY 10017
Fax: (212) 963–7878
Email: Security Council Affairs
www.un.org/docs/scinfo.org

The UN Security Council has primary responsibility under the UN Charter for maintaining international peace and security. It is organized to function continuously,

and a representative of each of its members must be present at all times at UN Headquarters. This website provides all of the Security Council's decisions and documents, as well as links to each UN website.

U.S. Department of Homeland Security

www.whitehouse.gov/homeland

The website for the U.S. Department of Homeland Security has information on terrorist threat levels, the organization, and functions of the department. It also enables you to find out who in your state is responsible for homeland security. News and information on cyberspace security positions are also available.

Endnotes

1. Moises Naim, "Collateral Damage," *Foreign Policy* 127 (November/December 2001), 108.
2. Condoleezza Rice, "Promoting the National Interest," *Foreign Affairs* 79, No. 1 (January/February 2000), 46–47.
3. Moises Naim, "The Five Waves of Globalization," *Foreign Policy* 134 (January/February 2003), 30.
4. "Education Chief Calls Teachers Union Terrorist Group," *Chicago Tribune*, 24 February 2004, Sect. 1, 5.
5. John Burns, "G.I.'s Battle in Falluja and Move South to Face Shiite Rebels," *New York Times*, 9 April 2004, A1.
6. Cindy C. Combs, *Terrorism in the Twenty-First Century* (Upper Saddle River, NJ: Prentice Hall, 2002), 15; and Peter Chalk, *West European Terrorism and Counter-Terrorism* (New York: St. Martin's Press, 1996), 12.
7. Chien-peng Chung, "China's War on Terror," *Foreign Affairs* 81, No. 4 (July/August 2002), 8–9.
8. Paul Wilkinson, *Terrorism Versus Democracy* (London: Frank Cass, 2000), 1.
9. Thomas L. Friedman, "The Humiliation Factor," *New York Times*, 9 November 2003, Sect. 4, 11.
10. Geneive Abdo, "Why Egypt Produces Extremists," *Christian Science Monitor*, 12 October 2001, 11.
11. Paul Blustein, "A Cradle of Terrorism," *Washington Post National Weekly Edition*, 25–31 March 2002, 8.
12. James Bennet, "Sharon Coup: U.S. Go-Ahead," *New York Times* 15 April 2004, A1.
13. Chester A. Crocker, "Engaging Failing States," *Foreign Affairs* 82, No. 5 (September/October 2003), 34.
14. Richard Bernstein, "Tape, Probably bin Laden's Offers 'Truce' to Europe," *New York Times*, 16 April 2004, A3.

15. Martha Crenshaw, "The Causes of Terrorism," in *The New Global Terrorism*, ed. Charles W. Kegley (Upper Saddle River, N. J: Prentice Hall, 2002), 97.
16. Jessica Stern, "The Protean Enemy," *Foreign Affairs* 82, No. 4 (July/August 2003), 33.
17. Martha Crenshaw, "Thoughts on Relating Terrorism to Historical Contexts," in *Terrorism in Context*, ed. Martha Crenshaw (University Park: Penn State University Press, 1995), 11.
18. Philip B. Heymann, *Terrorism and America* (Cambridge, MA: MIT Press, 1998), 11.
19. Ian O. Lesser, et al., *Countering the New Terrorism* (Santa Monica; CA: Rand, 1999), 41.
20. Jessica Stern, *The Ultimate Terrorists* (Cambridge, MA: Harvard University Press, 1999), 8–10.
21. Dana Milbank and Kathleen Day, "A Cash-Flow Crackdown," *Washington Post National Weekly Edition*, 12–18 November 2001, 17.
22. Patrick E. Tyler, "Blair Visits Qaddafi, Ending Libya's Long Estrangement," *New York Times*, 26 March 2004, A3.
23. Douglas Farah, "Diamonds Tainted by Terror," *Washington Post National Weekly Edition*, 12–18 November 2001, 15.
24. "Airline Losses Hit $14 Billion Worldwide," *Chicago Tribune*, 7 January 2003, Sect. 3, 3.
25. Paul R. Pillar, *Terrorism and U.S. Foreign Policy* (Washington, DC: Brookings Institution Press, 2001), 27.
26. Stanley Hoffmann, "Clash of Globalizations," *Foreign Affairs* 81, No. 4 (July/August 2002), 113.
27. Mike Tharp, "Thunder on the Far Right," *U.S. News and World Report*, May 1, 1995, 36; and Tore Bjorgo,

"Introduction," in *Terror From the Extreme Right*, ed. Tore Bjorgo (London: Frank Cass, 1995), 4.

28. "Italian Policeman Is Killed in Gunfight With Terror Suspects," *New York Times*, 3 March 2003, A3.

29. Frank Bruni and Anthee Carassana, "Greece to Begin Trial Involving Long-Elusive Terror Group," *New York Times*, 3 March 2003, A3.

30. Bruce Hoffman, *Inside Terrorism* (London: Victor Gollancz, 1998), 51.

31. Hoffman, *Inside Terrorism*, 68.

32. Gal Luft, "The Palestinian H-Bomb," *Foreign Affairs* 81, No. 4 (July/August 2002), 2.

33. Wilkinson, *Terrorism versus Democracy*, 31.

34. Wilkinson, *Terrorism versus Democracy*, 31.

35. Jonathan Stevenson, "Peace in Northern Ireland: Why Now?" *Foreign Policy* 112 (Fall 1998), 41–46.

36. Brian Lavery, "Northern Ireland: Party Linked to IRA," *New York Times*, 21 April 2004, A6.

37. Goldie Shabad and Francisco Ramo, "Political Violence in a Democratic State: Basque Terrorism in Spain," in *Terrorism in Context*, ed. Martha Crenshaw (University Park: Penn State University Press), 411.

38. Shabad and Ramo, "Political Violence," in *Terrorism in Context*, 411.

39. Susanne Daley, "Fear Spreads as Spanish and Basque Blood Flows," *New York Times*, 11 August 2000, A3.

40. Ray Moseley, "Divides Run Deep and Long in Spain's Basque Conflict," *Chicago Tribune*, 10 September 2000, Sect. 1, 3.

41. Carlta Vitzthum, "Basque Separatists Escalate Terrorism," *Wall Street Journal*, 4 December 2000, A20.

42. Dale Fuchs, "Huge Basque Arsenal Found in Southwestern France," *New York Times*, 5 April 2004, A3; and Alberto Letona, "Basque ETA Offers Spain a Total Truce," *Chicago Tribune*, 23 March 2006, Sect. 1, 1.

43. Hoffman, *Inside Terrorism*, 94–95.

44. David E. Kaplan and Andrew Marshall, *The Cult at the End of the World* (New York: Crown Publishers, 1996), 1.

45. Robert Worth, "The Deep Intellectual Roots of Islamic Terror," *New York Times*, 13 October 2001, A13.

46. Wilkinson, *Terrorism versus Democracy*, 34.

47. Wilkinson, *Terrorism versus Democracy*, 43.

48. Combs, *Terrorism*, 67.

49. Combs, *Terrorism*, 73.

50. David E. Kaplan and Lucian Kim, "Nazism's New Global Threat," *U.S. News and World Report*, 25 September 2000, 34.

51. Karen DeYoung and Michael Dobbs, "The Architect of a New Global Terrorism," *Washington Post National Weekly Edition*, 24–30 September, 2001, 20; and Jason Burke, "Al Qaeda," *Foreign Policy* 142 (May/June 2004), 18.

52. Pillar, *Terrorism and U.S. Foreign Policy*, 61.

53. George W. Bush, "The National Security Strategy of the United States," *New York Times*, 20 September 2002, A10.

54. Suzanne Daley, "NATO Quickly Gives the U.S. All the Help That It Asked," *New York Times*, 5 October 2001, B6.

55. Don Van Natta and Desmond Butler, "How Tiny Swiss Cellphone Chips Helped Track Global Terror Web," *New York Times*, 4 March 2004, A1.

56. Richard K. Betts, "Fixing Intelligence," *Foreign Affairs* 81, No. 1 (January/February 2002), 46.

57. John Deutch and Jeffrey H. Smith, "Smarter Intelligence," *Foreign Policy* 128 (January/February 2002), 64–69.

58. Tim Weiner, "U.S. Law Puts Honduran Port on Notice," *New York Times*, 24 March 2004, A6.

59. Elizabeth Bumiller, "President Urges Renewal of the Antiterrorism Law," *New York Times*, 3 March 2004, A12.

60. Kenneth Roth, "The Law of War in the War on Terror," *Foreign Affairs* 83, No. 1 (January/February 2004), 2.

61. Thomas Carothers, "Promoting Democracy and Fighting Terror," *Foreign Affairs* 82, No. 1 (January/February 2003), 84.

CHAPTER 6

Global Trade

INTRODUCTION

The origins of global trade are as old as human society. Lacking complete self-sufficiency, human beings traded goods and services within their communities and gradually expanded trade with people in distant areas. Global trade clearly shows the political, economic, and cultural aspects of globalization. Global trade is so integral to our daily lives that we are generally oblivious to how it links us to the rest of the world. Some of our most important agricultural crops are not native to North America. In fact, it is difficult to think of a country that has not been affected by the transfer of food crops from some distant area. The story of *sugar cane* vividly illustrates this point. More than 8,000 years ago, inhabitants of New Guinea, located north of Australia, discovered that grass, similar to bamboo, was not only sweet but could be easily cultivated by planting segments of it. This was the beginning of the global sugar trade, a development that would profoundly affect most of the world. Human craving for sweet foods facilitated the spread of sugar cane from New Guinea across Southeast Asia to India, which began producing crystal sugar around 500 B.C. Traders soon took sugar cane from India to China and Persia (now Iran). The spread of Islam from Saudi Arabia to Egypt, across North Africa, and into the Mediterranean and Spain was accompanied by the spread of sugar cultivation. Spanish and Portuguese colonization of the Americas marked a turning point in the cultivation, production, and consumption of sugar. Widely regarded by Europeans as a luxury product, sugar cane was soon cultivated on a massive scale throughout the Caribbean and Latin America. Requiring intensive labor, sugar cane cultivation fueled the trans-Atlantic slave trade and numerous conflicts among European countries for control of the sugar-producing Caribbean islands. For example, France gave its territory in Canada to Britain partly in exchange for the two sugar-growing islands of Martinique and Guadeloupe under the **Treaty of Paris of 1763**, which ended the Seven Years' War between the two European powers. By the 1830s, sugar cultivation spread to Hawaii, thereby completing its journey around the world and becoming a significant part of our diet. Our lives are increasingly affected by the webs of global interdependence that are integral parts of global trade. What's more, the ability of countries to control their economic activities is steadily being eroded by economic globalization.[1]

Many scholars have concluded that global trade and other aspects of globalization are transforming the functions of states. They see a shift in power away from countries to transnational or global companies and point to taxing power, an essential component of national sovereignty, to illustrate their point. Many countries, including the United States, attract foreign investments by offering numerous concessions. As Lester Thurow put it, "High profile multinational companies no longer pay taxes to

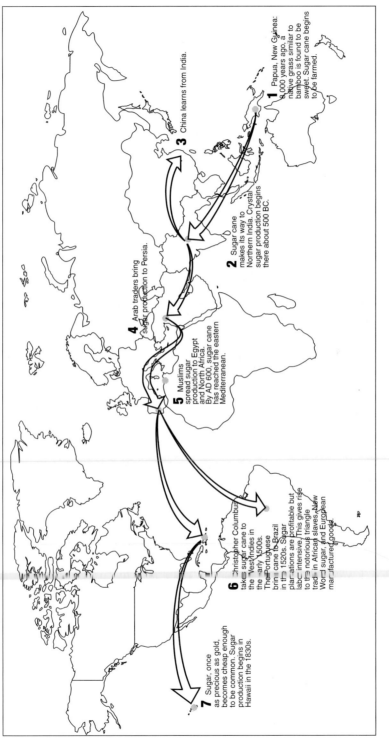

1 Papua, New Guinea: 8,000 years ago, a native grass similar to bamboo is found to be sweet. Sugar cane begins to be farmed.

2 Sugar cane makes its way to Northern India. Crystal sugar production begins there about 500 BC.

3 China learns from India.

4 Arab traders bring sugar production to Persia.

5 Muslims spread sugar production to Egypt and North Africa. By AD 600, sugar cane has reached the eastern Mediterranean.

6 Christopher Columbus takes sugar cane to the West Indies in the early 1500s. The Portuguese bring cane to Brazil in the 1520s. Sugar plantations are profitable but labor intensive. This gives rise to the notorious triangle trade in African slaves, New World sugar, and European manufactured goods.

7 Sugar, once as precious as gold, becomes cheap enough to be common. Sugar production begins in Hawaii in the 1830s.

FIGURE 6.1 The Global Spread of Sugar

Sources: Kenneth Kiple and Kriemhild Omelas, eds. The Cambridge World History of Food (Cambridge: Cambridge University Press, 2000; and Christian Science Monitor 5 August 2003, 18.)

Treaty of Paris

Ended the Seven Years' War between France and Britian

governments. Governments pay taxes to them."[2] Even more important is the weakening of traditional bonds between citizens and governments, a development that is partly due to the state's retreat from providing essential services and the growing trend toward privatization of even national security functions, such as housing and feeding military forces. One scholar, Kenichi Ohmae, contends that "the nation-state has become an unnatural, even dysfunctional, unit for organizing human activity and managing economic endeavor in a borderless world."[3] Instead of traditional states based on Westphalian sovereignty, Ohmae sees the development of *region states*. The boundaries of the region state are not determined by geopolitical considerations. Instead, they are drawn by "the deft but invisible hand of the global market for goods and services and follow real flows of human activity. Region states are natural economic zones."[4]

This chapter examines the growth of free trade, concerns about trade deficits and surpluses among countries, and how budget deficits and the relative value of currencies affect global trade. For example, a strong U.S. dollar, compared with other currencies, can increase American exports and make imports more expensive. However, the economic consequences of a strong U.S. dollar are complex and have both negative and positive implications for Americans. One of the most controversial areas of global trade is the emergence of global factories and global companies that depend on low production costs. An important component of global trade is the growth of economic integration and regional trade blocs, such as the European Union (EU) and the North American Free Trade Agreement. We will discuss these trade groups, various trade disputes among them, and how those disputes are resolved by emerging global institutions. Finally, we will discuss the impact of trade on the environment and the global spread of diseases and their implications for global trade. There is growing recognition in all countries that the global marketplace, left to itself, will not automatically produce wealth and prosperity for developing countries and poorer regions within developed countries unless there is rule-making and new structures diminish the potential for destructiveness.[5]

THE GLOBALIZATION OF FREE TRADE

Silk Road

Trade route linking China to the West

Mercantilist Model

Trade model stressing the role of government in trade and emphasizing the importance of balance-of-payment surpluses

Although discussions of free trade generally start with the repeal of the Corn Laws in Britain in 1846, trade among different groups and countries started much earlier. As early as the third century B.C., various nomadic groups and Chinese merchants established a trading route, known as the **Silk Road**. Linking China with the West, the Silk Road served as a commercial and cultural bridge between the two regions. The spread of Islam from Saudi Arabia to North Africa and the Middle East and across Asia, and reaching as far as Indonesia (the most populous Muslim country) was accompanied by trade. But trade in Europe, Asia, and elsewhere was often restricted by protectionist measures imposed by governments. Many governments adopted the **mercantilist model** of trade. It stressed the role of government in trade and emphasized the importance of balance-of-payment surpluses in trade with other countries. At the extreme is **autarky**, which promotes economic national self-sufficiency and focuses on eliminating economic interaction with other countries and foreigners.

Removing impediments to the free flow of goods and services among countries is the foundation of *free trade*, or *trade liberalization*. The consensus among advocates of free trade is that it reduces prices, raises the standard of living for more people, makes a wider variety of products available, and contributes to improvements in the quality of goods and services. Adam Smith, David Ricardo, and other economists believed that by removing barriers to the free movement of goods among countries, as well as within them, countries would be encouraged to specialize in producing certain products, thereby contributing to the optimum utilization of resources, such as land, labor, capital, and entrepreneurial ability. If countries focused on what they do best and freely trade their goods with each other, all of them would benefit. David Ricardo (1772–1823), a British economist, best articulated this concept, known as **comparative advantage**. Ricardo explained, for example, how it was more economically advantageous for Britain to produce cloth and for Portugal to produce wine, as long as they engaged in free trade, given their natural abilities to produce cloth and wine, respectively.

The theory of comparative advantage has been undermined by major developments that are integral to the current wave of economic globalization. The growth of transnational or multinational corporations complicates global trading. Production of goods and services is strongly influenced by costs, arbitrary specialization, and government and corporate policies. These developments mark a shift from the conventional theory of comparative advantage to what is known as **competitive advantage**.[6] Despite global acceptance of the concept of free trade, governments continue to engage in protectionism. For example, the EU and the United States each support their own commercial aircraft industries so that those industries can compete more effectively in a market dominated by a few companies. The idea of assisting such industries, which represents a departure from free trade, is known as the **strategic trade theory**.[7]

Current debates about the merits of free trade mirror previous concerns about how the free flow of goods among countries affects groups and individuals. However, movement toward free trade occurs because of a consensus that free trade is more beneficial to more countries and individuals than its alternatives. This is demonstrated by Britain's repeal of its Corn Laws and the United States' retreat from protectionism. In 1815, the British Parliament passed the *Corn Laws* to protect the wealthy producers of grain from foreign competition, thereby ensuring that the landed upper classes would receive high prices for their crops. Simultaneously, Britain promoted exports of its manufactured products to Europe, the United States, and its colonies. However, it became increasingly apparent that Britain could not produce sufficient food to feed its population and that the United States and European countries were adopting their own protectionist policies to safeguard their infant industries from British manufactured products. The Irish potato blight and the accompanying famine highlighted the dangerous and deadly consequences of Britain's policy of keeping food prices artificially high to protect upper-class interests. Outraged by widespread starvation,

Autarky

Ideology promoting economic national self-sufficiency and an end to economic interaction with other countries

Comparative Advantage

Theory that each country specializes in producing specific products, in order to better trade with other states

Competitive Advantage

Shift toward production of goods and services based on cost considerations, arbitrary specialization, and government and corporate policies

Strategic Trade Theory

Supports government subsidies of private industry

Britain's trade liberals, inspired by Ricardo's theory of comparative advantage, formed the *Anti-Corn Law League* to influence Britain to repeal the Corn Laws and to unilaterally adopt free-trade policies, regardless of whether other countries reciprocated. To a large extent, Britain's global leadership enabled it to induce other countries to adopt free-trade practices by setting the example. Britain's repeal of the Corn Laws and the *Navigation Acts* in 1846, which restricted the transport of goods to British ships, brought about the first period of relatively free trade among Western countries.

Trade protectionism did not retreat completely, however. By the end of the nineteenth century, many countries engaged in trade protectionism. The outbreak of World War I radically altered the global economic system and led to increased international economic instability. Widespread international economic problems that came with the onset of the *Great Depression* in 1929 influenced many countries to pursue autarky and protectionism. The enactment of the *Smoot-Hawley Tariff Act* in the United States in 1930, designed to protect American industries and trade, ultimately influenced other countries to increase their own tariffs. This development worsened global economic conditions. Attempting to diminish the negative economic consequences, the United States moved away from its protectionist policies by enacting the **Reciprocal Trade Agreement Act** of 1934, which authorized the president to negotiate substantial tariff reductions on a reciprocal and *bilateral* (i.e., between two countries) basis with other countries.[8] The rapid decline in global trade between World War I and World War II strongly influenced the United States and Western Europe to embrace freer trade.

At the *Bretton Woods Conference* in New Hampshire in 1944, the United States and its allies created (1) the **International Monetary Fund (IMF)** to manage exchange rates and payments imbalances among nations, and (2) the **International Bank for Reconstruction and Development (World Bank)** to supplement private capital for international investment, with an emphasis on the reconstruction of Western Europe. American and European concerns about the negative consequences of protectionism and their strong desire to promote free trade led to the establishment of the **General Agreement on Tariffs and Trade (GATT)** in 1947 to serve as a negotiating forum for the reduction of tariffs and other barriers to trade. The original goal was to establish the International Trade Organization (ITO). However, American dissatisfaction with restrictions the ITO placed primarily on the United States led the U.S. Senate to reject it. GATT was then established as a second-choice organization that did not require the same degree of Senate support as did the treaty establishing the ITO. GATT was not a treaty.

There were several *premises*, or assumptions, of *GATT*. These included

1. Multilateral negotiations (involving many countries) are preferable to bilateral negotiations (between two nations) on the trade issues.
2. Private economic actors are preferable to governments for conducting and managing international trade.
3. Free trade ultimately benefits the global society.
4. Governments distort the operation of the free market and should minimize their involvement.

Reciprocal Trade Agreement Act

Authorized the president to negotiate tariff reductions on a bilateral basis

IMF

Created to manage exchange rates and payment imbalances among nations

World Bank

Created to supplement private capital for international investment, originally with the intent of reconstructing Europe

GATT

Created in 1947 to promote free trade and to reduce tariffs and other trade barriers

Between 1947 and 1992, various meetings of GATT (known as rounds) resulted in significant reductions in tariffs and freer trade. However, GATT covered manufactured products, but excluded trade in agriculture and services. The **Uruguay Round** (meetings of GATT held in Uruguay from 1986 to 1992) added services and agriculture to the global trade framework and replaced GATT with the World Trade Organization (WTO) in 1993.

Although the premises of GATT continue to be the foundations of global trade liberalization, the *WTO differs significantly from GATT.* To a much greater extent than GATT, the WTO directly challenges fundamental aspects of national sovereignty by diminishing both the national barriers to global trade and governments' economic activities. For example, when China joined the WTO in 2001, it was required to make its domestic market more accessible to foreign competition and to privatize its state-owned industries. On the other hand, China benefited from provisions of the Most-Favored Nation Clause that was a key component of GATT. This clause reduces trade discrimination among members. WTO rules apply to activities generally regarded as domestic policies and beyond the reach of international regulations. Compared with GATT, the WTO is much more powerful in terms of governing global commerce and is empowered to settle trade disputes among countries. For example, tariffs imposed by President George W. Bush on steel imports in 2002 were judged by the WTO to violate global trade rules. Agreements establishing the WTO extended GATT rules to cover agriculture, consumer services (restaurants, hotels, travel agencies, and so on), producer services (investment, banking, insurance, **intellectual property rights**, or the control people have over their artistic, creative, scientific, industrial, and educational inventions, and data processing), textiles, clothing, telecommunications, labor standards, and the environment. They also call for greater transparency in writing product standards and testing procedures and in soliciting bids on government contracts.[9] For example, when the United States decided to limit bids on contracts for rebuilding Iraq in 2003 to countries that supported the war, countries that opposed the war, such as Germany and France, complained that America was violating WTO rules. WTO regulations also reduced or eliminated many import quotas and subsidies. For example, the *Multifiber Agreement*, an international arrangement concluded in 1974, used import quotas to regulate the more than $350 billion world trade in garments to benefit many developing countries and to protect domestic industries. Because such arrangements violate WTO rules, the Multifiber Agreement was allowed to expire in 2004.

The 142 member countries of the WTO met in Doha, Qatar, in 2001 to further reduce barriers to trade. The **Doha Agreement**, which reflected the growing power of developing countries regarding trade issues, relaxed patent protection for brand-name drugs by giving poor countries the right to make inexpensive generic medicines patented by global pharmaceutical corporations. Brazil, India, and many other developing countries, especially those ravaged by AIDS, viewed this concession as an important victory.[10] However, resistance to certain aspects of trade globalization in the developing world led to the collapse of the 2003 WTO meeting in Cancun, Mexico. At the heart of the controversy was the extent to which domestic industries should be protected from foreign competition. In 2006 the Doha Round of WTO negotiations ended in failure.

Uruguay Round

Meetings that replaced the GATT with the WTO

Intellectual Property Rights

Control that people and corporations have over artistic, creative, scientific, industrial, and educational inventions

Doha Agreement

Relaxed patent protection for band-name drugs by allowing poor countries to manufacture generic medicines

Exchange Rates, Budget Deficits, and Trade

As signs of spring appear, Josephine Zimmerman begins to think of traveling through Europe during the summer. She is keenly aware that she needs to save more dollars so that she will have sufficient money after she exchanges her dollars for euros when she arrives in Europe. The **exchange rate** for a currency is how much of one country's money can be bought with a specified amount of another country's currency.[11] The business section of major newspapers show that the values of currencies fluctuate constantly as a result of trading in foreign exchange markets, just as the values of stocks fluctuate on stock markets. Most currency trading is conducted by individuals and companies involved in international business transactions. The strength or weakness of currencies is determined by supply and demand, as is the case with commodities. Supply and demand can often be influenced by deliberate actions of governments and their central banks to buy or sell currencies, thereby affecting the price of currencies.

Exchange Rate

How much of one country's money can be bought with a specified amount of another country's money

The relative values of currencies directly affect global trade and domestic economies. A weak dollar (weak relative to other currencies) increases prices for imports in the United States. But a weak dollar also makes American exports less expensive in foreign markets, which stimulates economic productivity in the United States. More jobs are created and trade deficits with other countries decline. It allows American manufacturers to more effectively compete with less expensive imported manufactured products. A weaker dollar means that tourists from Europe, for example, are attracted to the United States because the strength of their currency enables them to get more for their money in America than what it could buy in Europe. But not all countries allow their currencies to fluctuate, which complicates the positive effects of a weak American dollar. China, for example, is likely to continue to have a trade surplus with the United States as long as its currency, which is somewhat pegged to the U.S. dollar, remains cheap compared with the dollar. Countries can also buy more dollars to increase the dollar's value relative to their own currencies, thereby protecting their exports to both the United States and Europe. A weak U.S. dollar can have substantial negative implications for America. Because the United States is so dependent on imported products—such as electronics, clothing, cars, and petroleum—a weaker dollar ultimately leads to higher consumer prices. Furthermore, huge U.S. budget deficits are funded by a *net inflow of capital* from abroad, meaning that the United States gets more money from other countries than it sends to them. It is estimated that the United States needed to attract $2.3 billion a day in 2006 to fund its budget deficit.[12] A weak dollar increases the cost of borrowing money from abroad and results in higher interest rates. The political, social, and economic ramifications of exchange rates are profound and far-reaching.

Mercantilism

Emphasized the need to accumulate trade surpluses in order to achieve greater economic and military power and national cohesion

Barriers to Free Trade

Even though most countries embrace *trade liberalization* (i.e., the movement toward unrestrained free trade), many governments engage in protectionist practices that impede the global free flow of goods and services. **Mercantilism**, which was widespread during the seventeenth and eighteenth centuries, emphasized the need to accumulate trade surpluses to achieve greater economic and military power, national cohesion, and an active role for government in this process implemented policies that discouraged imports while simultaneously protecting their infant industries. Many contemporary opponents to free trade essentially embrace *neomercantilism* (i.e., a new and more modern version of mercantilism). They argue that protectionism is essential to protect national security. Similarly, many developing countries argue that their need to achieve economic development, which includes economic diversification, justifies implementing protectionist policies. Finally, many antiglobalization activists view free trade as a threat to both the environment and respect for human rights.[13]

For more than forty years, the United States has maintained a trade embargo against Cuba to end the Castro regime and promote democracy that has effectively impeded free trade between the two countries. Furthermore, the United States attempted to pressure other countries, such as Canada and members of the EU, to refrain from engaging in commercial relations with Cuba. These efforts have largely failed. By 2001 domestic pressure influenced the U.S. government to permit the export of surplus American grain and meat to Cuba.[14] Another barrier to free trade is the formation of natural resource cartels, such as the *Organization of Petroleum Exporting Countries (OPEC)*, which deliberately limit supplies to increase prices or impose sanctions on importers to influence their political decisions or to punish them for particular actions. Many developing countries believe that developed countries exert strong influence over global trade through such organizations as the **Group of 8 (G–8)** industrial countries. Composed of the United States, Japan, Germany, France, Britain, Italy, Canada, and Russia, the G–8 routinely holds economic meetings or summits to discuss trade and financial issues that directly affect them. Because of these countries' power in the global economy, decisions made by their political and economic leaders at these summits significantly influence global trade.

Group of 8

Powerful developed countries: the United States, Japan, Germany, France, Britain, Italy, Canada, and Russia

Protests Against Free Trade and Globalization

From Jessica's perspective, Seattle was one of the most beautiful cities in the world. Its moderate climate, extensive connections with Pacific countries, location on Puget Sound and Lake Washington, views of the spectacular Cascade and Olympic mountains, great universities, and abundant cultural activities make it one of America's most attractive cities. Jessica and her friends walked slowly in the light mist to their favorite coffee shop not far from Pike Market to take a break from their classes. Given Seattle's dependence on global trade and technology, Jessica and her colleagues routinely observed the effects of global trade and frequently discussed both the positive and negative aspects of globalization. But they could not imagine that Seattle, one of the most tolerant, diverse, and economically prosperous cities in the country, would become the scene of such destructive protests against economic globalization during the WTO's meeting in November 1999. Protestors—a combination of antiglobalists, members of environmental groups, trade union members, and anarchists—had come to the city to shut down the WTO meetings. Anarchists threw bricks through storefronts and damaged property throughout downtown Seattle. As Jessica reflected on

Peruvian workers
protesting free
trade
*Source: New York
Times,* 19 July
2002, A1.

what had happened to her beloved city, it became increasingly apparent that the problem had been brewing slowly for some time.

Adam Smith argued that markets, particularly in global free trade, are guided by an invisible hand. Many developing countries, most of which were colonized by European powers, believe differently. They argue that global trade rules and practices have been largely engineered by rich countries to perpetuate their economic advantages. As early as 1967, developing countries formed the **Group of 77** to promote cooperation among themselves and to strengthen their bargaining power in trade negotiations with rich countries. In 1974, developing countries advocated the creation of the *New International Economic Order (NIEO)* in which they would enjoy increased economic benefits. Given the imbalance of economic power between rich and poor countries, developing countries were not taken seriously in global trade negotiations. The United States, Japan, Canada, and the members of the EU made trade decisions with which developing countries were expected to comply.[15] However, the expansion of global trade and the evolution of GATT into the more powerful and inclusive WTO enhanced the bargaining power of developing countries in global trade negotiations.

Even in the United States there is a growing uneasiness with the negative impact of free trade, especially the loss of manufacturing jobs and employment insecurity. Developing societies find themselves exposed to increased competition from other developing societies. For example, Rodrigo Hernandez from Isla, Mexico, joined hundreds of other farmers to protest globalization by dumping 400 tons of pineapples that they were unable to sell. For more than twelve hours, pineapple farmers blocked roads. Like other farmers who produce corn, oranges, cotton, and sugar, the pineapple farmers are threatened by less expensive imports. Thailand increased its exports of pineapples to Mexico from 692 tons in 1999, to 4,474 tons in 2000, a development that sent prices plummeting.[16] Similarly, the expansion of global trade has transformed Africa and other places into a dumping ground for discarded clothes, cars, furniture, tools, and even weapons from industrialized countries. Zambia, for example, once had a very successful clothing industry. However, when the government agreed to open up the country's economy to free trade in order to receive loans from international donors, Zambia was flooded with inexpensive secondhand clothing. Zambia's clothing industry collapsed, resulting in the loss of roughly 30,000 jobs.[17] At the heart of antiglobalization protests is the perception of an imbalance between the power of corporations and that of most countries.

Do Trade Deficits Matter?

Like millions of Americans who work in the manufacturing sector, Sharon and Michael grew up in families that had a long history of securing reliable jobs that provided enough income to keep them out of poverty. By the time they were 18 years old, both Sharon and Michael were employed by the local textile company, *Pillowtex*, in Kannapolis, North Carolina. They spent more than twenty years producing sheets and towels with the household names of Cannon and Fieldcrest. Similar to other manufacturing businesses, from electronics to furniture, the textile industry is moving much of its production to China, Mexico, and other developing countries. When Pillowtex decided to join the exodus, more than five thousand employees lost their jobs.[18] From the company's perspective, the move made financial sense. Why pay American workers roughly $35,000 a year when Chinese workers are paid as little as 50 cents an hour for doing the same job? While many economists and international trade analysts are not overly concerned about the loss of manufacturing jobs because companies such as Pillowtex are outsourcing their operations, many ordinary Americans strongly believe that U.S. companies should protect American jobs by keeping their manufacturing plants in the United States.

Business consolidations and increasing mechanization contribute to higher worker productivity and decrease the need for many employees. However, huge American trade deficits, especially with China, have linked the loss of manufacturing jobs to trade deficits in the minds of many Americans. The persistent rise in the U.S. trade deficit emerged as a potent social and political issue in the 2004 presidential election campaign. The U.S. trade deficit climbed to a record $800 billion in 2006, compared with $80 billion in 1990. The **trade deficit** is the difference between the value of goods and services that a country buys from overseas and the value of goods and services it sells to other countries. America's trade deficit with China reached a record $204 billion in 2006.[19]

Apart from the loss of manufacturing and service jobs in the United States, trade deficits have other significant consequences. Higher levels of unemployment mean less revenue for the government and higher government expenditures on social

Trade Deficit

Difference between the value of goods and services that a country buys overseas and the value of what it sells to other countries

TABLE 6.1 THE STRUCTURE OF GLOBAL TRADE

Country	Imports of goods and services (as % of GDP)		Exports of goods and services (as % of GDP)		Primary exports (as % of merchandise exports)		Manufactured exports (as % of merchandise exports)	
High Human Development	1990	2002	1990	2002	1990	2002	1990	2002
Norway	34	27	41	41	67	74	33	22
Sweden	29	37	30	43	16	13	83	81
Australia	17	22	17	20	73	65	24	29
United States	11	14	10	10	22	14	74	81
Netherlands	55	56	54	62	37	26	59	74
Japan	9	10	10	11	3	3	96	93
France	22	25	21	27	23	16	77	81
United Kingdom	27	28	24	26	19	16	79	79
Germany	25	32	25	35	10	9	89	86
Medium Human Development								
Mexico	20	29	19	27	56	16	43	84
Russian Federation	18	24	18	35	–	69	–	22
Venezuela	20	17	39	29	90	91	10	13
Thailand	42	57	34	65	36	22	63	74
Saudi Arabia	32	23	41	41	93	91	7	10
Brazil	7	14	8	16	47	44	52	54
China	14	26	18	29	27	10	72	90
India	9	16	7	15	28	22	71	75
Low Human Development								
Pakistan	23	19	16	19	21	14	79	85
Bangladesh	14	19	6	14	–	9	77	91
Nigeria	29	44	43	38	–	100	–	–
Zambia	37	42	36	29	–	86	–	14
Senegal	30	41	25	31	77	49	23	50
Angola	21	70	39	77	100	–	–	–

Source: Human Development Program, *Human Development Report 2004* (New York: Oxford University Press, 2004), 192–195.

Trade Surplus

Occurs when the value of exported goods and services is larger than the value of imported goods and services

services and other benefits for the unemployed. Trade deficits are closely related to budget deficits, although many other factors contribute to the large U.S. budget deficit. In order to pay for its trade and budget deficits, the United States borrows money from foreign investors, such as China and Japan, and global financial institutions. This reliance on foreign capital to pay for debt makes America vulnerable to pressure from abroad. The IMF warned that "America's voracious appetite for borrowing could push up global interest rates and thus slow global investment and economic growth."[20] Having a trade deficit in the United States means that other countries have a **trade surplus**; that is, the value of the goods and services they export is greater than the value of goods and services they import. From a neomercantilist viewpoint, trade deficits and surpluses directly affect a country's economic and military power. Countries with a trade surplus produce more engineers and scientists, attract more talent, and accumulate more financial resources to continue having high levels of productivity and innovation. This means that they acquire greater manufacturing capacity, higher levels of employment, and improvements in the development of intellectual property. For example, China's unprecedented economic growth, which was 10.3 percent in 2006, is attracting investments from around the world. Although China is best known for its factories that produce low-tech manufactured goods, foreign direct investment is rapidly flowing into high-technology industries. By 2000, China had emerged as the world's third largest producer of information technology hardware, after the United States and Japan.[21]

What a country imports or exports helps to determine if trade deficits or trade surpluses really matter. Also important is the extent to which these imports or exports can be substituted with suitable alternatives. With only 5 percent of the global population, America consumes more than 25 percent of the world's crude oil, much of which is imported. In the coming decades, there is likely to be increased competition for petroleum resources as China, India, Brazil, and other developing countries consume more energy due to their growing prosperity and larger populations. Political instability in oil-producing countries, more than trade embargoes, impede oil exports. Given modern societies' heavy reliance on petroleum, countries that depend on imports are extremely vulnerable economically and militarily to major interruptions in supplies. For example, instability in Iraq, combined with damage to oil operations in the Gulf of Mexico caused by hurricanes, pushed oil prices above $70 a barrel in 2005. Chaos in Iraq and increasing violence in Nigeria influenced oil prices to remain around $78 a barrel in 2006. The following tables indicate where the oil is and the major exporters and importers.

Contrary to the view that trade surpluses are positive and deficits are negative, some scholars, such as Joseph Quinlan and Marc Chandler, argue that this thinking is outdated and does not reflect contemporary global trade realities.[22] A fixation on imports and exports ignores how global companies operate. Many American companies pioneered the practice of establishing foreign affiliates and subsidiaries through which they sell goods and services instead of exporting them from the United States.

TABLE 6.2 OIL RESERVES BY COUNTRY (2006)

Rank	Country	Barrels, Billions
1	Saudi Arabia	264.3
2	Canada	178.8
3	Iran	132.5
4	Iraq	115.0
5	Kuwait	101.5
6	United Arab Emirates	97.9
7	Venezuela	79.7
8	Russia	60.0
9	Libya	39.1
10	Nigeria	35.9
11	United States	21.4
12	China	18.3

Source: U.S. Energy Information Administration and *Oil and Gas Journal* 103, No. 47 (December 2005).

TABLE 6.3 LEADING OIL PRODUCERS AND CONSUMERS (2006)

Oil Producers	Barrels/Day, Millions	Oil Consumers	Barrels/Day, Millions
1. Saudi Arabia	9.4	1. United States	20.4
2. Russia	9.4	2. China	6.6
3. United States	5.1	3. Japan	5.5
4. Iran	4.1	4. Germany	2.5
5. China	3.7	5. Russia	2.47
6. Mexico	3.3	6. India	2.4
7. United Arab Emirates	2.6	7. Korea	2.2
8. Venezuela	2.57	8. France	2.0
9. Norway	2.5	9. Mexico	2.0
		10. Brazil	1.95
10. Nigeria	2.35	11. Canada	1.9
11. Britain	2.24	12. Italy	1.8

Sources: Cambridge Energy Research Associates; and Joint Oil Data Initiative. JODIDB.ORG.

Most global companies follow the rule of "make where you sell" because of growing competition for global markets. While most Americans think of trade in national terms, American companies focus less on national ties and more on global market considerations. Consequently, they decide to compete not just through trade but also by moving production overseas. Furthermore, what are regarded as imports from other countries are actually transfers from American companies operating abroad. For example, American factories in China produce goods for export to the United States. Almost two-thirds of U.S. imports from Mexico are counted as *related-party trade* (i.e., trade between U.S. companies and their affiliates). In other words, slamming the door on imports from Mexico means slamming the door on corporate America.[23] Many foreign companies establish subsidiaries in the United States to gain access to U.S. markets. In the case of Japanese companies, they seek to reduce production costs and diminish anti-Japanese sentiment in America, but they also export cars from America to Japan and elsewhere. Given the growing partnerships among global companies and their global reach, the distinctions between imports and exports and between foreign and American are increasingly blurred.

GLOBAL COMPANIES AND GLOBAL FACTORIES

At the heart of trade globalization is the emergence of global companies that transcend national boundaries. Some companies, such as the British East India Company and the Dutch West India Company, collaborated with European countries to expand their power into distant areas, thereby creating an early period of globalization that continues to influence the contemporary period of globalization. These companies were predecessors to modern multinational corporations (MNCs). MNCs are closely associated with what some scholars calls *Fordism* (i.e., the manufacturing system that stressed mass production of standardized products, and the centralization and vertical integration of production processes). Initially, these companies' factories were located in a major industrial city in Europe or the United States. Between World War II and the early 1970s, many of these companies expanded their operations into industrialized countries but remained characterized by large-scale fixed investments and large structures. They were relatively immobile and vulnerable to sudden interruptions of production due to material shortages or strikes by workers.[24] *Post-Fordism* refers to the period after the mid-1970s when companies became more decentralized in virtually all aspects of production. Corporations became more transnational, or more global, in both their outlook and operations.

Revolutions in communications and computer technologies and transportation radically altered the way companies organize and conduct business. Communication within corporations occurs almost effortlessly, regardless of where various operations of the corporation are located. Financial globalization also contributes to the growth of global companies because it enables them to gain access to investment capital from around the world. McDonald's corporation is perhaps the most obvious example of a global company. Based in Oak Brook, Illinois, it operates in more than a hundred countries and continues to expand daily. In sharp contrast with the Fordist model, McDonald's is highly decentralized. In India, for example, where cows are sacred to the Hindu majority, McDonald's does not serve beef. On the other hand, it promotes aspects of American culture in other countries. McDonald's promoted birthday parties in China and other parts of Asia that have no tradition of having festivities to celebrate children's birthdays.[25] Another global company is Wal-Mart.

Global companies establish global factories that produce a wide range of goods. Most likely the labels on our clothes indicate that they were made in Mexico, China, Malaysia, Bangladesh, Singapore, Indonesia, or Fiji. Eddie Bauer, Kmart, Sears, Target, Mervyn's, Wal-Mart, and many other companies have their clothing manufactured in global factories. Most consumers are not overly concerned about where these

TABLE 6.4 WAL-MART'S GLOBAL REACH

Country	Total Stores	Total Employees	Year Entered Market
United States	3,499	1,200,000	1962
Mexico	633	100,164	1991
Britain	266	127,800	1999
Canada	225	58,000	1994
Puerto Rico	53	11,600	1992
China	31	16,000	1996
Brazil	25	6,600	1995
South Korea	15	2,800	1998
Argentina	11	4,200	1995

Sources: Wal-Mart; and *New York Times*, 6 December 2003, A1.

products are made. Distance is less of a factor in determining where factories are located. The fact that transportation by water is so much less expensive than by land encourages global trade and gives certain countries a definite advantage. The invention of the container ship in 1956 by *Malcolm P. McLean* revolutionized the shipping industry. The sealed cargo containers are unloaded in about a tenth of the time it took to unload conventional ships and at a fraction of the cost.[26] These containers are easily transferred from ships to trucks and trains. The low cost of transportation reduces the significance of location in achieving comparative or competitive advantage.

GLOBAL TRADE AND LOW WAGES

Founded in 1887, Rawlings Sporting Goods has had an exclusive contract to supply the major leagues with baseballs since 1977. All of the baseballs used in the major leagues are made in Turrialba, Costa Rica, by workers who earn roughly thirty cents for each ball. The average worker produces four balls an hour. The work is hard, often causing carpal tunnel syndrome. But Rawlings is the major source of employment in a town that has few economic opportunities. Rawlings moved to Costa Rica from Haiti in 1986 due to Haiti's political instability, alleged human rights abuses, and criticisms of Rawling's working conditions. Workers in Haiti earned even less than the Costa Rican Workers: approximately $15 to $25 a week.[27] The relentless search for lower production costs in politically stable countries has led to what is known as a *race to the bottom*. The constant loss of manufacturing jobs in the United States, Japan, and Europe as companies move production to countries with low wages and competent workers has motivated coalitions of labor union members, consumers, and environmentalists to try to slow this race to the bottom. However, from the perspective of many developing countries, these efforts are thinly disguised protectionist measures aimed at safeguarding jobs in the developed countries. This is a common theme in the outsourcing debate. Consequently, at the 1999 WTO meeting in Seattle, developing countries rejected a proposal to include a social clause in the global trade agreement. The *social clause* covers freedom of association; freedom to organize and bargain collectively; and freedom from forced labor, child labor, and job discrimination.[28]

China has an almost inexhaustible supply of skilled workers who are willing to work for low wages. In many ways, China is rapidly becoming a factory to the world. Japanese apparel companies, such as Fast Retailing, have built factories in China to avoid paying high wages in Japan. Japanese electronic companies—such as Toshiba Corporation, Sony, Matsushita Electric Industrial Company, and Canon—are expanding operations in China. Like many American workers, Japanese workers accuse these companies of exporting jobs to China.[29] China is also taking jobs away from developing countries, such as Mexico. The termination of the 1975 Multifiber Agreement at the end of 2004 removed protections for apparel producers in many developing countries, thereby enabling China to gain an even larger share of the apparel market. The sharp increase of apparel exports from China in 2005 generated stiff opposition in the United States and Europe. In other words, despite very low wages in most poor countries, China is able to produce quality products at lower prices. The implications for labor unions are profound.

LABOR UNIONS AND GLOBAL TRADE

At both the domestic and global levels, unions confront an almost Herculean task. In this section, we will discuss some of the reasons for the relative decline of the power of unions, as well as strategies unions use to enhance their bargaining power as trade becomes increasingly globalized. *Several factors contribute to labor unions' decline*. These include

1. **Public Perceptions of Unions.** Prior to the 1980s, unions throughout the industrialized world exerted great pressure on industries to obtain better wages and benefits. Often, they became forces of conservatism, resisting much-needed changes. Consequently, they were perceived by many citizens as being responsible for the economic problems that resulted from this rigidity.
2. **Political Change.** During the 1980s, many European countries, the United States, and Canada elected leaders who were strongly committed to free trade, including the operation of free-labor markets. Combined with a wave of privatization and the declining role of government in the economy, the embrace of economic neoliberalism undermined unions' power.[30]
3. **The Shift From Manufacturing to a Knowledge-Based Economy.** Most unions are in the manufacturing and public sectors. The rise of information technology and a knowledge-based economy radically shifted power away from manufacturing to industries that rely on highly educated employees.
4. **The Globalization of Individualism.** A growing sense of individual autonomy and the weakening of loyalties to organizations and institutions worldwide helped to undermine the power of unions, which depend on group solidarity.
5. **Demographic Changes.** Rapid population growth in the developing world and women's unprecedented levels of participation in the labor force in industrialized countries sharply increased the labor supply. Demand for labor was held in check by increased automation and higher labor productivity, thereby weakening the bargaining power of labor unions.
6. **The Global Spread of Manufacturing Centers.** As corporations moved production to countries with lower labor costs, union members in developed countries, who are relatively immobile, were forced to make major concessions in order to remain employed. The global dispersal of production makes it very difficult for unions to organize workers.
7. **Global Competition for Employment.** Workers in developing countries realize that their low wages give them an advantage in their competition with workers in rich countries.

Facing these formidable obstacles, labor unions have attempted to demonstrate that globalization is detrimental to too many people and beneficial to too few. Labor leaders view globalization as a leading cause of both domestic and global inequality and environmental degradation. Consequently, they have formed alliances with environmentalists, consumer advocates, students, and human rights groups to counteract global trade's negative impact on them. At the 1999 WTO meeting in Seattle, organized labor worked with its allies in an attempt to influence trade negotiations. Another strategy widely used by labor unions is to organize workers in developing countries to establish acceptable labor conditions. By getting workers in other countries to work toward establishing an internationally recognized set of labor standards, union leaders from developed countries hope to create a *win-win* situation for workers in both rich and poor nations. However, competition among countries for employment diminishes the chances that this strategy will be successful. Linking labor standards to global trade agreements would, in the view of poor countries, effectively undermine their competitive advantage, which is essential for them to achieve their own economic development.[31] Unions are also forming global links to counteract global companies' power. In this regard, they are more successful in Europe and Canada than in developing countries.[32] These countries have stronger unions that are generally accepted by these societies and corporations.

The globalization of production clearly reduces labor unions' power. However, the movement of goods on container ships from where they are produced to where they are consumed and the widespread practice of *just-in-time production* (which avoids maintaining an inventory and gets products only when they are needed) strengthen the power of a few labor unions. For example, global trade is very beneficial to dockworkers who unload and load ships in major ports. Compared with most workers, they occupy a very strategic position. Management is reluctant to use inexperienced people to operate cranes that move containers. The just-in-time delivery system used by factories means that delays can be extremely costly. Furthermore, many products are perishable and must be unloaded or loaded quickly. Above all, dockworkers control the chokepoints that can impede the flow of goods that consumers and businesses need. Compared with many union workers who have seen their wages decline in the face of global competition, dockworkers earn about $100,000 a year and have benefit packages averaging $42,000 a year.[33] To consolidate their control over these chokepoints, American dockworkers have created alliances with dockworkers in Canada, Europe, Japan, and elsewhere. For example, Japanese dockworkers refused to unload fruit shipped from a nonunion port in Florida at the request of American dockworkers who are unionized. Overall, global trade has weakened the power of trade unions, but has helped to influence the growth of regional trade blocs.

REGIONAL TRADE BLOCS

There are several *reasons for the formation of regional trade blocs*, which vary from one trade group to another.[34] These reasons include

1. **Economic Development.** Many countries attempt to achieve economic growth by creating their own industries and by embracing a policy of imports substitution. However, many industries encounter problems related to limited domestic markets and the inability to achieve economies of scale. Under

these circumstances, many countries pool their resources and create larger markets by integrating their economies.

2. **Managing Trade Regionally.** Many countries regarded global trade institutions as too bureaucratic and slow in responding to both trade opportunities and trade problems. As organizations expand their membership, they tend to become less responsive to their members, ideological differences proliferate, negotiations take forever, and reaching consensus is often very difficult. Neighboring countries usually have similar cultures and philosophical outlooks. The smaller group can respond faster than the global groups to problems and trade opportunities.

3. **Economic Competition.** Countries can become far more economically prosperous by forming trade blocs. European countries, for example, viewed economic integration as a way to stimulate trade in Europe. But Europeans also believed that economic growth in Europe would enhance their ability to compete with the United States and Japan.

4. **Political and Strategic Considerations.** Although trade appears to be the primary reason for economic integration, many countries form trade blocs for political and security reasons. The EU, for example, originated because of concerns about Germany's aggression in both World Wars. Governments gain greater credibility for their political and economic goals by cooperating with countries widely regarded as reliable, credible, and able to honor commitments. This was a major reason for Mexico's decision to join NAFTA.

Trade blocs vary widely in their objectives and levels of political and economic integration. Trade organizations range from free-trade areas to economic unions. We will briefly discuss the *main types of regional trade groups*, going from the most basic to the most complex. **Free-trade areas** are characterized by the removal of trade barriers among members. However, each country in the free-trade area maintains its own trade policies toward other countries, which often include significant trade barriers. *Customs unions* are free-trade areas that have a common external commercial and trade policy. Imports to the customs union are treated the same regardless of where they enter. This requires more cooperation and centralization of administrative tasks than in free-trade areas. The **Southern African Customs Union**—formed in 1910 and composed of South Africa, Botswana, Lesotho, Swaziland, and Namibia—is the world's oldest customs union. *Common markets* embrace the characteristics of free-trade areas and customs unions. They go further by providing for the free movement of people and capital, more harmonization of taxation and domestic policies, and more extensive administration. Finally, *economic unions*, which encompass all the features of common markets, represent the highest form of political and economic integration of sovereign countries. Besides harmonization of government spending and taxation (*fiscal policy*), they have a central bank, a common currency, and numerous political institutions to achieve greater cohesion in foreign as well as internal affairs.[35] The most powerful and recognized trade bloc is the European Union.

Free-Trade Areas

Characterized by the removal of trade barriers among members

Southern African Customs Union

World's oldest customs union, formed in 1910

The European Union

As you travel through Europe, you see that the euro is the common currency (with the notable exceptions of Sweden, Denmark, and Britain) and that passports are not required to cross national boundaries. In fact, common administrative regulations, the free movement of people across national boundaries, and the creation of numerous political, economic, and legal institutions are creating a stronger European identity. Stretching from Ireland and Britain in the west to Poland in the east, and from Finland in the north to Cyprus in the south, the EU is the most advanced trade bloc in the world. With roughly 450 million citizens and an economy of $9 trillion, close to that of the United States, the EU is widely seen as an emerging global power. Beginning with the European Coal and Steel Community (a treaty signed in 1951 that came into effect in 1952), European integration evolved into the European Economic Community (EEC) or Common Market in 1957 with the signing of the Treaty of Rome. Two steps toward transforming the EEC into the EU in 1993 under the **Maastricht Treaty** of 1991 were, first, the establishment of the *European Monetary System (EMS)* in 1979 to stabilize monetary affairs in Western Europe and to safeguard against fluctuations in the value of the U.S. dollar. The second was the signing of the **Single European Act** in 1986, which set the objective of building a unified European trade system by 1992.[36] As we discussed in Chapter 2, European integration focused primarily on political objectives, despite the emphasis on trade. In mid-2002, in an effort to create a union that would resemble the United States, European leaders completed a draft constitution. The proposed constitution provides for EU citizenship for nationals of member states, stresses the supremacy of EU law over those of member states, and designates certain areas (e.g., trade and foreign policy) over which the EU will have full authority and other areas (e.g., justice, transportation, and economic and social policy) over which authority is to be shared between the EU and the countries that belong to it.[37] In an attempt to counter the power of the EU, the United States, Canada, and Mexico formed the North American Free Trade Agreement.

Maastricht Treaty

Established the European Monetary System to stabilize monetary affairs in Western Europe

Single European Act

Set the objective of building a unified European trading system

The North American Free Trade Agreement

In sharp contrast with the EU, NAFTA continues to be a very controversial arrangement, with discontent on both sides of the U.S.-Mexican border. Canada, the other participant, has been largely silent. Unlike the EU, which was formed primarily in response to the consequences of war, NAFTA is predominantly concerned with economic issues. Signed on November 18, 1993, NAFTA entered into force on January 1, 1994. It brought together three different economies, with the United States the dominant power, Canada in the middle, and Mexico on the bottom. These divergent levels of economic development motivated the United States, Canada, and Mexico to form the agreement. Mexico, burdened with debt, regarded a trade agreement with the United States as essential to achieving economic development. The United States desired to maintain stability in Mexico and saw abundant and inexpensive Mexican labor as beneficial to U.S. companies that were anxious to gain a competitive advantage over the Japanese and Europeans. Canada, wanting to retain its favorable trading

You DECIDE | Costs and Benefits of NAFTA

When the United States, Canada, and Mexico signed NAFTA in 1993, it was assumed by many that the accord would generate millions of jobs, diminish illegal immigration, and raise living standards from the Yukon to the Yucatan. This optimistic view was countered by the assumption that Mexico would attract jobs away from Americans, wages would decline, and drugs and illegal immigrants would cross the U.S.-Mexican border. Ten years after NAFTA went into effect, Mexicans complain of the devastating impact it has had on small farmers in Mexico. The Carnegie Endowment for International Peace, a research institute in Washington, D.C., issued a report in 2004 concluding that NAFTA failed to generate substantial job growth in Mexico, hurt hundreds of thousands of subsistence farmers there, and had miniscule net effects on jobs in the United States. Income inequality is greater and illegal immigration continues unabated. The World Bank, on the other hand, found that NAFTA brought significant economic and social benefits to Mexico and argued that Mexico would have been worse off without the agreement.

Do you think NAFTA's benefits outweigh the costs? In your view, which country has benefited most from NAFTA?

Source: Celia W. Dugger, "Report Finds Few Benefits for Mexico in NAFTA," *New York Times,* 19 November 2003, A9.

relationship with the United States, viewed economic integration in North America as a way of countering U.S. dominance of the Americas.[38]

The level of integration among the United States, Canada, and Mexico differs significantly from that achieved by the EU. NAFTA, unlike the EU, does not provide for the free movement of people across borders. NAFTA countries pursue their own independent trade, foreign, domestic, and defense policies. Compared with the Europeans, who have given up some aspects of national sovereignty in exchange for European political and economic unification, NAFTA members jealously guard their sovereignty. Consequently, there are few institutions in NAFTA that are comparable to those in the EU, (e.g., the European Court of Justice, the Council of Ministers, the European Parliament, and the European Commission) that would diminish the autonomy of the United States, Canada, and Mexico. However, NAFTA has a significant supranational institution, the *Free Trade Commission*, which consists of cabinet-level officials or their designated representatives and is responsible for formulating policies dealing with trade.[39]

The Association of Southeast Asian Nations

China's rapid economic growth has helped to focus increased attention on the **Association of Southeast Asian Nations (ASEAN)**. Although we generally perceive Asia primarily in terms of its pivotal role in global trade and think of organizations such as ASEAN as trade blocs like the EU, ASEAN's origins were more strongly influenced by political and strategic considerations than by trade competition. The establishment of ASEAN in 1967 resulted primarily from the political and military concerns of

Indonesia, Thailand, the Philippines, Malaysia, and Singapore. Southeast Asia had become ground zero in the Cold War. The United States, perceiving nationalist movements in Vietnam as part of the Soviet Union's strategy to expand communism throughout Asia, inexorably militarized the conflict in Vietnam. But while America's policies in Vietnam are now regarded as having been seriously flawed, the threat of communism was real to ASEAN. The various countries, despite significant political differences among them, perceived communist expansion to be a growing danger, both within their own societies and in the region in general. Only a united front against communism could effectively counteract this threat.

Despite their obvious preoccupation with defeating communism, ASEAN members emphasized that their organization's purpose was to promote economic, cultural, and technological cooperation.[40] As the Vietnam conflict receded, ASEAN membership expanded to include Brunei, Vietnam, Cambodia, Laos, and Burma. In 2003, China and India joined ASEAN's *Treaty of Amity and Cooperation*, a nonaggression agreement designed to promote regional stability. They also agreed to collaborate in the fight against regional terrorism. But the focus has clearly shifted from traditional security issues to trade. ASEAN members believe that only through economic cooperation can they attract foreign investment and effectively compete with China. Apart from their reluctance to make the political compromises essential for forming an economic community similar to the EU, ASEAN countries face other serious obstacles in establishing a trade bloc. China, India, and Japan—the region's leading powers—are determined to participate in ASEAN. China, for example, is interested in creating, by 2010, a free-trade area that would combine its huge market with that of ASEAN, making it the world's most populous market.[41]

Asia-Pacific Economic Cooperation

Formed in 1989, the **Asia-Pacific Economic Cooperation (APEC)** is primarily a trade bloc composed of the leading trading countries in the region. These include the United States, Japan, Canada, China, Australia, the Republic of Korea, New Zealand, Taiwan, Indonesia, Singapore, Thailand, Malaysia, and the Philippines. APEC's administrative offices are in Singapore, and leaders from the member countries meet once a year. Most of the work is done by specialized groups that focus on the main trade issues, such as trade liberalization, energy, investment regulations, technology transfers, and telecommunications. APEC collaborates with the **Pacific Economic Cooperation Council (PECC)**, which was founded in 1980 to serve as a forum for Asia-Pacific countries to share information and ideas on investment, regulation, trade, technology, intellectual property rights, and nontariff barriers to global trade. In addition to APEC members, Mexico, Chile, and Peru participate in PECC.[42] The formation of both APEC and PECC emanated from the rapid economic growth of the Asia-Pacific region in the 1980s. Japan's economic power, widely perceived as a challenge to the United States, contributed to the growing regionalization of trade and investment. The economic success of the *Asian Tigers* (Singapore, Taiwan, Hong Kong, and South Korea) created stronger regional economic ties. The western coasts of the United States and Canada are economically integrated with Asia, a reality that makes the United States and Canada leading members of APEC. Another factor that influenced the formation of APEC was obvious competition with the EU and the United States. The South American Common Market was formed partly in response to the other blocs, especially NAFTA.

The South American Common Market

Latin Americans have made numerous attempts to integrate their economies to achieve economic development and to balance the economic and political power of the United States in the region. The formation of the **South American Common Market (Mercosur)** in 1991 represents a culmination of these efforts. Economic problems plaguing Latin America and historical cultural, economic, political, and border disputes between Brazil and Argentina impeded economic integration efforts. Furthermore, authoritarianism and military dictatorships throughout the region created such antagonism, competition, and distrust among the countries, especially Brazil and Argentina, that economic cooperation was virtually impossible. Not until these countries had resolved their economic and border disputes and had abandoned dictatorship and started to democratize were they able to begin integrating their economies.

> **Mercosur**
> Trade group created to integrate Latin American economies and foster stronger trading ties with the U.S.

Brazil and Argentina, the dominant countries in the region, were cognizant of growing economic regionalization and competition for investments and markets among trade blocs. They initiated the development of closer economic and political ties by signing the **Program for Integration and Economic Cooperation (PIEC)** in 1986. Given the economic competition between them, they decided to negotiate integrating specific sectors, such as capital goods, food, iron and steel, and the automotive industry. This allowed them to diminish business losses in both countries and to consolidate industrial processes.[43] This effort to open trade between Brazil and Argentina was consolidated by the signing of the *Treaty of Integration, Cooperation, and Development* in 1988. In 1991, Brazil, Argentina, Paraguay, and Uruguay signed the *Treaty of Asunción*, creating Mercosur. Bolivia, Peru, Chile, and Venezuela later joined the trade group as associate members. Barriers to trade among the members were removed; common external tariffs (against nonmembers) were adopted; and a commitment was made to coordinate trade, agricultural, industrial, fiscal, and monetary policies. In addition, they agreed to work toward harmonizing their domestic legislation to facilitate economic integration. Despite initial success, economic problems in Argentina and Brazil have undermined Mercosur's effectiveness. Furthermore, the United States has aggressively pursued bilateral trade agreements with Chile and other Latin American countries to create the **Free Trade Area of the Americas (FTAA)**, which would essentially engulf Mercosur.[44] Brazil supported the free-trade area to diminish the U.S. influence on trade in the region and to minimize damage to its own economic interests. As several Latin American countries elected more leftist leaders in 2006, Mercosur became increasingly politicized. President Hugo Chavez of Venezuela, for example, envisioned Mercosur as a powerful rival of the United States.

> **PIEC**
> Agreement to develop closer economic and political ties between Brazil and Argentina

> **FTAA**
> Attempt to unify North and South America under one free-trade agreement

GLOBAL TRADE DISPUTES

Throughout the 1980s, when Japan was widely perceived as an economic powerhouse that would eventually surpass the United States, trade disputes were passionate and frequent. Imagine members of the U.S. Congress smashing a Japanese car to demonstrate their displeasure with growing imports of Japanese automobiles. Many American companies complained that Japanese economic and trade policies, directed by the *Ministry of Trade and Industry (MITI)*, were deliberately designed to give Japanese companies an unfair advantage and to keep foreign companies at a disadvantage by closing Japan's markets to many foreign goods. For example, Japanese trade negotiators, who generally regarded Western companies as being too lazy to study Japanese consumers, argued that foreign meat was unsuitable for Japanese intestines and that foreign skis did not suit Japanese snow. French trade officials responded by refusing to allow imports of Japanese motorcycles, claiming that they were unsuitable for French roads. Although such disputes have declined after clearer and more binding trade rules were enacted with the creation of the WTO, many countries continue to find ways to protect their economic interests from foreign competition.

Controversy is an inevitable part of life. Global trade is no exception. Each country tries to influence other countries to abide by free trade rules while simultaneously trying to find ways to avoid following free-trade rules that undermine their own economic interests. Although Europeans and Americans steadfastly provide subsidies for their farmers, they routinely accuse each other of engaging in unfair trade because of those subsidies. Trade disputes are often complicated by divergent interests within countries. For example, while Japanese companies are protected from foreign competition by MITI, Japanese consumers pay extremely high prices for food. Inexpensive imports from China benefit many Americans who are raising families on tight budgets but deprive others of their jobs and thus their ability to provide for themselves and their families. Imposing higher tariffs on steel imports benefits steel workers but hurts auto workers and others whose jobs depend on imports of relatively inexpensive steel. Trade disputes are intertwined with domestic politics in virtually all countries and with cultural preferences. For example, disputes between Europeans and Americans about genetically modified foods are political, economic, and cultural. European political leaders are constrained by the reluctance of European consumers to eat such foods, while American political leaders are pressured to secure export markets by industries producing genetically modified food and are supported by most Americans who are more receptive to scientific advances and less concerned about consuming genetically modified food.

Global trade is sometimes controversial because it directly affects national security. During the Cold War, the United States and its allies restricted trade in products with *dual use*; that is, products that could be used for both civilian and military purposes. Computers, for example, could help students but could also be used by the military. Trade with China is generally perceived in this broader context. The United States has deliberately tried to keep China behind technologically by adopting export controls that restrict the sale of computer chip-making technologies. But China—with the world's largest cellular telephone market and the second largest personal computer market—is determined to achieve greater self-sufficiency in the manufacturing of computer chips. From a military viewpoint, China's access to the most sophisticated chip-making technologies gives it many military advantages and limits America's ability to maintain its military superiority over China in the long run. Competition inherent in global trade means that, despite U.S. efforts, other technologically advanced countries willingly sell to China what it needs to expand its semiconductor industry.[45]

Tariffs

In May 2002, U.S. Treasury Secretary Paul O'Neill traveled to Africa with Bono, the Irish rock star, to discuss trade issues with African leaders. While stressing that the United States and other industrialized countries had taken steps to promote trade with Africa—such as America's passage of the *Africa Growth and Opportunity Act*, which eliminated tariffs on many African exports—government officials, trade representatives, and nongovernmental organizations (NGOs) concerned with fighting poverty and promoting economic development expressed disappointment with the existence of many tariffs that stifle trade. For example, Ghana sells cocoa beans to Europe without having to pay customs tariffs. However, when Ghana processes cocoa beans to make chocolate and other products, which are far more profitable and beneficial to that country's economy than exporting beans is, its exports of processed cocoa are subject to a 50 percent tariff. Despite their emphasis on both global free trade and economic development, the United States, Europe, and Japan impose very high tariffs on basic exports—such as sugar, textiles, and fruits and vegetables—in which developing countries enjoy a comparative advantage because of their low labor costs. The United States imposes a 244 percent tariff on sugar imports and 174 percent tariff on peanuts. The EU has a 213 percent tariff on wheat. Canada restricts imports of butter by charging a 360 percent tax.[46] Nontariff barriers—such as imposing food safety restrictions and limiting exports to certain times of the year when they do not compete with domestic products—continue to be controversial trade issues.

That tariffs are frequently employed for both economic and political reasons is illustrated by America's decision to impose high tariffs (30 percent) on steel imports. Concerned about the loss of manufacturing jobs, especially in the steel industry, President Bill Clinton promised in 2000 to take aggressive new steps to protect domestic steel producers from **import surges** (sudden increases in imports) and **dumping**, (the selling of exports below production costs). However, the complicated political and economic aspects of protecting domestic steel producers influenced President Clinton to avoid imposing higher tariffs on imported steel. When George W. Bush was elected president with a slim majority of electoral votes but with fewer popular votes than his opponent, Al Gore, the politics of tariffs emerged as a major trade dispute. Steel-producing states—such as Pennsylvania, West Virginia, and Ohio—were regarded as essential for consolidating President Bush's political base. In 2002, the United States imposed temporary tariffs that increased the cost of imported steel by as much as 30 percent. This trade protectionist measure influenced the EU, Japan, Brazil, South Korea, Russia, and other steel exporters to petition the WTO to rule on the legality of the tariffs.

Import Surges

Sudden increases in imports

Dumping

Selling of exports below production costs

In November 2003, the WTO ruled that the tariffs were illegal and that the Europeans could impose sanctions totaling $2 billion on imports from the United States.

The dilemma confronting President Bush was both political and economic. As we mentioned earlier, disagreements arose within the United States because the tariffs had both negative and positive economic consequences for different groups of Americans. By refusing to comply with the WTO ruling, President Bush could have pleased some voters while displeasing others. Furthermore, in a globalized economy, other countries strongly influence both American politics and trade. Ironically, China's strong demand for steel in 2004 and 2005 made U.S. steel tariffs unnecessary. Similar to the U.S. strategy in its conflict with Europeans over their banana quotas, which involved selectively targeting countries to inflict maximum hardship, the Europeans decided to target industries in politically strategic parts of the United States. Tariffs were aimed at fruits, vegetables, and nuts from California and Florida and clothing from Southern states with ailing textile industries. They also targeted steel and metal products, including Harley-Davidson motorcycles.[47]

Quotas

A trans-Atlantic banana war raged between Europe and the United States for eight years following Europe's decision to erect barriers against imports of bananas grown by Chiquita and Dole (American companies) in Latin America in an effort to protect banana imports from its former colonies in the Caribbean and Africa. Beginning in 1993, when Europe formed a single agricultural market, banana quotas were imposed. The United States challenged Europe's preferential system in the WTO. The WTO concluded that the European banana quota violated trade rules and authorized the United States to impose retaliatory sanctions on $191 million worth of EU exports. The United States targeted high-end European imports, such as Louis Vuitton plastic handbags, Palais Royale bed linens, and peconino cheese. It imposed 100 percent tariffs on them to make them so costly that consumers would not purchase them. However, Americans continued to purchase Louis Vuitton handbags, which normally sold for around $400 before the tariffs, at twice their usual price after the tariffs went into effect. Exhausted by this relatively insignificant trade dispute that was negatively affecting far more important aspects of their relationship, Europeans and Americans decided to compromise. The Europeans agreed to a transition period of modified quotas and tariffs that lasted until 2006. The United States, which had originally demanded an immediate end to all quotas, agreed to remove its punitive tariffs.[48] The banana war was over.

Now that China has emerged as the country with which America has the largest trade deficit, Chinese exports are becoming a source of dispute between the two countries. In 2003, the United States imposed import quotas on selected Chinese textiles and clothing, largely in response to pressure from elected officials, businesses, and workers in North Carolina. While China claimed that such quotas violate free trade, the United States invoked a *safeguard clause*, which allows countries facing a sharp increase in textile or apparel imports, combined with job losses, to limit such imports.[49] However, industrialized countries agreed to eliminate all quotas and tariffs on textile and apparel imports from developing countries by 2005. China's apparel exports to Europe, the United States, and other countries increased dramatically in 2005. As Figure 6.2 shows, job losses in the textile industry have occurred steadily since the late 1980s. As in many other trade disputes, quotas protect some Americans while driving up consumer prices for all Americans.

Subsidies

In March 2002, about sixty impoverished Haitian rice farmers and their families, unable to compete with rice imports from the United States that are heavily subsidized by the U.S. government, decided to make a dangerous journey to the United States in search of better economic opportunities. They pooled the little money they had managed to save to purchase an unseaworthy boat and headed north toward the Turks and Caicos Islands, their first scheduled stop on their perilous trip to America. Halfway into the first leg of their voyage, their boat capsized, killing all of them.[50] Although government subsidies to various industries create trade disputes among nations, nothing evokes more controversy and conflict than agricultural subsidies in Europe, the United Sates, Japan, and other rich countries. At the heart of the problem is the unrelenting pressure used by developed countries to get developing countries to embrace globalization, especially free trade, while simultaneously engaging in trade protectionism. Even as these rich countries prohibit governments in the developing world from subsidizing farming—an occupation that provides a livelihood for roughly two-thirds of the population in poor countries—they continue to spend more than $300 billion to subsidize their own farmers and to give them an unfair advantage in the global market.

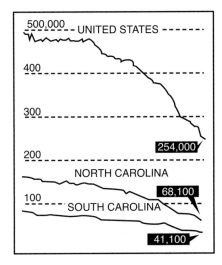

FIGURE 6.2 Declining Employment in the U.S. Textile Industry
Source: New York Times, 20 November 2003, C1.

Agricultural subsidies in developed countries originated largely to assist farmers and to provide more food security. In Europe and the United States, these subsidies contribute to overproduction and waste. In both Europe and the United Sates, huge amounts of grain, butter, cheese, wine, and other agricultural products are in storage. This overproduction problem is solved partly by encouraging Americans and Europeans to consume more food and by dumping agricultural products in developing countries' markets, selling them for below-cost prices. The EU provides subsidies to agriculture under the **common agricultural policy (CAP)**. The original objectives of CAP included (1) improving agricultural productivity, (2) improving living standards for those engaged in agriculture, (3) stabilizing markets, (4) guaranteeing regular food supplies, and (5) providing food at reasonable prices to consumers.[51] However, agriculture has changed significantly since CAP was established in 1968. Only about 5 percent of Europeans are engaged in agriculture, and agricultural science has contributed to dramatic increases in productivity.

Common Agricultural Policy
Supports agricultural subsidies to EU member countries

Influenced by the devastating impact of the Great Depression on farmers, the United States enacted *agricultural legislation in 1929* as part of the New Deal in order to stabilize farm prices and to save family farming. At that time roughly 21 percent of the American population engaged in farming, compared with less than 2 percent today.

Improved seeds, better farm machinery, and general advances in agricultural science and technology have raised the productivity of an acre planted in corn from thirty-four bushels then to more than 137 bushels now. Despite revolutionary developments in farming and the success of American farmers, the U.S. government continues to subsidize agriculture. The larger the farm, the greater the amount in subsidies it will receive. This system influences farmers to expand their acreage by buying their neighbors' farms. Instead of being governed by the law of supply and demand, which would encourage them to produce less, they are protected by government subsidies that encourage them to overproduce. As is the case in Europe, American agricultural subsidies are maintained through what is known as the *iron triangle*; that is, the political relationship among members of congressional committees who are affected by farm issues, interest groups, and government agencies whose existence is closely linked to farming interests.[52]

**Group of
21 Nations**

Developing countries that united to block discussion of many trade issues important to the U.S. and Europe

Agricultural subsidies in Europe and the United States encountered strong resistance from developing countries during the 2003 WTO meeting in Cancun, Mexico. Opposition to subsidies was strongly supported by some antiglobalization groups and various NGOs, such as Oxfam. The World Bank also stressed the negative economic implications of agricultural subsidies for developing counties. Pressured by their powerful domestic constituencies, the United States and the EU attempted to avoid addressing the issue of subsidies. But the developing countries, which formed the **Group of 21 Nations** (composed of China, India, Brazil, Mexico, South Africa, Argentina, and other major agricultural producers), effectively blocked discussion of issues important to the United States and Europe. Developed countries' resistance to reducing or eliminating agricultural subsidies and tariffs that block agricultural exports from the developing world contributed to the failure of WTO talks in Cancun in 2003 and again in Geneva in 2006.

Genetically Modified Food

As global trade facilitates transferring food from one country to another and as consumers become more aware of health risks associated with food, trade disputes based on real and perceived health problems are proliferating. Unlike the other trade disputes we have discussed so far, food disputes are more about cultural (or more precisely, culinary) differences than they are about protecting jobs and financial gains. We are aware of the growing emphasis on consuming organic foods, ranging from milk to eggs. The outbreak of mad cow disease in Washington State in 2003 reinforced the reluctance among consumers to have full confidence in the safety of food supplies. In general, Europeans tend to be more concerned than Americans are about consuming genetically modified foods, partly because they are more skeptical of science. Their confidence in scientists has been undermined by outbreaks of mad cow disease, during which scientists initially assured consumers that they faced no health risks. Also, knowledge of dioxin-infested chickens in Belgium was not reassuring.

An example of a dispute relating to food safety is Europe's decision in 1996 to ban imports of American beef produced from cattle that had been fed growth hormones. These hormones, used to accelerate beef production, are generally accepted by American consumers. However, Europeans, especially the extremely food-conscious

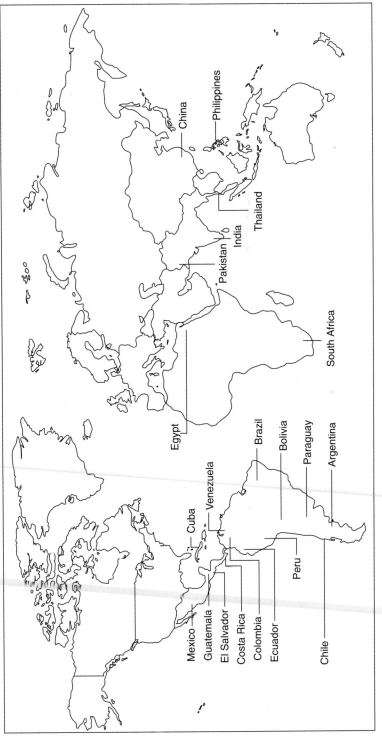

FIGURE 6.3 Group of 21 Nations (opposed to agricultural subsidies)

French and Italians, prefer beef that has not been fed hormones. These cultural differences became the source for a trade dispute between Europe and the United States. Under global trade agreements, countries are allowed to ban imports of foods if there is scientific evidence to support concerns about safety. Americans argued that scientific evidence showed that beef hormones did not endanger human health. The WTO agreed with the United States and authorized the imposition of punitive tariffs of $117 million a year against European exports. Despite high tariffs on Danish ham, Italian tomatoes, and other European products, Europe refused to lift the ban, citing its own scientific findings that showed that high doses of hormones cause cancer.[53]

Far more controversial than the beef hormone issue is the dispute concerning genetically modified foods. Although human beings have engaged in genetic modifications for centuries, experiments conducted by *Gregor Mendel* with pea plants in his monastery garden in 1866 represented a breakthrough in this area and set the stage for more advanced genetic research. While advances in agricultural science have been embraced globally, the ability to transfer isolated genes into the DNA of another organism is widely viewed as a threat. The idea that a trait for cold resistance can be transferred from a fish to a plant has encountered resistance from environmentalists, consumers, and farmers in Europe and elsewhere. From the other perspective, genetically modified crops, developed by *Monsanto*, solve many problems that plague farmers, such as pest control, soil preservation, and weed control. Most American farmers embraced genetically modified crops, such as "Roundup Ready" soybeans, that required fewer chemicals. Commercial use of genetically modified seeds was made available to farmers in 1996. By 1999, about half of the U.S. soybean crop and about one-third of the corn crop were grown from genetically modified seeds.[54]

In a world awash in grain, there was no sense of urgency in Europe to consume genetically modified crops. Environmental groups, such as Greenpeace, launched a global campaign against them, stressing not only the dangers they posed to consumers but also the dangers they posed to the natural environment. This campaign and others reinforced Europeans' concerns about eating genetically modified foods. Public pressure influenced the European Parliament to enact a food labeling law requiring merchants to clearly indicate if packaged foods contain any amount of genetically modified ingredients. Major food-importing countries, such as Japan and South Korea, also resisted consuming genetically modified crops. American grain exporters and various food companies—such as Gerber, H. J. Heinz, and Frito-Lay—decided to abandon genetically modified crops to maintain their sales in Europe, Japan, and other countries. Many supermarkets in Europe removed genetically modified products from their shelves. The United States, on the other hand, viewed Europe as using the genetically modified food issue to exclude American exports.[55]

GLOBAL TRADE AND THE ENVIRONMENT

The growing link between global trade and the environment can be seen daily and in fundamental ways. The notebooks and textbooks you use are likely to be made from recycled paper. The Chiquita banana and the coffee you had for breakfast were probably produced under conditions that met environmental standards determined by environmental NGOs, such as the Better Banana Project and the Rainforest Alliance. The Body Shop, the British cosmetics producer and retailer that has stores in most American shopping centers, makes protecting the environment an integral component of its global business. Many global companies—such as the Ford Motor Company, BP Amoco, Royal Dutch Shell, Dow Chemical, Sunoco, DuPont, Boeing, and United Technologies—are involved in global efforts to reduce emissions of greenhouse gases in order to diminish global warming and climate change. Home Depot, the world's largest home improvement business, requires its wood suppliers to meet international environmental standards.

Many environmentalists, trade analysts, and antiglobalization activists believe that relentless competition in global trade inevitably leads to a disregard for environmental standards. Global trade advocates, on the other hand, tend to believe that economic globalization is instrumental in improving and safeguarding the global environment.[56] As is generally the case in such debates, both sides are correct to some extent. Global trade provides both opportunities to internationalize sound environmental standards as well as significant threats to maintaining these standards and promoting sustainable development. As we see throughout this book, poverty is often both a cause and a result of environmental degradation. Economically developed societies usually enforce higher environmental standards, partly because they have adequate resources to enable them to do so. Several factors combine to make *environmental issues components of global trade*. These include

1. **Public Support for the Environment.** Growing awareness of environmental problems in the United States, Canada, Western Europe, and other industrialized countries has led to the passage of extensive environmental protection legislation.
2. **Global Political Pressure.** Public support for efforts to safeguard the environment, the growth of telecommunications and computer technologies, and inexpensive transportation have facilitated the efforts of environmental activists to organize on a global scale and to exert pressure on governments and international organizations.
3. **Corporate Action.** Many global companies are sensitive to consumer pressure. Many business leaders also believe that complying with global environmental standards makes good business sense in an extremely competitive market.
4. **Economic Integration.** The globalization of trade and the emergence of regional trading blocs have contributed to the growing acceptance of environmental practices. Leading members of trade blocs usually have higher environmental standards that often become the yardstick against which the practices of other members of the bloc are measured.

Environmental protection is sometimes used as a barrier to free trade. A coalition of environmental, labor, and consumer groups mounted strong opposition to changing the U.S. policy of excluding Mexican trucks from operating in the United States. Their basic argument was that Mexican trucks were unable to comply with the higher

American environmental standards and that they posed a serious threat to public health.[57] Given the interest of labor groups in limiting competition from Mexican trucks, these environmental concerns could not be entirely separated from tangible economic interests. Growing competition from shrimp producers in developing countries was also a factor in the U.S. decision to use environmental laws—requiring shrimp nets to have turtle extruder devices to protect endangered turtles that are often caught in fishing nets—against shrimp exporters. The WTO ruled against the United States, viewing the application of the environmental laws as an illegal barrier to free trade.

Global trade creates many environmental problems. The sharp increase in the number of global factories has contributed to higher levels of pollution in many countries. The maquiladoras along the U.S.-Mexican border have increased pollution. *China's phenomenal economic growth is closely linked to widespread pollution.* It is apparent to anyone visiting China that economic progress has contributed to the country's environmental problems. The air and water in many of China's major cities rank among the dirtiest and most dangerous in the world. China is the world's largest consumer of coal as well as the world's fastest-growing importer of petroleum. As an expanding middle class demands more energy for appliances, cars, and air conditioners, pollution will increase. The International Energy Agency predicts that between 2000 and 2030 China alone will produce the same amount of greenhouse gas emissions as the rest of the world combined.[58] Another aspect of trade that contributes to environmental degradation is the growing demand for inexpensive food and the view in many developing countries that agricultural development is essential to achieving economic growth. Brazil, for example, continues to clear large areas of the Amazon for soybean cultivation and for cattle ranches. There is a direct connection between the rising global demand for soybeans, especially in China, and deforestation in Brazil.[59]

Diseases and Global Trade

The spread of diseases is as old as human civilization. As people and products cross national boundaries more frequently in an increasingly global society, diseases that were once generally confined to a particular country or region now often spread to many other countries. The speed of international travel and the expansion of free trade make diseases in almost any part of the world an immediate threat to other places, as was made evident in 2002 when a previously unknown deadly respiratory disease, severe acute respiratory syndrome **(SARS)**, emerged in China's Guangdong Province. An American businessman who went to Hanoi contracted this mysterious disease. As the death toll began to climb, the impact of SARS on worldwide trade, especially in the Asia-Pacific region, was immediate and far-reaching. China, Taiwan, and Singapore experienced sharp declines in airline flights as businesspeople and tourists canceled trips. Although China's factories continued production, many workers fled the major cities to return to rural areas where the transmission of SARS was less rapid and devastating. Afraid of contracting the disease, customs officials in Europe and elsewhere delayed entry to ships coming from Asia.[60] Toronto and Vancouver, which have large Asian communities, were also affected. China, worried about the negative impact of

SARS on its economy, downplayed the seriousness of the problem for as long as possi-ble. Another threat, the spread of avian flu (H5N1) would also most likely severely curtail global trade. Although AIDS and many other infectious diseases impede economic development and trade, they are known and are taken into consideration in global trade decisions. But sudden outbreaks of highly contagious infectious diseases, such as SARS, tend to generate widespread fear that undermines business confidence.

Many products purchased at the grocery store are imported. Economic globaliza-tion and global migration help to create global cities that are characterized by great ethnic diversity. Demographic changes in the United States, Canada, Western Europe, and Australia have been accompanied by the proliferation of agricultural products available in grocery stores. At the same time, however, the relentless march toward reducing governments' involvement in the economy has resulted in a smaller number of food inspectors. Furthermore, the globalization of many aspects of the food industry means that there is much mixing of products from different countries, which facilitates the spread of food-related diseases. An outbreak of foot-and-mouth disease in Britain in early 2001 illustrates the impact of diseases on global trade. The United States and Canada quickly banned imports of animals and animal products from the EU.[61] Similarly, an outbreak of bovine spongiform encephalopathy (BSE), commonly known as mad cow disease, in Britain in the same year demonstrates how global trade spreads diseases. The problem was soon discovered in countries that imported British cattle, beef, and animal feed. Because animal feed is globally traded like any other commodity, and mixed in with other feed, it is difficult to identify the source of many food-related diseases. In the case of mad cow disease, Belgium, France, and the Netherlands imported infected animal feed from Britain and shipped it to the Middle East and North Africa. In late December 2003, mad cow disease was discovered on a farm in Washington State. The impact on global markets was immediate. Japan, South Korea, Venezuela, and many other countries banned imports of beef and beef by-products from the United States. Japan's refusal to lift the ban became a major issue for the United States in 2005. Although Japan eventually lifted the ban in late 2005, it decided to reimpose the ban in 2006 due to concerns over the safety of U.S. beef. Japan lifted the ban, once again, later in 2006. On the other hand, Brazil, which has the most beef cattle in the world and is the main competitor of the United States, viewed America's problems as presenting an opportunity for its own beef industry to increase exports. These examples show how globalization creates greater interdependence as well as greater vulnerability to problems that originate in distant places. Rapid transportation, global travel, migration, and the integration of markets increase our risk of being infected with diseases that develop anywhere in the world.

Summary and Review

This chapter focused on the growth of and challenges to global trade, and free trade as a way of increasing each country's economic prosperity. It shows how trade is intricately linked to politics, economics, and culture. In an era of global trade and interdependence, we are seeing the power to formulate trade policies shift away from countries and national sovereignty toward multinational corporations. Accompanying this shift is another: a shift toward increased privatization of national industries and services, and a smaller role for the state in providing social services and social welfare programs. Lower prices provided by companies like Wal-Mart, however, have been accompanied by an increase in corporate reliance on sweatshops that demand employees work long hours for relatively low pay. Such a "race to the bottom," where corporations disregard labor protections and rights in pursuit of the cheapest bottom line, has been a main factor in the backlash against corporate globalization and free trade.

In this chapter we also looked at the history of the globalization of free trade. As global trade became more important, we saw the development of various trade models distinguishing between the benefits of comparative and competitive advantage. In recent years, we have seen a trend toward increased liberalization in the transition toward free trade and global capitalism. In this transition, we witnessed the conflict between protectionist policies and state socialism and increasingly popular notions of free trade and corporate globalization. With the emergence of the Bretton Woods System after World War II, we saw a strengthening of free trade as promoted by such organizations as the World Bank, the IMF, GATT, and most recently, the WTO. Under the WTO, we have seen the growing importance of reducing trade barriers and protecting intellectual property rights as valuable components of global capitalism.

There is widespread debate about the virtues and drawbacks of corporate globalization and global capitalism. This debate is likely to turn to conflict, as it did in the 1999 Seattle WTO protests. Whatever happens in the future, issues relating to free trade and globalization are likely to incite passion and disagreement between supporters and opponents of global capitalism for years to come.

Key Terms

Treaty of Paris of 1763 182
Silk Road 184
mercantilist model 184
auturky 185
comparative advantage 185
competitive advantage 185
strategic trade theory 185
International Monetary Fund (IMF) 186

International Bank for Reconstruction and Development (World Bank) 186
General Agreement on Tariffs and Trade (GATT) 186
Uruguay Round 187
intellectual property rights 187
Doha Agreement 187
mercantilism 188
Group of 8 (G-8) 189
Group of 77 190

trade deficit 191
trade surplus 192
Maastricht Treaty 200
Single European Act 200
Association of Southeast Asian Nations (ASEAN) 201
Asia-Pacific Economic Cooperation (APEC) 202
Pacific Economic Cooperation Council (PECC) 202

South American Common Market (Mercosur) 203
Program for Integration and Economic Cooperation (PIEC) 203
Free Trade Area of the Americas (FTAA) 203
import surges 205
dumping 205
common agricultural policy (CAP) 207

Discussion Questions

1. What exactly is the mercantilist model?
2. What is the difference between comparative advantage and competitive advantage?
3. Can you distinguish between the global roles of the IMF and the World Bank?
4. What are the premises and principles of GATT addressed in this chapter?
5. What are intellectual property rights? Do intellectual property rights potentially violate principles of free trade? Please explain.
6. What is fair-trade coffee? What are the benefits of buying fair-trade coffee?
7. Do you think regional trade agreements, such as NAFTA and the FTAA, are more beneficial or harmful in the long term? Please explain.
8. What are some of the objectives behind the European common agricultural policy?
9. What factors discussed in this chapter have helped environmental issues become a concern in global trade?
10. Can you briefly explain why many European countries decided to stop importing American beef?

Suggested Readings

Aaronson, Susan. *Taking Trade to the Streets*. Ann Arbor: University of Michigan Press, 2001.

Barton, John, et al., *The Evolution of the Trade Regime*. Princeton: Princeton University Press, 2006.

Bhagwati, Jagdish. *The Wind of the Hundred Days: How Washington Mismanaged Globalization*. Cambridge, MA: MIT Press, 2001.

Elliott, Kimberly. *Delivering on Doha: Farm Trade and the Poor*. Washington, DC: Institute for International Economics, 2006.

Gilpin, Robert. *The Challenge of Global Capitalism*. Princeton: Princeton University Press, 2000.

Ingco, Merlinda D., and John D. Nash. *Agriculture and the WTO*. New York: Oxford University Press, 2003.

Klein, Naomi. *No Logo: Taking Aim at the Brand Bullies*. Toronto: Knopf Canada, 2000.

Krumm, Kathie, and Homi Kharas. *East Asia Integrates*. New York: Oxford University Press, 2004.

Little, Daniel. *The Paradox of Wealth and Poverty*. Boulder, CO: Westview Press, 2003.

Lofdahl, Corey L. *Environmental Impacts of Globalization and Trade*. Cambridge, MA: MIT Press, 2002.

Rosen, Ellen. *Making Sweatshops: The Globalization of the U.S. Apparel Industry*. Berkeley: University of California Press, 2002.

Tonelson, Alan. *The Race to the Bottom*. Boulder, CO: Westview Press, 2002.

Addresses and Websites

United Nations Conference on Trade and Development
UNCTAD Press Office
Palais des Nations
1211 Geneva 10
Switzerland
Tel.: 4122–907–5828
Email: press@unctad.org
www.unctad.org

The UNCTAD is the main UN body that deals with trade, development, and investment. Its goal is to assist nations in reaching their potential on these topics. This website offers information on current and past meetings, technical cooperation, publications, and related sites. It provides links to other UN offices, as well as economic commission information on the different regions.

World Trade Organization
Rue de Lausanne 154
CH 1211 Geneva 21
Switzerland
www.wto.org

The World Trade Organization is the only international organization that deals with trade between nations. It helps producers, importers, and exporters to trade their goods. Its goal is to maintain peaceful trade relations among nations, as well as to break down barriers between nations to help them develop. The website offers statistics, databases on issues such as trade law, and economic research.

International Confederation of Free Trade Unions
ICFTU/ITS Washington Office
1925 K St. NW, No. 425
Washington, D.C. 20006
Tel.: (202) 463–8573
Fax: (202) 463–8564
Email: pbakvis@earthlink.net

Contact: Mr. Peter Bakvis
www.icftu.org

This website is home to the International Confederation of Free Trade Unions. It offers a varied and detailed webpage on every issue relating to trade unions, as well as up-to-date news stories and links to other sites.

The European Union
Europa
www.eu.org

Europa is the portal site of the European Union (http://europa.eu.int/). It provides up-to-date coverage of EU affairs and essential information on European integration. Users can also consult all legislation currently in force or under discussion, access the websites of each of the EU institutions, and find out about the policies administered by the EU under the powers devolved to it by the treaties. This website is available in a variety of languages.

Endnotes

1. Richard Devetak and Richard Higgott, "Justice Unbound? Globalization, States, and the Transformation of the Social Bond," *International Affairs* 99, No. 3 (July 1999), 486.
2. Lester Thurow, "Globalization: The Product of a Knowledge-Based Economy," *Annals of the American Academy of Political and Social Science* 542 (July 2000), 20.
3. Kenichi Ohmae, "The Rise of the Region State," *Foreign Affairs* 72, No. 2 (Spring 1993), 78.
4. Ohmae, "The Rise of the Region State," 78.
5. Louis Uchitelle, "Globalization Marches On, As U.S. Eases Up on the Reins," *New York Times*, 17 December 2001, C12.
6. Robert Gilpin, *The Challenge of Global Capitalism* (Princeton: Princeton University Press, 2000), 95.
7. Gilpin, *The Challenge*, 96.
8. Thomas D. Lairson and David Skidmore, *International Political Economy* (Forth Worth, TX: Holt, Rinehart, and Winston, 1993), 57.
9. Peter Morici, "Export Our Way to Prosperity," *Foreign Policy* 101 (Winter 1995–1996), 12.
10. Celia W. Dugger, "A Catch-22 on Drugs for the World's Poor," *New York Times*, 16 November, W1.
11. Lairson and Skidmore, *International Political Economy*, 24.
12. Edmund L. Andrews, "Cheapening the Dollar," *New York Times* 9 February 2004, A5; and Martin Feldstein, "The Return to Savings," *Foreign Affairs* 85, No. 3 (May/June 2006), 90–91.
13. W. Raymond Duncan, et al., *World Politics in the 21st Century* (New York: Longman, 2002), 501; and Gilpin, *The Challenge*, 92.
14. David Gonzalez, "Cuba Receives U.S. Shipment, First Purchase Since Embargo," *New York Times*, 17 December 2001, A10.
15. David E. Sanger, "A Grand Trade Bargain," *Foreign Affairs* 80, No. 1 (January/February 2001), 69.
16. Chris Kraul, "Thai Pineapples Threaten Mexico Farmers' Livelihood," *Chicago Tribune*, 16 September 2001, Sect. 5, 6.
17. Jon Jeter, "The Price of Open Markets," *Washington Post National Weekly Edition*, 29 April–5 May 2002, 17.
18. Ron Scherer and Patrik Jonsson, "Beginning China Trade Rankles U.S.," *Christian Science Monitor*, 5 August 2003, 1.
19. Floyd Norris, "Europe's Trade Gap with China: Behind U.S. but Catching Up," *New York Times*, 29 April 2006, B3.
20. Elizabeth Becker, "U.S. Trade Deficit Reaches a Record $489.4 Billion, "*New York Times*, 14 February 2004, B5.
21. Nicholas R. Lardy, "Sweet and Sour Deal," *Foreign Policy* 129 (March/April 2002), 21.
22. Joseph Quinlan and Marc Chandler, "The U.S. Trade Deficit: A Dangerous Obsession," *Foreign Affairs* 80, No. 3 (May/June 2001), 87–97.

23. Quinlan and Chandler, "The U.S. Trade Deficit," 97.

24. Alessandro Bonanno and Douglas Constance, *Caught in the Net: The Global Tuna Industry, Environmentalism, and the State* (Lawrence: University Press of Kansas, 1996), 3–4.

25. James L. Watson, "Introduction," in *Golden Arches East*, James L. Watson, ed. (Stanford: Stanford University Press, 1997), 19.

26. Don Phillips, "The Modern Merchant Mariner," *Washington Post National Weekly Edition*, 3–9 September 2001, 18.

27. Tim Weiner, "Low-Wage Costa Ricans Make Baseballs for Millionaires," *New York Times*, 25 January 2004, A3.

28. Robert J. S. Ross and Anita Chan, "From North-South to South-South," *Foreign Affairs* 81, No. 5 (September/October 2002), 8; and Daniel W. Drezner, "Bottom Feeders," *Foreign Policy* 121 (November/December 2000), 64.

29. Clay Chandler, "Workers of the World," *Washington Post National Weekly Edition*, 10–16 December 2001, 17.

30. Kathleen Newland, "Workers of the World, Now What?" *Foreign Policy* 114 (Spring 1999), 53.

31. Wayne Arnold, "Translating Union Into Khmer," *New York Times*, 12 July 2001, C1.

32. Jay Mazur, "Labor's New Internationalism," *Foreign Affairs* 79, No. 1 (January/February 2000), 86.

33. Steven Greenhouse, "A Union Wins the Global Game," *New York Times*, 6 October 2002, Sect. 4, 1.

34. May T. Yeung, et al., *Regional Trading Blocs in the Global Economy* (Cheltenham, UK: Edward Elgar, 1999), 3–5.

35. Yeung, et al., *Regional Trading*, 18–19.

36. Gilpin, *The Challenge*, 195.

37. Elaine Sciolino, "Seeking Unity, Europe Drafts a Constitution," *New York Times*, 15 June 2003, A1.

38. Gustavo Vega-Canovas, "NAFTA and the EU: Toward Convergence?" in *Regional Trading Blocks in the Global Economy*, 230.

39. Lloyd Gruber, *Ruling the World: Power Politics and the Rise of Supranational Institutions* (Princeton: Princeton University Press, 2000), 96.

40. Andrew Mack and John Ravenhill, *Pacific Cooperation* (Boulder, CO: Westview Press, 1995), 3.

41. Jane Perlez, "Southeast Asian Nations Meet to Tighten Economic Bonds," *New York Times*, 6 October 2003, A4.

42. Frank B. Gibney, "Creating a Pacific Community," *Foreign Affairs* 72, No. 5 (November/December 1993), 22.

43. Lia Valls Pereira, "Toward the Common Market of the South," in *Mercosur: Regional Integration, World Markets*, ed. Riordan Roett (Boulder, CO: Lynne Rienner, 1999), 9.

44. Larry Rohter, "South American Trade Bloc Under Siege," *New York Times*, 24 March 2001, B2.

45. Craig S. Smith, "China Finds Way to Beat Chip Limits," *New York Times*, 6 May 2002, C4.

46. William Drozdiak, "Protectionism in a Golden Age," *Washington Post National Weekly Edition*, 21–27 May 2001, 17.

47. Elizabeth Becker, "U.S. Tariffs on Steel Are Illegal, World Trade Organization Says," *New York Times*, 11 November 2001, A1.

48. Anthony DePalma, "U.S. and Europeans Agree on Deal to End Banana Trade War," *New York Times*, 12 April 2001, C1.

49. Keith Bradsner, "China Protests U.S. Limit on Textiles," *New York Times*, 20 November 2003, A1.

50. Michael Dobbs, "The Price of Global Reforms," *Washington Post National Weekly Edition*, 23 April–1 May 2002, 8.

51. John S. Marsh and Pamela J. Swanney, "The Common Agricultural Policy," in *Institutions and Policies of the European Community*, ed. Juliet Lodge (New York: St. Martin's Press, 1983), 57.

52. Robert Samuelson, "Paying Off America's Farmers," *Chicago Tribune*, 10 May 2002, Sect. 1, 13.

53. Edmund L. Andrews, "Europe Refuses to Drop Ban on Hormone-Fed U.S. Beef," *New York Times*, 25 May 2000, C4.

54. Robert Paarlbert, "The Global Food Fight," *Foreign Affairs* 79, No. 3 (May/June 2000), 26.

55. Lizette Alvarez, "Consumers in Europe Resist Gene-Altered Foods," *New York Times*, 11 February 2003, A3.

56. Elizabeth Dowdeswell and Steven Charnovitz, "Globalization, Trade, and Interdependence," in *Thinking Ecologically*, ed. Marian R. Chertow and Daniel C. Esty (New Haven: Yale University Press, 1997), 92.

57. Steven Greenhouse, "Suit Seeks to Halt Bush Plan on Entry of Mexican Trucks," *New York Times*, 2 May 2002, A19.

58. Keith Bradsher, "China's Boom Adds to Global Warming Problem," *New York Times*, 22 October 2003, A1.

59. Larry Rohter, "Relentless Foe of the Amazon Jungle: Soybeans," *New York Times*, 21 2003, A1.

60. Keith Bradsher, "Economies Sickened by a Virus, and Fear," *New York Times*, 21 April 2003, A1.

61. Christopher Marquis, "Meat From Europe Is Banned as Illness Spreads," *New York Times* 14 March 2001, A1.

CHAPTER 7

Global Inequality

INTRODUCTION

Discussions about wealth and poverty and how to achieve greater equality are as old as human society. They demonstrate a perennial concern about the implications of inequality for the security and well-being of communities. Given the persistence of inequality among individuals, groups, and nations over centuries, this debate is interminable. Struggles to achieve equality are also endless. Issues pertaining to global inequality permeate almost every significant global problem, from trade to the environment, from terrorism and criminal activities to democratization and human rights, and from ethnic conflicts to the proliferation of weapons of mass destruction. Consequently, as our discussion shows, inequality is closely connected to politics, economics, and culture.

This chapter examines the controversial issue of global and domestic inequalities. One temptation that students encounter in studying this problem is trying to find a dominant cause for such economic disparities. Similar to other global issues, inequality is the result of a combination of complex causes, many of which cannot be measured accurately. For example, many scholars argue that colonialism and its legacies contribute to the growing gap between rich and poor countries. However, several countries that were colonized in Asia and Latin America are much better off than most countries in Africa. While some causes of inequality are comparatively concrete, many are nebulous. For example, values and attitudes are extremely important in determining success in life. Ways of thinking have direct and far-reaching consequences for the global distribution of wealth. But we also know that location and social, economic, and political connections are crucial determinants of success. Although the centrality of the human spirit and will to succeed are widely recognized as factors that contribute to achieving economic prosperity, we have seen in Chapter 2 how widespread fears and resentment of the pursuit of wealth and knowledge threatened conservative religious, political, and economic elites in Europe, China, and the Muslim world.

A central question addressed in this chapter is whether inequality matters. Human societies are inherently unequal due to variations of abilities, opportunities, geographic location, luck, personal characteristics, and so on. Empirical evidence shows that inequality is a constant feature of human societies. But why is it important to address issues of inequality, something that societies have struggled with historically? Globalization is widely perceived as the major cause of global inequality. Yet, as we have noted, unequal distributions of wealth existed independent of the current wave of globalization and are present in societies little affected by it. This chapter analyzes the globalization and inequality debate, and the current state of global inequality. In addition to focusing on inequality between rich and poor countries and inequality within both developed and developing societies, we will examine the issue of gender inequality. Finally, this chapter discusses the enduring issues of global poverty, hunger, and malnutrition and concludes with an analysis of various efforts to close the gap between rich and poor and reduce the negative effects of global and domestic inequality.

DOES INEQUALITY MATTER?

The existence of inequality is not automatically a major problem, especially when the economy is growing and there are many opportunities for upward mobility. As long as the standard of living is improving for those on the bottom of the economic ladder, concerns about inequality tend to diminish. The last two decades of the twentieth century were characterized by a widening gap between rich and poor and the proliferation of millionaires and billionaires. While economic disparities remained a serious problem in developing countries, the forces of globalization created conditions that helped widen the gap between rich and poor in industrialized societies. When the economy deteriorates, the gap between the rich and poor tends to be narrower but concerns about inequality are heightened. As the *Economist* pointed out, "In bad economic times, the rich may lose the most money but the poor lose their jobs, their houses, and even their families."[1] The perception that economic inequality is essentially transitory when opportunities for economic advancement are widely available mitigates negative effects of actual inequality. However, persistent inequality and enduring poverty challenge beliefs in the equality of opportunity and the possibility of upward mobility. Eventually, the legitimacy of the economic system and political and social institutions are challenged. The legitimacy of the global economic system is likely to be strengthened if a larger number of countries and individuals are benefiting from it. Extreme inequality perpetuates poverty and the concentration of economic and political power and reduces economic efficiency. It strengthens inequality-perpetuating institutions in *three ways*:

1. Inequality discourages the political participation of poor people, which, in turn, diminishes their access to education, health care, and other services that contribute to economic growth and development.
2. Inequality often prevents the building and proper functioning of impartial institutions and observance of the rule of law.
3. Inequality enables the wealthy to refuse to compromise politically or economically, which further weakens poor societies in a global society that requires relatively fast responses to economic developments.[2]

These consequences of inequality combine to ensure that poor societies will remain poor and unequal, trapping most of their inhabitants in a destructive cycle of poverty. Growing inequality among as well as within nations has direct and indirect implications for globalization. Inequality could undermine globalization by influencing countries to adopt protectionist policies and disengage, to the extent possible, from the global economy. But the ramifications extend beyond economic issues to problems such as terrorism, the environment, and the spread of infectious diseases. As Joseph S. Nye observed, "It would be ironic if current protests curtailed the positive aspects of globalization while leaving the negative dimensions untouched."[3]

As Chapter 4 shows, the democratization process and the effective functioning of consolidated democracy depend largely on a significant degree of economic and social equality. The legitimacy of any democratic system is contingent upon the voters' belief that they have a vested interest in its preservation. Their allegiance to the democracy is influenced partly by the benefits they derive from the economic system. The unequal distribution of wealth is often mitigated by government redistributive policies. Extreme inequality sometimes results in the voters pressuring governments to enact trade protection legislation to safeguard their employment and livelihoods. In this case, voters exercising their democratic rights could inadvertently undermine the economic system that supports democracy. The erosion of democracy also has implications for national, regional, and global security. Although democracies are not always peaceful, they are less likely than nondemocratic societies to engage in conflicts.

Given the increasing levels of globalization, global and domestic inequalities often directly affect many areas. The 2001 terrorist attacks in the United States were widely linked to poverty within developing nations, especially Afghanistan. Huge inequalities often fuel resentment, which finds expression in global crime and a general disregard for the rules and norms of global society. Those who are extremely poor are often excluded from participation in decisions that negatively impact their lives. Lacking democratic means of expression, they become vulnerable to being influenced by radical minorities who are committed to violent change. An increasingly interdependent world is characterized by porous borders that cannot effectively impede the transmission of the infectious diseases that accompany poverty. Poverty contributes to global and regional problems by fueling ethnic and regional conflicts, creating large numbers of refugees, and inhibiting access to resources, such as petroleum. Finally, global and domestic inequality is perceived as stimulating the global drug trade. For example, poor farmers in Bolivia regard the cultivation of coca as essential to their survival. In 2006, Evo Morales, a former coca farmer, a socialist protest leader, and an Indian, became Bolivia's first indigenous president. More than three-quarters of the heroin sold in Europe is refined from opium grown in Afghanistan by poor farmers whose survival and that of their families depends on the cultivation of poppies. The costs of fighting the war against drugs in poor countries, such as Colombia and Afghanistan, are extremely high. Global criminal activities, including terrorism, are often intertwined with the production and global distribution of drugs. In many significant ways, inequality matters in an increasingly global society.

THE GLOBALIZATION AND INEQUALITY DEBATE

Throughout the world, from meetings of the World Trade Organization (WTO) to discussions in classrooms, the impact of globalization on income distribution and living standards is a controversial topic. Studies by the World Bank, the United Nations

(UN), and other international organizations also concentrate on this issue. Various analyses by academics and nongovernmental organizations (NGOs) are similarly divided into contending camps about the effects of globalization on wealth and poverty. Such preoccupation with globalization to the exclusion of other factors often muddles the debate about globalization and inequality. Would less globalization produce more equality and would more equality among and within nations result in an improved quality of life for the poor? There are two dominant, but sometimes overlapping, viewpoints on this issue. The **globalists** argue that globalization has increased economic growth and decreased global inequality and poverty. The **antiglobalists** generally perceive globalization as a negative and destructive force that is responsible for the increasing global inequality and poverty and the declining levels of human welfare.[4]

Globalists Make Their Case

From the globalists' perspective, the basic cause of inequality and poverty is the relatively low level of globalization in some countries. In other words, the poorest societies are the least integrated into the global economy and the richest countries are the most integrated into it. Openness to foreign trade, investments, and technology—combined with such reforms as privatization of the domestic economy—will ultimately accelerate economic growth. **The Organization for Economic Cooperation and Development (OECD)** calculated that countries that are relatively open to trade grew about twice as fast as those that are relatively closed to trade.[5] China's rapid economic growth is an obvious example. But Ireland is also a country that became relatively prosperous due to its participation in the global economy, particularly in the European Union (EU). In 1985, significant poverty in Ireland was, in many ways, comparable to poverty in the developing world. Ireland today is one of the wealthiest and most globalized countries. Spain, Portugal, South Korea, Taiwan, and India are other beneficiaries of globalization. On the other hand, North Korea, Myanmar (formerly Burma), and Kenya are on the margins of globalization and remain impoverished.

OECD
Organization focusing on global economic development

Globalists also argue that globalization has contributed to the decline of inequality. Furthermore, poverty can be reduced even as inequality increases. David Dollar and Aart Kraay found that "a long-term global trend toward greater inequality prevailed for at least 200 years; it peaked around 1975. But since then, it has stabilized and possibly even reversed."[6] The accelerated economic growth of China and India, the world's two most populous countries, which is seen as directly linked to globalization, is given as the principal reason for the change. Much of the inequality that persists within countries is due less to globalization and more to policies dealing with education, taxation, and social problems. Moreover, more inequality in China, for example, has been accompanied by a spectacular reduction in poverty.[7]

Globalists emphasize that the number of people moving out of poverty has increased. The World Bank calculated that 800 million people abandoned the ranks of absolute poverty in the last decade of the twentieth century. The number of people living on less than one U.S. dollar a day remains high—around 1.2 billion. But given rapid population growth rates in the poorest countries, the decline in global poverty is impressive. The world's poor are seen as getting to be less poor in both absolute and relative terms. The more globalized poor nations become, the better off their populations are in both absolute and relative terms.[8] Globalization has generally helped the poor by contributing to reductions in the cost of numerous consumer products. Wal-Mart, for example, is so competitive and growing so fast that it is forcing other companies to reduce their prices. Lower labor costs, increased global competition for markets, low transportation costs, the overproduction of goods, and less government regulation of economies have benefited the poor. Less money has higher purchasing power in a globalized economy. Finally, by facilitating migration, establishing small businesses that rely on the Internet, and improving access to jobs in telecommunications and computer technologies in countries like India and China, globalization improves the quality of life for the poor. Migration, for example, is a major factor in the development of Mexico, as remittances from migrants account for that country's second largest source of income. Overall, from the globalists' perspective, globalization is a positive force that improves people's lives.

Antiglobalists Make Their Case

Antiglobalists believe that globalization is widening the gap between the haves and the have-nots. Concerned with making global capitalism more equitable, they view globalization as primarily benefiting the rich while making life more difficult for the poor. Unlike the globalists, who tend to view globalization as a *win-win* phenomenon, antiglobalists argue that globalization is a *zero-sum* game, meaning that the rich are winning at the expense of the poor. Contrary to the globalists, who believe that all countries participating in global markets are better off than nonparticipants, antiglobalists argue that globalization benefits rich countries, such as the United States. China is one of the few developing countries that is generally regarded as profiting from free trade and open markets. The United States, the locomotive of globalization, benefits the most from open markets worldwide. **George Soros**—a leading financier, philanthropist, and critic of globalization, though not an antiglobalist—believes that globalization drains surplus capital from periphery or developing countries to the United States, thereby allowing Americans to spend more than they save and import more than they export.[9] Similarly, Jack Beatty contends that the foundation of inequality resulting from globalization is that rich countries do not play by the rules that they made to govern the global economic system. Basically, the United States and other Western countries require developing countries to open their markets without reciprocating commensurably. To support this argument, Beatty points out that although global rules on trade discourage governments from subsidizing industries, rich countries continue to provide more than $245 billion in subsidies to agriculture. He calculates that developing countries lose about $100 billion a year due to Western countries' export subsidies and trade barriers.[10]

George Soros

Leading financier, philanthropist, and critic of corporate globalization

Critics also argue that globalization is like an "economic temptress," promising riches but not delivering.[11] Global communications have heightened awareness of the vast disparities between rich and poor within the same society and especially between rich and poor countries. Simultaneously, global communications spawn aspirations of escaping poverty and enjoying the good life. Unfortunately, globalization is unable to make these dreams real. Countries integrated into the global economic system are the most severely affected by downturns in the economy. For example, Southeast Asia, which depends on exports of steel, textiles, and electronic components, suffers significantly in global economic crises and is unable to generate enough jobs and sufficient wages for a population with aspirations nurtured by television programs that depict prosperity.[12] A sluggish global economy depresses demand for luxury items, such as diamonds, thereby causing countries that depend primarily on diamond exports, such as Botswana, to be negatively affected. While conceding that globalization is not entirely responsible for global poverty, antiglobalists generally view globalization as a tide that lifts a few boats while leaving the majority mired to the bottom. For example, 50 percent of Mexico's population lived in poverty in 1980; today 50 percent of all Mexicans are still in poverty. Even when global companies create jobs within societies, the race to the bottom in labor standards and wages inevitably results in the poor in developing countries being unable to escape poverty while, at the same time, reducing the wages for workers in rich countries or depriving them of employment.

Antiglobalists contend that globalization compounds existing inequalities and creates more inequality. By giving priority to privatization, globalization weakens governments' commitment to the public sector.[13] As Vito Tanzi states, "Even as the forces of globalization boost the demand for strong social safety nets to protect the poor, these forces also erode the ability of governments to finance and implement large-scale social welfare policies."[14] Instead of really improving the lives of poor people, the emphasis on integrating poor nations into the global economy diverts resources from more urgent development needs, such as education, public health, industrial capacity, and social cohesion. Many trade agreements impose tight prerequisites on developing countries in exchange for crumbs of enhanced market access. The **African Growth and Opportunity Act,** signed by U.S. President Clinton in May 2000, is an example. It provides increased access to the U.S. market only if African apparel manufacturers use fabric and yarns produced in the United States, instead of using their own or supplies from less expensive sources. In other words, the antiglobalists perceive globalization as perpetuating inequality by impeding development.[15] Furthermore, they argue, countries, such as South Korea and Taiwan, frequently held up as models for the benefits of globalization by the globalists, developed under radically different conditions. These countries were not required to pay the costs that are now an integral component of integration into global markets. During the 1960s and 1970s when they were rapidly growing, Taiwan and South Korea did not face contemporary globalization's pressures to privatize their economies and open their borders to capital flows. The demands of globalization undermine efforts essential for a comprehensive development agenda.[16]

African Growth and Opportunity Act

Trade agreement to strengthen apparel trade between the U.S. and African states

TABLE 7.2 HEALTH INEQUALITIES

Country	Physicians (per 100,000 people) 1990–2003	Life Expectancy at Birth (years) 2000	2002	Under Age 5 Mortality Rate (per 1,000 live births) 2000	2002
High Human Development					
Norway	367	79	78.9	5	4
Sweden	287	80	80.0	4	3
Canada	187	79	79.3	7	7
United States	**279**	**77**	**77.0**	**9**	**8**
Netherlands	328	78	78.3	7	5
Japan	202	81	81.5	5	5
France	330	79	78.9	6	4
United Kingdom	164	77	78.1	7	7
Germany	363	77	78.2	6	4
Italy	607	79	78.7	7	6
Spain	329	78	79.2	6	6
Israel	375	78	79.1	7	6
Greece	438	78	78.2	8	5
Medium Human Development					
Mexico	156	73	73.3	36	29
Cuba	596	76	76.2	9	9
Russian Federation	420	65	66.7	19	21
Colombia	94	72	72.1	23	23
Venezuela	200	73	73.6	24	22
Thailand	30	69	69.1	33	28
Saudi Arabia	153	73	72.1	23	28
Brazil	206	68	68.0	39	36
Philippines	115	69	69.8	39	38
Turkey	123	70	70.1	43	42
Jamaica	85	79	75.6	7	20
India	51	63	63.7	88	93
Low Human Development					
Pakistan	68	63	60.8	110	107
Sudan	16	55	55.5	108	94
Bangladesh	23	61	61.1	83	77
Haiti	25	53	49.4	111	123
Nigeria	27	47	51.6	153	183
Chad	3	48	44.7	188	200

Sources: World Bank, *World Development Report 2003* (Washington, DC: The World Bank, 2003), 234–235; and United Nations Development Program, *Human Development Report 2004* (New York: Oxford University Press, 2004), 139–142; 156–159.

combined with the structures of partnership law, kept Middle Eastern enterprises small. That, in turn, limited the pressure to evolve new economic forms."[20]

A final factor undergirding Europe's economic success and setting the foundation for global inequality is the *separation of the secular from the religious*. Whereas Islam became inseparable from the state, the origins of Christianity and its spread to Rome forced it to compromise with secular authority, a compromise encapsulated in the warning that Christians should give to Caesar what belongs to him and give God what is God's. However, Muslim societies prospered when religion was less restrictive. Muslims, commanded by the Koran to seek knowledge, became leading scientists, physicians, artists, mathematicians, philosophers, architects, and builders. For more than five hundred years, Arabic was the language of scholars and scientists. The Muslims transmitted Chinese scientific inventions, Greek and Persian texts, and their own impressive scientific discoveries and inventions to Europe. From the tenth to the thirteenth centuries, Europeans translated Arabic works into Hebrew and Latin, thereby giving impetus to a rebirth of learning that ultimately transformed Western civilization.[21]

Inequality Between Developed and Developing Countries

Despite rising living standards throughout most of the world in the last century, the gap between rich and poor countries has steadily widened. Historic trends suggest that most of the richest countries will maintain their lead over most of the poorest countries. The gap between the richest country and the poorest country was 3 to 1 in 1820, 11 to 1 in 1913, 35 to 1 in 1950, 44 to 1 in 1973, and 72 to 1 in 1992. By the end of the twentieth century, the richest 20 percent of the world's population had 86 times as much income as the poorest 20 percent. At the beginning of the twenty-first century, the average income in the richest 20 countries was 37 times that in the poorest 20 countries.[22] As Table 7.1 indicates, income disparities between developed and developing countries are very wide. To illustrate this disparity, let us imagine that John Cook lived in Britain in 1820 and Taye Selassie now lives in Ethiopia. Cook's income in 1820 would be roughly six times that of Selassie today, more than 185 years later. Despite rising incomes in most developing countries, the gap between rich and poor countries is likely to remain. Economic development, while dramatically improving the standard of living in most countries, has not significantly closed the gap because of differential growth rates between rich and poor countries. Rich countries have experienced higher economic growth rates than poor countries. Furthermore, per capita income actually declined in more than 100 of the world's poorest countries, many of them in Africa. Even developing countries that have enjoyed unprecedented economic growth, such as China and India, have failed to close the gap between themselves and rich countries. It is estimated that it would take China and India a hundred years of constant growth rates higher than those now experienced by industrialized countries just to reach current American income levels.[23] However, given the extraordinarily high standard of living in the United States, both China and India would be relatively prosperous if they achieved half the income level of Americans. Furthermore, globalization is profoundly altering many old assumptions. Because the income gap between rich and poor countries has widened historically, it does not necessarily follow that this will always be the case. Singapore and Kuwait, two high-income countries, illustrate that poor countries can become prosperous by implementing astute political, social, and economic policies (in the case of Singapore) or by having valuable natural resources (in the case of Kuwait). Economic disparities between the developed and the developing world have

Global Digital Divide

Contrast between those who have and those who don't have access to the Internet and other forms of digital communication

focused on the **global digital divide**. But access to the Internet and improved telecommunications are not automatic panaceas for solving the problems of developing societies.

Causes of Inequality Between Rich and Poor Countries

In this section we will briefly discuss some causes of the widening gap between rich and poor countries. It is important to remember that *several factors combine to contribute to inequality*: (1) geography, (2) colonialism and its legacies, (3) the structure of the global economy, (4) population growth, (5) government policies, (6) political instability, and (7) natural disasters.

Intergovernmental Organizations

Organizations that are composed of different national governments

Geography For more than fifty years, various **intergovernmental organizations**—such as the UN, the World Bank, the Conference on Trade and Development, regional development banks, and NGOs—have focused on closing the gap between developed and developing countries. Nevertheless, as we have seen, the gap persists and is widening. Countries that are poor, some argue, have certain geographic characteristics that contribute to their economic problems. For example, they are in tropical regions or face high transportation costs in accessing global markets because of their location. Apart from the prevalence of tropical diseases, which have been controlled to a large extent by modern medicines and practices, countries in the Southern Hemisphere also tend to suffer from being landlocked. Countries with extensive coastlines and good harbors tend to be better off economically than landlocked countries that lack the physical **infrastructure** (i.e., a system of roads and railroads) essential for gaining access to navigable rivers and the sea. Landlocked countries or countries located far from global markets are disadvantaged by high transportation costs.[24]

Infrastructure

Essential systems, such as education, roads, and hospitals, needed by nation-states in order to provide necessary public services

Colonialism Many argue that European colonization of Africa, Asia, and Latin America laid the foundation for economic disparities between rich and poor nations. Inequality breeds inequality. Just as wealth tends to perpetuate wealth, poverty tends to perpetuate poverty. Countries that grew rich two hundred years ago, partly because of their colonization of the developing world, are generally still rich today. European groups that migrated to Australia, Canada, the United States, South Africa, New Zealand, and throughout Latin America continue to enjoy significant advantages over indigenous populations. However, it is also argued that colonization is not the main reason for ongoing global inequality. In fact, colonization had many positive effects on Africa, Asia, and Latin America. It produced an educated elite in India, for example. Colonialism also brought modern medicines, contributed to the development of an infrastructure, and nurtured economic and cultural links to industrialized countries. Furthermore, some states, such as Singapore, South Korea, and Taiwan, that were colonized are now relatively rich.

Structure of the Global Economy Colonialism and historical experiences, as well as contemporary economic practices, are widely perceived as creating an unfair global economy that keeps poor countries poor and rich countries rich. The Scottish economist **Adam Smith**, who wrote *An Inquiry Into the Nature and Causes of the Wealth of*

Nations, believed that governments should not interfere with the functioning of markets and that business persons would be led by an invisible hand to do the best for society. However, many leaders of poor countries argue that governments and multinational corporations in rich countries cooperate to maintain an unfair global economy. They generally subscribe to the **dependency theory**, which holds that poor countries' reliance on exports of primary commodities, many of which were started during colonization for the benefit of Europeans, puts them at a severe economic disadvantage. The prices obtained from their exports decline relative to the prices of manufactured imports from industrialized countries. For example, Botswana depends on diamonds for almost 80 percent of its revenues; Nigeria receives 90 percent of its income from petroleum; and El Salvador relies on coffee exports for more than half of its revenues. Economic globalization blurs distinctions between domestic and global economies and makes national borders more porous and less significant. For example, global companies manufacture products in poor countries, such as China, Mexico, and India, thereby exporting jobs from rich countries. By intensifying competition among as well as within states, globalization helps engender economic success or failure for groups in both rich and poor countries. But to compete effectively, as we have discussed earlier, governments adopt policies that lead to greater inequality within their societies. Open markets often operate to disadvantage poor countries while benefiting rich states.

Adam Smith
Scottish economist and historic proponent of the capitalist system

Dependency Theory
Concept that poor countries' over-reliance on exports puts them at an economic disadvantage

Population Growth Rapid population growth in most developing countries plays a central role in perpetuating the economic chasm between rich and poor countries. Population growth decreased in the industrialized countries as the economic gap was widening. Since 1950, the population in rich countries grew by about 50 percent. In sharp contrast, the population grew by 250 percent in poor countries. Despite the devastating impact of HIV and AIDS on developing states, poor countries continue to experience high population growth rates. Large families, often perceived as a form of social security for parents, perpetuate poverty in most cases. Children are usually malnourished and unable to learn even if they have access to education because hunger destroys brain cells and retards development. Forced to seek menial employment to support the family, children fail to acquire the skills essential to escaping poverty. Their own children are likely to face similar circumstances, thus ensuring the continuation of poverty. Lester C. Thurow argues that "people who are poor in poor countries with rapid rates of population growth are going to die in poor countries. Whatever one believes about the world's ability to provide enough food, huge income gaps will emerge not just with the first world but within those parts of the third world that have their populations under control and those that do not."[23]

Government Policies Discussing causes of poverty in the Arab world, Alan Schwartz observed that many of these countries are poor because of the policies they pursue. For example, Saudi Arabia tolerates monopolies that help to sustain an elite clan that all too often opposes technological, economic, and social change. Many Arab countries use import duties to discourage trade and impede the flow of investment by disregarding the rule of law. Furthermore, many of these governments emphasize religion instead of science and technology and therefore do not adequately develop human capital. Perhaps the most serious policy failure is the lack of adequate investment in women's education and opposition to allowing women to have equal employment opportunities.[26] When Korea was divided in 1948, South Korea adopted capitalist policies that fostered economic success, while North Korea isolated itself from the global community and adopted a communist system of government. Today, South Korea is prosperous and North Korea routinely faces starvation. The People's Republic of China, India, Malaysia, and Singapore, for example, implemented policies that have a positive impact on their economies. Latin America, on the other hand, allocates resources disproportionately to the wealthy. The poor there remain trapped in the cycle of poverty.[27]

Political Instability Angola, a country twice the size of Texas, has abundant supplies of petroleum, diamonds, fish, and fresh water. However, life expectancy there is 45 years, infant mortality is among the highest in the world, and Angolans are extremely poor. For twenty-seven years, the country was devastated by ethnic conflicts. Political instability directly contributes to economic disparities between developed and developing countries. When rich countries engage in conflicts, they usually fight in poor countries, thereby avoiding many of the costs of war. Even though stability is not always conducive to development, as we have seen in North Korea and many nondemocratic societies, countries torn apart by civil war have little hope of escaping poverty. Conflict not only discourages foreign investment, it also influences the best educated, most talented, and most financially successful citizens to flee or to

Earthquake survivors in Pakistan.

invest their money outside the country. Instability clearly reinforces the vicious cycle of poverty and widens the economic gap between rich and poor countries.

Natural Disasters At the beginning of this section we discussed how geographic location directly affects the wealth and poverty of countries. Drought, earthquakes, volcanic eruptions, hurricanes, and other natural disasters are closely linked to geography. The tsunamis that caused widespread destruction in Asia in late 2004 and in July 2006, hurricanes Katrina and Rita in the United States in 2005, and the earthquake in Pakistan in 2005 are the most obvious examples. These natural disasters routinely destroy important economic sectors, increase severe infrastructure problems, force the relocation of a large number of people, and lead to greater impoverishment. It generally seems that the poorest countries are also the most severely affected by natural disasters. This is partly due to poor planning by governments and the settlement of vulnerable areas. The cyclones that regularly plague many parts of Asia—especially Bangladesh, the Philippines, and India—help to perpetuate global inequality by eliminating much of the progress achieved through years of economic development.

INEQUALITY WITHIN RICH COUNTRIES

History and literature are replete with examples of the difficulties endured by the poverty-stricken citizens of Britain and the United States and how the lives of the poor sharply contrasted with those of the wealthy. Theories of socialism and communism, articulated by **Karl Marx** who was living in Britain, underscore the durability of inequality within rich countries. Great economic disparities have existed in the United States throughout its history, with the *Gilded Age* of the nineteenth century, the Roaring Twenties, and the *Roaring Nineties* bringing unprecedented levels of both prosperity and economic inequality. The stock market crash of 1929, the Great Depression of the 1930s, implementation of the **New Deal** programs designed to help the poor, and the outbreak of World War II combined to redistribute wealth in the United States. The concentration of income declined dramatically, and the middle class grew rapidly. Income distribution remained relatively equal until the 1970s. In virtually all industrial countries, income inequality grew between the 1970s and the early twenty-first century. Globalization, new technologies, and other factors contributed to this development.

Karl Marx

German thinker who pioneered the theories of socialism and communism

New Deal

Social welfare system created in the 1930s in order to help the poor and restore trust in capitalism and government

The United States

As Table 7.3 shows, the United States has the greatest degree of income inequality among industrialized countries. The richest country on earth also has pockets of poverty that are similar to many parts of the developing world. Out of a population of 300 million, 37 million Americans lived below the **poverty line**, which was defined as an income of roughly $19,806 a year for a family of four in 2006. The poorest 10 percent of Americans receive 1.8 percent of the total income, while the richest 10 percent gets almost a third. The average for rich countries is 2.9 percent for the poorest 10 percent of the population. Economic statistics support the general perception of unprecedented

Poverty Line

The income level under which people cannot adequately sustain themselves. A measure of need.

TABLE 7.3 INCOME INEQUALITY WITHIN RICH COUNTRIES

Country	Survey Year	Share of Income (%)			
		Poorest 10 %	Poorest 20 %	Richest 20 %	Richest 10 %
High Human Development					
Norway	2000	3.9	9.6	37.2	23.4
Sweden	2000	3.6	9.1	36.6	22.2
Canada	1998	2.5	7.0	40.4	25.0
United States	**2000**	**1.9**	**5.4**	**45.8**	**29.9**
United Kingdom	1999	2.1	6.1	44.0	28.5
Germany	2000	3.2	8.5	36.9	22.1
Italy	2000	2.3	6.5	42.0	26.8
Chile	2000	1.2	3.3	62.2	47.0
Costa Rica	2000	1.4	4.2	51.5	34.8

Source: United Nations Development Program, *Human Development Report 2004* (New York: Oxford University Press, 2004), 188.

Center for Budget and Policy Priorities

A nonprofit research organization advocating tax spending to benefit the poor

inequality in the United States, with most of the income concentrated at the very top of society. The top 20 percent of households earned 56 percent of the nation's income and controlled 83 percent of the nation's wealth, which includes stocks, bonds, real estate, businesses, savings insurance, and other assets. In 2003 the *top one percent* owned about 57 percent of the country's wealth. Incomes in the top 1 percent of households ranged from $237,000 to several billion dollars.[28] According to the **Center for Budget and Policy Priorities**—a nonprofit research organization in Washington, D.C., that advocates tax and federal spending policies to benefit the poor—the richest 2.8 million Americans had $950 billion after taxes, or 15.5 percent of the $6.2 trillion economic pie in 2000. In contrast, the poorest 110 million Americans, or roughly 39 percent of the population, received 14.4 percent of all after-tax money.[29]

The tax cuts passed in 2001 and 2003 were widely regarded as creating an even wider gap between the rich and poor in the United States. While most Americans received modest increases between 1979 and 2000, averaging 10 percent, compensation for the nation's top one hundred CEOs climbed from $1.3 million, or 39 times the pay of an average worker, to $37.5 million, or more than 1,000 times the pay of ordinary workers. For example, Lee R. Raymond, chairman and chief executive of Exxon got $144,573 for each day he led the company between 1993 and 2005.[30] Various corporate scandals, including Enron, influenced U.S. leaders to more closely examine these disparities in 2006. Think of the salaries of major athletes compared with what the average American makes. In 1998, the top 0.01 percent of Americans received more than 3 percent of all income in the United States. In other words, the richest 13,000 families had almost as much income as the 20 million poorest households and roughly 300 times the incomes of average American families.[31] The devastation caused by Hurricane Katrina in August 2005 underscored the gap between rich and poor in the United States. The vast majority of the victims were poor.

You **DECIDE** | **Inequality and Democracy**

Income inequality in the United States is likely to be perpetuated for reasons discussed earlier in this chapter. Wealth, as opposed to income, can be passed on to future generations. One of the most controversial issues in the United States is the influence that those with large amounts of money have on the political process, especially on democracy. Politicians generally concentrate on raising money from wealthy constituents, while largely ignoring the poor. Inequality of incomes often translates into inequality in politics.

Do you think that economic inequality in the United States threatens democracy? What are some implications of inequality in America for U.S. foreign policy, especially in relation to promoting democracy?

Perhaps one of the most overlooked aspects of inequality is the growing income gap between urban areas and rural America. As one drives through the numerous small towns in Illinois, Iowa, North Dakota, Alabama, and elsewhere, these income disparities become obvious. Homes, businesses, barns, and grain elevators have been abandoned and are decaying, creating what are referred to as **rural ghettos**. Two New York academics, Frank and Debra Popper, have suggested that, given the relentless decay of rural towns, the federal government should accelerate the depopulation of the entire Great Plains region and turn it into a vast **"Buffalo Commons,"** a refuge for large mammals, hikers, and a reviving Native American population.[32]

Rural Ghettos
Poverty-stricken rural areas

Buffalo Commons
Proposed refuge for wildlife and Native American populations

Income disparity between men and women in the United States is an integral component of economic inequality in the country. (We will discuss global gender inequality later in this chapter.) The gender gap continues to be a contentious issue. Data gathered by the U.S. Internal Revenue Service showed that although women are earning more money than a generation ago, men continue to earn higher salaries than women. Men outnumbered women in the $1 million-plus category by more than 13 to 1. Men also outnumbered women 10 to 1 in the $500,000 to $1 million category. As Table 7.4 indicates, women earn as much as men only in the $25,000 to $30,000 salary range.

Britain, Japan, and Ireland, for example, are also experiencing high levels of income inequality. Britain's rural areas have higher poverty rates than urban areas, and schools, railroad stations, and post offices are closing, just as they are in rural parts of the United States. The gap between the prosperous South-East and the poorer North has steadily expanded. Londoners enjoy a higher share of the country's income than people living in the northern part of England, Wales, and Scotland.[33] Japan's long economic recession has heightened the problem of inequality. Unlike the United States, which is more tolerant of huge economic gaps among different groups, Japan emphasizes the oneness of its society. Although about 90 percent of Japan's citizens regard themselves as middle class, the economic recession that began in the early 1990s has weakened the middle class and sharpened distinctions between rich and poor. Income disparities grew by nearly 50 percent between 1995 and 2000, and more Japanese are now homeless.[34] Improvements in Japan's economy in 2005 and 2006 helped to diminish some of this inequality.

TABLE 7.4 GENDER INEQUALITY IN AMERICA

Annual Salary	People in Each Range, Millions	Share That Are Women (%)
Under $5,000	19.81	59.8
$5,000–$10,000	15.22	58.8
$10,000–$15,000	14.43	58.9
$15,000–$20,000	13.75	57.1
$20,000–$25,000	12.65	51.9
$25,000–$30,000	11.01	48.0
$30,000–$40,000	16.45	41.6
$40,000–$50,000	10.05	34.4
$50,000–$75,000	10.06	34.4
$75,000–$100,000	13.23	24.9
$100,000–$200,000	2.27	17.4
$200,000–$500,000	0.67	9.9
$500,000–$1 million	0.11	9.2
Over $1 million	0.05	6.9

Sources: U.S. Internal Revenue Service; and David Cay Johnston, "As Salary Grows, So Does a Gender Gap," *New York Times*, 12 May 2002, Sect. 3, 8.

Rapid economic growth in Ireland, fueled largely by an influx of investments in technology and the country's increased globalization, has contributed to significant income inequality. Ireland is one of the most unequal societies in the developed world. Wage inequality grew in the late 1980s, the gap widening between middle and the top of the income distribution. Those at the bottom of society, the poorest 40 percent, have seen their incomes remain essentially unchanged. On the other hand, high-technology industries have generated high-paying jobs for many in Ireland.

Globalization

The worldwide spread of ideas, values, markets, technology, and other developments

Globalization is generally seen as a major cause of the rapid rise in inequality in the last two decades of the twentieth century. Integral to globalization is the proliferation of new telecommunications and computer technologies. Individuals with technical skills have outperformed those who have few or no technical skills. The globalization of trade also contributed to shifting employment patterns, with low-wage workers in industrial countries losing out to workers in the developing world. Closely related to globalization and technology is *education*. The knowledge-based economies of rich countries give educated individuals an advantage over those who are less educated, less skilled, and less entrepreneurial. The interdependence of economies enables educated people to be more mobile and marketable. This disparity in income between those with a high school education on the one hand and those with a college education on the other became obvious between 1979 and the early 1990s. In 1979, the average American male college graduate earned 49 percent more than a male high school graduate. By 1993 the gap had grown to 89 percent.[35] The *weakening of labor unions* also contributed to rising inequality. Compared with most European countries, where unions remain relatively strong and where governments influence wage regulations, the United States has weak unions and relies on market forces to a much greater extent to determine wages. Significant job cuts and plant closings by Ford Motor Company and General Motors in 2006 only underscored the weakness of unions in a competitive global economy. Richard B. Freeman points out that distributions of wages set by institutions, including bargaining, are invariably more compressed than distributions of wages set by markets.[36] The *declining role of governments* in an age of growing globalization is therefore seen overall as a major cause of inequality within rich countries.

INEQUALITY WITHIN POOR COUNTRIES

Although leaders of the developing world consistently stress the inequality between rich and poor countries, very little emphasis is put on the gulf that separates rich and poor in developing countries. One persistent characteristic of the developing world is the lack of a large enough middle class to bridge the extremes of wealth and poverty. In most poor countries, there are basically two distinct worlds: one inhabited by the middle and upper classes that comprise a small percentage of the population and the other by the poor majority. Traveling in the developing world one observes high walls around the homes of the wealthy people to protect them from the poor. One also notices that the lifestyles of the rich are virtually identical to those of rich individuals in the developed countries. As Table 7.5 shows, the gap between rich and poor in poor

TABLE 7.5 INCOME INEQUALITY WITHIN POOR COUNTRIES

Country	Survey Year	Share of Income (%)			
		Poorest 10 %	Poorest 20 %	Richest 20 %	Richest 10 %
Medium Human Development					
Mexico	2000	1.0	3.1	59.1	43.1
Russian Federation	2000	1.8	4.9	51.3	36.0
Colombia	1999	0.8	2.7	61.8	46.5
Venezuela	1998	0.8	3.0	53.2	36.5
Brazil	1998	0.7	2.2	64.1	48.0
Philippines	2000	2.2	5.4	52.3	36.6
Paraguay	1999	0.6	2.2	60.2	43.8
China	2001	1.8	4.7	50.0	33.1
South Africa	1995	0.7	2.1	66.5	46.9
Honduras	1999	0.9	2.7	58.9	42.2
Nicaragua	2001	1.2	3.6	59.7	45.0
Low Human Development					
Pakistan	1998–99	3.7	8.8	42.3	28.3
Bangladesh	2000	3.9	9.0	41.3	26.7
Zambia	1998	1.1	3.3	56.6	41.0
Burkina Faso	1998	2.0	4.6	60.4	46.8
Mozambique	1997	2.5	6.5	46.5	31.7

Source: United Nations Human Development Program, *Human Development Report 2004* (New York: Oxford University Press, 2004), 189–190.

NAFTA

Trade agreement signed by Canada, the U.S., and Mexico aiming at economic integration under the capitalist system

Apartheid Laws

Laws that legally and forcibly separate people of different ethnic and racial backgrounds

Black Empowerment Initiative

South African government effort to encourage the expansion of black-owned businesses

Caste System

Religiously driven ideology and social system that promotes hierarchy and inequality

countries is wider than the gap between rich and poor in industrialized states. Disparities between rural and urban areas, women and men, castes, ethnic groups, and regions are pronounced. And what is inescapable to the observer of developing countries is the widespread indifference shown by many of the rich toward the poor within their own societies.

Some of the world's most unequal countries are in Latin America. In Brazil, for example, the richest 20 percent of the population receives 64.1 percent of the wealth, and the poorest 20 percent gets 2.2 percent. As is the case in rich countries, the gap between rich and poor in Brazil is widening. In 1960, the poorest 50 percent of the population received 18 percent of the national income; their share dropped to 11.6 percent by 1995. Regional inequalities are large and growing. In the Northeast region, only 50 percent of the children are enrolled in school, compared with 98 percent of the children in the Central-West region.[37] The distribution of income in Mexico is similar to that of Brazil. Whereas the richest 20 percent of the population gets 57.4 percent of the income, the poorest 20 percent receives 1.3 percent of the income. Despite significant economic progress made under the **North American Free Trade Agreement (NAFTA)**, formed in 1994 to integrate trade among the United States, Canada, and Mexico, more than 54 million Mexicans are mired in poverty. About 24 million Mexicans are extremely poor and unable to afford adequate food. Many of them earn less than $1.40 a day. By contrast, the richest 10 percent controls about half of the country's financial and real estate assets.[38]

In some developing societies, inequality is institutionalized. Some groups are severely disadvantaged because of ethnicity and social class. During the period when South Africa was ruled by **apartheid laws**—which rigidly segregated blacks, whites, Asians, and mixed-race people and distributed resources according to a racial hierarchy—whites enjoyed a privileged position and blacks faced widespread and persistent discrimination. The economic chasm between whites and blacks still exists. However, since apartheid was abolished in 1991, an economic gap within the black group has grown as more opportunities have opened up for blacks. The number of black households earning as much as or more than the average white household income of $20,708 has risen from fewer than 1,000 to more than 1.2 million. But the average income of the poorest 40 percent of black South Africans has declined from $601 to $510. The government's **Black Empowerment Initiative**, which uses lucrative government contracts as leverage to encourage the expansion of black-owned businesses, has created black millionaires in a relatively short period of time, further widening inequality among blacks.[39]

India's **caste system** is the most obvious and pervasive example of structured inequality. The caste system is a rigid hierarchical system of social classes in *Hinduism*, which determines the status, rights, privileges, occupations, and social interactions of each person from birth. One inherits one's caste or social standing in the community. Each child is born into one of four main castes: Brahman, Ksatriya, Vaisyas, and Sudras. Even though the caste system has been outlawed and is constantly challenged, it is widely adhered to in Indian society. **Brahmans** (the priests and scholars) stand at the top, the **Ksatriya** (the military, lawmakers, and rulers) are second, the **Vaisyas** (merchants, landowners, industrialists, and artisans) are third, and the **Sudras** (laborers and farm workers) are at the bottom of the caste system. The lowest group in India is the **untouchables**, who are literally regarded as outcasts. This means that they do not belong to a caste or class. Each caste is divided into many subcastes, or **Jatis**. The untouchables perform tasks deemed too polluted to be done by caste Hindus. According to 2002 data, the poorest 10 percent of India's population controlled 3.5 percent of the country's wealth compared with 33.5 percent controlled by the richest 10 percent. The richest 20 percent of Indians received 46 percent of the country's income, compared with 8.1 percent for the poorest 20 percent.[40]

Regions of the developing world that are relatively integrated into the global economic system have generally grown faster than other regions. The same set of factors that have contributed to the widening gap between rich and poor in the developed world are also present in developing countries. China is an example of this phenomenon. Economic benefits of China's rapid growth are most concentrated in urban coastal areas. Small towns, rural areas, and the interior experience much slower growth rates and are poorer than coastal industrial centers. About 84 percent of foreign investment is in the eastern coastal cities, 9 percent in the central region, and 4.6 percent in the western part of China. Similarly, 57 percent of the country's income is generated on the east coast, compared with 17 percent in the west.[41] Finding ways to diminish economic disparaties became a major priority of the Chinese government in 2006.

Gender Inequality

Women worldwide experience various degrees of inequality. At the heart of the issue of gender inequality are widely held perceptions, by both men and women, about the roles and status of women in society, especially in economic life. In all countries the poorest of the poor are women, the majority of those at the bottom of society. Perceptions of women and the reality of inequality are mutually reinforcing, creating a vicious cycle of inequality. Clearly, women are not a monolithic group. Some enjoy great wealth, power, and high positions in society. More women, especially in the industrialized countries, are gaining equality with men of similar educational achievement. Based on our previous discussion about the economic advantages college-educated people enjoy over those who do not attend college, women are likely to surpass men in terms of income in the next generation because women now comprise 58 percent of college students. Observing gender composition of college classes, it is obvious that women outnumber men by a significant margin. Leadership roles in society twenty years from now are likely to be dominated by women. Education is a major factor contributing to the changing roles and status of women in society.

Status refers to one's position in the social, economic, and political hierarchy. These positions are largely *socially constructed* primarily by men to safeguard their own power and privileged positions. This means that societies use subjective standards to determine who will have higher or lower status. Status can be based on gender, skin color, sexual orientation, physical appearance, and so on. These standards are subject to change as societies change. Women in societies dominated by religion invariably have a lower and more permanent status. For example, women in the Muslim world, where

Brahmans
Priests and scholars at the top of the caste system

Ksatriya
Second highest group in the caste system, includes those in the military, lawmakers, and rulers

Vaisyas
Third highest group in the caste system, includes merchants, landowners, industrialists, and artisans

Untouchables
Outcasts excluded from the caste system

TABLE 7.6 INCOME INEQUALITY BETWEEN MEN AND WOMEN

Country	Estimated Earned Income (US$) 2002		Ratio of Female to Male Earned Income
	Female	Male	
High Human Development			
Norway	31,356	42,340	0.74
Sweden	23,781	28,700	0.83
Canada	22,964	36,299	0.63
Australia	23,643	33,259	0.71
United States	**27,338**	**43,797**	**0.62**
Netherlands	20,358	38,266	0.53
Japan	16,977	37,208	0.46
France	19,923	33,950	0.59
United Kingdom	19,807	32,984	0.60
Germany	18,763	35,885	0.50
Ireland	21,056	52,008	0.44
Italy	16,702	36,959	0.45
Spain	13,209	29,971	0.44
Greece	10,892	25,601	0.43
Chile	5,442	14,256	0.38
Bahamas	13,375	20,700	0.65
Costa Rica	4,698	12,197	0.39
Kuwait	7,116	20,979	0.34
Medium Human Development			
Mexico	4,915	12,967	0.38
Panama	3,958	7,847	0.50
Russian Federation	6,508	10,189	0.64
Venezuela	3,125	7,550	0.41
Thailand	5,284	8,664	0.61

Source: United Nations Development Programs, *Human Development Program 2004* (New York: Oxford University Press, 2004), 217–224.

religion is inseparable from politics, have a lower status than women in industrialized societies where church and state are separated. An extreme example of religion and tradition combining to reinforce the low status of women was Afghanistan under the rule of the Taliban, prior to their removal from power by U.S. and British forces in 2002. The Taliban's conservative views and strict interpretation of the Koran led it to prevent girls from attending school and women from working outside their homes.

Gender Ideology

Beliefs, values, perceptions, and ideas about the roles of men and women and power relations between them

Closely related to status are roles. *Roles* are expectations regarding the skills, rights, and duties of individuals or groups that are rooted in perceptions, values, beliefs, and customs. Many of these perceptions, values, beliefs, and customs are legitimized by laws and policies made by governments. Roles determine how we should behave. The beliefs, values, perceptions, and ideas about the roles of men and women and power relations between them is referred to as **gender ideology**. Gender ideology is based on

Afghan girls
in school.

the assumption that women are naturally suited for particular jobs. In Afghanistan, for example, cultural beliefs and practices make family planning very difficult, and many women have ten or more children. Women's role as child bearers reinforces their unequal status, trapping them and their children, especially girls, in a cycle of poverty. In many parts of the world, women are perceived as being naturally suited for factory jobs that are part of globalization. In Mexico, China, Thailand, and elsewhere women are concentrated in low-wage employment.

Globalization and other developments have also contributed to greater gender equality globally. Countries that are the least globalized tend to have higher levels of inequality. For example, the gender gap in education is concentrated largely in the developing world, particularly in Africa, which is the least globalized continent. Women in the United States, by contrast, are experiencing increased equality with men. For decades following World War II, income inequality remained relatively unchanged. Women received about three-fifths of what men received for similar work. However, as we mentioned previously, the gap is closing as more women attend college and abandon lower paying professions (such as teaching) for more lucrative employment in business, engineering, and the sciences. Generational change and the enactment of civil rights legislation in the 1960s facilitated women's access to employment outside the home and equalized pay for men and women to a greater degree than previously. Nevertheless, women's pay still lags behind men's in almost every sector of the economy. Full-time female workers earned 77.5 percent of what men earned in 2002.[42] In 2006, the gap narrowed, with women making 81 percent of what men were paid. Globalization, particularly the Internet, created

Searching a garbage dump for food in East Jakarta, Indonesia.

new ways of conducting business as well as new opportunities for women, who are increasingly able to integrate family responsibilities and business endeavors. Trends toward gender equality are being consolidated in every field, including the military. For example, in 2002, Kathleen McGrath, a mother of two, became the first woman to command a U.S. Navy warship, the USS *Jarrett*.[43] Gender equality is increasing across the developed world. For example, in 2001, the London Stock Exchange appointed Clara Furse as the first female chief executive in its 200-year history.[44] There are also many examples of women gaining greater equality with men in the news media.

Global Poverty

Poverty, the most obvious indicator of global and domestic inequality, is an enduring reality for more than two-thirds of the world's population. Although poverty in developing countries is readily apparent, poverty is a growing reality in the richest countries, including the United States. Poverty persists despite improvements in living standards. But improvements—such as increases in per capita income, declining infant mortality rates, increased access to clean water, and decreases in illiteracy—are often counteracted by rapid population growth rates in the developing world. Nonetheless, the percentage of people living in **extreme poverty**, defined as living on less than $1 a day, has declined. Even the absolute number of very poor people declined between 1980 and 1998 by at least 200 million, to almost 1.2 billion in 1998. Economic growth in China and India contributed to this decrease in extreme poverty.[45] In 2000, the UN adopted the Millenium Declaration, which aimed at reducing extreme poverty by half

Extreme Poverty

The very poorest of the poor, or those living on less than $1 a day

and child mortality by two-thirds by 2015. But the struggle to further reduce poverty must take into consideration some powerful realities. These include

1. *Weak political support for foreign assistance* in most rich countries, including the United States;
2. *Uncertainty of commitment* from the World Bank, the International Monetary Fund (IMF), the WTO, and other multilateral agencies; and
3. *Ongoing armed conflicts* that impede efforts to help the poor in many parts of the developing world.[46]

These realities are compounded by the diminished role of governments worldwide in efforts to alleviate poverty.

Defining poverty is to some extent subjective. There are basically two aspects to poverty: **absolute poverty** (i.e., the absolute number of poor people below the defined poverty line) and **relative poverty** (which reflects the distribution of income in society). For example, in relative terms, many Americans are poor. However, a much smaller number of Americans are poor in absolute terms. Although poverty is not always easily defined, an important aspect of poverty is a subjective feeling of being poor either absolutely or relative to others.[47] The concept of the poverty line is not always a reliable indicator of poverty. The poverty line in the United States was developed in 1963–1964 by the Social Security Administration on the basis of a 1955 household food consumption survey by the U.S. Department of Agriculture. The poverty line is adjusted each year to reflect changes in the **Consumer Price Index**. The CPI measures changes over time in the cost of purchasing the "market basket" of goods and services used by a typical family. But the poverty line does not adequately reflect higher costs for transportation, child care, health care, and other costs associated with employment. Unlike the 1960s, when many mothers stayed home, both parents now work, thereby incurring expenses that were not taken into consideration when the poverty line was developed. Furthermore, the poverty level measurement assumes that costs are the same across the Untied States, with the exception of Alaska and Hawaii, where the poverty level is higher.[48] Global measurements of poverty are in reality estimates, despite the certainty conveyed by statistics.

Regardless of where poor people live, there are at least *six dimensions of poverty*:[49]

1. **Hunger:** Poverty throughout the world is about inadequate food supplies.
2. **Psychological Dimensions:** Poverty is usually characterized by a sense of powerlessness, dependency, humiliation, and shame.
3. **Inadequate Infrastructure:** Poor people generally lack access to roads, electricity, clean water, and transportation.
4. **Low Levels of Literacy:** Educational opportunities are often unavailable.
5. **Health Problems:** Poor people everywhere generally suffer from illness, which further impoverishes them.
6. **Inadequate Income:** Poor people stress managing physical, human, social, and environmental assets to cope with their vulnerability. Incomes receive less emphasis.

Absolute Poverty
The absolute number of poor people below the defined poverty line

Relative Poverty
Level of poverty based on the society in question

CPI
Released by the U.S. Department of Labor to measure the price of consumer goods and services as well as the rate of inflation

These dimensions of poverty are closely intertwined. Hunger, low literacy rates, and health problems, for example, combine to reinforce poverty. Having few resources to allocate to literacy programs, poor countries find themselves in a downward spiral of poverty. In Haiti, the poorest country in the Western Hemisphere, almost half of all school-age children have never attended school. In India, where females have limited access to education, less than half of all women are literate. African countries are not only the poorest in the world, they also have the lowest literacy rates. Chronic poor health drains individuals of the energy needed to take care of themselves and their families, find and keep employment, and protect their environment. These problems are usually made more burdensome by governments' inability or unwillingness to provide adequate sanitation and access to clean water. Infectious diseases thrive in these unsanitary conditions.

Hunger and Malnutrition

Malnutrition

Poor nutrition resulting from an insuffient or unbalanced diet

Hunger and malnutrition are obvious and important indicators of poverty and are at the foundation of both domestic and global inequality. **Malnutrition** causes impaired vision, an inability to concentrate and to learn, greater vulnerability to disease and poor health, and a shorter life expectancy. In its report on the state of food insecurity in the world in 2003, the UN Food and Agriculture Organization set a goal of reducing world hunger by half by 2015. There is evidence to suggest that this goal, set in 1996, is unlikely to be achieved. Between 1999 and 2001, the number of hungry people globally climbed, especially in Africa. More than 840 million people, or one-seventh of humanity, experienced hunger. Between 1995 and 2001, the number of malnourished people grew by an average of 4.5 million a year.[50] China and Mozambique reduced hunger and malnutrition, whereas India, Nigeria, Zimbabwe, North Korea, Ethiopia, and Eritrea faced growing starvation. Violence, AIDS, and natural disasters contribute to increased hunger in many parts of Africa, the continent most seriously affected by food shortages. For example, a civil war in the Democratic Republic of the Congo left more than 75 percent of the population undernourished. Similarly, violence in Afghanistan and Burundi contributed to the malnutrition of roughly 70 percent of their populations. Malnutrition also spread across Central America's drought corridor, which has experienced declining rainfall during the crucial planting and growing periods. The **World Food Program**, the UN agency and the world's largest food distribution organization, estimated that 1.5 million people were threatened with malnutrition in Honduras, Nicaragua, El Salvador, and Guatemala in 2002.[51]

World Food Program

UN agency that is also the world's largest food distribution organization

Closing the Gap

The 2001 terrorist attacks in the United States and subsequent U.S.-led invasions of Afghanistan and Iraq heightened global awareness of global inequality as a major threat to global peace and security. Poverty in the developing world in an age of global interdependence is widely perceived as engendering and supporting global terrorism, undermining democratization efforts, threatening freedom in established democracies, and contributing to many other global problems. Speaking at the UN conference in Monterrey, Mexico, in March 2002, President George W. Bush stressed that while poverty does not

TABLE 7.7 PERCENTAGE OF POPULATION LIVING ON $2 OR LESS A DAY

Country	Population Below $1 a Day (%)	Population Below $2 a Day (%)
Medium Human Development		
Costa Rica	12.6	26.0
Trinidad and Tobago	12.4	39.0
Mexico	15.9	37.7
Panama	14.0	29.0
Colombia	19.7	36.0
Venezuela	23.0	47.0
Brazil	11.6	26.5
Peru	15.5	41.4
Jamaica	3.2	25.2
Sri Lanka	6.6	45.4
Paraguay	19.5	49.3
Ecuador	20.2	52.3
China	18.8	52.6
Indonesia	7.7	55.3
Egypt	3.1	52.7
India	44.2	86.2
Zimbabwe	36.0	64.2
Ghana	44.8	78.5
Kenya	26.5	62.3
Low Human Development		
Pakistan	31.0	84.6
Nigeria	70.2	90.8
Zambia	63.6	87.4
Mali	72.8	90.6
Central African Rep.	66.6	84.0
Ethiopia	31.2	76.4
Sierra Leone	57.0	74.5

Source: United Nations Development Program, *Human Development Report 2004* (New York: Oxford University Press, 2004), 147–49.

cause terrorism, "persistent poverty and oppression can lead to hopelessness and despair. And when governments fail to meet the most basic needs of their people, these failed states can become havens for terror."[52] At their meeting in the United States in 2005, the Group of Eight (G–8) industrial countries also emphasized the urgent need to reduce poverty. Globalization not only makes national borders less significant, it also links the fates of rich and poor nations in an unprecedented web of interdependence. This section offers some suggestions for diminishing both global and domestic inequality.

Education and Family Planning Education and family planning are essential for diminishing inequality. The most prosperous societies have generally placed a high priority on education, freedom of thought, and the exchange of ideas. Societies that

TABLE 7.8 POVERTY IN DEVELOPING COUNTRIES

Country	Adult Literacy Rate (% Age 15 and Above) 2002	Population Without Access to Clean Water (%) 2000	Underweight Children Under Age 5 (%) 2000
Medium Human Development			
Mexico	90.5	14	8
Cuba	96.9	5	4
Belize	76.9	24	6
Colombia	92.1	9	7
Venezuela	93.1	16	5
Saudi Arabia	77.9	5	14
Brazil	86.4	13	6
Turkey	86.5	17	8
China	90.9	25	10
Egypt	56.6	5	12
India	61.3	12	47
Low Human Development			
Pakistan	41.5	12	38
Bangladesh	41.1	3	48
Haiti	51.9	54	28
Nigeria	66.8	43	37
Uganda	68.9	50	26
Senegal	39.3	22	18
Burkina Faso	12.8	—	34
Niger	17.1	41	40

Source: United Nations Development Program, *Human Development Report 2000* (New York: Oxford University Press, 2002), 157–59; and United Nations Development Program, *Human Development Report 2004* (New York: Oxford University Press, 2004), 140–142.

make education available to as many people as possible, such as the United States, are also the most prosperous societies. Because education affects ways of thinking, perceptions, and creativity, it is at the foundation of any effort to alleviate poverty. Education, especially for women, has a direct impact on the number of children women have, their level of education, and their quality of life. Educated women are more likely than uneducated women to use birth control, thereby reducing overpopulation, which is a major cause of inequality. Countries that make education and family planning priorities usually have healthier, more productive, and more economically and technologically competitive populations. These countries—which include Taiwan, Singapore, South Korea, and China—have effectively reduced domestic inequality as well as narrowed the gap between themselves and industrialized nations.

Democracy May Help India, the world's largest democracy, is also one of the world's poorest and most unequal societies. Nevertheless, democratic societies offer poor people an opportunity to improve their lives through their voting power. Democratic

TABLE 7.9 MALNUTRITION

Country	Undernourished People (% of Population) 1999–2001	Children Under Weight for Age (% Under Age 5) 1995–2002	Infants With Low Birthweight (%) 1998–2002
High Human Development			
Norway	–	–	5
Sweden	–	–	4
Canada	–	–	6
United States	–	1	8
Netherlands	–	–	–
Japan	–	–	7
France	–	–	6
United Kingdom	–	–	8
Germany	–	–	7
Medium Human Development			
Mexico	5	8	9
Cuba	11	4	6
Russian Federation	4	3	6
Venezuela	18	5	7
Thailand	19	19	9
Brazil	9	6	10
Philippines	22	28	20
China	11	11	6
India	21	47	30
Kenya	37	21	11
Low Human Development			
Pakistan	19	38	19
Bangladesh	32	48	30
Nigeria	8	36	12
Zambia	50	28	10
Ethiopia	42	47	15
Burundi	70	45	16

Source: United Nations Development Program, *Human Development Report 2004* (New York: Oxford University Press, 2004), 160–163.

governments may be pressured to reduce economic inequalities by interest groups and political parties. Furthermore, as we have discussed in Chapter 4, the effective and efficient functioning of democracies depends to a large extent on an educated, politically engaged middle class.

Government Policies and Free Trade Could Make a Difference Decisions made by governments have profound implications for inequality within and among nations. Government priorities, reflected in the allocation of resources in national budgets, directly affect chances of reducing inequality. For example, Brazil's government suspended a $760 million purchase of twelve jet fighters for its air force to use the money to alleviate hunger. This choice of spending money on guns or butter confronts most governments, and most of them place military expenditures ahead of poverty-reduction programs. China's government has tried to diminish regional inequalities by investing more money in economically depressed areas. Brazil decided to address inequality by "democratizing" land titles and expanding poor people's access to credit. Granting formal property rights to millions of slum dwellers is viewed as a way creating greater economic opportunities for the poor.[53] Korea, Brazil, and India have implemented various forms of affirmative action programs to diminish regional, racial, or caste inequalities. As we have seen from the debate between the globalists and antiglobalists, there is disagreement on free trade's role in reducing inequality. However, it is clear that countries that are marginalized from the global economy are generally the poorest. China, on the other hand, is an example of a country that dramatically improved its technology, encouraged foreign investment, and implemented far-reaching economic reforms to participate in the global economy. As a result, China has a rapidly growing middle class and fewer poor people than it had.

Reduce Corruption The poorest countries in the world are invariably the most corrupt countries. One of the most obvious and formidable obstacles to reducing poverty and enhancing equity is widespread corruption. Corruption drains scarce resources away from vital public services and infrastructural projects, rewards incompetence and stifles innovation and change, and discourages foreign investment. At a more fundamental level, corruption infuses society with cynicism, which is detrimental to efforts to achieve economic development and greater equality. Much of the illegally obtained money is invested abroad, instead of being invested at home.

Pay Attention to Women Societies that reward women for their participation in economic, political, and social life benefit from the talents of more than half of their population. Because women play a crucial role in raising, educating, and encouraging children to achieve, their treatment directly influences economic development and equality issues. The UN, the World Bank, and other international organizations recognize that women must be included in the decision-making process. Governments are paying attention to **gender budgeting**, which is essentially an analysis of national budgets to determine how spending priorities affect women. Gender-responsive budgets were developed to hold public officials accountable for promoting gender equity.[54]

Gender Budgeting

Analysis of national budgets to determine how spending priorities affect women

Improve Agriculture in Poor Countries Poverty and inequality are reinforced by the inability of the poor to produce sufficient food. The poorest countries routinely suffer from food shortages and malnutrition. Many of the world's poorest people live in societies where land is concentrated in the hands of a relatively small number of powerful families. Land redistribution in places like Brazil and Venezuela is regarded as a major step toward reducing hunger and creating greater equality of opportunity. Large subsidies to farmers in North America, Europe, and Japan are widely believed to be detrimental to the efforts of poor countries to develop agriculture and become self-sufficient in food production. **The Green Revolution**—which dramatically increased agricultural production through the development of high-yielding hybrids and faster growing plants, and the application of large amounts of fertilizers and insecticides—enabled countries like Mexico and India to produce more food and reduce starvation. In 2006 the Bill and Melinda Gates Foundation and the Rockefeller Foundation allocated $150 million to increase agricultural productivity in Africa. Genetically modified crops are viewed as being capable of improving on the achievements of the Green Revolution. These crops would reduce the need for chemical spraying, improve the nutritional value of agricultural products, and make crops more resistant to diseases and pests. Both food subsidies and genetically modified crops are controversial issues in global and domestic politics.

Think Small Fighting poverty and reducing inequality require global, local, and individual efforts. In the final analysis, individuals must provide some of the solutions to these problems. Personal choices that reinforce poverty within families will eventually reinforce national poverty and global inequality. Many college students are involved in volunteer efforts, and some think that joining the Peace Corps can help improve living conditions in an African or Latin American village. Similarly, poor people in Brazil have decided to help people even poorer than themselves by volunteering. Volunteers work in soup kitchens, homeless shelters, legal-aid clinics, and antiviolence organizations.[55] Another example of how thinking small can help to close the gap between rich and poor is **microlending**, or the granting of small loans to help the smallest entrepreneurs, who do not have access to conventional financial services, expand their businesses and climb out of poverty. Started in Bangladesh by **Muhammad Yunus**, founder of the Grameen Bank, microcredit is now a global phenomenon. Both Yunus and the Grameen Bank won the Nobel Peace Prize in 2006.

Foreign Aid Helps During the 1980s, the prevailing view in industrialized countries was that economic globalization offered greater benefits to poor countries than official development assistance did. Consequently, foreign aid declined sharply. However, in the aftermath of the 2001 terrorist attacks in the United States, a global consensus emerged around the need to increase economic assistance to the poorest countries, especially those that are democratizing and have relatively low levels of official corruption. In their *Global Monitoring Report 2005*, the IMF and the World Bank proposed doubling foreign aid to poor countries to reduce global poverty and inequality. Increasingly, individuals are providing significant aid to poor countries. For example, in 2006 George Soros gave $50 million to assist efforts to alleviate poverty in Africa.

Discussions of development assistance generally concentrate on contributions from countries. However, consistent with our discussion in Chapter 1 on the proliferation of nonstate actors and their growing influence in global politics and economics, various foundations, private voluntary organizations, corporations, universities, religious groups, and individuals provide an increasing proportion for foreign economic assistance. Although it is difficult to determine how much money NGOs provide, it is estimated that they give $35 billion each year, a figure that is more than three and a half

Green Revolution

Dramatic increase in agricultural production involving hybrids, fast-growing plants, and the use of fertilizer and insecticides

Microlending

Practice of granting small loans to help those who do not have access to conventional financial loan services

Muhammad Yunus

Founder of the Grameen Bank microlending institution

Kapstein, Ethan B. *Economic Justice in an Unfair World* (Princeton: Princeton University Press, 2006).

Krugman, Paul. *Development, Geography, and Economic Theory.* (Cambridge, MA: MIT Press, 1995).

Landes, David S. *The Wealth and Poverty of Nations: Why Some Are So Rich and Some So Poor.* (New York: W. W. Norton, 1997).

Micklethwait, John, and Adrian Wooldridge. *A Future Perfect: The Challenge and Hidden Promise of Globalization.* (New York: Times Books, 2000).

Milanovic, Branko. *Worlds Apart: Measuring International and Global Inequality.* (Washington, DC: Carnegie Endowment, 2005).

Runge, C. Ford, et al. *Ending Hunger in Our Lifetime.* (Baltimore: John Hopkins University Press, 2003).

Sachs, Jeffrey D. *The End of Poverty* (New York: Penguin, 2006).

Smith, Stephan. *Ending Global Poverty.* (New York: Palgrave, 2005).

Addresses and Websites

United Nations Development Program/SEPED
One UN Plaza, DC-1, 20th Floor
New York, NY 10017
Fax: (212) 906–5313
www.undp.org/poverty

This website, which is a part of the larger UN Development Program website, contains information on the UNDP's programs, initiatives, and experiences, as well as a place for discussions.

Association for Women's Rights in Development
96 Spadina Ave., No. 401
Toronto, ON MSV 256
Canada
Tel.: (416) 594–3773
Fax: (416) 594–0330
www.awid.org

The Association for Women's Rights in Development is an international membership organization connecting, informing, and mobilizing people and organizations committed to achieving gender equality, sustainable development, and women's human rights. Its website is divided into four themes: feminist organizations development, gender equality and new technologies, women's rights and economic change, and young women and leadership.

Women Watch

www.un.org/womenwatch/

This United Nations website discusses the UN's work with women and provides information on its conferences

for women. News, speeches, archives, and databases are available, and there is a special section that breaks down information regionally.

Office of High Commissioner for Human Rights
8-14 Avenue de la Paix
1211 Geneva 10
Switzerland
Tel.: 4122 917–9000
www.unhchr.ch/women

The Office of the High Commissioner for Human Rights attaches importance to practical and creative measures to realize the human rights of women—civil, cultural, economic, political, and social. This website has information on human rights, offers information on conferences on women, and provides links to other websites relating to women's issues.

World Health Organization Headquarters
Avenue Appia 20
1211 Geneva 27
Switzerland
Tel.: 4122 791 21 11
Email: info@who.int
www.who.int/frh-whd

The World Health Organization is a United Nations agency whose main goal is to provide health care to everyone. It has leading experts in a variety of health-related subjects, including humanitarian emergencies and disease outbreaks from around the world. This website offers information on women's topics, links, and conferences.

UNICEF
Email: netmaster@unicef.org
www.unicef.org

UNICEF is a United Nations organization responsible for mainstreaming a gender perspective throughout all its programs, and promoting the equal rights of girls and women, assisting governments and partners to use participatory approaches and communication to promote

behavior change and development, promoting effective participation of communities in decision-making in all phases of programs that affect their well-being, with special attention to marginalized or disadvantaged communities. UNICEF also works to strengthen partnerships with civil society organizations and governments to further the global agenda for children. This site also offers information, data, and profiles relating to current women's issues.

Endnotes

1. "Leaders: Does Inequality Matter?" *Economist*, 16 June 2001, 9.

2. World Bank, *World Development Report 2003* (New York: Oxford University Press, 2003), 89.

3. Joseph S. Nye, "Globalization's Democratic Deficit," *Foreign Affairs* 80, No. 4 (July/August 2001), 2.

4. Nancy Birdsall, "That Silly Inequality Debate," *Foreign Policy* 130 (May/June 2002), 92; and Nancy Birdsall, et al., "How to Help Poor Countries," *Foreign Affairs* 84, No. 4 (July/August 2005), 136–152.

5. John Micklethwait and Adrian Wooldridge, "The Globalization Backlash," *Foreign Policy* 126 (September/October 2001), 22.

6. David Dollar and Aart Kraay, "Spreading the Wealth," *Foreign Affairs* 81, No. 1 (January/February 2002), 120.

7. Dollar and Kraay, "Spreading the Wealth," 121.

8. Robert Wright, "Will Globalization Make You Happy?" *Foreign Policy* 120 (September/October 2000), 58.

9. Joseph Kahn, "Losing Faith: Globalization Proves Disappointing," *New York Times*, 21 March 2002, 24.

10. Jack Beatty, "Do As We Say, Not As We Do," *The Atlantic Monthly*, February 2002, 24.

11. Kahn, "Losing Faith," A6.

12. Wayne Arnold, "Globalization Stirs Asian Dreams, But Rural Poverty Grows Endemic," *New York Times*, 17 December 2001, C14.

13. Caroline Thomas, "Globalization and the South," in *Globalization and the South*, Caroline Thomas and Peter Wilkin, eds. (London: Macmillan Press, 1997), 6.

14. Vito Tanzi, "Globalization Without a Net," *Foreign Policy* 125 (July/August 2001), 78.

15. Dani Rodrik, "Trading in Illusions," *Foreign Policy* 123 (March/April 2001), 78.

16. Dani Rodrik, "Trading in Illusions," 59.

17. UN Development Program, *Human Development Report 2002* (New York: Oxford University Press, 2002), 19.

18. UN Development Program, *Human Development Report 2002*, 13.

19. David S. Landes, *The Wealth and Poverty of Nations* (New York: W. W. Norton, 1998), 56.

20. Virginia Postrel, "Economic Scene: The Decline of the Muslim Middle East," *New York Times*, 8 November 2001, C2.

21. Dennis Overbye, "How Islam Won, and Lost, the Lead in Science," *New York Times*, 30 October 2001, D1.

22. UN Development Program, *Human Development Report 1999* (New York: Oxford University Press, 1999), 38; and The World Bank, *World Development Report 2003* (New York: Oxford University Press, 2003), 2.

23. Nancy Birdsall, "Life Is Unfair: Inequality in the World," *Foreign Policy* 111 (Summer 1998), 76.

24. Ricardo Hausmann, "Prisoners of Geography," *Foreign Policy* 122 (January/February 2001), 46–47.

25. Lester C. Thurow, *The Future of Capitalism* (New York: William Morrow, 1996), 91.

26. Alan Schwartz, "Getting at the Roots of Arab Poverty," *New York Times*, 1 December 2001, A27.

27. Kwan S. Kim, "Income Distribution and Poverty: An Interregional Comparison," *World Development* 25, No. 11 (1997), 1916; and Nancy Birdsall and Juan Luis Londono, "No Tradeoff: Efficient Growth Via More Equal Human Capital Accumulation," in *Beyond Tradeoffs*, ed. Nancy Birdsall, et al. (Washington DC: Inter-American Development Bank, 1998), 1.

28. Ray Boshara, "The $6,000 Solution," *The Atlantic Monthly*, January/February 2003, 94; and David Cay Johnston, "Corporate Wealth Share Rises for Top-Income Americans," *New York Times*, 29 January 2006, A21.

29. Lynnley Browning, "U.S. Income Gap Widening," *New York Times*, 25 September 2003, C2.

30. Paul Krugman, "For Richer: How the Permissive Capitalism of the Boom Destroyed American Equality," *New York Times Magazine*, 20 October 2002, 64; and Jad Mouawad, "For Leading Exxon to Its Riches, $144,573 a Day," *New York Times*, 15 April 2006, A1.

31. Krugman, "For Richer," 65.

32. Joel Kotkin, "The Withering of Rural America," *Washington Post Weekly National Edition*, 29 July–4 August 2002, 22.

33. "Getting Wider," *The Economist* 2 December 2000, 57; and Sarah Lyall, "Grumbles Grow Louder in Quiet Rural Britain," *New York Times*, 2 October 2002, A3.

34. Doug Struck and Kathryn Tolbert, "Economic Gap in Japan," *Chicago Tribune*, 6 January 2002, Sect. 1, 6.

35. "Winners and Losers," *Economist*, 28 September 1996, 24.

36. Richard B. Freeman, "The New Inequality in the United States," in *Growing Apart: The Causes and Consequences of Global Wage Inequality*, ed, Albert Fishlow and Karen Parker (New York: Council on Foreign Relations Press, 1999), 37.

37. UN Development Program, *Human Development Report 1998* (New York: Oxford University Press, 1998), 29.

38. Mary Jordan and Kevin Sullivan, "Very Little Trickles Down," *Washington Post National Weekly Edition*, 31 March–6 April 2003, 15.

39. John Jeter, "In South Africa, a New Apartheid," *Washington Post National Weekly Edition*, 10 July 2000, 15.

40. UN Development Program, *Human Development Report 2002*, 196.

41. David Hale and Lyric Hughes Hale, "China Takes Off," *Foreign Affairs* 82, No. 6 (November/December 2003), 41.

42. David Leonhardt, "Wage Gap Between Men and Women Closes to Narrowest," *New York Times*, 17 February 2003, A1.

43. Justin Brown, "A Crack Appears in the Navy's Brass Ceiling," *Christian Science Monitor*, 31 March 2000, 1.

44. Bruce Stanley, "New Leader for London Exchange," *Chicago Tribune*, 25 January 2001, Sect. 3, 5.

45. The World Bank, *World Development Report 2003*, 2.

46. Moises Naim, "Missing in Monterrey," *Foreign Policy* 130 (May/June 2003), 104.

47. A. M. Khusro, *The Poverty of Nations* (New York: St. Martin's Press, 1999), 5.

48. Deepak Bhargava and Joan Kuriansky, "Drawing the Line on Poverty," *Washington Post National Weekly Edition*, 23–29 September 2002, 23.

49. Deepa Narayan, et al., *Can Anyone Hear Us: Voices of the Poor* (New York: Oxford University Press, 2000), 5.

50. Somini Sengupta, "Hunger Worsens in Many Lands," *New York Times*, 26 November 2003, A3.

51. Daniel B. Schneider, "Flash Points Loom in War on Hunger," *New York Times*, 18 November 2002, A27.

52. Tim Weiner, "More Entreaties in Monterrey for More Aid to the Poor," *New York Times*, 22 March 2002, A10.

53. Larry Rohter, "Brazil to Let Squatters Own Homes," *New York Times*, 19 April 2003, A7.

54. UN Development Program, *Human Development Report 2002*, 80.

55. Stephen Buckley, "In Brazil, The Poor Help the Poorer," *Washington Post National Weekly Edition*, 15–21 January 2001, 17.

56. Carol C. Adelman, "The Privatization of Foreign Aid," *Foreign Affairs* 82, No. 6 (November/December 2003), 9.

57. Adelman, "The Privatization of Foreign Aid," 12; and Eduardo Porter, "Flow of Immigrants' Money to Latin America Surges." *New York Times*, 19 October 2006, A23.

58. Celia W. Dugger, "World Bank and IMF Seek Doubling of Aid to Poor Lands," *New York Times*, 13 April 2005, A12; "Finance Chiefs Cancel Debt of 18 Nations," *New York Times*, 12 June 2005, A12; and Lydia Polgreen, "Nigeria Pays Off Its Big Debt," *New York Times*, 22 April 2006, A6.

CHAPTER 8

Environmental Issues

INTRODUCTION

China's impressive industrial growth, improved agricultural productivity, and rapidly growing Gobi desert have undoubtedly created environmental problems for China and the neighboring countries. But pollution from China is also creating problems in the United States and Canada. In fact, in an unusually severe dust storm in the spring of 1998, pollution levels in Oregon, Washington, and British Columbia were unprecedented. Air quality control officials in Seattle were astonished to see measurements showing that 75 percent of the pollution came from China.[1] Poor Africans, Asians, and Latin Americans clear forests for farmland and firewood, thereby contributing to an already serious problem of deforestation. Many burn coal to cook their food and to keep warm. Wealthy Americans and Europeans drive gas-guzzling sports utility vehicles, air condition their homes and offices in the summer and heat them in the winter, maintain perfect lawns, rely on numerous labor-saving appliances, and discard industrial and household wastes. In many ways, both affluence and poverty have devastating environmental consequences. Environmental problems underscore global interdependence and illustrate connections among political, economic, and cultural aspects of globalization.

Environmental problems demonstrate how vulnerable we are to developments in distant places and how much we need to cooperate across national boundaries to deal with them. They also illustrate how difficult it is to separate local, regional, and national environmental concerns from those at the international and global levels and to implement unilateral measures to diminish or eliminate them. Environmental issues remind us that the earth is a single biosphere, and that problems in one country are other countries' problems as well. Imagine that you are a resident of Boston in 1676 and that your cows are grazing the **commons**, which is land used by the entire community. Overgrazing would eventually destroy the commons and the cattle. But overgrazing is a problem that cannot be solved by restraining only a few members of the community. It is only through the cooperation of all members that overgrazing can be avoided. On a larger scale, environmental problems underscore the reality of global interdependence. Where these problems originate is less important than their global impact. A Soviet nuclear power plant in **Chernobyl** that exploded in 1986 illustrates this point. The power plant explosion released extensive radioactive material that spread to Europe, killing thirty people, damaging crops and animals, and polluting the environment for thousands of miles from the explosion.

Environmental issues are at the heart of debates about preserving life on earth. They are also intertwined with many other global concerns. Increasingly, scholars, politicians, leaders of international organizations and nongovernmental organizations

Commons

Land designated for use by the entire community

Chernobyl

Soviet nuclear power plant that suffered a melt-down in 1986

Environmental Security

A concept placing protection of the environment on equal ground with national security

Mesopotamia

An ancient civilization between the Tigris and Euphrates rivers, now known as Iraq

John Evelyn

Naturalist who criticized London for its high levels of pollution

(NGOs), and ordinary citizens worldwide are linking environmental security to human security (i.e. the challenges ordinary people face every day) and to traditional concerns about national security. The **environmental security** approach to international relations emphasizes that the ecological crisis we face is also a threat to national security. Environmental degradation is perceived to be as serious a threat to human societies as the traditional military threat.[2]

Throughout history, environmental factors have had serious implications for all aspects of human existence, including the rise and fall of great civilizations, the spread of infectious diseases, war and peace, economic prosperity and hunger, migration and resettlement, population growth, and global inequality. The destruction of Mayan civilization on the Yucatan peninsula in southern Mexico in the tenth century shows how climate change and population pressures can dramatically alter human societies. This chapter discusses how environmental problems became central concerns of the global community and the role of NGOs in making people more aware of environmental problems.

THE GLOBALIZATION OF ENVIRONMENTAL PROBLEMS

Ancient civilizations confronted some of the environmental challenges that are familiar to modern societies. For example, almost 3,700 years ago, Sumerian cities in the southern part of **Mesopotamia** (now modern Iraq) prospered because high levels of agricultural productivity supported permanent human resettlements. But these agricultural surpluses that helped develop the cradle of civilization came at a cost: extensive irrigation, which ultimately resulted in fields that were saline and waterlogged. Environmental decay forced people to abandon the Sumerian cities. Similarly, roughly 2,400 years ago, Plato was concerned about the impact of deforestation and overgrazing on soil erosion in the hills of Attica. Shipbuilding by the ancient Italian maritime states contributed to deforestation along the Mediterranean coasts. And air pollution from burning coal in medieval England was so bad that by 1661 the naturalist **John Evelyn** compared London with the "Court of Vulcan or the Suburbs of Hell."[3] Despite obvious environmental problems, the environmental movements did not germinate until 1865, when a private group called the Commons, Footpaths, and Spaces Preservation Society was founded in Britain. By the late 1890s and the turn of the century, groups in the United States that were committed to wilderness preservation and resource conservation emerged, strongly supported by President Theodore Roosevelt.

Contemporary ecological challenges differ significantly from those of earlier periods in *four main ways*:

1. Contemporary environmental problems are predominantly global in their cumulative consequences.
2. Whereas our current environmental problems represent biodegenerative products of humanity—such as air and water pollution, deforestation, overfishing, and soil erosion—our ancestors faced environmental constraints that

were primarily related to the biophysical parameters of nature, such as access to water, soil fertility, and temperature.

3. Natural forces created environmental problems for our ancestors. Today, however, some populations are more vulnerable to environmental crises principally because of human activities and government policies.

4. Ancient societies had more time and space to deal with environmental threats than we do today.[4]

Globalizing environmental issues is always a gradual, controversial, and complex process. In the past, most attempts to diminish environmental damage were primarily at the local and national levels. Before World War II, concerns about endangered wildlife and growing threats of ocean oil pollution led to bilateral and limited international environmental agreements. The globalization of environmental issues reflects the growth of global interdependence after World War II and the emergence of the United States as a superpower. The global environmental movement emerged principally in Western Europe, the United States, and Canada. A catalyst for growing concerns about how we are destroying our environment, and ultimately ourselves, was the publication of Rachel Carson's book *Silent Spring* in 1962. The book focused on how the widespread use of pesticides was devastating birds and other wildlife. Furthermore, space exploration reinforced perceptions of the oneness of the earth as well as its fragility. Exploding population growth and rapid industrialization, often with reckless disregard for environmental ramifications, focused more attention on resource scarcity, deforestation, and deteriorating health standards. Nuclear weapons proliferation, especially by the United States and the Soviet Union, also helped to reinforce our vulnerability to environmental threats resulting from our activities.

Silent Spring
A book that focused on the negative effects of pesticides

Earth as seen from Apollo space craft.

Images of "spaceship earth" facilitated a deeper understanding of global interdependence of environmental issues by illustrating that national boundaries are artificial and national issues are ultimately global issues. Like our example of the Boston common, the world was increasingly being perceived as a global common. Oil pollution, because of its immediate and drastic impact on coastal areas, clearly showed the

Torrey Canyon

Oil tanker that crashed off the coast of England in 1967

dangers of environmental disasters. When the oil tanker *Torrey Canyon* was wrecked on the coast of England and spilled about 875,000 barrels of crude oil in 1967, public opinion worldwide generated support for globalizing environmental issues. Globalization of the economy further reinforced environmental globalization by stimulating trade in endangered species, tropical hardwoods, and various metals. The production and distribution of chlorofluorocarbons (CFCs) around the world for use as a propellant in spray cans, as a refrigerant, and as cleaning solvents caused significant damage to the protective ozone layer in the earth's upper atmosphere.[5] European integration, a component of globalization, enabled animal rights groups in Europe to pressure the European Union (EU) to ban inhumane treatment of animals as well as international trade that contributed to the destruction of endangered species.

Biosphere Conference

Held in 1968, focused on the degradation of the environment from human activities

International agreements were made in response to specific environmental problems. The earliest ones concentrated on protecting wildlife in Africa and in the Western Hemisphere, Pacific fur seals, and whaling. Ocean oil pollution and the proliferation of nuclear weapons became major priorities of the environmental movement after 1945. **The Biosphere Conference**, held in Paris in 1968, focused on how human activities—such as air and water pollution, deforestation, the drainage of wetlands, and overgrazing—affected the biosphere. **The UN Conference on the Human Environment** (also known as Stockholm Conference), held in Stockholm in 1972, is often viewed as the beginning of serious global cooperation on the environment. Developed countries in particular acknowledged that multilateral efforts were essential in order to adequately address transboundary environmental problems.[6] The Stockholm Conference created the **United Nations Environmental Program (UNEP)**, an institutional framework to address the issues discussed in the conference. The 1992 UN Conference on Environment and Development (also known as the **Rio Summit** or the Earth Summit) and the 2002 **World Summit on Sustainable Development** (known as the Johannesburg Action Plan) emphasized priorities of developing countries, including concerns about sustainable development and its consequences for the environment and the reduction of poverty.

UN Conference on the Environment

Held in 1972, aimed at international cooperation in environmental protections

World Summit on Sustainable Development

Focused simultaneously on economic growth and environmental protections

States may join international agreements as a way of pressuring neighboring states into doing the same, thereby enhancing chances of widespread cooperation to protect the environment. Domestic political and economic considerations also play a role. Governments often respond to pressure from environmental activists. Industries that must comply with environmental laws in their home countries often support international agreements to prevent companies in other countries from gaining a competitive advantage.[7] Even though states recognize the need to cooperate, *political and economic considerations often weaken the effectiveness of environmental agreements.* These include

1. The lack of centralized authority in a world of sovereign states;
2. The gap between agreements and actual practice;
3. Disagreements between rich and poor countries about the economic implications of environmental agreements;

TABLE 8.1 MAJOR INTERNATIONAL ENVIRONMENTAL AGREEMENTS

Year	Agreement
1900	Convention for the Preservation of Animals, Birds, and Fish in Africa
1909	International Congress for the Protection of Nature
1911	The North Pacific Fur Seal Treaty
1913	Consultative Commission for the International Protection of Nature
1940	Convention on Nature Protection and Wildlife Conservation in the Western Hemisphere
1946	International Convention for the Regulation of Whaling
1954	International Convention for the Prevention of Pollution of the Sea by Oil
1958	Convention on the High Seas (provisions on maritime pollution)
1959	Antarctic Treaty (banning weapons tests and dumping nuclear waste in the Antarctic)
1963	Partial Test Ban Treaty
1968	Biosphere Conference
1972	London Dumping Convention (ocean pollution)
1972	The UN Conference on the Human Environment (the Stockholm Conference)
1973	International Convention for the Prevention of Pollution From Ships
1975	Convention on International Trade in Endangered Species and Wild Fauna and Flora
1979	Geneva Convention on Long-Range Transboundary Air Pollution
1985	Vienna Convention for the Protection of the Ozone Layer
1987	Montreal Protocol on Substances That Deplete the Ozone Layer
1989	Basel Convention on the Control of Transboundary Movements of Hazardous Wastes and Their Disposal
1991	Convention on Biological Diversity
1992	UN Conference on Environment and Development (Rio Summit or Earth Summit)
1992	UN Framework Convention on Climate Change
1997	Kyoto Protocol to the UN Framework Convention on Climate Change
2001	Stockholm Convention on Persistent Organic Pollutants
2002	World Summit on Sustainable Development (Johannesburg Action Plan)

4. Efforts by economic interests and governments to avoid compliance; and
5. A general perception that it is better to have an agreement, even if it is unworkable, than not to have an agreement, largely to satisfy demands for action.[8]

The implementation of and compliance with environmental agreements are influenced by at least four factors.[9] *One is the nature of the substances or activities that are regulated.* At the heart of many environmental debates is how international agreements will affect economic activities, and the costs and benefits of complying with the agreements. *Two is the characteristics of the agreement.* This relates to the process of reaching the agreement. Who initiates the treaty? What is required of the countries that sign it? Is the agreement vague or does it spell out clearly the conditions for compliance? *Three is the global environment.* How major countries, international organizations—such as World Bank, the United Nations, and the World Trade Organization (WTO), and environmental NGOs—view the agreement will impact its implementation. *Fourth is domestic factors.* Ultimately, the effectiveness of an environmental agreement depends on the nature of the society in which it is being implemented.

Nongovernmental Organizations and the Environment

Older environmental groups, such as the National Wildlife Federation and the National Audubon Society, were joined by numerous other environmental organizations, many having originated on college and university campuses in the 1960s and 1970s. The Environmental Defense Fund, the Natural Resources Defense Council, Greenpeace, Environmental Action, and Friends of the Earth were among them. Scientific groups, such as the Union of Concerned Scientists and Physicians for Social Responsibility, strengthened and broadened the environmental movement.[10] While most environmental groups operate on a local or national level and concentrate on specific problems facing particular communities, many of them have a global reach. They develop working relationships with governments, international organizations, global companies, and the national and global media. For example, many NGOs participate in global conferences on behalf of small, ecologically vulnerable islands of the Pacific. There are also NGOs—such as the Global Climate Coalition and the Alliance for Responsible CFC Policy—that represent industries and attempt to limit the effectiveness of other environmental organizations.[11]

Women and the Environment

The connection between women and environmental issues is acknowledged by **UNEP**, which has held conferences on women and the environment and established a committee of senior women advisers on sustainable development. The general emphasis on the gendered nature of environmental issues arises from the leading roles women have in environmental NGOs and numerous grassroots movements worldwide.

Green Belt Movement

Kenyan movement focusing on preventing further deforestation

Women in Kenya organized the **Green Belt Movement** to prevent further deforestation and to restore the land through reforestation. In 2004, Wangari Maathai, an environmentalist involved in the planting of more than 30 million trees, was awarded the Nobel Peace Prize for her work. Women's participation in environmental NGOs and at the grassroots level has resulted in *three main arguments about the connection between women and the environment*: (1) women are disproportionately disadvantaged by environmental problems, (2) gender bias is an impediment to achieving sustainable development, and (3) women's participation is vital to efforts to achieve sustainable development.[12]

Wangari Maathai.

Strategies Used by Nongovernmental Organizations

Regimes

Rules for governing state and nonstate actors

At the global level, NGOs must spend considerable resources to develop **regimes**; that is, the rules, codes of conduct, principles, and norms necessary to govern the behavior of both states and nonstate actors. Environmental NGOs that operate primarily on the global level encounter *three major impediments*. First, there is no common authority or power that can effectively force members of the global community to comply with rules. Second, the decentralized nature of international bureaucracies and their dependence on states make it difficult for NGOs to get international rules implemented. Third, global agreements and organizations are primarily produced by governments. Environmental NGOs are required in many cases to work though those governments to influence agreements and global institutions.[13] Many of the strategies environmental NGOs use to influence global environmental issues are familiar to those of you who have taken courses on American government and politics. There are *ten major strategies* that environmental NGOs use to accomplish their objectives:

1. Get media coverage and publicity for their issues. Generating domestic and global public awareness and support is crucial to NGOs' efforts to persuade policymakers to take action.
2. Educate the public on the issues by publishing research findings. One of the best examples of this approach is how saving whales became a major environmental concern.
3. Share information among groups in order to educate each other on the issues, coordinate strategies and activities, and provide each other with needed support.
4. Campaign and protest to advance their cause.
5. Raise money. This strategy is essential to the other strategies.
6. Lobby government officials and intergovernmental organizations, such as the World Bank.
7. Organize grassroots activities.
8. Litigate. Many NGOs see **litigation** as a principal way of getting governments to implement and comply with environmental laws.
9. Acquire and manage property to protect the environment.
10. Pressure companies to protect the environment.[14]

Litigation

Using national courts in environmental campaigns

BIODIVERSITY

Biodiversity is defined as the number and the variety of living organisms on earth. It includes genetic diversity, species diversity, and ecosystem diversity. Crucial to biodiversity is the interdependence of species and ecosystems and how their complex relationships affect the environment. In Chapter 1, we saw that what makes an issue global is not where it originates but the extent and significance of its impact. Biodiversity is an excellent example of a global issue. Biodiversity is concentrated in the forests of developing countries, especially Brazil, China, Colombia, Ecuador, India, Indonesia, Madagascar, Zaire, Peru, Mexico, Costa Rica, and Malaysia. Australia is the only developed country that has a large variety of species. The United States, Canada, and Europe are relatively poor in biodiversity. Biodiversity is at the heart of environmental globalization because it affects so many groups and individuals, including those interested in deforestation, agriculture, biotechnology, anthropology, pharmaceuticals, sustainable development, global trade, and ethics.[15]

Biodiversity

The large number and diversity of organisms on earth

Biodiversity provides many benefits. Ecosystem functions—such as carbon exchange, watershed flows of surface and ground water, the protection and fertility of soils, and the regulation of surface temperatures and local climates—are influenced by biodiversity. Diversity lessens the vulnerability of agricultural crops to diseases and pests. This is increasingly important for large-scale specialized agriculture. Through crossbreeding of diverse genetic stock, crops become more resistant to disease and pests. Biodiversity is especially important for medicinal and pharmaceutical product development. Preserving biodiversity is regarded as an ethical obligation. The basis of the ethical argument is that biodiversity is an intrinsic value and people should avoid destroying other species.[16] The destruction of rain forests in Brazil, for example, directly affects biodiversity, especially since Brazil alone contains almost 25 percent of the world's plant species. Perhaps the most widespread cause of damage to biodiversity is pollution and global environmental change.[17] Because the economic benefits derived from biodiversity, especially involving pharmaceuticals, are significant and potential benefits are even greater, governments are imposing strict controls on medicinal plants. In 2002, the **Group of Allied Mega-Biodiverse Nations** was created to certify the legal possession of biological material and to negotiate terms to transfer it. The group—composed of Brazil, China, India, Mexico, and nine other developing countries—controls roughly 70 percent of the world's biodiversity.

Convention on Biological Diversity

Designed to establish an international regime to protect biodiversity

North/South Divide

Refers to the large economic divide between many Northern and Southern states

Developed countries, especially the United States and members of the European Union (EU), attempted to reduce the destruction of the world's biodiversity by calling for the establishment of an international regime. Negotiations for such a regime, known as the **Convention on Biological Diversity**, began in 1991. Whereas the developed countries viewed genetic resources as belonging to all, as common heritage, developing countries saw these resources as national resources belonging to the states in which they are located. Both sides attempted to define the issues in ways that would protect their economic interests. The rich countries of the **North** wanted unimpeded access to these resources, particularly for their pharmaceutical and agricultural resources. The poor countries of the **South** wanted to control genetic resources to derive economic benefits from them. The Convention on Biological Diversity provides for: (1) national identification and monitoring of biological diversity; (2) the development of **national** strategies and programs for conserving biological diversity; (3) environmental assessment procedures to take into account the effects of projects on biological diversity; (4) sharing of research findings in a fair and equitable way; (5) the provision of technology for the conservation and use of genetic resources by the industrial countries; and (6) the facilitation of participation in biotechnology research by countries that provide genetic resources.[18]

Endangered Species and Wildlife Protection

At Taruichi restaurant in Tokyo's trendy Shijuku district, business executives, domestic workers, and ordinary Japanese gather to dine on whale meat. Among the thirty-six choices on the menu are fried whale, raw whale, whale bacon, whale heart, whale testicle, whale kidney, and ice cream made from whale fat.[19] Many governments, environmental NGOs, and most Americans oppose whale hunting and eating whales—especially after Greenpeace's successful campaign, "Save the Whales." In Japan, however, eating whales is viewed as part of the national culture, especially by older Japanese who survived on whale meat provided by the government after World War II.

Whales have received widespread attention partly because of the popularity of *Moby-Dick*, a book by Herman Melville about the whaling industry in the first half of the nineteenth century. At that time, Americans sailed the Pacific for up to four years at a time searching for whales. They returned to America with great wealth, since whales provided oil for lubricating industrial machinery, baleen for manufacturing corsets and umbrellas, oil for making soap and margarine, and food. Whaling was also important for making glycerin, which was an essential component in nitroglycerin that was used in manufacturing dynamite. Military competition among European countries and the outbreak of World War I created a great demand for glycerin. This, in turn, led to an expansion and intensification of whaling. The development of the harpoon cannon between 1864 and 1868 and the invention of factory ships that could process whales at sea hastened the depletion of whales.[20]

One of the earliest attempts by the international community to prevent the decline and extinction of whales, especially the widely hunted blue whale, came in 1935 when the **League of Nations** tried to regulate their exploitation. By 1946, the International Convention for the Regulation of Whaling, called for by nations involved in the whaling industry, established the **International Whaling Commission (IWC)** to protect the price of whale oil. For the most part, whales remained unprotected until 1964, when the IWC specifically advocated for the preservation of humpback whales. Blue whales were designated as a protected species a year later. The 1975 **Convention on International Trade in Endangered Species of Wild Fauna and Flora (CITES)** effectively prohibited trade in whale products. By 1982, the IWC had agreed to a moratorium on whaling, except whaling done by the **Inuit** of Alaska and Canada, whose diet and culture depended on hunting whales. An exception was also made for catching whales for scientific purposes, a provision that provides a loophole for Japan to continue harvesting a limited number of whales for consumption. In 1986, the moratorium came into effect, and in 1994 the IWC created a whaling sanctuary in the Southern Atlantic and Antarctica.[21] However, in 2006 Japan was able to secure a majority on the International Whaling Commission, a development that facilitated Japan's resumption of commercial whaling.

Dolphins, considered an endangered species, especially by the United States, are widely regarded as having human-like qualities. Environmental campaigns, movies and other media, and aquariums have strengthened the perception of dolphins as friendly creatures that must be protected. Threats to dolphins were a by-product of fishing with purse seine nets for tuna that schooled beneath the dolphins. Many dolphins drowned or were severely injured in the nets. Global environmental NGOs pressured consumers to boycott tuna that was caught in such nets. Because the United States is the world's largest market for tuna, environmentalists in America used the power of consumers to force tuna producers to adopt dolphin-safe measures for catching tuna. **The Inter-American Tropical Tuna Commission (IATTC),** under American leadership, adopted regulations to prevent the endangerment of dolphins, a development that has helped to protect dolphins globally.[22]

International Whaling Commission
Established to protect the price of whale oil

CITES
Convention prohibiting trade in whale products

IATTC
Commission devoted to protecting dolphins, among other things

Sea turtles are also listed as an endangered or threatened species under the U.S. Endangered Species Act. While overfishing of turtles and harvesting their eggs continue to be serious concerns, one major threat to turtles comes from shrimp trawlers. Turtles caught in shrimp nets usually drown. To eliminate this problem, the U.S. government required shrimp trawlers to use **turtle extruder devices (TEDs)** on their nets. Essentially, these devices are trap doors through which turtles can escape if caught in the net. Apart from arguing that TEDs were a financial burden and that they were losing almost half of the shrimp they caught, shrimp fishers pointed out that foreign fleets did not face similar restrictions, a fact that put U.S. shrimpers at a competitive disadvantage.[23] American environmentalists ultimately succeeded in getting foreign shrimpers to comply with U.S. laws protecting turtles by agreeing with domestic shrimpers that all shrimpers should play by the same rules to ensure fair competition. Another threat to endangered turtles—especially the leatherback turtle, which can weigh up to 1,400 pounds and grow to a length of seven feet—comes from long-line fishing. **Long-line fishing** involves a main line that can be as long as thirty miles. The line has branch lines that are roughly 200 feet apart and are equipped with baited hooks. Some turtles swallow the hooks or become entangled in the lines. Environmentalists view long-line fishing as posing excessive risks to sea turtles.[24]

The African elephant, hunted mostly for ivory tusks for export, is also an endangered species, a designation that drew opposition from some countries, such as Botswana, Malawi, Mozambique, South African Zambia, and Zimbabwe. These countries had carefully managed their elephant herds and believed that restrictions on ivory exports would unfairly penalize them economically. Compared with African states that depleted their elephant herds, Botswana and the other countries had too many elephants. In 1997, Botswana, Namibia, and Zimbabwe were granted permission to sell stockpiled ivory tusks to Japan. Other animals in peril are gorillas and chimpanzees. Roughly 80 percent of the world's gorillas and most of its chimpanzees inhabit Gabon and the Republic of Congo. These great apes, our closest relatives, face severe threats from hunting, deforestation, and infectious diseases. It is estimated that the gorilla and chimpanzee populations declined by more than 50 percent between 1983 and 2000 and that they are likely to drop by an additional 80 percent in the next thirty years.[25] Worldwide, rare and exotic animals are threatened with extinction because of escalating exotic animal trade in them, aided by the Internet and a global network of traffickers. In fact, sales of exotic animals comprise the third largest global illegal trade—behind illegal drugs and weapons—and generate between $5 billion and $20 billion a year.[26] The same forces of globalization that help to protect the environment are also working to destroy it.

DEFORESTATION

One of the principal threats to biodiversity is the accelerating rate of global deforestation. The Amazon rainforest is estimated to be disappearing at the rate of 3 million acres a year. The **Congo basin**—comprised of Cameroon, Gabon, the Central African Republic, Republic of Congo, the Democratic Republic of Congo (former Zaire), and Equatorial Guinea, which had the second largest tropical forests in the world—is

Congo Basin

Tropical area in central Africa

Is Environmental Protection Endangering Humans?

Charles Geisler argues that about 70 percent of the world's protected areas are inhabited by people, who are generally regarded by some environmentalists as a barrier to environmental conservation. Africa has long been viewed as a natural preserve, with more emphasis placed on the environment than on people. In 1985, Africa had 443 publicly protected areas, encompassing 217 million acres of land. Due to global pressure, African countries increased the protected areas to 1,000, covering about 380 million acres of land. More land is reserved for environmental conservation where hunger seems to be endemic.

How do you balance the emphasis on environmental protection with human needs?

Source: Charles G. Geisler, "Endangered Humans," *Foreign Policy*, No. 130 (May/June 2002): 80–81.

loosing about 8.9 million acres a year to deforestation. Similarly, Russia, which has roughly 22 percent of the world's forests, is depleting its natural forests. Deforestation is also a major concern in many parts of Asia, especially in light of China's rapid economic growth and its demand for forest products. Forests are essential in biodiversity and to preserve the quality of life, and life itself, for human beings. Forests, especially large rain forests such as the Amazon, have an impact on the global climate. Air quality, water supplies, climate stability, agricultural productivity, and countless human communities are affected by deforestation. It is widely believed that protecting existing forests and planting more trees are essential to diminishing some environmental problems, such as global warming and climate change, because forests soak up between 10 and 20 percent of the heat-trapping carbon dioxide released by industrial smokestacks and automobiles.[27]

Causes of Deforestation

The most pervasive cause of deforestation is the combination *of population pressures and poverty*. Throughout most of the world, poor people rely on forests for fuel, shelter, agricultural land, and grazing for their animals. The relationship between population pressure, poverty, and deforestation is demonstrated by developments in **Chiapas**, the poorest state in Mexico. Destitute villagers in hundreds of communities in Chiapas cut down trees and burn the undergrowth to create fields for cultivation and grazing cattle. Soon after, the thin layer of topsoil is planted with corn, the land is left to return to pasture, which is often overgrazed. The exposed soil becomes vulnerable to erosion during heavy tropical rains. Somalia, on the Horn of Africa, provides another example of how poverty accelerates deforestation. Somalia, which lacks an effective central governmental authority to protect the environment, exports tons of charcoal to Middle Eastern countries.

Deforestation is also caused by the *deliberate setting of fires* by small farmers, commercial farmers, cattle ranchers, logging companies, and governments. **Selective logging** involves cutting down large and particular types of trees in an effort to manage exploitation of forest resources and to promote sustainability. Selective logging

Chiapas
The poorest state in Mexico

Selective Logging
Cutting specific trees in order to promote forest sustainability

Somalia's charcoal exports.

contributes to forest fires because, as forests are thinned out, humidity decreases and drier conditions in the forest facilitate the spread of both natural and human-made fires. The forces of **economic development** play a significant role in global deforestation. Development involves building an extensive **infrastructure**, which includes roads, highways, electrical plants, airports, harbors, railways, large reservoirs, and dams. Another cause of deforestation is the **commercial logging** practices that disregard sustainable development of forest resources. The demand for tropical hardwoods, such as mahogany and teak, is contributing to deforestation in Southeast Asia, Central America, Africa, and elsewhere in the developing world. **Government policies** have aggressively promoted deforestation in an effort to relocate people to less crowded areas in order to diminish population pressures and encourage economic development. Brazil has used this strategy. Opening up the Amazon was viewed in Brazil as important for national economic growth as well as a way to strengthen the country's strategic position in South America. Environmental protection was not a priority of the military governments that ruled Brazil. Consequently, between 1970 and 1974, the government implemented its **Plan for National Integration**. This plan included the construction of the Trans-Amazon Highway and offered incentives to agribusiness enterprises and lenders peasants, especially from the northeast, to encourage them to settle in the Amazon and to clear the land for cultivation, cattle grazing, and industrialization.[28]

Infrastructure

Necessary elements of a stable society

Commercial Logging

Process disrupting sustainable development

Plan for National Integration

Brazil's efforts to encourage the development of the Amazon.

Efforts to Prevent Deforestation

Efforts to slow down the rapid pace of global deforestation appear to be largely ineffective. Nonetheless, governments, NGOs, and grassroots organizations are making some progress. In Brazil, the transition from military rule to democracy has been accompanied by government programs aimed at halting deforestation. Since the 1990s, the Brazilian government's perception of the environment has shifted from frontier development toward environmental protection. This change is partly due to growing global awareness of the Amazon's importance to environmental health and increased global and domestic pressures for change. In 1989, the Brazilian government announced the development of its **Nossa Natureza (Our Nature) Program** to reduce the destruction of the Amazon rain forests. The program included (1) suspending fiscal incentives for developing forest resources; (2) limiting log exports; (3) creating national parks; (4) and increasing the emphasis on environmental protection and research. An important component of this effort was the formation of **IBAMA**, the federal environmental protection agency, to monitor environment problems and to enforce environmental laws.[29] But loggers, ranchers, and farmers continue to destroy the forests and wildlife and to threaten the livelihoods of the indigenous inhabitants. The murder of Sister Dorothy Stang, an American nun opposed to deforestation, in February 2005, underscores the ongoing conflict in the Amazon. Another example of government involvement in efforts to diminish deforestation is the agreement reached in 2000 by logging companies, the government of Gabon, and several environmental NGOs to preserve 1,900 square miles of forests that comprise **Gabon's Lope Reserve**. This area contains very valuable trees and the highest density of large animals, including elephants and gorillas, ever recorded in a tropical rain forest.[30]

One of the most successful grassroots reforestation efforts is by the Green Belt Movement of Kenya. Its objectives include:

1. *Raising awareness* of the connection between the environment and poverty;
2. *Promoting the planting of multi-use trees* to meet fuel needs, provide employment, protect the environment, and provide food for the community;
3. *Protecting indigenous trees* from being replaced by foreign commercial trees;
4. *Promoting women's leadership roles* in economic development;
5. *Alleviating poverty* by creating jobs; and
6. *Disseminating information* on environmental protection through research, seminars, and workshops.[31]

Another approach to addressing the problem of deforestation is **forest certification**. The basic idea is to inform consumers about the origin of wood products and how their production affects the environment. This approach, which aims to promote eco-friendly lumber, has been championed by the **Forest Stewardship Council**, a coalition of environmentalists and lumber executives. The guidelines for gaining certification include complying with national laws aimed at (1) protecting forests, (2) protecting the rights of indigenous peoples, (3) preserving species, (4) eliminating waste, (5) promoting economic development, and (6) preserving the forests.[32]

Ocean Resources—Fishing

Concerned about proper nutrition, more people around the world—especially in Europe, Canada, and the United States—are eating more seafood. The modernization of fishing fleets has made more fish available to global markets. This modernization involves

Nossa Natureza Program

Designed to reduce destruction of the Amazon

IBAMA

Brazilian environmental protection agency

Gabon's Lope Reserve

Area in Gabon containing rich biodiversity

Forest Certification

Required in order to protect against deforestation

Forest Stewardship Council

Group of environmentalists and lumber companies dedicated to protecting forests

using such technology as electronic fish locators, satellite navigation, temperature-depth gauges, purse-seine nets, and long-line fishing gear. More than any other food commodity, seafood crosses national boundaries daily. Most fish are exported from Africa and Southeast Asia to Europe and the United States, making it very likely that the fish you had for dinner came from another country. In fact, it is estimated that the United States exports $2 billion but imports $9 billion in seafood each year.[33]

Fish remained abundant throughout much of the world until relatively recently. John Cabot, the fifteenth century explorer, claimed that cod were so abundant off the coast of Newfoundland, Canada, that he caught them simply by putting a bucket over the side of his ship. The cod fishing grounds in that area supported the fishing fleets of the United States and Canada for hundreds of years after John Cabot was there. By 1992, however, the cod had essentially disappeared. A ban on cod fishing, imposed to rejuvenate the stock, appeared to be futile. There are numerous examples of overfishing and the eventual collapse of fisheries. California's sardine industry, popularized by John Steinbeck, declined rapidly in the early 1940s and died out three decades later. In 1996, the **UN Food and Agriculture Organization (FAO)** estimated that more than half of global fisheries were overexploited and were facing a collapse.[34]

FAO

UN organization focusing upon world food and agriculture supplies

Apart from the growing awareness of the health benefits derived from consuming seafood, *there are several reasons for overfishing*. At the heart of the problem is that there are so many fishing fleets operating that fish stocks are not harvested in a way that is environmentally sustainable. For example, many fish are caught before they are old enough to reproduce and replenish fish supplies. The most important cause of overfishing is **government subsidies**. The subsidies include

1. Grants, low-cost loans, and tax incentives to promote the construction and repair of fishing fleets.
2. Price supports for fish and fish products,
3. Export promotion programs,
4. Construction and maintenance of port facilities,
5. Subsidization of payments for access to foreign fisheries, and
6. Support of the development of fishing technology.[35]

Faced with declining catches of fish, communities have historically attempted to regulate fishing. Countries that share North Sea fisheries have been very aware of the dangers of overfishing and have tried to adopt measures to limit the problem. Coastal states with rich fishing grounds often clash with countries that support long-distance fishing fleets. To protect their resources, coastal states successfully pushed for the establishment of **exclusive economic zones**, which extend to 200 miles and over which coastal states exercise jurisdiction. These sovereign rights of coastal areas are recognized by the **Law of the Sea Treaty**, which came into effect in 1994. In early 1999, the FAO's Committee on Fisheries attempted to mobilize global support for reducing overcapacity in the fishing industry by adopting the **International Plan for the Management of Fishing Capacity (IPMFC)**. But this is a nonbinding agreement. Most states have few incentives to comply with it. Another approach to protecting

Exclusive Economic Zones

Coastal waters exclusive to each state

global fisheries is boycotting restaurants that serve fish that are being severely depleted. Environmentalists and scientists believe that by educating consumers about fisheries and by monitoring the global market for seafood, they can save endangered species such as swordfish and Chilean sea bass. An important group supporting this effort, which demonstrates collaboration between environmentalists and businesses, is the **National Chefs Collaborative**. This organization is composed of more than 1,500 environmentally conscious restaurant owners throughout the United States who refuse to serve endangered species of fish.[36] Although controversial, because of environmental concerns and its impact on wild fish, the most promising approach to slowing the depletion of wild fisheries is **aquaculture**, or fish farming.

INVASIVE SPECIES

Fascinated by William Shakespeare, **Eugene Scheiffelin** imported sixty starlings from Europe and released them in Central Park in 1890 in order to give the birds mentioned in Shakespeare's plays an American home. As starlings blacken the summer skies and invade once quiet and pristine neighborhoods in the Midwest and elsewhere, it is difficult to believe that the original sixty starlings claim more than a billion descendants. When the population of imported European zebra mussels exploded in the Great Lakes in the 1980s and clogged industrial intake pipes, the issue of invasive species gained national attention. Although invasive species are as old as human migrations, the rapid growth of economic and cultural globalization has made this issue extremely important. Invasive species, often referred to as exotic aliens, are generally perceived as dangerous, threatening, and unacceptable. These exotics are more aggressive, prolific, competitive, and predatory than the indigenous species. They often threaten the survival of native species listed as endangered or threatened under the Endangered Species Act. Ecologists generally define an **invasive**, or **alien, species** as one that people inadvertently or deliberately carried to its new location. European contacts with the Americas in 1492 marked a major shift in the spread of species, including crops and animals. Think of the beneficial invasive species that we now consider American: corn, wheat, rice, potatoes, cattle, and poultry. Although exotics received a lot of negative attention, only a small percentage of invasive species create problems in their new habitats.[37]

Many species now regarded as detrimental to the environment were initially perceived as solutions to problems or as providing economic opportunities. Millions of kudzu seedlings were planted by the **Civilian Conservation Corps** during the Great Depression to prevent erosion and to provide employment. Kudzu is now a serious threat to the environment in parts of the American South. The multicolored Asian ladybugs—which many people now regard as pests, especially as they migrate indoors for winter—were brought from China to control aphids and other agricultural pests. Water hyacinth, native to the Amazon, was transported to East Africa to decorate a garden pond. Vast sheets of water hyacinth now cover parts of Lake Victoria, impeding travel, destroying fish, and ensnaring fishing boats. African honeybees, imported by Brazil in 1956, escaped and are resolutely advancing into the United States. When disturbed, the

Law of the Sea Treaty

Recognizes state rights over territorial coastal waters

IPMFC

FAO plan to reduce overcapacity in the fishing industry

Invasive/Alien Species

A species that invades other ecosystems

Civilian Conservation Corps

Created in the U.S. during the Great Depression to protect the environment and provide employment

bees attack in larger numbers and pursue victims for great distances and long periods of time. Their aggressiveness has earned them the designation of "killer bees."

Globalization is accelerating the spread of invasive species. China's exports have resulted in serious environmental damage in New York, and Illinois, for example. The population of the Asian longhorn beetle, native to China, exploded in fields of poplar planted to reverse deforestation in China. Wood from the trees, infested with Asian longhorns, was used for packaging products being exported to the United States. But America also exports invasive species. A tiny beetle, known as the western corn root-worm, is native to the United States. After boarding a plane at Chicago's O'Hare International Airport, the beetle landed in Belgrade and began to invade cornfields across Europe, with devastating consequences.[38] Since most global trade relies on shipping, invasive species often arrive at distant places in ballast water releases, in containers, in used tires, and on the ships themselves. The Leidy's comb jellyfish, native to the East Coast of the Americas, made its way to the Black Sea in ballast water and began eating zooplankton. Facing no natural competition, the jellyfish represents one of the most significant massive invasions in history and has caused severe damage to the Black Sea ecosystem.[39] The Asian tiger mosquito, which was largely confined to the Indian and Pacific regions, arrived into the United States and elsewhere in containers of used tires. This mosquito—which transmits dengue fever, yellow fever, and various forms of encephalitis—is now established in Brazil, Southern Europe, South Africa, Nigeria, New Zealand, and Australia.[40] Invasive species, those exotic aliens, are fast becoming natives.

OCEAN POLLUTION

Beaches worldwide are routinely closed, including in areas that depend heavily on tourism, because of dangers to human health posed by pollution. Long perceived as an almost bottomless sink, the seas have been used as dumping grounds for centuries. Major oil spills, rapid development of coastal areas, increased use of petroleum products, the dramatic increase in shipping to meet demands for global trade, and economic globalization and the rise of leisure travel on cruise ships, among other factors, have contributed to significant increases in the pollution of the oceans by oil. Oil spills by tankers, such as the one caused by the ***Exxon Valdez*** in 1989 off the Alaskan Coast, often generate a sense of urgency about actions to prevent ocean pollution. Israel's invasion of Lebanon in 2006 and its bombing of oil facilities caused major problems in the Mediterranean. Despite global concerns, oil spills due to tanker accidents continue to be a serious threat to the global environment.

The toxic and carcinogenic properties of petroleum and the damage it causes to sea life, most of which is immobilized when soaked with oil, are the most obvious negative effects of oil spills. But the longer oil remains on the surface of the oceans, the more it blocks sunrays and oxygen essential for the health and survival of marine life. The impact on biodiversity is always a major concern. Numerous businesses and individuals depend on the ocean for their incomes. When an Ecuadorian tanker spilled

Exxon Valdez

Oil tanker that spilled off the coast of Alaska

TABLE 8.2 MAJOR OIL TANKER SPILLS

Name of Tanker	Place	Date	Oil Spilled (Thousands of Tons)
Atlantic Empress	Trinidad/Tobago	1979	287
ABT Summer	Angola	1991	260
Castillo de Bellver	South Africa	1983	252
Amoco Cadiz	France	1978	223
Haven	Italy	1991	144
Odyssey	Canada	1988	132
Torrey Canyon	Britain	1967	119
Urquiola	Spain	1976	100
Hawaiian Patriot	Northern Pacific	1977	95
Independenta	Turkey	1979	95
Jakob Maersk	Portugal	1975	88
Braer	Britain	1993	86
Khark 5	Morocco	1989	80
Prestige	Spain	2002	77
Aegean Sea	Spain	1992	74
Sea Empress	Britain	1996	72
Katina P.	Mozambique	1992	72
Exxon Valdez	United States	1989	37

Sources: "An Ecological Disaster, Or Maybe Not," *Economist*, 23 November 2002, 75; and Emma Daly, "Oil Tanker Splits Apart off Spain, Threatening Coast," *New York Times*, 20 November 2002, A6.

243,000 gallons of diesel and bunker fuel in the **Galapagos Islands**, located about 600 miles off the Pacific Coast of South America, there was global concern about the impact of the spill on the environment. Apart from the economic consequences, environmentalists, scientists, and others worried about the effects of oil pollution on the species of marine iguanas, giant tortoises, and penguins that are found nowhere else.[41] The unusual diversity of wildlife in the Galapagos Islands was popularized by **Charles Darwin**, who visited the area in 1835 and developed his theory of **natural selection**.

Although major oil spills receive global attention, these accidents account for around 20 percent of global oil pollution at sea. Far more damaging and widespread is pollution caused by the deliberate dumping of oil used in shipping operations in the oceans. Oil tankers, container ships, and cruise ships, for example, use ballast water, which is sea water that is pumped into the bottom of the ship to keep it stable on the sea when it is not loaded with cargo. Because cargo serves as ballast, ballast water is pumped out when a ship is being loaded. Large ships carry thousands of cubic meters of ballast water, which is often contaminated by oil. Much of the 400 million pounds of waste generated annually by cruise ships is dumped into the oceans, according to the **Ocean Conservancy**, an organization that focuses on protecting the oceans, from pollution.[42]

The most important source of marine oil pollution is from land-based activities in which most of us engage. As your car drips oil onto the driveway, the streets, and the parking lot, you are likely to think of it as a minor inconvenience. Small amounts of oil

Charles Darwin

The leading proponent of evolution theory

Natural Selection

A prevalent theory regarding the evolution of plant and animal species

Ocean Conservancy

Focus on protecting the oceans from pollution

National Research Council

Conducts environmental studies for the U.S. government

ICPS

First international agreement aimed at reducing ocean pollution

ICPPS

Limited the discharge amounts of land and sea pollutants

from your outboard motorboat and jet skis are responsible for roughly 70 percent of marine pollution. These tiny amounts of oil are washed into lakes, streams, and rivers and eventually make their way to the sea, where they damage coastal ecosystems and marine life far beyond the coasts. The problem of pollution from land-based sources is pronounced along the densely populated East Coast of the United States, especially in the area extending from Boston to Washington, D.C. A study by the **National Research Council**—the branch of the National Academy of Sciences in Washington, D.C. that conducts independent studies for the U.S. government—concluded that, globally, people release about 210 million gallons of petroleum a year into the sea.[43] Oil spills have influenced the development of international law on environmental pollution. The first significant international agreement aimed at reducing ocean pollution was **the International Convention for the Prevention of Pollution of the Sea (ICPS) by Oil** in 1954. The **1973 International Convention for the Prevention of Pollution by Ships (ICPPS)** limited the amount of discharges from both land and sea for specific pollutants, including oil.

GLOBAL WARMING AND CLIMATE CHANGE

Despite much controversy surrounding the issues of global warming and climate change, there is a consensus among scientists that greenhouse gases are altering the atmosphere in ways that ultimately contribute to climate change and higher temperatures. The basic

TABLE 8.3 GLOBAL WARMING

Effects of Global Warming	Implications	Areas Most Affected
Floods	• Rising sea levels and heavy rains could displace millions of people and leave many areas under water • More refugees	Coastal U.S., Australia, Pacific Islands, Holland, Philippines, Bangladesh, China, Mozambique, Nigeria
Heat Waves	• Increase in deaths from heatstroke, forest fires, and skin cancer	Southern Europe, U.S., China, Brazil, Indonesia, Russia
Diseases	• Warmer, wetter weather could increase insect-transmitted and water-borne illnesses	U.S., Central, and South America, Africa, Asia
Coral Bleaching	• Depleting fisheries • Coastal flooding • Decline of tourism	Caribbean, Australia, Philippines, India
Pollution	• More respiratory problems, cancer, lung and heart diseases	U.S., Mexico, India, China, Egypt, Russia
Drought	• Crop failure • Malnutrition • Forest fires • Water-related conflicts	U.S., Mexico, Brazil, China, India, Africa, Middle East

Sources: U.S. News and World Report, 5 February 2001; National Center for Atmospheric Research, World Meteorological Organization, and the National Climatic Data Center.

TABLE 8.4 REGIONAL CLIMATE CHANGE IN THE UNITED STATES

Region	Likely Climate Changes
Northeast	Decline in winter weather extremes; more flooding; hotter summers; changes in forest species
Southeast	Rising sea levels; disappearance of some coastal wetlands, barrier islands and beaches; increase in water quality problems
Great Lakes	Declining water levels due to increased evaporation; increased transportation and shoreline problems due to lower water levels; warmer weather will keep shipping lanes open longer
Midwest—Great Plains	Extreme summer heat; milder winters; longer growing season; heavier rainfall; flash flooding; more droughts
Mountain West	Warmer winters; less snow; water problems; drier mountain regions; loss of mountain ecosystems
Southwest	Increased moisture; increased crop diversity; more flooding and fire risks; changes in desert ecosystem
Northwest—Alaska	Warmer water temperatures in the Pacific could cause salmon to migrate northward; more rain in summer; rising sea levels; warmer weather in Alaska will increase permafrost thawing and damage roads and buildings; warmer weather will keep shipping lanes open longer

Sources: "Temperature Increase to Change American Life," *Pantagraph*, 9 June 2000, A17; and Andrew C. Revkin, "Report Forecasts Warming's Effects," *New York Times*, 12 June 2000, A1.

assumption is that human activities are the main causes of these climatic developments. But determining human influence on global warming and climate change is complicated by a relative lack of accurate information about climate change over past centuries. Historically, climate has varied significantly. Natural forces such as volcanic eruptions can create climate changes, as was evidenced by the eruption of **Mount Pinatubo** in the Philippines in 1991. Ocean currents also change temperatures. Apart from greenhouse gases, factors such as deforestation, urbanization, and agricultural activities also affect the climate.[44]

Mount Pinatubo
Erupted in the Philippines in 1991

When our ancestors discovered how to make fire and how to use it, they set into motion a chain of events that would ultimately alter their environment and ours. However, it was the **Industrial Revolution** that marked a radical step toward the current problems of global warming and climate change because of its use of massive amounts of fossil fuels—coal, oil, and natural gas. More than a hundred years ago, **Svante Arrhenius**, a Swedish chemist, and **T. C. Chamberlain**, an American geologist, independently discovered that industrialization could lead to increasing levels of carbon dioxide in the atmosphere. This could ultimately raise the atmosphere's temperature by trapping solar radiation that would otherwise be reflected back into space, creating a **greenhouse effect**.[45] The U. S. government issued a report in 1965 that raised concerns about global warming and climate change. However, national security during the Cold War took precedence over more distant threats like environmental problems. Congress, under the leadership of Representative Al Gore, held hearings in the early 1980s on global warming. In 1988, after NASA scientist James Hansen told

Greenhouse Effect
Rise in Earth's temperature from greenhouse gases

Congress that he was 99 percent certain that the greenhouse effect had been detected and that it was already changing our climate, Congress established the **U.S. Global Change Research Program (USGCRP)** to study human-induced climate change and stratospheric ozone depletion from industrial emissions.[46]

Acid rain and ozone depletion preceded global awareness and concern about global warming. Air pollution from Europe's industrial societies, especially Britain and Germany, was identified by **Svante Oden**, a Swedish scientist, as a leading cause of the increasing acidification of precipitation, known as acid rain, in the Scandinavian countries in the late 1960s. Acid rain caused by industrial activities in the United States was

also a major concern for Canada, where more than 16,000 lakes were affected. **Acid rain,** composed of sulfur dioxide, nitrogen oxide, and volatile organic compounds, is caused primarily by burning coal. By increasing the acidity of lakes, rivers, and streams, acid rain damages animal and plant life. It has also destroyed buildings in Greece, Italy, and other parts of Europe. Ozone depletion was also identified as a serious environmental problem resulting from air pollution. The **ozone layer** of our atmosphere pro-

tects us from ultraviolet radiation that causes skin cancers, genetic changes in animals and plants, eye disorders, and suppression of our immune systems. Agricultural productivity and fisheries are also affected. Ozone depletion is most severe in Antarctica and the Northern Hemisphere. The major cause of ozone depletion was discovered to

be **chlorofluorocarbons (CFCs)**, synthetic products developed by DuPont and used in a wide range of products, including air conditioning, refrigeration, foam packaging, and aerosols. CFCs, when released into the atmosphere, react with ultraviolet light to form chlorine. It is this chlorine that destroys the ozone.

Reductions in the production of greenhouse gases are widely perceived to be the solution to diminishing global warming and climate change and their effects. The Kyoto Protocol to the UN Framework Convention on Climate Change, generally known as the **Kyoto Protocol**, is clearly the most important global environmental agreement and reflects an increasing awareness of environmental globalization. But economic, scientific, and ideological disagreements have weakened the Kyoto Protocol's effectiveness. The

United States, the leading producer of greenhouse gases, opposed the agreement on the grounds that the imposition of emission controls would be detrimental to the American economy. India and China are also responsible for significant shares of global carbon dioxide emissions. Developing countries that are energy exporters give *four main reasons* for opposing global efforts to reduce emissions: (1) emission controls will reduce their revenues by decreasing energy consumption, (2) imports from industrialized countries would be more expensive because of measures taken to reduce carbon dioxide emissions, (3) the development of new fuels to help cut down emissions are likely to reduce demand for their exports, and (4) oil, gas, and coal resources are part of their heritage.[47] In 2003, following the ratification of the Kyoto Protocol by more that ninety-six countries, many developing countries supported **the Delhi Ministerial Declaration on Climate Change and Sustainable Development**, which supports the right of poor countries to develop their own appropriate strategies to reduce carbon dioxide emissions. This position was endorsed to the United States. In November 2006, the global community met in Nairobi, Kenya to address the issues of global warming and climate change.

TABLE 8.5 GLOBAL CARBON DIOXIDE EMISSIONS (2006)

Country	Percent of Total Global Emissions	Millions of Metric Tons Per Year
United States	23	1,407
China	14	871
Russia	8	496
Japan	5	308
India	4	248
Germany	4	228
Britain	2	148
Ukraine	2	120
Canada	2	119
Italy	2	112
South Korea	2	102
Mexico	2	98

Source: United Nations Framework on Climate Change, 2006.

The Kyoto Protocol allows countries to use market forces to reduce carbon dioxide emissions. Targets are determined for lower levels of emissions and then permits are issued for that set level. Companies that exceed their target by not producing so much pollution can sell extra permits to companies that need to meet their targets. This approach is referred to as **emissions trading**. Many European countries use this approach. Britain and Denmark, for example, trade greenhouse gases to reduce climate change. The **Chicago Climate Exchange** is the first attempt to decrease greenhouse gases with a market approach. Participants in this effort include DuPont, Motorola, Ford Motor Company, American Electric Power, and the City of Chicago. Another approach, favored by the United States, is to rely primarily on forests to reduce the effects of emissions from industries and automobiles. But the long-term effectiveness of using forests instead of taking other major steps to reduce greenhouse gases is debatable. Research conducted at Duke University concluded that forests are likely to be a modest, if not disappointing, sink for carbon dioxide.[48]

Emissions Trading
Trading of greenhouse gases to reduce climate change

Chicago Climate Exchange
Attempts to decrease greenhouse gases through a market approach

HAZARDOUS WASTES

International concern about transporting toxic wastes across national boundaries was heightened in the early 1980s and continued to grow as more people, governments, and environmental NGOs became more aware of the extent of the problem and the dangers involved. Greenpeace played a leading role in focusing global attention on **toxic terrorism** (i.e., deliberate efforts to export very dangerous chemicals to poor countries). Several notorious cases galvanized support in the global community to address the problem of hazardous wastes. In one case, called the **Seveso Affair**, forty-one missing drums of topsoil contaminated with highly toxic dioxin were found in a barn in France. The toxic material came from the Seveso chemical plant in Italy that had exploded in 1976. Another case

Toxic Terrorism
Deliberate efforts toward spreading dangerous chemicals

PCBs

A highly toxic, radioactive, industrial waste

that received global attention was the discovery of 150 tons of **polychlorinated biphenyl (PCBs)**, a highly toxic and radioactive waste, on a farm in Koko, Nigeria.[49] Finally, the disintegration of Soviet Union in 1991 drew global attention to the large amount of radioactive materials and toxic wastes that were produced by the Soviet military. In 2006 a tankership owned by a Dutch firm dumped several tons of toxic wastes in the Ivory Coast. Shipbreaking in countries such as Bangladesh and India results in significant amounts of toxic wastes. Although many leaders and groups in developing countries facilitated the transfer of hazardous wastes, the general perception was that the rich countries were circumventing their own costly regulations regarding toxic wastes by simply dumping these toxic materials in economically vulnerable developing societies. Poor countries endorsed a comprehensive global approach to dealing with the problem for three main reasons: (1) they were unable to monitor and enforce their own policies restricting imports of hazardous wastes, (2) they lacked the technical and scientific expertise to deal with hazardous wastes, and (3) they believed that the global community had an ethical obligation to prevent the rich countries from using poor countries as toxic dumps.[50]

Cairo Guidelines

Developed to ensure regulation of hazardous waste

The first concrete action to address the problem was taken by the UNEP committee in 1985, which developed the **Cairo Guidelines**. These guidelines included the following: (1) prior notification of the state receiving any export of hazardous wastes, (2) consent by the receiving state prior to export, and (3) verification by the sending country that the receiving state's disposal requirements were as stringent as those of the state exporting hazardous wastes. These guidelines were strengthened by the **Basel Convention on the Control of Transboundary Movements of Hazardous Wastes and Their Disposal**, concluded in Basel, Switzerland in 1989. The main provisions of the Basel Convention are

Basel Convention

Strengthened the Cairo Guidelines on hazardous waste

1. A commitment was made to reducing the production of hazardous wastes.
2. Controlling and decreasing transboundary movements of hazardous wastes is to be accomplished by taking care of the problem at the source.
3. Obtaining prior informed consent by the importing country is required.
4. The receiving state must have the capability to dispose of hazardous wastes in ways that do not damage the environment.
5. States have the sovereign right to ban hazardous wastes imports.
6. Developing countries are entitled to receive technical assistance from industrialized states to deal with hazardous wastes.[51]

Fourth Lome Convention

Prohibited the export of hazardous wastes to ACP states

In addition to these global responses, developing countries have signed several regional agreements to combat the transfer of hazardous wastes. The African, Caribbean, and Pacific (ACP) states included a clause in the **Fourth Lome Convention** of 1989 that requires the EU to ban exports of hazardous wastes to ACP countries. It also prohibits ACP states from receiveing hazardous wastes. In 1992, the **Central American Regional Agreement on the Transboundary Movement of Hazardous Wastes** prohibits member states from importing dangerous wastes. Similarly, members of the South Pacific Forum signed an agreement in 1995, the **Waigani Treaty on Hazardous and Toxic Wastes (WTHTW)**, to control the movement of wastes generated within the Pacific region and to ban hazardous wastes imports by Pacific states. Finally, the African countries, dissatisfied with the Basel Convention's decision not to impose a total ban on exporting toxic and radioactive wastes, concluded the **Bamako Convention** in 1996. This agreement prohibits the import of all hazardous wastes.[52]

Bamako Convention

Prohibits the import of hazardous wastes in many African states

WATER SCARCITY

At the foundation of human existence and life on earth is water. The most common and abundant liquid in the world, water is at the heart of global environmental issues. Water, particularly potable water, is fueling conflicts globally. Increasing demands for water by the world's growing and increasingly more affluent populations threaten to create widespread shortages of freshwater. Water, in many ways, defines how we live and determines the limit of sustainable development. Imagine life without adequate water. Think of all the adjustments you would have to make just to survive. Water usage has grown by 600 percent over the past seventy years. Worldwide, an estimated 54 percent of the annual available freshwater is being used. Based solely on population growth, the UN Population Fund estimated that by 2025, we would use 70 percent of available freshwater.[53] Rivers throughout the world are drying up or no longer reach the sea year round. Parts of the United States—especially Arizona, Colorado, Utah, Nevada, and Wyoming—experience severe water shortages as they continue to be some of the fastest growing areas of the country. Tensions routinely flare up between the United States and Mexico over water rights to the Rio Grande and the Colorado rivers. Water is becoming a serious source of conflict in the Middle East, an area that already endures sustained violence. Increasing urbanization, industrialization, and the environmental problems we have discussed are likely to accelerate these problems. India faces severe water problems that seriously threaten to undermine its economic growth and public health.

Water scarcity—defined as a lack of secure, uninterrupted, and long-term availability of adequate amounts of freshwater of required quality[54]—is becoming an important component of the broader issues of environmental and global security. As we saw in Chapter 1, security issues go beyond traditional military threats. Water scarcity is likely to lead to direct military confrontation. Unlike oil, which can be replaced by several substitutes, there is no viable substitute for water at reasonable prices. When a country that is extremely dependent on water coming from rivers or streams in another country perceives that its supplies are threatened, it could use military force to resolve the problem. For example, when Lebanon decided to begin pumping water from the Wazzani Springs in late 2002, tensions with Israel intensified. The Wazzani Springs supply the Hasbani River, which is a tributary of the Jordan River. Israel depends on the Jordan River for water. Concerned about tensions over water erupting into war, the United States dispatched a water expert from the U.S. Department of State to try to resolve the conflict.[55] The struggle to control water supplies is an important component of the Palestinian-Israeli conflict. While Israel controls water supplies in Palestinian lands and Israeli settlers in Palestinian territories

Water Scarcity

A lack of secure, uninterrupted, long-term availability of adequate clean freshwater

have water for spriklers and swimming pools, Palestinian water supplies are controlled by Israel and are severely restricted and polluted. As we discussed earlier in this chapter, global warming and other environmental changes are already threatening water supplies. In coastal areas and on islands worldwide, rising seawater, due in part to global warming, is likely to contaminate freshwater supplies.

MILITARY ACTIVITIES AND THE ENVIRONMENT

From the beginning of civilization, our ancestors have enlisted the environment in their conflicts, with destruction of the environment being the inevitable outcome. The Romans sowed salt on Carthaginian farms during the Third Punic War (149–146 B.C.), thereby destroying the land's agricultural productivity. Water supplies have been contaminated, infectious diseases inflicted on the enemy, and forests destroyed to make war and as a consequence of war. Bombs remain unexploded in fields around the world. The overwhelming preoccupation with the survival of the sovereign state, to be achieved by developing lethal military weapons, relegated environmental concerns to the back burner. But growing environmental awareness and increased activism have heightened concerns about the impact of military activities on the ecosystems. The long-term environmental damage caused by war and training for war is increasingly being taken into consideration by the U.S. military, among others. In addition to analyzing the economic, political, cultural, and religious consequences of war, there is now a global recognition of the need to also consider environmental implications of conflict.[56]

Agent Orange

Highly toxic defoliant used by the U.S. in the Vietnam War

Environmental Security Program

Pentagon environmental program

South Pacific Nuclear Weapon Free Zone

Created in 1985 to reduce the risk of nuclear contamination

Links between military activities and the environment became a prominent issue during the Vietnam War, partly because of the fusion of the antiwar protests and the emerging environmental movement. During the Vietnam War, many Americans were directly affected by exposure to America's use of millions of gallons of **Agent Orange**, a herbicide that defoliated the forests as part of a strategy designed to deprive Vietcong forces of forest cover. Decaying ordnance, nuclear wastes, chemicals, and other toxic pollutants created long-term environmental problems. The Pentagon allocates about $5 billion a year to its **environmental security program,** designed to protect and rehabilitate the environment. Environmentalists have launched campaigns to get the military to protect endangered species that inhabit military bases. They also succeeded in getting the U.S. Navy to abandon the Puerto Rican island of Vieques, which was used for a firing range and various military exercises. The Pacific islanders linked nuclear testing directly to environmental issues, partly because radiation on some islands forced their inhabitants to abandon them. After many years of U.S., British, and French nuclear testing in the Pacific, the islanders, together with New Zealand and Australia, created the **South Pacific Nuclear Weapon Free Zone** in 1985 to reduce the risk of nuclear contamination.

Numerous conflicts in the developing world and recent wars in the Persian Gulf, Serbia, Chechnya, and elsewhere have created major environmental problems. During the first Persian Gulf War in 1991, retreating Iraqi soldiers ignited Kuwaiti oil fields, causing 3 to 6 million barrels of oil a day to burn and contaminate Kuwait and surrounding countries. Similarly, Russian soldiers deliberately ignited oil wells in Chechnya, making a large part of that area an ecological disaster zone. When NATO forces bombed oil refineries, industrial plants, electrical transformers, and other parts of the Serbian infrastructure in 1999, toxins—such as polychlorinated biphenyl's (PCBs), liquid mercury, and vinyl chloride monomer (VCM)—were released into the Danube River, the air, and the soil. The environmental consequences are significant and will last for a long time.[57]

A more common and devastating environmental problem related to war is the proliferation of landmines in conflicts around the world. Landmines, like toxic chemicals and unexploded bombs, continue to kill long after wars end. Vietnam, Angola, Afghanistan, Mozambique, and other developing countries have abandoned forests and agricultural areas because of the dangers posed by landmines. As conflict escalated between India and Pakistan, farmers were forced to abandon their land by the military so that landmines could be planted. While it is easy to plant mines, removing them is very difficult, time-consuming, and dangerous. Numerous civilians are killed or injured daily in many countries by landmines laid in wars that are largely forgotten in countries not affected by them. Environmentalists have focused their attention on not only removing landmines but also on banning their production and use in wars. Their efforts resulted in the signing of the **Ottawa Treaty** in 1999. Israel's use of cluster bombs during its invasion of Lebanon in 2006 shows how difficult it is to prevent countries from using weapons that kill innocent civilians indiscriminately.

Ottawa Treaty
Addressed the danger of land mines

ECO-TERRORISTS

Although the overwhelming majority of environmentalists adopt conventional methods to achieve their objectives, there is a small group of environmentalists who are extremists and anarchists. This fringe radical group believes that violence, the destruction of property, and arson are legitimate instruments of political protest. Because their goal is to effectuate change by creating a climate of fear and intimidation, radical environmentalists are indistinguishable from terrorists and are widely regarded as **eco-terrorists**. There has long been an extremist wing of the environmentalist movement that destroyed property. Many threw paint on fur coats to demonstrate their opposition to slaughtering animals. Others drove metal spikes into trees in the American Northwest to impede logging by lumber companies. But the eco-terrorists are much more radical and operate in small cells that are not part of a hierarchical organization. These groups include the **Earth Liberation Front (E.L.F.), the Strawberry Liberation Front, Seeds of Resistance, Cropatistas, Reclaim the Seeds,** and the **Anarchist Golfing Association**.

Eco-terrorists
Extremist wing of the environmental movement

Environmental militancy spread from Britain to the United States and elsewhere. Strong opposition in Europe to genetically modified foods, known there as Frankenfoods, spilled over into the United States. Eco-terrorists are also responding to the significant loss of farmland, wetlands, and forests to urban sprawl, and to what they view as excessive energy consumption. Experimental agricultural crops have been destroyed, and research centers involved in genetic engineering have been vandalized and burned. For example, arsonists destroyed a genetic-research faculty at Michigan State University in 2000. Lumber companies, such as Boise Cascade Corporation, have also suffered from arson. Eco-terrorists are increasingly burning large homes and resorts that they believe contribute to environmental degradation. They have also firebombed SUVs because of their high energy consumption. Many eco-terrorists are convinced that governments are unwilling or unable to protect the environment. Ironically, high oil prices in 2005 and 2006 effectively reduced the sales of SUVs and declining real estate prices slowed building of large homes in particular and new construction in general. Several eco-terrorists were arrested and convicted in 2006.

Summary and Review

Environmental problems illustrate how much developments in other parts of the world can impact our lives. Environmental problems cannot be contained by arbitrary national boundaries. Environmental factors have played an important historical role in the rise and fall of great civilizations, the spread of infectious diseases, war, economic prosperity, and many other international issues. Environmental problems are intertwined with politics, economics, and culture. Despite the importance of the environment in our lives, however, movements to protect the environment are relatively new. The global environmental movement emerged principally in Western Europe, the United States, and Canada. Attention to the environment was spurred, in large part, by a tremendous population growth and rapid industrialization that took place with little regard for the serious environmental ramifications, such as deforestation and deteriorating health standards. Nuclear weapons proliferation in the United States and Soviet Union also increased concern for environmental issues.

Biodiversity is a fundamental preoccupation of environmentalists and NGOs. This is such an important issue because the destruction of some species could upset the balance of the ecosystem, resulting in the loss of other species and the alteration of the ecosystem. Biodiversity affects many groups and individuals, such as those interested in deforestation, agriculture, biotechnology, anthropology, pharmaceuticals, sustainable development, global trade, and ethics. Another major concern of environmentalists is water, the foundation for human existence. The planet's increasing population is threatening to create widespread shortages of freshwater. Roughly two-thirds of freshwater consumed each year goes to irrigate farms. Compared with other environmental problems, global warming is sometimes perceived as being a less immediate issue. While there is evidence that human activities cause most climate changes, determining how much human activity influences global warming and climate change continues to be debated, partly because there is little information about climate change over past centuries. However, global warming is clearly contributing to rising oceans, and more destructive hurricanes, such as Katrina and Rita in 2005.

Key Terms

commons 253
Chernobyl 253
environmental
   security 254
Silent Spring 255
World Summit on
   Sustainable
   Development 256
Green Belt
   Movement 258
biodiversity 259
North/South
   Divide 260

CITES 261
selective logging 263
commercial logging 264
Nossa Natureza
   Program 265
Gabon's Lope
   Reserve 265
forest certification 265
Forest Stewardship
   Council 265
FAO 266
exclusive economic
   zones 266

Law of the Sea
   Treaty 266
invasive/alien
   species 267
Exxon Valdez 268
Charles Darwin 269
natural selection 269
National Research
   Council 270
greenhouse effect 271
acid rain 272
ozone layer 272
CFCs 272

Kyoto Protocol 272
emissions trading 273
Chicago Climate
   Exchange 273
toxic terrorism 273
PCBs 274
Cairo
   Guidelines 274
Agent Orange 276
environmental security
   program 276
eco-terrorists 277

Discussion Questions

1. The global environmental movement emerged primarily in Western Europe and North America. What were some of the issues that led to the creation of this movement?

2. Because of the global nature of environmental problems, international agreements are often used to address environmental issues. What are some factors that influence these agreements?

3. What are some of the domestic factors that influence a country's effectiveness in enforcing strong environmental standards?

4. As discussed in previous chapters, revolutions in technologies have played an important role in a number of global issues. How have these developments both helped and hindered the current environmental movement?

5. What are some examples of how environmental problems more negatively affect women than men?

6. What are some of the strategies that environmental NGOs use to achieve their objectives?

7. What are the impediments that global NGOs often encounter?

8. What are some of the groups of people affected by the loss of biodiversity? How are these groups affected?

9. What were some of the approaches discussed in the chapter to solving the problem of deforestation?

10. What is an eco-terrorist? How are eco-terrorists groups different from other mainstream environmental groups?

Suggested Readings

Barrett, Scott. *Environment and Statecraft*. New York: Oxford University Press, 2006.

Bell, Ruth Greenspan. "What to Do About Climate Change," *Foreign Affairs* 85 No. 3 (May/June 2006): 105–114.

DeSadeleer, Nicolas. *Environmental Principles*. New York: Oxford University Press, 2005.

DeSombre, Elizabeth R. *Domestic Sources of International Environmental Policy*. Cambridge, MA: MIT Press, 2000.

Diamond, Jared. *Guns, Germs, and Steel*. New York: W. W. Norton, 1999.

Dryzek, John, and David Schlosberg. *Debating the Earth*. New York: Oxford University Press, 2005.

Elhance, Arun P. *Hydropolitics in the Third World.* Washington, DC: U.S. Institute of Peace Press, 1999.

Elliott, Lorraine. *The Global Politics of the Environment.* New York: New York University Press, 1998.

McNeill, J. R. *Something New Under the Sun: An Environmental History of the Twentieth-Century World.* New York: W. W. Norton, 2000.

Shabecoff, Philip. *Earth Rising: American Environmentalism in the 21st Century.* Washington, DC: Island Press, 2000.

Victor, David. *Climate Change: Debating America's Policy Options.* New York: Council on Foreign Relations, 2005.

Addresses and Websites

Department of Economic and Social Development
E-mail: esa@un.org
www.un.org/esa/sustdev

This site offers ten links to topics such as sustainable development, environment, and population. These are all United Nations sponsored links that provide much information and other links on a variety of topics. It also offers details of current and past meetings relating to economic and social development topics.

United Nations Environment Programme

www.unep.org

This organization's main goal is to encourage sustainable development through environmental practices. Their mission statement is: "To provide leadership and encourage partnership in caring for the environment by inspiring, informing, and enabling nations and people to improve their quality of life without compromising that of the future generations."

World Health Organization Headquarters
Avenue Appia 22
1211 Geneva 27
Switzerland
Tel.: 4122 791 21 11
E-mail: info@who.int
www.who.int

The World Health Organization is a United Nations agency whose main goal is to provide health care to everyone. It has leading experts in a variety of health-related subjects, including humanitarian emergencies and disease outbreaks from around the world. The website offers links to other health-related topics, as well as UN information on health topics. It also offers information on pollution and the environment.

Secretary of the Publications Board
United Nations
New York, NY 10017
E-mail: cunninghama@un.org
Fax: (212) 963–0077
www.un.org

The purpose of the United Nations, as set forth in its Charter, is to maintain international peace and security; to develop friendly relations among nations; to cooperate in solving international economic, social, cultural, and humanitarian problems in promoting respect for human rights and fundamental freedoms; and to be the center for harmonizing the actions of nations in attaining these ends. This website offers links to all UN-sponsored websites on a variety of topics, including UNICEF and UNDP.

Food and Agriculture Organization
Viale delle Terme di Caracalla
00100 Rome
Italy
Tel.: +39 06 5705 3152
Fax: +39 06 5705 3152
Telex: 625852/610181 FAO I/
Cable address: FOODAGRI ROME
E-mail: FAO-OH@fao.org
www.fao.un

The Food and Agriculture Organization of the UN was created to raise traditions and standards of living, improve agricultural productivity, and better the lives of rural populations. It works to end poverty and hunger and to offer food security, which is access to food at any time for any person. This website includes information on food and agriculture topics.

EarthAction
30 Cottage St.
Amherst, MA 01002

Tel.: (413) 549–8118
Fax: (413) 549–0544
www.earthaction.org

EarthAction strives to get people of the North and the South to protect the planet. This website is for those who want to get involved. You can send a letter to the president, get updates, and read special reports on this website.

IUCN USA Multilateral Office
1630 Connecticut Ave. NW, 3rd Floor
Washington, DC 20009–1053
Tel.: (202) 387–4826
Fax: (202) 387–4823
www.iucn.org

The World Conservation Union (IUCN) focuses on species and biodiversity conservation and the management of habitats and natural resources. It also helps countries prepare national conservation strategies. This website provides information on its work and news stories.

WWF-US
1250 24th St. NW
Washington, DC 20037–1175
Tel.: (202) 293–4800
Fax: (202) 293–9211
www.panda.org

The WWF, formerly known as the World Wildlife Fund, deals not only with preservation of species but also with issues like toxins and global warming. This website provides information on WWF projects, fact sheets, and news items.

Endnotes

1. Gary Poakoric, "Pollution From Asia Drifting Over the U.S.," *Chicago Tribune*, 28 April 2002, Sect. 1, 8; and Keith Bradsher and David Barboza, "Clouds From Chinese Coal Cast a Long Shadow," *New York Times*, 11 June 2006, A1.
2. Lorraine Elliott, *The Global Polities of the Environment* (New York: New York University Press, 1998), 219; and David G. Victor, "Recovering Sustainable Development," *Foreign Affairs* 85, No.1 (January/February 2006), 91.
3. John McCormick, *Reclaiming Paradise: The Global Environmental Movement* (Bloomington: Indiana University Press, 1989), vii.
4. Barbara Johnson, *Life and Death Matters: Human Rights and the Environment at the End of the Millennium* (Walnut Creek, CA: Alta Mira Press, 1997), 13–14.
5. Elizabeth Economy and Miranda A. Schreurs, "Domestic and International Linkages in Environmental Politics," in *The Internationalization of Environmental Protection*, ed. Miranda A. Schreurs and Elizabeth Economy (Cambridge: Cambridge University Press, 1997), 6.
6. Elliott, *The Global Politics of the Environment*, 7.
7. Jacqueline Vaughn Switzer and Gary Bryner, *Environmental Politics* (New York: St. Martin's Press, 1998), 201; and Scott Barrett, *Environment and Statecraft* (New York: Oxford University Press, 2006), 1–3.
8. Elliott, *The Global Politics of the Environment*, 28.
9. Harold K. Jacobson and Edith Brown Weiss, "A Framework for Analysis," in *Engaging Countries: Strengthening Compliance With the International Environmental Accords*, ed. Edith Brown Weiss and Harold K. Jacobson (Cambridge, MA: The MIT Press, 1998).
10. Philip Shabecoff, *Earth Rising: American Environmentalism in the 21st Century* (Washington, DC: Island Press, 2000), 7.
11. Paul Wapner, "The Transnational Politics of Environmental NGOs," in *The Global Environment in the Twenty-First Century*, ed. Pamela S. Chasek (Tokyo: United Nations University Press, 2000), 93.
12. Elliott, *The Global Politics of the Environment*, 148.
13. John McCormick, "The Role of Environmental NGOs in International Regimes," in *The Global Environment*, ed. Norman J. Vig and Regina S. Axelrod (Washington, DC: Congressional Quarterly Press, 1999), 69.
14. McCormick, "The Role of Environmental NGOs," 67–68; and Wapner, "The Transnational Politics of Environmental NGOs," 100.
15. Marian Miller, A. L., *The Third World in Global Environmental Politics* (Buckingham: Open University Press, 1995), 109.
16. OECD, *Trade Measures in Multilateral Environmental Politics* (Paris: OECD, 1999), 11; and Elliott, *The Global Politics of the Environment*, 75.
17. OECD, *Trade Measures*, 11.
18. Miller, *The Third World*, 115; and Elliott, *The Global Politics of the Environment*, 78.
19. Calvin Sims, "Japan, Feasting on Whale, Sniffs at Culinary Imperialism of U.S.," *New York Times*, 10 August 2000, A1; and Bruce Wallace and Corol J. Williams, "Japan Gains Support on Whaling, Sparking Fears of New Seaughter," *Chicago Tribune*, 18 June 2006, Sect. 1, 14.

20. J. R. McNeill, *Something New Under the Sun: An Environmental History the Twentieth-Century World* (New York: W. W. Norton, 2000), 241.

21. McNeill, *Something New*, 242; and Elliott, *The Global Politics of the Environment*, 135.

22. Elizabeth R. DeSombre, *Domestic Sources of International Environmental Policy* (Cambridge, MA: MIT Press, 2000), 1.

23. DeSombre, *Domestic Sources*, 64.

24. Judith Graham, "Fear for Turtles' Fate Prompts Proposed Hawaii Fishing Ban," *Chicago Tribune*, 16 July 2000, Sect. 1, 6.

25. James Gorman, "Gorillas and Chimps in Peril," *New York Times*, 7 April 2003, A8.

26. Patrice M. Jones, "Brazil Grapples With Animal Trade," *Chicago Tribune*, 20 August 2001, Sect. 1, 1.

27. Andrew C. Revkin, "Report to Endorse Expanding Forests to Fight Global Warming," *New York Times*, 10 February 2001, A1.

28. Anthony Hall, *Sustaining Amazonia* (Manchester: Manchester University Press, 1997), 47; and Jane Perlez, "Forests in Southeast Asia Fall to Prosperity's Ax," *New York Times*, 29 April 2006, A1.

29. Hall, *Sustaining Amazonia*, 56.

30. Andrew C. Revin, "Pact is Reached to Save a Rich Tropical Forest," *New York Times*, 1 August 2000, D3.

31. The Greenbelt Movement, Nairobi, Kenya.

32. Dan Murphy, "The Quest for Certifiably Eco-friendly Lumber," *Christian Science Monitor*, 23 August 2001, 13.

33. William Mullen, "Popularity Tips Scales Against Fish," *Chicago Tribune*, 27 August 2000, Sect. 1, 1.

34. David K. Schorr, "Fisheries Subsidies and the WTO," in *Trade, the Environment, and the Millenium*, ed. Gary P. Sampson and W. Braduee Chambers (New York: UN University Press, 1999), 144.

35. Schorr, "Fisheries Subsidies," in *Trader, The Environment, and the Millenium*, 145.

36. Mullen, "Popularity Tips Scales Against Fish," 11.

37. Mark Derr, "Alien Species Often Fit In Fine," *New York Times*, 4 September 2001, D4.

38. Tom Hundley, "Midwestern Pest Is Eating up Europe," *Chicago Tribune*, 26 August 2001, Sect. 1, 3.

39. Christopher Bright, *Life Out of Bounds: Bioinvasion in a Borderless World* (New York: W. W. Norton, 1998), 157.

40. Bright, *Life Out of Bounds*, 169.

41. Larry Rohter, "Oil Spills Shift in Course Aids Galapagos Mop-up," *New York Times*, 24 January 2001, A3.

42. Edwin McDowell, "For Cruise Ships, a History of Pollution," *New York Times*, 16 June 2002, Sect. 5, 3.

43. Andrew C. Revkin, "Offshore Oil Pollution Comes Mostly as Runoff," *New York Times*, 24 May 2002, A14.

44. Daniel Sarewitz and Roger Pielke, "Breaking the Global Warming Gridlock," *Atlantic Monthly*, July 2000, 61.

45. Sarewitz and Pielke, "Breaking," 56.

46. National Research Council, *Global Environmental Change* (Washington, DC: National Academy Press, 1999), 2.

47. Peter Kassler and Matthew Paterson, *Energy Exporters and Climate Change* (London: Royal Institute of International Affairs, 1997), 7–8.

48. OECD, *Trade Measures*, 98; and Ruth Greenspan Bell, "What to Do About Climate Change," *Foreign Affairs* 85, No. 3 (May/June 2006), 105.

49. OECD, *Trade Measures*, 102.

50. OECD, *Trade Measures*, 90.

51. OECD, *Trade Measures*, 103.

52. OECD, *Trade Measures*, 102–103.

53. "Report: Too Many People, Too Little Freshwater," *Pantagraph*, 11 November 2001, A6.

54. Arun P. Elhance, *Hydropolitics in the Third World* (Washington, DC: U.S. Institute of Peace Press, 1999), 4.

55. Somini Sengupta, "In Israel and Lebanon, Talk of War Over Water," *New York Times*, 16 October 2002, A10.

56. Brad Knickerbocker, "Military Rediness vs. the Environment," *Christian Science Monitor*, 4 October 2001, 13.

57. Joan McQueeney Mitric, "The War Is Over, But the Damage is Spreading," *Washington Post National Weekly Edition*, 11–17 July 2000, 21.

CHAPTER 9

Population and Migration

INTRODUCTION

Population and migration issues, perhaps more than any other global problem, demonstrate the reality of globalization. Hunger, inequality, ethnic conflicts, environmental degradation, sustainable development, the treatment of women, global security, economic development, trade, poverty, democratization, human rights concerns—all aspects of globalization are intertwined with population. To a large extent, population factors will determine the future of humanity and the world. Rapid population growth is a silent threat to both human and global security, making it as grave a concern as the proliferation of weapons of mass destruction. Population problems have undermined great civilizations in the past and, as we saw in Chapter 2, a healthy, well-managed population is essential to the rise of great powers and the maintenance of hegemony. Demographic disparities among countries generally influence the distribution of economic, military, and political power among states. For example, France dominated continental Europe for a long time partly because of its relatively large population, although Britain used its geographic location and its navy to counter French power. America's growing population is likely to consolidate its power, whereas Europe's aging and declining population is likely to diminish its power in the global system. Russia's population decline has contributed to its loss of power globally. High population growth rates continue to be a significant impediment to economic growth in developing countries, a reality recognized by China and India, the world's most populous countries. Both countries recognize the need to reduce population growth rates to become more powerful economically, politically, and militarily. As countries' populations become more ethnically diverse and as globalization continues to erode boundaries that have distinguished "us" from "them," the traditional concept of nation-states is being challenged. Demographic changes also profoundly alter societies. Population is at the heart of the Palestinian-Israeli conflict, struggles between Catholics and Protestants in Northern Ireland, and many ethnic conflicts worldwide. The United States also confronts challenges of demographic shifts, as it has for most of its history. Population changes often produce intergenerational conflicts over allocating resources and distributing responsibility for providing those resources. Population and migration issues further strengthen globalization by influencing countries to cooperate to manage the numerous problems they generate.

Migration makes population issues an even more pressing global concern. Each wave of globalization has been accompanied by migration. The movement of capital, technology, and products across national boundaries is inseparable from the migration of people. The current period of globalization is marked by an unprecedented movement of people around the world. The creation of global institutions and the globalization of human rights and democracy have facilitated migration as well as given rise to a global human rights regime that protects migrants, independent of their nationality.[1] Prior to the consolidation of nation-states, migration was not a major problem. Migration issues became more important as nation-states strengthened their boundaries and forged a deeper sense of national identity. But migration has always challenged the concept of national sovereignty and the billiard ball view of international relations. Despite using the most sophisticated detection equipment in the world, the United States cannot prevent Mexicans and others from crossing its borders. Between 1.5 million and 2 million people migrate, legally and illegally, to the United States each year. A similar number migrate to Western Europe. Terrorist attacks on the United States, Spain, and Britain have raised serious concerns about global migration in the United States, Western Europe, and elsewhere. While immigrants from Muslim countries were the primary targets of more restrictive U.S. immigration policies and procedures, an impending agreement between the United States and Mexico that would have facilitated Mexican migration to America was abandoned.

This chapter focuses on population growth and its global implications. Although we will concentrate on global migration as an integral component of population issues, we will also see that most migration occurs within countries and among countries of particular regions. While the emphasis is on migration from poor to rich countries, this chapter stresses that the vast majority of migrants and refugees come from the developing world. The different kinds of migrants and migrations are discussed. The role of gender in migration, rural-to-urban migration, transcontinental migration, forced migration, refugees, reform migration, and the global smuggling of immigrants are all examined. The causes of migration are as old as human civilization. After analyzing them, we will look at case studies that illustrate the dynamics of global—as opposed to regional and internal—migration. The countries examined in the case studies are the United States, Canada, Australia, France, Germany, and Japan. Finally, we will assess the impact of migration on both the sending and the receiving countries.

POPULATION

Overpopulation

Excessive population within an area that lacks enough resources for long-term sustainment

Replacement Rate

Rate at which a population remains stable

At the heart of population as a global issue is the extent to which population growth threatens the earth's carrying capacity. **Overpopulation** (i.e., too many people living in an area that has inadequate resources to support them) has been a global preoccupation for centuries. Population problems must be seen in the context of consumption. In this context, the population of the developed world, which consumes much, is seen as a bigger problem for the world's resources than the population of the developing world, which consumes little. Often, population problems can be avoided if population growth remains stable, assuming that resources are also carefully managed. The rate at which the population remains relatively stable is referred to as the **replacement rate**. To achieve this, fertility rates must average 2.1 children per couple. Fertility rates that exceed the replacement rate lead to population decline. Migration influences the replacement rate, population growth, and population decline.

Thomas Malthus (1766–1834), an English economist, sociologist, and pioneer in demographics, wrote **An Essay on the Principle of Population** in 1798. In it, he argued that because population increases by a geometrical ratio and food supplies increase by an arithmetical ratio, the world would have high rates of population growth and suffer from poverty and starvation. The widespread practice of family planning and technological and scientific revolutions in food production, transportation, and storage essentially rendered these dire predictions false. The invention of genetically modified crops and other agricultural scientific breakthroughs further challenge Malthus' argument. Nevertheless, high population growth remains a serious threat to most developing countries and, as we discussed in Chapter 7, frustrates efforts to reduce global poverty and economic inequality. Malthus was concerned about the earth's carrying capacity. **Carrying capacity** refers to the maximum number of humans or animals a given area can support without creating irreversible destruction of the environment and, eventually, of humans and animals themselves. In Chapter 8, we saw how the commons can be destroyed by individuals who make decisions about expanding their own cattle herds without considering how all of their decisions, when combined, can have catastrophic effects on the carrying capacity of the commons. This also applies to population. Carrying capacity depends not just on the amount of available resources, but also on the values of the population. This means that high population growth rates are a problem for rich countries as well as poor countries, depending on how they utilize their resources. High consumption rates in developed societies exert great pressure on global resources and the environment, threatening sustainability and carrying capacity. As less developed countries, especially China and India, achieve higher levels of economic growth and adopt consumption patterns similar to those in rich countries, they will also demand more global natural resources, thereby further straining the earth's carrying capacity. The rapid increase in the elderly population globally and population growth in the developing world, even at slower rates, also threaten the earth's carrying capacity.

Carrying Capacity
The maximum number of humans or animals that can survive within a given area

Population problems create conflicts, especially in areas where the carrying capacity is strained and where people who have different political, cultural, and economic interests are competing for diminishing resources. Combined with fervent nationalism and a perception that survival itself is at stake, population pressures often result in military conflict. The Palestinian-Israeli struggle is an example of how demographic changes are perceived as determining destiny. Jews now comprise roughly 50.5 percent of the population in Israel and the Palestinian territories. By 2020, the proportion of Jews will decline to 42.1 percent, whereas the Palestinians, who now make up 44.3 percent of the population, will see their share of the population grow to 52 percent. Poverty, lower levels of education, gender inequality, religious beliefs, and the ongoing violence between Palestinians and Israelis influence Palestinians to have more children. Larger families are not only viewed as insurance or a safety net for parents, but also as potential fighters in the struggle against Israel. The birthrate for Palestinians in the West Bank and Gaza is forty for every 1,000 people. The birthrate for Palestinians in Israel is thirty-six per 1,000 people. Compare this with a birthrate for Jews of 18.3 per 1,000 and you will see why demographic changes are perceived as threats to Israel's security.[2] These demographic realities influenced Israel's decision to dismantle Jewish settlements in Gaza in 2005. This process was reversed in 2006 when conflicts escalated between Palestinians and Israelis and after Israel invaded Lebanon to fight Hezbollah following Hezbollah's seizure of two Israeli soldiers.

Population Issues in Developing Countries

Most developing countries have high population growth rates and suffer from vast differences in income. Inadequate education, low rates of contraception usage, cultural norms that value large families and male virility, the need for labor in subsistence economies, and the need to have children to support parents are some of the reasons population growth is higher in poorer countries. As Table 9.1 shows, most of the countries with the largest populations and the highest growth rates are in the developing world. Roughly 97 percent of the increase in the global population is occurring in Africa, Asia, the Middle East, and Latin America, with the more prosperous countries in these regions experiencing declining growth rates. Industrialized countries, on the other hand, are experiencing declining growth rates and even depopulation in some cases. Poverty is clearly a major cause of high population growth rates.

In India, more than 360 million people—roughly the combined populations of the United States, Britain, and Canada—live in dire poverty. In addition, an estimated 400 million Indian people are illiterate. Nonetheless, the population in India grows by about three people a minute, or 2,000 an hour, or 48,000 per day. In other words, the growth of India's population each day is equivalent to that of a medium-size American city. By 2025, Indian is projected to surpass China as the world's most populous country, with about 1.5 billion people, compared with China's 1.4 billion people. China and India alone account for one out of every three children added to the global population.[3]

Problems arising from rapid population growth have influenced governments, nongovernmental organizations (NGOs), and women to take action to limit population growth. It is generally agreed that *women's level of education strongly influences fertility rates*. Education helps to determine factors that affect population growth rates, such as contraceptive usage, the age of marriage and childbearing, social status and self-perception, employment opportunities outside of the home, and residence. It is widely accepted that educational achievement is a crucial factor in lowering fertility rates, even in countries with relatively low levels of economic development. Educated women usually postpone childbearing, become more aware of their economic opportunities and social options, are generally less constrained by prevailing

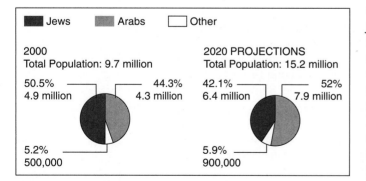

FIGURE 9.1 Population Projections in Israel and the Palestinian Territories

Sources: The Washington Institute for Near East Policy; and *Chicago Tribune*, 21 April 2002, Sect. 1,15.

TABLE 9.1 DEMOGRAPHIC TRENDS

Country	Total Population (millions)			Population Growth Rate (%)		Population Under Age 15 (as % of total)		Population Aged 65 and Above (as % of total)	
	1970	2000	2015	1975–2000	2000–2015	2000	2015	2000	2015
High Human Development									
Norway	4.0	4.5	4.7	0.4	0.3	19.8	15.8	15.4	18.2
Sweden	8.2	8.8	8.6	0.3	-0.2	18.2	12.4	17.4	22.3
Canada	23.1	30.8	34.4	1.1	0.8	19.1	15.9	12.6	16.1
United States	**220.2**	**283.2**	**321.2**	**1.0**	**0.8**	**21.7**	**18.7**	**12.3**	**14.4**
Japan	111.5	127.1	127.5	0.5	0.5	14.7	13.3	17.2	25.8
France	52.7	59.2	61.9	0.5	0.3	18.7	17.4	16.0	18.6
United Kingdom	56.2	59.4	60.6	0.2	0.1	19.0	15.1	15.8	18.9
Germany	78.7	82.0	80.7	0.2	-0.1	15.5	12.1	16.4	21.0
Italy	55.4	57.5	55.2	0.1	-0.3	14.3	12.0	18.1	22.4
Medium Human Development									
Mexico	59.1	98.9	119.2	2.1	1.2	33.1	26.3	4.7	6.8
Russian Federation	134.2	145.5	133.3	0.3	-0.6	18.0	13.6	12.5	13.8
Romania	21.2	22.4	21.4	0.2	-0.3	18.3	15.2	13.3	14.6
Brazil	108.1	170.4	201.4	1.8	1.1	28.8	24.3	5.1	7.3
Philippines	42.0	75.7	95.9	2.4	1.6	37.5	29.6	3.5	4.9
Turkey	40.0	66.7	79.0	2.0	1.1	30.0	24.1	5.8	7.2
China	927.8	1,275.10	1,410.20	1.3	0.7	24.8	19.4	6.9	9.3
Algeria	16.0	30.3	38.0	2.5	1.5	34.8	26.8	4.1	4.9
South Africa	25.8	43.3	44.6	2.1	0.2	34.0	30.5	3.6	5.4
Indonesia	134.6	212.1	250.1	1.8	1.1	30.8	24.7	4.8	6.4
Egypt	38.8	67.9	84.4	2.2	1.0	35.4	26.9	4.1	5.2
India	620.7	1,008.90	1,230.50	1.9	1.3	33.5	26.9	5.0	6.4
Low Human Development									
Pakistan	70.3	141.3	204.3	2.8	2.5	41.8	38.4	3.7	4.0
Bangladesh	75.6	137.4	183.2	2.4	1.9	38.7	32.9	3.1	3.7
Nigeria	54.9	113.9	165.3	2.9	2.5	45.1	41.4	3.0	3.3
Ethiopia	32.8	62.9	89.8	2.6	2.4	45.2	44.4	3.0	3.2

Source: United Nations Development Program, *Human Development Report 2002* (New York: Oxford University Press, 2002), 162–165.

You DECIDE

Declining Populations and the Decline of Civilizations

Visit any major American city, or even some rural areas, and you will see significant ethnic and racial diversity. Since the mid-1960s, when changes in U.S. immigration policies allowed more people from developing countries to migrate legally to the United States, the proportion of Americans of European ancestry has declined relative to the proportion of Americans of Asian, Latin American, Middle Eastern, and African backgrounds. The

demographic shift has created serious concerns among many Americans. Some argue that the growing number of immigrants is threatening American culture and giving rise to the dominance of an anti-Western culture. These changes are viewed as contributing to the death of American civilization.

Is immigration a serious threat to the United States?

beliefs and practices, and exercise more control over their economic and reproductive lives. Educated women have fewer children because they realize that in order to provide their offspring with a standard of living similar to or higher than their own, they will have to carefully budget their resources and concentrate them on a small family. Where women live also influences their fertility rates. Urban residents generally have fewer children, whereas women engaged in agriculture and those who live in rural areas tend to have larger families. In addition to the constraints of tradition, women in rural areas are less likely to be educated than women who live in cities, and have less access to family planning information and services.

An interesting development is the declining birthrates in Brazil, Mexico, Bangladesh, India, the Philippines, Iran, Vietnam, Indonesia, and Egypt, where poverty and illiteracy remain serious and pervasive problems. Even women who are less educated have become more assertive about their reproductive choices. Factors influencing this change include economic and cultural globalization, greater access to education, increasing urbanization, the declining influence of religion on women's reproductive lives, greater access to medical technologies, and the cumulative effects of satellite television and other media that stress the advantages of having fewer children. In Brazil, for example, the fertility rate dropped from 6.15 to 2.27 in the last half-century.[4]

Sexism

Discrimination against an individual or group based on sex or gender classifications

Son Complex

Preference for male children

Sexism strongly influences population decisions in developing countries. In many societies, tradition supports having large families by praising the fertility of women and the virility of men. The **son complex**—the preference for having boys instead of girls—influences many parents worldwide to continue having children until a boy is born. For example, a Chinese farmer dreamed of having a son. After seven daughters, he finally had a son and stopped having children. As one woman put it, "A woman without a son will be cursed by her mother-in-law and laughed at by the village. Everybody thinks it is the duty of a woman to bear a boy."[5] Parents, especially mothers, are demeaned in many societies if they do not produce boys. In many traditional

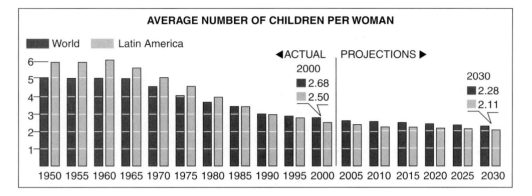

FIGURE 9.2 Declining Fertility Rates
Sources: UN World Population Division; and *Chicago Tribune*, 8 September 2002, Sect. 1,10.

South Asian families, a boy is expected to live with his parents, be employed, inherit property, provide financial security for aging parents, and light their funeral pyres. A daughter, by contrast, is widely perceived as a financial and social liability. When she marries, her family is required by tradition to provide the bridegroom's family with a substantial **dowry**, which can be money, property, or both. Parents often incur significant debt to provide dowries. Women are frequently abused or even killed by their husbands (or their husband's relatives) if they are unhappy with the size of the dowry. Furthermore, the woman is expected to live with her husband's family, thereby depriving her own parents of a potential source of support. The tradition in India was for women to throw themselves on their husband's funeral pyres, a practice known as **suttee** in India, before the British outlawed it during their colonial rule of the country. Faced with the reality that women are generally considered liabilities in some societies, parents invest less in girls' education, health care, and their general well-being. Sexism also conspires with advanced medical technology to reduce the number of girls in some countries, such as India and China. With the use of ultrasound machines to determine the sex of the fetus, many parents often decide to abort female fetuses. Combined with the practice of female infanticide, ultrasound technology has contributed to a widening divergence in the ratio of females to males in many parts of India and China.[6]

Confronted with the challenges of rapid population growth, most countries rely on educational programs that emphasize family planning. During the 1970s, **Prime Minister Indira Gandhi** of India implemented policies that allowed forced mass sterilization, an approach that Indians violently rejected. Although these coercive policies were quickly abandoned, Indians are now experimenting with aggressive approaches to limit population growth because of the increased concern that India's population is impeding economic development, generating more competition for resources (such as water and land), and frustrating efforts to reduce poverty and illiteracy. Some states in India encourage civil servants to choose sterilization after having one or two children by providing incentives, such as salary increases or access to land or housing.[7]

Dowry
Financial gift given to the husband's family by the wife's family at marriage in many traditional societies

Suttee
Past practice where a wife threw herself on her husband's funeral pyre

Indira Gandhi
Prime minister of India in the 1970s

One-Child Policy

Imposed on families in China to limit population growth

China's **one-child policy**, initiated in 1979 by Deng Xiao Ping, China's leader, to reduce China's population growth is the most controversial approach to dealing with rapid population growth. China established the **state family planning bureau** to formulate policies and procedures for enforcing the one-child policy. **Family planning committees** at the local level, a part of the Communist Party, are responsible for rewarding those who comply and punishing those who violate the one-child policy. Those who comply receive a monthly stipend until the child is 14 years old and get preferential treatment when applying for housing, education, and health benefits for the child; they are also granted a pension when they are old. Those who fail to comply with the one-child policy risk the loss of benefits for the first child; jeopardize their employment with the government; their property is subject to seizure; and women are often forced to be sterilized, especially after the birth of a second child. *Exceptions to the one-child policy* include the following cases: (1) if the first child has a defect; (2) in the case of a remarriage, one partner does not have a child; (3) if couples are involved in jobs, certain such as mining; or (4) if both partners come from families with one child. Although the one-child policy is officially in place, it has been weakened because it is largely unenforceable in a society that is highly mobile and relatively free and one in which the government's control over the economy is weakening. Implementation of the one-child policy has varied from the countryside, where it is routinely ignored, to the cities, where it is rigorously enforced.

Population Issues in Developed Countries

Compared with the developing world, Europe has always had a smaller population. Among the *reasons for this disparity* are:

1. Europe was settled by humans who migrated from Africa into Asia. In other words, it started out with a smaller population.
2. Geography and climate discouraged large numbers of people from settling in Europe. This was in sharp contrast to the population density in Asia, especially in the rich agricultural plains of major river systems, such as the Euphrates, Tigris, Ganges, and Yangtze.
3. Abstinence and the growing use of birth control, combined with high mortality rates, kept Europe's population relatively small.
4. Confronted with overpopulation, Europe was able to conquer, colonize, and settle North America, South America, parts of Africa, parts of Asia, Australia, and New Zealand.

The Industrial Revolution and scientific advances in agriculture made Europeans prosperous and diminished the need to have large families.

Subreplacement Fertility Regimes

Patterns of childbearing resulting in population decline

Europe is faced with the spread of **subreplacement fertility regimes**; that is, patterns of childbearing that would eventually result in indefinite population decline.[8] The sharpest dip in population is in Russia. Communicable diseases, widespread environmental problems, alcohol poisoning, sexually transmitted diseases, and an abortion rate that is twice as high as live births have combined to decrease Russia's population by roughly 700,000 each year. If current demographic trends continue, Russia will see its current population of 142.7 million drop precipitously to between 50 million and 60 million by 2075.[9] Such long-range predictions are often highly speculative and turn out to be inaccurate. Nevertheless, it is clear that Russia is going through a population implosion. Though immigration has slowed the decline of Western Europe's populations, immigration levels are not high enough to alter the demographic realities. The United States, Canada, and Australia are actually gaining population largely due to increased immigration and rising fertility rates.

It is estimated that by 2050, the median age in the United States will be 35.4, compared with 52.3 in Europe, due to the rapid growth in the number of the elderly and the subreplacement problem. For example, in 1950, about 30 percent of Germany's population was under 20 years and only 2 percent exceeded 80 years. By 2050, however, it is estimated that only 16 percent will be under 20 years, whereas those who are 80 years and older will constitute 12 percent of Germany's population.[10] Three major reasons account for Europe's aging societies:

1. Life expectancy has climbed due to medical advancements, a healthier environment, improved nutrition, and greater concerns about safety and public health.
2. The huge baby boom generation of the 1940s and 1950s is now entering middle-age and moving into the old-age category.
3. Declining fertility rates, below the replacement rate, increase the proportion of the population that is old.[11]

America's aging population, while growing, will comprise a smaller percentage of the overall population because of the number of young immigrants and higher fertility rates. Japan faces not only an aging population, but also subreplacement fertility rates.

Population challenges in the developed world differ significantly from those in poor countries. Rich countries will have to support a larger number of older people, some of whom will retire in their mid-fifties and receive pensions for the rest of their lives, which could be as long as they worked to accumulate their pensions. Subreplacement fertility rates deprive most rich countries of a younger population capable of supporting the elderly. The United States faces the problem of an aging population and a younger population; both require

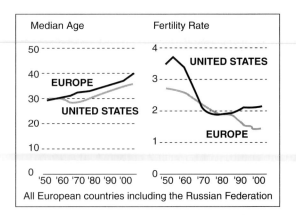

FIGURE 9.3 Demographic Contrasts Between Europe and the United States
Sources: United Nations World Population Division; and *New York Times*, 29 June 2003, A3.

substantial resources. Concerned about their own welfare, many older people in the United States are reluctant to support the young, and many young people, worried about financial security when they retire, strongly favor private retirement systems that allow them to invest their money for themselves instead of contributing to a public retirement system that they believe will soon be bankrupt. Developed countries face many challenges that require the implementation of difficult and controversial strategies.[12] These strategies include

1. Substantially increasing immigration from the developing world to offset declining fertility rates,
2. Postponing, or abandoning retirement,
3. Encouraging higher fertility rates (which is extremely difficult because richer and well-educated women have fewer children),
4. Investing more in the education of future workers to make them more productive,
5. Strengthening intergenerational responsibilities within families,
6. Targeting government-paid benefits to those who need them most, and
7. Requiring workers to invest for their own retirements.

The economic, social, and political implications of these changes are far-reaching. Significant tensions within rich countries over such strategies are already evident in many European countries.

GLOBAL MIGRATION

Migration

Movement of people from one place to another

Migrant

A person who moves from one country or area to another country or location

Refugees

Migrants living outside their country of origin who are unwilling or unable to return

Migration—the movement of people from one place to another—is an integral component of human behavior. Our ancestors moved out of curiosity and a sense of adventure; to find food; to search for better grazing and agricultural lands; to seek protection from adversaries; to conquer land for new settlements; and to obtain religious, political, social, and economic freedoms. Contemporary migration is rooted in the earlier periods of political, military, economic, and financial globalization that we discussed in Chapter 1. Migration includes the movement of people within a country's geographical boundaries as well as movement across national boundaries. People who migrate fall into several categories. A **migrant** is a person who moves from one country or area to another country or location. Migrants often move from one part of a country to another location within that country. The broad category of migrant is subdivided into refugees, displaced persons, and immigrants. **Refugees** are essentially migrants who live outside their country and are unable or unwilling to return because of documented cases of persecution or a well-founded fear of persecution. Historically and today, conflicts, famine, natural disasters, and political, religious, and economic oppression have been dominant factors contributing to the creation of refugees. In many ways, globalization has made determining who is a refugee extremely difficult. Refugees who attempt to obtain permanent residence in the country to which they

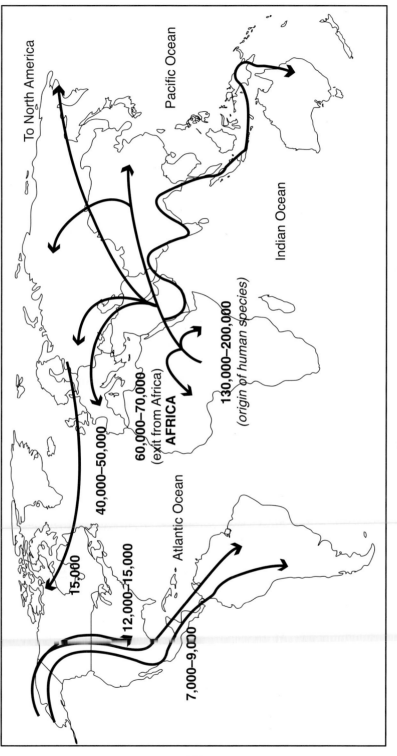

FIGURE 9.4 Early Human Migration. Figures indicate number of years ago that migration took place.
Source: New York Times, 12 November 2002, 03.

Asylum-Seekers

Refugees attempting to obtain permanent residence in the country to which they fled

Displaced Person

One who has fled his or her home but has not left the home country

Immigrant

One who travels to a foreign country, often to become a permanent resident

Transcontinental Migration

Movement of people from one continent to another

fled are referred to as **asylum-seekers**. The immigration laws of most countries distinguish asylum-seekers from other categories of migrants and generally grant them preferential treatment, in accordance with international law. A **displaced person** is someone who has been forced to leave his or her home because of violence, conflict, persecution, or natural disaster, but has not crossed an international border. Many displaced people eventually cross national boundaries, thereby becoming refugees. An **immigrant** is someone who goes to a foreign country to become a permanent resident. Many immigrants, both legal and illegal, tend to cross national boundaries frequently and do not perceive themselves as permanent residents in the foreign country. This trend is increasing with the spread of globalization and fundamental challenges to the concept of citizenship. Most migration occurs in a relatively limited geographical area, despite growing **transcontinental migration** (i.e., the movement of people from one continent to another).

Gender and Migration

Men are more likely than women to migrate under ordinary circumstances. There are several reasons for this. Who migrates is determined to a large extent by the requirements imposed by countries, companies, or individuals who need labor. Much of the work to be done is culturally defined as work for men. Large numbers of men from Turkey, North Africa, and the Caribbean migrated to Germany, France, and Britain, respectively, after World War II to help rebuild these countries. Men throughout the world have been recruited to work in industry, construction, and mining. Cultural norms and sex roles within sending countries also determine whether men are more likely than women to migrate. Gender roles also influence men to migrate in search of employment. Men are generally perceived as breadwinners in most countries, whereas women are viewed as being responsible for taking care of the home. Economic development and greater access to education for women change cultural views of gender roles and provide more employment opportunities for women. Demographic changes and greater employment opportunities for women in developed countries are transforming gender migration. Women migrate to rich societies to work in factories, tourism, education, hospitals, businesses, and private homes. As more women work outside the home in rich countries, more women from poor countries are hired to do domestic work. In Hong Kong, for example, women from the Philippines care for children. In nursing homes across the United States, one can find migrants from the Philippines, Latin America, and the Caribbean taking care of the elderly. In fact, for people living on the West Coast of the United States, their nurse is likely to be from the Philippines. More than half of those migrating from the Philippines are women.

Types of Migration

Regional Migration

Movement of people within a specified region

Although migration as a contemporary global issue is often thought of primarily as movement from developing countries to rich countries, far more common is the movement of people within countries and from one country to another within a particular geographical or cultural region. **Regional migration** is fueled by increasing economic opportunities in a country or group of neighboring countries. For example, people in North Africa move to Spain, France, and Italy to find employment, and people from Zimbabwe, Mozambique, Botswana, and Lesotho have migrated to South Africa to work in mining and other industries. **Rural-to-urban migration** is the dominant pattern of migration in both rich and poor countries. Many rural areas across the United States are losing population as residents seek better opportunities in urban areas. Much of the migration in the developing world is from rural areas to cities. **Rural-to-rural migration** (i.e., the movement of people from one rural area to another) is common in many parts of the world, despite the relatively limited economic opportunities found in most small towns or agricultural areas. Many migrants follow the planting, cultivation, and harvesting of various crops. **Urban-to-urban migration** is common in most countries. Families and individuals move from one city to another to find employment, to pursue a college degree, or to be in a culturally dynamic area. **Urban-to-rural migration** is usually designed to encourage the economic development of the countryside and to relieve population pressures on urban centers. Brazil, China, Indonesia, and Nigeria are countries that have used this strategy. Another type of migration is **seasonal migration**. People often move from one area to another because of the seasonal demand for labor. Agricultural industries often demand more labor at certain times of the year than at others. Harvesting fruit, sugar cane, coffee, and other crops requires intensive labor for a short period of time. Seasonal migration is also driven by other industries, such as tourism. Many vacation areas employ people from the United States, Europe, the Caribbean, and Latin America.

Another type of migration is **transit migration**. In this case, those seeking to enter a specific country pass through another country or stay there temporarily. For example, migrants use Mexico as a transit point for illegal entry into the United States. Visiting Mexico's main immigration detention center, you see migrants from Ecuador, India, Cuba, China, Albania, Russia, Ukraine, Tanzania, Sierra Leone, Sri Lanka, Bangladesh, and other countries.[13] Similarly, migrants attempting to enter Western Europe use such countries as Bosnia, Croatia, Serbia, Bulgaria, Hungary, Poland, and the Czech Republic as transit points. Many migrants also stop temporarily in Europe on their way to the United States and Canada. Within Europe, France is used as a transit point for migrants attempting to enter Britain in order to take advantage of its asylum policies.

Forced and induced migration is an integral component of human history. This involuntary movement of people is usually due to deliberate government actions. Various minorities have been routinely expelled from countries because of political, social, ethnic, and religious differences. The Spanish crown forced Jews to leave Spain in 1492; Africans were forcibly removed from their homeland and enslaved in the Americas, the Middle East, and other parts of the world; and the Cuban and Chinese governments have used forced migration to achieve various political and economic objectives. Another type of migration—one that is becoming common in an age of globalization—is **return migration**. For example, many American citizens retain meaningful ties with another country. Throughout history some migrants have returned to the places they left. In the late nineteenth century roughly a third of European migrants to the United States were returning after a few years. Immigrants from Southern

Seasonal Migration
Movement of people based on seasonal demand for labor

Transit Migration
Movement of people to one country on the way to another

Forced and Induced Migration
Involuntary movement of people, often due to a government initiative

Return Migration
Movement of people back to the country from which they originally emigrated

Europe, particularly Italy, were most likely to return after saving enough money to build homes, start small businesses, or buy farms. This trend of migration was strengthened by the relative newness of migration from Southern Europe and by declining transportation costs and faster and more reliable means of transportation.[14] Economic and political problems in Venezuela, Argentina, Colombia, and Ecuador have contributed to increased return migration to Italy, Spain, and Portugal. Many of those returning are eligible for citizenship in the country of their ancestors.

Economic success in the new country also motivates people to return to their country of origin. India and China, for example, encourage return migration to assist economic development. The Indian diaspora is one of the world's largest, most productive, and most economically successful. India offers incentives to Indians living in the United States, Britain, Australia, Canada, Singapore, and elsewhere to return. Similarly, China, which received about $60 billion in investments from roughly 55 million overseas Chinese, perceives return migration as an essential component of its development strategy.[15] Growing economic opportunities in China, India, and other countries, combined with the forces of globalization, facilitate the trend toward return migration.

Global migration is manifested in several ways. These include

1. **Global networks of immigrant business organizations.** Immigrant groups have developed extensive business and social contacts that enable them to provide mutual assistance and to cooperate on a global scale.
2. **New forms of global employment.** Globalization reinforces the well-established practice of people working in different countries on a temporary basis.

You
DECIDE | **Return Migration**

Debates about immigration problems in the United States generally focus on how to prevent illegal immigrants from entering the country. Given the historical reality of migration, many of the policies designed to keep illegal immigrants out have the opposite effect. Even when it was dangerous to cross the Atlantic Ocean in ships, many migrants, estimates range from 25 to 30 percent, returned home eventually. Revolutions in transportation and communications clearly make it much easier for people to cross national boundaries quickly and frequently. It is argued that when migrants are free to come and go as they wish, not as many of them migrate. Tougher border controls and restrictive immigration policies deter illegal migrants from returning home. When Mexicans were free to migrate to the United States to work in agriculture under the Bracero Program, many of them returned to Mexico. Ending the Bracero Program in the early 1960s actually contributed to a sharp increase of illegal immigrants from Mexico. The high costs involved in entering the United States illegally and the low probability of an illegal immigrant being caught once in the United States encourage migrants to remain in the country.

Do you think that relaxing immigration controls would encourage return migration?

3. **Formation of global communities.** Growing interdependence has contributed to the growth of global cities. The ethnic diversity of most major cities worldwide reflects the reality of migration. Immigrant communities maintain much of the culture of their homelands and face relatively little pressure to conform to the dominant culture.

4. **The formation of collective identities not confined by territory.** As immigrants maintain more of their culture and interact more frequently with their original country, their psychological and emotional bonds to their nation-state weaken. Collective identities are increasingly separate from a common national identity.[16]

Causes of Migration

Although the causes of migration are diverse and vary from one individual to another, demographers generally divide them into two categories: namely, push factors and pull factors.[17] **Push factors** are negative developments and circumstances that motivate or force people to leave their homes. These include widespread abuses of fundamental human rights; political oppression; forced resettlement programs and expulsion; high levels of violence and endemic political instability; rapid population growth; high rates of unemployment; poverty; natural and environmental disasters; the relative lack of educational and cultural opportunities; globalization; and discrimination that excludes specific groups and individuals from competition for resources and power. **Pull factors** are positive developments and circumstances in other areas or countries that attract people away from their homes. These include economic opportunities, higher wages, political and cultural freedom and stability, a comparatively healthy environment, educational and cultural opportunities, and family reunification. Push and pull factors are strongly influenced by geographic proximity; individual initiative; technology; transportation; and social, political, and economic beliefs. Pull and push factors are interrelated and often difficult to distinguish.

Push Factors

Negative developments leading many people to leave their homes

Pull Factors

Positive developments inducing people to move from their homes

PUSH FACTORS

Widespread *abuses of fundamental human rights*, discussed in Chapter 3, have traditionally pushed people from their homes. The United States was settled by many individuals who were deprived of basic human rights. Many Jews, political dissidents, homosexuals, and others fled Nazi Germany because of the government's systematic and profound violations of the most basic human rights, including the right to life. During the Cold War, many Central and Eastern Europeans fled oppression in the communist countries. Cubans migrated in large numbers when Fidel Castro came to power and imposed severe restrictions on fundamental freedoms. Dictatorships worldwide, despite their efforts to regulate and control the movement of people within their own countries, are generally so odious and disrespectful of human rights that many individuals take extreme risks to leave their country.

Forced resettlement programs and expulsion are a significant push factor. Governments have both forced and encouraged people to migrate for several reasons. These include

Huguenots

French Protestants expelled from France in the sixteenth century

Han Chinese

China's dominant ethnic group

Cultural Revolution

Zedong's forced implementation of communist economy, politics, and culture in China

Mao Zedong

China's repressive, former communist leader

Saddam Hussein

Iraq's former dictator

1. **To achieve cultural homogeneity.** This is particularly the case in newly independent countries that were faced with incompatible ethnic groups living in their artificially constructed boundaries. Yet the practice of achieving cultural homogeneity by expelling people perceived as different has deep historical roots. Catholic Spain expelled the Jews in the fifteenth century and Catholic France expelled the **Huguenots**, (i.e., French Protestants, and followers of John Calvin) in the sixteenth century.

2. **To subdue a region or a people.** China has sent millions of **Han Chinese**, the country's dominant ethnic group, to settle areas occupied by minority ethnic groups that challenge its authority. China's occupation of **Tibet** in 1950 was followed by the mass migration of Chinese settlers. This influx of non-Tibetans has essentially transformed virtually all aspects of Tibetan society. During the **Cultural Revolution** (1966–1976), **Mao Zedong**, China's leader, sent his Red Guard stormtroopers to subdue Tibet. They destroyed temples, imprisoned Tibetan monks, desecrated Buddhist sacred objects and scriptures, and punished those who practiced Buddhism.

3. **To evict dissidents and opponents of the government.** Many governments have resorted to forced migration to evict those who are hostile to their policies or who are perceived as threats to their existence. Fidel Castro, determined to build a communist society, influenced and coerced almost a million people to leave Cuba. **Saddam Hussein**, who ruled Iraq from 1979 until he was overthrown and captured by American military forces in 2003, pushed more than a million Kurds out of Iraq into the hills of neighboring Turkey following his country's defeat in the 1991 Gulf War.

4. **To achieve foreign policy objectives.** Forced emigration is sometimes implemented as a component of broader foreign policy objectives. Governments use forced emigration to exert pressure on neighboring countries.[18] For example, Castro has used emigration as an instrument of his foreign policy toward the United States.

5. **To achieve economic and national security objectives.** Several governments have forcibly removed people from one area of the country to another as part of an overall economic development or national security strategy. China, for example, has forcibly removed people from urban to rural areas, from developed coastal areas to underdeveloped interior regions, and from its huge urban centers to remote regions that border other countries.

High levels of violence and political instability are factors that push people away from home. Violence, endemic in many parts of the developing world, routinely motivates people to emigrate. Another push factor is rapid population growth, as we have seen in our previous discussion. Declining population growth rates in rich countries facilitate migration that is driven by high population growth rates in the developing world. High rates of unemployment and poverty are widely regarded as dominant and constant push factors that are strongly connected to population problems. *Natural disasters, environmental problems, and famines* push people away from their homelands or force them to relocate within their countries.

Globalization and discrimination are also push factors. Globalization has contributed to the creation of strong economic regions within, as well as among, countries. Globalization's emphasis on economic liberalization, free trade, and diminished government involvement in the economy has resulted in the displacement of millions of small farmers in the developing world. Thousands of farmers in Mexico, unable to compete with subsidized agriculture in the United States and Europe, move to urban areas in Mexico or make the dangerous journey to the United States. Migration is often induced by governments that fail to provide adequate support for rural communities or alternative sources of employment.[19] These problems are compounded by **competitive exclusion**, which occurs when governments allow more land to be taken by large agro-export companies to create megafarms. This generally drives up land prices and decreases the amount of land available to small subsistence farmers. Discrimination also contributed to emigration. Successful ethnic minority groups have historically been scapegoated for problems within societies, the most obvious being the Jews in Nazi Germany. Idi Amin forced Ugandans of Asian descent to leave Uganda because of their economic success. Ethnic Chinese in Indonesia and other Asian countries have had similar experiences.[20] Marginalized groups, often victims of discrimination, are forced to emigrate by a majority that is less successful economically and unable or unwilling to engage in fair and open competition.

Competitive Exclusion

Process by which government allows agro-corporations to monopolize productive land

Refugees

In 2001, the European Union (EU) decided to recognize as refugees women and homosexuals fleeing violence or sexual abuse.[21] Cubans, experiencing poverty and repression, flee to the United States, for example. Distinguishing refugees from other migrants grows increasingly complicated in an age of globalization and heightened awareness of human rights abuses. The **1951 United Nations Geneva Convention** stressed that individuals or groups persecuted on the grounds of race, religion, nationality, membership in a particular social group, and holding certain political opinions would be recognized as refugees and granted asylum. However, these categories have been expanded to reflect a growing awareness of other forms of persecution. In many ways, the interaction of economic problems, political instability, and violence makes it difficult to separate economically motivated migrants from refugees.

United Nations Geneva Convention

Stressed the importance of granting asylum to refugees who have been persecuted

Refugees are individuals who left their homes because of violence, death threats, and well-founded fears of persecution, and have moved across national boundaries to seek safety. They believe that their government is unable or unwilling to protect them from violence or that their government is directly responsible for the violence against them. As we have seen in Chapter 3, governments are often the worst violators of fundamental human rights. Refugees enjoy certain rights, such as resettlement and legal protection from deportation or being returned to the country they fled. Refugees who seek to become permanent residents of the country in which they settle are known as asylum-seekers. Immigration officials in the United States and immigrant advocacy groups often disagree about who is entitled to refugee status. Complicating the refugee problem is the growing number of **internally displaced people**, who are differentiated from refugees only by the fact that they remain within the boundaries of their country. Displaced persons do not enjoy the same international legal safeguards and protections as those accorded to refugees. Most governments are reluctant to accept large numbers of refugees and generally prefer to provide humanitarian assistance to displaced persons to stem the flow of refugees. As Table 9.2 shows, the number of refugees worldwide is astounding. Yet global attention is often focused on migration as a problem of developed countries. Neighboring countries, mostly in the developing world, receive most of the refugees and are often too poor to provide them with adequate food, water, shelter, education, and sanitary conditions.

NGOs play a major role in helping refugees and displaced people obtain basic requirements for survival. Many refugees are often resented by local residents, who perceive them as competitors for scarce resources and as intruders. Ironically, refugees—who fled violence and persecution—often become victims of crime, sexual exploitation, political harassment, and political violence in areas they settle. Although refugees are generally thought of as temporary residents, many refugees have lived and died in refugee camps. As we will see, many Palestinians have been refugees since 1948, when the state of Israel was established in Palestine.

TABLE 9.2 REFUGEES

Country	Internally Displaced People (Thousands) 2003	Refugees by Country of Asylum (Thousands) 2003	Refugees by Country of Origin (Thousands) 2003
High Human Development			
Norway	–	56	–
Sweden	–	142	–
Canada	–	133	–
Australia	–	99	–
United States	–	**453**	–
Netherlands	–	148	–
Japan	–	2	–
Finland	–	13	–
Switzerland	–	49	–
France	–	132	–
United Kingdom	–	277	–
Denmark	–	74	–
Austria	–	14	–
Germany	–	960	–
Italy	–	12	–

(Continued)

TABLE 9.2 REFUGEES (CONTINUED)

Country	Internally Displaced People (Thousands) 2003	Refugees by Country of Asylum (Thousands) 2003	Refugees by Country of Origin (Thousands) 2003
Medium Human Development			
Mexico	–	6	2
Cuba	–	1	3
Malaysia	–	50	–
Russian Federation	368	10	67
Colombia	2,040	–	16
Thailand	–	119	–
Georgia	260	4	10
Azerbaijan	572	–	284
Sri Lanka	386	–	81
China	–	299	100
Iran	–	985	57
Algeria	–	170	6
Vietnam	–	16	331
Indonesia	–	–	9
India	–	165	3
Myanmar	–	0	141
Kenya	–	239	1
Low Human Development			
Pakistan	–	1,124	10
Sudan	–	328	567
Nepal	–	129	–
Uganda	–	231	24
Tanzania	–	650	–
Zambia	–	227	–
Congo, Dem. Rep.	–	234	428
Eritrea	–	4	11
Angola	–	13	313
Ethiopia	–	130	26
Burundi	100	41	525
Sierra Leone	–	61	78

Source: United Nations Development Program, *Human Development Report 2004* (New York: Oxford University Press, 2004), 211–213.

Widespread refugee problems in Europe and elsewhere during and after World War II influenced the United States, Western Europe, the Soviet Union, and China to develop institutions, such as the office of the **United Nations High Commissioner for Refugees (UNHCR)**, to help with refugees. Established in 1950, the UNHCR is funded primarily by governments, NGOs, and individuals. Because the proliferation of ethnic conflicts and natural disasters has severely restrained UNHCR's resources, other UN agencies, the **International Committee of the Red Cross**, and various NGOs are involved in helping refugees globally. Their task is often made even more

International Committee of the Red Cross

Organization involved in humanitarian operations worldwide

difficult by the inability or unwillingness of some countries to separate fighters from innocent civilians in refugee camps, despite international legal guidelines for doing so. Increasingly, the UN is pressured to take measures to prevent the outbreak and escalation of ethnic conflicts, which are a major cause of the refugee problem. More countries, including the United States, favor selective **humanitarian intervention** (i.e., the military invasion of a country) to prevent or diminish human rights abuses that drive people away from their homes.

Humanitarian Intervention

Use of military force in defense of human rights

Numerous ethnic conflicts and civil wars in Africa have left that continent with more than 4 million refugees. In the Middle East, violence against the Kurds has not only led to the growth of Kurdish refugees in the region, but has also influenced many Kurds to seek refuge in Europe and North America. There are more than 500,000 Kurds in Western Europe, with Germany and France receiving most of them. Germany has about 400,000 and France has 60,000. America's invasion of Iraq in 2003 led to a large number of refugees and internally displaced persons by 2006. The Vietnam War produced a mass exodus of Vietnamese, with most of the refugees settling in the United States. As economic conditions deteriorated, and as the communist government consolidated its power, many Vietnamese also sought refuge in neighboring countries. More than 200,000 ethnic Chinese who lived in Vietnam fled to China when conflict erupted between China and Vietnam in 1978 and 1979. Another 70,000 Vietnamese arrived in Hong Kong in small boats or were rescued from small boats by ocean-going ships on their way to Hong Kong.[22]

Women and children, who comprise the majority of the world's refugees, are the most vulnerable to violence. Even though women leave their country for many of the same reasons as men, women are often victims of human rights abuses and violence. In most wars and ethnic conflicts around the world, women are victims of rape. In some cases, such as in Bosnia and Kosovo, rape was part of a broader strategy designed to intimidate people and force them to leave their homes. Women also flee their homelands because they fear persecution and death in countries that practice honor killings or permit the abuse of women who violate traditions and religious beliefs. An increasing number of women from Africa and the Middle East have fled their countries and sought asylum to escape such practices as female genital mutilation. Many women are sexually abused when they try to escape from war and ethnic conflicts and when they reach refugee camps.

Palestinian Refugees

The Palestinian refugee problem is one of the oldest, most serious, and most intractable global refugee cases. The creation of the state of Israel in 1948 as well as wars and low-intensity conflicts between the Israelis and Arabs led to the creation of roughly 3.5 million Palestinian refugees. Many Palestinians have lived in refugee camps throughout the Arab World for more than half a century. Many of them were born and raised in these camps, and many have also died in these camps. Between 1947 and 1948, approximately 800,000 Palestinians became refugees. The 1967 war, during which all of Palestine was occupied by Israel, created a second wave of Palestinian refugees. Roughly 400,000 Palestinians, out of a population of 2.5 million,

Palestinian refugee hoping to return home.

left Palestine to seek refuge in Jordan, Lebanon, Kuwait, Syria, and other Arab countries. The civil war in Lebanon in the 1970s and 1980s and Israel's invasion of Lebanon in 1982 forced more Palestinians to become refugees again. Roughly 5.1 million Palestinians live abroad, mostly in Jordan, which has 3 million of them. Some of them left for Europe, the United States, and Canada. There are more than 200,000 Palestinians living in the United States and Canada, and roughly 200,000 in Europe.[23] Many Palestinian refugees migrated to oil-producing Arab countries that needed both skilled and unskilled labor. However, when Iraq invaded Kuwait in 1990, many Palestinians supported Saddam Hussein. The Gulf War in 1991 contributed to the expulsion of about 350,000 Palestinians from Kuwait alone. Palestinians also left Iraq and Saudi Arabia. Although many Palestinians hope to return to their homes in Israel and the Palestinian territories, the Palestinian refugee problem is at the heart of the Palestinian-Israeli conflict and is likely to remain unresolved in the near future. The **United Nations Relief Works Agency for Palestinian Refugees in the Near East (UNRWA)** was established in 1949 to provide relief, education, and welfare services to Palestinian refugees.

UNRWA

UN agency established to aid in relief, education, and welfare services for Palestinian refugees

PULL FACTORS

Our discussion of push factors in relation to migration focused on negative developments and circumstances that induce people to leave their homelands. Pull factors are developments and circumstances that attract people to specific areas or countries.

Freedom has always been a significant pull factor, both within countries and across international boundaries. Freedom, associated with cities, enticed many individuals to leave the countryside with its relative lack of freedom. *Freedom* in Britain, Holland, and the United States has served as a magnet for European migrants and, more recently, for migrants from the developing world. Religious, artistic, economic, political, and scientific freedoms remain almost irresistible pull factors, which, in turn, usually enhance the degree of freedom that existed. New York, London, Paris, Sydney, Toronto, Los Angeles, Seattle, Chicago, Miami, and Boston are vibrant and dynamic because of the freedom that characterizes them and attracts talent and financial resources from around the world.

Economic opportunities are one of the most powerful pull factors. People have historically migrated to industrial areas that offered employment and financial and entrepreneurial opportunities. Income inequality between rural and urban areas or between developing and developed countries generally induces people to migrate to seek higher income. Economic opportunities of an earlier period of globalization, between 1870 and 1910, influenced roughly 10 percent of the world's population to immigrate. Millions of Europeans migrated from poor countries to industrialized societies on the continent and to the United States, Canada, Australia, Argentina, Brazil, and other Latin American countries. It is estimated that 12 million Chinese emigrated between 1815 and 1914, many of them from the south of China.[24] Economic opportunity as a pull factor become even more powerful when wages for essentially the same skills differ dramatically. For example, Mexicans are motivated to migrate to the United States partly because many of them can earn much more money doing similar jobs in the United States. This is a global phenomenon. Higher wages in Britain, France, and Germany, combined with labor shortages in those countries following World War II, attracted immigrants from the Caribbean, India, Africa, and Turkey. Similarly, higher wages in the mining industry in South Africa induced people from neighboring countries to migrate to South Africa. Oil wealth and jobs in the Persian Gulf countries pulled more than 3.5 million Asians to the region.[25] Demand for inexpensive and reliable labor contributed to the development of an Indian diaspora that covers sixty-three countries and has more than 20 million people. A **diaspora** is a community of people living outside their original or ancestral country.

Diaspora

A community of people living outside their original or ancestral country

Colonization and financial globalization combined to create a very powerful pull factor between 1820 and 1920. European colonization of the Americas, Asia, and Africa was accompanied by massive flows of capital. Industrialization in Europe generated a significant supply of capital, which stimulated an expansion of industrialization overseas. Colonization opened up some new territories for European settlement and, combined with various development schemes in the new lands, enticed millions of Europeans and others to emigrate. Many of these areas had been settled long before the arrival of Europeans, a reality that often resulted in the forceful removal and even death of native populations. More than 60 million Europeans emigrated to the Americas, Asia, and East and Southern Africa.[26] As we mentioned earlier, the demand for inexpensive labor in the European colonies led to the emigration of roughly 12 million Chinese and 30 million Indians to areas conquered and colonized by

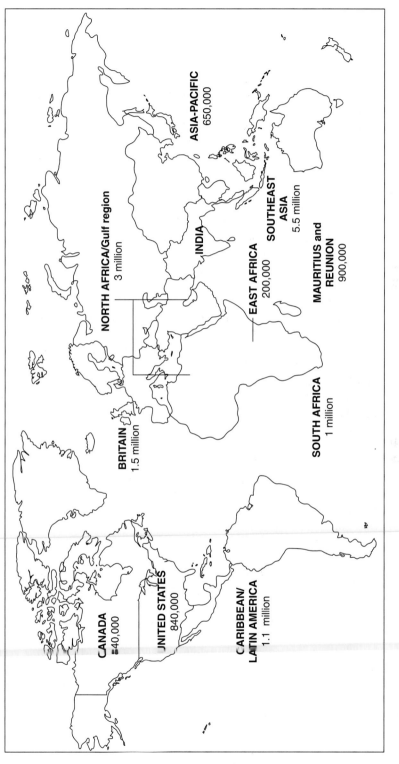

FIGURE 9.5 The Indian Diaspora

Sources: Government of India; and *New York Times*, 12 January 2003, A4.

CANADA
840,000

UNITED STATES
840,000

CARIBBEAN/
LATIN AMERICA
1.1 million

BRITAIN
1.5 million

NORTH AFRICA/Gulf region
3 million

INDIA

EAST AFRICA
200,000

SOUTHEAST
ASIA
5.5 million

ASIA-PACIFIC
650,000

MAURITIUS and
REUNION
900,000

SOUTH AFRICA
1 million

Europeans. The British, who colonized India, encouraged Indians to migrate to British colonies, including Burma, Malaysia, Singapore, Australia, Fiji, Trinidad and Tobago, British Guyana, Kenya, South Africa, Uganda, and other African countries between 1834 and 1937. Many Indians returned to India eventually, but a significant number, estimated to be 6 million, remained abroad.[27]

Globalization is widely viewed as one of the most significant pull factors in relation to migration. As we saw earlier, globalization is also a push factor. Globalization erodes national boundaries, weakens the ability of governments to control many aspects of national life, and strengthens the interdependence of countries, nonstate actors, and individuals. Globalization, especially economic and cultural globalization, enables poor people to see prosperity in rich countries. Movies, magazines, television, and tourism contribute to promoting glamorous and desirable lifestyles in developed countries. Globalization shrinks the world, thereby making it easier for people to compare themselves not only with their immediate neighbors but also with people around the world.[28] Globalization creates dreams that many individuals in poor countries find irresistible. The global system of communication provides individuals with information about economic and social opportunities in other countries and how to get there. Low-cost transportation and the increasing flow of people across national borders facilitate movement from one part of the world to another. As financial globalization spreads capital around the world, we also see a restructuring of global production and economic activities. Just as global companies migrate to find the lowest production costs and higher profits, people migrate in search of jobs and other economic opportunities. If globalization makes rich countries richer and poor countries poorer, then it also serves a powerful magnet for poor people to migrate to rich countries. **Global cities** enable immigrants to blend into the population and become low-wage workers in hotels, restaurants, sweatshops, homes of American families, manufacturing and retail companies, and in agro-business.

Global Cities

Cities that contain enough migrants to make them international in scope and appeal

Family Reunification

Major pull factor encouraging global migration

Cultural Ties

Major pull factor in promoting global migration

Family reunification and **cultural ties** are major pull factors. In many parts of the world, people migrate to places where they know someone, which gives rise to a concentration of immigrants from a particular country or a region of a country in certain areas. For example, many early Scandinavian immigrants went primarily to the United States and settled in Midwestern agricultural states, including Minnesota, Wisconsin, Nebraska, Illinois, and Iowa. Many Italians who left Italy for other European countries settled principally in southern France, Germany, and Austria-Hungary. Italians who came to the Americas were divided into two main groups: those from Northern Italy, who settled mainly in South America, and those from southern Italy, who favored the United States. Emigrants from Spain and Portugal, because of cultural, historical, and family ties, went primarily to South American countries. Emigrants from Ireland and Britain settled in English-speaking countries, such as the United States, Canada, Australia, and New Zealand.

These preferences were often reinforced by actions of the receiving countries that encouraged or discouraged the immigration of different groups.[29] Many immigrants live in particular parts of the countries they settle. For example, many Polish immigrants settled in Chicago, making it the city with the largest number of people of Polish ancestry in the United States and second only to Warsaw, Poland. The largest group of migrants is composed of relatives of individuals who are already living in a specific country. Family reunification is a leading objective of immigration policies in several countries. Roughly 75 percent of legal immigrants in the United States have relatives in that country and about 80 percent of legal immigrants in Sweden have family members in Sweden. In many cases, one family member will emigrate to a particular country and, once relatively economically secure, will encourage family members to join him or her. This phenomenon is known as **chain migration**.

Sparsely populated areas, as we have seen, provide a significant pull factor. As we mentioned earlier, European conquest and colonization of the Americas, Asia, and Africa provided opportunities for certain parts of Europe to relieve their population pressures. North America and Australia attracted millions of European emigrants. However, anthropological evidence supports the view that the Americas had vast human populations when the Europeans arrived. Today, many European countries have declining population growth, a development that is inducing the growth of both legal and illegal migration to that region. Many countries have large areas that have few inhabitants. In Brazil, for example, the vast and sparsely settled Amazon region continues to attract settlers from other parts of Brazil and other countries. Earlier we pointed out how many states in the American Midwest have been losing population. To ease this population decline, Iowa, for example, has responded by creating an **immigration enterprise zone**. Iowa hopes to become a priority destination for refugees and foreigners who are willing to migrate in search of economic opportunities. Low population growth or decline is widely perceived as a serious threat to Iowa's economy.[30]

Closely related to freedom and economic opportunities as pull factors is the *availability of educational and cultural opportunities*. Western Europe, Canada, and the United States have long been magnets for students, artists, and professionals from many countries. Globalization has facilitated educational and cultural exchanges to an unprecedented degree and, in the process, is creating a global community of individuals who are connected by common educational and cultural experiences. Many foreign-born students and professionals achieve great success in the United States, which encourages more students and professionals to emigrate to that country. For example, the unpopularity of careers in science among American students reinforces the demand for foreign students to study science and engineering and to become part of the science and engineering workforce in the United States. From 1990 to 2000, the percentage of foreign-born workers in science and engineering with doctoral degrees rose from 24 percent to 38 percent, reflecting the country's growing dependence on immigration to sustain its technologically advanced economy.[31] On the other hand, this means that many developing countries experience brain drain,

Chain Migration
Process by which one family member immigrates to a country and then encourages other family members to join him or her

Immigration Enterprise Zone
Areas created to attract immigrants due to under-population problems

CASE STUDIES

The following case studies provide examples of how specific countries are affected by global migration. The case studies show that both developed and developing societies are being transformed, to varying degrees, by the influx of people from different countries and that governments and nonstate actors regard migration and population issues as extremely important components of human, national, and global security.

The United States

More than any country in the world, the United States is known as an immigrant country. Consequently, most Americans—with the exception of Native Americans and Americans of English and African descent—are descendents of people who migrated to the United States less than three hundred years ago. The demand for labor in the United States, together with poverty, conflict, and oppression in Europe, led to the migration of millions of Europeans to America. Rapid westward expansion and the need for a growing population to develop agriculture as well as industry attracted immigrants primarily from Western and Northern Europe until the early 1900s. Agricultural problems in Scandinavia, for example, prompted Swedes, Danes, Norwegians, and Finns to emigrate and settle in agricultural states in the Midwest.[32] By 1901, most immigrants came from Southern and Eastern Europe. Chinese and Japanese immigrants came to California in the 1850s to work in the gold mines, on the railroads, and in agriculture.

National Quota System

System to limit immigration into the United States

The United States adopted policies that excluded Asians and restricted immigrants from non-European countries. Growing fears about America's changing ethnic composition and about competition from new arrivals among "old stock" Americans led to the passage of legislation in 1921 that initiated the national quota system, which remained in place until 1965. The **national quota system** was designed to preserve the ethnic or national composition of the United States as of 1920. Quotas for immigrants from any one country were calculated in terms of 1/6 of 1 percent of persons of that national origin already in the United States. There was an absolute ceiling of 2,000 immigrants from the Asia-Pacific region.[33] Improved economic conditions in Europe and the abolishment of the national quota system in 1965 changed the pattern of U.S. immigration. Most of the new arrivals are from the developing world, with various groups dominating particular parts of the country. For example, Mexicans comprise the majority of new immigrants in California, Texas, and Illinois; Dominicans, Chinese, and Indians are prominent in New York; and Cubans are the leading group in Florida. Immigrants make up a large proportion of America's population, and demographic projections indicate that they will be largely responsible for the country's population growth.

Mexico's geographic proximity to the United States and historical factors combine to make the growing number of Mexican migrants in the United States a contentious issue. Many Mexicans were already living in Texas, California, Arizona, New Mexico, Utah, Nevada, and Colorado when these areas were taken by the United States from Mexico during the **Mexican-American War**, which lasted from 1846 to 1848. The annexation of these territories by the United States did not significantly alter migration across the newly established borders.

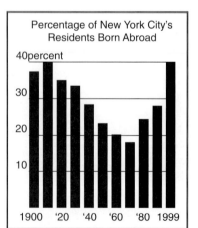

FIGURE 9.6 New York City's Immigrant Population
Sources: U.S. Bureau of the Census; and *New York Times*, 24 July 2000, A18.

Economic and political problems in Mexico have traditionally served as push factors, and the demand for labor and economic opportunities in the United States functioned as pull factors. For example, the demand for labor in the United States during World War II brought Mexicans to America under the **Bracero Program**. The Bracero Program was a set of agreements between the United States and Mexico that facilitated the migration of Mexican workers, on a temporary basis, to work principally in agriculture. The increase in legal migration under the program was accompanied by the growth of illegal immigration. From 1942 to 1952, roughly 900,000 Mexican workers entered the United States under the Bracero Program, compared with more than 2 million illegal workers during the same period. In response to economic competition as well as fears about communists entering the country through Mexico, the United States launched **Operation Wetback** (from 1954 to 1959) in which hundreds of thousands of Mexicans were arrested and deported. However, by the time the Bracero Program had ended in 1964, the relationship between Mexican workers and American employers was so well established that controlling the flow of migrants across the U.S.-Mexican border was almost impossible. Immigration from Mexico, both legal and illegal, became a reality of American life. Mexican immigrants throughout the United States are employed in all sectors of the economy. More than a million immigrants boycotted work and classes to demonstrate in favor of immigration reform in 2006. These protests, however, engendered popular opposition to illegal immigration. Apart from stationing the National Guard along the U.S.–Mexican border, the United States government decided to build a fence along its borders with Mexico.[34]

Mexican-American War

(1846–1848) War in which U.S. seized half of Mexico's territory, which is now Texas, California, Arizona, New Mexico, Utah, Nevada, and Colorado

Bracero Program

Agreements between U.S. and Mexico to promote migration of Mexican workers to the U.S. on a temporary basis (ended in 1964)

Operation Wetback

U.S. operation that deported hundreds of thousands of Mexican migrants

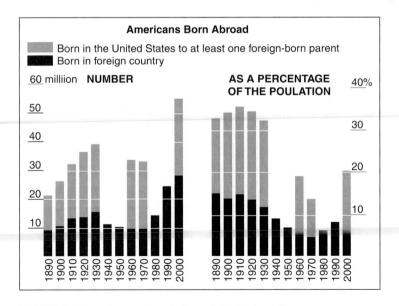

FIGURE 9.7 Immigrant Population of the United States

Sources: U.S. Census Bureau, *Current Population Survey*, 2002; and *New York Times*, 7 February 2002, A18.

Mexican guest worker harvesting oranges in Florida.

Canada

Toronto, Montreal, and Vancouver are three of the most ethnically diverse cities in the world. Perhaps Canada's relatively small population of 31 million and its geographic and cultural proximity to the United States often obscure the reality of Canada as an immigrant country that is extremely ethnically diverse. Settled by the English and French, Canada became a refuge for escaped enslaved Americans as well as Americans who refused to participate in the American Revolution and the Vietnam War. Canada has always encouraged immigration from Europe and parts of the developing world to populate its vast territory. Canada's per capita immigration rate is twice that of the United States, and roughly 17 percent of Canada's population was born abroad. Similar to many Western European countries, Canada is experiencing depopulation in such areas as Newfoundland, the Yukon, Northwest Territories, New Brunswick, and Saskatchewan. Most of the new immigrants settle in Toronto, Vancouver, and Montreal. To reverse depopulation of other parts of Canada, both federal and provincial governments have adopted policies to aggressively recruit immigrants, especially skilled workers from the developing world and Eastern Europe.[35]

Australia

Settled by large numbers of convicts and sheep farmers from Britain, Australia encouraged immigration to develop a relatively sparsely populated continent. The original inhabitants, Australian aborigines, numbered roughly 300,000 at the time of

European colonization. Invasion by the British and resistance on the part of native Australians led to the systematic massacre of native people by the technologically superior Europeans. These early experiences laid the foundation for the country's **White Australia policy**, which effectively barred Asians, Africans, and other nonwhites from immigrating to Australia, while deliberately encouraging white Europeans to become immigrants. Although Australia abandoned its controversial immigration policy in the mid-1970s and allowed Asians and others to immigrate, the growing number of migrants attempting to enter the country and a widespread desire to limit population growth have influenced the government to adopt relatively restrictive immigration policies, especially when compared with Canada and the United States. Australia admits roughly 80,000 immigrants each year on the basis of ethnicity, professional skills, and financial assets. About 12,000 refugees are also selected, based on their ability to integrate into the society.[36] The global smuggling of migrants complicates refugee issues. Australia has refused to accept smuggled refugees and has kept asylum-seekers in detention camps.

White Australia Policy

Government policy prohibiting Asians, Africans, and other nonwhites from immigrating to Australia

Western Europe

The growing unification of Europe, manifested in the creation and strengthening of the European Union (EU), also enables illegal immigrants to move from one country to another once they enter a member country of the EU. Italy's extensive coastline provides many entry points for migrants desperate to settle in Western Europe. Despite numerous tragic accidents involving migrants on unseaworthy and overcrowded vessels, migrants continue to enter Italy. Europe has surpassed the United States as a magnet for refugees and asylum-seekers. Illegal immigrants come from North Africa, Eastern and Central Europe, the Middle East, Latin America and the Caribbean, China, Sub-Saharan Africa, India, Russia, the former Soviet Republics, and elsewhere. Variations in immigration policies among EU members make some countries more attractive than others to migrants. For example, thousands of refugees gather in France at the entrance of the English Channel tunnel waiting for an opportunity, often fatal, to hide in trains and trucks going to Britain, which has more generous refugee policies than France. Hardships endured by migrants do not deter others from trying to enter Europe. Many Europeans believe that uncontrolled immigration is threatening their culture and national or European identities. Furthermore, they perceive immigrants as being responsible for high crime rates, violence, and general threats to security. These fears intensified after the 2001 terrorist

TABLE 9.3 MUSLIMS IN EUROPEAN UNION COUNTRIES

Country	Muslim Population	% of Total Population
France	4–5 million	7.1–8.9
Germany	3 million	3.7
Britain	1.4 million	2.6
Italy	700,000	1.2
Netherlands	696,000	4.4
Belgium	370,000	3.6
Greece	270,000	0.7
Spain	300,000–400,000	0.7–1
Austria	300,000	3.7
Sweden	250,000–300,000	2.8–3.4

Sources: F. Buijs and J. Rath, *Muslims in Europe* (New York: Russell Sage Foundation, 2002); and *The Christian Science Monitor*, 16 May 2003, 6.

attacks in the United States, in Spain in 2004, and in Britain in 2005. Muslims in particular came under increased scrutiny. Riots by Muslim youths in France in 2005 and 2006 reinforced such fears across Europe.

France The influx of large numbers of immigrants from developing countries into France must be seen in the broader context of French colonialism and the demand for labor. As our discussion of the rise and fall of great powers (Chapter 2) showed, global powers usually try to generate feelings of belonging among people under their influence and control. Britain is a multicultural society today partly because its colonial activities set into motion a set of dynamics that brought people from the colonies into Britain. America's rise to a global power has also been accompanied by significant demographic changes. France, like the United States, views its revolution as having universal significance and has developed a tradition of respecting the civil and human rights of foreigners. Its self-perception as a champion of the developing world reinforced its policy of accepting immigrants from poor countries. France adopted a **policy of assimilation** toward its colonies in Africa, Asia, the Caribbean, and the Pacific, under which many residents of French colonies gained French citizenship and were free to migrate in France. Many Africans, Asians, and people from the Caribbean found employment in France, especially following World War I, which had such a devastating impact on the French population that the country had to import labor for its industries. As was the case in Britain, World War II also created demand for labor from the colonies. Algeria's struggle for independence from France (1954–1962) resulted in hundreds of thousands of Algerians gaining asylum in France because of their support for France. More immigrants from France's former colonies arrived in the 1960s to meet the labor needs of France's growing economy. The largest number of immigrants came from Muslim countries—such as Algeria, Tunisia, Morocco, and Senegal—a development, as we have seen, that resulted in the large number of Muslims in France today.[37]

Policy of Assimilation

French policy allowing many people from its colonies to become residents and citizens of France

As in other parts of Europe, rising immigration is fueling political and social extremism in France. **Jean-Marie Le Pen**, leader of the extreme right-wing National Front party, has consistently advocated ending legal immigration and deporting illegal immigrants. There was strong popular support for Le Pen in French presidential elections in 2002. In those elections he received the second highest percentage of votes in the preliminary and runoff elections and qualified to run against President Jacques Chirac in the runoff elections. This popular support for Le Pen demonstrated widespread French opposition to immigration. On the other hand, strong French opposition and strong negative reactions from other European countries to Le Pen following his unexpected political success led to his defeat in the runoff elections.[38] However, in 2006 France began deporting illegal immigrants.

Jean-Marie Le Pen

Right-wing, anti-immigration leader who ran against Jacques Chirac in the 2002 French elections

Germany Unlike the United States, Canada, and Australia, Germany is not traditionally an immigrant country. Instead, Germany encouraged its citizens to emigrate to North America, Eastern Europe, Latin America, and elsewhere in order to diminish population pressures and economic problems at home. Between 1920 and 1950, almost 7 million Germans settled in the United States, many of them in the midwestern agricultural states.

This pattern of migration was radically altered by Germany's initiation of World War II and the devastation it experienced in that conflict. Similar to Britain and France, Germany lost so many of its citizens in the war that it was forced to import labor to help in its economic reconstruction. This was especially so after the construction of the **Berlin Wall**, built by the Soviet Union to divide East Germany from West Germany. The Berlin Wall effectively reduced to a trickle the flow of migrants from communist East Germany to the more prosperous capitalist West Germany.

The growing domestic and global market for West Germany's cars, machine tools, appliances, and other manufactured products influenced the government to recruit foreign workers, primarily from Spain, Greece, Turkey, and Portugal. The government and trade unions agreed that Germans and foreigners would receive equal wages. Under the **Gastarbeiter rotation system**, foreign workers were regarded as guest workers who would remain in Germany for one to three years and then return to their home countries.[39] While economic development in Spain, Greece, and Portugal influenced many workers from those countries to return home, many of them sent for family members and more Turks migrated to Germany. Employers in Germany wanted these temporary workers to remain because of the significant investments they had made in training them and for the economic benefits they derived from them.

Today, almost 3 million Turks live in Germany. The fall of the Berlin Wall in 1989 and the reunification of Germany complicated immigration issues as millions of East Germans migrated to West Germany for economic opportunities and as Germany struggled to develop the former East Germany. Unemployment became a major issue as Germany's economy weakened. Faced with the influx of migrants from Eastern Europe, the former Yugoslavia, and other countries, Germans began to perceive immigrants as economic competitors and threats to their country's cultural values. These developments have been compounded by what Ralph Rotte calls "a permanent latent potential of culturally and ethnically oriented xenophobia,"[40] or Germany's reluctance to include people who are not of German ancestry. Terrorist activities by Muslims in Europe, the United States, and elsewhere after September 11, 2001 reinforced this tendency.

Japan

Historically an insular nation and a strong proponent of ethnic homogeneity, Japan has not encouraged immigration. However, as we discussed earlier, Japan is confronting a significant demographic and economic crisis as its population continues to decline while the proportion of its citizens over 65 years is continuing to grow. Depopulation in Japan is the most severe of all the industrialized countries, largely because Japan's restrictive immigration policies are preventing it from replenishing its population. Without higher birthrates and immigration, Japan will be unable to support its elderly population and to grow economically. Despite Japanese opposition to immigration, immigrants are arriving from Asia and Latin America, especially Brazil. During World War I, labor shortages in Japan prompted manufacturers and mine operators to import Korean workers. Although more than 2 million Koreans were brought to Japan during World War II to meet the demand for labor, most of them were sent back to Korea after the war. Japan's industrial growth after World War II was fueled largely by highly trained and industrious workers from the countryside. As Japanese citizens became prosperous, they discouraged their children from doing manual labor, encouraging them instead to obtain a university education. As we saw at the beginning of this chapter, prosperity and education combine to be an effective contraception. In general, educated women worldwide have smaller families or decide not to have children. Japan's high standard of living is attracting workers from Thailand, the Philippines, Malaysia, South Korea, Vietnam, China, Indonesia, and Bangladesh. Since 1989, Japan has allowed Latin Americans of Japanese ancestry (or **Nikkeijin**) to gain virtually unrestricted access to employment. As we mentioned earlier, economic problems in Japan forced many Japanese to migrate to the United States and Latin America at the beginning of the twentieth century. Brazil, for example, has 1.3 million people of Japanese ancestry, the largest such population outside Japan.[41] Return migration is unlikely to solve Japan's problems arising from depopulation and an aging society.

Nikkeijin

Latin Americans of Japanese ancestry

THE IMPACT OF MIGRATION ON SENDING COUNTRIES

This movement of people within countries and across national boundaries tells various stories that underscore the growing interdependence of nation-states, NGOs, and individuals. Because globalization is a manifestation of complex relationships among states and nonstate actors, migration as a central component of this process is also complicated. Both gains and losses result when large numbers of people migrate, especially since those who leave are usually the best educated, the most ambitious, and enterprising individuals. However, by leaving, these individuals also position themselves to make significant contributions to their original homes.

Brain Drain

Migration of highly educated, skilled, and trained people from one country to another

   Brain drain (i.e., the migration of highly educated and trained people) is widely regarded as a serious problem and a major impediment to development in poor countries. Many doctors, nurses, teachers, and university professors leave poorer countries and rural areas for higher paying jobs and better opportunities in neighboring countries as well as in rich industrial countries. As many as 70,000 educated and skilled Africans migrate to Western Europe, Canada, the United States, and elsewhere each year. This brain drain has significant implications for poor countries. So many medical problems in countries that are most negatively impacted by a shortage of medical personnel. For example, countries such as Tanzania, Malawi, and Sierra Leone had three or fewer doctors per 100,000 people, compared to 256 doctors per 100,000 people in the United States in 2006. Many European countries, especially following World War II, were concerned about losing talented individuals who were attracted to better opportunities in the United States. Canada faces brain drain to the United States, a problem that is solved partly by encouraging brain drain from developing countries. Many small towns in the United States suffer from the loss of their most talented residents to urban areas. By looking at the growing diversity of the United States, Europe, and Canada, we can see how migration contributes to brain drain. We can also observe this phenomenon in our immediate surroundings, such in the universities, hospitals, and various industries. The porousness of national boundaries, the ease of global communication and transportation, and changing attitudes about belonging to a geographic entity make brain drain a reality of globalization. In fact, many individuals who remain in their home countries contribute to brain drain by working for companies in the United States and Europe. For example, global communications technologies enable someone in India to answer consumer calls from the United States. The person sitting in an office in India could as easily be sitting in an office in the United States.

It is estimated that half of the recent graduates from the prestigious Indian Institute of Technology migrate to the United States. They are driven out by push factors, such as overregulation, higher taxes, stagnant career paths, and numerous impediments to entrepreneurship. Many are attracted to the United States by better economic opportunities and a dynamic environment conducive to economic success and personal growth.[42] The fact that most Indian immigrants speak English enables them to easily integrate into American society. It is estimated that one-third of the engineers in Silicon Valley are of Indian origin. About 7 percent of Silicon Valley's high-tech firms are managed by Indians. Sabeer Bhatia, for example, founded Hot-Mail and sold it to Microsoft, and Vinod Khosla is a co-founder of Sun Microsystems.[43] But the migration of talented individuals is seen as detrimental to India's economic development. On the other hand, many countries have a problem of **brain overflow**, which is essentially an oversupply of skilled individuals. Many poor countries, such as the Philippines, India, and Egypt, have become exporters of highly educated people because of their inability to utilize their talents. In fact, India views the migration of such individuals as an integral component of global trade. Many skilled migrants maintain contacts with their home countries and often take back investment capital, advanced technologies, and technical knowledge acquired abroad. For example, China and India strongly encourage migrants to return and contribute to economic development, a trend that is strengthening with increased migration and globalization.

Remittances (i.e., money earned abroad that is sent by migrants to their home countries) play a crucial role in the economic development of poor societies. Given the fact that remittances are transferred by millions of migrants in various ways, it is extremely difficult to know how much money migrants send to their families or invest in their home countries. Remittances clearly create networks of interdependence among countries, NGOs, and individuals. The growing number of migrants challenges traditional international relations theories of citizenship. It also forces many poorer countries to embrace dual citizenship, which enables their citizens to find better jobs abroad and to send even more money home.[44] Some organizations—such as the **Inter-American Development Bank (IDB)** and the **U.S. Agency for International Development (USAID)**—have developed strategies to assist migrants to transmit remittances more economically. This development reflects the growing economic impact of remittances on developing countries. For example, it is estimated that Mexican migrants and Mexican-Americans send approximately $10 billion a year to Mexico, which is twice the value of Mexico's agricultural exports and over a third more than Mexico's tourist revenues. In 2006, immigrants from Latin America in the United States sent a total of $45 billion to their respective countries.[45] The complexity of migration in an increasingly global age makes it difficult to assess its costs and benefits for sending countries.

Brain Overflow
When countries retain an over-supply of skilled individuals

Remittances
Money earned abroad sent by migrants to their home countries

THE IMPACT OF MIGRATION ON RECEIVING COUNTRIES

Migration is transforming many receiving countries, a reality that generates both accommodation and resistance. Large-scale migration is directly influencing the economics, culture, and politics of Western Europe, the United States, Canada, and other countries. Controversy over immigrants in the United States, for example, underscores society's ambivalence about their economic impact. The estimated 12 million illegal immigrants in the United States continue to be a source of debate among politicians, business leaders, and ordinary citizens. European societies and Japan face daunting challenges due to aging populations on the one hand and the growing number of immigrants on the other. Migrants in these societies not only help to support an aging population but also radically alter the demographics and cultures of these countries.

Migrants are in demand in rich countries because they make significant economic contributions, despite the costs associated with educating their children, providing them with economic assistance, and addressing their health and social problems. As we have seen in our discussion on brain drain, developing countries provide well-educated and highly trained individuals at relatively little or no cost to rich countries, which is a major economic contribution to receiving countries. America's scientific and technological dominance is strengthened by immigrants. On the other hand, immigrants provide numerous services that few Europeans or Americas are willing to perform. Many sectors of the American economy—especially agriculture, the service industry, and construction—depend heavily on migrant labor. Few consumers are willing to threaten the bountiful supply of inexpensive food and services, despite their opposition to immigration in theory. Migrants generally dampen inflationary pressures by providing wage competition.

Cultural challenges emanating from migration are widespread in Europe and, to a lesser degree, in the United States and Canada. Many European societies are now experiencing what could be termed a **reverse globalization**, which is characterized by large flows of immigrants from countries colonized by European powers during an earlier period of globalization. Most receiving countries are concerned about the social and political implications of this development. Nowhere is this apprehension more obvious than in France. A predominantly Catholic country, France worries about the large number of Muslims from North Africa. Unlike earlier generations of migrants who adopted French culture, the recent migrants are determined to maintain their own distinct ethnic identities. Many children of migrants, who were born in France, reject much of French culture, regard Islam as essentially incompatible with French morality, and are increasingly separating themselves from mainstream French society. France, which has stressed the separation of church and state and the importance of a secular society, has reacted strongly to Islamic symbols, such as wearing a scarf, in public schools. In late 2003, France banned wearing overtly religious symbols in public schools, thereby giving rise to debates across Europe about integrating immigrants in a changing continent. This debate intensified in late 2005 and 2006 following widespread rioting by French Muslim youths. Terrorist activities in Britain

Reverse Globalization

Large flows of immigrants from countries colonized by European powers during an earlier period of time also influenced some prominent British leaders to suggest that Muslim women should not be allowed to cover their faces in public.

Germany continues to wrestle with cultural challenges represented by large numbers of guest workers from Turkey. Although Turks comprise about one-fourth of Germany's immigrants, their relative poverty, lack of education, practice of Islam, and perceptions of them as economic competitors by former East Germans make them the focus of Germany's concern about migration. Even though many Turks were born and raised in Germany, they were not granted German citizenship. Germany's refusal to see itself as a country of immigration contributes to the Turks' reluctance to fully integrate into German society. Christian churches and labor unions have consistently urged the government to treat guest workers the same as German citizens. In 1996, Germany changed its policy on citizenship for the Turks, and made 46,300 Turks German citizens.

Migration is rapidly changing cultural, economic, and political aspects of American society, a development you can observe in any major U.S. city and, increasingly, in smaller towns. As our discussions indicated, prior to 1965 most immigrants came from Europe. Today, most immigrants come from Mexico, the Philippines, China, Cuba, India, Vietnam, Dominican Republic, and other developing countries. The large number of Hispanics in the United States, is profoundly altering American political and social institutions. It is estimated that Hispanics will constitute 25 percent of America's population by 2050. Politicians are increasingly aware of the growing and potential political power of Latinos and focus on their interests and concerns. Latinos have great potential political power because they are concentrated in states with large numbers of **electoral votes** (i.e., the votes that actually elect the president of the United States) as opposed to the popular vote. These states include California, Texas, Florida, New York, and Illinois. President George W. Bush's proposals in 2004 and 2006 to grant temporary worker status to millions of illegal immigrants was widely perceived not only as recognizing the reality of their contributions to the American economy but also as a strategic political calculation. The popularity of Spanish in America's schools and universities as well as a general perception of Spanish as America's second language underscore the growing influence of Latinos in American society. On the other hand, several groups in the United States advocate limiting immigration and making English the country's official language.

Summary and Review

Migration is an important issue throughout many countries and regions of the world today. It has greatly contributed to globalization and to an increased interdependence among many countries and peoples. This chapter illustrates how population and migration issues are essentially about politics, economics, and culture. Population issues are an increasing problem in the developed and developing countries, as they hinder economic growth and place great pressures on already strained populations. Underpopulation has become a major problem due to a rapid increase in aging populations throughout developed countries. In an attempt to rectify this problem, some states have attempted to increase fertility rates domestically and encourage immigration from abroad. High rates of population growth have had devastating consequences in the developed world as well. In an effort to ease overpopulation, many developing countries have resorted to strict population controls, an example is China's one-child policy. Other countries have encouraged their citizens to migrate to other states.

Migration has various forms. It can be forced or induced. Sometimes it is temporary, as when workers return to their countries of origin. Migration can be regional or transcontinental, and it can be seasonal or permanent. Many factors have contributed to increased migration. Push factors—such as environmental disasters, high unemployment, high population growth rates, state repression, and discrimination—have encouraged many to look for safer homes where they can pursue prosperous futures. Pull factors have also enticed many to migrate, seeking economic and political freedoms, a safer environment for themselves and their families, educational opportunities, and a chance to earn higher wages.

Key Terms

replacement rate 284
carrying capacity 285
one-child policy 290
subreplacement fertility regimes 290
refugees 292
asylum-seekers 294
displaced persons 294
transcontinental migration 294
regional migration 294
rural-to-urban migration 295
rural-to-rural migration 295

urban-to-urban migration 295
urban-to-rural migration 295
seasonal migration 295
transit migration 295
forced and induced migration 295
return migration 295
push factors 297
pull factors 297
Cultural Revolution 298
competitive exclusion 299

United Nations Geneva Convention 299
internally displaced people 300
humanitarian intervention 302
UNRWA 303
diaspora 304
global cities 306
family reunification 306
chain migration 307
immigration enterprise zone 307
national quota system 308

Mexican-American War 308
Bracero Program 309
Operation Wetback 309
White Australia policy 311
policy of assimilation 312
Nikkeijin 314
brain drain 314
brain overflow 315
remittances 315
reverse globalization 316

Discussion Questions

1. How has migration challenged the traditional divisions between nation-states?
2. What are some of the causes, as well as negative consequences, of high and low population growth rates?
3. In what ways have governments attempted to tackle population problems?
4. What is the difference between return migration and a reverse wave of migration?
5. Name some initiatives discussed in this chapter that have been used by governments to limit immigration and prevent noncitizens from gaining citizenship.
6. In what way do remittances help strengthen the ties between economies and people? Do you think remittances are a positive thing?
7. What is a diaspora? Can you give an example from this chapter?

8. What is the difference between a refugee and someone who is internally displaced?
9. Can you identify some of the push and pull factors that traditionally lead to increased regional and global migration?
10. Does the migration of businesses across national borders harm national sovereignty or national prosperity

in any way? Does business migration (downsizing, outsourcing) put citizens of different countries at a disadvantage when they are forced to compete for the jobs made available by multinational corporations? If so how?

Suggested Readings

Adams, Richard J. *International Migration, Remittances, and Brain Drain*. Washington, DC: World Bank, 2003.

Bhagwati, Jagdish. "Borders Beyond Control," *Foreign Affairs* 82, No. 1 (January/February 2003): 98–104.

Bloom, David E., et al. *The Demographic Dividend: Perspectives on the Economic Consequences of Population Change*. Santa Monica, CA: Rand, 2003.

Giry, Stephanie. "France and Its Muslims," *Foreign Affairs* 85, No. 5 (September/October 2006): 87–104.

Hanson, Gordon. *Why Does Immigration Divide America?* Washington, DC: Institute for International Economics, 2005.

Massey, Douglas, and J. Edward Taylor. *International Migration*. New York: Oxford University Press, 2005.

Papademetriou, Demetrios G., and Kimberly A. Hamilton, *Reinventing Japan: Immigration's Role in Shaping Japan's Future*. Washington, DC: Carnegie Endowment for International Peace, 2000.

Schiff, Maurice, and Caglar Ozden, eds. *International Migration, Remittances, and the Brain Drain*. London: Palgrave Macmillan, 2005.

Skerry, Peter. "How Not to Build a Fence," *Foreign Policy* 156 (September/October 2006): 64–67.

Sterett, Susan. *Immigration*. Burlington, VT: Ashgate, 2006.

UN High Commissioner for Refugees. *The State of the World's Refugees*. NewYork: Oxford University Press, 2006.

Addresses and Websites

Center for Migration Studies of New York
209 Flagg Pl.
Staten Island, NY 10204–1199
Tel.: (718) 351–8800
Fax: (718) 667–4598
www.cmsny.org

The Center for Migration Studies of New York was founded in 1964 as an institute for migration study. Its goals are simple: to educate the world on migration and refugees, and their issues. This website provides resources and information on current projects, publications, migration, and refugee movements. It also has a library of archives.

IRSA
1717 Massachusetts Ave. NW, No. 200
Washington, DC 20036
Tel.: (202) 347–2460
Fax: (202) 797–2105
www.irsa-uscr.org

The IRSA acts to defend human rights, build communities, foster education, promote self-sufficiency, and forge partnerships through an array of programs. It manages education and other services to refugees relocating to the United States. This website offers information on refugees relocating to America and news about refugees. It also provides a way for individuals to help refugees.

Migration and Refugee Services (MRS)
1900 South Acadian Thruway
P.O. Box 4213
Baton Rouge, LA 70821–4213
Tel.: (225) 346–0660
Fax: (225) 346–0220

www.brmrs.org

The primary mission of Migration and Refugee Services (MRS) of Catholic Community Services is to develop and provide resettlement opportunities to incoming refugees and immigrants. The major objective of the program is to assist them to achieve economic self-sufficiency by providing social services, including teaching English as a second language, employment services, immigration, and family reunification.

Office of High Commissioner for Human Rights
8-14 Avenue de la Paix
1211 Geneva 10
Switzerland
Tel.: 4122–917–9000
www.unhcr.org

This website offers databases on human rights, as well as education and training in the prevention of human rights. The Office of the High Commissioner for Human Rights attaches importance to practical and creative measures to realize the human rights of women—civil, cultural, economic, political, and social rights. This website has comprehensive information on human rights.

Migration Information Source
Migration Policy Institute
1400 16th St. NW, No. 300
Washington, DC 20036–2257
Tel.: (202) 266–1940
Fax: (202) 266–1900
www.migrationinformation.org/index.cfm

The Migration Information Source provides fresh thought, authoritative data from numerous global organizations and governments, and global analysis of international migration and refugee trends. The website contains news, global data, country profiles, and refugee information. It has a special section on the United States.

Endnotes

1. Christian Joppke, "Why Liberal States Accept Unwanted Immigration," *World Politics* 50, No. 2 (1998), 268.
2. Tom Hundley, "Foes' Births Alarm Israel," *Chicago Tribune*, 23 April 2002, Sect. 1, 1.
3. Gurcharan Das, "The India Model," *Foreign Affairs* 85, No. 4 (July/August 2006), 16.
4. Barbra Crossette, "Population Estimates Fall as Poor Women Assert Control," *New York Times*, 10 March 2002, A3.
5. "More Girls Being Abandoned in China's Countryside," *Pantagraph*, 23 November 2001, A11.
6. David Rohde, "India Steps Up Effort to Halt Abortions of Female Fetuses," *New York Times*, 26 October 2003, A3.
7. Amy Waldman, "States in India Take New Steps to Limit Births," *New York Times*, 7 November 2003, A1.
8. Nicholas Eberstadt, "The Population Implosion," *Foreign Policy*, 123 (March/April 2001), 44.
9. John Dillin, "The Incredible Shrinking Russia," *Christian Science Monitor*, 22 February 2001, 15; and C. J. Chivers, "Russians, Busy Making Shrouds, Are Asked to Make Babies," *New York Times*, 14 May 2006, A4.
10. Richard Bernstein, "Aging Europe Finds Its Pension Is Running Out," *New York Times*, 29 June 2003, A3.
11. Peter G. Peterson, *Gray Dawn* (New York: Random House, 1999), 5.
12. Peter G. Peterson, "The Global Aging Crisis," *Foreign Affairs* 78, No. 1 (January/February 1999), 53.
13. Kevin Sullivan and Mary Jordan, "World's Refugees Deluge Mexico on Way to U.S." *Chicago Tribune*, 8 June 2001, Sect. 1, 4.
14. Tim Hatton, "The Age of Mass Migration," in *Migration and Mobility*, ed. Subrata Ghatak and Anne Showstack Sassoon (New York: Palgrave, 2001), 25.
15. Amy Waldman, "India Harvests Fruits of a Diaspora," *New York Times*, 12 January 2003, A4.
16. Oliver Schmidtke, "Transnational Migration," *World Affairs* 164, No. 1 (Summer 2001), 4.
17. Kimberly A. Hamilton and Kate Holder, "International Migration and Foreign Policy," *Washington Quarterly* (Spring 1996), 196.
18. Myron Weiner, "Security, Stability, and Migration," in *Conflict After the Cold War*, ed. Richard K. Betts (New York: Longman, 2002), 470.
19. David Gonzalez, "Central America's Cities Grow Bigger, and Poorer," *New York Times* 17 March, 2002, A3.
20. Myron Weiner, *The Global Migration Crisis* (New York: HarperCollins, 1995), 30.

21. "Europe Urges Wider Definition of Refugees," *New York Times*, 12 September 2001, B4.

22. Ronald Skeldon, "Hong Kong's Response to the Indochinese Influx," *Annals of the American Academy of Political and Social Science* 534 (July 1994), 92; and UN High Commissioner For Refugees, *The State of the World's Refugees* (New York: Oxford University Press, 2006).

23. Samih K. Farsoun and Christina E. Zacharia, *Palestine and the Palestinians* (Boulder: Westview Press, 1997), 138–139; and Michael Fischbach, *The Peace Process and Palestinian Refugee Claims* (Washington, DC: U.S. Institute of Peace Press, 2006).

24. David Held, et al. *Global Transformations* (Stanford: Stanford University Press, 1999), 294.

25. Cameron W. Barr, "Kuwait Shifts Welfare Costs to Immigrants," *Christian Science Monitor*, 18 April 2001, 7.

26. Martin Wolf, "Will the Nation-State Survive Globalization? *Foreign Affairs* 80, No. 1 (January/February 2001), 181.

27. Held, et al., *Global Transformation*, 294.

28. Peter Stalker, *Workers Without Frontiers* (Boulder; CO: Lynne Rienner, 2000), 100.

29. Hatton, "The Age of Mass Migration," in *Migration and Mobility*, 24–25.

30. Pam Belluck, "Short of People, Iowa Seeks to Be Ellis Island of Midwest," *New York Times*, 20 November 2003, A24.

31. James Glanz, "Study Warns of Lack of Scientists as Visa Applications Drop," *New York Times*, 20 November 2003, A24.

32. Hans Norman, "Swedes in North America," in *From Sweden to America*, ed. Harald Runblom and Hans Norman (Minneapolis: University of Minnesota Press, 1976), 246.

33. Henry J. Steiner and Detlev F. Vagts, *Transnational Legal Problems* (Mineola, New York: Foundation Press, 1976), 19; and Gordon H. Hanson, *Why Does Immigration Divide America?* (Washington, DC: Institute for International Economics, 2005).

34. Kitty Calavita, "U.S. Immigration and Policy Responses," in *Controlling Immigration: A Global Perspective*, ed. Wayne Cornelius, et al. (Stanford: Stanford University Press, 1994), 59; Michael Martinez; "Rallies Draw Over 1 Million," *Chicago Tribune*, 2 May 2006, sect. 1, 7; and Peter Skerry, "How Not to Build a Fence," *Foreign Policy* 156 (September/October 2006), 64.

35. Clifford Krauss, "Canada Courts Migrant Families to Revive a Declining Hinterland," *New York Times*, 2 October 2002, A1.

36. Jane Perlez, "Deep Fears Behind Australia's Immigration Policy," *New York Times*, 8 May 2002, A3.

37. Milton Viorst, "The Muslims of France," *Foreign Affairs* 75, No. 5 (September/October 1996), 78; James F. Hollifield, "Immigration and Republican France," in *Controlling Immigration*, 153; and Stephanie Giry, "France and Its Muslims," *Foreign Affairs* 85, No. 5 (September/October 2006), 89–91.

38. Suzanne Daley, "French Political Leaders Rally Around Chirac," *New York Times*, 23 April 2002, A1.

39. Herman Kurthen, "Germany at the Crossroads," *International Migration Review* 29, No. 4 (Winter 1995), 922.

40. Ralph Rotte, "Immigration Control in United Germany," *International Migration Review* 34, No. 2 (Summer 2000), 358.

41. James Brooke, "Sons and Daughters of Japan, Back From Brazil," *New York Times*, 27 November 2001, A4.

42. Stephan-Gotz Richter, "The Immigration Safety Valve," *Foreign Affairs* 79, No. 2 (March/April 2000), 15.

43. Anthony Spaeth, "The Golden Diaspora," *Time*, 19 June 2000, B28.

44. Devesh Kapur and John McHale, "Migration's New Payoff," *Foreign Policy* 139 (November/December 2003), 50.

45. Kapur and Hale, "Migration's New Payoff," 50; and Maurice Schiff and Caglar Ozden, eds., *International Migration, Remittances, and the Brain Drain* (London: Palgrave Macmillan, 2005); and Eduardo Porter, "Flow of Immigrants' Money to Latin America Surges," *New York Times*, 19 October 2006, A23.

CHAPTER 10

Global Crime

INTRODUCTION

Global criminal activities have proliferated with the rapid growth of globalization. **Global crime** is intricately intertwined with revolutionary technological, financial, communications, economic, cultural, and political changes that characterize globalization, and it is increasingly difficult to separate criminal activities from legitimate global transactions. As national boundaries become more porous and as different legal and political systems are more closely integrated, uncertainties about the legality of various activities abound. What some countries regard as serious problems are often viewed as lower priorities for others. Furthermore, different countries—influenced by divergent cultural attitudes and beliefs—adopt different approaches to solving problems. An example is the European and American strategy for dealing with illegal drugs. The multiplicity of values, conflicting interests, inadequate resources, ineffective global cooperation, the cumbersomeness of national sovereignty, rapid economic and political change, ethnic conflicts, and the existence of weak states help to fuel the growth of global crime and militate against efforts to reduce it. Further contributing to the growth and spread of global crime are the forces of cultural globalization that have eroded traditional values and have influenced people everywhere to experiment with new lifestyles, which often incorporate using illegal drugs.

Global crime is a paramount issue because it is so closely connected with so many other global issues. The disintegration of the Soviet Union contributed to the strengthening and unleashing of criminal organizations that have constructed global networks involved in drug trafficking, human trafficking, money laundering, illegal arms sales, and other criminal activities. Global crime is also linked to global poverty and inequality, the spread of infectious diseases, global migration, growth of global cities, the expansion of free trade, rapid communications and computer technologies, easy global financial transactions, spread of democratic freedoms, the proliferation of weapons, human rights abuses, terrorism, and ethnic conflicts.

This chapter examines the globalization of crime, the perpetual global drug problem, the global smuggling of migrants, contemporary slavery and human trafficking, criminal gangs and kidnapping, money laundering, illegal trade in exotic animals and plants, illegal trade in human organs, cybercrimes and piracy, and stolen art and antiquities. It concludes with a discussion of various global responses to crime. The lucrative nature of these crimes and the ease with which most of them are committed ensure their continuation and growth. The social, economic, and political costs of global crime are incalculable.

THE GLOBALIZATION OF CRIME

Global crime has existed with legal commerce for centuries. In fact, crime has been an integral component of human society. However, fundamental changes resulting from globalization, as we discussed in Chapter 1, have intensified and expanded crime and given rise to complex global criminal networks. Communications, transportation, computer technologies, the liberalization of trade, migration, and the openness of many societies that facilitate economic, cultural, environmental, and other forms of globalization have worked to the advantage of global criminals. By diminishing the significance of geographic distance, globalization enables criminal networks to grow alongside legal global activities and to establish connections within many different countries. As we will discuss, alliances are common among criminal organizations involved in trafficking in humans, drugs, weapons, and various illicit products. Moises Naim observed that criminal networks have benefited more than nation-states from the information revolution, economic links, and other aspects of globalization.[1] An essential component of globalization is speed. Information, products, money, and people move quickly across national boundaries. Delays would increase costs, create uncertainties, diminish competitiveness, undermine confidence, and reduce reliability. In other words, slowing down global trade to reduce global crime would effectively impede global trade.

Although globalization has contributed to increased economic equality among and within nations, as **Thomas Friedman** argues in *The World Is Flat*, globalization is widely perceived as contributing to more inequality. To an unprecedented degree of poignancy, globalization heightens the awareness of the economic and social disparities between the rich and the poor within nations and between rich and poor countries. Not only do poor people perceive themselves as losers in the process of globalization, they have little incentive to adhere to rules that they perceive to be adverse to their interests. For example, convincing coca farmers in Peru, Columbia, and Bolivia that they should not participate in illegal drug production has been difficult. Similarly, small farmers in Afghanistan continue to produce poppies used to make heroin. While organized crime imposes excessive burdens on society, particularly the poor, many criminal groups, in order to gain political influence and legitimacy, invest in social services, athletic facilities, housing, and medical services. These areas have been largely neglected by many governments as part of the privatization process required by economic globalization. Ultimately, global crime is integrated into the fabric of these societies and enjoys significant official and unofficial protection.

Global crime generally flourishes in weak states. As we discussed in Chapter 1, the forces of globalization have played a major role in diminishing the power of states, especially when compared with the power of global nongovernmental organizations (NGOs). Due to their institutional weaknesses, many states in the developing world are vulnerable to pressure from global criminal enterprises. Corrupt officials often participate in illegal activities, such as drug trafficking and money laundering. Given the relentless competition brought about by globalization, many weak governments enable criminal groups to take advantage of their sovereignty in order to conduct illegal activities. In some cases, weak institutional capabilities have prevented governments from reducing global crime. Consequently, there has been an unprecedented escalation in such crimes as trade in pirated goods, illegal arms, human trafficking, stolen art, and illegal drugs.[2] Political instability and ethnic conflicts within many developing countries and regions provide opportunities for global crime to consolidate and expand.

The disintegration of the Soviet Union in 1991 was one of the most important developments contributing to the emergence and growth of global crime. Rapid political and economic changes in Eastern and Central European countries further enhanced opportunities for widespread criminal activities. Exploiting weakness of the Russian government, organized criminal groups consolidated their power domestically and built strategic alliances with global criminal organizations in Latin America and the Caribbean. Russian criminal groups proliferated throughout Central Europe, in countries such as the Czech Republic, as successful revolutions against communism ushered in social disorganization, poorly guarded national borders, free-market economies, and a willingness of young people to experiment with drugs. Furthermore, as we discussed in Chapter 1, the expansion of the European Union (EU) into Central and Eastern Europe and the removal of many national barriers to the movement of people and products facilitated the growth of criminal activities.[3] The global drug problem, so intertwined with other crimes, receives more attention from the global community than any other global crime.

THE GLOBAL DRUG PROBLEM

From Shanghai to San Francisco, from London to Buenos Aires, in Christian, Jewish, Islamic, Hindu, and Buddhist societies, in small towns and in big cities, and in rich countries and poor countries, the use of illegal drugs is a serious problem. Norway—which generally ranks first in the world in terms of income, health care, life expectancy, and education—is widely regarded as having one of Europe's worst drug problems. For many years, Oslo has been ranked as Europe's drug overdose capital.[4] Illegal drug use is one of the most important global issues. No society has managed to escape the consequences of the global drug trade, largely because the global drug problem is so closely intertwined with other areas of globalization. Many aspects of the current period of globalization—such as communications, travel, tourism, migration, transportation, financial transactions, and trade—facilitate the globalization of illegal drugs. As we have emphasized throughout this book, the privatization and deregulation of many governmental functions in an increasingly borderless world have contributed to the weakening of governments' ability to effectively police their borders. It has become more difficult to separate legal from illegal trade. Given the huge profits that are obtained from drugs, estimated to be $320 billion a year worldwide, global and domestic inequalities often motivate the poor to participate in the production, transportation, and distribution of illegal drugs. Powerful drug cartels often exercise significant control within weak and unstable states, largely because weak governments often engage in corruption and are unable to control many parts of their countries. The foundations of the contemporary global drug problem were laid during an earlier period of globalization that was marked by European expansion, colonization, and trade.

The discoveries of tobacco in the Caribbean, chocolate in South America, coffee in the Middle East and Africa, and tea in Asia marked the beginning of a global trade that eventually included opium. The growth of the opium trade was influenced partly by China's huge trade advantage with Portugal, Holland, and Britain. Whereas China had silk, teas, pottery, and other items that Europeans wanted, Europe had little to trade with China, thereby creating a trade deficit in China's favor. Europeans, who had trafficked in opium in parts of Asia, decided to sell it to China in order to reduce the trade imbalances.[5] The **British East India Company**, for example, paid Asian farmers to produce opium, which it then sold to independent wholesalers. Opium cultivation in India grew steadily, and the British pressured China to import it. Chinese resistance to the importation and consumption of opium ultimately led to the **Opium Wars** with Britain in 1839 and 1842, in which Britain forced China to import opium, despite an already horrendous drug addiction problem in China. British military power was instrumental in the legalization of opium in China in 1858. The Portuguese, French, Spanish, and Dutch also participated in the trade, creating opium addicts in their colonies as well as in Europe. The Spanish, for example, promoted the use of coca leaves to enable enslaved Indians to endure harsh physical labor. Toward the end of the nineteenth century, *the demand for opium in Europe and America was on the rise, due to several factors. These included*

British East India Company

British company that dominated Indian trade

Opium Wars

Fought so that the British could force the opium trade onto the Chinese people

1. *The advancement in medical practices*, especially the discovery of morphine and heroin (both obtained from opium) and the invention of the hypodermic needle to administer them;
2. *Significant cultural and economic changes* that resulted from the Industrial Revolution, particularly the consumption of natural stimulants;
3. *The migration of Chinese*, many of whom used opium, to America and elsewhere;
4. *The growth of global trade*;
5. *The rise of mass-consumption habits*, influenced by marketing and mass communication;[6] and
6. *Military conflicts*, including the U.S. Civil War, which increased the demand for drugs to diminish pain.

Globalization combined with major cultural changes worldwide—especially in the United States, Canada, and Europe—are driving the global drug trade. Most experts agree that widespread use of illegal drugs in western societies during the 1960s and 1970s created a global demand for drugs, which in turn stimulated worldwide illegal drug production. Heroin was smuggled in from areas that cultivated opium poppies, primarily the **Golden Triangle** countries (Burma/Myanmar, Thailand, and Laos) and the **Golden Crescent** countries (Afghanistan, Pakistan, and Iran). Cocaine came primarily from Colombia, Peru, Bolivia, and other South American countries. Marijuana, now increasingly grown within consuming countries, came primarily from Mexico, Jamaica, Colombia, and Thailand. Global trafficking networks quickly developed or were expanded to produce, distribute, and sell illegal drugs. Global commerce and migration have helped to consolidate the global drug trade. For example, Mexican

Golden Triangle

Countries that cultivate opium poppies (Burma/Myanmar, Thailand, and Laos)

Number of users in 2002, age 12 and older	
Drug	
Marijuana	14.6 million
Prescription drugs	6.2
Cocaine or crack	2.0
Ecstasy	0.7
Methamphetamine	0.6
Inhalents	0.6
Heroin	0.2
LSD	0.1

FIGURE 10.1 Most Abused Drugs in the United States
Source: U.S. Substance Abuse and Mental Health Services Administration.

drug traffickers took advantage of the growing number of Mexican immigrants in Dalton, Georgia, to turn that area into a distribution center for methamphetamine and other drugs.[7] Industrial countries are now themselves major sources of illegal drugs. Nightclub crowds worldwide routinely use **Ecstasy**, a euphoria-producing psychedelic drug that was initially used in Europe around 1912 as an appetite suppressant. What's more, distinctions between legal and illegal drugs are diminishing as more people abuse prescription medications. As Figure 10.1 shows, while marijuana remains the most widely used drug, prescription drugs, such as OxyContin and Vicodin, rank second.

Efforts to Control the Drug Problem

War on Drugs

Stresses supply-side control and harsh treatment of drug users

The reality of the global drug trade and the inability of governments to prevent drugs from entering countries have spawned essentially two different approaches to dealing with the drug problem. The first approach, the **war on drugs**, stresses supply-side control and harsh treatment of drug users. The second approach, *drug prevention and harm reduction*, emphasizes the need to keep drugs out of society and to treat drug abuse as a disease. The first approach is strongly embraced by the United States; the second approach is widely practiced in Europe. Before discussing these two strategies, we will briefly examine historical efforts to control the use of illegal drugs. As is currently the case, drug-exporting countries usually become major drug-consuming societies. As we saw earlier, European countries openly and aggressively built a global drug trade. By the beginning of the twentieth century, the widespread use of cocaine-based tonics, heroin, opium, and other narcotics in Europe, the United States, Japan, and China raised concerns about their negative impact on public morals. Religious groups, temperance societies, and others in Britain and the United States advocated ending the opium trade. As the United States expanded its power into Asia, especially after the **Spanish-American War** in 1898 (which resulted in the end of Spain's empire and America's acquisition of the Philippines), Americans became more concerned about drug abuse. The Philippines had a large population of drug addicts, and China, as we saw earlier, had been forced by Britain to allow millions of its citizens to become opium addicts.

Hague Convention

Broadened the international drug-fighting effort by cracking down on morphine and cocaine

Partly because of its interest in gaining greater influence in China, the United States collaborated with China to persuade other countries to participate in an international conference designed to convince drug-exporting countries to reduce their production of drugs. The conference, held in Shanghai in 1909, created the **International Opium Commission**. Although the twelve countries involved agreed to gradually suppress opium smoking in their territories, very little progress on controlling drugs was made. The **Hague Convention** of 1911 broadened the drug-fighting effort by including morphine and cocaine, and committed the signatories to reducing their production and

Colombia's president destroying coca plants.

distribution of drugs. However, the Hague Convention was ineffective, partly because some countries—such as Germany, which at the time was the world's largest cocaine producer—insisted that implementation of the treaty be made conditional on its world-wide acceptance.[8] Given the lucrativeness of drugs, few countries were willing to comply with the restrictive agreements. A turning point in the effort to control the drug trade was America's enactment of the **Harrison Act** in 1914, which required distributors and medical prescribers of specified drugs to be registered and pay taxes. Britain and other European countries enacted similar legislation. The **League of Nations** (1919) helped to consolidate drug-control efforts by stressing the development of mandatory international controls to be supervised by international organizations. The **Opium Control Board** was established by the League of Nations to monitor countries' compliance with international agreements on controlling drugs. The rapid spread of drug usage in the 1960s and 1970s influenced the United Nations (UN) to sponsor the International **Conference on Drug Abuse and Illicit Traffic** in 1987 in order to discuss strategies for dealing with the problem. In 1988, strongly influenced by America's emphasis on the war-on-drugs approach, the global community signed the **UN Convention Against Illicit Traffic in Narcotic Drugs and Psychotropic Substances**. This convention stressed sharing law enforcement evidence, providing mutual legal assistance, controlling the sale of chemicals used in producing drugs, and escalating the eradication of drug crops.[9] Founded in 1990, the **UN International Drug Control Program (UNDCP)** stressed the need for both demand reduction and alternative development. In 1998, the UN General Assembly Special Session on Drugs advocated the goal of a drug-free world by 2008.

Harrison Act

U.S. act requiring distributors and prescribers of drugs to be registered and pay taxes

Opium Control Board

Established under the League of Nations to monitor countries' compliance with international drug agreements

Confronted with the rapid rise in drug abuse, the United States mobilized financial, law enforcement, and military resources to combat the problem. The war on drugs concentrates primarily on reducing global drug trafficking and drug use by eliminating supplies and implementing punitive drug laws. It is estimated that between 50 and 80 percent of Americans who are imprisoned have committed a drug-related offense. The United States has cooperated with governments throughout Latin America to eradicate drug crops, implement crop-substitution programs, and destroy trafficking networks. In 2000, for example, the United States and Colombia launched **Plan Colombia**, an antidrug program that had the goal of reducing Colombia's coca crop in half by 2005. The plan involved aerial spraying, promoting crop substitution, destroying cocaine labs, and disrupting transportation routes. The United States allocated $1.3 billion to Plan Colombia.[10] By 2006, that figure had increased to $4 billion. Given how lucrative it is, the war on drugs has not significantly reduced the drug trade. Poverty and tradition motivate many small farmers in Latin America and Asia to grow drug crops. The money they earn from crop substitution is only a fraction of what they can earn from drug crops. Ironically, success in removing drugs from the market increases the demand for declining supplies, thereby driving up prices. This, in turn, influences people to cultivate drug crops. Corrupt law enforcement officials worldwide also undermine the war on drugs. Most importantly, the war on drugs largely ignores the demand for drugs within the United States, Europe, and elsewhere. Coca production in Colombia was not significantly reduced in 2006, despite the $4 billion pumped into that effort by the United States.

By contrast, Europeans concentrate on treating drug addiction more as a medical problem, while supporting efforts to reduce drug supplies. **Harm-reduction approaches** acknowledge the weaknesses of the war-on-drugs approach. Holland became a pioneer in implementing the harm-reduction approach. It decriminalize possession and use of small amounts of "soft" drugs (such as marijuana), provides "safe injection rooms" so that addicts can avoid public places, distributes sterile syringes to reduce the spread of HIV and AIDS, and supports medical treatment for drug addicts.[11] Europeans strongly oppose Plan Colombia and the U.S. war on drugs. The EU voted 474 to 1 to oppose the large-scale use of chemical herbicides and biological agents to eradicate coca plants because of the consequences for human health and the environment.

Plan Colombia
U.S. sponsored antidrug campaign implemented to eradicate Colombia's cocaine production

Harm-Reduction Approach
Aims at drug prevention and drug treatment

Global Smuggling of Migrants

In June 2000, British customs officials discovered the bodies of fifty-eight illegal Chinese immigrants in a sealed compartment of a Dutch-registered tomato truck. They had been smuggled into Dover after a five-hour journey across the English Channel from the Belgian port of Zeerbrugge. France is also a transit point for illegal immigrants who pay global smuggling operations to get them into Britain and, in many cases, eventually to the United States and Canada. The migrants wait on the French coast to be smuggled across the English Channel into Britain. The extensive U.S.-Mexican border provides smugglers with a relatively easy way to get migrants to the

You DECIDE

Strategies to Reduce Global Drug Use

Whereas the United States stresses eliminating the growth of drug crops, cutting off supplies, and punishing drug abusers, the Europeans treat drug addiction as a medical problem, do not arrest people for possessing or using small amounts of drugs, and generally believe that focusing primarily on the supply of drugs and declining to acknowledge that demand for drugs is a major part of the problem will not reduce global drug usage. Most Americans, however, view Europe's permissive drug policies as promoting drug abuse. But America continues to have serious drug problems, and drug supplies have not been significantly reduced. Methamphetamine labs can be found across the United States and prescription drugs are widely abused.

Evaluate the effectiveness of the European and American approaches to drugs. Do you think the war on drugs is counterproductive?

most popular destination. Immigrant communities along the border, the existence of criminal organizations that operate between the countries, the well-established drug trade, and the flow of people and products across the U.S.-Mexican border facilitate the successful smuggling of migrants from around the world. It is estimated that more than a million migrants are smuggled across this border each year. But the tragic deaths of nineteen migrants who were being smuggled across the border in May 2003 refocused national attention on the illegal and brutal nature of global smuggling. At least seventy-seven migrants were packed into an unconventional tractor-trailer without

TABLE 10.1 GLOBAL SMUGGLING OF MIGRANTS

Payments to Traffickers for Selected Migration Routes

Route	Payment ($ Per Person)
China to New York	35,000–60,000
China to Europe	10,000–30,000
Turkey to Austria	6,000
Iraq to Europe	4,100–5,000
Middle East to the United States	1,000–15,000
Philippines to Malaysia	3,500
Pakistan to the United States	25,000
India to the United States	25,000
Kurdistan to Germany	3,000
Arab States to United Arab Emirates	2,000–3,000
North Africa to Spain	2,000–3,500
Mexico to Los Angeles	200–400

Sources: "Migrant Trafficking and Human Smuggling in Europe," International Organization for Migration, 2000; and *Economist*, 2 November 2002, 6.

water for a 325-mile journey across the scorching desert. Some who survived had body temperatures as high as 105 degrees. The person in charge of the smuggling operation had been smuggled across the border about ten years before this deadly tragedy.[12]

Chinese global smuggling organizations are generally regarded as the most sophisticated and most brutal. Many migrants come from the Fujian province in Southern China and take advantage of connections with family members and friends already established in the United States, Canada, and European countries. Chinese communities worldwide, especially those in large cities, provide extensive networks of connections that enable global smuggling operations to be efficient and lucrative. Chinese migrants pay smugglers between $30,000 and $60,000 to be transported to Europe, the United States, and Canada. They travel across many countries or across 9,000 miles of the Pacific Ocean for five weeks in unsanitary, unseaworthy ships. Many of them land in Central America and make a long and perilous journey across Mexico and into the United States, where they find employment in Chinese communities to repay their debt for being smuggled. Often, they pay an initial 10 percent of the smuggling cost and relatives pay the rest once the migrants arrive at their destinations. One of the most famous smuggling cases involved Cheng Chui-Ping, known affectionately in New York City's Chinatown as Sister Ping. She sold clothes and operated a restaurant that served dishes from her native Fujian province. She also used her entrepreneurial skills to build a global smuggling network that brought Chinese migrants to Mexico, Belize, and other Central American countries and eventually to the United States. She was able to bribe immigration officials and obtain false documents for migrants. Once migrants arrived in the United States, they usually found employment in restaurants and garment factories, which enabled them to repay her. By the time she was arrested by an undercover U.S. police officer, she had built a global smuggling network from which she received more than $40 million, making her a major player in the roughly $7 billion to $12 billion global smuggling business.[13]

CONTEMPORARY SLAVERY AND HUMAN TRAFFICKING

Contemporary Slavery

Transporting people from one area to another, where they are subjugated to forced labor or prostitution

Human trafficking (i.e., the forced or coerced movement of people across national borders as well as within countries) is probably as old as human civilization. Throughout history, human beings have enslaved each other, and forced each other to work under the most inhumane conditions, justifying this exploitation in many ways. From ancient Egypt to the present-day United States, slavery was and is an integral component of economic life. While old-fashioned slavery has been abolished, slavery continues to exist in the twenty-first century. **Contemporary slavery** is the transporting of victims under false pretenses from one nation, or province, to another, where they are subjugated to forced labor or prostitution.[14] Compared with the global drug trade, human trafficking receives much less attention. Nonetheless, it is a growing problem, partly because it combines high profits, increasing demand, abundant supply, relatively low risks of punishment, increasing sexual tolerance worldwide, and varying perceptions of the problem in the global community. Although the U.S.

Central Intelligence Agency estimates that almost a million people worldwide are enslaved each year, including 20,000 in the United States, it is impossible to know how many people are actually trafficked.[15]

The exponential growth in contemporary slavery and human trafficking is inseparable from increasing levels of economic and cultural globalization. As we discussed in Chapter 9, global migration is extremely difficult to manage. The porousness of borders that are inadequately monitored facilitates human trafficking. Because much of the trafficking is conducted by individuals and small groups, often in cooperation with large criminal organizations, it is difficult to detect and control. Global inequality and demographic factors contribute to the rapid growth of labor migration, a development in which most countries participate. Migrants are employed to do the most strenuous and undesirable jobs in most countries, including the United States. Globalization and changing attitudes about women have led to a dramatic increase in women migrants. Many women are employed as domestic helpers, in service industries, and in the entertainment industry as dancers, strippers, and sex workers. This **feminization of migration**, (i.e., the increasing percentage of women in the migrant population), complicates the human trafficking problem.[16] As we mentioned earlier, globalization enables criminals to operate alongside the legal global economy. Massive migration flows, mostly illegal, provide an effective cover for human traffickers. At a fundamental level, human trafficking is fueled by socioeconomic conditions that make so many people desperate and vulnerable. Furthermore, globalization, by shrinking geographic distances and spreading cultural values that promise an escape from poverty and a better life in richer countries, enhances the ability of criminals to engage in human trafficking.

Feminization of Migration

The increasing percentage of women in the migrant population

Despite the global emphasis on women and girls being trafficked for sexual exploitation, labor trafficking of males as well as females is more prevalent. In 2005, the **International Labor Organization (ILO)** found that of the estimated 9.5 million victims of forced labor in Asia, less than 10 percent were trafficked for commercial sexual exploitation. Globally, less than half of all trafficking victims are involved in the sex trade.[17] Forced labor exists worldwide. In early 2006, the deaths of twelve workers who had been trafficked from Nepal to Iraq demonstrates the pervasiveness of human trafficking. The workers, who came from one of the most impoverished areas of the world, became entangled in a trail of deceit, fraud, coercion, and negligence. Contractors and subcontractors, employed directly or indirectly by the U.S. government at American facilities in Iraq, put the workers in the war zone. All twelve workers were kidnapped on their way to work on a U.S. military base and were subsequently executed by militants.[18]

Women and girls are generally perceived as replaceable commodities by human traffickers. Globalization has added news dimensions to this ancient human practice. Although virtually all societies have experienced human trafficking for sexual purposes, this practice seems to be more prevalent in several Asian countries. Prior to the Russian Revolution in 1917, Russian and Eastern European women were trafficked into China and Argentina. Between the 1970s and today, there have been *four distinct waves of sexual human* trafficking, all of which are manifestations of increasing globalization. The *first wave* began in the 1970s and was primarily composed of trafficked women from Southeast Asia, particularly Thailand and the Philippines. The *second wave* started in the early 1980s, and involved trafficked women mostly from Africa, especially Ghana and Nigeria. The *third wave*, from the 1980s to the 1990s, was made up of Latin Americans, with most of the women coming from Colombia, Brazil, and the Dominican Republic. The *fourth wave*, which mirrors the rapid expansion and growing complexity of globalization, is closely connected to the demise of the Soviet Union. The women are coming from Eastern and Central Europe.[19] The fact that human trafficking is escalating globally, underscores the reality of the continuation of all four waves of trafficking.

While women are trafficked globally, the Netherlands, Germany, Japan, the United Arab Emirates, Israel, Greece, South Korea, Turkey, Austria, Belgium, Bosnia, the United States, and Canada are the principal destinations. Reflecting the complex networks and alliances that characterize globalization, discussed in Chapter 1, criminals collaborate to maximize their profits from human trafficking. Groups in the Russian Far East cooperate with Japanese and Korean organized crime to transport women to China, Japan, Korea, Thailand, and other countries of the Pacific Rim. Groups in the Caucuses collaborate with human traffickers in Turkey to transport women to brothels in Turkey, Cyprus, and countries in the Middle East. Women from Kazakhstan are trafficked to Bahrain, where the Muslim links of the traffickers provide women for this free-trade zone.[20]

The explosive growth in human trafficking largely reflects the general changes associated with globalization. Although the vast majority of trafficked women are forced into prostitution, cultural globalization has also facilitated this global crime. Many young women worldwide are seduced by romantic images of the West to take risks that often result in their sexual exploitation. Poverty has usually been a major factor influencing human trafficking. Radical economic changes that accompanied the fall of communism in the Soviet Union and the transition from a centralized economy to a market-based economy undermined economic security for many women, even as these changes provided the impetus for increased globalization. The rapid privatization process, required for Russia to participate in the global economy, contributed to the elimination or reduction of employment opportunities, especially for women. Women became more vulnerable to trafficking as they attempted to find employment in other countries to support their families.

Economic deprivation also facilitates trafficking of orphans throughout Eastern Europe and elsewhere. Forced to leave orphanages at age 16 or 17, many of them become homeless. Other children, abandoned by impoverished families, are unable to even find places in overcrowded orphanages in some countries, such as Russia, the Ukraine, and Romania. Furthermore, as the role of the state shrinks and privatization becomes dominant, financial support for social services has diminished globally, thereby rendering the poor even more vulnerable to global crime. Finally, revolutions in communications and transportation that are the hallmarks of globalization facilitate the proliferation of matchmaking services, many of which are owned and operated by organized crime.[21] Women who participate in them often find themselves trapped in brothels.

Although trafficking across national boundaries for sexual exploitation is a significant component of global crime, most trafficked women and girls remain within their countries or regions. In India alone, for example, more than half a million girls are in brothels, more than any other country in the world. The rapid growth of sex tourism in Asia and elsewhere reinforces the sexual exploitation of women and girls within their own societies. What's more, the AIDS pandemic is influencing human traffickers to find younger women and girls, especially virgins, because customers believe they are less likely to be infected with HIV and AIDS.[22] Eventually, many of these young women contract the disease and become disease carriers and drug addicts.

The global response to human trafficking has been largely ineffective, as evidenced by the rapid increase of this crime. Several efforts to address this problem have been made at both the national and global levels. In 1989 the European Parliament adopted a resolution that called for tough measures to eradicate human trafficking. Meeting in Beijing at the **Fourth World Conference on Women** and declaring that women's rights are human rights, delegates from 189 countries unanimously adopted a **platform for action**, which called on governments to dismantle criminal networks engaged in trafficking women. In response to the unprecedented growth in human trafficking, the **UN Protocol Against the Trafficking in Women and Children** was adopted along with the UN Convention on Transnational Crime in 2000. At a world summit on organized crime in 2000 in Palermo, Italy, leaders from eighty countries signed the UN protocol. Also in 2000, a coalition of Democrats, Republicans, feminists, and evangelical Christians pressured the U.S. Congress to enact the **Victims of Trafficking and Violence Protection Act** to prosecute traffickers in the United States and to take action abroad against this global crime. This law recognized human trafficking as a federal crime for the first time and requires the U.S. Department of State to publish an annual report on the state of human trafficking globally.[23]

While the global community was responding to the problem of human trafficking, several countries were legalizing the sex trade, which consists predominantely of foreign women in most European countries. For example, roughly half a million women are trafficked as prostitutes in Europe every year. In Germany, three out of four sex workers are foreigners, and in the Netherlands one out of two sex workers comes from another country. In 2000, the Netherlands legalized prostitution, which is a $1 billion-a-year industry and represents roughly 5 percent of that country's economy. Germany legalized prostitution in 2001. The sex trade contributes approximately $4.5 billion to Germany's economy.[24] Many countries in Europe, Asia, Latin America, and Africa tolerate the sex trade, a reality that complicates and weakens efforts to find a solution to global human trafficking. Very few traffickers are prosecuted and convicted. Furthermore, the illegal immigration status of trafficked women becomes an impediment to punishing criminals involved in trafficking. Some success in efforts to reduce human trafficking came in 2006, when John R. Miller, a senior adviser to U.S. Secretary of State Condoleezza Rice, persuaded Japan to reduce the number of entertainment visas for young women from the Philippines from 80,000 to 5,000 a year.[25]

Fourth World Conference on Women

Called on governments to prevent trafficking in women

Victims of Trafficking and Violence Protection Act

Requires the U.S. to prosecute human traffickers and to publish an annual report on global trafficking

Victim of gang vio-
lence in Guatemala.

CRIMINAL GANGS AND KIDNAPPING

Carmen Toro stops by the morgue in Guatemala City on her way to work to see if her
son's body is there. A member of the extremely violent **Maria 18 street gang**, he disappeared after being abducted by three masked gunmen who forced him into an
unmarked car. Such experiences are increasingly common in Central America and
around the world as violent gangs proliferate to create an upsurge in global crime.
While gangs have existed in many societies throughout history, globalization has
intensified their activities and expanded their territory. The same communications
and technological revolutions that drive globalization also help gangs to grow. The
Internet enables them to form alliances, to learn from each other, and to terrorize.[26]
Repeated exposure to cultural globalization—especially violent television programs,
movies, video games, and magazines—reinforces their violent behavior. Ethnic conflicts and civil wars, combined with easy access to guns, provide fertile ground for
gang violence to flourish. Aspects of globalization—especially global migration,
global inequality, and fewer government-provided public services due to privatization
and trade liberalization—contribute to the growth of gangs. Demographic factors also
play an important role. Young people between the ages of 16 and 24 tend to commit
most of the crimes, especially in densely populated areas. As we discussed earlier in
this chapter, the decline of social services and poverty often combine to influence parents to abandon their children, making them vulnerable to gangs. Gang violence
increases political instability, weakens democratic institutions, increases human rights
violations, and impedes economic development. Kidnapping is often an integral

component of gang violence, and it is generally fueled by poverty and economic inequality. Gang violence usually generates counterviolence by vigilante groups, the military, and police officers who are frustrated by the government's inability to provide security and deliver justice.

Foundations for rising gang violence in Central America were laid during the civil wars that devastated the region in the 1980s, driven partly by military and political rivalry between the United States and the Soviet Union. The Cold War in Central America was accompanied by widespread human rights abuses, rape, torture, extrajudicial executions, kidnappings, and drug production and trafficking. In Guatemala alone, more than 200,000 people were killed or missing (out of a population of 14 million) during these conflicts. Civil wars also bring with them the proliferation of weapons. As we discussed in Chapter 9, violence is a factor that pushes people to migrate. Many Central Americans came to the United States and settled in the ghettos of Los Angeles and other major American cities. Many young migrants soon became involved in street gangs, committed violent crimes, including murder, and participated in drug trafficking. When the U.S. Congress decided to enact very punitive immigration laws in 1996, noncitizens who were sentenced to a year or more in prison could be repatriated to their country of origin. Foreign-born U.S. citizens who committed felonies could lose their American citizenship and be expelled from the country after serving their sentences. Consequently, roughly 20,000 young Central American criminals were deported to El Salvador, Guatemala, Honduras, Nicaragua, and elsewhere.[27] Gang members recreated their violent lifestyles in Central America, drug trafficking escalated, "crack babies" became more common, and murder rates rose sharply. Gang members rule many parts of Central America through violence and intimidation. They routinely force residents of poor neighborhoods to pay what they call protection fees, demand war taxes from businesses, and often murder individuals who refuse to or cannot pay them. Rapes of young women have increased, homes are robbed, schoolchildren are turned into drug addicts, and kidnappings occur frequently. Gang violence generates more violence by gang opponents.

The kidnapping in Iraq heightened global awareness of a very old criminal activity. Previously, most victims of kidnappings were wealthy individuals who could arrange to pay large ransoms. Today, however, ordinary individuals are being kidnapped for a variety of reasons. Terrorists have used kidnappings as bargaining chips and to create widespread fear. Islamic terrorists in the Philippines routinely kidnap foreigners, especially Westerners, to extract money to finance terrorism. Kidnappings are an integral component of violence and drug trafficking in Colombia. Colombia is by far the world's leader in kidnappings, despite an increase in kidnappings in China in 2006. In Mexico, Brazil, and other places, most kidnappings are fueled by glaring economic inequalities and poverty. As the gap between the rich and poor widens with China's rapid economic growth, kidnappings, extortion, and related crimes have increased dramatically. Kidnappings, like so many other global crimes, have exploded with the current period of globalization. Criminal gangs are primarily responsible for most kidnappings. These crimes are very lucrative, generating hundreds of millions of dollars each year in ransoms.[28] Economic inequality and poverty also motivated Nigerians in the Niger Delta region to kidnap petroleum workers employed by Royal Dutch Shell in January 2006.[29] Kidnapping is essentially a part of the global economy.

MONEY LAUNDERING

Money Laundering

The act concealing money obtained from illegal activities

When you open a bank account, you are usually required to show some identification. However, many criminals open bank accounts without having to face any financial scrutiny. The globalization of financial services, the growth of "megabyte money," the proliferation of small states with corrupt officials and weak economies, and the ease with which money is transferred electronically have facilitated the practice of money laundering.[30] **Money laundering** is the concealment of money obtained from illegal activities and finding ways to make the money appear as though it was derived from legitimate sources. Many banks in the Bahamas, Bermuda, Cayman Islands, Nauru, Liechtenstein, Panama, and elsewhere have strict secrecy laws designed to conceal money and allow it to be easily transferred and invested in legal activities. Among the islands that promote offshore banking, Grand Cayman stands out. With a population of approximately 36,000, Grand Cayman is one of the largest financial centers in the world. While generally perceived as a tourist destination, Grand Cayman is dominated by banking and financial industries. It is estimated that more than 2,200 mutual funds, 500 insurance companies, 60,000 businesses, and 600 banks and trust companies with almost $800 billion in assets are located in Grand Cayman.[31] As Grand Cayman illustrates, many legitimate businesses routinely incorporate in countries that are also used by money launderers to reduce their tax burdens and avoid regulations in rich countries. For many years, the United States expressed little interest in preventing money laundering, partly because it viewed such efforts as impediments to free markets and financial globalization. Many American banks sheltered money from dictators and others from around the world. For example, Riggs Bank in Washington, D.C., was caught in a scandal in 2005 that involved sheltering funds from Augusto Pinochet, the former dictator of Chile. The ease with which terrorists could launder money became a major U.S. preoccupation only after the 2001 terrorist attacks in the United States.

The issue of money laundering is complicated by the very nature of financial globalization and the speed and complexity of financial transactions in a global economy. Technological revolutions facilitate concealing both legitimate income from taxation authorities and financial gains from drug trafficking and other global criminal activities. Furthermore, the proliferation of financial institutions globally makes government regulation of them extremely difficult. In most countries, less government regulation is regarded to be an important component of economic globalization. Criminal groups take advantage of this development. Many societies have always found informal ways to hide money received from illegal activities and to invest it in legitimate businesses. So have many traditional underground banks, which have operated in several Asian countries for centuries, and beneficiaries of revolutions in telecommunications and computer technologies.[32] Divergent interests and values among countries complicate dealing with money laundering. Many small countries in the Caribbean, Latin America, and the Pacific that have fragile economies and very little manufacturing often perceive their sovereignty as an asset that can assist in their economic development. Consequently, their financial institutions actively promote both the legal and illicit sheltering of financial assets.

ILLEGAL TRADE IN ENDANGERED ANIMALS AND PLANTS

Similar to other global crimes, the illegal trade in **endangered species** coexists with legal transactions, thereby making it difficult to ascertain the magnitude of the problem. Nevertheless, there is general agreement that many of the factors we discussed earlier about the globalization of crime combine to sustain and expand both the legal and illicit aspects of this trade. Local and individual decisions directly affect trade in endangered animals and plants and, cumulatively, these decisions have significant global consequences. For many individuals, the trade liberalization that characterizes globalization augments perceptions that almost anything can be traded, regardless of long-term consequences for the environment. The economic inequality between conservationists in rich countries and poor people in the developing world, where most animals and plants are located, often give rise to divergent perceptions of and approaches to illegal trade. For example, while elephants are generally regarded as exotic by many residents in rich countries, many Africans in farming areas view them as threats to their safety and their crops. On the other hand, carefully managed animals and plants can play a major role in eco-tourism and other aspects of economic development. It is estimated that one elephant in Kenya generates $1 million in tourist revenue over its lifetime. Political instability and ethnic conflicts in many countries often facilitate both trade in and the destruction of many endangered animals and plants. Illicit trade fuels many conflicts. Illegal wildlife trade also raises such issues as **sustainability and biological diversity**, discussed in Chapter 8. Because of conflicting interests and priorities, implementing the agreements states reach on wildlife protection and issues is often difficult. Also, imports of animals and plants sometimes contribute to problems associated with invasive species that threaten native species.

Given the global reach of traffickers in endangered animals and plants and the numerous small illegal transactions that occur daily by individuals worldwide, ascertaining the financial gains from this global crime is extremely difficult, if not impossible. However, estimates of illegal trade revenues range from $5 billion to $20 billion annually, and are usually ranked in the same category as illegal drugs, weapons, and human trafficking in terms of revenue.[33] While global attention was drawn to illicit trade in endangered animals by large sales of African elephant tusks to Japan and elsewhere, the expansion of legal trade and the Internet have significantly broadened this criminal activity. The most endangered species—such as tigers, Asian bears, rhinoceros, hyacinth macaws from the Amazon, Australian palm cockatoos, Saiga antelopes, and hawksbill turtles—command high prices. For example, the gall bladder of a bear can be sold for as much as $15,000, the palm cockatoo for $10,000, and the hyacinth

Endangered Species

Animals and plants vulnerable to extinction

[Text on torn overlapping page fragment, partially legible:]

...ng and distributing ...rtificates that indi- ...Many patients in ...ors with commu- ...he problem from

...logies, particu- ...of interdepen- ...he Internet is ...s are increas- ...g the Internet ...lobal society. ...crime as well ...ct, a national ...ternet users ...cal crime.[38] ...that is con- ...smuggling...ple, the average seller is a...

age buyer is roughly 48 years old.[35] Rapid com... play a role in the global trade in organs. In many... ents travel abroad for the operation. South Afric... until 2003, when South African authorities broke u... ing South Africans, Israelis, and Brazilians. The gl... makes removing and transplanting organs relativel... Return migration, discussed in Chapter 9, has contri... tise in many developing countries.

Many organs are obtained from nonconsenting do... operations. This practice is increasingly prevalent in i... the world's poorest countries where human life is viewe... human rights abuses abound, and where weak political... ruption exist. Organs are also illegally obtained from m... and the developing world, a ghoulish practice that... deceased traumatized. Medical centers in Germany, for... valves obtained illegally from cadavers of poor South... famous are not exempt from organ theft. **Alistair Co**... *Masterpiece Theater* and author of a weekly radio commen... died at the age of 95 in 2004. Investigators found that Coo... sold for $7,000 by organ traffickers in the United States.[36] ...ernment officials ordered **Biomedical Tissue Services**,

macaw for $8,00
have medicinal p
Many traditional (
bile, deer musk gla
worldwide. Produc
ornaments, and tou
ization, has also led
countries around the
gal trade in caviar ha
involved in criminal ac
by illegal logging ope
Africa, the Amazonian
medicinal plants that a
include **hoodia** (which
Chinese yew tree (whi
associated with wealth ge
these products, thereby fa

Concerned about anir
by signing the **Conventic**
Wild Flora and Fauna (C
within which countries adop
at the national level. Comba
integral component of effort
ability, and diminish defores
endangered species, including
Nature, Fauna and Flora Inter
Commerce, and the World Cor
degrees of protection to roughl
global community has achieved
A worldwide ban on ivory in 198
a sharp decline in the price of iv
importer of parrots for pets, en
bans imports of all wild-caught th
parrot imports dropped sharply.
countries to regulate hunting certai
and economic benefits. However, d
demand for endangered animals and

Wild Bird Conservation Act

Bans imports of all wild-caught threatened parrots listed in CITES

ILLEGAL TRADE IN HUMAN OF

Global trade in human organs has been
these transactions are legal, illicit trade i
seen throughout this chapter, separating

---

linked to a national organ looting scandal, to refrain from recover
organs. Biomedical Tissue Services produced inauthentic death c
cated the wrong ages and causes of death for several organ donor
Chicago received organs that were believed to have come from do
nicable diseases. The globalization of illegal organ trading spread
the United States to Germany, the Netherlands, and China.[37]

CYBERCRIMES AND PIRACY

Worldwide, the growth of telecommunications and computer techno
larly the **Internet**, has engendered unprecedented complex networks
dence. At the heart of globalization is interconnectedness. Because
global, geographic distance, national boundaries, and legal jurisdictio
ingly irrelevant. This also means that criminal activities that involve usi
can lead to extremely costly, if not catastrophic, consequences for the
Just as individuals use the Internet to conduct legal business, organized
as individuals take advantage of this technology to commit crimes. In fa
survey commissioned by IBM Corporation in 2006 found that most I
believe that they are more likely to be victims of cybercrime than a phys
Cybercrimes are standard crimes committed online or harmful behavior
nected to computers. Examples of cybercrimes are fraud, pornography,
copyright and software piracy, identity theft, and extortion.[39] The proliferation of
online shopping has been a boon for cybercriminals. **E-Bay,** the biggest online marketplace, has roughly 180 million members worldwide who are connected to the
Internet and more than 60 million items for sale at any particular moment. Both distance and anonymity conspire to render these global online shopping centers perfect
places for fraudulent activities. As a marketplace that links buyers and sellers, e-Bay
has very little control over transactions.[40]

The essential role of computer software in global computer operations makes it a
prime target for cybercriminals. So pervasive is software piracy that many ordinary individuals do not perceive stealing software as a crime, thereby further blurring the boundaries between legal and illegal behavior. Like other global crimes we have discussed, it is
impossible to determine the exact value of pirated software. However, it is estimated
that the global market for pirated computer software is around $30 billion. This crime is
concentrated in Western countries, where computer technologies are most prevalent.
China, with its rapid industrialization and technological growth is also involved to a significant degree in software piracy. As Table 10.3 illustrates, the estimated market for
software piracy in the United States is twice as large as the market in China.

The global expansion of the Internet, the widespread use of credit cards, and the
growth of electronic banking combine to facilitate a wide array of fraudulent activities.
From Mattoon, a small town in central Illinois, Clyde Hood ran an investment scam
that brought in roughly $12.5 million from people worldwide by promising that each
dollar invested would generate $50 in profit. The **Nigerian scam** is one of the most

Cybercrimes

Standard crimes committed online

E-Bay

The biggest online marketplace

Nigerian Scam

One of the most common cybercrimes

different cellphones (to avoid being detected) to send instructions during what Austrian police called a scavenger hunt. He had purchased the cellphones months in advance. Irritated by what he perceived to be police in an unmarked car flouting his instructions, Mang used a recently purchased cellphone to call off arrangements to pick up the ransom money. The cellphone was traced to a store in Vienna, which uses a hidden video camera to record all purchases. This enabled the police to obtain Mang's picture, which was made public. Mang immediately contacted the police to identify himself as the man in the picture but denied that he had stolen the sculpture. He was so upset about the publication of his picture that he asked the police to refrain from further publication of it. Naturally, police were even more convinced that Mang was the thief. Searching his apartment, police found notes about the scavenger hunt Mang had conducted with them. That was how they caught him.[45] The sculpture was recovered. But not all art thieves appreciate sculpture to that extent. More than twenty large bronze sculptures were taken from museums, sculpture gardens, and private collections in an around London in late 2005. Art thieves simply put them in trucks and drove away. These criminals are believed to have melted down the sculptures and sold the bronze for scrap. It is estimated that a two-ton sculpture by Henry Moore, **Reclining Figure,** valued at $18 million as a work of art, was worth about $9,000 as scrap metal.[46]

Partly influenced by increased sales in art during the 1980s and 1990s, many Jewish families and organizations renewed their efforts to have numerous artworks that were stolen by the Nazis in World War II or acquired by art museums under dubious circumstances returned to their legitimate owners. In 2006, in one of the largest restitutions of art seized by the Nazis, the Dutch government announced that it would return more than 200 Old Masters paintings to the heir of **Jacques Goudstikker**, a wealthy Dutch Jewish dealer and collector who fled Amsterdam ahead of advancing German troops in May 1940. Due partly to an eight-year campaign led by Marei von Saher of Greenwich, Connecticut, the widow of Goudstikker's son, the Dutch government formed a restitution commission to investigate the provenance of all of the art in its museums. The restitution committee eventually recommended returning the art to its rightful owners.[47]

Similarly, various governments have reinvigorated their efforts to have art and antiquities returned to them. In early 2006 the **Metropolitan Museum of Art** in New York decided to relinquish claims to ownership of a 2,500-year-old Greek vase, regarded as one of the finest artworks in the world. The vase, known as the **Euphronios Krater**, had long been claimed by the Italian government, which contended that the vase had been stolen from an Etruscan tomb near Rome and smuggled from Italy.[48] University museums are also confronted with charges that they have stolen art and antiquities. Yale University's exhibition about **Machu Picchu** attracted more than a million visitors while traveling to six cities in the United States. The exhibition returned to Yale's Peabody Museum of Natural History in 2005, only to be mired in a dispute with the government of Peru. Peru argues that the artifacts excavated at Machu Picchu in 1912 by a Yale University professor and explorer, Hiram Bingham III, were loaned to the University, which has failed to return them. Yale University contends that it is the rightful owner of the artifacts.[49] This struggle to obtain what many countries regard as their indigenous heritage is likely to intensify.

Saliera

A rare gold-plated sculpture made by Benvenuto Cellini between 1540 and 1543

Jacques Goudstikker

A wealthy Dutch Jewish art dealer and collector

Machu Picchu

Fortress city of the Incas in Peru, site of valuable artifacts and antiquities

GLOBAL RESPONSES TO CRIME

Viewing themselves and the world predominantly through the prism of Westphalian sovereignty, countries are ill equipped to effectively respond to global criminal activities. As we pointed out earlier in this chapter, globalization has been far more beneficial to nonstate actors, including smugglers, drug traffickers, and other global criminal networks, than it has been to nation-states. The hierarchical structure of countries is a liability in an increasingly decentralized, global society. Furthermore, globalization has diminished the ability of states to exercise effective jurisdiction over their territories and to regulate trade and other activities. The nature of globalization makes it difficult to determine where the crimes occurred and which country or countries have jurisdiction over them. Few governments have the resources to effectively control global crime, especially in light of reduced government budgets for public services. Furthermore, divergent views among countries about crime and different priorities render effective collaboration among states difficult to achieve.

Interpol

Global clearing-house for police information that assists countries in criminal cases

The International Criminal Police Organization, commonly known as **Interpol**, is a global clearinghouse for police information. Based in France, Interpol had a miniscule budget of roughly $25 million in 2001.[50] Compared to the resources available to Interpol, global criminal organizations make more than $1.5 trillion a year. The global drug trade alone generates in excess of $320 billion a year. As we have seen, global crime is proliferating so rapidly and on such a vast scale at a time when cultural attitudes are generally much more tolerant of many global criminal activities that global efforts to reduce the crimes we have discussed are significantly undermined. Nevertheless, Interpol's role in combating drug trafficking and other global crimes is important. Interpol collects and analyzes data obtained from member countries for strategic and tactical intelligence reports, supports global crime investigations, organizes operational working meetings among countries, and organizes regional and global conferences on a wide range of criminal activities. Despite support from Interpol, fighting crime is essentially a local activity, and states themselves are ultimately responsible for reducing global crime. But as with many domestic crimes, states confront many serious obstacles in fighting global crime. Bureaucracies have serious communication problems that prevent them from using information in a timely fashion. Global criminal activities overwhelm law enforcement agencies within countries. Attempting to be more effective in countering global crime, 178 countries have joined Interpol. In 2000, most of these countries signed the **UN Convention Against Transnational Organized Crime**, a global agreement that outlaws bank secrecy, keeps prosecutors worldwide in contact by e-mail, allows international arrest warrants to be sent by e-mail, provides for videoconferences to allow witnesses to testify without having to travel around the world, and creates international witness protection programs.[51] The challenge confronting the global community is the ability to implement these provisions. The forces of globalization are likely to give global criminals the advantage in the worldwide struggle to reduce global crime. However, progress can be made by tackling problems such as poverty, global inequality, immigration policies, environmental degradation, women's rights, and unfair trading practices.

UN Convention Against Transnational Organized Crime

Global agreement aimed at reducing crime through global cooperation

Summary and Review

Global criminal activities have proliferated with the rapid growth of economic, financial, technological, cultural, and other forms of globalization. Increased global migration, global inequality, the growth of global cities, the explosion of global trade, inexpensive communications, revolutions in computer technologies, and the disintegration of the Soviet Union have contributed to the spread and intensification of global crime. As we saw, global crime is intricably intertwined with politics, economics, and culture. This chapter shows how illegal activities occur alongside legal activities and how difficult they sometimes are to separate. Furthermore, there are divergent perceptions about global crimes as well as different approaches to dealing with them. Globalization has weakened states in ways that prevent them from effectively combating many global crimes. We discussed major global crimes, such as drug trafficking, human trafficking, illegal trade in endangered species, money laundering, cyber-crimes, and trade in human organs. Throughout history, the world has experienced an increase in the global drug trade, accompanied by growing drug use and addiction. This global crime commands the attention of the global community, although countries adopt divergent approaches to dealing with illegal drugs. There are global responses to all of the crimes discussed. Organizations such as Interpol provide information on criminal activities and cooperate with countries in an effort to reduce global crime.

Key Terms

global crime 322
British East India
    Company 325
Opium Wars 325
Golden Triangle 325
war on drugs 326
Opium Control
    Board 327

Plan Colombia 328
harm-reduction
    policy 328
human
    trafficking 330
contemporary
    slavery 330

feminization of
    migration 331
Fourth World
    Conference on
    Women 333
money
    laundering 336

endangered species 337
Cybercrimes 340
global piracy 341
intellectual property
    rights 341

Discussion Questions

1. Discuss ways in which globalization facilitates the growth of global crime.
2. How and to what extent has globalization affected the ability of states to diminish global criminal activities?
3. Compare European and American approaches to dealing with illegal drugs.
4. What is Plan Colombia? Is America losing the war on drugs?
5. What specific steps can states take to reduce the smuggling of migrants?
6. Discuss how legalizing prostitution affects the crime of human trafficking

7. Discuss the growth of criminal gangs, the causes, and possible ways to reduce violence.
8. How has globalization contributed to the global trade in human organs?

9. What can individuals do to reduce the growth of cybercrime?
10. What, in your view, should be done to make Interpol more effective in responding to global crime?

Suggested Readings

Andreas, Peter, and Ethan Nadelman. *Policing the Globe*. New York: Oxford University Press, 2006.

Arana, Ana, "How the Street Gangs Took Central America," *Foreign Affairs* 84, No. 3 (May/June 2005): 98–110.

Crandall, Russell. *Driven by Drugs*. Boulder, CO: Lynne Rienner, 2002.

Cukier, Wendy, and Victor Sidel. *The Global Gun Epidemic*. Westport, CT: Praeger, 2005.

Kshetri, Nir. "Hacking the Odds," *Foreign Policy* 148 (May/June 2005): 93.

McAllister, William B. *Drug Diplomacy in the Twentieth Century*, London: Routledge, 2000.

Morton, David, "Gunning for the World," *Foreign Policy* 152 (January/February 2006): 58–67.

Naim, Moises. *How Drug Smugglers, Traffickers, and Copycats Are Hijacking the Global Economy*. Washington, DC: Carnegie Endowment, 2005.

Papachristos, Andrew. "Gang World," *Foreign Policy* 147 (March/April 2005): 49–55.

Reuter, Peter, and Edwin M. Truman. *Chasing Dirty Money*. Washington, DC: Institute for International Economics, 2004.

Van Schendel, Willem, and Itty Abraham. *Illicit Flows and Criminal Things*. Bloomington: Indiana University Press, 2006.

Addresses and Websites

The Interdisciplinary Center Herzlia
P.O. Box 167,
Herzlia 46150
Israel
Fax: 972–9–9513073
www.ict.org.il

The International Policy Institute seeks to foster international cooperation in the global struggle against terrorism, paving the way for multilateral action against terrorist networks, benefactors, and states sponsoring terrorism. ICT is a research institute and think tank dedicated to developing innovative public policy solutions to international terrorism. This website provides information on Arab-Israeli terrorism as well as international terrorism.

United Nations
Security Council Affairs Division
Room S-3520

New York, NY 10017
Fax: (212) 963–7878
Email: Security Council Affairs
www.un.org/docs/scinfo.org

The UN Security Council has primary responsibility under the UN Charter for maintaining international peace and security. It is organized to function continuously, and a representative of each of its members must be present at all times at UN Headquarters. This website provides all of the Security Council's decisions and documents, as well as a link to each UN website.

European Monitoring Center for Drugs
and Drug Addiction
Rua da Cruz de Santa Apolonia 23–25
PT-1149-045 Lisbon
Tel.: (+351) 21 811 3000
Fax: (+351) 21 813 1711
www.emcdda.org

The mission of the EMCDDA is to provide the community and its member states with objective, reliable, and comparable information at the European level concerning drugs, drug addiction, and their consequences. The agency focuses on monitoring the drugs situation and analyzing the **responses** to it. The agency also plays a key role in implementing the **EU joint action on new synthetic drugs,** as well as monitoring national and Community **strategies and policies** and their impact on the drug situation.

Centre for International Crime Prevention
Office for Drug Control and Crime Prevention
P.O. Box 500
A-1400 Vienna
Austria
www.uncjin.org

The Vienna-based UN Center for International Crime Prevention is collaborating with member states to strengthen the rule of law, promote stable and viable criminal jutice systems in postconflict societies, and combat the growing threat of transnational organized crime.

Europe Against Drugs
Grainne Kenny
International Resident
8 Waltersland Rd.
Stillorgan County
Dublin, Ireland
Tel.: 353 1 2756 766/7
www.eurad.net

Europe Against Drugs is a grassroots movement composed of European parents, youth, and other citizen organizations concerned about limiting the spread of drug abuse. The website has information on EURAD, legalization, and decriminalization of drugs.

Endnotes

1. Moises Naim, "Five Waves of Globalization," *Foreign Policy* 134 (January/February 2003), 29.
2. Moises Naim, "It's the Illicit Economy, Stupid," *Foreign Policy* 151 (November/December 2005), 96.
3. Bruce Michael Bagley, "Globalization and Transnational Organized Crime," in *The Political Economy of the Drug Industry*, ed. Menno Vellinga (Gainesville: University Press of Florida, 2004), 261; and Miroslav Nozina, "Crossroads of Crime: The Czech Republic Case," in *Transnational Organized Crime*, ed. Emilio C. Viano, et al. (Durham: Carolina Academic Press, 2003), 147.
4. Warren Hoge, "In Scenic Norway, A Death Scene of Addictions," *New York Times*, 8 August 2002, A3.
5. William B. McAllister, *Drug Diplomacy in the Twentieth Century* (London: Routledge, 2000), 11.
6. Paul B. Stares, *Global Habit: The Drug Problem in a Borderless World.* (Washington, DC: Brookings Institution Press, 1996), 16.
7. Tim Golden, "Mexican Drug Dealers Turning U.S. Towns Into Major Depots," *New York Times*, 16 November 2002, A1.
8. Stares, *Global Habit*, 17.
9. Stares, *Global Habit*, 36.
10. Juan Forero, "No Crops Spared in Colombia's Coca War," *New York Times*, 31 January 2001, A1.
11. Ethan A. Nadelmann, "Commonsense Drug Policy," *Foreign Affairs* 77, No. 1 (January/February 1998), 114.
12. Kate Zernike and Ginger Thompson, "Deaths of Immigrants Uncover Makeshift World of Smuggling," *New York Times*, 29 June 2003, A1.
13. Edward Barnes, "Two-Faced Woman," *Time*, 31 July 2000, 48; and Jeffrey Bartholet, "The New People Trade," *Newsweek*, 3 July 2000, 32–33.
14. Joel Brinkley, "A Modern-Day Abolitionist Battles Slavery Worldwide," *New York Times*, 4 February 2006, A4.
15. Brinkley, "A Modern-Day Abolitionist," A4.
16. Elena Tiuriukanova, "Female Labor Migration Trends and Human Trafficking," in *Human Traffic and Transnational Crime*, eds. Sally Stoecker and Louise Shelley (Lanham: Rowman and Littlefield, 2005), 98.
17. David A. Feingold, "Human Trafficking," *Foreign Policy* 150 (September/October 2005), 26.
18. Cam Simpson, "U.S. to Probe Claims of Human Trafficking," *Chicago Tribune*, 19 January 2006, Sect. 1, 1.
19. Victor Malarek, *The Natashas: Inside the Global Sex Trade* (New York: Arcade Publishing, 2004), 6.
20. Louise Shelley, "Russian and Chinese Trafficking," in *Human Traffic and Transnational Crime*, 70.
21. Malarek, *The Natashas*, 14.
22. Nicholas D. Kristof, "Slavery in Our Time," *New York Times*, 22 January 2006, A17.

23. Feingold, "Human Trafficking," 30.

24. Malarek, *The Natashas*, 255.

25. Brinkley, "A Modern-Day Abolitionist," A4.

26. Andrew V. Papachristos, "Gang World," *Foreign Policy* 147 (March/April 2005), 51.

27. Ginger Thompson, "Guatemala Bleeds in Vise of Gangs and Vengeance," *New York Times*, 1 January 2006, A4; and Ana Arana, "How Street Gangs Took Central America," *Foreign Affairs* 84, No. 3 (May/June 2005), 100.

28. Evan Osnos, "Kidnapping Industry Is Booming in China," *Chicago Tribune*, 27 January 2006, Sect. 1, 4.

29. Lydia Polgreen, "Poor Nigerian Villages Become Oil Battleground," *New York Times*, 1 January 2006, A1; and "Delta Villages Fear Troops in Nigeria," *New York Times*, 26 January 2006, A10.

30. William F. Wechsler, "Follow the Money," *Foreign Affairs* 80, No. 4 (July/August 2001), 43.

31. Naim, *"Five Waves of Globalization,"* 34.

32. Peter Grabosky and Russell Smith, "Telecommunications Fraud in the Digital Age," in *Crime and the Internet*, ed. David S. Wall (London: Routledge, 2001), 32.

33. Patrice M. Jones, "Brazil Grapples With Animal Trade," *Chicago Tribune*, 20 August 2001, Sect. 1, 1.

34. Nancy Scheper-Hughes, "Organs Without Borders," *Foreign Policy* 146 (January/February 2005), 26.

35. Scheper-Hughes, "Organs Without Borders," 27.

36. Jeremy Manier and Tonya Maxwell, "Tissue Fraud Fears Spread," *Chicago Tribune*, 3 February 2006, Sect. 1, 1.

37. Jeremy Manier, "FDA Orders Firm to Stop Tissue Recovery," *Chicago Tribune*, 4 February 2006, Sect. 1, 3.

38. Jon Van, "Computer Crimes Seen as More Likely Than Physical Ones," *Chicago Tribune*, 28 January 2006, Sect. 2, 3.

39. David S. Wall, "Cybercrimes and the Internet," in *Crime and the Internet*, ed. David S. Wall (London: Routledge, 2001), 3.

40. Katie Hafner, "Seeing Fakes, Angry Traders Confront E-Bay," *New York Times*, 29 January 2006, A1.

41. Nir Kshetri, "Hacking the Odds," *Foreign Policy* 148 (May/June 2005), 93.

42. Robert Manor, "Primitive Computer Virus Hits Few So Far," *Chicago Tribune*, 4 February 2006, Sect. 2, 1.

43. Robert Marquand, "China's Pirate Industry Thriving," *Christian Science Monitor*, 9 January 2002, 6.

44. Jack Hitt, "Bandits in the Global Shipping Lanes," *New York Times Magazine*, 20 August 2000, 37.

45. Richard Bernstein, "For Stolen Saltcellar, A Cellphone Is Golden," *New York Times*, 26 January 2006, B1.

46. Sarah Lyall, "Thieves Fond of Heavy Lifting Are Making Off With England's Bronze Sculptures," *New York Times*, 26 January 2006, B7.

47. Alan Riding, "Dutch to Return Art Seized by Nazis," *New York Times*, 7 February 2006, B1.

48. Randy Kennedy and Hugh Eakin, "The Met, Ending 30-Year Stance, Is Set to Yield Prized Vase to Italy," *New York Times*, 3 February 2006, A1.

49. Hugh Eakin, "Inca Show Pits Yale Against Peru," *New York Times*, 1 February 2006, B1.

50. "Meet the World's Top Cop," *Foreign Policy* 122 (January/February 2001), 32.

51. Peter Ford, "A Treaty to Counter Global Crime," *Christian Science Monitor*, 13 December 2000, 1.

CHAPTER 11

The Globalization of Disease

INTRODUCTION

Globally, infectious diseases remain the leading killers of human beings. More than a quarter of all deaths today are linked to infectious diseases, with the developing world facing the brunt of the problem. More than 40 million people live with HIV, and more than 3 million die of AIDS each year. Infectious diseases—such as malaria, influenza, tuberculosis, dengue, and yellow fever—claim millions of lives in the developing world each year, with the very young and the very old being the primary victims. In the case of AIDS, more women are becoming victims due to poverty, discrimination, violence, traditional values and beliefs about women's roles in relation to men's roles, and women's involvement in **survival sex** (i.e., having sex to feed their families and to protect themselves from physical abuse and economic deprivation). Diseased populations are vulnerable to contracting other diseases due to compromised immune systems. For example, many individuals who suffer from HIV/AIDS die from tuberculosis, a highly infectious disease. The emergence and reemergence and spread of infectious diseases demonstrate both the reality and the dangers of globalization. As we discuss various infectious diseases, it will become increasingly obvious that our fate is determined to a large extent by developments that are largely beyond our control, that national boundaries are essentially meaningless, that human beings share a common destiny, and that the concerns about national security are increasingly inseparable from global and human security, or the well-being of ordinary individuals.

Infectious diseases are intertwined with numerous global issues and are inseparable from political, economic, and cultural components of globalization. Ethnic conflicts make populations vulnerable to infectious diseases. Fighting contributes to the collapse of public services, which means that many people die from what would ordinarily be treatable diseases, such as diarrhea and respiratory infections. Conflicts also create refugees, overcrowding, and unsanitary conditions, thereby creating environments conducive to the spread of infectious diseases. Many infectious diseases are closely linked to poverty, global inequality, and low levels of economic development. Environmental degradation and deforestation expose humans to a variety of infectious diseases. They also contribute to global warming and flooding, which facilitate the emergence of infectious diseases. Rising temperatures in winter enable germs to survive in large numbers, and flooded areas become potent breeding grounds for mosquito-related diseases and cholera. Rapid population growth and urbanization bring more people closer together and into contact with infectious diseases. Illegal drug use, especially intravenous drug use, spreads diseases, such as HIV/AIDS. As we will discuss, AIDS contributes to a growing number of orphans; many of them become street children who are vulnerable to human trafficking and recruitment into

Survival Sex

Having sex to feed families and for self-protection

criminal gangs. Finally, trade has long been a major facilitator of the spread of infectious diseases. Consequently, trade suffers greatly when outbreaks occur, as we will see with the spread of SARS in 2003. In many ways, trade liberalization contributes to the spread of infectious diseases by reducing the role of many governments in providing essential basic health care and other services. Infectious diseases have far-reaching social, economic, demographic, security, and political consequences.

This chapter first examines the globalization of infectious diseases, the concept of human security, and the nature and spread of infectious diseases. Next we will analyze specific diseases: influenza and avian flu, malaria, dengue fever and yellow fever, tuberculosis, cholera, SARS, and the Marburg virus. Given the global significance and far-reaching consequences of HIV/AIDS, this chapter focuses on AIDS, particularly in Africa. Africa is the epicenter of the AIDS pandemic. Within Africa, South Africa is the most adversely affected country. Globalization is also contributing to the rapid growth of AIDS in Asia, Eastern Europe, and Russia. This chapter concludes with a discussion of global responses to the growth, persistence, and transmission of infectious diseases.

GLOBALIZATION OF INFECTIOUS DISEASES AND HUMAN SECURITY

Although infectious diseases dominated the daily existence of almost all human societies throughout history, the ability of rich countries to eliminate many leading diseases diminished global concern and the sense of urgency about eradicating the diseases that were concentrated in the developing world. The rapid spread of globalization, especially starting in the 1980s, underscored links between infectious diseases in poor countries and outbreaks of these diseases in rich countries. The most dramatic development was the discovery of HIV/AIDS in the United States, Western Europe, and other rich countries. While perceived initially as a disease limited primarily to homosexuals, HIV/AIDS began to spread to the general population through blood transfusions, intravenous drug usage, and heterosexual practices. Furthermore, prominent people who were suffering from the disease fought to put it on both the domestic and global agendas. By the 1990s, there was a definite shift toward recognizing the globalization of infectious diseases. Many of the diseases that were believed to have been eradicated in rich countries reemerged and were placed on the global agenda. Two factors explain this reemergence: (1) *growing resistance to common antibiotics*; and 2) *the devastating impact of new epidemics*. The new epidemics included cholera in Latin America, particularly in Peru; plague in India; the Ebola virus in Africa; dengue fever in Asia; West Nile virus in the United States; and **bovine spongiform encephalitis** (mad cow disease) in Europe.[1] The globalization of infectious diseases is linked to the global issues discussed throughout this book, including global travel and communications, trade, migration, environmental changes, population growth, the global sex trade, changing cultural behaviors, ethnic conflicts and wars, poverty, intravenous drug use, modern medical practices, accelerating urbanization, and the growth of global cities. Of all the factors

TABLE 11.1 OUTBOUND TOURISM BY GENERATING REGION

Region	International Tourist Arrivals (million)						
	1990	**1995**	**2000**	**2001**	**2002**	**2003**	**2004**
World	441.0	538.1	680.6	680.4	700.4	689.7	763.2
From:							
Europe	252.5	307.2	389.5	390.4	401.6	406.7	431.3
Asia and the Pacific	59.8	88.8	118.3	120.6	130.8	120.6	151.2
Americas	99.3	108.0	130.7	125.5	121.2	115.4	127.7
Middle East	8.5	10.4	15.2	16.3	18.3	17.9	22.0
Africa	9.9	13.0	16.5	16.5	17.6	17.6	18.2
Origin not specified*	11.1	10.8	10.5	11.2	10.9	11.5	12.8
Same region	351.9	430.5	537.9	546.0	566.8	560.2	617.2
Other regions	78.0	96.8	132.2	123.3	122.7	118.0	133.2

Source: World Tourism Organization, ©2005.

associated with the globalization of infectious diseases global travel and communications have the most impact.

Global Travel and Communications Human beings are the most efficient transmitters of diseases that have historically affected relatively small isolated parts of the world. In the past, large proportions of populations were killed by plagues as people traveled to distant places. The Plague of Justinian, which occurred in 541 A.D., devastated Europe. In the twelfth and thirteenth centuries, the bubonic plague, known as the Black Death, killed 25 million (or one of every three) Europeans. The decimation of Native American populations by European diseases is another example of how travelers spread infectious diseases. More recently, China and other Asian countries have spawned deadly infectious diseases, which have spread quickly to the rest of the world because of travel and excellent global links. In 1968, the Hong Kong flu, originating in South China, spread from Hong Kong to other countries. About 700,000 people died worldwide. In 1997, the avian flu (bird flu) was transmitted by chickens imported by Hong Kong from South China. The global spread of **severe acute respiratory syndrome (SARS)** originated in South China in November 2002.[2] Consider, too, how the West Nile virus outbreak started in the United States. Most European airlines linking the developing world with rich countries routinely use insecticides to destroy mosquitoes. Airlines from the United States, by contrast, hesitate to use sprays to control mosquitoes, partly due to fears about lawsuits by passengers. The **West Nile virus** was transported to the United States on airplanes. It is believed that African mosquitoes that transmit yellow fever and dengue fever arrived in South America and other parts of the New World aboard ships engaged in the trans-Atlantic slave trade. Since then, the speed of air transportation and communications have combined to rapidly spread infectious diseases and information about them worldwide.

SARS

Deadly viral disease that originated in South China in 2002

Trade Trade has also been a major facilitator in the globalization of infectious diseases. The bubonic plague (Black Death) was transmitted to Europe through trade with Asia. Today, the rapid expansion of trade with China exposes the world to many diseases, as we discussed in Chapter 6. The global trade in agricultural products has also escalated the risk of the global transmission of diseases. Mad cow disease has become a contentious issue between the United States and Japan, for example, because of fears among the Japanese about being infected by imports of American beef.[3]

Environmental Factors As we saw in Chapter 8, human activities have profoundly affected the natural environment. People have migrated to areas that bring them into contact with animals and soils that play a role in the spread of infectious diseases. Furthermore, gradual increases in the earth's temperature, (i.e., global warming), are conducive to the global spread of diseases.

Ethnic Conflicts and Wars Ethnic conflicts, widespread violence, and wars have always contributed to the outbreak of disease and often the spread of infectious diseases. Combatants are often more likely to die from infectious diseases than from actual fighting. It is estimated that more than two-thirds of the roughly 600,000 deaths in the **American Civil War** were caused by infectious diseases. Furthermore, the movement of troops and mass migrations of civilians as a consequence of war contributed to the wider transmission of infectious diseases.[4] During the Spanish flu pandemic of 1918–1920, many American soldiers who were transported on trains and troop ships perished. On the battlefields of Vietnam and Iraq, American troops have suffered from infectious diseases, many of which are drug-resistant. Endemic ethnic conflicts in Africa play a leading role in that continent's struggle with infectious diseases.

Refugees and Migration Conditions that influence people to leave one area to settle in another initiate the downward spiral leading to infectious diseases. The deterioration of health services, the destruction of infrastructure, food shortages, and the lack of proper sanitation make refugees susceptible to communicable diseases. For example, following the Gulf War in 1991, roughly 400,000 Kurdish refugees fled Iraq and ended up in squalid camps in adverse weather conditions on the border with Turkey. More than 70 percent of the deaths there were attributed to diarrhea and cholera. Malaria has also been a killer of refugees in the border regions of Thailand, Cambodia, Ethiopia, and Sudan. As we will discuss, migrants are primarily responsible for transmitting diseases, such as tuberculosis, in the United States and Western European countries.

Poverty The poorest countries, like poor individuals, are generally more vulnerable to contracting infectious diseases. Poverty is usually a reliable incubator of disease. Overcrowding, malnutrition, inadequate medical care, and unsanitary conditions facilitate the growth and transmission of infectious diseases. Given the complex networks of interdependence that characterize globalization, diseases associated with poverty become global threats.

Modern Medical Practices A growing problem that assists the spread of infectious diseases is overuse and misuse of antibiotics. The increasing use of antibiotics in agricultural products has contributed to a process of pathogenic natural selection, which promotes the emergence of more virulent, resilient, resistant, and powerful disease strains.[5]

Changing Social and Behavioral Patterns Globalization, especially cultural globalization, profoundly affects behavioral patterns worldwide. Pervasive and instant communications, television programs, movies, and the Internet facilitate the global spread of information about social practices that were once limited to smaller groups within societies. The global sex industry is an example of how changing behavior contributes to the globalization of infectious diseases, such as HIV/AIDS. The spread of infectious diseases has focused attention on human security.

HUMAN SECURITY AND INFECTIOUS DISEASES

As we discussed in Chapter 1, the forces of globalization have strengthened the concept and reality of **global security**, which stresses a common and comprehensive security. The concept of global security moves us beyond the narrow traditional view of national security with its emphasis on military force and war to emphasize the global dimensions of emerging threats and problems and the need to achieve security with others.[6] Within the broader context of global security is the concept of **human security**, derived from the globalist school of thought. Human security focuses on the individual as the primary object of security. It embraces a people-centered approach of anticipating and coping with the multiple threats ordinary individuals face in an increasingly globalized society.[7] The emergence of the concept of human security during the 1990s is attributed to *three developments*: (1) *the end of the Cold War*, which radically altered the global political and security environment; (2) *a better understanding of the everyday insecurities* experienced by the world's poor, the vast majority of the world's population; and (3) the process of globalization, which ushered in *unprecedented changes and uncertainty*, thereby influencing a reevaluation of traditional views of security.

Links between human security and human health were reinforced by anthrax bioterrorism in the United States shortly after the 2001 terrorist attacks and the unrelenting spread of the HIV/AIDS pandemic. These developments are augmented by links between health and economic development on the global agenda, especially the **UN Millennium Development Goals**. In fact, four of the eight Millennium Goals concentrate on health-related issues. The *globalization of infectious diseases threatens human security in several ways. First*, diseases kill far more people than wars. *Second*, disease undermines public confidence in the state, thereby eroding its legitimacy. *Third*, disease weakens the economic foundations of human security. *Fourth*, disease profoundly affects social order and stability. *Fifth*, the spread of infectious diseases contributes to regional instability. *Sixth*, disease can be used in biowarfare and

Global Security

Stresses a common and comprehensive security worldwide

Human Security

Focuses on the individual as the primary object of security

UN Millennium Development Goals

Four concentrate on health-related issues

TABLE 11.2 INFECTIOUS DISEASES

Disease	Description
Influenza (flu)	Viral infection of the respiratory tract that is highly contagious. Three major outbreaks killed 25 million people.
Tuberculosis (TB)	Highly contagious disease associated with poverty, HIV, and overcrowding.
Malaria	Spread by mosquitoes, primarily in Africa; affects between 300 million and 500 million people globally.
HIV/AIDS	Virus spread through exchange of bodily fluids; destroys the immune system. 28 million deaths.
Dengue Fever	Spread by mosquitoes; is characterized by sudden fever, headache, and shock. Affects 50 million to 100 million people each year.
Yellow Fever	Spread by mosquitoes. Serious cases can affect the blood, liver, and kidneys.
Nipah Virus	Spread by fruit bats and infected pigs in Malaysia.
Encephalitis	Numerous viral strains, including West Nile virus, spread by mosquitoes. Can cause fatal inflammation of the brain.
SARS	Originated in China. Civit cat believed to be the host. Causes pneumonia that leads to death.
Ebola	Virus spread by human contact with infected primates. Kills quickly. No cure.
Gonorrhea	Sexually transmitted disease that is becoming drug-resistant.
Marburg Virus	Spread by contact with bodily fluids. Kills 9 out of 10 people infected.

Sources: Centers for Disease Control and Prevention; World Health Organization (WHO); and *New York Times*.

bioterrorism.[8] The heightened sense of vulnerability in rich countries to terrorism has focused increased attention on the ongoing problems of infectious diseases that dominate the lives of the vast majority of the world's population. We will now examine infectious diseases in general as well as specific diseases.

INFECTIOUS DISEASES

Pathogens

Organisms capable of causing disease

Epidemics

When infectious diseases spread to a large number of people

Pandemics

Long-lasting, catastrophic global epidemics

The microbes (such as bacteria) viruses, parasites, and fungi that are the agents of infectious diseases are integral components of the natural and human environments. Throughout recorded history, our ancestors have been extremely vulnerable to and mostly defenseless against infectious diseases. **Pathogens** (i.e., organisms capable of causing disease) have routinely demolished societies. In many cases, there are **outbreaks** of diseases; that is, essentially localized, endemic occurrences. When infectious diseases spread to a relatively large number of people, they are classified as **epidemics**. Although epidemics generally impact populations worldwide, **pandemics** are long lasting, catastrophic, and truly global in their consequences. Two factors that have always been at the root of infectious disease threats to human populations are (1) social, economic, and environmental conditions that enable infectious diseases to exist among human hosts; and (2) various means of transmission to new populations. As our ancestors developed agriculture and moved from isolated villages to more densely populated areas, they were exposed to more diseases.[9] Altering the natural environment enables microbes to infect humans. Humans are infected when they come into contact with natural **hosts**, (i.e., organisms that carry diseases). The hosts are not negatively affected by the disease. Transmission of infectious diseases can occur within a single species or from one species to another. Humans often infect other humans. But host animals also infect humans, a transmission known as **zoonosis**. Infectious diseases are transmitted through air, water, direct contact with the host's bodily fluids, sexual activity, as well as through **vectors**, such as mosquitoes and other insects.

To better understand contemporary concerns about infectious diseases, we will discuss the problem within the framework of **epidemiologic transition theory**. Each transition is characterized by "a unique pattern of diseases that is ultimately related to modes of subsistence and social structure."[10] There are basically *three distinct epidemiologic transitions*. The **first transition**, as we mentioned earlier, occurred when our ancestors established agricultural communities. Think about sanitation problems in permanently settled areas and the close interaction of humans and their domesticated animals. Both of these situations provided favorable environments for the dispersal of infectious diseases. Cattle, goats, sheep, pigs, and fowl transmitted tuberculosis, anthrax, and other diseases. Large proportions of populations were routinely killed by plagues, especially as trade among communities increased and people traveled to distant places. An example of an early pandemic is the **Plague of Justinian**, named after the Roman emperor, which devastated Europe around 541 A.D. Increased trade and migration between Asia and Europe and the Medieval Warm Period of the twelfth and thirteenth centuries contributed to the proliferation of rats and fleas that transmitted bubonic plague. Believing that cats were witches, Europeans inadvertently helped to spread the plague by killing cats. Known as the **Black Death**, the bubonic plague killed roughly 25 million people, or one of every three Europeans.[11] Individuals who manage to survive infectious diseases acquire immunity to them but transmit them to others. For example, most Europeans survived such diseases as tuberculosis and smallpox. West Africans lived with malaria and yellow fever. However, groups that lived in isolation from Europeans or Africans became quickly infected with their diseases. Millions of Native Americans were killed by diseases brought to the Americas by Europeans.[12] Many Europeans died of malaria and yellow fever in Africa, Asia, and the Americas.

The **second epidemiologic transition** coincided with the Industrial Revolution in Europe. Various inventions that accompanied the Industrial Revolution contributed to declining rates of infectious diseases. But overcrowding, environmental degradation, and unsanitary conditions led to the rebounding of cholera, smallpox, and tuberculosis. Developments in medical science and technology diminished epidemics, not only in Europe but also in places affected by European migration, colonization, and commercial relations. We are now experiencing the **third epidemiologic transition** Just in the past three decades we have seen an unprecedented emergence of new diseases and a reemergence of infectious diseases that were thought to have been eliminated. Another characteristic of this third transition is growing antimicrobial resistance, due primarily to the frequent use and misuse of antibiotics and other antimicrobials. Incomplete drug treatment for various diseases also contributes to antimicrobial resistance. Global trade, migration, and international travel effectively remove barriers to

Hosts

Organisms that carry diseases

Zoonosis

Transmission of diseases from host animals to humans

First Transition

Related to the establishment of agricultural communities

Plague of Justinian

Named after the Roman emperor, it devastated Europe around 541 A.D.

Black Death

Bubonic plague that killed roughly 25 million people throughout Europe

Second Transition

Coincided with the Industrial Revolution

Third Transition

The current wave of infectious diseases

the global spread of infectious diseases. As we discuss the following infectious diseases, we will see the urgency and magnitude of this global challenge in a fragmented international health system.

INFLUENZA AND AVIAN FLU

The spread of H5N1 **avian flu** (bird flu) in 2006 to areas beyond Asia galvanized global efforts to prevent or diminish the impact of an influenza pandemic. Of all the major infectious diseases, influenza demands the unique and urgent attention of the global community because of its lethality and the speed with which it is transmitted. Of the more than 1,500 microbes known to cause disease in humans, influenza continues to dominate in terms of overall mortality. Ever year, 5 to 10 percent of the American population gets the flu and about 36,000 of them die. Even in normal times, an estimated 1.5 million people worldwide die from influenza infections or related complications each year.[13] **Influenza**, which is a viral infection of the respiratory tract, is very contagious and poses serious threats to children, the elderly, and individuals with compromised immune systems. It is estimated that three influenza pandemics in the twentieth century killed more than 50 million people. The **Spanish flu** pandemic of 1918–1920 is generally regarded as the most lethal plague in history, causing roughly 50 million deaths worldwide. Pandemics in 1957 and 1968, which originated in China and Hong Kong, together killed more than 2.5 million people.[14] Given the efficiency with which flu is transmitted through the air, close contact is not required for people to become infected. Furthermore, it is very difficult to identify and quarantine infected people who are spreading the disease. Because the last two influenza pandemics originated in China, where people live in close contact with birds and swine, the emergence of the avian flu in China in 2003 is now a major global issue.

Throughout the world, large commercial poultry farms, as well as the *proliferation of chickens kept by families, have provided ideal conditions for the avian flu to spread.* Furthermore, rapid population growth, especially in Asia, has given rise to densely populated urban areas. For example, during the 1968–1969 influenza pandemic, China had 790 million people and 12.3 million chickens and other poultry. China now has 1.3 billion people and 13 billion chickens.[15] Poultry, pigs, and people living together or in close proximity enhances the transmission of avian flu from animals to humans. Although the avian flu had caused eighty-eight deaths out of a total of 165 cases globally by early 2006, transmission from human to human had not occurred. The global community feared that the virus would undergo changes enabling it to **reassort** (i.e., mix genes with other human influenza viruses that are also present). This process can produce an entirely new viral strain, capable of sustained human-to-human transmission. If such a virus has never existed, humans will lack immunity and the global population will be vulnerable to contracting the disease. The new strain would be easily transmitted from person to person, thereby causing a new pandemic. Approximately 1.7 million Americans would die, and there would be roughly 180 million to 360 million deaths globally.[16] The young and elderly would be the primary vic-

Influenza

A contagious viral infection of the respiratory tract

Spanish Flu

Most lethal influenza pandemic

Reassort

Mutation of viruses that enhance chances of human-to-human transmission of disease

tims. On the other hand, it is possible that the avian flu will not develop into a pandemic.

By 2006, humans had been infected in several countries outside Asia, such as Turkey, Iraq, India, and Iran. Dead birds infected with the H5N1 virus have been discovered in Russia, Romania, France, Croatia, Austria, Greece, Germany, and Nigeria. Migratory birds are believed to be primarily responsible for spreading the disease to other birds. The migratory route over East Asia overlaps with the Central Asian flyway, which overlaps with flyways to Africa and Europe. The deadly form of the H5N1 strain in Asia had not been found in North and South America, where migratory patterns are separate from those in Europe, Africa, and Asia.[17] However, when the H5N1 virus was detected in Nigeria in early 2006, the global community became increasingly concerned about the ability of the virus to spread from human to human, given Africa's widespread poverty and the inability of the governments to deal with any health crisis. Furthermore, impoverished people were unlikely to destroy their chickens, knowing that governments were unable or unwilling to compensate them for their poultry.

Responding to the threat of a pandemic, governments, international organizations, and nongovernmental organizations (NGOs) have concentrated on quarantine and the extensive culling of birds in affected areas. European countries were advised by the **Animal Production and Health Division** of the **UN Food and Agriculture Organization** to require travelers to fill out forms detailing their travel history and the agricultural products in their possession, which is the practice in the United States. Increased checks of airline passengers and their belongings are also regarded as effective countermeasures.[18] A major obstacle to an effective global response is the weakness of governments and poverty, which will eventually undermine global cooperation. As we will see, poor countries lack adequate resources to deal with routine health problems, and fighting avian flu is not their principal priority. Within rich countries, governments have allocated resources to develop vaccines, primarily **Tamiflu**, to deal with a pandemic. However, even in rich countries, there is insufficient medication for all of their inhabitants. Poor societies would remain extremely vulnerable to an avian influenza pandemic.

Tamiflu

Medicine used to treat patients infected with the avian flu

MALARIA, DENGUE, AND YELLOW FEVER

Malaria, dengue, and yellow fever are found primarily in the Tropics and are transmitted by mosquitoes. These are the most common vector-borne diseases. The spread of human settlements and various activities in forested areas have led to increased contact with mosquitoes that carry the viruses that cause these diseases. Global transportation and global warming have enabled these diseases to spread and grow outside tropical areas. Discarded tires, bottles, cans, and other containers that collect water become fertile breeding grounds for mosquitoes. Humans contract **malaria** when bitten by female mosquitoes. Malarial parasites infect red blood cells, causing chills, fever, and often death. Of the estimated 300 million to 500 million people infected with malaria each

You
DECIDE

Pharmaceutical Companies' Role in Fighting Infectious Diseases

The increasing globalization of infectious diseases has contributed to a growing awareness of the connectedness among rich and poor countries and the need for increased cooperation between them to deal with these problems. Diseases are closely linked to a variety of global concerns, including malnutrition, inadequate education, poverty, and inequality. Roughly 460 million people are affected by HIV/AIDS, tuberculosis, and malaria, which together are responsible for an estimated 5.6 million deaths each year. While there is an abundance of expensive drugs available in wealthy societies, more than a third of the world's population lacks adequate access to essential medications. Pharmaceutical companies are primarily concerned with developing drugs that are profitable. This means that most medical research focuses overwhelmingly on diseases in rich countries. In 2006, Bill Gates, chairman of

Microsoft, decided to concentrate less on leading his company and more on working with the Bill and Melinda Gates Foundation to find ways to reduce the spread of infectious diseases. Between 1999 and 2006, the Bill and Melinda Gates Foundation gave $908.5 million to the Global Alliance for Vaccines and Immunization to fight infectious diseases. During the same period, governments worldwide contributed a total of $791.5 million. Pharmaceutical companies have largely resisted providing inexpensive drugs that would cure those suffering from infectious diseases in developing countries.

What policies do you think the global community could develop and implement to influence pharmaceutical companies to produce medicines for poor countries?

Source: Erika Check, "Quest for the Cure," *Foreign Policy* 155 (July/August 2006): 28–37.

year, roughly 1.5 million die from the disease.[19] **Dengue**, a viral disease, is transmitted by mosquitoes that acquire the virus when they suck blood from an infected person, replicate the virus in their system, and transmit it to the next person they bite. Dengue is marked by fever, severe headaches, muscle and bone pain, shock, and fatal hemorrhaging. There are roughly 50 million cases of dengue infection worldwide each year.[20] **Yellow fever** is endemic in Africa, Asia, Latin America, and several Caribbean islands. It is estimated that 30,000 people die each year of yellow fever. Symptoms include fever, muscle pain, backaches, headaches, shivering, loss of appetite, nausea, and vomiting. After a few days most people who are infected improve and their symptoms disappear. However, approximately 15 percent of infected individuals experience a toxic phase, in which they develop jaundice, abdominal pains, bleeding, and kidney failure. Roughly half of those who enter the toxic phase die within ten to fourteen days.[21] Malaria is by far the most pervasive and deadly of these three diseases, and is the focus of the rest of this section.

Malaria Globally, Africa suffers the most from malaria. More than 90 percent of malaria deaths occur there, despite the relative ease with which the disease can be prevented and cured. In many ways, the prevalence of malaria in Africa is a manifestation of that continent's endemic poverty. Malaria was once believed to be caused by swamp air. The role that mosquitoes play in transmitting the disease was not discovered until 1898. Several factors have contributed to the increase of malaria in different parts of the world. As *population pressures* have influenced farmers to cultivate areas bordering on swamps and as agroforestry has grown, mosquitoes have multiplied and have more opportunities to infect humans. The *construction of dams and irrigation systems* for agriculture has radically altered the natural environment and provided breeding places for mosquitoes. **Natural disasters**, such as earthquakes, often destroy sanitation facilities, cause severe flooding, and allow standing water to accumulate in which mosquitoes breed. Natural disasters can also destroy the habitats of natural hosts of diseases or disease vectors, bringing these organisms into closer contact with humans. Finally, **global warming** is widely believed to be responsible for increased rainfall and higher temperatures, which can result in flooding. These environmental conditions facilitate the spread of malaria.[22]

The poor suffer disproportionately from malaria, and pregnant women and children bear the heaviest burdens. Malaria during pregnancy threatens the child's development, both in the uterus and as an infant. Mothers who have had limited exposure to malaria parasites and therefore less immunity are extremely vulnerable during pregnancy when their immunity is generally lower. Often, malaria infections cause anemia, which often results in maternal mortality. Malaria usually causes low-birth-weight babies, brain damage, and cognitive impairment.[23]

Efforts to eradicate malaria began in 1898, when the connection between mosquitoes and the disease was discovered. In addition to draining swamps and removing standing water from around homes, insecticides and larvicides were used. Quinine was also used to treat infections. A major breakthrough in fighting malaria came after World War II when DDT was applied. DDT was first used in 1939 as an agricultural insecticide in Switzerland. However, it was during the war that its public health applications were discovered. The Allies had used DDT to control typhus epidemics. Complete eradication of malaria was achieved in such places as the United States, Southern Europe, Sri Lanka, and much of Brazil by massive DDT spraying.[24] Success in reducing malaria problems influenced the **World Health Organization (WHO)** to initiate its **Global Malaria Campaign** in 1955 to intensify the use of DDT to control malaria. However, by the 1960s malaria began to reemerge in countries that had made significant progress in eliminating it because many countries were unable to continue the highly organized and costly spray program essential for success. Furthermore, widespread use of DDT engendered resistance to it at a time when more people were becoming aware of its danger to human health and the environment. As we discussed in Chapter 8, the toxicity of pesticides was stressed by **Rachael Carson** in her influential book, *Silent Spring*. The WHO adopted a more comprehensive approach that included strengthening basic health services, focusing on the unique social and economic conditions in each region, and concentrating on treating malaria patients. Known as the **horizontal approach**, this new strategy emphasized control and containment, as opposed to complete eradication.[25] This change was due partly to limited supplies of DDT and escalating costs, as efforts to ban the use of

Global Malaria Campaign

Intensified the use of DDT to control malaria

Horizontal Approach

Strategy that emphasized the control and containment, as opposed to the eradication, of malaria

DDT were increasingly successful. Both interest in and funding for malaria control declined during the 1970s, which enabled the disease to spread.

Concerned about the proliferation of infectious diseases, the **U.S. Agency for International Development (USAID)** in 1997 cooperated with the World Bank, the WHO, and other international agencies to form the **Africa Initiative for Malaria Control (AIM)**. AIM was expanded to become a more comprehensive global initiative known as **Roll Back Malaria (RBM)** in 1998. A major objective of the RBM campaign was to reduce malaria-related mortality in half by 2012. Given the increase in malaria, meeting this goal remains a challenge.

The globalization of infectious diseases has contributed to increased global awareness of malaria and has engendered renewed efforts to eradicate it. Furthermore, many individuals and NGOs are involved in these efforts. Rotarians worldwide have made eradicating malaria a major goal. In 1993, Drake Zimmerman of the Rotary Club of Normal, Illinois, played a leading role in distributing bed nets treated with safe insecticides to reduce malaria problems. The emphasis on bed nets was influenced by the growing ineffectiveness and health hazards of other approaches, such as indoor spraying and the use of chloroquine. Other organizations, such as the United Nations Children's Fund (UNICEF), play a leading role in providing bed nets. An insecticide-treated bed net costs around $3. However, even at that price many poor families cannot afford to purchase them. Based on recommendations of Jeffrey Sachs, the UN Secretary General's special adviser on the Millenium Development Goals, these bed nets are heavily subsidized or given away. A special initiative to eradicate malaria in Zambia was launched in 2006. Using $35 million donated by the **Bill and Melinda Gates Foundation**, Zambia's objective is to provide bed nets to 80 percent of its population by 2009. An additional $82 million was donated by international organizations and governments to supply the most effective malaria drugs to every public clinic and to pay for coordinated spraying programs across Zambia.[26] These efforts are likely to significantly reduce malaria infections.

Bill and Melinda Gates Foundation

Provides bed nets to Zambia to control the spread of malaria

TUBERCULOSIS

Links between tuberculosis and the HIV/AIDS pandemic reinvigorated global interest in diminishing the spread of tuberculosis. The combination of tuberculosis and AIDS is lethal, with each disease contributing to the rapid progress of the other. HIV weakens the immune system, making it easier for an HIV-positive person to contract tuberculosis. In Africa, the epicenter of the HIV/AIDS pandemic, HIV is the single most important factor determining the increased incidence of tuberculosis.[27] The resurgence of tuberculosis underscores how globalization is instrumental in the transmission of infectious diseases and how increasing numbers of societies are unable to avoid the consequences. Migration from poor countries is a significant cause of the reemergence of tuberculosis in rich countries. In the United States, Sweden, Norway, Canada, Australia, Denmark, France, and other European countries, a large proportion of new cases of tuberculosis, as high as half in some countries, is found in immigrants. In fact,

TABLE 11.3 ESTIMATED TB INCIDENCE AND MORTALITY, 2003

WHO region	Number of Cases (thousands)		Cases per 100,000 population		Deaths from TB (including TB deaths in people infected with HIV)	
	All Forms %	Smear-positive	All forms	Smear-positive	Number (thousands)	Per 100,000 Population
Africa	2372 (27)	1013	345	147	538	78
The Americas	370 (4)	165	43	19	54	6
Eastern Mediterranean	634 (7)	285	122	55	144	28
Europe	439 (5)	196	50	22	67	8
South-East Asia	3062 (35)	1370	190	85	617	38
Western Pacific	1933 (22)	868	112	50	327	10
Global	**8810 (100)**	**3897**	**140**	**62**	**1747**	**28**

Source: World Health Organization, April 2005.

Mexico, the Philippines, China, India, and Vietnam—countries that are major sources of migrants to the United States—have some of the highest rates of tuberculosis in the world. High rates of illegal immigration reduce the ability of governments to screen and exclude infectious migrants. Tuberculosis is also rampant in refugee camps. For example, during the **Balkan conflict** (between 1992 and 1995), tuberculosis cases quadrupled. Similarly, famine and civil war throughout Africa have spawned significant growth in tuberculosis cases. Overcrowding in urban areas, rapid growth of prison populations (particularly in the United States), the rapid growth in global travel on airplanes with limited air circulation, and the global trend towards privatizing public health care systems (which generally deprives the poor of adequate medical treatment) have contributed to the reemergence of tuberculosis in affluent countries. In 2006 the WHO reported that the existence of virulent strains of tuberculosis that are resistant to all standard drugs had killed fifty-three patients in a rural hospital in South Africa.

Balkan Conflict
Occurred from 1992 to 1995 and contributed to the quadrupling of tuberculosis in the Balkans

Tuberculosis, prevalent in overcrowded poor areas with unsanitary conditions and malnutrition, is one of the most deadly infectious diseases. The WHO estimates that someone in the world is newly infected with tuberculosis bacilli every second and that one-third of the world's population is infected with tuberculosis.[28] More than 1.7 million die from tuberculosis each year, with the highest number of deaths in Southeast Asia. However, the highest mortality rate per capita is in Africa, due primarily to the prevalence of HIV/AIDS. In the mid-nineteenth century, tuberculosis was the leading cause of death in Europe and North America. It was a terrifying disease because it could not be prevented from spreading and it was incurable. Being transmitted through the air, changing one's behavior provided no protection. As social, economic, and sanitary conditions improved in Europe and North America, tuberculosis began to recede. Furthermore, survivors of the disease developed greater immunity to it. The discovery of effective medicines starting in 1944 to control tuberculosis diminished the epidemic, with wealthier countries experiencing steady declines in tuberculosis-related deaths.[29] By 1991, pharmaceutical companies had abandoned manufacturing **streptomycin**, a drug commonly used to treat tuberculosis, and many developed countries sharply reduced spending on programs designed to combat the disease. Sanitariums, which had proliferated to treat tuberculosis patients, were closed, giving the perception that tuberculosis was no longer a major public concern. Although many poor areas within rich countries continue to experience cases of tuberculosis, the gap between rich and poor had created a general sense of indifference to the disease. *Four factors have contributed to the tuberculosis as a global disease:*

1. Whereas tuberculosis declined in rich countries, it increased in the developing world.
2. Many policymakers and the general population in wealthy countries underestimated the degree to which their health was intertwined with that of people in other parts of the world.
3. The emergence of the HIV/AIDS pandemic rejuvenated tuberculosis, creating new concerns for wealthy countries.
4. The world was unprepared for an increase in outbreaks of multi-drug-resistant tuberculosis.[30]

Faced with the spread of tuberculosis in an increasingly global society, various governmental and nongovernmental organizations rejuvenated efforts to diminish the transmission of the disease.

DOTS Strategy

Introduced in 1991 by the WHO to control tuberculosis

In 1991, the WHO introduced the **DOTS strategy** to control tuberculosis. This *strategy is composed of five elements*: (1) government commitment to sustained tuberculosis control, (2) detection of tuberculosis cases through sputum-smear microscopy among people with symptoms, (3) regular and uninterrupted supply of high-quality antituberculosis drugs, (4) six-to-eight months of regularly supervised treatment, and (5) reporting systems to monitor treatment progress and program performance.[31] The DOTS strategy has achieved treatment success rates as high as 90 percent in some countries, a decline in the incidence of tuberculosis infections, and the prevention of an estimated 70 percent of deaths among infectious cases between 1991 and 2000. Nonetheless, the 2004 WHO report on **global TB control** concluded that governments must do more to meet global targets in order to eradicate and control tuberculosis. It recommends that governments and national tuberculosis control programs must adopt a more strategic approach to planning, match budgets more closely to plans, and match fundraising activities to realistic budgets.[32] The emergence of the avian flu, HIV/AIDS, and other infectious diseases will engender even stiffer competition for limited financial resources.

HIV/AIDS

HIV/AIDS

Evolved from SIV found in chimpanzees in Southwestern Africa

When AIDS was first recognized in 1981, the general assumption was that this deadly disease was essentially limited to homosexuals and West Africans. Today, however, **HIV** (the virus that causes AIDS) and **AIDS** have become a pandemic. By 2006, more than 40 million people worldwide, 60 percent of them women, had been infected.

Roughly 3 million people die every year from AIDS. Although Africa remains the epicenter of the AIDS pandemic, the disease is rapidly growing in China, India, Russia, Latin America and the Caribbean, Eastern and Central Europe, and elsewhere. India, with more than 5 million cases of HIV, ranks second in the world, behind South Africa. Homosexuals, heterosexuals, bisexuals, intravenous drug users, recipients of infected blood transfusions, and children are victims of AIDS. In many ways, AIDS is a weapon of mass destruction, one that occupies the attention of people everywhere and institutions at all levels of the global community.

HIV (human immunodeficiency virus) is probably as old as human society. It is generally accepted that HIV evolved from the **simian immunodeficiency virus** (SIV) found in chimpanzees in southwestern Africa. It is believed that individuals acquired the disease from exposure to blood in the process of handling the meat of a chimpanzee that carried the virus. Compared with other infectious diseases, HIV/AIDS—while devastating—is transmitted in very specific ways and is thus more controllable. The virus is passed from one individual to another through the exchange of bodily fluids during sexual intercourse, through blood transfusions, from mother to fetus, through intravenous drug use, and other activities in which infected blood is transmitted from one person to another. Early symptoms of HIV infection include chronic fatigue or weakness, noticeable and sustained weight loss, extensive and persistent swelling of the lymph glands, routine diarrhea, and sustained deterioration of the central nervous system. These conditions make HIV-positive patients vulnerable to contracting many other infectious diseases, especially tuberculosis.

Globalization is a major factor contributing to the spread of HIV/AIDS. As global tourism continues to grow and people venture to all corners of the world, they increase their risk of contracting infectious diseases. **Sex tourism**, which is traveling to specific countries to participate in the local sex industry, is a potent source of infectious diseases, especially HIV/AIDS. Furthermore, as we discussed in Chapter 10, the growth in human trafficking and the sex trade in many parts of the world helps to spread HIV/AIDS. Poverty, ethnic conflicts, and wars facilitate the transmission of HIV/AIDS. Refugees and other misplaced people are vulnerable to sexual abuse. Conflicts generally destroy social organizations as well as health care systems. And, as we will see in the case of South Africa, traditional values and perceptions of women are also important factors that assist the transmission of HIV/AIDS.

The HIV/AIDS pandemic has disastrous consequences. Eurasia, home to five out of every eight people on the planet, is an area with substantial economic power. It is also the location of countries that have nuclear weapons. Rapid increases in AIDS are likely to have profound global demographic, economic, political, and military strategic implications.[77] Compounding the problem is widespread poverty and the unwillingness or inability of governments to adequately address the AIDS crisis. The South African government was strongly criticized at the 16th International AIDS Conference in Toronto in 2006 for its refusal to take a more serious approach to the problem and to use available antiretroviral drugs. Nowhere are the devastating consequences of HIV/AIDS more prominent than in Africa, a continent estimated to have 70 percent of the people infected with the disease globally. Just as previous plagues

Simian Immuno-deficiency Virus
Believed to be the source of HIV/AIDS

Sex Tourism
Traveling to countries to participate in the sex industry

radically altered European and Asian societies, AIDS is currently reshaping Africa. In some southern African countries, such as South Africa, Botswana, and Zambia, more than a third of the adults are infected with HIV. This means that many children become orphans and are abandoned. They are extremely vulnerable to sexual exploitation and drug abuse, as well as to being used to fight in Africa's numerous conflicts. The AIDS epidemic in Africa deepens the continent's economic and health care problems and facilitates the spread of other diseases, including tuberculosis, that severely strain medical resources. Because AIDS kills more women than men, and because women are primarily responsible for farming and child care, starvation increases. Economic life is severely affected as employees become more disabled and die of AIDS.[34] Perhaps one of the most severe economic and social aspects of HIV/AIDS is the nature of the disease itself. Unlike previous pandemics, HIV/AIDS is a slow and deliberate killer. The Black Death and Spanish flu were devastating but quick. HIV/AIDS, by contrast, is long term and consequently more destructive in many ways. Since its discovery in 1981, the HIV/AIDS pandemic has been characterized by waves of infection, followed years later by waves of debilitating illness, and years after that followed by waves of death and family disruption.[35]

Africa

Africa bears the burden of the HIV/AIDS pandemic. Because of its poverty, which is exacerbated by debilitating infectious diseases. Africa is marginalized in the process of globalization. Within the continent, southern Africa, especially **South Africa**, has become the epicenter of HIV/AIDS. More than 5.3 million South Africans, out of a population of 45 million, are living with the virus, making it the country with the largest number of HIV/AIDS cases in the world. All aspects of South African life are affected by the pandemic. By examining South Africa, we can get a deeper understanding of the gravity of this global issue for South Africa and other developing countries. South Africa is experiencing only the first phase of the pandemic.

South Africa

The epicenter of the global HIV/AIDS crisis

Apart from the fact that HIV/AIDS originated in Africa, several other factors have contributed to its rapid growth in South Africa. Economic, cultural, and political factors combine to make South Africa a special case. Settled by Europeans, primarily from Holland and Britain, South Africa experienced racial conflicts and endured

TABLE 11.4 HIV/AIDS IN AFRICA (2005)

HIV/AIDS	Sub-Saharan Africa	World
New infections	3,200,000	4,900,000
Children (under age 15) infections	630,000	700,000
Deaths	2,400,000	3,100,000
Child deaths	520,000	570,000
People living with HIV/AIDS	25,800,000	40,300,000

Sources: WHO, UNAIDS, and Africa Renewal, January 2006, 3

forced racial segregation under the system of **apartheid**. The political and social components of apartheid provided the breeding ground for the HIV/AIDS problem. Apartheid laws required men who worked in the gold, diamond, and other mines; the factories; and all sectors of the economy to leave their families. **Rural-to-urban migration** occurs throughout Africa, as we discussed in Chapter 9. Under various colonial administrations, Africans were forced to leave rural areas in search of employment in urban centers, in mining, and in agriculture. The majority of these migrant workers returned home periodically. This pattern of migration was firmly rooted in South Africa and it continues. As in other parts of Africa, HIV/AIDS cases were initially concentrated along major trading routes and areas frequented by long-distance truck drivers. Bars and hotels along these routes became centers for the sex trade. HIV prevalence is often extremely high among the women, with documented rates up to 76 percent prevalence in Uganda.[36] The men transmit the virus to women in rural areas, making HIV/AIDS a predominantly heterosexual disease in Africa. Women in rural areas who are infected continue to spread the disease to their sexual partners.

Another factor that facilitates the spread of HIV/AIDS in South Africa is the casual, unsafe, and abusive nature of sexual relationships. Cultural attitudes and behaviors influence many South Africans to accept having multiple partners and engage in unprotected sex, rejecting the use of condoms. Traditional sexual practices (such as **dry sex**, which involves the use of powders and herbs to prevent vaginal

Apartheid

South Africa's system of rigid, legal, racial segregation that was violently enforced

Rural-to-urban migration

Facilitates the spread of HIV/AIDS in South Africa

Dry Sex

A practice that facilitates the transmission of AIDS

TABLE 11.5 ESTIMATED HIV PREVALENCE AMONG SOUTH AFRICANS, BY AGE

Age (years)	Male prevalence (%)	Female prevalence (%)
2–4	4.9	5.3
5–9	4.2	4.8
10–14	1.6	1.8
15–19	3.2	9.4
20–24	6.0	23.9
25–29	12.1	33.3
30–34	23.3	26.0
35–39	23.3	19.3
40–44	17.5	12.4
45–49	10.3	8.7
50–54	14.2	7.5
55–59	6.4	3.0
60+	4.0	3.7
Total	**8.2**	**13.3**

Among females, HIV prevalence is highest in those between 25 and 29 years old; among males, the peak is in the group aged 30–39 years. According to these results, males aged 15–49 years old are 58% as likely to be infected as are females in the same age group (11.7% in men vs. 20.2% in women).

Source: The South African National HIV Survey, 2005

Catholic leaders, as well as overseas missionaries who worked in countries devastated by HIV/AIDS, Graham focused national attention on the problem. Perceptions of the disease as affecting primarily heterosexuals, as opposed to only homosexuals, enabled many conservatives to take action instead of disregarding the pandemic because they believed it was God's punishment of homosexuals. In his 2003 State of the Union address, President George W. Bush, influenced by Graham and the evangelicals, announced the **Emergency Plan for AIDS Relief** and committed $15 billion over five years to preventing HIV infections and treating of patients.[45] However, political pressure from conservatives influenced the U.S. government to allocate a third of the money to abstinence-promoting programs and to avoid spending money on sterile syringes and needles for intravenous drug users. Essentially, the U.S. government adopted Uganda's **ABC** (Abstinence, Be Faithful, and Use Condoms) program, which helped to significantly reduce the prevalence of HIV/AIDS in that country. In 2003, the **William J. Clinton Presidential Foundation HIV/AIDS Initiative** concluded an agreement with generic drug manufacturers to lower the price of triple combination antiretroviral drug regimens to less than $140 per patient per year. The Clinton Foundation has concentrated its efforts against HIV/AIDS in Mozambique, Rwanda, Tanzania, South Africa, and several Caribbean states.

Confronted with the emergence of HIV/AIDS, the global community responded. The WHO and U.S. government agencies—including the U.S. Food and Drug Administration (FDA), and the Alcohol, Drug Abuse, and Mental Health Administration—convened the **First International AIDS Conference** in Atlanta, Georgia, in 1984. This was followed by the initiation of **WHO's Special Program** on HIV/AIDS in 1985, which set the objective of reducing the growth of HIV/AIDS globally and to lessen the disease's impact on the countries most seriously affected. Concerned about HIV/AIDS patients' inability to afford drugs to treat the disease, members of the World Trade Organization (WTO) ratified the **Agreement on Trade-Related Aspects of Intellectual Property Rights (TRIPS)** in 1994. TRIPS included a provision to allow states to wave patent protections without authorization from the patent holder in national emergencies for noncommercial use.[46] This provision facilitated the ability of governments, such as Brazil's, to manufacture generic drugs used to treat HIV/AIDS patients. A major breakthrough in the fight against the pandemic came in 1996, when the **Joint United Nations Program on AIDS (UNAIDS)** was founded. UNAIDS's main objective is to be the leading advocate for global action against HIV/AIDS. Several organizations, reflecting UNAIDS's comprehensive approach to the problem, participate in the program. These

UNICEF, the UN Development Program; the UN Population Fur Educational, Scientific, and Cultural Organization (UNESCO); the V UN Office on Drugs and Crime; and the International Labor C organizations have been joined by the eight leading industrial co G-8), various NGOs, and pharmaceutical companies (such as Boo Bristol-Myers Squibb, GlaxoSmithKline, Merck, and F. Hoffmann-x in to global pressure to lower drug prices to make them accessible to maceutical companies responded by discounting their antiretroviral n.

diarrhea. Typhoid fever—which affects roughly 17 million people worldwide every year and causes 600,000 deaths—has been basically eliminated in countries with proper sanitation. However, imported food from poor areas has caused occasional outbreaks in developed counties. Untreated victims transmit the disease, and a small percentage of them (between 2 and 5 percent) become permanent carriers of the bacteria.

In early October 2004, medical personnel in the Angolan town of Uige observed an escalation in deaths among children who had what appeared to be treatable diseases. The suddenness of their deaths was initially downplayed, partly because many countries in Africa are routinely plagued with infectious diseases. The WHO and Doctors Without Borders, which assumed leading roles in investigating the causes of these deaths, found that they were due to an outbreak of the Marburg virus. The **Marburg virus** is spread by contact with bodily fluids and is fatal in nine out of ten cases. It kills its victims within a week, and there is no effective treatment. By April 2005, of the approximately 214 people who had been infected, 194 of them had died. Marburg virus victims were found in Luanda, Angola's capital city, which is 180 miles away from Uige.

POLIO

Polio, an acute viral infection found mainly in children, is transmitted primarily through contact with infected persons. It causes severe physical disabilities, including paralysis, and death. **President Franklin Delano Roosevelt** was disabled as a result of polio. The discovery of the **Salk vaccine** in 1955 significantly diminished polio cases in Western countries. It was the development of the oral vaccine by Dr. Albert Sabin in 1961 that made immunization possible for the masses in the developing world. The case of polio clearly demonstrates that problems can become global if one country fails to cooperate with efforts to prevent them. The global community was confident that polio, unlike smallpox, would be eradicated. However, religious and political leaders in predominantly Muslim northern Nigeria, believing that the polio vaccine made girls infertile and that the WHO and Western countries were using it to reduce the Muslim population, forced the suspension of the immunization program. Muslims who had access to the Internet found websites questioning the safety of the vaccines. Many Muslims were also suspicious of the Rotary International's involvement because they saw the group as another religion. By 2000, Nigeria was the last country in the world with polio cases.

The global community was on the verge of eradicating this disease in 2004. Opposition to polio vaccination in Nigeria led to a reemergence of the disease in neighboring Ivory Coast, Benin, Burkina Faso, Cameroon, the Central African Republic, Togo, Sudan, Ethiopia, and Chad. Even as the WHO, Rotary International, and the other groups struggle to secure resources to combat the spread of polio, the migration of Muslim pilgrims from Africa to Mecca led to the outbreak of polio in Yemen and Saudi Arabia in 2005. Polio can be spread everywhere when there is a single infected person anywhere.[51] Each country must be free of the disease for three years before eradication is certified.

Salk Vaccine

Vaccine that helped diminish the number of polio cases

GLOBAL RESPONSES TO INFECTIOUS DISEASES

The global community has long recognized that preventing, treating, and controlling the spread of infectious diseases can be accomplished only through cooperation among individuals, NGOs, governments, and international organizations. As early as 1851, European countries convened the **International Sanitation Conference** in an effort to prevent the spread of infectious diseases from developing countries to Europe, primarily through travel and trade. Significant improvements in sanitation, nutrition, and medical technology in Europe have reduced outbreaks of infectious diseases. But Europe remained vulnerable to the importation of diseases. Shortly after the United Nations was founded, the WHO was created as a specialized agency to develop international rules concerning infectious disease control. Under the **International Health Regulations** developed by the WHO, countries are required to report outbreaks of yellow fever, cholera, plague, and other diseases. This information is disseminated to other countries and surveillance strategies are implemented to help prevent transmission. Countries are also required to provide safe drinking water, food, and disposal of refuse, wastewater, and other things dangerous to health at their airports and ports. International health regulations also require counties to provide health services, equipment, and services for isolating infected persons and for disinfecting, disinsecting, and deratting ships and aircraft.[52] The U.S. **Centers for Disease Control and Prevention (CDC)**, based in Atlanta, Georgia, also plays a leading role in preventing and controlling the transmission of infectious diseases into the United States. Both the CDC and the WHO emphasize the importance of research and the development of medicines to prevent the emergence and spread of infectious diseases. One major problem relating to health issues in the developing world is access to medical information. The WHO persuaded six major publishers of medical journals to reduce their prices so that doctors and researchers in poor societies could have increased access to information to improve health care systems and develop new treatments.[53]

As we have seen, an important component of the global response to the emergence and reemergence of infectious diseases is stressing **preventive measures**. These include protecting and chlorinating water supplies, disposing of human feces in a sanitary manner and maintaining fly-proof latrines, paying special attention to cleanliness in food preparation and food handling, stressing the importance of frequent hand washing, and eliminating potential mosquito breeding sites. Routine preventive immunization programs have effectively reduced outbreaks of many infectious diseases. The WHO launched the **3 by 5 anti-AIDS initiative**, which aimed to provide anti-AIDS drugs to 3 million people in poor countries by the end of 2005. Of the roughly 42 million people infected with AIDS in 2004, only 400,000 of them received the necessary drugs.[54] In 2006 WHO launched the *universal access initiative* to bring an even greater sense of urgency and commitment to HIV prevention and treatment. The United States made a commitment to spend $15 billion on efforts to prevent and control the spread of AIDS. In 2006 the Bill and Melinda Gates Foundation gave $287

International Sanitation Conference

Effort to prevent the spread of infectious diseases from developing countries to Europe

Centers for Disease Control and Prevention

U.S. organization devoted to preventing and controlling the transmission of infectious diseases into the United States

million to researchers to develop an HIV vaccine. A basic challenge was persuading pharmaceutical companies to lower drug prices and to permit developing countries, such as India and Brazil, to be exempt from patent restrictions so that they could produce relatively inexpensive anti-AIDS drugs. By 2006, as we have seen, many major pharmaceutical companies had agreed to arrangements allowing poor countries to have access to relatively inexpensive drugs. The SARS virus, the growing concern about terrorists using biological weapons, and the emergence of avian flu contributed to a greater awareness of the globalization of infectious diseases and the need to act promptly and decisively to prevent both infections and transmission. As we saw, the global response to SARS is widely regarded as the model of both current and future pandemics.

Summary and Review

This chapter discussed the globalization of infectious diseases; rapid increases in global travel, trade, and migration; growing use of illegal drugs; human trafficking for sexual purposes; rapid population growth; environmental changes; widespread poverty; and inadequate medical resources—all factors that have facilitated the global spread of infectious diseases. These diseases pose significant threats to humans as well as to global security. By discussing infectious diseases—such as influenza, avian flu, malaria, tuberculosis, HIV/AIDS, and SARS—we were able to see the social, economic, and political challenges these diseases pose and the ease with which they are spread globally. Special emphasis was given to HIV/AIDS because of its grave threats to the global society. We discussed various responses to globalization of infectious diseases. The case of SARS demonstrates that rapid transportation and instantaneous communications have raised global awareness of how quickly infectious diseases are transmitted worldwide. The global response to SARS is widely regarded as a model for how to deal with emerging as well as current infectious diseases. Some organizations, such as the WHO, play a pivotal role in reducing the expansion of infectious diseases. NGOs as well as individuals are also actively involved in fighting pandemics. However, many governments have inadequate resources to deal with multiple infectious diseases. Furthermore, countries have different priorities. Cultural values and practices also complicate global efforts to prevent the emergence and spread of infectious diseases.

Key Terms

SARS 351
human security 353
UN Millennium
    Development
    Goals 353
pathogens 354
epidemics 354

pandemics 354
hosts 355
zoonosis 355
epidemiologic transition
    theory 355
Plague of Justinian 355
avian flu 356

WHO 359
Global Malaria
    Campaign 359
HIV/AIDS 362
sex tourism 363
100 Percent Condom
    Program 368

intellectual property
    rights 369
Samaritan's
    Purse 369
UNAIDS 370
Marburg virus 373
polio 373

Discussion Questions

1. Discuss the role of globalization in the spread of infectious diseases.
2. What are the differences between an epidemic and a pandemic? Give examples of each.
3. Discuss the three epidemiologic transitions.
4. Discuss the emergence of SARS and the global response to it.
5. Discuss the role of the WHO in preventing the spread of infectious diseases.
6. Discuss the factors that facilitate the spread of HIV/AIDS and various efforts to deal with this pandemic.
7. Compare domestic and global approaches to malaria and tuberculosis.
8. Discuss how conflicts, global warming, and poverty contribute to the emergence and spread of infectious diseases.

Suggested Readings

Brower, Jennifer, and Peter Chalk. *The Global Threat of New and Reemerging Infectious Diseases.* Santa Monica; CA: Rand, 2003.

Burkhalter, Holly. "The Politics of AIDS," *Foreign Affairs* 83, No. 1 (January/February 2004): 8–14.

Fidler, David P. *International Law and Infectious Diseases.* Oxford: Clarendon Press, 1999.

Garrett, Laurie. *The Coming Plague.* New York: Penguin Books, 1994.

Garrett, Laurie. "The Lessons of HIV/AIDS," *Foreign Affairs* 84, No. 2 (July/August 2005): 51–64.

Greenfeld, Karl. "The Virus Hunters," *Foreign Policy* 153 (March/April 2006): 42–55.

Knobler, Stacey. *Learning From SARS.* Washington DC: National Academies Press, 2004.

Koplow, David A. *Smallpox: The Fight to Eradicate a Global Scourge.* Berkeley: University of California Press, 2004.

Marlink, Richard G., and Alison G. Kotin. *Global AIDS Crisis,* Santa Barbara. CA: ABC-CLIO, 2004.

Stillwagon, Eileen. *AIDS and the Ecology of Poverty.* New York: Oxford University Press, 2005.

Whitman, Jim. *The Politics of Emerging and Resurgent Infectious Diseases.* New York: St. Martin's Press, 2000.

Addresses and Websites

World Health Organization
Avenue Appia 20
1211 Geneva 27
Switzerland
Tel.: 4122 791 2111
Email: info@who.int
www.who.int

The World Health Organization, the UN specialized agency for health, seeks to have all people worldwide attain the highest level of health. The WHO website contains news, reports, and information on emergencies and disease outbreaks.

United Nations AIDS Organization
20 Avenue Appia CH
1211 Geneva 27
Switzerland
Tel.: 4122 791 3666
Email: unaids@unaids.org
www.unaids.org

UNAIDS is a UN organization that deals with the global AIDS epidemic. This website offers information on AIDS, new research, publications, and provides links to other AIDS websites.

Centers for Disease Control
and Prevention
1600 Clinton Rd.
Atlanta, GA 30333
Tel.: (800) 311–3435
www.cdc.org

The Centers for Disease Control and Prevention is sponsored by the U.S. Department of Health and Human Services. Its website provides information on diseases and how to prevent them.

European AIDS Treatment Group
Mindener Strasse, 33
Germany
Tel.: 490 211 7883481
http://www.eatg.org

Made up of representatives from twenty-eight countries in Europe, EATG's mission is to increase access to anti-retroviral medications, technological advances, and treatment for opportunistic infections for people living with HIV and AIDS.

Global AIDS Alliance
1225 Connecticut Ave. NW No. 401
Washington D.C. 20036
Tel.: (202) 296–0260
www.globalaidsalliance.org

The Global AIDS Alliance works with governmental and nongovernmental partners worldwide to educate policymakers about HIV and AIDS in order to "catalyze" improvements to human rights, access to care and treatment, and funding.

Global Fund to Fight AIDS, Tuberculosis,
and Malaria
53 Avenue Louis-Casai
1216 Geneva-Cointrin
Switzerland
Tel.: 41 22 791 1700
www.theglobalfund.org

The Global Fund supports HIV and AIDS care, treatment, and prevention programs proposed by governments and NGOs in developing countries worldwide. The Global Fund is financed by donations from national governments, individuals, and private foundations, and is administered independently from any national government or international organization.

Endnotes

1. Lincoln Chen and Vasant Narasimhan, "A Human Security Agenda for Global Health," in *Global Health Challenges for Human Security*, ed. Lincoln Chen, et al. (Cambridge, MA: Global Equity Initiative, 2003), 8.
2. Tommy Koh, "The New Global Threat," in *The New Global Threat*, ed. Tommy Koh, et al. (London: World Scientific, 2003), 147.
3. Vikas Bajaj, "Japan Again Suspends Shipments of Beef from U.S.," *New York Times*, 21 January 2006, B3.
4. Michael J. Toole, "Refugees and Migrants," in *The Politics of Emerging and Resurgent Infectious Diseases*, ed. Jim Whitman (New York: St. Martin's Press, 2000), 110.
5. Jennifer Brower and Peter Chalk, *The Global Threat of New and Reemerging Infectious Diseases* (Santa Monica: Rand, 2003), 17.
6. Brower and Chalk, *the Global Threat*, 4.
7. Chen and Narasimhan, "A Human Security Agenda," in *Global Health Challenges*, 3.
8. Brower and Chalk, *The Global Threat*, 10.
9. David P. Fidler, *International Law and Infectious Diseases* (Oxford: Clarendon Press, 1999), 9.
10. Ronald Barrettt, et al., "Emerging and Reemerging Infectious Diseases: The Third Epidemiologic Transition," *Annual Review of Anthropology* 27 (1998), 247.
11. Paul R. Epstein, "Climate, Ecology, and Human Health," in *Plagues and Politics*, ed. Andrew T. Price-Smith (New York: Palgrave, 2001), 49.
12. Alfred W. Cosby, *The Columbian Exchange: Biological and Cultural Consequences of 1492* (Westport, CT: Greenwood Press, 1972), 37.
13. Michael T. Osterbolm, "Preparing for the Next Pandemic," *Foreign Affairs* 84, No. 2 (July/August 2005), 26.
14. National Research Council, *Under the Weather: Climate, Ecosystems, and Infectious Disease* (Washington DC: National Academy Press, 2001), 54.
15. Osterbolm, "Preparing for the Next Pandemic," 37.

16. Osterbolm, "Preparing for the Next Pandemic," 26.

17. Howard Markel, "If the Avian Flu Hasn't Hit, Here's Why, Maybe," *New York Times*, 1 January 2006, A10.

18. Elizabeth Rosenthal, "Europe Urged to Check Travelers to Prevent Spread of Bird Flu," *New York Times* 17 January 2006, A3.

19. National Research Council, *Under the Weather*, 48.

20. National Research Council, *Under the Weather*, 47.

21. World Health Organization, *Yellow Fever: Fact Sheet No. 100*, December 2001, 1.

22. Lisa Sattenspiel, "The Evolution, Transmission, and Geographic Spread of Infectious Diseases," in *The Changing Face of Disease*, ed. Nick Mascie-Taylor, et al. (London: CRC Press, 2004), 44.

23. S. W. Lindsay, et al., "Protecting Pregnant Women From Malaria," in *The Changing Face of Disease*, 104.

24. Roger Bate, "Testimony on Fighting Malaria," *Congressional Quarterly*, 13 May 2005, 3.

25. Bate, "Testimony on Fighting Malaria," 3.

26. Laurie Goering, "Zambia Expands Effort to Control its Biggest Killer," *Chicago Tribune*, 14 February 2006, Sect. 1, 5.

27. World Health Organization, *Tuberculosis*, April 2005, 2.

28. World Health Organization, *Tuberculosis*, 1.

29. Kraig Klaudt, "The Political Causes and Solutions of the Current Tuberculosis Epidemic," in *The Politics of Emerging and Resurgent Infectious Diseases*, 87.

30. Klaudt, "The Political Causes," in *The Politics of Emerging and Resurgent Infectious Diseases*, 89.

31. World Health Organization, *Tuberculosis*, 2.

32. World Health Organization, *Tuberculosis*, 4.

33. Nicholas Eberstadt, "The Future of AIDS," *Foreign Affairs* 81, No. 6 (November/December 2002), 23.

34. "The Cost of AIDS: An Imprecise Catastrophe," *Economist*, 22 May 2004, 68.

35. Laurie Garrett, "The Lessons of HIV/AIDS," *Foreign Affairs* 84, No. 2 (July/August 2005), 52.

36. Richard G. Marlink and Alison G. Kotin, *Global AIDS Crisis* (Santa Barbara; CA: ABC-CLIO, 2004), 28.

37. Brower and Chalk, *The Global Threat*, 39.

38. Brower and Chalk, *The Global Threat*, 42.

39. Brower and Chalk, *The Global Threat*, 50.

40. Marlink and Kotin, *Global AIDS Crisis*, 19.

41. Evan Osnos, "AIDS Travels Fast on Ancient China Road," *Chicago Tribune*, 5 February 2006, Sect. 1, 1.

42. Marlink and Kotin, *Global AIDS Crisis*, 17.

43. Marlink and Kotin, *Global AIDS Crisis*, 79.

44. Lawrence O. Gostin, *The AIDS Pandemic* (Chapel Hill: University of North Carolina Press, 2004) 279.

45. Holly Burkhalter, "The Politics of AIDS," *Foreign Affairs* 83, No. 1 (January/February 2004), 10.

46. Marlink and Kotin, *Global AIDS Crisis*, 123.

47. Donald G. McNeil, "Bristol-Myers Allows Two Major AIDS Drugs to Be Sold Cheaply," *New York Times*, 15 February 2006, A6.

48. Stacey Knobler, et al., *Learning From SARS*, (Washington, DC: National Academies Press, 2004), 6.

49. Aileen J. Plant, "SARS and Public Health," in *The New Global Threat*, 4.

50. Knobler, et al., *Learning From SARS*, 260.

51. Lawrence K. Altman, "Polio in Ivory Coast Started in Nigeria," *New York Times*, 1 March 2004, A13; and Donald G. McNeil, "Polio Back in Yemen After 6-Year Absence," *New York Times*, 22 April 2005, A8.

52. Fidler, *International Law and Infectious Diseases*, 62.

53. Melody Peterson, "Medical Journals Plan to Offer Far Lower Rates in Poor Nation," *New York Times*, 9 July 2001, A3.

54. "The Global Effort Against AIDS is Changing Gear," *Economist*, 15 May 2004, 78.

CHAPTER 12

Cultural Clashes and Conflict Resolution

INTRODUCTION

While some groups and individuals promote globalization as a positive force to advance their own interests, others perceive globalization as threatening. Global integration is increasing while, simultaneously, national cohesion is weakening as smaller groups seek increased political and cultural autonomy. As we have seen, globalization is widely equated with Americanization. The dual forces of globalization and antiglobalization are reflected in the contradictory trends of Americanization and anti-Americanism. Progress toward global order and security is accompanied by persistent outbreaks of violent conflicts and insecurity. Most cultural clashes, as this chapter shows, are inseparable from politics and economics.

Globalization attracts and repels, unifies and divides, integrates and separates. Western tourists in predominantly Islamic Zanzibar find their preference for bikinis colliding with Zanzibar's cultural values that require women to be covered from head to toe. Western ideals of beauty conflict with those found in many African societies. In Kenya, a former British colony, lawyers and judges debate wearing horsehair wigs. In Ireland, which has experienced rapid economic development as a consequence of European economic integration and economic globalization, Gaelic is being revitalized. Once regarded as the language of poverty, this ancient Irish language now represents Irish self-confidence and economic success. Throughout Europe, the removal of national boundaries is spawning a resurgence of local cultures and languages. Globalization is both an integrative and a disintegrative force.

Globalization challenges traditional certainties, conservative values, and parochialism; it also erodes identities based on nationality, geographic location, religion, social status, and ethnicity. Global financial markets, a borderless world, the growth of transnational elites, and weakening national institutions fuel insecurity. Insecurity gives rise to global, international, and domestic conflicts. That these clashes occur at different levels (global, international, regional, national, and local) and often operate interdependently manifest the complexity of global society. Benjamin R. Barber, for example, envisions two possible global futures, both of them negative: (1) the McDonaldization or interdependence of the world, and (2) a **"jihad"** or (struggle) in the name of a hundred narrowly conceived faiths against every kind of interdependence, every kind of artificial social cooperation and civic mutuality.[1] Barber's view of a jihad is essentially synonymous with ethnic conflicts. Another perspective, best articulated by Samuel P. Huntington, is that the world is divided into distinct civilizations that inevitably clash.[2]

This chapter examines the role of culture in global conflicts, focusing on civilization clashes, international conflicts, and ethnic conflicts. Dividing the world into

Jihad

Arabic word symbolizing a religiously based inner struggle between "good" and "evil" that exists within all people

Hybridization

Stresses cultural mixing due to increasing globalization

distinct and mutually exclusive civilizations and races is deeply rooted in the academic world, which facilitates a general acceptance of the clash-of-civilizations perspective. The **hybridization** theory emphasizes cultural mixing due to complex global interdependence. Jan Nederveen Pieterse argues that "hybridization has been taking place all along but has been concealed by religious, national, imperial, and civilization chauvinisms."[3] Think about the most violent conflicts in recent history. Most of these clashes have occurred among countries belonging to the same civilizations. In fact, many wars have been civil wars. The conflict in Iraq in 2006 between Sunnis and Shiites represented the larger and growing conflict within Islam. Sharp distinctions between religions, especially Islam on the one hand and Christianity and Judaism on the other, are stressed by proponents of the **clash-of-civilizations theory.** This view holds that civilizations are separate and distinct—like billiard balls and that conflicts between them are almost inevitable. The rise of Islamic fundamentalism and terrorism by Islamic groups, such as al-Qaeda, are marshaled to buttress this view. Pope Benedict's quotation in 2006 of a 14th century scholar who linked Islam to violence reinforced perceptions of clashing civilizations. However, these three monotheistic religions are closely related.[4]

Cultural influences on international conflicts are generally analyzed as one component of a complex set of factors that motivate countries to go to war.[5] This approach takes into consideration the influence of culture on perceptions and how perceptions provide a foundation and motivation for action, including the use of force. Perceptions of cultural proximity and similarity generally diminish the tendency to resort to military means to settle disputes. Conversely, perceptions of cultural distance and differences enhance the likelihood of conflict among nations when significant interests are at stake. Cultural differences are also used to justify inaction in the face of serious problems when major national interests are not involved. American policy toward the Palestinian-Israeli conflict and America's failure to respond forcefully to prevent genocide in Rwanda illustrate these two different approaches.

Ethnic Conflicts

Generally understood as violent clashes between or among groups within a particular country

The end of the Cold War brought a renewed focus on **ethnic conflicts,** generally understood as violent clashes between or among groups within a particular country. As we mentioned earlier, while some analysts view clashes between civilizations as the dominant feature of global politics, others see increased fragmentation of the world into violent ethnic groups. Both perspectives share the common assumption that world conflicts are fueled by ancient hatreds and irreconcilable cultural differences. Another assumption is that ethnic identities motivate people to persecute and kill. A third assumption is that ethnic diversity, enhanced by globalization, inevitably leads to ethnic conflicts.[6]

CULTURAL INFLUENCES ON CONFLICTS

Culture and nationalism have generally been closely intertwined. In fact, culture has been synonymous with nations, races, and ethnic groups. Nations have traditionally been defined in terms of their common identity, values, customs, languages, and geographic boundaries. How nations and nonstate actors, such as ethnic groups, interact and resolve disagreements is determined largely by the cultural reservoirs created among them, or the lack of them. A **cultural reservoir** may be defined as an accumulation of goodwill and understanding that emanates from a common set of values, beliefs, attitudes, historical experiences, and racial and ethnic links. Similarities are augmented by international exchanges, military alliances, interpersonal connections, and economic interdependence. When disputes between countries or ethnic groups occur, cultural reservoirs, or the lack of them, play a pivotal role in how differences are resolved. Leaders usually draw upon cultural similarities to diminish tensions and, conversely, on cultural differences and hatreds to promote conflict. Cultural reservoirs strengthen the perception that friendly relations between culturally similar countries or groups are the norm, and that a particular disagreement is a deviation from an otherwise peaceful and amicable relationship. On the other hand, absence of strong cultural links and of significant economic interaction between states often facilitates indifference or hostility.[7] Yet culturally similar countries have clashed militarily and culturally distant countries have been allies when significant interests were perceived to be at stake. For example, Russia cooperated with the United States during the Napoleonic Wars in an effort to keep an emerging America from formally joining France, and again during both World Wars. On the other hand, Britain and the United States fought each other in the American Revolution and in the War of 1812, with Russia acting as a mediator in the latter.[8]

Anthropologists, sociologists, and political scientists define culture in different ways. A distinction can be made between **material culture** (i.e., the tangible products of human society) and **nonmaterial culture** (i.e., the intangible products of society, such as value, and rules of right and wrong behavior). Nonmaterial culture is the learned ideational aspects of human society.[9] In most countries, culture is generally equated with civilization. The clash-of-civilizations theory adopts this definition of culture. **Culture** is generally defined as a set of shared learned values, beliefs, perceptions, attitudes, modes of living, customs, and symbols. According to Clifford Geertz, "The concept of culture denotes an historically transmitted pattern of meanings embodied in symbols, a system of inherited conception expressed in symbolic form by means of which men communicate, perpetuate, and develop their knowledge about and attitudes toward life."[10] The concept of culture is understood in a **pluralist sense** as differentiation within a collectivity. Subcultures are the bedrock of a pluralist view of culture. A **subculture** "is the way of defining and honoring the particular specification and demarcation of different interests of a group of people within a larger collectivity."[11] Emile Durkheim, in ***Division of Labor***, articulated the view that as societies become more complex, cultural consensus is weakened. Divergent attitudes and values develop, and beliefs and attitudes are modified in ways that are significantly different from those prescribed or proscribed by the collective conscience or a strongly defined moral consensus.[12]

One of the first questions we tend to ask someone who appears to be different is: Where are you from? This question, though routine, goes to the heart of identity and belonging. Do you belong to this society? Are you foreign? All societies, directly and indirectly, promote their values as positive and desirable while, simultaneously, devaluing those of other societies. This behavior is referred to as **ethnocentrism.** Positive images

Cultural Reservoir

An accumulation of goodwill and understanding that emanates from a common set of values, beliefs, attitudes, experiences, and racial and ethnic links

Material Culture

Tangible products of human society

Nonmaterial Culture

Intangible products of society, such as values and rules of right and wrong behavior

Culture

A set of shared learned values, beliefs, perceptions, attitudes, modes of living, customs, and symbols

Subculture

A subgroup that exists within a larger cultural group

Ethnocentrism

Practice of societies promoting their values as positive and desirable while simultaneously devaluing those of other societies

of one's society are developed and reinforced by rewards for conformity. Ken Booth for example, contends that each society views itself as the center of the world, perceives and interprets other societies within its peculiar frame of reference, and invariably judges them to be inferior.[13] The more culturally distinct the other society is perceived to be, the more inferior it is often deemed to be, and thus suitable to be treated negatively.

Cultural beliefs, attitudes, and values of ordinary people help to shape decisions to engage in conflicts, the objectives of conflicts, how wars are fought, how they are terminated, and postconflict relations among combatants. Leaders often tap into their cultures to find ways to dehumanize and demonize those designated as enemies. The greater the distance between cultures in conflict, the easier it is for leaders to mobilize public support for war and to dehumanize others. **Dehumanization** of others is designed not only to destroy their humanity, but also to reassure those who dehumanize of their own presumed goodness. Dehumanization facilitates justification of the inhumane treatment of those regarded as enemies by diminishing empathetic faculties.[14] **Empathy**, viewed as the emotional cornerstone of moral judgment, enables us to feel with other human beings, to cognitively and effectively put ourselves in their place, and to become more aware of others' needs and concerns.[15] Personalizing the injurious effects experienced by others makes their suffering much more noticeable and troubling. It is therefore difficult to kill people we do not dehumanize without risking personal distress and self-censure.[16] Dehumanization is closely related to **moral exclusion**, a practice that is intertwined with cultural values. Those who are morally excluded are perceived as being outside the boundary within which moral values, rules, and considerations of fairness apply. Because those who are morally excluded are regarded as expendable, subhuman, threatening, and undeserving, harming them often appears acceptable, appropriate, and just.[17] We will frame our discussion at three levels of analysis: civilizations, nations, and ethnic groups, bearing in mind the interdependence of these levels in an age of globalization.

CLASHING CIVILIZATIONS

According to the clash-of-civilizations perspective, global conflicts occur due to cultural differences. Although nation-states will continue to be the most powerful actors in global affairs, civilizations will be the dividing lines. A civilization is broadly defined as a cultural entity that, despite variations within it, is distinct from another civilization. For example, despite differences between Spain and Britain, they belong to the same Western civilization and are distinguished from Arab or Chinese civilizations. Huntington states that "a civilization is the highest cultural grouping of people and the broadest level of cultural identity people have short of that which distinguished humans from other species. It is defined by common objective elements, such as language, history, religion, customs, institutions, and by the subjective self-identification of people.[18] From Huntington's perspective, *there are seven or eight major civilizations:* Western, Confucian, Japanese, Islamic, Hindu, Slavic-Orthodox, Latin American, and African.[19] The clash-of-civilizations theory stresses conflict instead of cooperation among civilizations. Huntington gives *six reasons why conflicts occur along the cultural fault lines* that separate civilizations:

1. People from different civilizations hold fundamentally divergent views on relations between God and man, the individual and the group, liberty and authority, and so on.
2. As globalization contributes to shrinking time and distance, increasing interactions among people from various civilizations highlight differences among them and intensify civilization consciousness.
3. Globalization weakens the nation-state as a source of identity and separates people from their cultural moorings. Religion, mostly fundamentalist in nature, has moved in to fill the gap. Religion serves as a basis for identity and commitment that transcends national boundaries.
4. Civilization–consciousness is enhanced by the power of the West, which is accompanied by a return to the past in other parts of the world.
5. Cultural differences are less mutable and less easily compromised than political and economic differences.
6. Economic regionalization is reinforcing civilization-consciousness.[20]

Many scholars have criticized the clash-of-civilizations perspective. For example, Fouad Ajami argues that "Huntington has found his civilization whole and intact, watertight under an eternal sky. Buried alive, as it were, during the Cold War, these civilizations rose as soon as the stone was rolled off, dusted themselves off, and proceeded to claim the loyalty of their adherents."[21] Similarly, Stanley Hoffmann criticized Huntington's concept of what constitutes a civilization as being hazy. From Hoffmann's perspective, Huntington "failed to take into account sufficiently conflicts within each so-called civilization, and he overestimated the importance of religion in the behavior of non-Western elites, who are often secularized and westernized. Hence he could not clearly define the link between a civilization and the foreign policies of its member states."[22] Civilizational bonds have not restrained countries from competing with each other for power. Furthermore, civilizations are products of cultural cross-fertilization. Their members are complex,

---

You DECIDE | **Clashing Civilizations**

Cultural influences have undoubtedly played a significant role in many conflicts. Samuel P. Huntington believes that globalization contributes to the emergence of increased tensions among civilizations. On the other hand, many scholars have argued that globalization lessens differences and promotes greater cooperation among nations, nonstate actors, and individuals.

In your view, which of these two future scenarios is likely to dominate? Why?

Hispanic Muslims mark the end of Ramadan.

and the lines separating civilizations are often blurred and messy. For example, music by Haydn, Mozart, and Beethoven have Turkish origins. The Ottomans used giant war drums and cannons to frighten their enemies on the battlefield and to terrify the population in places like Vienna, Austria. Eventually, West Europeans adopted many Turkish cultural practices, including its military music for its marching bands. Haydn wrote his *Military Symphony* and Mozart composed the piano sonata *Rondo Alla Turea* under the influence of Turkish music.[23]

Religion, a foundation of civilizations, is regarded by Huntington as essentially pure and unaffected by other religions. The mixing of religions is as old as human civilization. As Susanne Rudolph observes, "Religious communities are among the oldest of the transnationals. Sufi orders, Catholic missionaries, and Buddhist monks carried word and practice across vast spaces before those places became nation-states. Religious communities have become vigorous creators of an emergent transnational civil society."[24] The forces of globalization are contributing to the spread of religions across national and civilizational boundaries. As you look around any major metropolitan area, you will see Protestant and Catholic churches, Muslim mosques, Hindu temples, Sikhguru-dwaras, Jewish synagogues, and Buddhist temples. More than 60 percent of Christians are found in Africa, Asia, and Latin America. The Republic of Korea has four times as many Presbyterians as America. While Christianity is growing rapidly in China, it is shrinking in Europe. Missionaries from Africa reinvigorate Christianity in the United States. Muslims, including some Latin American immigrants, are an integral component of American culture and society.

The West and the Muslim World

Dhimmis

People of the Book who believe in the God of Abraham

At the heart of the theory of the inevitability of cultural clashes between the West and the Muslim world is the assumption that the two civilizations are inherently incompatible and hostile. But Western perceptions of Islam, like perceptions in general, are rooted in selective historical memories. Cooperation and similarities between these cultures are overlooked or downplayed while historical conflicts are stressed. Despite the Muslim conquest of part of Spain in the eighth century, Muslims were largely tolerant of Jews and Christians, regarding them as **Dhimmis**, (i.e., people of the Book who also believed in one God, the God of Abraham). The advent of the Crusades in 1096 aided the foundation for the clashes between the West and Islam. The Crusades became a potent experience that continues to influence many Muslims' perceptions of the West and their own self-perceptions. The Crusaders' brutality symbolized Western hatred not only of Muslims but also of Islam.

A small number of European Christians had regularly made pilgrimages to the Holy Land (then Palestine) since the fourth century without encountering systematic or widespread violence. However, in 1009 the Egyptian **caliph** (religious ruler) **Hakim** ordered the destruction of the **Holy Sepulcher** in Jerusalem (where Christians believed that Jesus was buried). This action engendered increased conflicts between Christian pilgrims and Muslims in Syria and Palestine. Hoping to unite European Christians, who were engaged in incessant feudal warfare against each other, and to terminate attacks on pilgrims, **Pope Urban II** (in 1095) called on European Christians to proclaim their faith by taking military action to force the infidels (primarily Muslims) out of Jerusalem. The First Crusade (1096–1099) represented unprecedented European cooperation as well as Europe's emergence from the Dark Ages. There were nine Crusades. The final Crusade (1271–1272) was followed by the Muslim reconquest of the last Christian stronghold in the Islamic world in 1291. Armstrong states, "The Christianity of the Angles, the Saxons, and the Franks was rudimentary. They were aggressive and martial people and they wanted an aggressive religion."[25] Crusaders, believing that Jews had killed Christ, slaughtered Jews in communities along the Rhine Valley and elsewhere on their 3,000-mile journey to fight Muslims, about whom they were largely unaware. Believing that they were "God's Chosen People," the Crusaders were unrestrained in their cruelty. When they conquered Jerusalem in 1099, "they fell on the Jewish and Muslim inhabitants with the zeal of Joshua and massacred them with a brutality that shocked even their contemporaries."[26] The ability of the less culturally sophisticated European Christians to plunder and defile Islam's holy sites, including the **Dome of the Rock** in Jerusalem, has been interpreted by many Muslims as a consequence of their religious shortcomings. Contemporary Muslim grievances are often linked to the Crusades. Believing that Islam continues to be attacked by the West, many Muslims feel an obligation to engage in jihad (or holy war) against unbelievers. The establishment of the state of Israel in 1948 and the Palestinian-Israeli conflict combine to reignite clashes between the West and Islam.

Pope Urban II
Initiated the Crusades

Dome of the Rock
One of Islam's holy sites in Jerusalem

The Palestinian-Israeli Conflict

The Palestinian-Israeli conflict is rooted in rampant anti-Semitism throughout most of Europe, culminating in the Holocaust in Nazi Germany. But Jewish interest in a homeland cannot be divorced from the destruction of Jerusalem by the Romans and the exile of the Jewish people. The tragedy of European Jews led ultimately to the Palestinian tragedy. In a very real sense, both Jews and Palestinians became victims of Hitler's hatred of the Jews. Contrary to popular assumptions, the Palestinian-Israeli problem and the wider Arab-Israeli conflict are not rooted in ancient hatreds between Jews and Muslims, as is evident from our discussion of the Moors in Spain and the Crusades. Circumstances in Europe influenced the emergence of Zionism and **Theodor Herzl's** determination to establish a Jewish state. Arab revolts against the Ottoman Empire in 1916, the capture of Jerusalem by the British from the Turks in 1917, and subsequent British control over Palestine under the League of Nations mandate system paved the way for establishing a

Theodor Herzl
Early Zionist proponent of the creation of a Jewish homeland and state

Jewish homeland in Palestine. As a **Class A mandate**, Palestine was technically an independent state under British supervision. The United States played a minor role in the critical events that became the roots of the Palestinian-Israeli conflict. U.S. President Woodrow Wilson endorsed the Balfour Declaration, issued by British Foreign Secretary Lord Balfour in 1917 in a letter to Lord Rothschild, an advocate of a Jewish homeland. The **Balfour Declaration** called for a Jewish homeland in Palestine that would not replace the Palestinian state. But British actions as well as clarifications of the Balfour Declaration added to confusion and angst among both Arabs and Jews. The **Churchill White Paper**, issued by Britain's Prime Minister Winston Churchill to clarify the Balfour Declaration, reaffirmed that Palestine was not to be converted into a "Jewish National Home." It further emphasized that the British government would not contemplate the disappearance or subordination of the Arab population, language, or culture in Palestine.[27] Compounding the misunderstanding and feelings of betrayal among Arabs was the rapidly increasing Jewish immigration to Palestine between 1922 and 1939, due to horrifying events in Nazi Germany and many countries' refusal to admit Jewish refugees from the impending Holocaust.

Frustrated by their inability to move the British more decisively toward establishing a Jewish state in Palestine, Zionists shifted their lobbying efforts to the United States. They organized the **Biltmore Conference** in New York in May 1942 to articulate their objectives and to pressure the United States to persuade Britain to act in their favor. But strategic considerations during the war forced U.S. President Franklin Delano Roosevelt to balance his sympathies toward Zionist aspirations against Allied military strategy. With German forces in North Africa and the eastern Mediterranean, the United States concluded that Arab support was essential to defending the Middle East.[28] American and Soviet opposition to British imperial designs in the Middle East led to a tacit alliance between Washington and Moscow in favor of the Jews at the end of World War II. Weakened by war and a terrorist campaign by the Irgun and other groups, Britain became more vulnerable to

Balfour Declaration

British statement calling for a Jewish homeland in Palestine

Churchill White Paper

Stated that the British were committed to Palestinian and Jewish coexistence in Palestine

Biltmore Conference

Zionist lobbying effort to pressure the United States to persuade Britain to act in favor of a Jewish homeland in Palestine

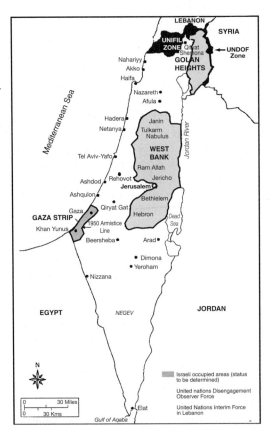

FIGURE 12.1 Israel and the Palestinian Territories

American pressure. Britain relinquished control of Palestine, turning over the Palestinian problem to the fledgling United Nations. While the United States supported the UN vote on the creation of Israel and recognized the new state literally minutes after it came into existence on May 14, 1948, Britain abstained on the UN vote and did not recognize Israel until a year later. Attempting to maintain Arab support, the United States embargoed arms sales to the Middle East in 1947 and did not play a major role in the first Arab-Israeli war of 1948–1949.[29]

Many of Israel's policies directly conflicted with America's new global responsibilities, including its efforts to prevent Communist expansion into the oil-rich and strategically important Middle East. Alienating the Arab states was contrary to America's strategy of **containment**, a policy of establishing a strategic alliance between NATO and Middle Eastern countries to frustrate Soviet ambitions in the region. Consequently, the United States opposed the attack by Israel, Britain, and France on Egypt in 1956. By the **Six-Day War** in 1967, however, the United States had moved away from its position of impartial friendship and neutrality in the Arab-Israeli conflict to overt support for Israel. The 1967 war resulted in the defeat of the Arab armies and Israel's occupation of Palestinian, Syrian, and Egyptian territories. The city of Jerusalem and other holy places of great significance to Jews, Muslims, and Christians came under Israel's control. When Egypt and Syria launched a surprise attack against Israel on Yom Kippur in 1973, the United States responded by organizing a massive airlift of military supplies to Israel and by engaging in unprecedented diplomatic efforts to end hostilities. The Arabs responded with an oil embargo against Israel's supporters, including the United States.[30] By 1979, the United States, led by President Jimmy Carter, had managed to persuade Egypt and Israel to sign the **Camp David Peace Accords**, which ended hostilities between the two countries, returned Egyptian territory, and promised Palestinian autonomy by May 26, 1980. Despite much effort to reach a negotiated settlement of the Palestinian-Israeli conflict, violence escalated. In 1987, the Palestinians launched an **intifada** (i.e., uprising) to improve their living conditions and gain a homeland.

Following the first Gulf War in 1991, President George H. W. Bush initiated a peace conference on the Palestinian-Israeli conflict that culminated in the Oslo Accord in 1993. This agreement called for Israel's gradual withdrawal from Palestinian territory in the West Bank and Gaza. Failure of the Oslo peace process was accompanied by violence throughout the 1990s, a development that influenced President Bill Clinton to persuade Ehud Barak (Israel's prime minister) and Yasser Arafat (head of the Palestine Liberation Organization and chairman of the Palestinian Authority) to attempt to resolve all of the major issues in the conflict at Camp David in 2000. This failed endeavor eventually contributed to the outbreak of a second intifada between 2000 and 2005, during which more than 3,000 Palestinians and 1,000 Israelis were killed. This upsurge in violence was also characterized by the widespread use of suicide bombers against Israelis by Hamas and other Palestinian groups as well as by increased Israeli military action against Palestinians, targeted assassinations of Palestinian militants, intensification of economic hardships for Palestinians, expansion of Jewish settlements in the West Bank and Gaza, and the construction of a barrier or wall that balkanized

Containment
U.S. policy of establishing strategic alliances with other countries in order to contain Soviet ambitions throughout the world

Camp David Peace Accords
1979 peace agreement between Egypt and Israel

Intifada
Palestinian uprising against Israeli occupation of the West Bank and the Gaza Strip

International conflicts that are influenced by cultural differences and divergent national interests are also prevalent in Asia. China's rapid economic expansion and growing U.S. dependence on imports from China have engendered both cooperation and conflict between the two countries. China is widely perceived as a rising power that will eventually compete with America for global hegemony. Its strong economy attracts advanced technology from around the world, which enables it to improve its military capabilities. Japan's historical rivalry with China is reinvigorated by Japan's economic problems and the transfer of some of its manufacturing industries to China. Nationalism in both China and Japan is resurging, even as economic cooperation between them strengthens. North Korea's decision to test a nuclear device in 2006 further reinforced Japan's nationalism and security concerns.

ETHNIC CONFLICTS

Horrific bloodshed in Rwanda, Bosnia, Sudan, Iraq, Chechnya, and elsewhere is widely publicized by the global media. The proliferation of humanitarian organizations and other nonstate actors has also helped to make the world more aware of ethnic conflicts. As our discussion of global terrorism in Chapter 5 demonstrates, European countries, such as Spain, are challenged by violent groups that claim separate ethnic identities. In fact, as Europe moves toward greater unification, minority groups—such as Catalans, Basques, Corsicans, Scots, and Flemish—are seeking more autonomy. However, most of these ethnic or nationalist groups are not violent.[44] Although the brutality and intractability of many ethnic conflicts tend to reinforce perceptions of escalating ethnic wars, there has actually been a decline in their number. Ted Robert Gurr identifies *four regional and global forces that help to explain the decline in the number of ethnic wars:*

1. The active promotion of democratic institutions and practices that protect minority rights.
2. Engagement by the UN, regional organizations, and nongovernmental organizations (NGOs) on behalf of minority rights.
3. The virtual consensus among the global foreign policy elite in favor of reestablishing and maintaining global and regional order.
4. The costs of ethnic conflicts, which have become evident to both governing elites and rebel leaders.[45]

While globalization contributes to cultural clashes, it also restrains them. Ethnic conflicts are much less pervasive or durable in areas that are integrated into the global economy than they are in countries that are relatively unaffected by global interdependence or regional integration.

Tribalism

Groups of indigenous people in Africa, Asia, Latin America, and North America

Ethnicity and Ethnic Identity

Tribalism, ethnicity, and ethnic nationalism are terms that are often used interchangeably. **Tribalism** is usually regarded as an anachronistic term that refers to groups of indigenous people. Most scholars prefer to refer to these groups as ethnic groups.

Sometimes ethnic groups are across the artificially created boundaries of several countries. Ethnic groups within states as well as those that straddle national boundaries may aspire to create their own country. To achieve this, they develop a strong sense of nationalism. For example, the **Kurds,** an ethnic group that has nationalistic aspirations, are scattered among Turkey, Iraq, Iran, Syria, and parts of the former Soviet Union. Most ethnic groups attempt to achieve more political and cultural autonomy within the boundaries of existing states.

Kurds

An ethnic group residing in Turkey, Iraq, Iran, and Syria

An **ethnic group** is composed of individuals who generally have a sense of common identity based on a common set of historical experiences, national sentiments, religious beliefs, geographic location, language and culture, and, in countries such as the United States, largely arbitrary racial categories. **Ethnicity** is a subjective perception of who belongs to a particular group. Ethnicity serves as a rallying point for mobilizing ethnic group members to compete for economic resources, positions in government and social and economic organizations, and social and religious status.[46] An essential component of ethnicity is a strong sense of identity. **Identity** may be defined as a concept of the self, a selection of physical, psychological, emotional, or social attributes of particular individuals.[47] Identity provides a framework within which people construct reality and determine their positions on a wide range of issues. Members of different ethnic groups are predisposed to hold certain stereotypes about each other and to act on the basis of these assumptions.

Ethnicity

A subjective perception of who belongs to a particular ethnic group

Identity

A concept of oneself based on physical, psychological, emotional, or social attributes

Identity is generally about drawing sharp distinctions among groups and building boundaries that separate one group from another. It contributes to developing a feeling of us versus them, insiders versus outsiders. We treat members of our own group differently from members of another group. **Discrimination** on the basis of ethnic identity is a common problem worldwide. Instead of seeing discrimination as being inherently wrong and unfair, discrimination becomes the norm. **Ethnic pluralism**, (i.e., ethnic diversity) is the presence of many different groups within a specific geographic boundary. *Several factors contribute to ethnic pluralism.* These include

Ethnic Pluralism

Also known as ethnic diversity

1. Conquest and annexation;
2. The decision by colonial powers to put different ethnic groups together in newly created countries;
3. The deliberate attempts by colonizers and others to divide people in order to control them; and
4. Migration.[48]

The Causes of Ethnic Conflict

Although conflicts between ethnic groups are often perceived as the result of "ancient hatreds," most ethnic conflicts are very complex and have little to do with ancient animosities. In all societies, generational change and economic and social developments generally modify ancient hatreds. Contemporary ethnic conflicts have more immediate causes. Although the Scots and the English fought each other for centuries, these ancient hatreds do not influence them to fight today. *Most ethnic wars occur in poor countries that have weak political institutions.* Paul Collier has found that once a country achieves a per capita income similar to those of rich countries, its risk of ethnic conflict is negligible. The potential for conflict is concentrated in the poorest countries with declining economies and a heavy reliance on natural resources for a large share of national income.[49] Think about the countries that suffer from perennial ethnic wars. These include Sudan, Angola, Rwanda, Sierra Leone, Afghanistan, and Turkey. While many rich countries experience ethnic tensions, these problems generally do not erupt into sustained or widespread violence.

Another cause of ethnic conflict is *the deliberate manipulation of negative perceptions* by leaders to mobilize group support for their own individual political, economic, and social objectives. Leaders rely on the emotional intensity and loyalty of ethnic group members. They know that distrust can be instrumental in fueling fears, and that fears usually override logical, objective thinking. Consequently, despite misgivings individuals may have about engaging in or condoning violence against another group, these fears and an emotional commitment to their own group generally influence ethnic group members to follow their leaders. The most terrifying example is the violence in Rwanda that claimed as many as 800,000 lives in 1994. Hutus killed more than three-fourths of Rwanda's Tutsi population because Hutu political leaders incited fear and hatred among the Hutus in order to remain in power.

Competition among groups for scarce economic resources is a major cause of ethnic violence. Growing economic disparities, resulting from economic development, may increase the fears and insecurities of those ethnic groups that are disadvantaged. On the other hand, ethnic conflict may emanate from attempts by an ethnic group to monopolize scarce resources. In Nigeria, for example, the **Ibos** fought to create a separate country (called Biafra) partly because of their experience with violence and discrimination and because they did not want to share their wealth from petroleum found in their region of the country. The discovery of oil in the Sudan has contributed to humanitarian crisis in Darfur and the inability of the global community to prevent the deaths of roughly 200,000 people and the displacement of more than two million. Even prosperous groups sometimes feel insecure because the same forces of modernization that enrich them also make them vulnerable. Their status could deteriorate in a volatile global economic environment. Ethnic Chinese in Indonesia and elsewhere in Southeast Asia are often victims of ethnic conflicts due primarily to their economic success.

Cultural globalization, evidenced by the Westernization of architecture, the proliferation of fast-food restaurants, the influx of consumer items, automobiles, television, movies, books, and magazines, and increased access to computers and telecommunications threaten ethnic groups' perception of the uniqueness and purity of their culture.[50] These forces of globalization help to destroy boundaries essential to ethnic group solidarity and identity. Many leaders' power is threatened, a development that often influences them to promote ethnic identity more zealously. *Weak political institutions* contribute to ethnic conflicts, especially when countries are experiencing economic transformation. The inabilities of political institutions to effectively regulate change and provide mechanisms through which differences can be managed frequently contribute to ethnic violence.

Ibos

Ethnic group in Nigeria that tried to create a separate state (called Biafra)

Systematic and widespread frustration of human needs may culminate in outbreaks of ethnic violence. Tensions are heightened by perceptions of favoritism toward other groups, compared with disadvantages suffered by the particular ethnic group. Ethnic group members are mobilized to articulate their grievances and to seek solutions to them.[51] In many cases, violence is seen as the most effective instrument to get the government to respond favorably to their demands. This, in turn, influences the government to respond with violence against the ethnic group. Finally *the proliferation of automatic weapons*, especially AK–47s, is a significant contributor to ethnic conflicts around the world. While it may be argued that these weapons do not cause conflict, their availability increases the potential for deadly clashes among ethnic groups or the use of violence by ethnic groups against governments.

Although ethnic violence is clearly more prevalent in poor countries, developed countries are also experiencing ethnic tensions and renewed ethnic nationalism. Since the end of the Cold War and the fall of the Berlin Wall, there has been a resurgence of anti-Semitism in Europe, especially in France. Mark Strauss states that "not since **Kristallnacht**, the Nazi-led pogrom [violent campaign] against German Jews in 1938, have so many European synagogues and Jewish schools been desecrated."[52] One of the oldest hatreds in Europe, anti-Semitism is strongest in **Alsace**, France, a region that has strong cultural ties to Germany. This traditionally German-speaking area was annexed by Germany in 1871, following the Franco-Prussian War, and remained under German control until the French conquered it in World War I. Alsace became a Nazi stronghold in the 1930s, and many Alsatians joined the Nationalist Socialist Party (Nazi Party) when Alsace was annexed by Adolf Hitler in 1940. The worst German atrocity in France against the Jews was the massacre at Oradour in Alsace in 1944. This historical affiliation with Nazism was rekindled by the rise of the **National Front**, an extremely conservative political movement led by Jean-Marie Le Pen. Both Jews and Muslims are targets of violence. There was a surge in 2004 in the number of Jewish and Muslim holy places, including tombstones, desecrated by neo-Nazis.[53]

The growing number of Muslims in countries across Europe is perceived as a threat to cultural institutions. This perception of threat escalated with the rise of Islamic terrorism and the terrorist attacks on the United States, Spain, and Britain between 2001 and 2006. But Germany, Austria, France, Britain, Spain, Italy, and other countries have been concerned about demographic changes brought about largely by Muslim immigrants. While many Europeans define their cultures in terms of Christianity, Muslims are making Islam a part of European culture. Religious symbols, especially the Muslim headscarf, have been politicized. France, stressing separation of church and state, has been the most aggressive European country in terms of banning headscarves in public schools. Most Muslim girls complied with the law banning scarves, which went into effect in September 2004. And when kidnappers in Iraq threatened to kill two French hostages if France did not revoke the ban, most French Muslims, who opposed the law, supported France's refusal to change its laws to appease terrorists.

Canada and the United States, two of the world's most ethnically diverse countries, have managed to reduce ethnic violence by bringing various ethnic minorities

Kristallnacht

Nazi-led pogrom against German Jews

National Front

Conservative French political movement led by Jean-Marie Le Pen

Desecration of Jewish tombstones.

into the democratic process and by outlawing discrimination. Canada was confronted with separatist movements in Quebec until recently. Quebec, colonized and settled by the French, was conquered by the British in 1759. The **Treaty of Paris** in 1763 officially transferred Quebec from France to Britain, making it part of British Canada. Many people in Quebec maintained close ties with France and nurtured French culture and language. Generational change, economic interdependence, political reforms, and increased immigration to Quebec combined to lessen nationalistic aspirations.[54] However, the growing numbers of Muslims in Canada, as well as that country's strong commitment to multiculturalism, have created new ethnic tensions. Autonomy granted to various Native American groups has inspired other ethnic groups to seek more cultural autonomy. Muslims, for example, point to Jews and their ability to use Jewish laws to govern their communities and argue that **Shari'a law** (Islamic law) should govern Muslim communities.

The fall of communism and the disintegration of the Soviet Union rekindled ethnic conflicts in Eastern Europe, Central Asia, the Balkans, and elsewhere. Ethnic conflicts in the former Yugoslavia produced widespread military confrontation in which ethnic identity literally became a matter of life and death. These conflicts also underscored how cultural links with various countries influenced both military actions and efforts to terminate the bloodshed. **The Croats** have been historically the most thoroughly integrated into European civilization, largely as a consequence of their domination by Austria-Hungary and Venice. **Serbs** identify with Eastern Orthodox countries, such as Greece and Russia; and the **Muslims**, though they are also

Treaty of Paris

Transferred Quebec from France to Britain in 1763

Shari'a Law

Islamic law used to govern Muslim communities

Europeans and Slavic, are regarded as remnants of the Ottoman Empire and identify with Turkey and other Islamic countries. Composed of six republics—Bosnia-Hercegovina, Croatia, Macedonia, Montenegro, Serbia, and Slovenia—and the two provinces of Kosovo and Vojvodina, Yugoslavia was an artificial nation-state held together by **Marshall Josip Tito's** domineering personality and the League of Communists of Yugoslavia (LCY) until Tito's death in 1980 and the fall of communism in the late 1980s. As Yugoslavia's disintegration became obvious, the Republic of Serbia intensified its efforts to arrest Yugoslavia's fragmentation and to continue Serbia's dominance. Bosnia's Serbs, led by **Radovan Karadzic**, favored increased centralization, while the Muslims and Croats opted for a loose confederation. Acting on their fears of each other and remembered historical experiences, Croats and Serbs began to dismember Bosnia. Muslims, aware that Bosnia had been divided between Croatia and Serbia prior to World War II, resisted reabsorption into those states.[55] Serbia clearly intended to use its superior military might to fashion Greater Serbia out of Croatia and Bosnia. **Slobodan Milosevic**, president of Yugoslavia (who was later tried for war crimes at the International Criminal Court at the Hague), boasted that the Serbs were on the threshold of "the final solution."[56] Milosevic died in prison in 2006.

Although Muslims and Croats engaged in their own campaigns of **ethnic cleansing**, the Serbs were primarily responsible for genocide, and Muslims were the principal victims. After depriving Muslims of their jobs and property, the Serbs began to destroy their villages and cities, and forced them to leave, thereby creating the greatest refugee crisis in Europe since World War II. Many refugees were shipped out of northern Bosnia in sealed freight trains, a practice reminiscent of Nazi Germany's treatment of the Jews. Atrocities included the massacre of villagers; the torture, rape, and killing of prisoners; the use of Muslims as human shields; and the taking of hostages. Many civilians, imprisoned in forty-five concentration camps, were executed. Serbian gunmen raped more than 50,000 Muslim women and children as

Marshall Josip Tito
Communist leader who ruled Yugoslavia until his death in 1980

Radovan Karadzic
Bosnian leader who favored continued Serbian dominance of Yugoslavia

Slobodan Milosevic
President of Yugoslavia who was tried for war crimes at the International Criminal Court

Ethnic Cleansing
Mass forced relocation or expulsion of one ethnic or religious group by another ethnic or religious group

---

You
DECIDE | ### Hispanic Challenges to America

Many Americans, concerned about growing public acceptance of multiculturalism and diversity, believe that the influx of Hispanics will create ethnic tensions and undermine American culture and national identity. Samuel P. Huntington, a Harvard University political scientist, argues that Mexican immigrants could divide the United States into a country of two languages and two cultures. They pose an unusual threat because they, unlike any other group, assert a claim to U.S. territory. Almost all of Texas, New Mexico, Arizona, California, Nevada, and Utah were Mexican territory conquered by the United States in 1835–1836 (the Texas War of Independence) and in 1846–1848 (the Mexican-American War). These areas have large numbers of Hispanic immigrants.

Will Hispanic immigration contribute to ethnic conflicts in the United States?

Source: Samuel P. Huntington, "The Hispanic Challenge," *Foreign Policy* 141 (March/April 2004), 32–36.

part of their program of ethnic cleansing. Echoing Nazi Germany's plan to extermi-
nate the Jews and eliminate all traces of Jewish culture, Serb nationalists attempted to
destroy the Muslims' culture. Mosques, central to Muslims' identity and society, were
principal targets. Historical monuments and libraries that were depositories for more
than five centuries of Muslim culture were reduced to rubble.[57]

Ethnic conflicts in Rwanda also demonstrate how ethnic differences are socially
constructed and how deadly the consequences of policies exaggerating and emphasizing small differences can be. Genocide in Rwanda and genocide in Sudan illustrate
that the decline in the number of ethnic conflicts globally is largely irrelevant to
Africa, the continent most marginalized from globalization. As we discussed earlier,
the world's poorest countries, most of which are in Africa, are the most vulnerable to
prolonged and widespread ethnic violence. Africa also has a very large number of ethnic groups, many of which live together in artificially created countries. When the
Germans conquered what is now Rwanda in 1899, they encountered two main groups:
the **Hutus**, who the comprised the majority of the population, and the **Tutsis**, a small
group of cattle herders who ruled the area. Many smaller groups spoke the same language and shared the same culture. Years of intermarriage made it difficult to neatly
separate them into distinct ethnic groups.[58] The Germans relied primarily on the ruling Tutsis to help them control the territory. They designated the Tutsis as the superior group, a perception reinforced by the Belgians who gained control of Rwanda in
1916, following Germany's defeat in World War I. Germany's and Turkey's colonies
became mandates under the League of Nations. Finding it difficult to distinguish
Hutus from Tutsis, the Belgians issued mandatory identity cards to all Rwandans,
placing each person into a fixed ethnic category. Eventually the Tutsi, who received
preferential treatment from the Belgians, believed that they were indeed superior to
the Hutus.[59] However, Belgian missionaries, believing in equality and social progress,
helped disadvantaged Hutus obtain an education. Educated Hutus, facing discrimination, challenged the system that gave Tutsis significant advantages and advocated ethnic separation. In 1959, the Hutus rebelled and killed more than 20,000 Tutsis. When
Rwanda became independent in 1962, the Hutu majority gained political control.

Ethnic rivalries escalated in 1990 when the Hutus's power was challenged by the
Rwanda Patriotic Front army, composed of Tutsis. To restore a measure of peace and
stability, moderate Hutus agreed to share power with the Tutsis. Hutu extremists
responded by killing both Tutsis and moderate Hutus. When a plane carrying
Rwanda's President Juvenal Habyarimana, a Hutu, crashed on April 6, 1994, ethnic
violence erupted with a force that stunned the global community. Believing that Tutsis
were responsible for destroying the plane, the Hutus circulated lists of names of
those favoring democracy and national reconciliation. They set up roadblocks and
demanded identity cards, and systematically killed Tutsis. Students were slaughtered by
their teachers, neighbors killed neighbors, and clergymen participated in the genocide.
In many cases, husbands killed their families and then committed suicide to avoid a
more terrible death.[60] About 800,000 people were slaughtered in thirteen weeks of
fighting in Rwanda. In the aftermath of this genocide, Rwandan authorities decided to
outlaw ethnic identity.[61]

Hutus

Majority group in
Rwanda who com-
mitted genocide
against the minority
Tutsi population

Tutsis

Small group of
cattle herders who
had ruled Rwanda
under German
and Belgian
colonization

RESOLVING CULTURAL CONFLICTS

In many ways, globalization was widely perceived as instrumental in creating a more harmonious world. Global markets and the promotion of democracy were believed to diminish violent clashes. Although the realization of Immanuel Kant's vision of perpetual peace seemed distant, many political scientists and others observed that democratic norms that emphasize compromise, persuasion, peaceful competition, protection of minority rights, and so on would move the global community closer to Kant's vision. In other words, they assert that democracies rarely fight each other.[62] But, as we have seen, democracies fight countries that are not democratic; and poor, marginalized, and undemocratic countries fight each other and are often plagued with ethnic conflicts. Nevertheless, the end of the Cold War and increasing globalization contributed to a stronger global emphasis on peacefully resolving conflicts. UN Secretary General Boutros Boutros-Ghali, in his **Agenda for Peace**, a 1992 report written at the request of the UN Security Council, emphasized various techniques for resolving conflicts, such as preventive diplomacy, confidence-building measures, fact-finding, and preventive deployment. We will examine **four interrelated approaches to conflict resolution:** (1) negotiation; (2) peacekeeping (which includes humanitarian intervention); (3) peacemaking; and (4) peacebuilding.

Negotiation

Negotiation is back-and-forth communication to reconcile contradictory positions and conflicting interests in order to reach an agreement acceptable to the parties involved. **Negotiation** is principally concerned with helping your opponent make a particular decision. An important impetus for advancing proposals and making concessions and compromises is that there are common interests that can be secured through cooperation.[63] Each side must be willing to make those adjustments that are essential to reaching a compromise, thereby creating what Roger Fisher and William Ury in *Getting to Yes* call a **win-win** situation (where both sides gain) instead of taking a **zero-sum** approach (where one side wins and the other loses). But negotiation is not entirely separated from the use of coercion or violence. Most conflicts cannot be resolved by relying on either negotiation or the threat of force. Negotiations involve both **carrots** (inducements) and **sticks** (punishments).

Carrots/Sticks
Practice by which states rely on inducements and punishments in their relations with other states

Raymond Cohen stresses that cultural values directly influence negotiation strategies and the success of negotiations in *Negotiating Across Cultures*. When individuals, countries, and ethnic groups focus primarily on their underlying interests and objectives, they have a better chance of resolving disputes than if they allow their emotions and beliefs to dominate. Learning the other side's real interests necessitates a careful and patient probing of the needs, hopes, fears, perceptions, and cultural values that form their sense of what is threatening or vital to protecting their identity.[64] This requires willingness on the negotiator's part to listen actively to the other side and to put himself or herself in the other side's shoes, as it were. **Active listening** involves trying to hear and absorb the other side's views of the facts as distinct from one's own, to seek further clarification through questioning, and to process the information received

Trade-offs

An exchange designed to address the interests of both groups involved in mediation

UN Security Council Resolution 242

Attempted to resolve the Palestinian-Israeli conflict by exchanging land for peace

in terms of the larger context of the situation and the issues of the movement.[65] In addition to active listening, negotiators must develop **formulas,** or **trade-offs.** A trade-off is essentially an exchange to address the fears and interests of those involved. An example of a trade-off is the 1967 **UN Security Council Resolution 242,** which attempted to resolve the Middle East conflict by exchanging land for peace. Israel would withdraw its armed forces from territories it conquered and occupied in exchange for the Arabs' termination of belligerency against Israel and recognition of Israel's sovereignty and territorial boundaries.

Numerous barriers impede successfully negotiating cultural conflicts. Perceptions often complicate negotiations between parties that have very different cultures. Information and facts that contradict our perceptions and images of ourselves and others are usually ignored or overlooked. **Stereotypes** impede the negotiating process between nations and ethnic groups that are culturally distant by fostering negative interpretations of motives behind actions that could be viewed as positive developments. **Public opinion** is also important. If citizens or ethnic group members believe that force is an effective and desirable means of dealing with disputes, leaders are likely to consider military action against the opponent. A society or group that perceives compromise as a sign of weakness is likely to produce leaders who devalue negotiations with adversaries.[66] Similarly, leaders and policymakers who perceive the world as hostile and conflict-ridden and who believe that only military force provides real security are generally likely to reject or downplay negotiations.

Peacekeeping and Humanitarian Intervention

Peacekeeping

International intervention designed to limit or end state interethnic violence

Just War

War fought for noble, humanitarian purposes

Increasingly, the United Nations and regional organizations intervene militarily to end international and interethnic violence or to prevent it from escalating. This is called **peacekeeping.** A principal objective is to create an environment that is conducive to both humanitarian operations and negotiations. Peacekeeping missions are generally supported by the global community as well as the combatants. Nonstate actors—such as Amnesty International, Catholic Relief Services, Oxfam, and the International Committee of the Red Cross—cooperate with the United Nations and regional organizations. However, as the cases of Rwanda, Bosnia, Sudan, and East Timor demonstrate, the global community is often slow in responding to ethnic conflicts. Another issue raised in humanitarian intervention is the concept of a **just war.** *A just war must meet certain criteria:*

1. Support a just cause,
2. Be just in intent,
3. Be of last resort,
4. Have limited objectives,
5. Be proportional,
6. Be declared by legitimate authorities, and
7. Not involve noncombatants.

Peacemaking

Peacemaking, which generally occurs after peacekeeping has made significant progress, involves the intervention of neutral third parties. Their objective is to get the combatants to reach a political settlement through negotiations. These intermediaries rely on certain methods, such as arbitration, mediation, and facilitation. **Arbitration** refers to "binding, authoritative third-party intervention in which conflict parties agree to hand the determination of a final settlement to outsiders."[67] **Mediation** is a process of facilitating communication between combatants to encourage them to brainstorm, invent options for mutual gains, try to see the other side's perception of reality and legitimate concerns, as well as to help them understand difficulties that might prevent the other side from meeting their demands. Mediators generally have some leverage over parties to a conflict and are generally seen as impartial. **Facilitation** is a cooperative, nonhierarchal, and noncoercive approach to conflict resolution. Facilitation attempts to get those involved in conflict to see the problem as a shared problem that requires cooperation to be solved. The third party's objective is to get the adversaries to engage in joint decision-making to reach a settlement that is self-sustaining.[68]

Peacebuilding

Peacebuilding is a long-term process of implementing peaceful social change through economic development and reforms, political reforms, and territorial compromises. Peacebuilding concentrates on improving conditions for a country's population or an ethnic group's members. By making economic reform, more equal distribution of economic opportunities, and economic development leading priorities, governments of ethnically torn countries can end the cycle of conflict. Ongoing violence in Afghanistan and the civil war in Iraq are widely perceived as partly due to the failure of the United States to provide essential economic change and help people with basic human security needs. Paul Collier observes that the postconflict period is a good time to reform because vested interests are loosened up.[69] Diaspora organizations can play a major role in the economic recovery of their original countries by providing money, skills, and valuable connections. Political reforms, including transitions to democracy, and power-sharing arrangements can be helpful. However, equating holding elections with democracy is a fallacy that is usually counterproductive. Building democracy takes time. This is clearly demonstrated by the failure of U.S. efforts to promote democracy in Iraq by stressing holding elections. **Power-sharing arrangements** divide political power among different ethnic groups. However, unless periodic adjustments are made to reflect changing demographics, these arrangements tend to disintegrate and ethnic conflicts erupt. In Lebanon, for example, government positions and political power were divided between the Maronite Christians and Sunni Muslims. But the power-sharing arrangement was not changed to reflect the rapid growth of the Muslim population. The country was plunged into a brutal civil war from 1975 to 1990. Israel's invasion of Lebanon in 2006 weakened the Lebanese government and exacerbated tensions among the various ethnic and religious groups. **Federalism** (i.e., the sharing of power between the central government and states, provinces, or regions) helps to solve ethnic conflicts. Ethnic groups can enjoy a degree of

Peacemaking
Intervention intended to convince combatants to reach a political settlement through peaceful negotiations

Arbitration
Negotiations under which a third party determines the final settlement between two conflicting groups

Mediation
Process of facilitating communication between combatants in order to reach a peaceful settlement of disputes

Facilitation
Cooperative, noncoercive approach to conflict resolution that seeks to get conflicting parties to acknowledge a shared problem that requires cooperation to be solved

Peacebuilding
Long-term process of implementing social change through economic development, political reforms, and territorial compromises

You DECIDE | Women and Peacemaking

The proliferation of women's peace groups in the 1980s reinvigorated the view that women have historically been leading proponents of nonviolent settlements of disputes. Such groups as the **Women's International League for Peace and Freedom** challenged World War I and supported the Comprehensive Test Ban Treaty. Swanee Hunt and Cristina Posa argue that women are more collaborative than men and are thus more inclined toward compromise. Furthermore, given their roles as family nurturers, women have a huge investment in the stability of their communities. They believe that allowing men who plan wars to plan peace is a bad habit. They stress the need to include more women, regarded as peace promoting, in efforts to negotiate peaceful solutions to conflicts.

Are women better than men at peacemaking?

Source: Swanee Hunt and Cristina Posa, "Women Waging Peace," *Foreign Policy* 124 (May/June 2001), 38–41.

Power-Sharing Arrangements

Divide political power among different ethnic groups

Partition

Forming of separate and independent countries between ethnic groups

autonomy while remaining within the existing country. Finally, **partition** (i.e., the forming of a separate and independent country from an ethnic group) is generally regarded as a last resort. Many Kurds in Iraq and Turkey have advocated creating separate states to solve ethnic conflicts. As ethnic violence escalated in Iraq in 2006, many Shiites advocated dividing the country along ethnic lines. States are extremely reluctant to agree to partition, as America's Civil War clearly demonstrates.

Summary and Review

Various periods of globalization have contributed to the cross-fertilization of cultures as well as to cultural clashes. This chapter focused on how the contemporary period of globalization is creating cultural homogenization and hybridization even as scholars and others believe that the world is divided into clashing civilizations. As we have seen throughout history, most of the violent conflicts have occurred within civilizations, within regions, and among groups within the same country. We see that culture and nationalism have often been closely intertwined. We discussed the problem of ethnocentrism as a major factor in civilizational, international, and ethnic conflicts. We challenged the dominant perspective that Western states and the Muslim world are inherently incompatible and hostile. However, the political, economic, and cultural forces of globalization heighten insecurities among states, groups, and individuals.

This chapter examined ethnic conflicts, several causes of ethnic conflicts, and some of the reasons for the decline in ethnic wars. The rising costs of ethnic conflicts, active global promotion of democracy, global concerns about human rights, and increased global efforts to find peaceful solutions to conflicts have contributed to the decline or limitation of many ethnic wars. Nevertheless, many leaders continue to manipulate ethnic differences to achieve their various objectives. Finally, we examined global and regional efforts to end conflicts. These include negotiation, peacekeeping, peacemaking, and peacebuilding.

Key Terms

jihad 379
clash-of-civilizations
   theory 380
material
   culture 381
nonmaterial
   culture 381

culture 381
subculture 381
ethnocentrism 381
containment 387
intifada 387
mujahedeen 389
tribalism 392

ethnicity 393
ethnic
   pluralism 393
Shari'a law 396
ethnic
   cleansing 397
peacekeeping 400

just war 400
peacemaking 401
arbitration 401
mediation 401
facilitation 401
peacebuilding 401
partition 401

Review Questions

1. How would you distinguish between material and nonmaterial culture?
2. How would you define subculture?
3. What is ethnocentrism? How has it contributed to national conflicts?
4. What were the intifadas? What ethnic/national groups were involved in these two conflicts?
5. What was the mujahedeen? What was its relationship to Osama bin Laden?
6. Who are the Kurds? In what states do they currently reside?
7. What is ethnic cleansing?
8. Can you give a short background on the Hutu/Tutsi ethnic conflict that resulted in the Rwandan genocide?
9. What are the four approaches to resolving cultural conflicts discussed in this chapter?
10. What is the difference between peacekeeping, peacemaking, and peacebuilding?

Suggested Readings

Barber, Benjamin R. *Jihad vs. McWorld*. New York: Ballantine Books, 1996.

Collier, Paul. *Breaking the Conflict Trap: Civil War and Development Policy*. Washington, DC: World Bank, 2003.

Durch, William J., ed. *Twenty-First-Century Peace Operations*. Washington, DC: U.S. Institute of Peace Press, 2006.

Fiscbatch, Michael. *The Peace Process and Palestinian Refugee Claims*. Washington, DC: U.S. Institute of Peace Press, 2006

Gorenberg, Gershom. *The Accidental Empire: Israel and the Birth of the Settlements*. New York: Times Books, 2006.

Gurr, Robert led. *Peoples Versus States: Minorities at Risk in the New Century*. Washington, DC: United States Institute of Peace Press, 2000.

Harff, Barbara, and Ted Robert Gurr. *Ethnic Conflict in World Politics*. Boulder, CO: Westview Press, 2003.

Haufman, Stuart J. *Modern Hatreds: The Symbolic Politics of Ethnic War*. Ithaca: Cornell University Press, 2001.

Holzgrefe, J. L., and Robert O. Keohane, eds. *Humanitarian Intervention*. Cambridge: Cambridge University Press, 2003.

Huntington, Samuel P. *The Clash of Civilizations and the Remaking of World Order*. New York: Simon and Schuster, 1996.

Huntington, Samuel P. *Who Are We?* New York: Simon and Schuster, 2004.

Klare, Michael T. *Natural Resource Wars*. New York: Henry Holt, 2001.

Kohnt, Andrew, and Bruce Stokes. *America Against the World*. New York: Times Books, 2006.

Nasr, Vali. "When the Shutes Rise," *Foreign Affairs* 85, No. 4 (July/August 2006): 58–74.

Nevins, Joseph. *A Not-So-Distant Horror: Mass Violence in East Timor*. Ithaca: Cornell University Press, 2005.

Pieterse, Jan Nederveen. *Globalization and Culture*. Lanham, MD: Rowman and Littlefield, 2004.

Power, Samantha. *A Problem From Hell: America and the Age of Genocide*. New York: Basic Books, 2002.

Prunier, Gerard. *The Rwandan Crisis*. New York: Columbia University Press, 1995.

Rubin, Barry. "Israel's New Strategy," *Foreign Affairs* 85, No. 4 (July/August 2006): 111–125.

Sapolsky, Robert. "A Natural History of Peace," *Foreign Affairs* 85, No.1 (January/February 2006): 104–120.

Zartman, I. William, ed. *Peacemaking in International Conflict*. Washington, DC: U.S. Institute of Peace Press, 2007.

Addresses and Websites

Office of High Commissioner for Human Rights
8-14 Avenue de la Paix
1211 Geneva 10
Switzerland
Tel.: 4122-917-9000
www.unhchr.ch

The goal of the UNHCHR is to protect and promote human rights worldwide. It is also responsible for implementing norms for human rights and enforcing those ideas throughout all member states. It provides technological assistance to members who are establishing human rights and responds to human rights violations. The website offers up-to-date information on work involving human rights. All other UN organizations can be linked from this page.

Human Rights Watch
350 Fifth Ave.; 34th Floor
New York, NY 10118-3299
Tel.: (212) 290–4700
Fax: (212) 736–1300
Email: hrwnyc@hrw.org
www.hrw.org

This organization stands with victims and activists to prevent discrimination, uphold political freedom, protect people from inhumane conduct in wartime, and bring offenders to justice. It also investigates and exposes human rights violations. Human Rights Watch is an independent, nongovernmental organization, supported by contributions from private individuals and foundations worldwide. This website provides links to current hot topics in human rights, as well as news and information on topics from around the world.

Human Rights Without Frontiers

www.hrwf.net

This site works to end religious persecution, intolerance, discrimination, human rights violations, and human trafficking. HRWF is independent of all political, ideological or religious movements. Its objective is to promote democracy, the rule of law, and the rights of the individual. This website provides links to recent documents published on human rights as well as information on human rights violations worldwide.

CIA World Factbook

www.cia.gov/cia/publications/factbook/index.html

The *CIA World Factbook* is available on this website for nearly every recognized nation in the world. It provides information on such topics as population, area, religious background, and foreign relations. The handbook is also available in hard copy.

United Nations Economic, Social, and Cultural Organization
7 Place de Fontenoy
75352 Paris 07 SP
France
Tel.: 33 1 45 68 10 00
www.unesco.org

The goal of UNESCO is to promote peace and stability through education, science, and culture. The website offers statistics, publications, and documents on educational, scientific, and cultural topics. It also offers a link to numerous other UN websites.

Association for the Study of Ethnicity and Nationalism
European Institute
London School of Economics
Houghton St.
London WC2A 2AE
England
Tel.: 44 020 7955 6801
Fax: 44 020 7955 6218
www.ac.uk/depts/european/asen

This website is home to the Association for the Study of Ethnicity and Nationalism. It collects information and offers conferences, seminars, lectures, and workshops relating to nationalism and ethnicity. It also provides information about ASEN and its activities.

Institution for International Mediation and Conflict Resolution
1424 K St. NW, No. 650
Washington, DC 20005
Tel.: (202) 347–2042
Fax: (202) 347–2240
www.iimrc.org

This organization offers information, programs, and services that promote peaceful conflict resolution. Its goal is to provide future leaders with skills for conflict resolution. The website provides information on the institute, publications, and programs. It also offers news and other links.

Conflict Resolution Center International
204 37th St.
Pittsburgh, PA 15201–1859
Tel.: (412) 687–6310
Fax: (412) 687–6232
Email: paul@ConflictRes.org
www.conflictres.org/info.html

The Conflict Resolution Center International is a nonprofit organization dedicated to the peaceful resolution of conflicts among nations, organizations, institutions, groups, and individuals worldwide: This website provides information on violence and conflict resolution.

Endnotes

1. Benjamin R. Barber, *Jihad vs. McWorld* (New York: Ballantine Books, 1996), 1.
2. Samuel P. Huntington, *The Clash of Civilizations and the Remaking of World Order* (New York: Simon and Schuster, 1996).
3. Jan Nederveen Pieterse, *Globalization and Culture* (Lanham, MD: Rowman and Littlefield, 2004), 82.
4. Karen Armstrong, *A History of God: The 4,000-Year Quest of Judaism, Christianity, and Islam* (New York: Ballantine Books, 1994).
5. Richard J. Payne, *The Clash With Distant Cultures: Values, Interests, and Force in American Foreign Policy* (Albany: State University of New York Press, 1995).
6. John R. Bowen, "The Myth of Global Ethnic Conflict," *Journal of Democracy* 7, No. 4 (1996), 3.
7. Payne, *The Clash With Distant Cultures*, 5.
8. Eugene V. Rostow, *Toward Managed Peace* (New Haven: Yale University Press, 1993), 104.
9. Chris Jenks, *Culture* (New York: Routledge, 1993), 8.
10. Clifford Geertz, *The Interpretation of Cultures* (New York: Basic Books, 1973), 89.
11. Jenks, *Culture*, 10.
12. Anthony Giddens, ed. *Emile Durkheim: Selected Writings* (Cambridge: Cambridge University Press, 1972), 5.
13. Ken Booth, *Strategy and Ethnocentrism* (New York: Pergamon Press, 1990), 343.
14. Payne, *The Clash With Distant Cultures*, 36–37.
15. Rafael Moses, "Empathy and Dis-Empathy in Political Conflict," *Political Psychology* 6, No. 1 (March 1985), 135.
16. Albert Bandura, "Selective Activism and Disengagement of Moral Control," *Journal of Social Issues* 46, No. 1 (1990), 1.
17. Payne, *The Clash With Distant Cultures*, 37.
18. Huntington, *The Clash of Civilizations*, 25.
19. Huntington, *The Clash of Civilizations*, 25.
20. Huntington, *The Clash of Civilizations*, 25–27.
21. Fouad Ajami, "The Summoning," *Foreign Affairs* 72, No. 4 (September/October 1993), 2.
22. Stanley Hoffmann, "Clash of Globalizations," *Foreign Affairs* 81, No. 4 (July/August 2002), 105.
23. "Invading Turks' Music Marched West," *New York Times*, 10 March 2002, A6.
24. Susanne Rudolph, "Introduction," in *Transnational Religion and Fading States*, eds. Susanne Rudolph and James Piscatori (Boulder, CO: Westview Press, 1997), 1.

25. Armstrong, *A History of God*, 197.

26. Armstrong, *A History of God*, 197.

27. Rosemary Hollis, "Great Britain," in *Powers in the Middle East*, ed. Bernard Reich (New York: Praeger, 1987), 186.

28. Dan Tschirgi, *The American Search for Mideast Peace* (New York: Praeger, 1989), 2.

29. Richard J. Payne, *The West European Allies, the Third World, and U.S. Foreign Policy* (New York: Greenwood Press, 1991), 76.

30. Payne, *The West European Allies*, 84.

31. Ken Ringle, "A Thousand Years of Bad Memories," *Washington Post National Weekly Edition*, 29 October–4 November 2001, 8.

32. Fouad Ajami, "The Falseness of Anti-Americanism," *Foreign Policy* 138 (September/October 2003), 53.

33. Richard J. Payne and Jamal R. Nassar, *Politics and Culture in the Developing World* (New York: Longman, 2003), 35.

34. Neil MacFarquhar, "Islamic Jihad, Forged in Egypt, Is Seen as bin Laden's Backbone," *New York Times*, 4 October 2001, B4.

35. Barry Rubin, "The Real Roots of Arab Anti-Americanism," *Foreign Affairs* 81, No. 6 (November/December 2002), 73.

36. "Findings on Abu Ghraib: Sadism, Deviant Behavior, and a Failure of Leadership," *New York Times*, 25 August 2004, A10.

37. Linda Colley, *Britons: Forging the Nation 1707–1837* (New Haven: Yale University Press, 1992), 5.

38. Michael W. Suleiman, *The Arabs in the Mind of America* (Brattleboro, VT: Amana Books, 1988), 147.

39. Payne, *The Clash With Distant Cultures*, 94–95.

40. Minxim Pei, "The Paradoxes of American Nationalism," *Foreign Policy* 136 (May/June 2003), 31.

41. Fareed Zakaria, "Hating America," *Foreign Policy* 144 (September/October 2004), 48.

42. Robert Jervis, "The Compulsive Empire," *Foreign Policy* 137 (July/August 2003), 85.

43. Parag Khanna, "The Metrosexual Superpower," *Foreign Policy* 143 (July/August 2004), 66.

44. Charles A. Kupchan, "Introduction," in *Nationalism and Nationalities in the New Europe*, ed. Charles A. Kupchan (Ithaca: Cornell University Press, 1995), 1.

45. Ted Robert Gurr, "Ethnic Warfare on the Wane," *Foreign Affairs* 79, No. 3 (May/June 2000), 59.

46. Donald Rothchild, *Managing Ethnic Conflict in Africa* (Washington, DC: Brookings Institution Press, 1997), 4.

47. Virginia R. Dominquez, *White by Definition* (New Brunswick: Rutgers University Press, 1986), 266.

48. Milton J. Esman, *Ethnic Politics* (Ithaca: Cornell University Press, 1994), 3.

49. Paul Collier, "The Market for Civil War," *Foreign Policy* 136 (May/June 2003), 40.

50. Robin Wright, "Ethnic Conflict: An Overview," in *National and Ethnic Conflict*, ed. Charles P. Cozic (San Diego: Greenhaven Press, 1994), 158.

51. Connie Peck, *Sustainable Peace* (Lanham, MD: Rowman and Littlefield, 1998), 16.

52. Mark Strauss, "Antiglobalism's Jewish Problem," *Foreign Policy* 139 (November/December 2003), 58.

53. Craig S. Smith, "Thwarted in Germany, Neo-Nazis Take Fascism to France," *New York Times*, 13 August 2004, A3.

54. Clifford Krauss, "Quebec Result: Solidly for Canada," *New York Times*, 16 April 2003, A8.

55. Josef Joffe, "The New Europe: Yesterday's Ghosts," *Foreign Affairs* 72, No. 1 (1993), 31.

56. James O. Jackson, "A Lesson in Shame," *Time*, 2 August, 1993, 38.

57. Roy Gutman, *A Witness to Genocide* (New York: Macmillan, 1993).

58. Yahya Sadowski, "Ethnic Conflict," *Foreign Policy* 111 (Summer 1998), 13.

59. Alain Destexhe, *Rwanda and Genocide in the Twentieth Century* (New York: New York University Press, 1995), 40; and Michael Ignatieff, *The Warrior's Honor: Ethnic War and the Modern Conscience* (New York: Metropolitan Books, 1997), 62.

60. Destexhe, *Rwanda and Genocide*, 31.

61. Marc Lacey, "A Decade After Massacres, Rwanda Outlaws Ethnicity," *New York Times*, 9 April 2004, A3.

62. Bruce M. Russett, *Controlling the Sword: Democratic Governance of National Security* (Cambridge, MA: Harvard University Press, 1990), 121–124.

63. Roger Fisher and William Ury, *Getting to Yes: Negotiating Agreement Without Giving In* (New York: Penguin, 1983).

64. Harold H. Saunders, "An Historic Challenge to Rethink How Nations Relate," in *Psychodynamics of International Relationships*, ed. Vamik Volkan, et al. (Lexington, MA: Lexington Books, 1990), 15.

65. George A. Lopez and Michael S. Stohl, "Diplomacy, Bargaining, and Coercion," in *International Relations*, eds. George A. Lopez and Michael S. Stohl (Washington, DC: Congressional Quarterly Press, 1989), 16.

66. Martin Patchen, *Resolving Disputes Between Nations* (Durham: Duke University Press, 1988), 107.

67. Raymond C. Taras and Rajat Ganguly, *Understanding Ethnic Conflicts* (New York: Longman, 2002), 95.

68. Taras and Ganguly, *Understanding Ethnic Conflicts*, 96.

69. Collier, "The Market for Civil War," 44.

BIBLIOGRAPHY

Acemoglu, Daron, and James A. Robinson. *Economic Origins of Dictatorship and Democracy*. Cambridge: Cambridge University Press, 2006.

Ackerman, Bruce. *Before the Next Attack: Civil Liberties in an Age of Terrorism*. New Haven: Yale University Press, 2006.

Adelman, Carol C. "The Privatization of Foreign Aid." *Foreign Affairs* 82, No. 6 (November/December 2003): 9–14.

Ajami, Fouad. *The Foreigner's Gift*. New York: Free Press, 2006.

Ali, Tariq. *Bush in Babylon: The Recolonization of Iraq*. New York: Verso, 2003.

Allison, Graham. "How to Stop Nuclear Terror." *Foreign Affairs* 83, No. 1 (January/February 2004): 64–74.

Andreas, Peter. *Border Games: Policing the U.S.-Mexico Divide*. Ithaca: Cornell University Press, 2002.

Andreas, Peter, and Ethan Nadelmann. *Policing the Globe*. New York: Oxford University Press, 2006.

Art, Robert J., and Louise Richardson, eds. *Democracy and Counterterrorism*. Washington, DC: U.S. Institute of Peace Press, 2006.

Aslund, Anders, and Michael McFaul. *Revolution In Orange*. Washington, DC: Carnegie Endowment Press, 2006.

Baldwin, Robert E. *The Decline of U.S. Labor Unions and the Role of Trade*. Washington, DC: Institute for International Economics, 2003.

Bales, Kevin. *Disposable People: New Slavery in the Global Economy*. Berkeley: University of California Press, 1999.

Barnett, Michael, and Martha Finnemore. *Rules for the World*. Ithaca: Cornell University Press, 2006.

Berretta, David. "Pirate Tactics." *Foreign Policy* 155 (July/August 2006): 92.

Birdsall, Nancy. "That Silly Inequality Debate." *Foreign Policy* 130 (May/June 2002): 92–94.

Bjorgo, Tore, ed. *Terror From the Extreme Right*. London: Frank Cass, 1995.

Bloom, Mia. *Dying to Kill: The Allure of Suicide Terror*. New York: Columbia University Press, 2005.

Boutwell, Jeffrey, and Michael T. Klare, eds. *Light Weapons and Civil Conflict*. Lanham, MD: Rowman and Littlefield Publishers, 1999.

Bowen, John R. "The Myth of Global Ethnic Conflict." *Journal of Democracy* 7, No. 1 (1996): 3–11.

Bright, Christopher. *Life Out of Bounds: Bioinvasion in a Borderless World*. New York: W. W. Norton, 1998.

Brittan, Leon. *Globalization vs. Sovereignty? The European Response*. Cambridge: Cambridge University Press, 1998.

Brown, Michael, et al., eds. *Primacy and Its Discontents*. Cambridge, MA: MIT Press, 2006.

Brown, Seyom. *Human Rights in World Politics*. New York: Longman, 2000.

Calder, Kent E. "China and Japan's Simmering Rivalry." *Foreign Affairs* 85, No. 2 (March/April 2006): 129–140.

Carothers, Thomas. "Promoting Democracy and Fighting Terror." *Foreign Affairs* 82, No. 1 (January/February 2003): 84–97.

Chung, Chien-peng. "China's War on Terror." *Foreign Affairs* 81, No. 4 (July/August 2002): 8–12.

Cohen, Daniel. *Globalization and Its Enemies*. Cambridge: Cambridge University Press, 2006.

Coleman, Isobel. "Women, Islam, and the New Iraq." *Foreign Affairs* 85, No. 1 (January/February 2006): 24–38.

Collier, Paul. "The Market for Civil War." *Foreign Policy* 136 (May/June 2003): 38–45.

Collier, Paul, and Nicholas Sambanis, eds. *Understanding Civil War*. Washington, DC: World Bank, 2005.

Covey, Jack, et al., eds. *The Quest for Viable Peace*. Washington, DC: U.S. Institute of Peace Press, 2005.

Cranston, Maurice. "Are There Any Human Rights?" *Daedalus* 112, No. 4 (Fall 1993): 1–18.

Crenshaw, Martha, ed. *Terrorism in Context*. University Park: Pennsylvania State University Press, 1995.

Crocker, Chester, et al. *Leashing the Dogs of War: Conflict Management in a Divided World*. Washington, DC: U.S. Institute of Peace Press, 2006.

Crocker, Chester A. "Engaging Failing States." *Foreign Affairs* 82, No. 5 (September/October 2003): 32–44.

Crosby, Alfred W. *The Colombian Exchange: Biological and Cultural Consequences of 1492*. Westport, CT: Greenwood Press, 1972.

Daalder, Ivo H., and James M. Lindsay. *America Unbound: The Bush Revolution in Foreign Policy*. Washington, DC: Brookings Institution Press, 2003.

Derleth, J. William. *The Transitions in Central and Eastern European Politics*. Upper Saddle River, NJ: Prentice Hall, 2000.

DeSombre, Elizabeth R. *Domestic Sources of International Environmental Policy*. Cambridge, MA: MIT Press, 2000.

Diamond, Jared. *Guns, Germs, and Steel*. New York: W. W. Norton, 1999.

Dunne, Tim, and Nicholas J. Wheeler, eds. *Human Rights in Global Politics*. Cambridge: Cambridge University Press, 1999.

Riemer, Neal, ed. *Protection Against Genocide*. Westport, CT: Praeger, 2000.

Rosenau, James N., and Mary Durfee. *Thinking Theory Thoroughly*. Boulder, CO: Westview Press, 2000.

Roth, Kenneth. "The Law of War in the War on Terror." *Foreign Affairs* 83, No. 1 (January/February 2004): 2–7.

Rotte, Ralph. "Immigration Control in United Germany." *International Migration Review* 34, No. 2 (Summer 2000): 357–389.

Rubin, Barry. "Israel's New Strategy." *Foreign Affairs* 85, No. 4 (July/August 2006): 111–125.

Rubin, Barry. "The Real Roots of Arab Anti-Americanism." *Foreign Affairs* 81, No. 61 (November/December 2002): 73–85.

Sachs, Jeffrey D. *The End of Poverty*. New York: Penguin, 2006.

Sapolsky, Robert M. "A Natural History of Peace." *Foreign Affairs* 85, No. 1 (January/February 2006): 104–120.

Schlesinger Jr., Arthur. "Has Democracy a Future?" *Foreign Affairs* 76, No. 5 (September/October 1997): 2–12.

Schmidtke, Oliver. "Transnational Migration." *World Affairs* 164, No. 1 (Summer 2001): 3–16.

Schraeder, Peter J., ed. *Exporting Democracy*. Boulder, CO: Lynne Rienner, 2002.

Schreurs, Miranda A., and Elizabeth Economy, eds. *The Internationalization of Environmental Protection*. Cambridge: Cambridge University Press, 1997.

Simes, Dimitri K. "America's Imperial Dilemma." *Foreign Affairs* 82, No. 6 (November/December 2003): 91–102.

Soros, George. *The Bubble of American Supremacy: Correcting the Misuse of American Power*. New York: Public Affairs, 2003.

Stares, Paul B. *Global Habit: The Drug Problem in a Borderless World*. Washington, DC: Brookings Institution Press, 1996.

Stern, Jessica. *The Ultimate Terrorists*. Cambridge, MA: Harvard University Press, 1999.

Stevenson, Jonathan. "Peace in Northern Ireland: Why Now?" *Foreign Policy* 112 (Fall 1998): 41–54.

Stillwaggon, Eileen. *AIDS and the Ecology of Poverty*. New York: Oxford University Press, 2005.

Tammen, Ronald, et al. *Power Transitions: Strategies for the 21st Century*. New York: Seven Bridges Press, 2000.

Taras, Raymond C., and Rajat Ganguly. *Understanding Ethnic Conflicts*. New York: Longman, 2002.

Todd, Emmanuel. *After the Empire: The Breakdown of American Order*. New York: Columbia University Press, 2003.

Tucker, Jonathan B., ed. *Toxic Terror: Assessing Terrorist Use of Chemical and Biological Weapons*. Cambridge, MA: MIT Press, 2000.

UN High Commissioner For Refugees. *The State of the World's Refugees*. New York: Oxford University Press, 2006.

Van Schendel, William, and Itty Abraham. *Illicit Flows of Criminal Things*. Bloomington: Indiana University Press, 2006.

Vig, Norman J., and Regina S. Axelrod, eds. *The Global Environment*. Washington, DC: Congressional Quarterly Press, 1999.

Von Hippel, Karin. *Democracy by Force: U.S. Military Intervention in the Post-Cold War World*. Cambridge: Cambridge University Press, 2000.

Wallerstein, Immanuel. "The Eagle Has Crash Landed." *Foreign Policy* 131 (July/August 2002): 60–68.

Walt, Stephen M. *Taming American Power*. New York: W. W. Norton, 2006.

Waltz, Kenneth. "Globalization and American Power." *National Interest* 59 (Spring 2000): 46–56.

Weimann, Gabriel. *Terror on the Internet*. Washington, DC: U.S. Institute of Peace Press, 2006.

Wiarda, Howard J., and Margaret Macleish Mott. *Catholic Roots and Democratic Flowers*. Westport, CT: Praeger, 2001.

Wilkinson, Paul. *Terrorism Versus Democracy*. London: Frank Cass, 2000.

Zachary, Pascal. "The Rage for Global Teams." *Technology Review* 101, No. 4 (July/August 1998): 33.

Zakaria, Fareed. "Hating America." *Foreign Policy* 144 (September/October 2004): 47–49.

Zakaria, Fareed. "The Rise of Illiberal Democracy." *Foreign Affairs* 76, No. 6 (November/December 1997): 22–43.

Zartman, I. William, ed. *Peacemaking in International Conflict*. Washington, DC: U.S. Institute of Peace Press, 2007.

INDEX